Household Portfolios

Household Portfolios

edited by Luigi Guiso,
Michael Haliassos, and
Tullio Jappelli

The MIT Press
Cambridge, Massachusetts
London, England

This book was set in Palatino in '3B2' by Asco Typesetters, Hong Kong, and was printed and bound in the United States of America.

Library of Congress Cataloging-in-Publication Data

Household portfolios / edited by Luigi Guiso, Michael Haliassos, and Tullio Jappelli.
    p. cm.
  Papers presented at the Conference on Household Portfolios, held in Florence, Italy, Dec. 17–18, 1999.
  Includes bibliographical references and index.
  ISBN 0-262-07221-1 (hc. : alk. paper)
  1. Portfolio management—Congresses. 2. Capital assets pricing model—Congresses. 3. Saving and investment—Congresses. I. Guiso, Luigi. II. Haliassos, Michael. III. Jappelli, Tullio. IV. Conference on Household Portfolios (1999 : Florence, Italy)
  HG4529.5 .H68   2002
  332.6—dc21   2001044321

To Angelika

Contents

Preface   ix

Contributors   xi

Introduction   1
Luigi Guiso, Michael Haliassos, and Tullio Jappelli

I   Theoretical and Methodological Issues   25

1   What Does Theory Have to Say About Household
     Portfolios?   27
     Christian Gollier

2   Calibration and Computation of Household Portfolio
     Models   55
     Michael Haliassos and Alexander Michaelides

3   Taxation and Portfolio Structure: Issues and Implications   103
     James M. Poterba

4   Econometric Issues in the Estimation of Household Portfolio
     Models   143
     Raffaele Miniaci and Guglielmo Weber

II   Issues and Trends in Household Portfolios   179

5   Household Portfolios in the United States   181
     Carol C. Bertaut and Martha Starr-McCluer

6   Household Portfolios in the United Kingdom   219
    James Banks and Sarah Tanner

7   Household Portfolios in Italy   251
    Luigi Guiso and Tullio Jappelli

8   Household Portfolios in Germany   291
    Angelika Eymann and Axel Börsch-Supan

9   Household Portfolios in the Netherlands   341
    Rob Alessie, Stefan Hochguertel, and Arthur Van Soest

10 Portfolios of the Rich   389
    Christopher D. Carroll

11 Portfolio Holdings of the Elderly   431
    Michael D. Hurd

    References   473
    Index   493

Preface

Preliminary versions of the chapters that appear in this book were presented at the Conference on Household Portfolios held in Florence, Italy, December 17–18, 1999. The conference was organized and financed by the Finance and Consumption in the EU chair, the research program on consumer credit and related issues sponsored by Findomestic SpA, and CETELEM at the European University Institute (EUI). We are indebted to the following distinguished academics who served as conference discussants: Giuseppe Bertola (EUI), Martin Browning (Copenhagen), Angus Deaton (Princeton), Arie Kapteijn (Tilburg), Ramon Marimon (EUI), Marco Pagano (Salerno), Steven Pischke (MIT), James Poterba (MIT), Nick Souleles (Wharton), Annette Vissing-Jørgensen (Chicago), and Steven Zeldes (Columbia). The quality of the book would not have been the same without their valuable input and advice. We are most grateful to all chapter authors for putting some of their best effort into preparing thoughtful and thought-provoking work and for submitting their manuscripts on time.

We are grateful to Stavros Zenios (HERMES Center, Cyprus), who at an early stage stimulated our interest in this project, and to Giuseppe Bertola, who facilitated interaction among contributors by arranging visits to the EUI over the past two years. The TMR Project on Savings, Pensions and Portfolio Choice, coordinated by Arie Kapteijn, has been instrumental in building research interaction among experts from both sides of the Atlantic. On the production side, we are indebted to Roger Meservey for professional editing, to Lia Ambrosio, who managed the manuscript submission, and to the MIT Press editors and staff for their high degree of professionalism, efficiency, and courtesy.

This book is dedicated to the memory of Angelika Eymann, who passed away too soon.

Contributors

Rob Alessie Department of Economics, Free University of Amsterdam

James Banks Institute for Fiscal Studies

Carol C. Bertaut Board of Governors of the Federal Reserve System

Axel Börsch-Supan Department of Economics, University of Mannheim

Christopher D. Carroll Department of Economics, Johns Hopkins University

Angelika Eymann Department of Economics, University of Mannheim

Christian Gollier Department of Economics, University of Toulouse

Luigi Guiso Department of Economics, University of Sassari

Michael Haliassos Department of Economics, University of Cyprus

Stefan Hochguertel European University Institute and Uppsala University

Michal D. Hurd Rand Corporation

Tullio Jappelli Department of Economics, University of Salerno

Alexander Michaelides Department of Economics, University of Cyprus

Raffaele Miniaci Department of Economics, University of Padova

James M. Poterba Department of Economics, Massachusetts Institute of Technology

Martha Starr-McCluer   Board of Governors of the Federal Reserve System

Sarah Tanner   Institute for Fiscal Studies

Arthur Van Soest   Department of Econometrics, Tilburg University

Guglielmo Weber   Department of Economics, University of Padova

Introduction

Luigi Guiso,
Michael Haliassos, and
Tullio Jappelli

The past decade has seen radical change in both financial markets and related academic research. Financial markets have experienced a policy-induced move toward greater international integration and coordination, liberalization, and product innovation. The European Union directives on financial integration, the removal of the remaining capital controls, the privatization of public utilities, and recent pension reforms in various countries are but a few examples of policies that have had a great impact on financial markets.

Some of the most striking effects are the broadening of the stockholder base, the growth in mutual fund participation, the increasing importance of private pension funds, and the enthusiastic employee response to retirement accounts, such as 401(k) accounts in the United States. On the liability side, there has been fast growth in credit card use and consumer indebtedness, debt often coexisting with asset holdings offering lower rates of return than loan rates.

In the face of such dramatic changes in portfolio behavior, it is not surprising that academic research has seen a resurgence of interest in macroeconomics and finance. A number of economists with interests in monetary economics, government finance, consumption and saving, public economics, and theory of choice under uncertainty have joined forces to provide a fresh perspective on finance. Their work is shifting attention from the simple consumption-saving choice to the simultaneous determination of spending plans and portfolio composition for households that perceive a richer asset-liability menu. Theoretical modeling in this area has been able to use the solid foundations provided by the theory of choice under uncertainty, but it has been helped considerably by the development of computational techniques to handle models of portfolio choice under nondiversifiable labor income risk. Empirical work in this field is now possible thanks to the development of extensive household-level surveys offering information on both portfolio composition and attitudes toward saving, borrowing, risk taking, and liquidity.

Despite this happy coincidence of developments in financial markets, theoretical tools, and databases, there has been no coordinated effort at bringing the tools and the data to bear on issues relating to household portfolio behavior. This book seeks to fill the gap with a comprehensive collection of chapters on theory, methodology, policy issues, and household-level data analysis in this exciting new field of research.

The book has four main objectives: first, to provide an up-to-date account of the status of our theoretical knowledge regarding the structure of household portfolios and to compare its predictions with empirical findings; second, to describe the main tools of analytical, numerical, and econometric analysis, as well as some of the key policy questions; third, to use microdata for in-depth study of portfolio composition of population groups of special policy interest, such as the young, the elderly, and the rich; finally, to offer an original comparative analysis of household portfolios in countries for which detailed data are available.

I The Current State of Portfolio Theory and Methodology

The study of household portfolios employs analytical methods, computational algorithms, and econometric tools. So far, economic theory has emphasized the decision between consumption and saving much more than household portfolio choices. Finance has emphasized the asset-pricing implications of models such as the capital asset pricing model (CAPM) and the consumption CAPM (CCAPM), combined with portfolio analysis aimed mainly at guiding institutional investors.

At least three factors contributed to the relative neglect of household portfolios: first, the persistent tendency of most households to hold very simple portfolios until the recent emergence of the equity culture, that is, willingness to participate in the stock market; second, the inability of the dominant asset pricing models—the CAPM and CCAPM—to account for household portfolio incompleteness; and third, the lack of detailed databases on household portfolios in many countries until the late 1980s or 1990s.

Theoretical analysis of household portfolios has emphasized mostly the choice between risk-free and risky financial assets, at least since the 1950s (Markowitz 1952; Tobin 1958). Early analysis contributed significantly to our understanding of how risk aversion influences the propensity of households to take financial risk. In the early 1990s, portfolio theory also dealt with the way in which uninsurable income risk influences the portfolio share of risky assets, leading to the development of notions such as "prudence" and "temperance."

Chapter 1 (by Christian Gollier) explicates these theoretical developments. It concludes by highlighting a number of theoretical predictions that can be confronted with the data—among them, that under decreasing relative risk aversion, wealthier people should invest a larger share of their wealth in risky assets, that younger investors should invest more in risky assets, and that investors with riskier human capital should invest less in risky assets. The chapter also points out that borrowing constraints, transaction costs, and information costs should tend to lower the demand for risky assets.

Despite the elegance of the analytical results, two limitations in applying them to the portfolios of households that face earnings risk have become evident. First, analytical results normally require restrictive assumptions on preferences.[1] Second, studying the age pattern of household portfolios requires multiperiod models in order to follow investors over their life cycle. With general preference specifications, analytical solution of portfolio models with more than two periods becomes essentially intractable, especially if, in addition to earnings risk, one also incorporates market frictions such as liquidity constraints and transaction costs. This bottleneck can be overcome by applying computational methods to household portfolio models. Chapter 2 (by Michael Haliassos and Alexander Michaelides) describes calibration and numerical solutions of household portfolio problems in multiperiod models with uninsurable income risk. The chapter illustrates the main numerical computation techniques available and provides a host of intertemporal models to isolate the contribution of each major factor affecting portfolio choice (such as age, wealth, information costs, and borrowing constraints).

Chapter 3 (by James Poterba) provides an overview of how taxation affects household portfolio structure. Most of the modern theory of portfolio choice was developed without reference to taxes. The chapter begins by summarizing the after-tax CAPM, then proceeds to outline six margins of portfolio adjustment where taxes can affect investor incentives: asset selection, asset allocation, borrowing, asset location in taxable and tax-deferred accounts, asset turnover, and whether to hold assets directly or through financial intermediaries. The analysis considers how ignoring tax considerations may bias estimates of how other variables, such as income or net worth, affect the structure of household portfolios. This chapter also reviews the existing evidence on how taxation affects household portfolio choice. A small but growing empirical literature suggests that taxes have a substantial impact on several aspects of portfolio choice. Further evidence about the importance of taxes is contained in a number of the country studies given here, notably for the United Kingdom and the Netherlands.

Chapters 1 through 3 highlight a number of theoretical results that are at variance with the data presented in part II. For instance, theoretical models and simulation results suggest that even under stringent borrowing constraints and considerable income risk, young people should invest in risky assets to take advantage of the equity premium. Furthermore, conditioning on participation, the share of wealth invested in risky assets should decrease with age. A famous economist once jestingly remarked that we ought not to let reality interfere with an elegant theory. Whatever the merits of this thought, this book takes a close look at detailed surveys of household portfolios in order to identify stylized facts and confront the theoretical models with observed behavior.

The empirical analysis of portfolio composition cannot do without state-of-the-art econometric techniques, mainly to allow for the fact that not all households participate in certain asset markets. Chapter 4 (by Raffaele Miniaci and Guglielmo Weber) provides an econometric tool kit for estimating household portfolio models with survey data. The emphasis is on estimating the decision to invest in risky assets and the conditional demand for risky assets when households are followed through time. The authors explain how to estimate the effect of time-varying characteristics, such as wealth, income, and age, on the decision to invest in risky assets. In principle, panel data allow one to disentangle state dependence from unobserved heterogeneity in the participation decision and to handle serial correlation in shocks. The chapter then describes how, given a specification for the participation equation, an equation relating the risky asset share to household characteristics can be estimated. Estimation methods (both parametric and semiparametric) suitable for both types of equations are introduced and evaluated. That concludes the methodological part of the volume.

II Trends and Patterns in Household Portfolios

Part II looks at household financial portfolios in five countries. Chapter 5 (by Carol Bertaut and Martha Starr-McCluer) covers the United States, Chapter 6 (by James Banks and Sarah Tanner) the United Kingdom, Chapter 7 (by Luigi Guiso and Tullio Jappelli) Italy, Chapter 8 (by Angelika Eymann and Axel Börsch-Supan) Germany, and Chapter 9 (by Rob Alessie, Stefan Hochguertel and Arthur Van Soest) the Netherlands. The book concludes by examining the portfolio choices of two population groups that warrant closer scrutiny. The behavior of the rich is the object of Chapter 10 (by Christopher Carroll), and the analysis of the elderly is taken up in Chapter 11 (by Michael Hurd).

Table I.1 lists the household assets and liabilities that each of these chapters attempts to cover, as well as groupings of assets by degree of riskiness.[2] Table I.2 highlights an initial problem in describing household portfolios: definitions. Whereas in theoretical models it is customary to partition assets into risky and risk free, in practice this is difficult and to some extent arbitrary. The simplest definition of risky assets is *direct stockholding*, but consider that many risky assets are held indirectly through mutual funds and retirement accounts (*direct and indirect stockholding*). A third definition that has been used in the empirical chapters is that of *risky financial assets*. In some countries, this coincides with direct and indirect stockholding, but in others it also includes foreign assets or long-term government bonds (exposed to exchange rate and interest rate risk, respectively) and excludes defined-benefit pension plans (part of which are invested in stocks, but which are arguably safe assets). An even broader measure of risky assets includes equity in own business and real estate (*total risky assets*).

Table I.3 lists the sample surveys used to analyze portfolio behavior in each of the five countries. There is unavoidable variability in reference periods and number of observations. In Germany and the U.K., two different surveys are needed to study portfolio decisions. In Italy and the Netherlands, panel data are available but are relatively short. Some surveys collect data only on participation,

Table I.1
Household portfolio components

Assets	Liabilities
Financial assets	Mortgage and home equity
Liquid accounts (checking, saving, money market deposit accounts)	Loans for investment real estate
	Credit card balances
Certificates of deposit (time accounts)	Other debt (home improvement loans,
Government bonds	student loans, vehicle loans, unsecured
Other bonds (including corporate and foreign bonds)	credit lines, loans against pension and life insurance policies)
Stocks (directly held)	
Mutual funds (excluding money market funds)	
Retirement accounts (individual and employer sponsored)	
Cash value of life insurance	
Trusts and other managed assets (including managed investment accounts)	
Other financial assets (e.g., royalties, futures contracts)	
Nonfinancial assets	
Primary residence	
Investment real estate (residential and nonresidential)	
Business equity (privately owned, with or without management role)	
Other nonfinancial (mainly vehicles and recreation tools, artwork, antiques, furniture, valuable collections)	

while others collect data on both participation and amounts; even so, to varying degrees, the aggregates computed from survey data tend to understate the aggregate financial accounts, suggesting measurement errors. The special features and problems of each survey are described in detail in the various chapters and should be kept in mind when trying to compare data across countries.

The empirical findings on the determinants of household portfolio choice fall into two main categories: those on the *participation decision*, that is, the decision to hold assets of a particular category, and those on the *portfolio shares* of either financial assets or total assets, financial and nonfinancial. As we shall see, the empirical findings here point to the importance of fixed costs of entering the stock

Table I.2
Risky asset definitions

Direct stockholding	Shares held directly.
Direct and indirect stockholding	Shares held directly, mutual funds, investment accounts, retirement accounts. Except for the United States, information on the specific types of mutual funds and investment accounts is unavailable, and one cannot disentangle indirect stockholding in mutual funds and managed investment accounts from investment in other financial assets. For this reason, the reported figures overestimate the true value of indirect stockholding. In Germany there is no information on pension funds.
Risky financial assets	In the United States, direct and indirect stockholding, plus corporate, foreign, and mortgage-backed bonds. In the United Kingdom, direct and indirect stockholding plus corporate bonds. In the Netherlands, direct and indirect stockholding but excluding defined-benefits pension funds. In Germany, direct and indirect stockholding plus foreign bonds. In Italy, direct and indirect stockholding plus long-term government bonds and corporate bonds.
Total risky assets	Risky financial assets, business, investment real estate. In Germany, there is no information on investment real estate, and information on business property is available only in 1983. In the United Kingdom, there is no information on real assets.

Table I.3
Data sources for international comparison of household portfolios

Country	Data source	Sample size	Data years
United States	Survey of Consumer Finances (for ownership and amounts)	4,000–4,500	1983, 1989, 1992, 1995, 1998
United Kingdom	Family Expenditure Survey (for ownership only)	7,000	1978–1996
	Financial Research Survey (for ownership and amounts)	58,000	1997–1998
Netherlands	CentER Savings Survey (for ownership and amounts)	2,000	1993–1998
Germany	German Income and Expenditure Survey	40,000–46,000	1978, 1983, 1988, 1993
	German Socioeconomic Panel (for ownership only)	5,000	1990–1997
	Spiegel-Verlag Survey *Soll und Haben* (for ownership only)	4,000–8,500	1980, 1985, 1989, 1995
Italy	Survey of Household Income and Wealth (for ownership and amounts)	7,000–8,000	1989, 1991, 1993, 1995, 1998

market, in the form of informational requirements and participation fees. This is a departure from the practice of traditional theoretical portfolio models of ignoring such costs. The empirical chapters take the view that the decision to invest and the decision on how much to invest are distinct, and they use a sample selection approach to disentangle the two empirically. Authors examine how participation choices and portfolio shares depend on various factors, such as wealth, age, education, and demographic characteristics.

The Participation Decision

Arguably, the most dramatic portfolio development in the past decade has been the spread of an equity culture. Table I.4 documents that in the countries we examine, the proportion of stockholders (direct and indirect) increased dramatically during the 1990s, although as of 1998, there was still no country in the world where the majority of households hold stocks. The United States and the United Kingdom are the countries where the proportion of households that hold stocks directly is highest (about 20 percent). Italy is at the other end of the spectrum, with only 7 percent.

In addition to an increase in direct stockholding, the key to the spread of the equity culture is the growing importance of investment through financial intermediaries, such as mutual funds and retirement accounts. Counting such indirect holdings more than doubles the fraction of households investing in stocks in most of the countries we consider. This pattern is observed despite the fact that some forms of indirect holdings, like mutual funds, involve substantial tax costs and other expenses imposed by financial intermediaries (as explained in Chapter 3 on taxation). In addition to facilitating the diversification of risk, mutual funds and other investment accounts considerably lower the informational requirements for asset management, since participation and trading decisions are delegated to professionals. Households also benefit from record keeping, financial education, and other services (Bayer, Bernheim, and Scholz 1996). The relative importance of these considerations in inducing households to participate in indirect asset holding vis-à-vis directly investing in stocks is worth further study.

A related issue, and one with a long tradition in portfolio analysis, is the extent of diversification in household portfolios. The country studies find that the extent of diversification between and within risk

Table I.4
Proportion of households investing in risky assets

Year	United States	United Kingdom	Nether-lands	Germany	Italy
Direct stockholding					
1983	19.1	8.9	n.a	9.7	n.a
1989	16.8	22.6	n.a	10.3	4.5
1995	15.2	23.4	11.5	10.5	4.0
1998	19.2	21.6	15.4	n.a	7.3
Direct and indirect stockholding					
1983	n.a.	n.a	n.a.	11.2	n.a.
1989	31.6	n.a.	n.a	12.4	10.5
1995	40.4	n.a.	29.4	15.6	14.0
1998	48.9	31.4	35.1	n.a.	18.7
Risky financial assets					
1983	n.a.	n.a.	n.a.	13.7	n.a.
1989	31.9	n.a.	n.a.	17.2	12.0
1995	40.6	n.a.	21.9	20.2	18.5
1998	49.2	32.4	27.7	n.a.	22.1
Total risky assets					
1983	n.a.	n.a.	n.a.	17.8	n.a.
1989	46.4	n.a.	n.a.	24.1	47.0
1995	51.6	n.a.	28.4	25.2	46.9
1998	56.9	n.a.	32.8	n.a.	43.8

Sources: United States: Survey of Consumer Finances. United Kingdom: Family Expenditure Survey. Netherlands: CentER Saving Survey. Germany: German Income and Expenditure Survey (1983) and *Soll und Haben* Survey (1989 and 1995). For comparison with earlier periods, all data refer to West Germany. Italy: Survey of Household Income and Wealth.
Note: All statistics use sample weights.

categories is typically quite limited. However, the growing popularity of mutual funds and indirect stockholding has certainly helped increase the degree of intracategory diversification of financial assets. For real assets, such as private businesses, there is a pronounced lack of diversification. The wealthy prefer to own one business rather than to divide up their wealth and own small parts of many businesses (see chapter 10). Evidently these real assets involve other features and may provide other services to compensate for this portfolio specialization. There are also other ways in which households are poorly diversified. For example, it is not uncommon for employees to

own stock in their own firms, resulting in a positive correlation between earnings shocks and financial portfolios. Although this makes
no sense in terms of diversification, firms have incentives to promote
it, as it can be a good mechanism to induce effort on the part of employees. In this book, we emphasize portfolio diversification across
risk categories, identifying households that hold only risk-free assets,
as well as the most popular portfolio combinations.

Table I.4 suggests that an increasing number of households now
include risky assets in their portfolios. By-products of this tendency
are the observed increases in the proportion of households that
combine riskless with risky assets and of those that have complete
portfolios combining all risk categories. However, in most countries,
the vast majority of households still hold only safe assets, despite
the return premiums expected on risky assets. This "participation
puzzle" is studied both theoretically and empirically in this book.
The proportion of households holding only very low-risk assets has
come down somewhat in some countries where it was quite high,
such as Italy and the Netherlands, but has remained relatively stable
in others, such as the United States (stabilized around 25 percent).

The country studies explore the factors that are most likely to
affect the decision to invest in risky assets and focus especially on
wealth, age, and education. Table I.5 reports, for each quartile of the
asset or wealth distribution and for the top 5 percent, the fraction of
households investing in risky assets. In all countries, participation
in the equity market and in risky assets is strongly correlated with
wealth. For instance, in the United States, the fraction of investors
with direct or indirect stockholding rises from 4.4 percent in the
bottom quartile to 86.7 percent in the top quartile, and to over 93
percent in the top 5 percent of the financial wealth distribution. One
of the most pronounced differences is the probability of owning a
private business, which is substantially higher for the wealthy than
for the nonwealthy. It is argued in chapter 10 that this is likely due
to a combination of the financing requirements for setting up a
business with the "capitalist spirit" that induces a "love of wealth"
for its own sake.

The finding that wealth matters in determining participation points
to an important reason that the portfolios of wealthy households are
not simply scaled-up versions of their less wealthy counterparts, as
in the classical portfolio model of chapter 1. Two important implications arise. First, understanding the relationship between wealth and

Table I.5
Proportion of households investing in risky assets, by asset quartiles

	Quar-tile I	Quar-tile II	Quar-tile III	Quar-tile IV	Top 5%	Average
Direct stockholding						
United States	1.4	6.9	20.6	47.9	70.1	19.2
United Kingdom	0.0	4.4	28.3	53.6	67.9	21.6
Netherlands	0.5	3.7	13.0	40.4	77.1	14.4
Germany	2.6	6.6	11.4	19.4	31.9	10.0
Italy	0.5	2.7	5.8	17.5	32.2	7.3
Direct and indirect stockholding						
United States	4.4	38.3	66.0	86.7	93.7	48.9
United Kingdom	4.9	11.9	37.8	71.1	83.9	31.5
Netherlands	4.4	16.9	36.8	75.9	92.3	33.5
Germany	6.6	17.6	22.1	29.3	41.6	18.9
Italy	3.4	10.8	19.6	38.9	54.6	18.9
Risky financial assets						
United States	4.4	38.6	66.4	87.2	93.8	49.2
United Kingdom	4.9	12.0	38.5	74.0	86.9	32.4
Netherlands	0.8	8.0	26.0	64.4	87.5	24.8
Germany	8.9	24.1	29.2	38.2	51.4	25.1
Italy	4.4	13.5	24.1	44.2	57.7	22.1
Total risky assets						
United States	15.4	48.0	70.8	93.2	98.8	56.9
United Kingdom	n.a.	n.a.	n.a.	n.a.	n.a.	n.a.
Netherlands	1.0	25.5	29.7	70.0	96.6	31.5
Germany	n.a.	n.a.	n.a.	n.a.	n.a.	n.a.
Italy	11.6	35.7	50.0	75.6	94.2	43.8

Sources: United States: 1998 Survey of Consumer Finances. United Kingdom: 1997–1998 Financial Research Survey. Netherlands: 1997 CentER Saving Survey. Germany (unified): 1993 data, drawn from the Income and Expenditure Survey. Italy: 1998 Survey of Household Income and Wealth.
Note: The first three panels report the proportion of investors by gross financial wealth quartiles. The last panel reports the proportion of investors by total asset quartiles. All statistics use sample weights.

the decision to hold particular assets provides insights into the likely distributional consequences of taxing particular asset categories. This is discussed at length in chapter 3. The second implication relates to surveys based on representative population samples. Since the wealthy segment tends to hold most assets but constitutes a very small proportion of the population (and hence of the sample), the only way to obtain a clearer picture of how aggregate holdings of various asset categories are related to household-level character- istics is to oversample wealthy households. Indeed, this is the ap- proach taken in some surveys, notably the U.S. Survey of Consumer Finances.

One feature that emerges from table I.5 is that differences in stockholding across countries are essentially due to differences in the propensity to hold stock in the wealthier segments of the population. In all countries, households in the bottom two quartiles of the wealth distribution behave very similarly in terms of ownership of stocks or other risky assets. While in the United States and the Netherlands the vast majority of households in the top 5 percent of the wealth distri- bution hold some risky assets, in Italy and Germany about half of this class of investors have no direct or indirect stock holding. This puzzling difference may be due in part to some combination of national differences in these households' background risk and in- formational and other entry costs. Heaton and Lucas (2000a) stress that wealthy households face considerable background risk through holdings of business wealth. Chapter 7 finds that even wealthy Italian households lack information on financial investment opportunities.

A fairly robust finding of these country studies is a hump-shaped age profile of participation in risky assets, reported in table I.6.[3] The fraction of investors in risky assets peaks in the 50–59 age bracket and declines during retirement.[4] Interpreting this stylized fact is a challenge, but a plausible story can be told in the context of a model with fixed costs of participating in the stock market (see chapters 1 and 2). The young typically have a small ratio of accumulated wealth to expected future earnings and should optimally borrow to con- sume and take advantage of the equity premium. Faced with bor- rowing constraints and with limited cash on hand, they tend to hold small amounts of assets or none at all. Thus, if stock market partici- pation entails any fixed costs in the form of entry fees, informational requirements, or time, the young will be more likely to abstain. As households age, they accumulate wealth, information, and experi-

Table I.6
Proportion of households investing in risky assets, by age

	Under 30	30–39	40–49	50–59	60–69	70 and over	Total
Direct stockholding							
United States	11.8	16.0	21.2	24.8	23.7	18.2	19.2
United Kingdom	10.8	19.6	24.5	28.1	26.2	18.5	21.6
Netherlands	4.7	6.8	13.4	18.4	17.8	21.2	14.4
Germany	8.5	11.3	12.1	11.2	10.1	6.1	10.0
Italy	3.4	9.9	8.4	9.3	6.4	4.2	7.3
Direct and indirect stockholding							
United States	34.3	51.8	58.3	61.4	47.1	32.4	48.9
United Kingdom	20.4	31.5	37.0	41.2	34.8	21.9	31.5
Netherlands	12.1	25.6	33.7	40.1	38.6	35.9	33.5
Germany	18.6	21.8	22.0	21.0	17.1	11.7	18.9
Italy	11.9	27.5	24.2	23.4	15.8	7.8	18.9
Risky financial assets							
United States	34.5	51.8	58.5	61.5	47.9	33.4	49.2
United Kingdom	20.9	32.0	37.7	42.2	36.4	23.1	32.4
Netherlands	8.7	15.6	21.0	31.1	31.1	35.1	24.8
Germany	23.9	28.2	28.0	27.8	23.1	18.0	25.1
Italy	17.3	30.3	26.9	26.3	20.6	10.3	22.1
Total risky assets							
United States	38.7	58.6	67.0	68.4	59.2	42.4	56.9
United Kingdom	n.a.	n.a.	n.a.	n.a.	n.a.	n.a.	n.a
Netherlands	12.8	22.9	29.6	41.2	32.8	38.8	31.5
Germany	n.a.	n.a.	n.a.	n.a.	n.a.	n.a.	n.a.
Italy	32.4	50.6	50.6	51.7	45.9	26.4	43.8

Sources: United States: 1998 Survey of Consumer Finances. United Kingdom: 1997–1998 Financial Research Survey. Netherlands: 1997 CentER Saving Survey. Germany (unified): 1993 data, Income and Expenditure Survey. Italy: 1998 Survey of Household Income and Wealth.
Note: All statistics use sample weights.

ence in handling their finances, and they are less likely to be deterred from entering the stock market. What happens after retirement depends on various factors, including the extent to which the elderly decumulate wealth, the ease with which stocks can be liquidated, and any tax incentives or disincentives for passing accumulated capital gains on to descendants.

Chapter 11 looks closely at the portfolio behavior of the elderly, drawing on U.S. data. A striking finding is that the incidence of stock holding has increased among virtually all age groups even in this segment of the population. Education is highly correlated with the propensity of the elderly to hold stocks, even after controlling for wealth, income, age, marital status, and the subjective probability of survival. This finding parallels similar results for the population as a whole and is consistent with the importance of informational considerations in the decision to invest in risky assets.

Insofar as informational considerations are important, we can expect further increases in the percentage of households holding risky assets. Informational requirements are being continually lowered through the proliferation of opportunities for indirect asset holding. Furthermore, knowledge about portfolio management and investment strategies spreads through observation of other household choices and advertising campaigns.

On the liability side, there is a general trend toward borrowing; higher fractions of households have some type of debt. In Italy, starting from a very low base, this fraction more than doubled in the 1990s. In the Netherlands, the increase in the use of debt results mainly from increases in the percentage of households with mortgages and checking account overdrafts. In the United States, where debt ownership was established earlier, the increase has been smaller and is associated with increased use of mortgages and credit card liabilities. A recently documented fact is that households often carry debt despite the generally high interest rates on credit card debt and even while they have positive holdings in liquid, low-interest accounts. These unexploited arbitrage opportunities form yet another portfolio puzzle in need of resolution.

Portfolio Shares

When comparing portfolio shares across groups of households, it is useful to examine them conditional on participation, since unconditional shares would not distinguish the effects of relevant variables on the participation decision from those on the portfolio share given that the asset is held. As we have argued, the two decisions may be determined by distinct factors. Furthermore, many of the theoretical predictions of the classical portfolio theory refer to asset shares, not participation decisions. An example is the classical prediction that, given preferences characterized by constant relative risk aversion, the portfolio share of risky assets, conditional on holding it, should be independent of the level of wealth.

Table I.7 reports portfolio shares of risky assets across the wealth distribution in various countries, conditional on holding such assets. It reveals some common patterns but also significant international differences. In all the countries, the portfolio shares of risky assets are larger for the rich than for the poorer households, in particular with respect to risky total assets. While in principle causality could be running from the household's propensity to hold risky assets to the high wealth levels of successful risk takers, the detailed study of rich households in this book strongly suggests the converse. However, the positive correlation between the conditional share and wealth is less marked than that between the probability of owning and wealth. Indeed, in some countries, the relation between wealth and the conditional share of risky financial assets in financial wealth is relatively modest. The conclusion that wealth affects mainly the asset ownership decision is strengthened by regression analysis showing that a large part of the positive correlation between (conditional) risky asset shares and net worth revealed by simple tabulations tends to disappear when other factors are controlled for. The residual positive correlation is consistent with decreasing relative risk-aversion preferences but it is also consistent with decreasing portfolio management costs as the size of the portfolio increases.

The age pattern of risky portfolio shares, so crucial to understanding portfolio behavior over the life cycle, proves to be perhaps the most controversial issue in the empirical chapters of this book. Table I.8 reports the age profile of the conditional share for the various definitions of risky assets. In most countries, while there is a definite hump-shaped profile for the ownership of risky assets, conditional on owning them, the age profile of the share of risky assets is relatively flat. In some countries, there does seem to be some moderate rebalancing of the portfolio away from risky securities, but often this tends to disappear when other factors that evolve with age

Table I.7
Conditional asset shares, by asset quartiles

	Quar- tile I	Quar- tile II	Quar- tile III	Quar- tile IV	Top 5%	Average
Direct stockholding						
United States	32.9	33.0	25.6	34.9	37.9	34.6
United Kingdom	–.–	73.1	64.3	28.8	23.3	42.7
Netherlands	68.3*	31.5	34.1	48.2	66.6	47.6
Germany	23.8	16.7	15.8	19.5	22.5	18.6
Italy	23.3*	36.8	21.0	24.1	22.1	23.0
Direct and indirect stockholding						
United States	40.7	45.0	49.0	60.4	64.0	59.6
United Kingdom	n.a.	n.a.	n.a.	n.a.	n.a.	n.a.
Netherlands	40.3*	32.7	37.3	55.2	66.1	53.6
Germany	26.7	21.9	20.6	22.0	24.5	21.8
Italy	53.4	50.9	50.2	50.0	65.1	57.3
Risky financial assets						
United States	40.7	44.9	49.0	61.3	65.2	60.5
United Kingdom	n.a.	n.a.	n.a.	n.a.	n.a.	n.a.
Netherlands	48.9*	31.0	36.4	50.6	61.7	49.7
Germany	28.9	25.0	24.8	27.2	30.2	26.3
Italy	51.4	54.2	53.1	56.4	77.1	65.4
Total risky assets						
United States	29.5	24.8	23.4	59.2	69.4	54.4
United Kingdom	n.a.	n.a.	n.a.	n.a.	n.a.	n.a.
Netherlands	20.9*	38.8	16.8	35.4	47.3	33.1
Germany	n.a.	n.a.	n.a.	n.a.	n.a.	n.a.
Italy	27.6	33.7	25.9	33.5	57.9	42.9

Sources: United States: 1998 Survey of Consumer Finances. United Kingdom: 1997–1998 Financial Research Survey. Netherlands: 1997 CentER Saving Survey. Germany (unified): 1993 data, Income and Expenditure Survey. Italy: 1998 Survey of Household Income and Wealth.
Note: The first three panels report asset shares, conditional on participation, by gross financial wealth quartiles. The last panel reports asset shares, conditional on participation, by total asset quartiles. All statistics use sample weights.
*The figure is based on fewer than twenty observations.

Table I.8
Conditional asset shares, by age

	Under 30	30–39	40–49	50–59	60–69	70 and over	Total
Direct stockholding							
United States	22.5	28.3	29.4	32.7	37.5	41.3	34.6
United Kingdom	57.1	51.3	46.7	38.9	33.0	37.6	42.7
Netherlands	24.2*	48.8	30.2	41.1	57.2	56.3	47.6
Germany	17.0	15.2	15.0	16.6	22.1	27.5	18.6
Italy	18.9*	22.3	23.4	23.7	22.8	22.7	23.0
Direct and indirect stockholding							
United States	52.0	53.4	61.0	61.4	60.8	57.9	59.6
United Kingdom	n.a.	n.a.	n.a.	n.a.	n.a.	n.a.	n.a
Netherlands	29.8*	37.5	42.9	54.9	61.6	59.1	53.6
Germany	20.6	19.3	16.9	19.0	26.2	32.6	21.8
Italy	47.9	52.5	52.2	56.2	53.2	59.1	57.3
Risky financial assets							
United States	52.1	53.7	61.8	62.1	61.4	59.4	60.5
United Kingdom	n.a.	n.a.	n.a.	n.a.	n.a.	n.a.	n.a
Netherlands	32.1*	40.0	37.0	43.2	56.6	64.0	49.7
Germany	24.8	23.2	20.7	22.3	30.2	40.8	26.3
Italy	46.4	58.0	58.3	67.0	71.4	71.1	65.4
Total risky assets							
United States	44.4	43.0	52.9	58.8	56.2	56.1	54.4
United Kingdom	n.a.	n.a.	n.a.	n.a.	n.a.	n.a.	n.a
Netherlands	24.2*	27.1	28.0	34.8	32.3	44.7	33.1
Germany	n.a.	n.a.	n.a.	n.a.	n.a.	n.a.	n.a.
Italy	42.8	43.9	38.6	46.5	44.3	40.5	42.9

Sources: United States: 1998 Survey of Consumer Finances. United Kingdom: 1997–1998 Financial Research Survey. Netherlands: 1997 CentER Saving Survey. Germany (unified): 1993 data, Income and Expenditure Survey. Italy: 1998 Survey of Household Income and Wealth.
Note: All statistics use sample weights.
*The figure is based on fewer than twenty observations.

are controlled for. On the whole, a fair summary of the evidence is that over the life cycle, most of the action concerns the decision to enter and exit the market for risky assets, not managing the portfolio share. This again suggests that considerable emphasis, in theoretical as well as in empirical research, should be put on ownership decisions. One exception to this pattern is the Netherlands, where both the ownership and the conditional share are increasing at all ages.

The different behavior of participation and of portfolio shares implies that an observed increase in risky assets in proportion to a group's assets does not allow one to distinguish the part due to increased participation from that due to an increase in portfolio shares of those already participating. Thus, whenever possible, one should distinguish between unconditional and conditional portfolio shares. In most countries, the unconditional portfolio share of risky assets increased during the 1990s. These trends reflect partly an increase in the proportion of stockholders (table I.4) and partly an increase in the share of risky assets among holders. Calculations done in the country chapters show that in some countries, the two increases are equally important.

The chapter on taxation provides some unexpected corroborating evidence for the thesis that there is an element of history in portfolios that prevents households from rebalancing too frequently. It finds that asset selection tends to be more sensitive to taxation of returns than does portfolio composition. As Jim Poterba puts it, "Portfolio rebalancing may be something that investors do less frequently than asking if they are holding the right kind of assets." If portfolio rebalancing is so infrequent as to render age irrelevant for conditional portfolio shares, then justifying this finding on the basis of either analytical or computational portfolio models will be some challenge indeed. Analytical models (chapter 1) stress the role of the length of the horizon for optimal choice of portfolio composition. Computational large-scale, finite-life models (chapter 2) similarly imply policy functions for portfolio shares that are sensitive to age, at least over some range of cash on hand. Moreover, professional advisers follow a sort of rule of thumb of encouraging investors to reduce their portfolio share of risky assets as they age. It is unlikely that such portfolio inertia can be explained by transaction costs alone. Perhaps habit persistence or some form of loss aversion with a reference point related to past consumption could contribute to some inertia in portfolio composition.

Even if further scrutiny reveals the age pattern of the conditional risky portfolio share to be hump shaped in the data, theory will still have difficulty in explaining the low portfolio shares of the young. The gist of the theoretical models is that young savers should choose relatively high shares of risky assets so as to take advantage of the equity premium, even though they may not be able to hold large amounts because of limited cash on hand. Chapter 2 shows that these results hold even when households are not allowed to borrow in any form and that if they can, households should borrow to invest in risky assets. Perhaps a low portfolio share in risky financial assets can be justified by lumpy investment in real assets, such as housing, which tends to be made at an early age and may force young households to adopt more conservative financial portfolios as they save toward accumulating a down payment.

III   The Road Ahead

Theory

The contrast between the implications of existing theory and the empirical findings points to a number of fruitful avenues for future theoretical work on household portfolios. On the portfolio choice between risky and risk-free financial assets, both the theoretical and empirical chapters support the thesis that fixed costs of participation in markets for risky assets play a crucial role. The exact nature of these costs and how they affect the decision to enter and exit the stock market need to be understood further, and they are the focus of ongoing research.[5]

The state of knowledge on optimal portfolio composition is less encouraging. It should not be too hard to rationalize the increased propensity of wealthier households to hold more types of assets in the context of models with fixed costs of asset market participation. Theoretical models, however, tend to imply that households with less cash on hand (and correspondingly lower ratios of accumulated financial wealth to labor income) should invest more in risky assets to exploit the wealth-generating potential of the equity premium, while richer ones should be able to sacrifice some of this potential in favor of risk-free assets. Yet this pattern is exactly the opposite of what is observed in the data: the tendency of poorer households to specialize in risk-free assets and of richer households to add risk. It remains to be seen whether the ease of risky investment through financial intermediaries, combined with the desire of poorer households to get rich, fueled by the recent success stories in international stock markets, will serve to reverse this pattern.

The apparent invariance with age of the conditional portfolio composition, and the apparent lack of sensitivity to tax treatment, suggest that households may be paying more attention to picking the right assets rather than to getting the right portfolio shares. If this is the case, the attempt to characterize household portfolios by means of models that assume frequent and costless portfolio rebalancing may be doomed to failure. Still, it would be surprising if this apparent neglect of portfolio composition persisted in the future, as entry and adjustment costs are steadily lowered.

Although risky financial assets have recently grown in significance as components of household portfolios without correspondingly clear effects on total risky assets, the interaction between financial and real assets is obviously of interest. This is influenced by liquidity constraints and events associated with the life cycle. For the young household, the natural desire to own a home is bound to influence their financial portfolio. The elderly who downsize from larger to smaller homes or move in with their children face the question of allocating their liquid funds, including the proceeds from the sale of the house, among alternative financial assets. At this stage, the taxation of inheritances and inter-vivos transfers may be an important factor. Finally, the rich who own a private business are bound to consider business returns in selecting their financial portfolio. Very little work has been done on such interactions, and much can be learned from work that models the contributions of real assets, not only in budget constraints but also in service flows, pride of ownership, and power of control.

Whether one studies financial or real assets, a host of unexplored issues relate to taxation. Dividend and interest taxation, though nontrivial, is likely to be the easiest theoretical topic. Others, such as taxation of capital gains accruing since purchase but paid only on dismissal, challenge the power of even modern computational algorithms. Moreover, the chapter on taxation reveals wide international differences in the treatment of assets and liabilities, which make theoretical generalizations more problematic.

Although this book is probably the first of its kind on household portfolios, a substantial body of literature on asset prices already

exists. Since prices are equilibrium outcomes of asset markets, research on household portfolios and asset pricing should eventually
be integrated, in the context of general equilibrium models with
portfolio choice. So far, asset pricing models have had limited success in explaining limited asset market participation and portfolio
diversification and have encountered asset pricing puzzles such
as the equity premium and interest rate puzzles. This book shows
that portfolio models also face puzzles with participation and conditional portfolio shares, even when they assume historically given
return processes. There is little doubt that the two literatures are des-
tined to merge, but the chances for a successful marriage will be
improved if each is given time to solve its own puzzles and ambig-
uities beforehand.

Empirical Research

Empirical research has revealed significant regularities in how households allocate their savings among assets. Some of the findings appear to be well established, while others need further applied
work. Perhaps the most important solid finding is that most households do not diversify but specialize in a few assets, mainly the safest
and most liquid. An important feature of the data is that few households, even among the richest segment of the population, hold complete portfolios. Can this feature be fully accounted for by entry and
management costs? Are other factors impeding diversification, and if
so what are they? One firm conclusion here is that some form of
participation costs is essential to understanding portfolio behavior,
but more empirical work is needed to determine whether they are
sufficient to account for the empirical regularities and how they interact with other factors.

   Another area that needs more work is the age-portfolio profile.
Overall, the chapters suggest that while the age-ownership profile is
hump shaped, the conditional share is poorly correlated with age.
One problem with this characterization is that the age-portfolio correlation is essentially identified by the cross-sectional variation,
while age may actually be picking up unobserved correlated factors
that are correlated with age. As is pointed out neatly in chapter 4, to
identify the effect of age on the portfolio, fixed-effects models should
be used to account for unobserved heterogeneity, which is somewhat
problematic in discrete-choice models with short panels. The future

availability of longer panels may enable us to sort out better the age effect of unobserved heterogeneity.

There remain a number of important issues that are only touched on in this book and that future research should clarify. As theory predicts, households that are more averse to risk should be more reluctant to hold risky assets. Barsky, Juster, Kimball, and Shapiro (1997) use survey responses to hypothetical lotteries to construct measures of Arrow-Pratt risk aversion and find that households differ markedly in their willingness to bear risk. Moreover, risk aversion has considerable predictive power on the actual risk-bearing choices of households. This implies that risk aversion may be an important omitted variable, which could bias empirical results.

A related issue is the role of background risk. Recent empirical research supports the theoretical prediction that households in risky environments tend to tilt their portfolios toward safe assets. An interesting question is whether international differences in households' exposure to uninsurable risks could explain the large differences in portfolio holdings documented in tables I.4 and I.5. Finally, one important task for future empirical research is to study the joint behavior of saving and portfolio decisions. While theorists have been working on such joint analysis at least since the seminal works of Merton (1969) and Samuelson (1969), empirical research on household savings and on portfolio choice has proceeded separately. It is time to rejoin the issues!

Financial Innovation and Education

A fairly robust finding here concerns the relevance of information and education to the participation decision. Better-educated households are more likely to hold diversified portfolios, appear to be better informed about the existence and properties of different assets, and are thus better able to take advantage of investment opportunities. The evidence for Italy and Germany suggests that many households are poorly informed about financial matters and that a large part of the population is even unaware of the existence of stocks and other basic financial assets. Lack of knowledge of investment opportunities and partial information on return and risk characteristics conflict with the full information hypothesis of most portfolio models. Empirically it seems that some households cannot hold diversified portfolios simply because they know only a subset of the full menu of assets. Applied work can help determine how important lack of knowledge is to understanding observed household portfolios and discover how households learn about asset types. The development of theoretical household portfolio models that incorporate partial ignorance, partial information, and learning would shed light on this issue. Lessons from this exercise are likely to be relevant not only to academic research but also to practitioners in the financial industry who are interested in marketing financial products to targeted groups.

IV Conclusion

The broadest message of this book is that taking the step from understanding saving to understanding portfolio behavior in a world with financial and real assets is not simple but is certainly worthwhile. Economists of different backgrounds, whether in macroeconomics, microeconomics, or econometrics, have a good deal to contribute to household portfolio analysis. This is especially so since, as this book shows, the number of puzzles is still quite high compared to that of stylized facts, and state-of-the-art econometric and computational techniques can be applied to resolve portfolio puzzles. Many doctoral dissertations and research papers are still to be written before these issues are cleared up.

Notes

1. Quadratic or exponential utility is often assumed to obtain closed-form solutions. Quadratic utility implies increasing risk aversion with wealth and rules out any precautionary wealth accumulation intended to buffer consumption against earnings shocks. Exponential utility implies precautionary wealth holdings but also zero wealth elasticity of risky investment.

2. Where the data available are less detailed, authors report broader aggregates.

3. The age profiles reported in table I.5 are derived from a single cross section and therefore might be contaminated by cohort effects. The issue of disentangling age, cohort, and time effects in asset participation and portfolio shares is discussed in detail in the individual country chapters, all of them using repeated cross-sectional data or panel data. In general, the authors find that the data are best described by a combination of age and time effects and that cohort effects in portfolio decisions are not of paramount importance. This implies that the cross-sectional profile reported in table I.5 provides a good approximation also to the individual profile.

4. Hump-shaped age profiles are not uniformly corroborated by econometric analysis. An increase in participation at early ages appears empirically more robust than a de-

cline in participation after retirement. For example, the age-participation profile for risky financial assets is positively sloped in the Netherlands, though the profile for total risky assets exhibits a hump shape.

5. Some recent work studies the interaction between adjustment costs and portfolio choices. Vissing-Jørgersen (2000) tries to identify empirically various forms of portfolio adjustment costs. Luttmer (1999) studies the effect of adjustment costs on optimal cash holdings.

I

Theoretical and Methodological Issues

1 What Does Classical Theory Have to Say About Household Portfolios?

Christian Gollier

This chapter examines what determines the structure of household portfolios. Owning risky assets is compensated by higher expected returns on one's portfolio. Risk-averse households must determine their best trade-off between risk and expected return. We can separate the determinants of households' portfolios into three broad categories. The first group is genetic: we cannot a priori exclude the possibility that risk aversion is heterogeneous in the economy, due to either different genes or different human capitals. The second group is linked to the type of objective pursued by households that invest in financial markets. Is it specifically to accumulate wealth for retirement or to finance lifetime consumption? Is it for their own consumption or for that of their children? The third group is a set of factors external to the decision maker: the distribution of returns, tax incentives, liquidity and short-sales constraints, access to credit, and so on.

In a static framework, the portfolio choice problem is classically formalized by introducing a concave utility function on final consumption. Under the standard axioms on decision under uncertainty (von Neumann and Morgenstern 1944), households will select the portfolio that maximizes the expected utility of their final consumption. The degree of concavity of the utility, as defined by Arrow (1971) and Pratt (1964), characterizes their degree of absolute risk aversion, which can be measured by answers to questionnaires on risk choices. When this information is combined with the specific distribution of returns to financial assets, one can compute the optimal portfolio. An increase in absolute risk aversion reduces the demand for risky assets. In the same spirit, an increase in wealth increases the demand for risky assets if absolute risk aversion is decreasing. This mechanism is well understood and is cited in most textbooks in market finance.

The temptation is to assert that this is the only mechanism that is well understood in this field. For example, important progress was made in the late 1960s by introducing time into portfolio strategies. Usually households have such long-term objectives as retirement when they invest in financial markets. How does the length of the time horizon affect the optimal structure of the portfolio? In other words, how does the option to purchase stocks tomorrow modify the attitude toward portfolio risk today? Pioneering work by Mossin (1968), Merton (1969), and Samuelson (1969) answered this question in a simple but intriguing way: the intrinsically dynamic structure of portfolio management has no effect on the solution. Under their assumptions, the sequence of portfolio structures that are statically optimal is also dynamically optimal. In other words, households should act as if each period of investment were the last before retirement. Myopia is optimal. But it is often forgotten that this result holds only under very restrictive conditions on the utility function. That is, myopia is optimal only if the utility function exhibits constant relative risk aversion. In this chapter, I explain why this is so and under what conditions households that can invest longer in risky assets should invest more in them.

Household portfolios do not serve only such long-term objectives as financing retirement. An important share of savings is invested in liquid funds that act as households buffer stocks. When they have been lucky on their previous investments, they can reduce their saving rate and cash in the benefits of the larger-than-expected portfolio returns immediately. They can also increase their saving rate against an adverse shock on portfolio returns. This means that households do not bear the accumulated lifetime portfolio risk at the time of retirement. Rather, they can spread this risk over their lifetime consumption pattern, which allows for some time diversification through consumption smoothing. The implication is a testable hypothesis: households that can adapt their contributions to their pension funds over time will select riskier portfolio structures.

Two other factors have important implications for household portfolios. First, the presence of liquidity constraints on the consumption-saving strategy should be taken into account to design portfolio strategies. Indeed, liquidity constraints, if binding sometime in the future, will preclude the transfer of capital risks over time through consumption smoothing. It will induce more conservative portfolio management for households that are most likely to face a binding liquidity constraint. Second, most risks borne by households are not portfolio risks but uninsurable risks affecting their human capital. Intuition suggests that households bearing a larger risk on their human capital should invest less in risky assets.

In examining several factors influencing the optimal portfolio composition, I present each factor in isolation in a simplified model that excludes the others in order to help readers understand the nature of this factor without obscuring the big picture. The analysis of how these factors can be combined is left for the calibrations that will be presented in the following chapter. Section 1.1 presents the classical static portfolio problem under uncertainty. It will be useful for the remainder of the chapter to note that this problem is symmetric to the dynamic consumption problem under certainty. In section 1.2, we derive the main properties of the optimal static portfolio. The effect of background risk is examined in section 1.3 and the repeated nature of portfolio management in section 1.4. The notion of time diversification is developed in section 1.5. Finally, in section 1.6, we examine the effect of the liquidity constraint before providing some concluding remarks.

1.1   The Basic Model and Its Applications

Most of the chapter deals with the properties of the following model:

$$\max_{C_1,\ldots,C_N} \sum_{i=1}^{N} p_i u(C_i) \tag{1.1}$$

$$s.t. \quad \sum_{i=1}^{N} p_i \pi_i C_i = X, \tag{1.2}$$

where $(p_1,\ldots,p_N)$ and $(\pi_1,\ldots,\pi_N)$ are two vectors of nonnegative scalars and u is a real-valued, increasing, and concave function. The only specificity of this model with respect to the basic problem of consumer theory is the additivity of the objective function. Under the concavity of u, the necessary and sufficient condition for program 1.1 under constraint 1.2 is written as

$$u'(C_i) = \xi \pi_i, \quad i = 1,\ldots,N, \tag{1.3}$$

where ξ is the Lagrangian multiplier associated with the constraint.

The most obvious application of program 1.1 is the static portfolio problem of a risk-averse investor in an Arrow-Debreu economy. More specifically, consider an economy in which investors live for one period. At the beginning of the period, the investor is endowed with a sure wealth X. He does not know the state of the world that will prevail at the end of the period. There are N states of the world indexed by i, $i = 1, \ldots, N$. The uncertainty is described by the probability p_i that state i occurs, with $\sum_i p_i = 1$. Consumption takes place only after the realization of i is observed. The agent invests his endowment in a portfolio of assets that will be liquidated at the end of the period to finance consumption. We assume that financial markets are complete. This implies that for each state i, there exists an associated state price (per unit of probability) $\pi_i \geq 0$. In other words, the agent must pay $p_i \pi_i$ at the beginning of the period to increase his consumption by one unit in state i. Vector $(C_1, \ldots, C_N)$ is the state-contingent consumption plan of the agent, and equation 1.2 is the budget constraint of the investor. This vector can also be seen as a portfolio of Arrow-Debreu securities. The objective function in equation 1.1 is the ex ante expected utility of the investor who selects this portfolio. This application has been extensively used in the theory of finance during the past three decades.

In this presentation, we assume that the agent has no income ex post. Introducing state-contingent incomes is not a problem when markets are complete. Indeed, X can also be seen as the ex ante market value of these state-contingent incomes, that is, $X = \sum_i p_i \pi_i Y_i$, where Y_i is the household's income in state i. This is the main feature of market completeness, as agents can transfer their individual risks to the market.

Another application of program 1.1 is the lifetime consumption-saving problem under certainty. Consider a household that lives for N periods, from period $i = 1$ to period $i = N$. There is no uncertainty about the net present value of its incomes. The household's net discounted wealth at the beginning of period $i = 1$ equals X. Vector $(C_1, \ldots, C_N)$ represents the time-dependent consumption plan, with C_i measuring consumption in period i. The objective function is to maximize the discounted utility of consumption over the lifetime of the household. Parameter p_i in equation 1.1 is the discount factor associated with period i. To avoid problems of time consistency in decision making, it is often assumed that $p_i = \beta^i$. People can finance their consumption in period i by purchasing in period 1 zero coupon bonds maturing in period i. The gross rate of return of such bonds is denoted $(p_i \pi_i)^{-1}$. Constraint 1.2 is the household's lifetime budget constraint. Program 1.1 has been a cornerstone of the permanent income hypothesis and of life cycle model in macroeconomics.

In spite of their technical equivalence, these two problems are different in nature. For example, in the portfolio problem, the concavity of the utility function represents risk aversion, whereas in the consumption-saving problem it implies aversion to consumption fluctuations. This means that the agent is simultaneously willing to insure risks perfectly if insurance prices are fair ($\pi_i = 1$ for all i) and to smooth consumption over time if the return on bonds equals the rate of impatience. This aversion to fluctuations of consumption across time or states is measured by the Arrow-Pratt index of absolute aversion, which is defined by $A(C) = -u''(C)/u'(C)$. It is more convenient in general to use an index of relative aversion, $\rho(C) = CA(C) = -Cu''(C)/u'(C)$. In the consumption-saving problem, ρ is the inverse of the well-known elasticity of intertemporal substitution.

These dual interpretations of the theoretical model suggest two ways to estimate ρ. Viewing it as a degree of risk aversion, one can estimate it by answering the following question: What is the share of that wealth that one is ready to pay to escape the risk of gaining or losing a share α of that wealth with equal probability? Let x be this (certainty-equivalent) share of wealth. Suppose that the agent has constant relative risk aversion (CRRA), which implies that

$$u(C) = \frac{C^{1-\rho}}{1-\rho}. \tag{1.4}$$

Normalizing wealth to unity,[1] this implies that x is the solution of the following equation:

$$0.5\frac{(1-\alpha)^{1-\rho}}{1-\rho} + 0.5\frac{(1+\alpha)^{1-\rho}}{1-\rho} = \frac{(1-x)^{1-\rho}}{1-\rho}. \tag{1.5}$$

Table 1.1 relates x to ρ, when $\alpha = 10$ percent or $\alpha = 30$ percent.

If we take on the risk of gaining or losing 10 percent of one's wealth, we would consider an answer $x = 0.5\%, \ldots, 2\%$ as sensible. This implies that it is reasonable to believe that relative risk aversion is somewhere between 1 and 4. In other words, a relative risk aversion superior to 10 seems foolish, because it implies very high relative risk premiums. In particular, note that a relative risk aversion of

Table 1.1
Relative certainty-equivalent loss x associated to the risk of gaining or losing a share α of wealth, with constant relative risk aversion ρ

Relative risk aversion	$\alpha = 10\%$	$\alpha = 30\%$
$\rho = 0,5$	0.3%	2.3%
$\rho = 1$	0.5	4.6
$\rho = 4$	2.0	16.0
$\rho = 10$	4.4	24.4
$\rho = 40$	8.4	28.7

40 implies that one would be ready to pay as much as 8.4 percent of one's wealth to escape the risk of gaining or losing 10 percent of it!

The other approach is to see ρ as the degree of relative aversion to consumption fluctuations. Consider an agent who consumes income $1 - \alpha$ in even years and $1 + \alpha$ in odd years. He is offered the chance to smooth his consumption by paying a premium x on his average income. What is the critical value of x that makes the agent indifferent between the two consumption plans? Under CRRA, the relationship between x, ρ, and α is governed by exactly the same formula, 1.5.[2] Looking at table 1.1, an interval $[1, 4]$ for the degree of relative aversion to consumption fluctuations over time seems to be reasonable. Barsky, Juster, Kimball, and Shapiro (1997) used experimental data from the Health and Retirement Study in the United States to measure risk aversion and aversion to consumption fluctuations for people older than 50. They reported values of ρ that are slightly larger than those suggested here.

The elegance of the model derives from the additivity of the objective function with respect to states of the world or time, depending on which application we have in mind. All the properties reported in the remainder of this chapter will be derived from this additive hypothesis. In the case of risk, we know that this hypothesis can be derived from the more fundamental independence axiom. A similar axiom can be built to derive an additive property for preferences with respect to time.

1.2 The Static Arrow-Debreu Portfolio Problem

After this discussion of the basic decision model, 1.1, we can now explore the main features of its solution. We consider an agent who lives for one period and has to invest his endowment X in a portfolio that will be liquidated at the end of the period to finance his final consumption. Of course, this model is completely unrealistic because it is static and because we assume market completeness. It is taken as a benchmark and will be extended to include dynamic strategies and market incompleteness in subsequent sections.

Condition 1.3 tells us that the demand C_i for asset i is a function of π_i alone: $C_i = \phi(\pi_i)$. This result is much more profound than appears at first. If there are two states i and j with the same state price per unit of probability $\pi_i = \pi_j$, the demand for the corresponding state-contingent claims should be the same: $C_i = C_j$. Otherwise it would be like purchasing a fair lottery ticket for gambling on the realization of states i or j. No risk-averse household wants to do that. This implies that all households' consumptions move in the same direction at the same time. All reduce consumption when an expensive state occurs, and all increase it when a cheap state is realized. Everyone is better off in a bull market, and everyone suffers in a bear market. This is possible because it is optimal to diversify away all diversifiable risks in the economy. This theoretical result is contradicted by the facts: some lose; others win. There are two reasons for this, both reflecting the fact that markets are incomplete. The first reason is that some individual risks, such as human capital risk, cannot be insured; we examine this problem in the next section. The other is that people do not diversify their portfolio enough. This remains a puzzle, as it means that people accept zero-mean risks.

We can measure the degree of risk exposure taken by a household with utility function u by the sensitivity of its consumption to difference in state prices. Fully differentiating condition 1.3 and eliminating the Lagrangian multiplier ξ yields

$$\phi'(\pi) = -\frac{\tau(\phi(\pi))}{\pi}, \tag{1.6}$$

where $\tau(C) = -u'(C)/u''(C) = (A(C))^{-1}$ is the degree of absolute risk tolerance of the agent. When ϕ' is zero, the agent takes no risk at all, since he has a consumption level ϕ that is independent of the state of nature. We see in equation 1.6 that this is the case only when absolute risk tolerance is zero, that is, the agent is infinitely risk averse. More generally, we see that the optimal exposure to risk, measured by ϕ', is increasing in the degree of absolute risk tolerance τ, as is intuitive.

Because state-dependent consumption is increasing in wealth, an increase in wealth induces the agent to take more portfolio risk if function τ is increasing. This is the case under decreasing absolute risk aversion (DARA).

An important question is whether all agents have the same portfolio structure. Consider two agents, respectively with utility function u_1 and u_2. We say that two portfolios, ϕ_1 and ϕ_2, have the same risk structure if the state-dependent final value of the first is a linear function of that of the second: $\phi_2(\pi) = a + b\phi_1(\pi)$ for all π. From condition 1.6, this is true for the optimal portfolios of agents u_1 and u_2 if and only if $\tau_2(a + b\phi_1(\pi)) = b\tau_1(\phi_1(\pi))$ for all π. This condition holds if and only if $\tau_i(c) = \alpha_1 + \theta c$, $i = 1, 2$, that is, when the two agents have linear absolute risk tolerances with the same slope. Thus, when all agents in the economy have linear absolute risk tolerances with the same slope, their final consumptions are linear with respect to each other; that is, their final consumption is linear in per capita gross domestic product.[3] This is possible only if all agents allocate their capital to two funds: one risk free and the other comprising all risky assets in the economy. The only difference in portfolio structure is the share of wealth invested in the risky fund. The standard two-fund separation theorem states that all agents allocate their wealth in that way when they have linear absolute risk tolerance with the same slope.

Let us assume that a two-fund separation result holds. Let R be the gross return of the risk-free asset. $\tilde{R}_s$ is the excess return of the risky fund. Let w denote the share of the initial endowment that is invested in the stock fund. The final consumption in this case equals $\tilde{C} = X(R + w\tilde{R}_s)$. The optimal share w of wealth invested in stocks is then obtained by the following condition:

$$E\tilde{R}_s u'(X(R + w\tilde{R}_s)) = 0. \tag{1.7}$$

What do we know about the properties of the optimal share of wealth invested in risky assets as a function of the parameters of the problem? As noted, an increase in absolute risk aversion reduces the optimal absolute risk exposure measured by Xw. Moreover, an increase in X increases the absolute exposure to risk if absolute risk aversion is decreasing ($A' < 0$). Consequently, an increase in initial wealth X always increases the optimal share w of wealth invested in the risky fund if the index of relative risk aversion $\rho(C)$ is decreasing in C. A substantial body of literature exists on the effect of a change in the distribution of excess returns on the demand for stocks. Contrary to intuition, it is not true in general that a first-order stochastically dominated shift in distribution of returns, or a Rothschild-Stiglitz increase in risk in returns, necessarily reduces the demand for stocks. This literature did not provide any testable property of optimal portfolio strategies and will therefore not be covered here.[4]

We can also estimate the optimal w by calibrating the model. Using a first-order Taylor approximation of the left-hand side of equation 1.7, we obtain the following formula:

$$w \simeq R \frac{E\tilde{R}_s}{\sigma_s^2} \frac{1}{\rho}, \tag{1.8}$$

where σ_s^2 is the variance of $\tilde{R}_s$, and ρ is the coefficient of relative risk aversion evaluated at wealth level XR. The approximation is exact when the utility function is CARA and $\tilde{R}_s$ is normally distributed.

Historically, the equity premium $E\tilde{R}_s$ has been around 6 percent per year over the century in U.S. markets.[5] The standard deviation of yearly U.S. stock returns over the same period is 16 percent. The real risk-free rate $R - 1$ averaged 1 percent per year. Combining this information with formula 1.8 yields an optimal relative share of wealth invested in risky assets that equals 220 percent and 55 percent for relative risk aversion of 1 and 4, respectively. This very large share with respect to observed portfolio compositions of U.S. households is commonly referred to as the asset allocation puzzle. It is probably better known, through its equilibrium interpretation, under the name of the equity premium puzzle, introduced by Mehra and Prescott (1985): in order to explain actual portfolio composition in the United States, one needs to assume a degree of relative risk aversion around 40 for the representative agent. From our discussion of the level of ρ, this is highly implausible. Kocherlakota (1996) surveys potential ways to solve the puzzle.

1.3 The Optimal Static Portfolio Composition with Background Risk

So far, we have assumed that the only source of risk that the household faces is portfolio risk. This is far from realistic, of course, since most of the observed volatility of households' earnings comes from variations in labor income. Typically risks related to human capital cannot be traded on Wall Street, and financial intermediaries such as insurers are not willing to underwrite such risks mainly because of moral hazard. Unemployment insurance is ineffective in most countries. This is particularly true of the risks of long-term unemployment, one of the central concerns of middle-class households in Europe. Thus, it appears to be important to adapt the basic portfolio problem to include an uninsurable background risk. The question is how the presence of a human capital risk affects the demand for stocks.

We will assume that the human capital risk is independent of portfolio risk. This is clearly unrealistic. Most shocks to the economy affect the marginal productivity of labor (wages) and the marginal productivity of capital (portfolio returns) in the same direction. This implies that human capital is usually positively correlated with asset returns. But allowing for statistical dependence is not a problem, at least in a mean-variance framework. In particular, a positive correlation makes human capital a substitute for stocks. Therefore, an increase in the correlation will reduce the demand for stocks. Baxter and Jermann (1997) observed that human capital risks are strongly closely correlated with the return on domestic assets but less closely related to the returns on foreign assets. Therefore, households should bias their portfolio in favor of foreign assets. The failure of the data to provide any evidence of such hedging strategy is another puzzle.

The rest of this section is devoted to the case of independent human capital risk. Intuition strongly suggests that independent risks are substitutes. By this I mean that the presence of one risk reduces the demand for other independent risks. This would mean that background risks have a tempering effect on the demand for stocks. Households that are subject to a larger (mean-preserving) uncertainty about their future labor incomes should be more conservative on their portfolio.

The theoretical model for treating this question is quite simple. Consider an agent with utility u on his final consumption. He is endowed with capital X at the beginning of the period, which can be invested in Arrow-Debreu securities as in the previous section. What is new here is that the final wealth of the agent equals the sum of the value of his portfolio and his labor income. Because the risk-free part of this income has been included, discounted, in X, we assume that this added sum has zero mean. This background risk is denoted $\tilde{\varepsilon}$ and is independent of the state of the world i. The portfolio problem is now written as

$$\max_{C_1,\ldots,C_N} \sum_{i=1}^{N} p_i Eu(C_i + \tilde{\varepsilon}), \tag{1.9}$$

subject to the unchanged budget constraint 1.2.

Let us define indirect utility function v, with $v(Z) = Eu(Z + \tilde{\varepsilon})$ for all Z. Thus, the above problem can be rewritten as

$$\max_{C_1,\ldots,C_N} \sum_{i=1}^{N} p_i v(C_i), \tag{1.10}$$

subject to equation 1.2. We conclude that the introduction of an independent background risk is equivalent to the transformation of the original utility function u into the indirect utility function v. This change in the attitude toward portfolio risk can be signed if and only if the degree of concavity of these two functions can be ranked in the sense of Arrow-Pratt. More specifically, the intuition that background risk negatively affects the demand for stocks would be sustained by the theory if v is more concave than u. Technically, this means that

$$E\tilde{\varepsilon} = 0 \Rightarrow \frac{-Eu''(C + \tilde{\varepsilon})}{Eu'(C + \tilde{\varepsilon})} \geq \frac{-u''(C)}{u'(C)} \tag{1.11}$$

for all C and $\tilde{\varepsilon}$. In general, this property does not hold. All utility functions that satisfy property 1.11 are said to be "risk vulnerable," to use the terminology introduced by Gollier and Pratt (1996). Using Taylor approximations, it is easy to prove that this property holds for small risks if and only if

$$A''(C) \geq 2A'(C)A(C), \tag{1.12}$$

where $A(C) = -u''(C)/u'(C)$ is absolute risk aversion. A simple sufficient condition for risk vulnerability is that A be decreasing and convex. Because the proof of this result is simple, we reproduce it here. The left-hand condition in equation 1.11 can be rewritten as

$$EA(C + \tilde{\varepsilon})u'(C + \tilde{\varepsilon}) \geq A(C)Eu'(C + \tilde{\varepsilon}). \tag{1.13}$$

But a decreasing and convex function A implies that

$$EA(C+\tilde{\varepsilon})u'(C+\tilde{\varepsilon}) \geq [EA(C+\tilde{\varepsilon})][Eu'(C+\tilde{\varepsilon})] \geq A(C)Eu'(C+\tilde{\varepsilon}). \tag{1.14}$$

The first inequality in equation 1.14 comes from the fact that both A and u' are decreasing in ε. The second inequality is an application of

Jensen's inequality, together with $A'' \geq 0$ and $E\tilde{\varepsilon} = 0$. Thus, the convexity of absolute risk aversion is sufficient.

Observe that the classically used power utility function (equation 1.4) has decreasing and convex absolute risk aversion, since $A(C) = \rho/C$. The conclusion is that the introduction of background risk in the calibration of household portfolios will imply a rebalancing toward the risk-free asset.

1.4 The Optimal Dynamic Portfolio Composition with Complete Markets

One of the main shortcomings of the standard portfolio problem examined in section 1.2 is that it is static. Technically, it is descriptive of the situation of an agent who invests his wealth for a retirement that will take place in one year. In this section, we examine the optimal portfolio composition for people who have more than one period before retirement. In other words, we examine the relationship between portfolio risk and time horizon.

In the formal literature, the horizon-riskiness issue has mainly been approached in addressing portfolios appropriate to age. Samuelson (1989) and several others have asked: "As you grow older and your investment horizon shortens, should you cut down your exposure to lucrative but risky equities?" The conventional wisdom says yes; long-horizon investors can tolerate more risk because they have more time to recoup transient losses.[6] This dictum has not received the imprimatur of science, however. As Samuelson (1963, 1989) in particular points out, this "time-diversification" argument relies on a fallacious interpretation of the law of large numbers: repeating an investment pattern over many periods does not make risk wash out in the long run. In the next section, we examine an alternative concept of time diversification.

To address this question, we consider the problem of an agent who has to manage a portfolio over time to maximize the expected utility of his consumption at retirement. We abstract from the consumption-saving problem by assuming that this portfolio is specific to retirement and that it cannot be used for consumption beforehand. Also, we normalize the risk-free rate to zero. This implies that a young and an old investor with the same discounted wealth today can secure the same level of consumption at retirement by investing in the riskless asset. If the risk-free rate were positive, the younger investor would implicitly be wealthier.

We can now understand why the age of the investor has an ambiguous effect on optimal portfolio composition. Unlike the old investor, the young agent has the option of investing in stocks in subsequent periods. This option has a positive value, which makes the younger agent implicitly wealthier, at least on average. Under DARA, that makes him less risk averse. This wealth effect increases positively the share of wealth invested in stocks. But taking a risk does not have the same comparative statics effect as getting its expected net payoff for sure, as is stressed in section 3. The fact that the younger agent will take a portfolio risk in the future plays the role of a background risk with respect to his portfolio choice problem in the present. This risk effect goes in the opposite direction from the wealth effect, under risk vulnerability. All this is made more complex by the dynamic aspect of the problem, in the sense that the portfolio risk that the young will take in the future can be made contingent on the accumulated portfolio value in previous periods.

This kind of dynamic problem is ordinarily solved by using backward induction. Let T denote the number of periods before retirement. Because we assumed that the decision maker's only concern is the welfare of the investor at the time of retirement, the objective is to maximize $Eu(\tilde{C}_T)$. Assuming complete markets for risks occurring during the last period, the problem is exactly the same as problems 1.1 and 1.2. Denoting X_{T-1} for the wealth that has been accumulated at the beginning of the last period, this problem is rewritten as

$$V_{T-1}(X_{T-1}) = \max_{C_{1T},\dots,C_{NT}} \sum_{i=1}^{N} p_i u(C_{iT}) \tag{1.15}$$

$$s.t. \quad \sum_{i=1}^{N} p_i \pi_i C_{iT} = X_{T-1}, \tag{1.16}$$

where C_{iT} is the demand for the Arrow-Debreu security associated with state i. Because we assume that there is no serial correlation in asset returns and that the random walk of returns is stationary, we do not index state prices π_i and probabilities p_i by T. In short, financial risks are assumed to be the same in each period. Again, with a negative serial correlation in asset returns, investing in stocks in the future may serve as partial insurance for portfolio risks taken today.

This would provide an additional incentive for young investors to increase the share of their wealth invested in stocks. We do not consider this possibility here.

Equation 1.15 brought the (Bellman) value function V_{T-1}. $V_{T-1}(X_{T-1})$ is the maximum expected utility of consumption at retirement that can be obtained when the household has accumulated capital X_{T-1} at the end of period $T - 1$. Then the portfolio problem at the beginning of period $T - 1$ when the accumulated capital at that date is X_{T-2} can be written as

$$V_{T-2}(X_{T-2}) = \max_{X_{1T-1},\ldots,X_{NT-1}} \sum_{i=1}^{N} p_i V_{T-1}(X_{iT-1}) \tag{1.17}$$

$$s.t. \quad \sum_{i=1}^{N} p_i \pi_i X_{iT-1} = X_{T-2}, \tag{1.18}$$

where X_{iT-1} is at the same time the demand at $T - 1$ for the Arrow-Debreu security associated with state i and the accumulated capital at the end of period $T - 1$ if state i occurs. The optimal portfolio strategy in period $T - 1$ is to maximize the expected value V_{T-1} (which is itself the maximal expected utility of final consumption) of the accumulated wealth at the end of the period. This will generate a dynamic portfolio strategy that is optimal, in the sense that it will maximize the expected utility of final consumption. Pursuing this method by backward induction, we obtain the full description of the optimal nonmyopic portfolio strategy, which is given by the set of functions $\{X_{it}(X_{t-1}) \mid i = 1, \ldots, N; \ t = 1, \ldots, T\}$, with $X_{iT}(X) = C_{iT}(X)$.

The question is to determine the impact of index t on the optimal portfolio composition $(X_{1t}(X), \ldots, X_{Nt}(X))$ for a given wealth X accumulated at the beginning of the period. To illustrate, we limit the analysis to the comparison between the optimal portfolio composition in periods $T - 1$ and T, assuming the same $X = X_{T-2} = X_{T-1}$. We see that the only difference between these two decision problems, 1.15 and 1.17, is the replacement of the original utility function u for retirement consumption by the value function V_{T-1} for accumulated wealth at the end of the period. We know that this is the case if and only if the degree of concavity of V_{T-1} is comparable to the degree of concavity of u in the sense of Arrow-Pratt. Thus, we need to evaluate the degree of concavity of V_{T-1}. This is done as follows. At the last period, the optimal portfolio composition, characterized by $C_{iT}(.)$, is the solution of

$$u'(C_{iT}(X)) = \xi(X)\pi_i, \tag{1.19}$$

subject to the budget constraint $\sum_i p_i \pi_i C_{iT}(X) = X$. Fully differentiating this condition with respect to X and eliminating π_i yields

$$C'_{iT}(X) = \frac{-\xi'(X)}{\xi(X)} \tau(C_{iT}(X)), \tag{1.20}$$

where $\tau(C) = -u'(C)/u''(C) = [A(C)]^{-1}$ is the degree of absolute risk tolerance of the agent. From the budget constraint, we have that $\sum_i p_i \pi_i C'_{iT}(X) = 1$. Using equation 1.20, this implies that

$$\frac{-\xi'(X)}{\xi(X)} = \left[\sum_i p_i \pi_i \tau(C_{iT}(X))\right]^{-1}. \tag{1.21}$$

On the other side, we know from the standard Lagrangian method that $V'_{T-1}(X) = \xi(X)$. This implies that

$$\frac{-V'_{T-1}(X)}{V''_{T-1}(X)} = \sum_i p_i \pi_i \tau(C_{iT}(X)). \tag{1.22}$$

The left-hand side of this equation is the weighted expectation of the absolute risk tolerance evaluated at the random final wealth. It is an expectation under the assumption that $\sum_i p_i \pi_i = 1$, which means that the risk-free rate is zero. Condition 1.22 means that the relative risk tolerance of the value function used to measure the optimal attitude toward portfolio risk at $T - 1$ is a weighted average of ex post absolute risk tolerance. This result was first obtained by Wilson (1968) in the context of static risk sharing. Suppose that function τ is convex. By Jensen's inequality, we then obtain that

$$\frac{-V'_{T-1}(X)}{V''_{T-1}(X)} \geq \tau\left(\sum_i p_i \pi_i C_{iT}(X)\right) = \tau(X) = \frac{-u'(X)}{u''(X)}. \tag{1.23}$$

Because this is true for any X, V_{T-1} is less concave than u in the sense of Arrow-Pratt. We conclude that other things being equal, the convexity of absolute risk tolerance is necessary and sufficient for younger people to take more portfolio risk. By symmetry, the concavity of absolute risk tolerance is necessary and sufficient for younger people to take less portfolio risk. This result was first obtained by Gollier and Zeckhauser (1998), who extended it to the more difficult case of incomplete markets.

The limit case is when absolute risk tolerance is linear, which corresponds to the set of functions exhibiting harmonic absolute risk aversion (HARA). For HARA preferences, the age of the investor has no effect on the optimal portfolio composition. Because this set of functions contains the only one for which a complete analytical solution for optimal portfolio strategies can be obtained, it is not a surprise that most economists specializing in this field recommend an age-independent portfolio strategy. It must be stressed, however, that there is no strong argument in favor of HARA functions except their simplicity. Whether absolute risk tolerance is concave, linear, or convex remains an open question for empirical investigation.

In this analysis, we have not considered an important factor: younger people usually face a larger background risk to human capital. As they grow older, the uncertainty over human capital is revealed by labor markets. From our discussion in section 1.3, this is likely to imply a tempering effect on the optimal demand for stocks.

1.5   Self-Insurance and Time Diversification

So far we have assumed that households have no control over deposits to and drawings on the fund of assets in each period. In other words, we assumed that capital is accumulated for a single objective: consumption in retirement. Obviously this is not a realistic assumption. Most households also use savings for precautionary motives. They increase their saving in case of an unexpected transitory increase in income and reduce it, or even become borrowers, in case of an adverse transitory shock to their incomes. Conversely, agents may decide to reduce their saving effort if they have been lucky on their portfolio. This means that agents can smooth shocks to their accumulated wealth by increasing or reducing consumption over several periods. As we will see, consumption smoothing plays the role of self-insurance, which implies more risk taking.

The simplest model that we could imagine for self-insurance over time is one model in which agents live for N periods $t = 1, \ldots, N$. They have cash-on-hand K prior to period 1. At each period, they receive noncapital income Y. They consume C_t from it in period t. The remainder they save in a risk-free asset whose gross return is R. Agents are allowed to take risk prior to period 1, but they are prohibited from doing so afterward. This simplified assumption is made here because we want to isolate the self-insurance effect of time. We will return to this point.

Let $\tilde{\varepsilon}$ denote the net payoff of the risk taken prior to period 1. In period 1, the aggregate wealth X will be the sum of cash on hand, the discounted value of future incomes, and the actual payoff of the lottery: $X = K + \sum_t R^{-t}Y + \varepsilon$. Given X, agents select the consumption plan that maximizes their discounted lifetime utility $V(X)$, which takes the following form:

$$V(X) = \max_{C_1,\dots,C_N} \sum_{t=1}^{N} \beta^t u(C_t) \tag{1.24}$$

$$s.t. \ \sum_{t=1}^{N} R^{-t}C_t = X, \tag{1.25}$$

where β is the discount factor on utility. This yields an optimal consumption plan $C_t(X)$, which is a function of the discounted wealth of the agent. To solve this problem, we can use the fact that it is equivalent to program 1.1 with $p_t = \beta^t$ and $\pi_t = (R\beta)^{-t}$. From equation 1.22, we directly infer that

$$\frac{-V'(X)}{V''(X)} = \sum_{t=1}^{N} R^{-t}\tau(C_t(X)). \tag{1.26}$$

Condition 1.26 characterizes the degree of tolerance toward the risk $\tilde{\varepsilon}$ taken prior to period 1. The absolute tolerance of wealth risk equals the discounted present value of future absolute tolerances of consumption risk. The simplest case is when $\beta R = 1$, when we know that it is optimal to smooth consumption perfectly. This yields

$$\frac{-V'(X)}{V''(X)} = \left[\sum_{t=1}^{N} R^{-t}\right] \tau\left(\frac{X}{\sum_{t=1}^{N} R^{-t}}\right) = \left[\sum_{t=1}^{N} R^{-t}\right] \tau\left(Y + \frac{K+\varepsilon}{\sum_{t=1}^{N} R^{-t}}\right). \tag{1.27}$$

Now compare two agents whose wealth levels per period $(X/\sum R^{-t})$ are the same, but one has one period to go ($N = 1$), and the other has $N > 1$ periods to go. Equation 1.27 tells us that the agent with time horizon N will be $\sum R^{-t} \approx N$ times more risk tolerant than the agent with only one period to go. Thus, we conclude that there is a strong time diversification effect in this model. The intuition is quite simple. Each dollar of loss or gain will be equally split into $1/N$ of a dollar reduction or increase in consumption in each period. This is an efficient risk-sharing scheme of the different future selves representing the household over time. This ability to diversify the single risk over time induces the agent to be more willing to take it.

Our ceteris paribus assumption above was that agents have the same wealth level per period. This means that a reduction in the time horizon does not affect the feasible consumption level per period. This is the case, for example, when the agent has no cash on hand in period 1, so that wealth X comes solely from discounting future incomes. We can alternatively compare two agents with different time horizons but with identical discounted wealth X. In this case, the agent with a longer time horizon will consume less in each period. Under DARA, that will induce more risk aversion, and it is not clear whether the time diversification effect or this wealth effect will dominate. The limit case is when absolute risk tolerance is homogeneous of degree 1 with respect to consumption. This is the case under CRRA, since we have $\tau(C) = C/\gamma$. In that case, equation 1.27 is rewritten as $-V'(X)/V''(X) = X/\gamma$. This is independent of the time horizon. Under CRRA, the wealth effect just compensates the time diversification effect: two CRRA agents with the same aggregate wealth but facing different time horizons will have the same attitude toward the single risk $\tilde{\varepsilon}$. When absolute risk tolerance is subhomogeneous., the agent will be more tolerant of a single risk if it is resolved earlier in his life.

Remember that equation 1.27 holds only under the assumption that constant consumption over the lifetime is optimal, that is, when $R\beta = 1$. When R and β^{-1} are not equal, we must use equation 1.26 with the optimal consumption plan $(C_1, \ldots, C_N)$. If absolute risk tolerance is convex, Jensen's inequality applied to this equation implies that

$$\frac{-V'(X)}{V''(X)} \geq \left[\sum_{t=1}^{N} R^{-t} \right] \tau \left(\frac{\sum_{t=1}^{N} R^{-t} C_t}{\sum_{t=1}^{N} R^{-t}} \right) = \left[\sum_{t=1}^{N} R^{-t} \right] \tau \left(\frac{X}{\sum_{t=1}^{N} R^{-t}} \right). \quad (1.28)$$

This is equation 1.27, except that the equality has been replaced by an inequality. Thus, under convex absolute risk tolerance, the time diversification effect is even stronger than above. Technically, this result has been obtained by following the same procedure as for the complementarity of repeated risks in section 4. Here, the optimal fluctuations of consumption over time, rather than across states, are complementary to risk taking if τ is convex.

The model presented in this section is not realistic because of the assumption that there is a single risk in the lifetime of the investor. We now combine the different effects of time horizon on the optimal instantaneous portfolio:

· The complementarity effect of repeated risks over time. The option to take risk in the future raises the willingness to take risk today under convex absolute risk tolerance;

· The time diversification effect. The opportunity to smooth shocks on capital by small variations of consumption over long horizons raises the willingness to take risk.

· The wealth effect. For a given discounted wealth, a longer horizon means less consumption in each period, which reduces the willingness to take risk under DARA.

We consider the following model. Investors can consume, save, and take risk at each period from $t = 1$ to $t = T$. At each period, there is some uncertainty about which state of the world $i = 1, \ldots, N$ will prevail at the end of the period. Within each period t, the agent begins with the selection of a portfolio. After observing the state of the world and the value X_t of the portfolio, the agent decides how much to consume (C_t) and how much to save for the next period (S_t). We can decompose the three effects of time horizon by using backward induction again. This is done in the following steps:

1. In period T, the agent selects his optimal portfolio of Arrow-Debreu securities by solving program 1.15, where X_{T-1} is replaced by S_{T-1}. The transformation from u to V_{T-1} describes the complementarity (or substitutability) effect of repeated risk.

2. At the end of period $T - 1$, after observing the state of the world and the associated value of the portfolio X_{T-1}, the agent solves his consumption-saving problem, which is written as

$$\hat{V}_{T-1}(X_{T-1}) = \max_C u(C) + \beta V_{T-1}(R(X_{T-1} - C)). \tag{1.29}$$

This operation describes the time diversification effect and the wealth effect of time horizon.

3. The agent determines the optimal composition of his portfolio at the beginning of period $T - 1$ by solving program 1.17, but with

function V_{T-1} being replaced by function $\hat{V}_{T-1}$, defined by equation 1.29 to take into account the possibility of smoothing consumption over time.

Going back to the original question of how time horizon affects the optimal structure of households' portfolios, we must compare the degree of concavity of $\hat{V}_{T-1}$ with respect to the degree of concavity of u. If $\hat{V}_{T-1}$ is less concave than u, it would imply that, ceteris paribus, one selects a riskier portfolio in period $T-1$ than in period T. The CRRA function is an instructive benchmark. Because CRRA is a special case of HARA, we know from section 1.4 that $V_{T-1}(.) \equiv hu(.)$: the option to invest in risky assets in period T does not affect the degree of concavity of the value function. This implies that program 1.29 is a special case of program 1.24, with β being replaced by βh. Because u is CRRA, we also know that the time diversification effect is completely offset by the wealth effect, so that $\hat{V}_{T-1}(.) \equiv \hat{h}u(.)$: $\hat{V}_{T-1}$ has the same concavity as u. We conclude that under CRRA, myopia is optimal. The optimal dynamic portfolio strategy is obtained by behaving as if each period were the last one before retirement. There is no effect of time horizon on the optimal portfolio, ceteris paribus. This result has already been shown in Merton (1969) and Samuelson (1969). Mossin (1968) showed that CRRA is also necessary for optimal myopia.

It is easy to combine our other results. For example, a longer time horizon induces riskier portfolios if absolute risk tolerance is convex and subhomogeneous. On the contrary, if absolute risk tolerance is concave and superhomogeneous, it induces more conservative portfolios.

1.6   Other Factors

The classical model presented in the previous sections is not realistic. In this section, we discuss the effect of various modifications.

1.6.1   Liquidity Constraints

We assumed earlier that markets are frictionless. There are no transaction costs for exchanging assets and no cap on the risk that can be taken on financial markets. Moreover, we assumed that the borrowing rate is equal to the lending rate on the credit market. Whereas the effect on the optimal portfolio of introducing market imperfections is easy to examine in a static model, the analysis becomes complex in a dynamic framework.

The qualitative effect of a liquidity constraint on the optimal portfolio is easy to grasp. Remember that it is optimal for households to smooth adverse portfolio return shocks by reducing consumption over a long period of time. This is done by reducing saving immediately after the adverse shock to finance short-term consumption. If the shock is large enough, some households may be short of cash; they may become net borrowers for a short period of time. Under the liquidity constraint, this is not allowed. Thus, these households must drastically reduce their short-term consumption. They will not be able to diversify their portfolio risk anymore, which will raise their degree of aversion toward portfolio risk. In short, liquidity constraints shorten the time horizon, thereby making consumers more averse to risk on wealth.

1.6.2 Transaction Costs

Trading and owning risky assets entails various costs, which affect the optimal portfolio structure. Proportional costs have complex and ambiguous effects on the optimal dynamic portfolio management and are not discussed here. Instead we examine pure participation costs: the fixed costs incurred in each period to invest in stocks. This kind of cost may be helpful in solving one of the most surprising puzzles of financial markets: the low proportion of households that hold stocks. In presenting the classical theory, I showed that it is always optimal to take some risk on financial markets if risk aversion is finite. But if households have to incur a fixed cost to own risky assets, it might be optimal for some of them not to invest at all in stocks. Under DARA, this would be the case for the poorer households, whose potential benefits from the portfolio are small given the size of their savings.

To determine the decision to participate, let us focus on the static Arrow-Debreu portfolio decision problem with CRRA preferences. To determine participation, households compare the certainty equivalent value $\hat{C}$ of their portfolio to the participation cost. $\hat{C}$ is given by

$$u(XR) = Eu(X(R + w\tilde{R}_s) - \hat{C}), \tag{1.30}$$

where w is the optimal portfolio structure if the agent participates. $\hat{C}$ can as usual be approximated by

$$\hat{C} \simeq 0.5(wX)^2 \sigma_s^2 \frac{\rho}{XR} \simeq 0.5 \frac{RX[E\tilde{R}_s]^2}{\rho \sigma_s^2}. \tag{1.31}$$

Using the parameter of the calibration presented in section 1.2, with $R = 1.01$, $E\tilde{R}_s = 0.06$, and $\sigma_s = 0.16$, we get that the certainty equivalent is somewhere between 3.5 percent ($\rho = 4$) and 14 percent ($\rho = 1$) of the wealth (per period) of the investor. In other words, we need to introduce a fixed participation cost amounting to as much as 14 percent of per capita GDP to explain the participation puzzle.

1.6.3   Predictability, Mean Reversion, and Learning

We have assumed so far that time brings no new information about future returns. In other words, future returns are not predictable. This is not compatible with the data. Campbell (1991), for example, showed some predictability in asset returns. In the real world, investors and econometricians can observe signals that are correlated with future returns. In that case, the investor's horizon may affect the optimal portfolio of the agent even in the HARA case, as Merton (1973) shows.

There is a simple intuition that mean reversion may induce investors with a long time horizon to take more risks. Indeed, future returns being negatively correlated to current returns, the option to take risk in the future is a way to hedge the current portfolio risk. However, this is not true in general, and the effect of mean reversion on the optimal portfolio structure depends on whether relative risk aversion is larger or smaller than unity, as Merton (1973) shows. This is because someone who has been lucky in period 1 wants to take more risk in period 2.

Information about future returns can also be obtained by learning, experimenting, or getting advice from relatives. The effect of information channels on the optimal portfolio is ambiguous in general. Consider, for example, an agent who believes that expected excess returns are zero in period 2. He will get information about the distribution of these future returns at the end of the first period. Before getting this information, he must decide about his first-period portfolio. Compare the situation with and without the anticipation of getting the information. In the absence of any information, the investor will not take any risk in period 2, because the unconditional distribution of excess return is zero. But when the agent anticipates that he will obtain some information about future return, he internalizes in period 1 that he will take some portfolio risk in the future, because the distribution of future returns conditional on the signal will in general not be zero. The effect of such information structure on the optimal first-period portfolio is thus equivalent to that of offering the investor the valuable option of purchasing risky assets in the future, which lengthens his time horizon. In the HARA case, this has no effect, and if absolute risk tolerance is concave, it reduces the first-period demand for risky assets.

1.6.4 Taxation

Arrow (1971) observes that the tax system has a potentially large effect on the optimal structure of the household's portfolio. Consider a static economy in which the two-fund separation theorem holds. Capital gains z from investment in stocks are taxed in such a way that after-tax gains are $\phi(z)$. The portfolio choice problem is written as

$$\max_{w} \; Eu(XR + \phi(wX\tilde{R}_s)). \tag{1.32}$$

The simplest case is when the tax is proportional to gains, with full deductibility for capital losses: $\phi(z) = (1 - t)z$. It is trivial that the optimal reaction to the introduction of such a tax is to raise the demand for the risky asset at a rate exactly equal to the tax rate. This means that investors completely offset the risk reduction generated by the tax by increasing their asset demand.

More generally, we can define an indirect utility function $V(.)$ such that $V(z) = u(XR + \phi(z))$ to measure the impact of the tax on the attitude toward risk on capital gains. It yields

$$-\frac{V'(z)}{V''(z)} = \frac{\tau(XR + \phi(z))}{-\dfrac{\phi''(z)}{\phi'(z)}\tau(XR + \phi(z)) + \phi'(z)}. \tag{1.33}$$

The after-tax capital gain function ϕ is concave when capital losses cannot be deducted from gross income. We see from equation 1.33 that this tends to reduce the demand for risky assets by reducing the tolerance of risk on capital gains.

1.6.5 Household Composition

The optimal portfolio is also a function of the number of members of the household who will share the portfolio risk. To examine this, suppose that there is a Pareto-efficient risk-sharing rule within the household. This is the case if, in each state of the world, the household shares wealth in such a way as to maximize a weighted sum of each member's utility, with prespecified weights. Suppose that the N members have all the same utility function u. If the household's wealth is X, the allocation $(C_1, \ldots, C_N)$ will solve

$$V(X) = \max \sum_{i=1}^{N} \lambda_i u(C_i) \quad s.t. \quad \sum_{i=1}^{N} C_i = X. \tag{1.34}$$

Because this problem is another illustration of program 1.1, 1.2, it has the same property that

$$-\frac{V'(X)}{V''(X)} = \sum_{i=1}^{N} \tau(C_i). \tag{1.35}$$

The degree of absolute risk tolerance of an efficient household is the sum of the absolute risk tolerance of its members. For example, if we compare two households having the same income per head, the larger one will be willing to take more portfolio risk.

1.7 Other Decision Criteria

The aim of this chapter is to present the classical theory of portfolio choices. Yet I cannot resist presenting a quick overview of a few nonclassical models of portfolio choice. Many of these alternative models depart from the assumption that the objective function of the investor is separable with respect to time and to states of nature.

1.7.1 Recursive Utility and Habit Formation

A problem arises when we try to mix risk and time in the classical model. When future consumption levels are uncertain, the objective function is usually defined as the discounted expected lifetime utility. This implies that the utility function simultaneously represents attitude toward risk and attitude toward time. But imagine an agent that does not give the same answer to the two questions posed in section 1.2 to measure relative risk aversion and relative aversion to consumption fluctuations. This agent may not have the discounted expected lifetime utility as an objective function. Kreps and Porteus (1978) and Selden (1979) suggested a model that would disentangle risk aversion from aversion to consumption fluctuations. In this model, additivity across states in each period is preserved with the additivity across period in each state. But additivity in the full space (risk, time) is not preserved, contrary to the situation with the discounted expected utility model. Again, we will not cover this generalization here. In fact, the relationship between the optimal portfolio risk and savings remains the same as in the classical model. The difference comes from changes in the optimal saving strategy over time. Applications of Kreps-Porteus preferences in macroeconomics are explored by Weil (1990).

There is another way to break the time separability of the objective function of the investor: assuming that the felicity of the agent at each period depends not only on consumption in that period but also on his past consumption. When past consumption affects current felicity negatively, we refer to "habit formation." These models with habit formation appear quite promising but will not be examined here (see, for example, Constantinides 1990).

1.7.2   Hyperbolic Discounting

Laibson (1997) argues convincingly that many consumers do not discount future felicity exponentially, as assumed in equation 1.24. Rather, they use a large discount rate for short-term substitution of consumption and a smaller rate when contemplating substitution of consumption in a distant future. This generates a problem of time consistency: the consumption plan that is optimal when considered today will not be optimal tomorrow. In this section, as in Harris and Laibson (1999), we explore whether this could affect the optimal portfolio. To do this, we first have to explain how agents may solve their time inconsistency problem.

Let us consider the simplest model with three periods. The consumer uses a discount factor β to discount next-period felicity and a discount factor $\beta^2 h$ for felicity two periods later. Case $h = 1$ is the classical one, but $h > 1$ corresponds better to observed behavior. As in section 1.5, we consider a pure consumption problem under certainty. We solve the problem backward. At the beginning of period 2, the agent has some wealth X_2 that he allocates over the last two periods in order to maximize $u(C_2) + \beta u(C_3)$, yielding a consumption plan $(C_2^*(X_2), C_3^*(X_2))$. Now, we solve the problem in period 1. If he could commit to a specific future consumption plan, the agent would like to implement the plan that maximizes $u(C_1) + \beta u(C_2) + \beta^2 h u(C_3)$ under the budget constraint $C_1 + R^{-1}C_2 + R^{-2}C_3 = X_1$. This yields an optimal consumption plan $(C_1^{**}, C_2^{**}, C_3^{**})$. The time-consistency problem comes from the observation that when $h > 1$, then $C_2^*(R(X_1 - C_1^{**}))$ is larger than C_2^{**}. Laibson (1997) proposes to solve this problem by playing a Stackelberg game between the self in period 1 (leader) and the self in period 2 (follower). The self in period 1 maximizes his lifetime utility under the constraint that the self in period 2 will allocate the remaining wealth in his own way. This gives the following problem:

$$V(X_1) = \max_S u(X_1 - S) + \beta u(C_2^*(RS)) + \beta^2 h u(C_3^*(RS)). \tag{1.36}$$

Our aim here is to determine the effect of such behavior on the attitude toward risk prior to period 1. How does time inconsistency of consumption affect risk taking? After tedious manipulations that are not reported here, we obtain that

$$-\frac{V'(X)}{V''(X)} = \frac{\tau_1 + R^{-1}\tau_2 + R^{-2}\tau_3 + R^{-1}\dfrac{\tau_1\tau_2\tau_3(\tau_2' - \tau_3')(h-1)}{(\tau_2 + R^{-1}h\tau_3)(\tau_2 + R^{-1}\tau_3)}}{1 + R^{-1}\dfrac{\tau_2\tau_3(\tau_2' - \tau_3')(h-1)}{(\tau_2 + R^{-1}h\tau_3)(\tau_2 + R^{-1}\tau_3)}}, \tag{1.37}$$

where $\tau_i = \tau(C_i)$, and $\tau_i' = \tau'(C_i)$ and C_i is the solution of program 1.36. Observe that in the classical case $h = 1$, we return to equation 1.26. But we also get the same solution in the HARA case, since this implies that $\tau_2' = \tau_3'$. Thus, if we believe that HARA utility functions are realistic, hyperbolic discounting has no effect on optimal portfolios.

1.7.3   Nonexpected Utility

Very impressive efforts have been made over the past two decades to devise a decision criterion under uncertainty to solve various paradoxes of the expected utility model. However, the applications to finance are rare. The most important effect of the departure from expected utility is probably the possibility of having first-order risk aversion, as defined by Segal and Spivak (1990). Under expected utility, the demand for risky assets is always positive when the expected excess return is positive. This is because under expected utility, risk aversion is a second-order effect. Indeed, using the Arrow-Pratt approximation, the risk premium is approximately proportional to the square of the size of this risk, whereas the expected value is proportional to the size of the risk. This implies that when the size of the random variable is small, the risk effect is always dominated by the expectation effect.

Some nonexpected utility models, like expected utility with rank-dependent probabilities (Quiggin 1982), do exhibit first-order risk aversion—preferences for which risk premia are proportional to the size of the risk, not to its square. This could explain why the stock market participation rate is low in spite of the positive expected excess return of stocks.

1.8 Conclusion

The theory of dynamic portfolio management is a fascinating field. The similarity between the static portfolio problem under uncertainty and the dynamic consumption problem under certainty helps to explain how risk and time interact to generate a dynamically optimal portfolio strategy. We have shown in particular that the concavity or convexity of the absolute risk tolerance with respect to consumption is important to characterize the effect of time on risk taking. This is because the absolute tolerance to portfolio risk in the static portfolio problem is a weighted average of ex post absolute risk tolerances on consumption. Similarly, the absolute risk tolerance in relation to wealth in the dynamic consumption problem under certainty is equal to the discounted value of future absolute risk tolerances in relation to consumption.

This very basic result is at the origin of our understanding of how portfolio risks at different points in time interact with one other. I have shown how the familiar notion of time diversification can be justified on theoretical grounds and presented several testable hypotheses using data on household portfolios:

• Wealthier people own more risky assets (under decreasing absolute risk aversion).

• Wealthier people invest a larger share of their wealth in risky assets (under decreasing relative risk aversion).

• Households with riskier human capital invest less in risky assets (under risk vulnerability).

• Households that can invest in risky assets over many periods will invest more in them (under convex absolute risk tolerance).

• Households that cannot smooth their consumption over time will invest less in risky assets. In particular, households that are more likely to be liquidity constrained in the future will invest less in risky assets.

Empirical evidence related to these hypotheses is presented in various chapters of this book.

Notes

I am grateful to Giuseppe Bertola, Chris Carrol, Luigi Guiso, Michael Haliassos, Tullio Jappelli, and Steve Zeldes for helpful comments on an earlier version of this chapter.

1. With constant relative risk aversion, the certainty-equivalent share x is independent of initial wealth.

2. To be more precise, one of the two terms on the left-hand side of equation 1.5 should be multiplied by the rate of impatience, depending on whether we start with an even year or an odd year.

3. Leland (1980) determines the characteristics of agents who should purchase call options on the aggregate risk in the economy. These agents have a consumption function that is convex with respect to per capita GDP.

4. Gollier (1995) obtained the necessary and sufficient condition on the change of distribution for a reduction in the demand for stocks by all risk-averse investors.

5. These summary statistics are from Kocherlakota (1996).

6. However, most empirical analyses, as in Guiso, Jappelli, and Terlizesse (1996), have documented a hump-shaped curve for the relationship between age and the share of wealth invested in stocks. Investors do not follow the recommendations of financial advisers.

2

Calibration and Computation of Household Portfolio Models

Michael Haliassos and
Alexander Michaelides

This chapter discusses calibration and numerical solution of household portfolio models in a variety of specifications. Interest in the computational approach has been generated mainly by the difficulties associated with obtaining exact analytical solutions in dynamic, intertemporal models of portfolio choice that allow for uninsurable background earnings risk. Our objective is threefold: (1) to illustrate the main conceptual, technical, and computational issues that arise in this context; (2) to explore the portfolio implications of alternative modeling choices, isolating the individual contribution of each major factor wherever possible and understanding the main mechanisms at work; and (3) to identify new and explore enduring puzzles, that is, discrepancies between the properties of optimal portfolios and econometric findings in empirical chapters of this book that future portfolio research should resolve. As in other areas where calibration is used, the main purpose of a calibrated model is not to mimic reality but to provide an understanding of the main economic mechanisms. Thus, puzzles should be viewed not as proof that existing portfolio models are irrelevant for the real world, but as an impetus to identify economic mechanisms sufficiently strong to modify the tendencies already captured in existing models.

Portfolio puzzles relate to either participation in the stock market or the portfolio composition of participants. The enduring participation puzzle is that despite premiums on equity, there is no country in the world where the majority of households hold stocks, directly or indirectly. In our calibration experiments, we do identify cases where zero stockholding is optimal. However, these typically involve a combination of low current cash on hand and constraints preventing households from borrowing. The former is unlikely to explain persistent zero stockholding by vast segments of the population; the latter may understate the true borrowing potential of most house-holds. We report on recent work, suggesting that fixed costs of entry and participation in the stock market could contribute significantly to explaining the participation puzzle.

We uncover three portfolio composition puzzles. One arises from the tendency of models to imply that it is optimal for small savers to hold all of their assets in the form of stocks so as to take advantage of the equity premium. Coexistence of positive holdings of stocks and riskless assets is optimal only for households with large amounts of cash on hand, which can afford to give up the equity premium on part of their savings in exchange for reducing portfolio risk. While the tendency of large savers to hold more diversified portfolios is present in the data, there is no corresponding tendency of small savers to be fully invested in stocks. Small savers tend to hold no stocks, and those who do tend to hold riskless assets. What is the economic force that overrides the incentive of small savers to put all of their savings in the most high-powered vehicle, other than risk aversion, earnings risk, and borrowing constraints, which are already incorporated in the calibration models?

A second participation puzzle is that for those predicted to hold the riskless asset, the share of risky assets in total financial wealth is decreasing in cash on hand. This is consistent with the view that richer households do not need to rely as much on the wealth-generating power of the equity premium and can afford to put a larger share of their wealth in the riskless asset. Yet in the data, financial wealth and current labor income contribute positively to the portfolio share of the risky asset, conditional on participation.

A third participation puzzle relates to the prediction that the port-folio share of risky assets, conditional on holding stocks, is strongly decreasing with age. Empirical studies in this book find a hump-shaped age profile for the probability of participation in the stock market but cast serious doubt on the sign and significance of age effects for portfolio composition conditional on stock market partici-pation (see chapter 7 on Italy, for example). In view of the strong tendency of models to yield age effects and of financial advisers to encourage households to reduce exposure to stockholding risk as they grow older, this is perhaps an area where the ball is in the court of empirical researchers. If the absence of age effects is indeed estab-lished across countries, time periods, and estimation methods, then this will not only provide a major challenge to model builders but may also imply that more emphasis should be placed on explaining the stock market participation decision than the age pattern of portfolio shares among stockholders.

Researchers who are building models to study household portfolio choice face numerous modeling choices. Should they build a partial equilibrium or a general equilibrium model? Would the (unrealistic) assumption of infinite investor horizons yield a good simplifying approximation to the portfolio behavior of an important subset of the population? Should a researcher who assumes finite horizons build a large-scale model that allows portfolio rebalancing every year, or can she obtain the key insights by solving variants of versatile, small-scale models that focus on long-term career risk and consider only the changes in portfolios associated with major landmarks in the economic life of a household? What aspects of preferences and of the environment are likely to be important in shaping household saving and portfolio behavior? Answers to such questions are unlikely to be unanimous, but they should be informed. As is true for good theory, good computation should deliver the most relevant results in the least complicated way. The wide range of calibration exercises reported in this chapter are intended to provide a guide not only as to how to build and solve models but also as to the likely relevance of each complication for optimal portfolios.

In section 2.1 we describe some key choices regarding model ingredients. Section 2.11 deals with preference specification, nesting expected utility, and two measurable departures from it (Kreps-Porteus preferences and rank dependent utility). Habit formation is also examined. Section 2.1.2 deals with modeling the economic environment of the household, potentially one with nondiversifiable labor income risk, borrowing and short-sales constraints, and fixed costs of entry and participation in the stock market. Section 2.2 describes calibration. This entails approximating continuous stochastic processes that govern labor incomes and stock returns with discrete processes, choosing values for preference parameters, and examining sensitivity of portfolios to them. This is followed in section 2.3 by a description of a generic household portfolio model, whose different variants we explore in the rest of the chapter. Our focus is on household behavior for given asset return and labor income processes. This avoids compounding portfolio puzzles with asset return puzzles still present in general-equilibrium models and provides a building block for future general equilibrium exercises that will extend promising early models discussed toward the end of the chapter. Section 2.4 deals with how to compute optimal household portfolios using different variants of the model in section 2.3. We derive policy functions and time series moments for consumption and portfolio components, and examine the influence of preferences and the economic environment. We first consider versatile three-period models and then turn to large-scale portfolio models with either infinite or finite horizons.[1] After a brief discussion of the prospects for building general equilibrium models with aggregate uncertainty, we offer concluding remarks.

2.1   Modeling Choices

2.1.1   Preferences

A popular saying among economists is that for each desired result, there is a preference structure that will justify it. Although this view discourages some from experimenting with alternative preference assumptions, we share the view that some exploration of flexible preference forms can be fruitful, as long as their performance is validated with reference to different aspects of behavior. Our preference specification is based on Epstein and Zin (1989). A household is assumed to maximize in each period t recursive utility U_t of the form:

$$U_t = W(C_t, \mu(U_{t+1}|I_t)) \tag{2.1}$$

where W is an aggregator function. Utility is a function of current consumption and of some certainty equivalent of the next period's uncertain utility, based on current information, I_t. We assume that the aggregator function is

$$W(C_t, \mu(U_{t+1}|I_t)) = [(1-\beta)C_t^\zeta + \beta\mu_t^\zeta]^{1/\zeta}, \quad 0 \neq \zeta < 1 \tag{2.2}$$

or

$$W(C_t, \mu(U_{t+1}|I_t)) = [(1-\beta)\ln C_t + \beta \ln \mu_t], \quad \zeta = 0, \tag{2.3}$$

where $\mu_t(\cdot)$ is an abbreviation for $\mu(\cdot|I_t)$. Our proposed functional form for $\mu_t(\cdot)$ nests alternative preference specifications:

$$\mu(U_{t+1}|I_t) = [f_t(U_{t+1}^\alpha)]^{1/\alpha}, \quad 0 \neq \alpha < 1 \tag{2.4}$$

or

$$\ln \mu(U_{t+1}|I_t) = f_t(\ln U_{t+1}), \quad \alpha = 0, \tag{2.5}$$

where f_t is a linear operator that uses information available in period t. The definition of f_t will vary depending on preference type. Suppose that the household chooses at time t some control variable h_{it}, where i indexes control variables (e.g., asset levels). The first-order conditions for utility maximization are of the form:

$$C_t^{\zeta-1}\frac{\partial C_t}{\partial h_{it}} + \beta[f_t(U_{t+1}^\alpha)]^{\zeta/\alpha-1}f_t\left[U_{t+1}^{\alpha-\zeta}C_{t+1}^{\zeta-1}\left(\frac{\partial C_{t+1}}{\partial h_{it}}\right)\right] = 0, \quad \forall i,t. \tag{2.6}$$

Expected utility (EU) is obtained under two restrictions: (1) $\alpha = \zeta$ and (2) $f_t \equiv E_t$; that is, the linear operator f_t is the mathematical expectation operator conditional on information in period t. A variant of EU allows for habit formation, that is, for a stock of habits to affect current utility; ceteris paribus, for a higher habit level, higher consumption will be necessary to achieve the same utility.[2] With "external" habit formation, an individual's habit depends on the history of aggregate consumption; this is Abel's (1990) "catching up with the Joneses" formulation or Duesenberry's (1949) "relative income" model. The felicity function is usually specified as $\frac{(C_t - H_t)^\alpha - 1}{\alpha}$, where H is the level of the habit. Defining the surplus consumption ratio as $SUR_t = \frac{C_t - H_t}{C_t}$, it is straightforward to show that the local curvature of the utility function equals $\frac{1-\alpha}{SUR_t}$ and is increasing in the level of the habit. Campbell and Cochrane (1999) show that in recessions, the agent requires a higher return to hold the claim to the risky asset, rationalizing a higher equity premium. The first-order condition now becomes

$$C_t^{\alpha-1}SUR_t^{\alpha-1}\left(\frac{\partial C_t}{\partial h_{it}}\right) + \beta E_t C_{t+1}^{\alpha-1}SUR_{t+1}^{\alpha-1}\left(\frac{\partial C_{t+1}}{\partial h_{it}}\right) = 0, \quad \forall i,t.$$

In the "internal" habit formulation, the habit is determined by past individual consumption (Constantinides, 1990), and current decisions affect the utility from future consumption.

Kreps-Porteus preferences (KP) disentangle the effects of risk aversion from those of the elasticity of substitution. Under KP, the linear operator f_t in equation 2.6 is still the expectations operator E_t, as under EU, but the risk-aversion parameter α is no longer tied to the intertemporal elasticity parameter ζ. Departures from expected utility are measured by the difference between the elasticity of substitution used in the KP model and the value used in the EU model— the inverse of risk aversion (see Haliassos and Hassapis 2001).

Under EU or KP preferences, households assign to each state a weight equal to its probability of occurrence. A literature pioneered by Quiggin (1982) and Yaari (1987) argues in favor of specifying weights that depend on the desirability ranking of each state. A simple example involves only two states, "bad" and "good," occurring with probabilities p and $1 - p$, respectively. Under rank-dependent utility, the bad state obtains a weight of p^γ, where $\gamma < 1$, and the good state obtains $1 - p^\gamma$. Given that both p and γ are below unity, this results in overweighting of the bad state relative to expected utility. When more than two states exist, the formula for assigning a weight w_j to the state ranked jth is

$$ w_j = \left(\sum_{i=1}^{j} p_i \right)^\gamma - \left(\sum_{i=1}^{j-1} p_i \right)^\gamma, \tag{2.7} $$

where i indexes states of the world. When $\gamma = 1$, these reduce to $w_j = p_j$, as in EU and KP models. When $\gamma < 1$ and $\alpha = 1$, that is, the degree of relative risk aversion is equal to zero, we have a version of Yaari's dual theory of choice.

The desirability ranking of states of the world that involve different labor income and asset return realizations can change, often repeatedly, as we vary the level of risky asset holdings. For example, in the absence of any other risk, including labor income risk, high stock returns are preferred when stockholding is positive, but low returns are preferred when the household has a short position in stocks. Whenever the desirability ranking changes, the weights attached to each state need to be recomputed using equation 2.7. Adjustment of weights alters the objective function, generating a point of nondifferentiability of indifference curves at each level of risky asset holdings where a switch in desirability rankings occurs. Epstein and Zin (1990) and Haliassos and Bertaut (1995) suggested that this property might help resolve the participation puzzle because of a kink at zero stockholding, where the household switches objective functions. Haliassos and Hassapis (2001) have since shown that kinks do not occur at zero stockholding in the presence of labor income risk and that such preferences cannot resolve the participation puzzle in the absence of other frictions and imperfections. Further improvements in predicted portfolio shares, conditional on participation, could result from experimentation with rank-dependent utility or more flexible forms of expected utility.

2.1.2   Market Frictions and Imperfections

Portfolio literature to date suggests that preferences alone are unlikely to resolve the stock market participation puzzle and may even have trouble accounting for the limited level of stockholding conditional on participation. Both tasks are facilitated, however, when certain types of market frictions and imperfections are incorporated in portfolio models. In this section, we describe such complications that have important portfolio consequences: labor income risk, borrowing constraints, and stock market participation costs.

Nondiversifiable Labor Income Risk
Background labor income risk is nondiversifiable because of moral hazard and adverse selection considerations. Analytical solutions for portfolio models with labor income risk are available for linear, quadratic, and exponential felicity, all of which have known questionable properties for consumption and portfolios. Preferences displaying constant relative risk aversion require solution using computational methods. We adopt the following exogenous stochastic process for income of household i:

$$Y_{it} = P_{it}U_{it} \tag{2.8}$$

$$P_{it} = G_tP_{it-1}N_{it}. \tag{2.9}$$

This process, first used in a nearly identical form by Carroll (1992), is decomposed into a "permanent" component, P_{it}, and a transitory component, U_{it}, where P_{it} is defined as the labor income that would be received if the white noise multiplicative transitory shock U_{it} were equal to its mean of unity.[3] Assume that the $\ln U_{it}$ and $\ln N_{it}$ are each independent and identically (normally) distributed with mean $-.5 * \sigma_u^2$, $-.5 * \sigma_v^2$, and variances σ_u^2, and σ_v^2, respectively. The log normality of U_{it} and the assumption about the mean of its logarithm imply that

$$EU_{it} = \exp(-.5 * \sigma_u^2 + .5 * \sigma_u^2) = 1, \tag{2.10}$$

and similarly for EN_{it}. The log of P_{it} evolves as a random walk with a deterministic drift, $\ln G_t$, assumed to be common to all individuals. Given these assumptions, the growth in individual labor income follows

$$\Delta \ln Y_{it} = \ln G_t + \ln N_{it} + \ln U_{it} - \ln U_{it-1}, \tag{2.11}$$

where the unconditional mean growth for individual earnings is $\mu_g - .5 * \sigma_v^2$, and the unconditional variance equals $(\sigma_v^2 + 2\sigma_u^2)$. The last three terms in equation 2.11 are idiosyncratic and average to zero over a sufficiently large number of households, implying that per capita aggregate income growth is given by $\ln G_t$. Individual labor income growth has a single Wold representation that is equivalent to the MA(1) process for individual income growth estimated using household-level data (MaCurdy 1981; Abowd and Card 1989; Pischke 1995).[4] An alternative specification with less persistent income shocks, not examined in this chapter, has been proposed by Hubbard, Skinner, and Zeldes (1994, 1995) and is explained in Haliassos and Michaelides (2000, henceforth referred to as HM).[5]

Borrowing and Short-Sales Constraints
In portfolio models, borrowing needs arise not only for current consumption but also for investment in assets with an expected return premium. Thus, constraints on borrowing could in principle limit investment in premium assets or even preclude participation in certain asset markets. Three types of borrowing constraints that can have important portfolio consequences are borrowing limits, interest rate wedges between borrowing and lending rates, and down payment requirements for major durables purchases.

In portfolio models incorporating N assets, a general form of borrowing limits is

$$\sum_{i=1}^{N} b_{it} A_{it} \geq 0 \quad \forall t, \tag{2.12}$$

where $0 \leq b_{it} \leq 1$. This allows short sales of any asset provided that certain collateral requirements are met, which depend on the asset used as collateral. The most frequently used quantity constraint in existing portfolio studies imposes no-short-sales restrictions on each asset:

$A_{it} \geq 0 \quad \forall i, t.$ (2.13)

It is also possible to incorporate borrowing limits that depend on household labor income, perhaps as a signal of the household's ability to meet repayment schedules:

$-B_t \leq kY_t, \quad k \geq 0,$ (2.14)

where B_t is the amount of riskless asset (bond) holding in period t and the negative of this is borrowing at the riskless rate.[6] Interest rate wedges and down payment requirements are not examined here but are explained in HM.

Stock Market Participation Costs

A promising avenue for explaining the stock market participation puzzle is fixed costs for entering the stock market, possibly coupled with subequent recurring costs for continued participation. Some such costs may be direct, such as brokerage or membership fees. Others may involve the value of the household's time devoted to keeping up with developments in the stock market and monitoring brokers and financial advisers. Value-of-time considerations imply costs proportional to household income. Whatever the objective size of such entry and participation costs, what matters for participation decisions is how they are perceived by the household. Misperceptions, ignorance, and even prejudice can contribute to inertia.

Rather than attempting to calibrate such unobservable costs, one can compute the minimum size of entry and participation costs required to keep a household with given characteristics out of the stock market. Consider the simplest case of a ticket fee, which applies only to first-time investors. If we denote the value function associated with participating in the stock market by V_s and the value function when using solely the bond market by V_B, the threshold ticket fee that would make a household indifferent between participating and not participating is a function of a state variable like cash on hand, $K(X)$, such that

$V_S(X - K(X)) = V_B(X).$ (2.15)

Value functions are monotonic in the state variable, and therefore the value functions can be inverted to derive the cost $K(X)$. This function must be greater than zero, since the investor has the right (but not the obligation) to participate in the equity market. Using methods we describe, one can determine the distribution of cash on hand in the population if households use only bonds as a saving vehicle. This distribution also represents the possible outcomes of cash on hand for a given household over time. One can then compute the maximum level of X that any household is likely to experience, $\hat{X}$, as that which satisfies $\Pr(X \leq \hat{X}) = 1$. Then a level of costs equal to $K(\hat{X})$ would ensure that nobody participates in the stock market, with the marginal investor being indifferent between participating or not. The lower the levels of such ceilings are, the more plausible are entry costs as explanations of the participation puzzle.

2.2 Calibration

Once the various components of the model have been chosen, the researcher needs to calibrate parameter values and approximate continuous stochastic processes, such as asset returns and labor incomes, using discrete approximations. Calibration of parameter values is normally based on empirical estimates when these are available. Even when they are available, but especially when they are not, it is instructive to examine the sensitivity of solutions to a range of parameter values.

A simple (binomial) method to approximate a continuous stochastic process is to postulate two possible outcomes, a "high" and a "low" realization, such that their mean and variance match those of the original stochastic process. In small-scale models (including overlapping-generations models), each period is thought of as lasting twenty to thirty years. While riskless rates are simply compounded over this longer interval, risky annual returns can be converted to a binomial process first, which can then be used to compute the mean and variance of multiyear compounded returns. Similarly, any continuous stochastic process for labor incomes can be simulated over a twenty-year period to derive the relevant moments to be matched by a binomial model.

More generally, a discrete approximation of $I = \int_a^b f(x)w(x)\,dx$, where $w(x)$ is a probability density function, can be found by considering N states and using $\sum_{i=1}^{i=N} \omega_i f(x_i)$. The quadrature nodes $\{x_i: i = 1, \ldots, N\}$ lie in the domain of x, and the quadrature weights $\{\omega_i: i = 1, \ldots, N\}$ are chosen appropriately so as to make the approximation of $\int fw$ a "good" one.[7] Gauss-Hermite quadrature is often used to evaluate numerically the integral over a function of a normal variable.[8] Tauchen (1986) showed that for univariate problems, a discrete approximation of the underlying random variable over ten points, for instance, works well in practice. Deaton and Laroque (1995) follow a similar procedure by replacing a standard normal variable with N discrete points $Z = (Z_1, \ldots, Z_N)$. The Z_i are chosen by first dividing the support of the normal distribution into N equiprobable intervals and then finding the conditional means within each interval. For $N = 10$, the 10 values are given by (± 1.75498333, ± 1.04463587, ± 0.67730694, ± 0.38649919, ± 0.12599747).[9] Tauchen and Hussey (1991) show how to extend these methods to evaluate expectations of functions of random variables that follow a Markov chain.[10] HM provide more detail, including methods for handling serially dependent processes.

When using discretization methods, a function is evaluated at, say, 100 grid points. It will often be necessary to interpolate the function at points not on the grid. There are two common procedures: linear interpolation and cubic splines (see Judd 1998, chap. 6). Linear interpolation works well in many portfolio problems where policy functions are well approximated by a piecewise linear specification. Cubic splines are continuously differentiable and have a nonzero third derivative, thus preserving the prudence feature of the utility function. The existence of a second derivative can also be a useful attribute when estimating the model with maximum likelihood, for instance.

Disastrous states of the world that result from the confluence of adverse realizations of random economic variables, such as labor incomes and stock returns, can have substantial effects on optimal portfolios even when they have a small probability of occurrence. This is obviously true in rank-dependent utility models, where utility in bad states receives a weight disproportionate to its probability of realization, but also in expected-utility or Kreps-Porteus frameworks under constant relative risk aversion, because marginal utility tends to infinity as consumption tends to zero. Inclusion of such states will induce households to choose portfolios that will not lead to a very low level of consumption even in the small-probability disastrous state. In practice, this means limiting both the extent of borrowing and the exposure to stockholding risk (see Carroll 1997 on saving effects of zero unemployment income and Rietz 1988 on the equity premium).[11]

2.3   A Model of Household Portfolio Choice

Consider now the problem of a household that lives for T periods, where T can be either finite or infinite. Household preferences are represented using the general Epstein-Zin formulation in section 2.1.1. In the first period of life, the household is faced with the recursive problem of choosing a sequence of bond and stockholdings, $\{B_t, S_t\}_{t=0}^{T}$, in order to maximize lifetime utility, U_0:

$$\max_{\{B_t, S_t\}_{t=0}^{T}} [U_0 = W(C_t, \mu(U_{t+1}|I_t))]. \tag{2.16}$$

In each period t, the household consumes C_t and chooses a portfolio of bonds and stocks to hold for one period, given the cash on hand, X_t, available to it in the current period:

$$C_t + B_t + S_t \leq X_t. \tag{2.17}$$

In finite-life variants, the household is assumed to have no bequest motive and thus to consume all cash on hand in the last period: $C_T = X_T$. Portfolio income in $t+1$ is determined by portfolio composition chosen in t, the random gross return on stocks, $\tilde{R}_{t+1}$, and the constant return on bonds, R_f. The excess return on equity is assumed independently and identically distributed except in section 4.2, where we discuss mean reversion of stock prices. Annual labor income follows the specification in section 2.1.2. Formally, cash on hand evolves as follows:

$$X_{t+1} = S_t \tilde{R}_{t+1} + B_t R_f + Y_{t+1}, \tag{2.18}$$

for given initial cash on hand, X_0. Consumption plans must satisfy the usual nonnegativity conditions:

$$C_t \geq 0, \quad \forall t. \tag{2.19}$$

In some model variants, we consider borrowing constraints in the form of no-short-sales restrictions (equation 2.13):

$$B_t \geq 0, \quad S_t \geq 0. \tag{2.20}$$

The most general forms of first-order conditions in $t = 1, \ldots, T-1$ for choice of B_t and S_t, respectively, are:

$$-C_t^{\zeta-1} + \beta[f_t(U_{t+1}^{\alpha})]^{\zeta/\alpha-1} f_t[U_{t+1}^{\alpha-\zeta} C_{t+1}^{\zeta-1} R_f] = \lambda_B \tag{2.21}$$

and

$$-C_t^{\zeta-1} + \beta[f_t(U_{t+1}^\alpha)]^{\zeta/\alpha-1} f_t[U_{t+1}^{\alpha-\zeta} C_{t+1}^{\zeta-1} \tilde{R}_{t+1}] = \lambda_S, \qquad (2.22)$$

where the Lagrange multipliers λ_B and λ_S are zero when short-sales constraints are either not imposed or not binding. For expected-utility variants, f_t is the expectations operator E_t, and $\alpha = \zeta$, thus yielding the familiar set of conditions for constant relative risk aversion (CRRA) preferences.

2.4   Solution

In this section, we derive and discuss solutions to variants of the basic household portfolio model. We examine three-period models, infinite-horizon, and multiperiod finite-horizon models, under various specifications of exogenous labor income and asset return processes, as well as market imperfections.

2.4.1   A Small-Scale Model Variant

Let us start with an end-of-period, three-period model ($T = 3$), which could also be used as a module within general equilibrium, overlapping-generations models of portfolio choice. At the end of the first two twenty-year time periods, the household consumes and chooses portfolios to hold over the second half of working life and during retirement, respectively. At the end of the retirement period, it consumes all cash on hand. Such models are solved by either constrained-optimization routines in software such as MATLAB or GAMS or the full nonlinear equation system. Since solutions are indexed by time period, state of the world, and history of past states, it is easy to handle cases where current policy is not only a function of realized cash on hand but also of prior portfolio composition (e.g., because of differential transactions costs or capital gains taxation).

Annual labor incomes follow the specification described in section 2.1.2. First-period income is the present value of labor incomes received between ages 21 and 40, and it is known prior to consumption or portfolio decisions. Starting from unity (a normalization), annual incomes grow exponentially at a known annual rate $\mu_g - .5 * \sigma_v^2$, with $\mu_g = 0.03$ and $\sigma_v = 0.08$. This rate is equal to the unconditional mean growth for individual annual earnings when earnings are stochastic. When second-period incomes (from age 41 to 60) are assumed nonstochastic, they are derived by extrapolation of this process for the next twenty years. When they are assumed stochastic, we set $\sigma_u = 0.1$ and $\sigma_v = 0.08$ to simulate 20,000 twenty-year sequences of annual labor incomes and compute the mean and variance of their present values. Our high- (low-) income state equals this expected value plus (minus) one standard deviation.[12] Third-period (retirement) income is assumed nonstochastic. To compute the twenty-year present value, annual retirement income is set to 70 percent of the annual labor income that would be obtained in the last year of working life if annual labor incomes were growing at $\mu_g - .5 * \sigma_v^2$ up to that point.[13]

The benchmark levels of preference parameters are set at $(\rho, \delta, \gamma) = (2, 0.05, 0.5)$, where ρ is relative risk aversion, δ is the annual rate of time preference, and γ is the degree of overweighting of inferior states in rank-dependent preferences (see section 2.1.1). The intertemporal elasticity of substitution, σ, is equal to the inverse of relative risk aversion in expected utility models, but it is set at 0.5 in nonexpected utility specifications.[14] The annual riskless rate is set at 0.02 and the annual equity premium at 0.042, with standard deviation equal to 0.18.[15]

First-period policy functions can be derived by solving the problem for a grid of first-period cash on hand and plotting solutions for real consumption, real stockholdings, and real bond holdings against cash on hand, all normalized by current labor income. Figure 2.1

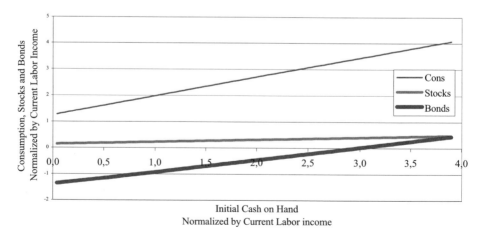

Figure 2.1
First-period policy functions for consumption, stock-, and bond holding as a function of cash on hand (expected utility specification): Risk aversion = 3

shows such policy functions for an expected utility specification with a risk aversion of 3 and without borrowing constraints, and the first panel of table 2.1 reports numerical results for a selected subset of the grid of normalized cash on hand.[16] In the absence of borrowing constraints, the model implies that it would be optimal for young expected-utility maximizers to hold stocks even at very low levels of normalized cash on hand. This finding is at variance with observed behavior of most young households, and an illustration of the stock market participation puzzle. As Haliassos and Bertaut (1995) showed, the theoretical result arises because stocks dominate bonds in rate of return and have zero covariance with the marginal utility of consumption at zero stockholding. At low levels of cash on hand, it is optimal for such young households that expect their labor income to grow over time to borrow at the riskless rate, so as to enhance consumption and purchase stocks that offer an equity premium. Since borrowing is devoted to both consumption and stockholding, the net financial worth of these households is negative, and this explains the negative portfolio shares of stocks in table 2.1. The marginal propensity to consume out of initial cash on hand is less than one, and households with higher initial resources tend to borrow less and invest more in stocks.

In addition to the participation puzzle, the model illustrates the three portfolio composition puzzles. The model implies that it is optimal for poorer households to hold only stocks in positive net amounts (portfolio specialization puzzle), to enrich their portfolios with positive net holdings of riskless assets only if their initial cash on hand exceeds a certain threshold (portfolio coexistence puzzle), and, for those with positive net worth, to have decreasing portfolio share of stocks as a function of initial cash on hand (decreasing portfolio share puzzle).[17] These puzzles occur despite a modest perceived equity premium of 4.2 percent. As we will see, they are surprisingly robust to augmenting the scale of the model through extensions in the household's horizon and the number of states of the world.

It may not be obvious how these theoretical predictions can be reconciled with the usual results of static two-asset models, surveyed in chapter 1. In static models, the investor is given a positive amount of initial wealth to allocate between risky and riskless assets and usually chooses a portfolio share of risky assets between zero and one, even in the presence of background labor income risk. Figure 2.2

Table 2.1
First-period policy functions for asset holdings under alternative preference specifications (three-period model, risk aversion = 3)

Normalized cash on hand	Expected utility			Kreps-Porteus preferences ($\sigma = 0.5$)			Quiggin preferences ($\sigma = 0.5, \gamma = 0.5$)		
	Stock-to-income ratio	Bond-to-income ratio	Stocks as a share of net worth	Stock-to-income ratio	Bond-to-income ratio	Stocks as a share of net worth	Stock-to-income ratio	Bond-to-income ratio	Stocks as a share of net worth
0.19	0.12	-1.01	-0.13	0.11	-1.05	-0.12	0.05	-0.93	-0.05
0.39	0.13	-0.94	-0.16	0.12	-0.98	-0.14	0.05	-0.85	-0.07
0.58	0.15	-0.87	-0.20	0.14	-0.92	-0.18	0.06	-0.78	-0.08
0.78	0.16	-0.80	-0.25	0.15	-0.85	-0.21	0.07	-0.70	-0.10
0.97	0.17	-0.73	-0.31	0.16	-0.79	-0.26	0.07	-0.63	-0.13
1.17	0.19	-0.66	-0.39	0.18	-0.72	-0.32	0.08	-0.55	-0.17
1.36	0.20	-0.59	-0.51	0.19	-0.66	-0.40	0.09	-0.48	-0.22
1.56	0.21	-0.52	-0.70	0.20	-0.59	-0.51	0.09	-0.40	-0.29
1.75	0.23	-0.45	-1.02	0.21	-0.52	-0.68	0.10	-0.33	-0.43
1.95	0.24	-0.38	-1.75	0.23	-0.46	-0.97	0.10	-0.25	-0.71
2.14	0.25	-0.31	-4.86	0.24	-0.39	-1.56	0.11	-0.18	-1.71
2.34	0.27	-0.23	8.10	0.25	-0.32	-3.41	0.12	-0.10	6.62
2.53	0.28	-0.16	2.37	0.26	-0.26	43.08	0.12	-0.02	1.23
2.73	0.29	-0.09	1.44	0.28	-0.19	3.21	0.13	0.05	0.71
2.92	0.31	-0.02	1.06	0.29	-0.12	1.74	0.14	0.13	0.51
3.12	0.32	0.05	0.85	0.30	-0.05	1.22	0.14	0.21	0.39
3.31	0.33	0.13	0.72	0.31	0.01	0.96	0.14	0.29	0.32
3.51	0.35	0.20	0.63	0.32	0.08	0.80	0.14	0.37	0.27
3.70	0.36	0.27	0.57	0.34	0.15	0.69	0.14	0.46	0.23
3.90	0.37	0.35	0.52	0.35	0.22	0.62	0.14	0.54	0.20

Note: Initial cash on hand consists of labor income and initial net financial assets. Cash on hand and asset holdings are normalized by current labor income. Solutions are shown for equal increments of normalized cash on hand and for relative risk aversion equal to 3. For nonexpected utility specifications, elasticity of intertemporal substitution is set at 0.5. For the Quiggin specification of rank-dependent utility, the gamma parameter is set at 0.5.

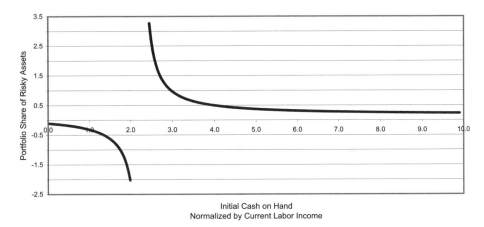

Figure 2.2
First-period share of net wealth in risky assets as a function of initial cash on hand:
Risk aversion = 3

and table 2.2 shed light on the apparent conflict by showing how the first-period share of risky assets in financial net worth varies with normalized cash on hand in the three-period model. In tracing this policy rule, we keep constant the process governing future labor income. Thus, we vary the ratio of initial cash on hand to human wealth. As can be seen in figure 2.2, the risky portfolio share is particularly sensitive to such variation. This suggests that the main source of difference between static and dynamic portfolio models lies in the type of question each asks. Static models postulate a wealth-allocation problem, often with no future labor income, implying a large (in the limit, infinite) ratio of initial resources to human wealth. Indeed, when normalized cash on hand is roughly greater than three, even the three-period dynamic model predicts an optimal portfolio share between zero and one, as in the static model. By contrast, dynamic computational models focus on young households with future earnings potential but with little or no inherited assets. Figure 2.2 shows that for a young household with no initial wealth and normalized cash on hand equal to one, the dynamic model predicts negative financial net worth and positive demand for stocks.

In small-scale models, second-period consumption and asset holdings in each state can be plotted against the corresponding level of second-period cash on hand. This gives us a visual impression of the subset of second-period policy functions relevant for each state.

Table 2.2
First-period portfolio shares of risky assets for various levels of initial normalized cash on hand (three-period expected-utility model, risk aversion = 3)

Normalized cash on hand	Share of risky assets	Normalized cash on hand	Share of risky assets
0.39	−0.16	5.07	0.37
0.78	−0.25	5.46	0.34
1.17	−0.39	5.85	0.32
1.56	−0.70	6.24	0.30
1.95	−1.75	6.63	0.29
2.34	8.10	7.02	0.28
2.73	1.44	7.41	0.27
3.12	0.85	7.80	0.26
3.51	0.63	8.19	0.25
3.90	0.52	8.58	0.25
4.29	0.45	8.97	0.24
4.68	0.40	9.36	0.23

Note: Initial cash on hand consists of labor income and initial net financial assets. Cash on hand is normalized by first-period labor income, and it is shown at equal increments. The share of risky assets in the model is the share of stocks in financial net worth.

Figure 2.3 shows solutions for the "best" state 1 that involves high labor incomes and high stock returns and the "worst" state 4 that involves the corresponding low realizations. Although the second-period consumption function has a lower intercept than that for the first, comparison with figure 2.1 shows that its marginal propensity to consume (MPC) is higher because of the shorter remaining lifetime. Similarly, the bond-holding function has a higher intercept but also a higher slope than in the first period. Since first- and second-period policy functions are quite similar in shape, we focus on policy functions for the young in the remainder of this section.

Although KP or Quiggin (Q) preferences have small effects on policy functions for consumption, table 2.1 shows that rank-dependent utility dramatically lowers stockholding (see also figure 2.4), borrowing, and the portfolio share of stocks in absolute value.[18] In unreported calibrations, we found that the size and sign of differences in stockholding predicted by an EU and a KP model depend on the relationship between risk aversion and the inverse of the elasticity of substitution in the KP model.[19] Positive correlation between earnings shocks and stock returns enhances the correlation between stock

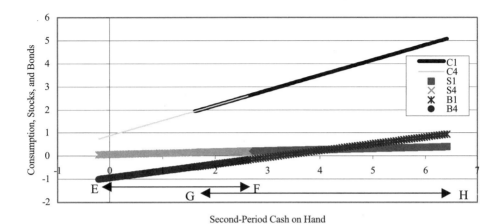

Figure 2.3
Second-period policy functions for consumption, stockholding, and bond holding (expected utility specification): Risk aversion = 3; 1: Best state (high earnings, high returns); 4: Worst state (low earnings, low returns); C: consumption; S: stockholdings; B: bond holdings

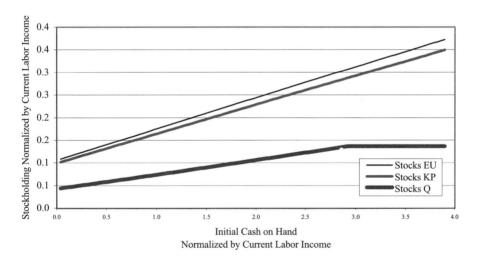

Figure 2.4
Policy functions for stockholding under expected utility (EU), Kreps-Porteus (KP), and Quiggin (Q) preferences: Risk aversion = 3

returns and consumption, thus making stockholding less desirable. Recent empirical research suggests that such correlation is relevant, especially for highly educated households (see Heaton and Lucas 2000a,b; Davis and Willen 2000). We have found that even combining positive correlation of 0.3, risk aversion of 8, and Q preferences does not justify zero stockholding in this model (see HM).

Precautionary effects are derived by comparing the above policy functions with those for an identical model that removes earnings risk and ensures labor incomes equal to the values that were expected when earnings risk was present. Table 2.3 presents precautionary effects on wealth, stocks, and bonds normalized by current labor income, for risk aversion of three and uncorrelated labor incomes and stock returns. Figures 2.5 and 2.6 plot precautionary wealth and effects on stockholding, respectively. Precautionary wealth is a decreasing function of initial cash on hand for all three preference specifications. This accords with intuition: since the marginal propensity to consume out of initial cash on hand is less than one, households with higher initial resources hold a larger amount of total wealth relative to future labor income and are able to accommodate future earnings shocks with a smaller precautionary buffer. Households that are particularly concerned about utility in the worst state (Q preferences) accumulate a larger precautionary wealth buffer than their EU counterparts with the same level of normalized cash on hand. Figure 2.6 confirms that normalized stockholding under EU or KP preferences is discouraged by the presence of uncorrelated background risk, but less so for households with higher initial resources. Although KP preferences yield larger precautionary responses in wealth and in stockholding than EU preferences in our benchmark calibration, we found in unreported calibrations that this ranking is reversed when risk aversion falls short of the inverse of the intertemporal elasticity of substitution. Even when reversals between EU and KP rankings were found, Q preferences continued to yield larger precautionary effects than either KP or EU. Thus, weighting of bad states by more than their probability of occurrence can exert considerable influence on precautionary portfolio behavior. Indeed, table 2.3 and figure 2.6 show that households with Q preferences accumulate such large precautionary wealth buffers that they end up holding more stocks as well as more riskless assets (or less riskless borrowing).[20]

Table 2.3
First-period precautionary effects on normalized wealth, stocks, and bonds under alternative preference specifications (three-period model, risk aversion = 3)

Normalized cash on hand	Expected utility			Kreps-Porteus preferences ($\sigma = 0.5$)			Quiggin preferences ($\sigma = 0.5$, $\gamma = 0.5$)		
	Effects on wealth-to-income ratio	Effects on stock-to-income ratio	Effects on bond-to-income ratio	Effects on wealth-to-income ratio	Effects on stock-to-income ratio	Effects on bond-to-income ratio	Effects on wealth-to-income ratio	Effects on stock-to-income ratio	Effects on bond-to-income ratio
0.19	0.072	-0.019	0.091	0.086	-0.018	0.104	0.117	-0.002	0.118
0.39	0.068	-0.018	0.086	0.081	-0.017	0.098	0.114	0.000	0.115
0.58	0.064	-0.018	0.081	0.077	-0.016	0.093	0.112	0.001	0.111
0.78	0.060	-0.017	0.077	0.073	-0.016	0.089	0.109	0.002	0.107
0.97	0.057	-0.016	0.073	0.069	-0.015	0.084	0.107	0.004	0.103
1.17	0.054	-0.015	0.069	0.066	-0.015	0.080	0.105	0.005	0.100
1.36	0.051	-0.015	0.066	0.063	-0.014	0.077	0.103	0.007	0.096
1.56	0.049	-0.014	0.063	0.060	-0.014	0.073	0.102	0.009	0.093
1.75	0.047	-0.014	0.060	0.057	-0.013	0.070	0.100	0.010	0.090
1.95	0.045	-0.013	0.058	0.055	-0.013	0.067	0.098	0.012	0.087
2.14	0.043	-0.013	0.055	0.053	-0.012	0.065	0.097	0.014	0.083
2.34	0.041	-0.012	0.053	0.050	-0.012	0.062	0.096	0.015	0.080
2.53	0.039	-0.012	0.051	0.049	-0.011	0.060	0.094	0.017	0.077
2.73	0.038	-0.011	0.049	0.047	-0.011	0.058	0.093	0.019	0.074
2.92	0.036	-0.011	0.047	0.045	-0.011	0.056	0.092	0.020	0.072
3.12	0.035	-0.011	0.046	0.043	-0.010	0.054	0.090	0.016	0.074
3.31	0.034	-0.010	0.044	0.042	-0.010	0.052	0.088	0.011	0.077
3.51	0.033	-0.010	0.043	0.041	-0.010	0.050	0.087	0.006	0.080
3.70	0.032	-0.010	0.041	0.039	-0.009	0.049	0.085	0.002	0.083
3.90	0.031	-0.009	0.040	0.038	-0.009	0.047	0.084	-0.003	0.087

Note: Initial cash on hand consists of labor income and initial net financial assets. Cash on hand and precautionary effects on asset holdings are normalized by current labor income. Solutions are shown for equal increments of normalized cash on hand and for relative risk aversion equal to 3. For nonexpected utility specifications, elasticity of intertemporal substitution is set at 0.5. For the Quiggin specification of rank-dependent utility, the gamma parameter is set at 0.5.

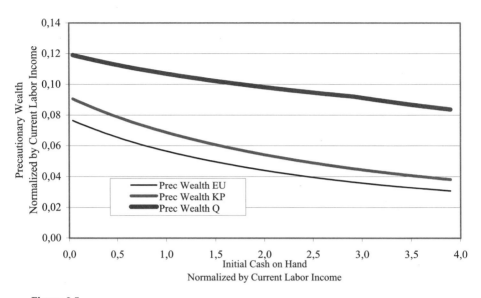

Figure 2.5
Precautionary wealth under expected utility (EU), Kreps-Porteus (KP), and Quiggin
(Q) preferences: Risk aversion = 3

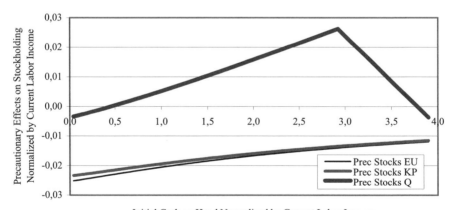

Figure 2.6
Precautionary effects on stockholding under expected utility (EU), Kreps-Porteus (KP),
and Quiggin (Q) preferences: Risk aversion = 3

Haliassos and Hassapis (1998) derive effects of income-based and collateral constraints. They compute precautionary effects as differences between models with and without earnings risk, when both incorporate borrowing constraints. They find that binding borrowing constraints of either type reduce precautionary effects on wealth relative to what would have been observed in the absence of constraints and can reduce or even reverse precautionary effects on stockholding. Such findings suggest that populations that contain a sizable proportion of borrowing-constrained households are likely to exhibit small or insignificant effects of earnings risk on wealth and on risky asset holdings.

2.4.2   A Large-Scale, Infinite-Horizon Model

The wealth of information provided by small-scale models comes at some cost: the number of equations increases rapidly as we add time periods, states of the world, and constraints (the dimensionality issue). Large-scale models adopt computational shortcuts that sacrifice some information but yield solutions for a much larger number of periods and states of the world. The remainder of this chapter is devoted to large-scale models that assume expected utility maximization, CRRA preferences, and short-sales constraints on bonds and on stocks. We first consider the limiting case of an infinite planning horizon by setting $T \to \infty$ in the model of section 2.3 (see Ramsey 1926 and Barro 1974 for motivation).[21]

A Solution Method Based on Euler Equations
We describe here an approach to solving based on the first-order conditions for bonds and stocks. (We later describe an alternative approach, based on the value function.) Analytical first-order conditions for bonds and for stocks, respectively, can be written as follows:

$$U'(C_t) = \frac{1+r}{1+\delta} E_t U'(C_{t+1}) + \lambda_B \qquad (2.23)$$

and

$$U'(C_t) = \frac{1}{1+\delta} E_t[U'(C_{t+1}), \tilde{R}_{t+1}] + \lambda_S, \qquad (2.24)$$

where λ_B and λ_S refer to the Lagrange multipliers for the no-short-sales constraints. Recalling the budget constraint $C_t = X_t - B_t - S_t$, where X_t is cash on hand, a binding short-sales constraint on bonds implies that $C_t = X_t - S_t$ since bond holdings are zero. Similarly, a binding constraint on short sales of stock implies $C_t = X_t - B_t$. The Deaton (1991) solution can be generalized to allow for portfolio choice by writing the two Euler equations as:

$$U'(C_t) = \max\left[U'(X_t - S_t), \frac{1+r}{1+\delta}E_t U'(C_{t+1})\right] \tag{2.25}$$

and

$$U'(C_t) = \max\left[U'(X_t - B_t), \frac{1}{1+\delta}E_t\tilde{R}_{t+1}U'(C_{t+1})\right]. \tag{2.26}$$

Given the nonstationary process followed by labor income, we normalize asset holdings and cash on hand by the permanent component of earnings P_{it}, denoting the normalized variables by lowercase letters (Carroll, 1992). Defining $Z_{t+1} = \frac{P_{t+1}}{P_t}$ and taking advantage of the homogeneity of degree $(-\rho)$ of marginal utility implied by CRRA preferences,

$$U'(x_t - s_t - b_t) = \max\left[U'(x_t - s_t), \frac{1+r}{1+\delta}E_t U'(c_{t+1})Z_{t+1}^{-\rho}\right] \tag{2.27}$$

and

$$U'(x_t - s_t - b_t) = \max\left[U'(x_t - b_t), \frac{1}{1+\delta}E_t\tilde{R}_{t+1}U'(c_{t+1})Z_{t+1}^{-\rho}\right]. \tag{2.28}$$

The normalized state variable x evolves according to

$$x_{t+1} = (s_t\tilde{R}_{t+1} + b_t R_f)Z_{t+1}^{-1} + U_{it+1}, \tag{2.29}$$

where the last term is the ratio of labor income in period $t+1$ to its permanent component, the transitory earnings shock. We use the identity $c_{t+1} = x_{t+1} - b_{t+1} - s_{t+1}$ where both b_{t+1} and s_{t+1} will be functions of x_{t+1} to substitute out c_{t+1} on the right-hand sides of equations 2.27 and 2.28. Given that conditions 2.30 and 2.31 (which follow) are satisfied, we can solve simultaneously for $\{s(x), b(x)\}$. Starting with any initial guess (say, $s(x) = .1 * x$ and $b(x) = .1 * x$), we use the right-hand side of the first Euler equation to get an update for b and continue doing so until b converges to its time-invariant solution b_1^* (see Deaton 1991). We then use the second Euler equation, with b_1^* taken as given, to find the solution for the time-invariant optimal s; call it s_1^*. We now have two updated functions $\{s_1^*, b_1^*\}$; the process can be repeated until these functions converge to their time-invariant solutions.

In order for the algorithm to work, the Euler equations, 2.27 and 2.28, must define a contraction mapping. Based on Deaton and Laroque (1992), sufficient conditions for a contraction mapping are

$$\frac{1+r}{1+\delta}E_t Z_{t+1}^{-\rho} < 1 \tag{2.30}$$

for equation 2.27 and

$$\frac{1}{1+\delta}E_t \tilde{R}_{t+1}Z_{t+1}^{-\rho} < 1 \tag{2.31}$$

for equation 2.28. If these conditions hold simultaneously, there will exist a unique set of optimum policies satisfying the two Euler equations. It can be shown that under a positive equity premium, these conditions translate into

$$\frac{\mu_r - \delta}{\rho} + \frac{\rho}{2}\sigma_n^2 < \mu_g + \mu_n. \tag{2.32}$$

Impatience must now be even higher than in a corresponding single-asset model to prevent the accumulation of infinite stocks (see HM). Note that a high expected earnings growth profile, μ_g, can guarantee that the individual will not want to accumulate an infinite amount of stocks or bonds but would rather borrow, expecting future earnings increases. Also, if the rate of time preference exceeds the expected stock return, more risk-averse (higher ρ) individuals will not satisfy the convergence conditions. We set the rate of time preference, δ, equal to 0.1, and the constant real interest rate, r, equal to 0.02. Carroll (1992) estimates the variances of the idiosyncratic shocks using data from the Panel Study of Income Dynamics, and our baseline simulations use values close to those: 0.1 percent per year for σ_u and 0.08 percent per year for σ_v. We set the mean aggregate labor income growth rate, denoted μ_g, equal to 0.03, and we consider various coefficients of relative risk aversion that meet sufficient condition 2.32 for the existence of a contraction mapping.

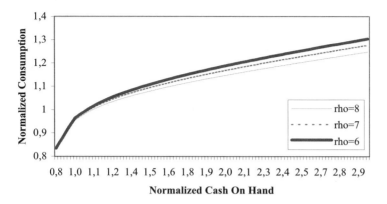

Figure 2.7
Normalized consumption (varying rho)

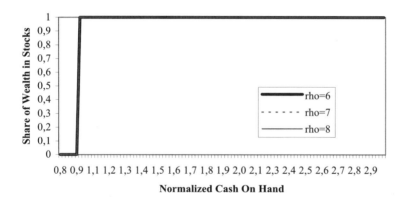

Figure 2.8
Share of wealth in stocks (varying rho)

Policy Functions and Time-Series Results
Figures 2.7, 2.9, and 2.10 show, respectively, consumption, stock-holdings, and bond holdings, normalized by the permanent compo-nent of income, as functions of similarly normalized cash on hand. Figure 2.8 plots the share of financial wealth held in the risky asset for different levels of cash on hand for relative risk-aversion co-efficients equal to 6, 7, and 8. Figure 2.7 shows that at levels of nor-malized cash on hand below a cutoff x^* (typically around 97 percent of the permanent component of labor income), the household wants to borrow but is bound by both short sales constraints (figures 2.9 and 2.10). Its stockholding is zero as a result. This suggests that

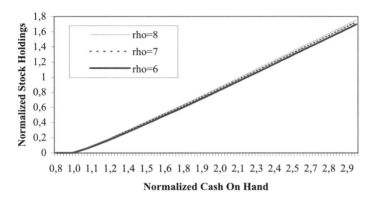

Figure 2.9
Normalized stockholdings (varying rho)

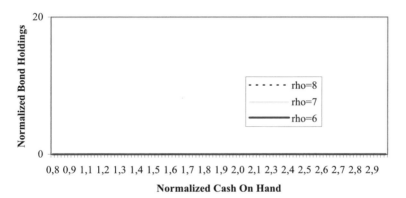

Figure 2.10
Normalized bond holdings (varying rho)

a combination of short-sales constraints on both assets and low current resources can provide a reason for not participating in the stock market, but only for those who have no other savings.

These figures also illustrate two of the three portfolio composition puzzles. Figure 2.7 demonstrates the portfolio specialization puzzle of Heaton and Lucas (1997). It shows that it is optimal for households with normalized cash on hand above x^* to start saving exclusively in stocks. Haliassos and Michaelides (1999) argue that this happens because, under no stockholding and no correlation between earnings and stock returns,

$$\frac{1}{1+\delta}E_t[U'(C_{t+1})]E_t[\tilde{R}_{t+1} - R_f] = \lambda_B - \lambda_S. \tag{2.33}$$

Given nonsatiation and an equity premium, the left-hand side of equation 2.33 is positive: $\lambda_B > \lambda_S$. Thus, households in the neighborhood of x^* would like to borrow risklessly to consume and invest in stocks that offer an equity premium and have zero covariance with consumption.[22] Prevented from borrowing, they devote all saving to stocks. Changes in the degree of risk aversion, rate of time preference, perceived size of (positive) equity premium, or even habit persistence cannot reverse this result.

Figure 2.8 shows that for those predicted to hold the riskless asset, the share of risky assets in total financial wealth is decreasing in cash on hand. Richer households do not need to rely as much on the wealth-generating power of the equity premium and can afford to put a larger share of their wealth in the riskless asset. Yet the country chapters in this book consistently find that both financial wealth and current labor income contribute positively to the portfolio share in the risky asset, conditional on holding stocks.

Figure 2.9 shows that normalized stockholdings are increasing in risk aversion at levels of normalized cash on hand that justify saving, and figure 2.8 shows that the portfolio share remains unaffected by risk aversion over a range of cash on hand. This surprising result is due to a conflict between risk aversion and "prudence" in the presence of binding short-sales constraints. Since prudence is positively related to risk aversion, households want to increase their net wealth when cash on hand is above x^* (figure 2.7), but none of this increase comes from changes in realized borrowing, which is still at zero because of the binding short-sales constraint (figure 2.10). Their desire to increase wealth dominates their motive to reduce exposure to stockholding risk, leading to increased stockholding for higher degrees of risk aversion. Interestingly, we have found in unreported calibrations that this feature persists even in a model that assumes there are no permanent earnings shocks but allows for transitory shocks to earnings.

When we are interested in either the aggregate or the time-series implications of a portfolio model, we can simulate individual life histories and optimal choices over time. In the current model, however, normalized cash on hand follows a renewal process, and therefore the aggregate or individual time-series implications of the

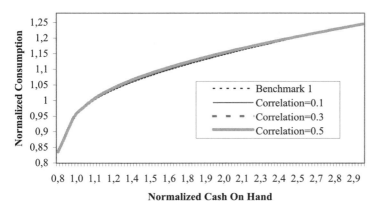

Figure 2.11
Normalized consumption

model can be derived by computing the time-invariant distribution of cash on hand. The method by which this can be done is explained in HM. The invariant distribution of normalized cash on hand can be used to show that mean and median bond holding are zero in the infinite-horizon model. Consistent with policy functions, mean and median normalized stockholdings are not only positive but also increasing in risk aversion. Such portfolio behavior by the more risk averse is justified, since it results in smaller standard deviation of normalized consumption, as well as in higher mean normalized consumption.

Can positive correlation between labor incomes and stock returns, which tends to lower demand for stocks, account for participation and portfolio composition puzzles? Figures 2.11 through 2.14 illustrate the effects of positive correlation equal to 0.1, 0.3, and 0.5. For correlation of 0.3, the household is still predicted to enter the stock market first, but the range of cash on hand for which the saver is predicted to hold both stocks and bonds is considerably expanded (figure 2.13). Thus, this level of correlation is consistent with both households that do not participate in any asset market because of low resources and binding constraints (relevant to the participation puzzle) and those that are better off and hold diversified portfolios (relevant to one portfolio composition puzzle). Positive correlation cannot handle the second composition puzzle. At a correlation of 0.5, we find that it will not be optimal for households to participate in the

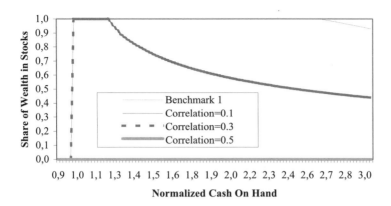

Figure 2.12
Share of wealth in stocks

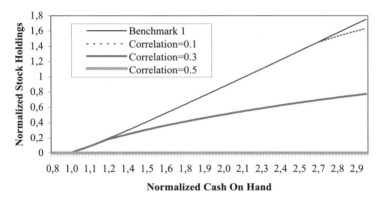

Figure 2.13
Normalized stockholdings

stock market for any level of cash on hand they are likely to experience, a rather extreme solution to the participation puzzle.

How plausible are such levels of correlation? Davis and Willen (2000) obtain correlation estimates ranging between .1 and .3 over most of the working life for college-educated males and around −.25 at all ages for male high school dropouts.[23] Heaton and Lucas (2000a) argue that entrepreneurial risk is positively correlated with stock returns and reaches levels around .2. These numbers appear smaller than needed to explain zero stockholding. Moreover, they come close to generating zero stockholding for college graduates or enterpreneurs who in fact tend to hold stocks, and they predict that

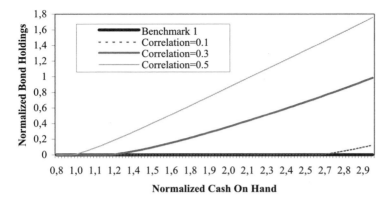

Figure 2.14
Normalized bond holdings

low-education households should actually be holding stocks as a hedging instrument when in fact they tend not to do so.

The positive probability of a disaster event (in either the labor income process or the realization of a very low stock market return) might substantially affect portfolio choices. We have found that even with a small probability (.5 percent)[24] of receiving a low labor income realization (the latter set at 25 percent of mean labor income), the complete portfolio specialization in stocks result is not reversed. The result is even more robust when disaster events in stocks are allowed (complete ruin with a small probability equal to .5 percent), but a positive floor in labor income exists with positive probability. More work is needed to explore the robustness of these preliminary results for different probabilities and specifications of disaster.

Effects of Stock Market Participation Costs   In this section, we report the normalized entry cost to the stock market that would make agents indifferent between entering the stock market or not participating computed in Haliassos and Michaelides (1999). For a household with rate of time preference $\delta = 0.1$ whose labor income is uncorrelated with stock returns, the threshold ranges from 4 percent of the permanent component of annual labor income when risk aversion is 2 to 16 percent when risk aversion is 8. The reason that higher costs are needed to discourage more risk-averse households is the conflict between prudence and risk aversion already noted. When risk aversion rises, prudence dominates risk aversion and dictates that more wealth be accumulated in the form of stocks. This in turn raises the entry costs needed to prevent stockholding. When permanent shocks to household labor income have correlation with stock returns equal to 0.3, the corresponding range is only from 3 percent to 6 percent, because of the reduced attractiveness of stocks. Raising the equity premium from the assumed 4.2 percent to 6 percent increases the thresholds by about 50 percent. Halving the rate of time preference to $\delta = 0.05$ roughly doubles the necessary fixed costs.

All in all, threshold fixed costs of entry needed to keep households out of the stock market tend to be quite small, given that they are paid only once and that we have constructed our experiment so as to overstate these costs in at least two other respects. First, we have assumed that once these costs are paid, they allow the household to access stocks over a (remaining) infinite horizon. Second, the reported level is what would be sufficient to keep all households out of the stock market, as opposed to the approximately 50 percent that do not undertake stockholding in the United States. Thus, the figures suggest that relatively small costs associated with information acquisition, commissions, time spent, and perhaps even inertia could keep households out of the stock market.

Indeed, one may wonder why threshold entry costs are so small, despite assumptions designed to overstate them. As shown by the invariant distributions, the reason is that even in the absence of entry costs, impatient households are likely to spend a substantial fraction of their time at levels of normalized cash on hand that justify none or very limited stockholding.[25] Since their use of the stock market will be limited in this sense, households require relatively small entry costs to be deterred from entering. The relevance of entry costs for the participation puzzle is the subject of ongoing research. A particularly troublesome feature of the data is the observed coexistence of zero stockholding with substantial holdings of essentially riskless liquid assets for some households.[26]

Stock Market Mean Reversion   This section, based closely on Michaelides (1999), highlights portfolio effects of predictability of the excess return of stocks over Treasury bills, now considered a stylized fact in finance (see Cochrane 1999).[27] Stock market predictability is interesting for our purposes because it can contribute to resolution of portfolio composition puzzles by rationalizing the observed coexistence of bonds and stocks. Letting $\{r_f, r_t\}$ denote the net risk-free rate

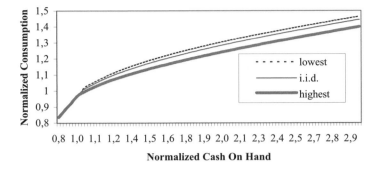

Figure 2.15
Normalized consumption. *Note:* Relative risk aversion is set at 3. There is zero correlation between ε and z, and between η and z.

and the net stock market return, respectively, and f_t being the factor
that predicts future excess returns, we have

$$r_{t+1} - r_f = f_t + z_{t+1} \tag{2.34}$$

$$f_{t+1} = \mu + \phi(f_t - \mu) + \varepsilon_{t+1}, \tag{2.35}$$

where the two innovations $\{z_{t+1}, \varepsilon_{t+1}\}$ are contemporaneously correlated. Mean reversion in the stock market is captured by the autoregressive nature of the factor (f_t) predicting stock market returns
$(\phi > 0)$. The autoregressive nature of the factor is captured by a ten-
point discretization scheme. Labeling the m factor states $i = 1, \ldots, m$,
there are m bond and stock demand functions, one for each currently
observed factor state.

Figures 2.15 through 2.18 depict some of the resulting policy
functions.[28] When the factor predicting stock returns follows an
AR(1) process, there is an incentive for the individual to "time the
stock market." A low current factor realization signifying lower
future returns induces a decrease in demand for stocks and in saving
relative to the i.i.d. case, in response to less favorable future investment opportunities and vice versa. When the current factor realization is above its mean, any additional demand for stocks is equal
to the increase in saving, since the borrowing constraint is already
binding in the i.i.d. model. For such factor realizations, the complete
portfolio specialization puzzle persists (figure 2.17). However, when
the current factor realization is below its mean, the demand for
stocks falls relative to the i.i.d. model, and so does their portfolio
share, thus generating portfolio coexistence of bonds and stocks at

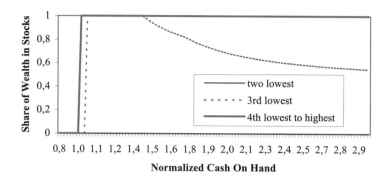

Figure 2.16
Share of wealth in stocks. *Note:* Relative risk aversion is set at 3. There is zero correlation between ε and z, and between η and z.

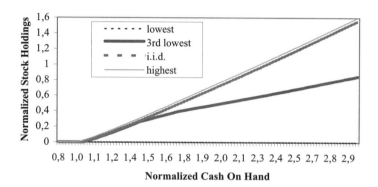

Figure 2.17
Normalized stockholdings. *Note:* Relative risk aversion is set at 3. There is zero correlation between ε and z, and between η and z.

lower levels of normalized cash on hand than in the i.i.d. case. Witness, for example, the policy functions for the third lowest factor in figures 2.17 and 2.18 compared to those for the i.i.d. case. Under the lowest realization of the factor, the investor stops participating in the stock market altogether because of the grim stock market prospects (figure 2.17), suggesting a further reason for stock market nonparticipation: the perception of bad outcomes.

Michaelides (1999) also shows that positive correlation between labor income innovations and stock returns increases the hedging demand for bonds. Time-series moments confirm the portfolio coexistence of bonds and stocks. On the negative side, the median

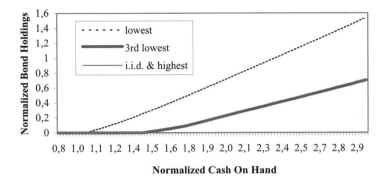

Figure 2.18
Normalized bond holdings. *Note:* Relative risk aversion is set at 3. There is zero correlation between ε and z, and between η and z.

stockholding share (counterfactually) remains equal to one, while the volatility of stock market trading that arises from the market timing activity is very high.

2.4.3 Large-Scale Models with Finite Horizons

Let us now turn to large-scale portfolio models that analyze household choices over the life cycle. Such models are useful even when the properties of solutions to infinite-horizon setups are fully understood. They yield predictions on the age pattern of asset market participation and portfolio composition, based on age-earnings profiles and on factors that are likely to vary over the life cycle, such as earnings uncertainty, demographic characteristics, and constraints facing the household.

We modify the objective function 2.16 of the model in section 2.3 to allow for a horizon of $T+1$ periods with a positive probability of death in each period:

$$\max_{\{S_{it}, B_{it}\}_{t=1}^{T}} E_1 \sum_{t=1}^{T} \beta^{t-1} \left\{ \prod_{j=0}^{t-1} p_j \right\} U(C_{it}), \qquad (2.36)$$

subject to constraints 2.17 through 2.20. E_1 is the mathematical expectations operator, and $\beta \equiv \dfrac{1}{1+\delta}$ is the constant discount factor. The probability that a consumer-investor is alive at time $(t+1)$ conditional on being alive at time t is denoted by p_t, with $p_0 = 1$, as in Hubbard, Skinner, and Zeldes (1995). We abstract from bequests, although they can be accommodated easily.

During working years, $1 \le t \le T - k - 1$, labor income is given by equations 2.8 and 2.9. In the k retirement years, $T - k < t \le T$, pension income is a fraction c of permanent income

$$Y_t = cP_t, \tag{2.37}$$

where c lies between zero and one.

The Value Function Approach
This approach involves the repeated use of backward induction on the value function. Assuming constant relative risk aversion felicity, the Bellman equation associated with the problem is

$$V_t(X_t, P_t) = \max_{\{S_t, B_t\}} \left[\frac{C_t^{1-\rho}}{1-\rho} + \beta E_t V_{t+1}([S_t \tilde{R}_{t+1} + B_t R_f + Y_{t+1}], P_{t+1}) \right], \quad (2.38)$$

where $V_t(\cdot)$ denotes the value function that depends on the age of the individual and thus has a time subscript, and the first argument of $V_{t+1}(X_{t+1}, P_{t+1})$ has been substituted using equation 2.18. Cocco, Gomes, and Maenhout (1999) use backward induction on equation 2.38 to derive the optimal policy functions.

Considerable simplification can be obtained by using the fact that the value function is homogeneous of degree $(1 - \rho)$.[29] This property can be used to reduce the number of state variables from three (X_t, P_t, Age_t) to two $(x_t \equiv \frac{X_t}{P_t}$ and $Age_t)$. Instead of computing $V_t(X_t, P_t)$, we can focus on $\hat{V}_t(x_t) \equiv V(x_t, 1)$; in view of equation 2.38 and the homogeneity property, this is given by

$$\hat{V}_t(x_t) = \max_{\{s_t(x_t), b_t(x_t)\}} \left[\frac{c_t^{1-\rho}}{1-\rho} + \beta E_t V_{t+1} \left(\frac{X_{t+1}}{P_t}, \frac{P_{t+1}}{P_t} \right) \right]$$

$$= \max_{\{s_t(x_t), b_t(x_t)\}} \left[\frac{c_t^{1-\rho}}{1-\rho} + \beta E_t \left(\left\{ \frac{P_t}{P_{t+1}} \right\}^{1-\rho} \hat{V}_{t+1}(x_{t+1}) \right) \right], \tag{2.39}$$

where $s_t = \dfrac{S_t}{P_t}$ and $b_t = \dfrac{B_t}{P_t}$ are the normalized holdings of stocks and bonds, respectively, and

$$x_{t+1} = [s_t \tilde{R}_{t+1} + b_t R_f] \frac{P_t}{P_{t+1}} + U_{t+1}. \tag{2.40}$$

Note that U_{t+1} is the transitory earnings shock, which enters as the ratio of Y_{t+1} to P_{t+1}.

Backward induction produces the value functions, $\hat{V}_t(x_t)$, and the policy functions, $b_t(x_t)$ and $s_t(x_t)$, for each period. In the last period and without a bequest motive, $c_T = x_T$ and the value function corresponds to the indirect utility function $\hat{V}_T(x_T)$. To compute the policy rules and the value function for the previous period $T - 1$, the set of admissible values for the decision variables is discretized using equally spaced grids and noting that the short-sales constraints (equation 2.20) bound b_t and s_t from below at zero. For each given level of cash on hand (which is also discretized), the optimal levels of decision variables are chosen by evaluating the value function at all possible pairs (b_t, s_t) and picking the maximands. This grid search is intended to avoid choosing local optima. Expectations of random variables are taken using quadrature methods, and interpolation is used to evaluate the value function for points not on the grid (see section 2.2). Once $\hat{V}_{T-1}(x_{T-1})$ is thus computed, the procedure is iterated backward to the beginning of working life.

The Euler Equation Approach
The model can also be solved using the first-order conditions 2.23 and 2.24 in their normalized form, 2.27 and 2.28, respectively, recognizing that policy functions are age dependent under finite horizons. Equations 2.27 and 2.28 comprise a system with two unknowns, $s(x_t)$ and $b(x_t)$, once a functional form for $c_{t+1}(x_{t+1})$ is given. In the absence of a bequest motive, $c_T = x_T$, and the functional form is determined for period T. For $t < T - 1$, the policy function $c_{t+1}(x_{t+1})$ is determined numerically, as a set of consumption levels each of which corresponds to a grid point for normalized cash on hand. Using $c_{t+1}(x_{t+1})$, we can begin solving simultaneously this system of Euler equations using backward induction.[30] The proposed algorithm takes the following form:

1. Given an initial guess about $s(x_t)$, find $b(x_t)$ from equation 2.27 using a standard bisection algorithm.[31]

2. Given $b(x_t)$, find $s(x_t)$ from equation 2.28 using the bisection algorithm.

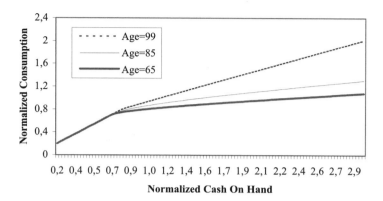

Figure 2.19
Normalized consumption (retirement)

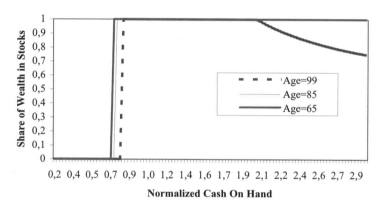

Figure 2.20
Share of wealth in stocks (retirement)

3. If the maximum of the absolute differences between the initial $s(x_t)$ and its update from step 2 is less than a convergence criterion (say, .0001), then the policy functions for normalized bonds and stocks are determined.

The policy function for normalized consumption can also be determined using $c_t = x_t - b_t - s_t$. We repeat for period $t - 1$, until we reach the first period of life.

Policy Function Results
Figures 2.19 through 2.22 report normalized consumption and the share of wealth in stocks during both retirement and working life.[32]

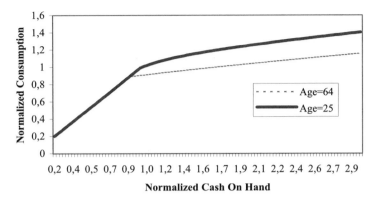

Figure 2.21
Normalized consumption (working life)

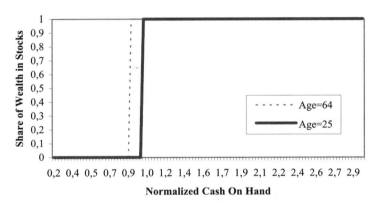

Figure 2.22
Share of wealth in stocks (working life)

They confirm that for parameter configurations that respect the contraction mapping condition, the backward recursion converges to the infinite horizon solution derived earlier using a different method. Policy rules for the younger agents (age 25 in figures 2.21 and 2.22) suggest that infinite horizon models are a good approximation to the behavior of the younger segment of the population.

The low level of prudence ($\rho = 3$) and the equity premium continue to generate complete portfolio specialization in stocks during working life (figure 2.22), illustrating that the puzzle is not unique to the infinite horizons model. Figure 2.21 illustrates how saving rises (consumption drops) as one ages once normalized cash on

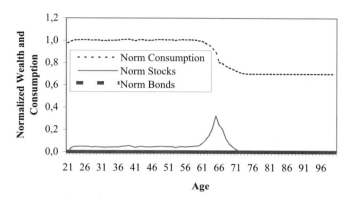

Figure 2.23
Stocks, bonds, and consumption: $g = 0.03$, delta $= 0.1$, rho $= 3$

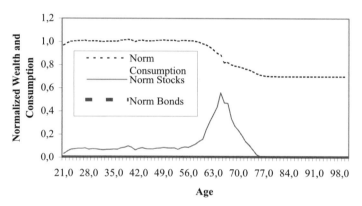

Figure 2.24
Stocks, bonds, and consumption: $g = 0.03$, delta $= 0.1$, rho $= 5$

hand exceeds a certain threshold (this is saving for retirement; see Gourinchas and Parker 1999). Moreover, older people tend to enter the stock market at lower levels of normalized cash on hand than the young (figure 2.22), because they have a higher saving rate than their younger counterparts, who anticipate growing labor income.

Given age-specific policy functions, the evolution of wealth over the life cycle can be analyzed either by simulation or by using the transition distribution of normalized wealth in the economy. Figures 2.23 through 2.26 report the average normalized consumption and bond and stockholdings of 10,000 simulated life histories under two alternative expected rates of income growth ($g = 0.1$ and $g = 0.3$),

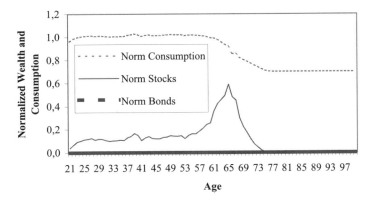

Figure 2.25
Stocks, bonds, and consumption: $g = 0.01$, delta $= 0.1$, rho $= 3$

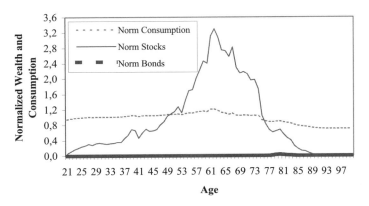

Figure 2.26
Stocks, bonds, and consumption: $g = 0.01$, delta $= 0.1$, rho $= 5$

and two degrees of relative risk aversion ($\rho = 3$ and $\rho = 5$). High impatience ($\delta = 0.1$) results in very low wealth accumulation, and consumption is very close to mean normalized labor income during working life (equal to one) and very close or equal to the normalized pension benefit (0.7) during retirement. Higher prudence generates higher wealth accumulation (compare figure 2.24 to 2.23, and figure 2.26 to 2.25), while a higher expected income growth rate acts as a higher discount factor and reduces wealth accumulation (compare figure 2.25 to 2.23 and figure 2.26 to 2.24). Not surprisingly, the highest wealth accumulation in the panel is observed when prudence is highest and income is expected to grow at the lower rate (figure

2.26). The portfolio specialization puzzle is evident in these simulations, which imply that wealth accumulation essentially occurs through holdings of stock.

2.4.4 Toward General Equilibrium Models

The small-scale models we described could in principle be embedded in general equilibrium, overlapping-generations models, in which each generation lives for three periods. A pioneering overlapping-generations model of this type has been proposed by Constantinides, Donaldson, and Mehra (1998), in order to study the likely effects of borrowing constraints on the equity premium. In their model, as in ours, the young are faced with earnings risk in the second period of their lives, and they would like to borrow in order to invest in stocks and thus take advantage of the equity premium. The middle-aged know that their income in old age will depend on their holdings of stocks and bonds, and they choose to hold positive amounts of both. A borrowing constraint on the young prevents them from financing stockholding through borrowing. This lowers the aggregate demand for stocks in the economy and raises the equity premium relative to what would be obtained in the absence of borrowing constraints. The result shows that equity premiums are likely to be higher when "junior can't borrow" and highlights the importance of undestanding the portfolio behavior of young households.

The large-scale models we examined are candidate building blocks for a different type of general equilibrium models. Aiyagari (1994) and Huggett (1993) were the first to study the equilibrium interest rate in heterogeneous agent models with labor income uncertainty and borrowing constraints but without aggregate uncertainty. Den Haan (1996), Rios-Rull (1996), and Krusell and Smith (1998) extend this line of research by solving general equilibrium models with aggregate uncertainty. In models with heterogeneous agents and aggregate uncertainty, the wealth distribution becomes an endogenously evolving state variable. Given that this is an infinite-dimensional state variable, the problem becomes intractable. A potential solution is to approximate the evolution of this distribution with its important moments. Consistency of rational expectations would then require that agents' expectations about the future evolution of the weatlh distribution moments materialize in reality. In a nonlinear model, however, there is no guarantee that the predicted evolution of the wealth distribution will match the actual wealth distribution, and there is no obvious choice of which moments should be followed. Surprisingly, Krusell and Smith find that (in their first-order Markov equilibrium) the mean of the wealth distribution and the aggregate productivity shock are sufficient statistics for the evolution of the wealth distribution, in the sense that the actual values of the wealth distribution are very close to the predictions agents use to solve their individual problems. Storeslettern, Telmer, and Yaron (1998) analyze the implications of the Krusell-Smith economy for the equity premium using similar techniques and find that their model can explain part of the equity premium.

2.5 Conclusion

This chapter has presented a set of computational techniques that can be used to solve models of household portfolio choice, the main features of solutions, and key puzzles when solutions are confronted with data in the empirical chapters. Household portfolios is an exciting area of research with many unanswered questions. Most existing models have explored implications of our standard choice models for portfolio choices between risky and riskless financial assets. Although this literature has contributed to our understanding of key factors influencing portfolio choice, it is fair to say that we do not yet have models that can account simultaneously for the limited incidence of stockholding in the population, the pattern of observed stockholding among different age, education, and other relevant demographic groups, and the positive (concave?) relationship between risky portfolio shares and cash on hand typically observed in country data. This is an important agenda for future portfolio research.

A second fruitful avenue for future research is to study the portfolio interaction between financial and real assets such as private businesses and housing. As chapter 10 on the rich illustrates, private businesses are a key portfolio component for wealthy households and an important determinant of their labor income. Housing, not covered in this book, is important for all households (though less so for the rich) as both a portfolio component and a source of housing services. The dual role of real assets, their usefulness as collateral for loans, and their lumpiness that often necessitates accumulation of down payments or start-up funds make them potentially fascinating objects of future analysis.

A third area for potential research lies in the analysis of tax effects on portfolios (see chapter 3 on taxation). One needs to explore the portfolio effects of the tax treatment of labor income, interest and dividend income, capital gains, bequests, and inheritances. Particularly exciting from a computational perspective is the analysis of capital gains taxation, in view of the requirement that capital gains be taxed at realization and of special tax provisions for capital gains bequeathed to descendants, such as "step-up-of basis" clauses. A fourth dimension, not covered in this book, deals with privatization of pension systems, new types of retirement accounts and their tax treatment, as well as the implications of such schemes for the rest of a household's portfolio.

From a methodological perspective, a challenge for future portfolio research is to move from partial-equilibrium to general-equilibrium models in an effort to account simultaneously for portfolio puzzles and asset return puzzles, such as the equity premium. This move will be much smoother if it takes place after we gain a clear understanding of optimal portfolios involving each of the various asset types discussed above. When asset returns are also successfuly endogenized, the stage will have been set for computer simulations of artificial economies with optimizing agents in which portfolio behavior and the wealth distribution play a key role. Perhaps this is as close as we are likely to get to controlled experiments in economics.

Notes

We are grateful to Carol Bertaut, Giuseppe Bertola, Christopher Carroll, Angus Deaton, Luigi Guiso, Tullio Jappelli, and Ramon Marimon for helpful discussions. We also thank participants at the European University Institute conference on household portfolios for insightful comments. None of those should be held responsible for any remaining errors in this chapter. We thankfully acknowledge financial support from the Project on Finance and Consumption in the European Union at the European University Institute, and from the HERMES Center at the University of Cyprus.

1. We cannot and do not do justice to the full array of existing computational algorithms and approaches to solving intertemporal models of household choice under uncertainty. In order to explore variants that differ only in the sense relevant to each section, we had to write and run numerous computer programs. We cannot claim that they are the only possible ways to solve such models. We describe them and use them because we know them best, and we are reasonably confident that they do not yield materially different solutions from other existing methods in the literature. Wherever possible, we also refer to work by other authors who follow different techniques from ours. We hope to offer enough information to the readers so that they can experiment with their own models and algorithms.

2. See Ryder and Heal (1973), Sundaresan (1989), Constantinides (1990), and Deaton (1992) for a recent overview.

3. Carroll (1992, 1997) assumes a very small probability (usually 0.5 percent) of an unemployment state with zero labor income.

4. Although these studies generally suggest that individual income changes follow an MA(2), the MA(1) is found to be a close approximation.

5. Portfolio effects of such processes in a variety of small-scale models are derived by Bertaut and Haliassos (1997) and Haliassos and Hassapis (1998, 2000, and 2001).

6. The consequences of such constraints have been empirically investigated by Ludvigson (1999) in the context of a single-asset model. The saving and portfolio effects of varying the constraint tightness parameter k have been analyzed computationally by Haliassos and Hassapis (1998). In view of accumulating evidence that lenders are unwilling to extend credit to households with highly variable income because of their high probability of default, an interesting extension would be to link borrowing limits to the variability of earnings.

7. For a more detailed discussion of the practical issues involved in the numerical evaluation of a definite integral, see Judd (1998, chap. 7).

8. For $N = 10$, the quadrature nodes and the quadrature weights are given in Judd (1998, table 7.4).

9. Assigning a probability of one-tenth for each of these nodes gives a mean equal to zero and standard deviation equal to .964, whereas if the Gauss-Hermite quadrature is used (with $N = 10$), the mean is again zero but the standard deviation is exactly one. In some instances (especially when estimation is involved), this approximation error is worth paying if a matrix programming language like GAUSS is being used.

10. Burnside (1999, pp. 106–107) provides an excellent discussion of the Tauchen and Hussey (1991) proposal and its relationship to the method described in the text.

11. Although this approach is potentially powerful and does away with the need to consider credit market frictions in the form of quantity constraints, it still requires assumptions regarding the institutional and legal framework. For example, would it be possible for households to choose not to repay their loans in such unlikely disastrous states? Alternatively, would it be possible for them to buy unemployment insurance to cover (at least partially) these unlikely events instead of modifying their entire portfolio to accommodate those states? If such unemployment insurance does not exist, then portfolio effects continue to arise from a market failure even though we have not imposed borrowing constraints.

12. Results are reported in terms of that level of annual labor income that, if received every year, would yield the same present value. This facilitates comparison with levels of annual incomes used elsewhere in the chapter.

13. The labor income levels used in our runs are $[y1, y2h, y2l, y3] = [1.2826, 2.7793, 1.7639, 1.9908]$. Models with income certainty set $y2h = y2l = 2.2716$.

14. Note that our benchmark expected utility specification with $\rho = 3$ is identical to a Kreps-Porteus specification with $\rho = 3$ and $\sigma = \frac{1}{3}$. See section 2.1.1.

15. The high and low twenty-year rates of return on stocks used are 5.2375 and −0.5768, respectively.

16. First-period income is set at 1.2826 because of the normalization described in the previous subsection.

17. Specifically, households hold positive financial net worth when their initial cash on hand is a bit less than 2.5 times their initial labor income in this calibration, and they start investing positive amounts in stocks and in bonds when it is about triple their labor income.

18. See Haliassos and Hassapis (2001) for the solution method for Quiggin models that involve kinks of the indifference curves at points not known a priori. The straight line in figure 2.4 is due to such a kink. A complete set of graphs is in HM.

19. When risk aversion is larger than the inverse of the intertemporal elasticity of substitution (as in figure 2.4, where risk aversion is $3 > \frac{1}{0.5}$), KP preferences imply lower stockholding than EU preferences. When risk aversion is smaller than the inverse, KP preferences actually enhance stockholding at a given level of normalized cash on hand. When the two are equal, the KP and EU model obviously coincide.

20. The peak is a consequence of the kink in the model with risky income (see HM).

21. This first section follows closely the analysis in Haliassos and Michaelides (1999).

22. Recall that this was also a finding of the unconstrained small-scale model above.

23. They use the Annual Demographic Files of the March Current Population Survey to construct panel data on mean annual earnings between 1963 and 1994.

24. Carroll (1997) uses an even lower probability equal to .05 percent to endogenously generate no borrowing in the single-asset version of the model.

25. The implication of the model that there is not only entry but also exit from the stock market is corroborated by the empirical findings of Bertaut (1998).

26. See King and Leape (1987), Mankiw and Zeldes (1991), and Haliassos and Bertaut (1995).

27. Recent articles on the effects of return predictability for saving and portfolios include Barberis (1999), Brennan, Schwartz, and Lagnado (1997), Campbell and Koo (1997), Campbell, Cocco, Gomes, Maenhout, and Viceira (1998), Campbell and Viceira (1999), and Balduzzi and Lynch (1999). See Michaelides (1999) for an extended bibliography.

28. Calibration settings are as follows: $\delta = 0.12$, $r = 0.01$, $\sigma_u = 0.1$, $\sigma_n = 0.08$, $\mu_g = 0.03$, $\rho = 3$. The high discount rate is chosen to accommodate the convergence conditions $\frac{r_f + f_t - \delta}{\rho} + \frac{\rho}{2}\sigma_n^2 < \mu_g + \mu_n$ for all factor realizations. The parameters describing the evolution of stock market returns are selected from Campbell (1999, table 2C), who reports parameter estimates for a VAR model based on annual U.S. data between 1891 and 1994. They are $\mu = .042$, $\phi = .798$, $\sigma_z^2 = .0319$, $\sigma_\varepsilon^2 = .9^2 * .001$, and $\sigma_{z,\varepsilon} = -.0039$. He estimates r_f to be .0199 and $\sigma_\varepsilon = .001$. We decrease both quantities so that the convergence condition can be satisfied for all factor state realizations.

29. Merton has shown that the value functions for problems with HARA felicity functions inherit the functional form of the felicity function. Homogeneity follows from the same arguments as in proposition 4 and lemma 1 in Koo (1995). Viceira (1999) uses a similar normalization (dividing by the level of earnings).

30. Two questions arise: (1) Do solutions for $\{s(x_t), b(x_t)\}$ that satisfy equations 2.27 and 2.28 exist? (2) Are these solutions unique? If we assume that c_{t+1} is an increasing function of cash on hand, then one can easily show that given $s(x_t)$, the right-hand side of equation 2.27 is decreasing in $b(x_t)$ while the left-hand side is increasing in $b(x_t)$, guaranteeing existence and uniqueness of a solution for $b(x_t)$ from the bond Euler equation. The argument works in exactly the same fashion for $s(x_t)$ by symmetry (given $b(x_t)$ now).

31. For more details on bisection, see Judd (1998, pp. 147–150).

32. Calibration settings are $\delta = 0.1$, $r = 0.02$, $\sigma_u = 0.1$, $\sigma_v = 0.08$, $\mu_g = 0.03$, $\rho = 3$, $c = .7$.

3 Taxation and Portfolio Structure: Issues and Implications

James M. Poterba

Tax rules are a potentially important determinant of household portfolio structure. While media reports typically focus on pretax returns, investors actually receive the after-tax returns associated with their investments. Tax rules are often cited as a significant influence on a wide range of household portfolio choices, including whether to hold stocks or bonds, how much to invest in owner-occupied housing, when to sell appreciated securities, and how to accumulate assets for retirement. There is substantial variation across major industrialized nations in the tax treatment of different portfolio assets and in the associated incentives for household portfolio structure.

There are several reasons for analyzing the impact of taxation on portfolio choice. The first is to understand the behavioral effects of the often complex tax rules that modern tax systems apply to capital income. Such an understanding could ultimately lead to estimates of the efficiency cost of various tax rules. The second justification for examining taxation and portfolio choice is to investigate whether taxation can help to explain some of the stylized patterns that emerge in studies of household portfolios. For some assets, there are clear patterns in the probability of ownership of the asset, and in the share of a household's portfolio invested in the asset, across income and net worth categories. Direct holdings of corporate equities in the United States, for example, are strongly positively correlated with both income and net worth. This pattern may reflect differences in risk tolerance across households in different income and net worth ranges, but it may also reflect the greater tax incentives for equity rather than debt ownership among high-income, high-marginal-tax-rate households. The tax system may also have important effects on the set of households that takes advantage of opportunities for

tax-deferred saving and portfolio accumulation. Finally, recognizing
the tax incentives for holding particular assets can be important for
interpreting empirical results on how nontax variables are correlated
with portfolio structure. Because household income and net worth
are often correlated with household tax rates, some of the effect of
these variables on observed portfolio holdings may operate through
their effect on tax rates, and therefore on after-tax rates of return.

While taxation may affect portfolio choice, relatively few empirical
studies have established a clear link between taxation and investor
behavior. This is largely because marginal tax rates are typically a
nonlinear function of household income, which makes convincing
identification of tax effects very difficult. In most countries and at
most times, all households face the same tax system. Differences in
the tax incentives facing different households therefore result from
differences in their economic circumstances, such as their incomes or
their family structures and associated tax deductions. When differences in these variables are the source of differences in marginal tax
rates, it is difficult to isolate a pure taxation effect on household
portfolios.

This chapter examines the channels through which taxation can
affect portfolio holdings, and it describes the tax incentives facing
investors in major industrialized nations. It seeks to develop a broad
perspective on the ways that taxation may affect portfolio structure
and provide a framework that can be used to integrate empirical
findings from different countries and different institutional environments. The chapter also summarizes previous work on the links
between tax rates and household portfolio structure, and it notes
several aspects of household portfolio structure that appear difficult
to reconcile with tax-efficient investor behavior. Most of this empirical work is based on data from the United States.

There are many aspects of taxation and portfolio structure that the
chapter does not explore. It does not consider the structure of employer-provided pensions and the choice between pension saving
and other saving, except in situations where pension saving is done
through individually directed accounts. The incentives for pension
provision typically depend on both the household and corporate
income tax structures. The chapter also stops short of considering
the detailed tax and other incentives for investment in specialized
financial products, such as the many products offered by insurance
companies, on the grounds that there is great heterogeneity across
nations in both the products that are available and their tax treat-

ment. It also focuses primarily on the incentives to hold financial assets, although nonfinancial assets such as owner-occupied housing constitute a major share of many households' portfolio.

The first section of this chapter describes the many different margins along which households may adjust their portfolios in response to tax incentives. It also notes the tax parameters that interact to determine investor incentives. Section 3.2 considers the consequences of omitting tax variables from cross-sectional studies of household portfolio choice, and it notes some of the difficulties that arise in measuring household marginal tax rates. Section 3.3 summarizes the differences across countries in the tax rates on interest and dividend income, the tax treatment of capital gains, and special tax incentives for retirement and other dedicated saving. Section 3.4 presents a brief summary of previous research on how taxes affect portfolio structure. The final section distills several key conclusions about how taxes appear to influence portfolio structure, and it suggests a number of directions that require future investigation.

3.1 Portfolio Choice in the Presence of Taxation

Most of the modern theory of portfolio choice was developed without reference to taxes. The key results therefore apply directly to the portfolio choices of nontaxable investors or to the choices of investors who face the same positive tax rate on all types of portfolio income. It is not clear that any taxable investors fall into the latter category, since even when all realized capital income is taxed at the same rate, accrued but unrealized capital gains are typically untaxed until realization.

A number of dimensions of household portfolio choice can be influenced by taxation. This section begins by summarizing the after-tax capital asset pricing model and its limitations and then outlines six margins of portfolio choice where taxes can affect investor incentives. The section closes with a discussion of the empirical difficulties that arise in trying to analyze the link between taxes and portfolio choice.

3.1.1 After-Tax Capital Asset Pricing Model

One way to develop a theory of portfolio choice in the presence of taxation is simply to redefine the returns and covariances of the standard model in after-tax terms. For any investor, the relevant tax rules can be summarized by five parameters: the tax rates on interest income (τ_{int}), dividend income (τ_{div}), realized capital gains (τ_{cg}), contributions to tax-deferred saving vehicles ($\tau_{contrib}$), and withdrawals from tax-deferred accounts ($\tau_{withdrawal}$). Many models consider portfolio choice in the absence of tax-deferred accounts, so only the first three parameters are important. Yet since tax-deferred accounts play an increasingly important part in the portfolio choices of many households, especially middle-income households, this may be an important omission. The limit on the amount of assets that can be held in these accounts is usually specified as a restriction on the annual contribution to the account, rather than as a constraint on the total amount that may be held in the account. In some countries, the relevant tax rate on a realized capital gain may depend on the length of time for which the asset has been held. This can expand the set of tax rate parameters that need to be considered, and it also raises additional portfolio choice problems of the type considered by Constantinides (1984).

A number of studies have considered the portfolio choice problem facing taxable investors when assets have inherent and immutable tax attributes. The dividend and capital gain components of the income from equities, for example, are assumed to face a given tax rate for a particular investor, while interest income may face a different tax rate for the same investor. Studies in this tradition include Auerbach and King (1983), Brennan (1970), Elton and Gruber (1978), and Long (1977). These studies consider investment in a range of different risky assets, under the assumption that risky assets (presumably equities) are taxed at a different tax rate from the riskless asset (presumably a bond). While these studies assume that all equities are taxed at the same rate, so that there are effectively only two types of capital income tax (one for bonds, one for equities), it is straightforward to generalize the analysis to consider a wider range of different tax rules.

The central findings of these studies can be summarized easily. Let W_0 denote a household's beginning-of-period investable wealth, S_i denote the household's investment in risky asset i, and assume that the riskless rate of return r_f takes the form of interest that is taxed at rate τ_{int}. All risky assets are taxed at a rate of τ_{eq}, which is a weighted average of the taxes on dividends and realized capital gains, and pretax returns on the N equity securities are given by r_i. The expected pretax return on equity security i is μ_i, the vector of mean returns on equity securities $\{r_1, \ldots, r_N\}$ is μ, and Ω denotes the N-

by-N covariance matrix of risky returns. The covariance between the pretax returns on risky assets i and j is σ_{ij}.

The individual investor is assumed to maximize a utility function that can be written in terms of the mean and variance of final wealth, $U(W, \sigma_W^2)$. The investor's expected end-of-period wealth, which depends on the amounts invested in each risky security, is

$$E(W) = [W_0 - \Sigma S_i] * (1 - \tau_{int})r_b + \Sigma S_i * (1 - \tau_{eq})\mu_i. \tag{3.1}$$

The variance of end-of-period wealth is

$$V(W) = \sum_i \sum_j S_i * S_j * (1 - \tau_{eq})^2 * \sigma_{ij}. \tag{3.2}$$

Manipulating the first-order condition for the asset allocation that maximizes expected utility yields

$$S^* = \delta * \Omega^{-1} * [(1 - \tau_{eq})\mu - (1 - \tau_{int})r_b * 1], \tag{3.3}$$

where 1 denotes a column vector of 1's. S^* is a column vector that contains the optimal asset allocation to each risky security. The term δ is related to the investor's risk aversion: $\delta = U_W/[2U_{\sigma 2} * (1 - \tau_{eq})^2]$. If there were no taxes on interest income or equity returns, this expression reduces to the standard expression for risky asset demands. Equation 3.3 generalizes the standard result from portfolio choice in the presence of taxes to allow for differential tax treatment of different assets, and it shows that the investor's optimal portfolio holdings will depend on after-tax expected returns and after-tax covariances.

Auerbach and King (1983) show that the optimal portfolio in the presence of taxes can be interpreted as a weighted average of two portfolios: the market portfolio and a portfolio chosen on the basis of tax but not risk considerations. The relative weights on these two basic portfolios depend on the investor's tax rates in comparison to the tax rates of other investors and on the investor's risk aversion. More risk-averse investors will place greater weight on the diversification portfolio and down-weight the portfolio that derives from tax specialization, relative to less risk-averse investors or investors whose tax rates diverge substantially from those of the investing population.

While the after-tax portfolio choice analysis of equation 3.3 is a useful starting point, it fails to describe the actual portfolio selection environment facing many households. Two factors are important in this regard. First, the analysis that underlies equation 3.3 assumes that households can take short as well as long positions in all securities. When short selling is costly, this may not be feasible for many investors. Second, and more important, equation 3.3 does not recognize the possibility of holding a given asset in either a taxable form or in a tax-deferred account. For investors in many nations, this is a very real possibility, and it leads to a richer portfolio choice problem.

3.1.2   Importance of "Asset Habitat"

One of the most important recent developments in the institutional environment facing investors is the potential separation between an asset's risk characteristics and its tax attributes. Most conceptual analyses of taxes and portfolio choice assume that tax differences across assets are inherent features of the assets, just like their return attributes. But as tax-deferred and tax-exempt saving vehicles become more important in many nations, it is necessary to recognize that an asset's tax attributes may be affected by the habitat in which the asset is held. Consider the case of corporate equities held by individual investors in the United States. When equities are held outside tax-deferred accounts, dividend income is taxed at the investor's ordinary income tax rate, unrealized capital gains are not taxed, and realized capital gains are taxed at either the long- or short-term capital gains tax rate. If the same assets are held in a tax-deferred saving account, however, then neither dividend income nor realized capital gains are taxed until the assets are withdrawn from the account. At that point, the entire amount of the withdrawal is taxed at the investor's ordinary income tax rate, which equals the dividend income tax rate. Depending on an investor's horizon and the share of the equity return that accrues in the form of dividend payments, the effective tax burden on equities may be greater inside or outside the tax-deferred account.

To illustrate the effect of asset habitat, consider an investor who has $1 of current earnings and is considering investing this money by holding stocks in a retirement account or a traditional taxable setting. Assume that a fraction λ of the return on corporate equities (r_{eq}) is generated in the form of dividends, and to simplify matters, assume that equity returns are certain. Let the tax rate on withdrawals from tax-deferred accounts equal that on dividend income, which equals the tax rate on earned income. If the investor chooses to invest in a taxable account, his current earnings will face a tax burden of τ_{div}, because the tax rate on earnings equals the dividend tax rate. The investor will therefore have $(1 - \tau_{div})$ dollars available for current investment. The investor's after-tax wealth in T years if the equity is held in a taxable account will be:

$$W_{\text{taxable}} = (1 - \tau_{\text{div}}) * \exp\{[(1 - \tau_{\text{div}})^* \lambda + (1 - \tau_{\text{cg}})^*(1 - \lambda)]^* T^* r_{\text{eq}}\}. \quad (3.4)$$

This outcome can be compared with the situation if the investor uses the same amount of pretax earnings to fund a tax-deferred retirement saving account, such as an Individual Retirement Account or a 401(k) plan. In this case, the investor will be able to allocate pretax earnings to the account, and the value of the equity in the account will grow to $\exp(T^* r_{\text{eq}})$ after T years. A tax of τ_{div} will be due when the assets are withdrawn from the account, assuming that the investor's ordinary income tax rate is the same at the time of withdrawal as at the time of contribution. (For many investors the former may be smaller than the latter, raising the tax benefit associated with tax-deferred investments.) The after-tax value of the tax-deferred account after T periods will be:

$$W_{\text{tax-deferred}} = (1 - \tau_{\text{div}})^* \exp(T^* r_{\text{eq}}). \quad (3.5)$$

The contrast between the values in equations 3.4 and 3.5 underscores the importance of asset habitat in considering the portfolio choices facing investors. When the assets are held in a traditional taxable format, the effective tax burden on equity income depends on the statutory tax rates on dividends and capital gains and on the fraction of equity returns that take the form of dividends. In the tax-deferred account, however, the equity return is untaxed, in the sense that the earnings used to fund the tax-deferred account are taxed only when the funds are withdrawn from the account.

The possibility of holding assets with the same pretax returns in different habitats, and thereby subjecting them to different tax treatment, complicates the household's portfolio optimization problem and makes it more difficult to describe how the tax system affects portfolio choices. In most settings, a household's optimal portfolio plan will involve maximal use of tax-deferred saving vehicles, with their correspondingly favorable tax treatment, before making investments in traditional taxable accounts.

3.1.3 Margins Along Which Taxation Affects Portfolio Structure

One way to organize the study of taxes and portfolio choice is to isolate the various margins of portfolio choice that may be affected by taxation. There are at least six such margins, and different aspects of the tax system may influence choices along each margin.

Asset Selection: Which Assets to Own
In simple models of portfolio choice, each household that holds any risky assets holds some of every risky asset, with the household's total holdings of risky assets determined by the household's risk tolerance. (This presumes that there are no dominated assets—those that offer a lower payoff in all states of nature than other assets available to investors.) This prediction is distinctly at odds with the patterns we observe in actual portfolios. Most households own an incomplete set of assets. Typically many asset categories are not represented in the portfolio of households with modest wealth. Asset ownership patterns show that many households choose not to own assets in each broad asset category.

Table 3.1 shows the fraction of households that report ownership of positive amounts of assets in a broad range of categories. Bertaut and Starr-McCluer 2000 present complementary information, including some results from the 1998 Survey of Consumer Finances. The table shows that less than 20 percent of households own corporate stock directly, that is, in a taxable account. Less than one-third of households held corporate equity in a tax-deferred account, although there has been substantial growth in this form of stock ownership in the last two decades. One word of caution is in order when analyzing results like those in table 3.1. The Survey of Consumer Finances does not provide definitive information on the

Table 3.1
Ownership probabilities for various assets, United States, 1983–1995

	1995	1992	1989	1983
Directly held equity	16.41	18.13	17.91	19.08
Equity mutual funds	11.26	8.35	5.86	3.03
Tax-deferred equity	30.40	25.67	20.42	19.51
Tax-deferred bonds	30.54	30.35	30.54	26.10
Tax-exempt bonds	6.44	6.79	6.40	3.31
Taxable bonds	26.17	27.29	28.14	23.99
Interest-bearing accounts	87.22	87.24	85.52	87.63
Other financial assets	42.96	44.56	48.29	36.52

Source: Tabulations from Survey of Consumer Finances surveys in various years, as reported in Poterba and Samwick (1999).

asset composition of tax-deferred accounts. Table 3.1 assumes that accounts that are invested "mostly in stock" are completely held in equities and that accounts invested in "combinations of stock and interest-bearing assets" are invested half in corporate stock. This approach follows Poterba and Samwick (1997). A very small fraction of households—slightly more than 6 percent—reports ownership of tax-exempt debt. Most households report positive ownership of some categories of assets, such as interest-bearing accounts. This asset class includes checking accounts and other financial instruments that households typically use to facilitate transactions.

Incomplete portfolio holdings do not appear to be confined to U.S. households. Hochguertel, Alessie, and van Soest (1997) report similar findings, for a broader set of asset classes, in a study of Dutch households. Banks and Tanner in chapter 6 present evidence for U.K. households that also suggests a lack of portfolio diversification.

The explanation for portfolio incompleteness is not clear. Leape (1987) argues that if there are fixed costs associated with the purchase of some assets, households may decide not to purchase some assets because their marginal contribution to the after-tax risk-adjusted expected portfolio return is not large enough to outweigh this fixed cost. Bertaut and Haliassos (1995), Haliassos and Michaelides (chapter 2, this volume), and Vissing-Jørgensen (1999b) also explore the issue of portfolio incompleteness. The costs of asset acquisition may be explicit transaction costs or the psychological costs associated with learning about various assets. Regardless of the source of these costs, the tax burden on an asset's returns should affect an investor's calculation of whether to hold an asset.

It is possible that the tax system contributes to the fixed cost of owning some asset classes. An investor who considers purchasing corporate stock or a mutual fund, for example, but does not have any other investments in similar assets, may face more complex tax reporting and tax calculation tasks as a result of the investment. This issue would apply to the first investment in a given asset category, but it would apply with less force to subsequent investments. (The tax system could also have the opposite effect: reducing participation costs. Financial costs of trading are usually a tax-deductible expense when an investor computes capital gains or losses. When there is a fixed cost associated with buying and selling securities, the after-tax cost is smaller than the pretax cost. A similar argument applies to the time that investors spend to learn about investments; the after-tax value of such time is smaller than the before-tax value.)

Another key feature of actual asset holding patterns is the presence of some puzzling patterns in asset cross-ownership. Table 3.2 shows the conditional probability of owning one asset, given that a household owns another, again using the 1995 Survey of Consumer Finances. Some findings are difficult to reconcile with the formation of strong tax-related clienteles. More than half of the households that own tax-exempt bonds also report holding taxable bonds, although only 14 percent of those that own taxable bonds report owning tax-exempt bonds. Of the households that own bonds in their tax-deferred investment accounts, 54 percent also hold equities in tax-deferred accounts. Forty percent of the households with tax-deferred bond holdings report holding taxable bonds as well.

Table 3.2 also shows interesting patterns with respect to investor specialization in different types of financial intermediaries. Less than one-third (28 percent) of the households that have direct holdings of corporate stock hold equity mutual funds, but 41 percent of the households with equity funds also have direct stockholdings. These patterns underscore the importance of considering portfolio choice as a decision to hold a collection of assets rather than just a set of stand-alone decisions about investing in particular assets.

Asset Allocation: How Much to Invest in Each Asset
The after-tax capital asset pricing model analysis is most directly targeted at this aspect of investor behavior. Investors who face different tax burdens on different securities will choose to invest different amounts in these securities. The key parameters for assessing this aspect of asset demand are the marginal tax rates that investors face on the income flows from each asset type. Because portfolio holdings depend on the full vector of returns available to investors, it is difficult to specify simple empirical models of portfolio choice with taxes.

Taxes influence the specification of the covariances across asset returns. One simple strategy for constructing after-tax returns is to multiply the pretax returns on a given asset, or the capital gain or loss component of these returns, by a $(1 - \tau_{cg})$ term that indicates that investors receive returns net of capital gains taxes. Poterba (1999) argues that the relevant capital gains tax rate might not be the statutory rate, but rather one based on a forecast of the future pattern of realizations and the associated effective tax burden on current accruing gains.

Table 3.2
Conditional probabilities of asset ownership, 1995 Survey of Consumer Finances

	Directly held equity	Equity mutual funds	Tax-deferred equity	Tax-deferred bonds	Tax-exempt bonds	Taxable bonds	Interest-bearing accounts	Other financial assets
Directly held equity	100.00	28.23	52.61	45.38	19.27	49.65	99.72	60.10
Equity mutual funds	41.13	100.00	58.86	45.85	29.36	57.08	99.56	57.28
Tax-deferred equity	28.40	21.81	100.00	54.36	11.26	41.58	97.63	53.13
Tax-deferred bonds	24.38	16.91	54.10	100.00	9.68	39.66	96.96	52.96
Tax-exempt bonds	49.11	51.35	53.14	45.92	100.00	55.60	98.84	67.27
Taxable bonds	31.13	24.56	48.30	46.28	13.68	100.00	98.00	58.10
Interest-bearing accounts	18.76	12.86	34.03	33.95	7.30	29.41	100.00	46.33
Other financial assets	22.96	15.02	37.60	37.66	10.09	35.40	94.08	100.00

Source: Poterba and Samwick (1999).
Note: Each entry is the probability that a household owns the asset in the column, conditional on owning the asset in the row. Households are weighted by sample weights.

This approach may understate the interdependence of returns across different assets, however, because an investor's tax rate may itself depend on realized returns. When asset markets generate high returns, investors may have higher-than-expected taxable income, and their marginal tax rates may be higher than they would otherwise have expected. If asset markets generate poor returns, investors may face substantial capital losses, and in nations where losses are not fully deductible against ordinary income, they may become loss constrained. These features have not yet been considered in models of asset allocation.

How Much to Borrow
While many discussions of taxation and portfolio structure concentrate on the assets that households own, taxes can have at least as much impact on whether households borrow to finance their asset holdings. In many nations, households are able to deduct their interest payments on loans used to finance asset purchase, as well as on loans for home purchase. In the United States until 1986, all consumer interest, even that used to purchase consumer durables, was tax deductible. Since then, only borrowing for financial or housing investment has been deductible.

Table 3.3 presents information on borrowing patterns for U.S. households, again drawing on data from the 1995 Survey of Consumer Finances. Just over 40 percent of households report some outstanding mortgage debt, with middle-aged households having the highest probability of such borrowing. The probability of mortgage borrowing is relatively insensitive to household net worth, despite the fact that higher-income households (which tend to be higher-net-worth households) face higher marginal tax rates and therefore a lower after-tax cost of mortgage borrowing.

Table 3.3 also shows that two-thirds of U.S. households report some nonmortgage borrowing, even though there is no tax subsidy to such borrowing. There is a pronounced decline in the likelihood of nonmortgage borrowing, and in the ratio of nonhousing debt to nonhousing assets, as one moves up the age distribution and up the net worth distribution. While nonmortgage debt represents more than one-third of the nonhousing assets of households with net worth of less than $100,000, it represents less than 5 percent of nonhousing assets for those with net worth of $500,000 or more.

Table 3.3
Household borrowing by net worth and age categories, United States, 1995

	Households with mortgage debt	Households with non-mortgage debt	Total debt/ total assets	Nonhousing debt/ nonhousing assets
Net worth category				
Less than $100,000	34.7%	71.6%	48.6%	34.9%
$100,000 to $250,000	52.3	67.3	20.9	10.2
$250,000 to $500,000	50.7	56.8	13.7	6.8
$500,000 to $1 million	53.7	55.8	10.3	5.2
$1 million to $2.5 million	58.9	50.1	8.0	4.2
More than $2.5 million	51.9	54.1	4.8	3.5
Age of household head				
Less than 34	32.9	80.0	44.1	24.3
35–49	56.7	80.6	23.9	9.3
50–64	51.3	68.2	12.5	6.9
65 and over	16.9	36.6	4.1	3.1
All	41.0	68.3	16.0	7.5

Source: Author's tabulations using 1995 Survey of Consumer Finances.

Asset Location

With the emergence of tax-deferred or tax-exempt retirement saving accounts and other specialized saving vehicles, in many nations, investors face a new decision about where to hold a given asset. Shoven (1999) and Shoven and Sialm (1999) consider the problem of bonds versus stocks in the tax-deferred account, with particular reference to equity mutual funds in the United States. The choice of which assets to hold in tax-favored accounts and which in traditional taxable format depends on the tax rate on each asset when it is held outside the tax-favored account and the tax rules that apply to withdrawals from the tax-deferred account.

Table 3.4 presents information from the 1995 Survey of Consumer Finances on the location of corporate stockholdings for U.S. households. The table shows the fraction of households in various age and net worth categories that report owning corporate stock directly (in a taxable format) as well as indirectly, through a 401(k) plan or Individual Retirement Account. The roughly one-third of households that own some corporate stock are approximately evenly distributed across the three different ownership possibilities. Roughly one-third

Table 3.4
Ownership of corporate equity in taxable and tax-deferred accounts, United States, 1995

	Only direct holdings	Only tax-deferred holdings	Both taxable and tax-deferred holdings	No corporate equity
Net worth category				
Less than $100,000	6.3%	14.0%	4.9%	74.8%
$100,000 to $250,000	16.9	16.7	14.1	52.4
$250,000 to $500,000	28.1	14.3	24.1	33.4
$500,000 to $1 million	25.8	12.9	35.4	25.8
$1 million to $2.5 million	35.8	12.0	38.8	13.4
More than $2.5 million	35.0	5.9	40.8	18.2
Age of household head				
Under 35	6.7	16.6	9.7	66.9
35–49	10.0	20.0	13.3	56.6
50–64	11.9	13.5	13.7	60.9
Over 64	20.5	4.1	4.6	70.9
All	11.9	14.4	10.6	63.1

Source: Author's tabulations using 1995 Survey of Consumer Finances.

of those that own any stock own stock both through a tax-deferred account and in a taxable format. At low net worth levels and at young ages, the probability of holding stock only through a tax-deferred account is significantly greater than the probability of holding stock directly or than the chance of owning stock through both mechanisms. This is consistent with a situation in which employer-provided saving plans, such as 401(k)s, are drawing young investors and investors with modest levels of net worth into the equity market.

Choice of Financial Intermediaries
Yet another aspect of portfolio choice that may be affected by tax rules is the decision of whether to hold securities such as stocks and bonds directly, by purchasing them in the securities market, or through intermediaries such as mutual funds or insurance companies. This choice is likely to depend on the transactions costs, such as expense ratios on mutual funds, that are charged by financial intermediaries, and on the relative tax treatment of assets held directly

and held through intermediaries. Dickson and Shoven (1995) describe the current tax rules on mutual funds in the United States, and they note that these rules typically make equity held through a mutual fund a more heavily taxed asset than equity held directly.

Taxes are not the only distinction between assets held directly and through intermediaries; there are typically differences in the pretax returns associated with the transactions costs and other administrative expenses associated with the intermediary. In the United States, for example, Rea, Reid, and Lee (1999) estimate that the average expense charge on equity mutual funds was 135 basis points in 1998. For load funds, the average was 200 basis points, and for no-load funds, it was 83 basis points. Charges of this magnitude are not trivial in comparison to the expected after-tax returns associated with many asset categories.

When to Trade Assets

The discussion so far has focused on portfolio decisions that concern which assets to hold. Investors must also make decisions, however, about when to sell the assets they hold. The tax treatment of capital gain realizations, and the treatment of losses, can affect this decision. When investors are taxed on realized gains but not on accruing gains, they may become locked in to the assets that they hold. Realization-based taxes discourage the sale of capital assets and the associated portfolio rebalancing that investors might undertake in a world without taxes.

There is no widely accepted theory of what motivates households to trade the assets that they hold. In many standard models of portfolio choice, all households hold a market portfolio, so they are not predicted to trade their holdings of one security for that of another. One can deviate from this structure by assuming that households have private information that leads them to value some securities more than other market participants do, but models of this type are often ad hoc. Further work on the factors that influence trading could be very helpful in guiding research on the efficiency cost of tax rules, such as realization-based capital gains taxes or securities transactions taxes, that make it more expensive for households to rebalance their portfolios.

Patterns of actual trading suggest that high-net-worth households are more likely to trade assets than are households with lower net worth. Table 3.5 reports data on ownership of and trading of

Table 3.5
Probability of trading corporate stock, United States, 1995

	Probability of owning stock directly	Probability of buying or selling in the last year, conditional on owning directly
Net worth category		
Less than $100,000	7.3%	39.0%
$100,000 to $250,000	21.0	38.7
$250,000 to $500,000	36.2	57.3
$500,000 to $1 million	39.8	96.4
$1 million to $2.5 million	55.1	88.3
Over $2.5 million	65.6	87.2
Age of household head		
Under 35	10.8	53.1
35–49	15.4	48.7
50–64	16.1	69.9
Over 64	19.1	49.3
All	15.2	54.1

Source: Author's tabulations using 1995 Survey of Consumer Finances.
Note: The question, "Over the past year, about how many times did you or anyone in your family living here buy or sell stocks or other securities through a broker?" is asked of anyone who reports having a brokerage account. Not all stockholders have brokerage accounts, and brokerage accounts are uncommon among those who own stock only indirectly, for example, through a retirement account. It is also possible that some households with brokerage accounts that are asked about their trading are not current stockholders.

common stocks by U.S. households in 1995. The table shows that the fraction of households that own corporate stock who have bought or sold stock in the last year rises in household net worth. This fraction is less than 40 percent for those with net worth of less than $250,000, compared with more than 85 percent for those with net worth of more than $2.5 million. Since the table shows the share of households that own stock in each net worth category that trade, the differences cannot be explained by the fact that more high-net-worth households own corporate stock.

3.2 Empirical Challenges Posed by the Taxation of Investment Income

The fact that investors are taxed on their investment income raises a number of difficult issues for econometric analysis of household portfolios. This section begins by noting how failure to include tax variables in reduced-form models that explain household portfolio choices could result in biased estimates of the true effect of other variables of interest. It then considers several empirical issues in measuring marginal tax rates and including these variables in econometric work.

3.2.1   Tax Rates as Omitted Variables

The standard model of household portfolio choice in an after-tax setting would define the amount that household h invests in asset I as a function of that household's expected after-tax returns, μ_{at}, and household net worth, W. Household income (Y) might also affect asset demands for reasons related to precautionary demands for wealth or because income may provide information about other household attributes that affect asset demand. Consider what happens when an investigator estimates a statistical model linking portfolio choices to income, net worth, and pretax returns. In this case, the derivative effects of asset demand with respect to income and net worth will reflect not just the effects of these variables on asset demand directly, but also their effects through their impact on marginal tax rates. Thus,

$$\{dA_i/dY\}_{measured} = (dA_i/dY)_{true} + \Sigma_j\, dA_i/d\mu_j * (d\mu_j/dY). \tag{3.6}$$

Since tax rates depend on income, there is a presumption that the $d\mu_j/dY$ terms will be nonzero for many assets. This means that omitting after-tax returns can yield results that are difficult to interpret. (Note that the second term in equation 3.6 is not limited to substitution effects across assets that are associated with tax-induced changes in rates of return. There may also be effects of tax rates, through after-tax returns, on the level of saving and hence of overall wealth accumulation.)

Evaluating the bias from omitted tax variables is complicated by the fact that $d\mu_j/dY$ is likely to differ across assets. In the United States, for example, the marginal tax rate on realized capital gains is relatively insensitive to a household's total income, while the marginal tax rate on dividend and interest income follows a progressive schedule that is influenced by total income. As noted in the discussion of the after-tax capital asset pricing model, changes in marginal tax rates can also affect the after-tax covariances for various assets.

This is another source of omitted variable bias when tax rates are not included in the specification.

3.2.2   The Problem of Measuring Marginal Tax Rates

The preferred alternative to excluding tax rates in defining after-tax returns is computing household marginal tax rates and including these variables in the analysis of portfolio choices. A number of operational problems arise in following this strategy. First, most household surveys do not include as much detailed information as tax returns about specific income flows. This means the data analyst is imputing some of the variables that determine marginal tax rates. The problem is likely to be most serious for high-income households with substantial net worth and substantial portfolio holdings, because their financial affairs are more complicated than those of lower-income households. They are also likely to hold a higher fraction of financial assets, and they are correspondingly more important for the study of portfolio choices.

Second, for most investment problems, it is necessary to measure not just a household's current marginal tax rate but its future marginal tax rates as well. Future tax rates matter because the decision to purchase an asset is often a long-term decision, since the asset may be illiquid or subject to trade only at a substantial discount. If there are costs of portfolio adjustment, decisions about which assets to hold at a given point in time will depend on both current and future marginal tax rates.

There are two sources of uncertainty in analyzing future marginal tax rates: aggregate tax policy risk and household-specific rate uncertainty. It is not clear that households forecast future changes in overall tax policy, or why there are differences across households in such forecasts. If there were differences, they could affect the empirical analysis of how current tax rates, or current income or net wealth, affect portfolio choice.

Consider a situation in which high-income households believe that future marginal tax rates will increase, while lower-income households do not expect that tax rates will change in the future. Such a situation would lead to differences in the portfolio choices across households in different income groups; the data analyst would attribute these to differences in income, but the differences would in fact be the result of different tax policy perceptions that are correlated with income. With respect to taxpayer-specific variation in marginal tax rates over time, there may be substantial correlation between taxpayer circumstances and projected future tax rates. Older households, for example, may anticipate a decline in their labor income and correspondingly expect that their marginal tax rates will fall in future periods. Households at the start of the life cycle may expect rising income and correspondingly rising marginal tax rates. These patterns imply that households may expect different future patterns in the returns on different assets, and they may affect the portfolio structure that we observe.

Uncertain future taxes raise difficult empirical issues for the analysis of any type of long-lived consumer decision, including occupation choice, intertemporal labor supply, and portfolio choice. However, portfolio decisions may be particularly sensitive to future tax rates. If an investor buys an asset that appreciates, particularly if the asset does not pay dividends, her after-tax return will be largely dependent on the capital gains tax rate that prevails when the asset is sold. Other decisions, such as labor supply choices, do not offer payoffs that are so sharply affected by the tax regime at one point in time.

A third complication for portfolio analysis that arises from the presence of taxes is linked to the formation of taxpayer clienteles for particular assets. The after-tax return that a given taxpayer receives from holding a particular type of asset depends on only the asset's pretax return and the taxpayer's marginal tax rate. Which taxpayers should hold particular assets, however, depends more generally on the structure of marginal tax rates facing all households. Generalizations of Miller's (1977) classic analysis of taxpayer clienteles, such as Auerbach and King (1983) and McDonald (1983), show that the set of taxpayers who should hold particular assets will depend on the relative tax treatment of different taxpayers with respect to different assets. The equilibration process should involve changes in the pretax return on different assets, so that investors in each investor type find their highest posttax return on the asset for which they have the greatest relative tax advantage.

The fact that optimal portfolio allocation across investors depends not just on the particular investor's tax rate, but on the tax position of other investors as well, is not especially troubling for analyzing cross-sectional patterns of portfolio holdings. The economy-wide aggregate tax situation should drop out in comparisons of portfolios and marginal tax rates across investors. However, this feature of the after-tax portfolio equilibrium makes it difficult to compare two cross sections or to analyze panel data on tax returns. That a given investor's marginal tax rate rises from one point in time to another does not imply that the investor has a smaller incentive to hold a heavily taxed asset. The investor's incentive to hold such an asset will depend on the change in the investor's tax treatment relative to the treatment of all other investors.

3.3 The Tax Rules Facing Investors in Different Nations: A Brief Summary

The discussion so far has considered taxation and portfolio choice at a general level, without reference to the specific tax rules that apply to investors in various nations. One of the difficult problems in studying how taxes affect investor behavior is the very detailed nature of many tax incentives. For example, in countries that tax capital gains realizations, the tax rate on a gain can depend on the specific nature of the transaction that generated the gain, with respect to both the underlying asset and the length of time that the asset was owned. In most countries, whether a taxpayer can deduct interest payments depends on the purpose for which the taxpayer borrowed.

This chapter is too short to provide a comprehensive introduction to the heterogeneous tax treatment of capital income in major industrialized nations. Nevertheless, it is useful to provide some information on the nature of the cross-national variation in tax incentives for household portfolio choice. This section reports on three sets of tax rules that may affect portfolio structure: the tax treatment of interest, dividends, and capital gains; the availability of tax-deferred retirement saving accounts; and the tax treatment of household borrowing. Poterba (1994b) offers a more detailed, if somewhat dated, discussion of the tax provisions in each nation, and more recent information is usually available from accounting firms that advise multinational firms and their employees.

3.3.1 Tax Rules on Interest, Dividends, and Capital Gains

Tax rules that apply to capital income differ substantially across countries. There are differences in the rules that middle-income households face and differences between the tax treatment of middle-income and high-income households across nations. Since many nations apply progressive income tax schedules to a household's taxable income, there is variation in marginal tax rates across different households within each nation. This makes it hard to select a single summary statistic for "the" tax rate on interest, or dividends, in a particular nation.

This difficulty notwithstanding, table 3.6 presents an overview of the tax treatment of capital income in eight major industrialized nations. The table shows that the level of marginal tax rates on each of the different income flows varies from country to country and that the relative tax burdens on different types of income also differ.

The tax treatment of capital gains provides a tractable starting point for analyzing the information in table 3.6. The last two columns of the table describe the general tax treatment of realized capital gains, along with the rules that affect the relationship between an asset's holding period and the tax burden on any gain. In two of the eight nations, Germany and the Netherlands, capital gains are effectively untaxed. None of the eight countries taxes accruing capital gains, and six tax gains at realization. (Germany taxes short-term capital gains but not long-term gains, so most realized gains are untaxed.) One nation, Italy, currently taxes accrued capital gains.

The United States has the most complicated set of rules for determining the tax treatment of capital gain. There are both short-term and long-term gains, with short-term gains more heavily taxed. There have been recent periods, such as 1997–1998, when there were three different capital gains tax rates in the United States. These rates applied to short-term gains (less than a twelve-month holding period), intermediate-term gains (twelve to eighteen months), and long-term gains (holding period of longer than eighteen months).

The United Kingdom, which levies a 40 percent capital gains tax on gains above a threshold, has the highest statutory tax rate on capital gains, although gains are defined in real rather than nominal terms. Of the countries that tax gains, Japan and Italy have the lowest rates; investors who realize gains can choose to pay a tax equal to 1 percent (Japan) or a roughly similar fraction (Italy) of their asset's value rather than pay tax on their realized gain. This set of tax rules effectively limits the capital gains tax rate to 1 percent.

Table 3.6 also shows substantial heterogeneity in the tax treatment of dividend income. It is important to consider the combined tax burden at the corporate as well as the investor level in analyzing

Table 3.6
Tax rules on investment income, major industrial nations

Country	Tax treatment of interest	Tax treatment of dividends	Tax treatment of capital gains	Short- versus long-term capital gain distinction
Canada	Provincial and federal tax; combined rates, 27–48%	Partial integration; dividends grossed up by 25%, then 13.3% tax credit	Taxable at 23.8% maximum rate; $100,000 lifetime capital gains exemption	No
France	Taxable at flat-rate withholding of 56.2%	Integrated corporate and personal tax systems	Taxable at 18.1% rate	No
Germany	Marginal tax rate up to 53% but generous exclusion; only those with very high income pay tax	Taxed as ordinary income (rates to 53%) *but* full integration with German corporate income tax (36%)	Long-term untaxed, short-term "speculative profits" taxed	Short term (less than 6 months) taxed at up to 53%
Italy	Subject to flat rate tax of 12.5%; higher tax rate on bank deposits	Partial integration system; Average marginal tax rate on dividends near 50%	Accrued gains taxed at 12.5% rate	No
Japan	15% flat rate tax	Partial integration with progressive degree of integration	Tax of 20% of gain *or* 1% of sale price; specific rules on housing, land	No
Netherlands	Taxed at progressive marginal rates—36.4%, 50%, and 60%	Partial integration; dividends included with other taxable income	Untaxed	No
United Kingdom	Taxable at marginal rate of 25% or 40%	Integration of corporate and personal income taxes	Real gains above indexed asset basis, in excess of £7,100, taxed at 40% rate	No
United States	Taxed at marginal rates of 15% to 39.6%	Taxed at marginal rates of 15% to 39.6%	39.6% top rate on short-term gains, 20% on long-term gains	Long-term gains and losses are held more than twelve months

Source: American Council on Capital Formation (1996); Poterba (1994).

dividend taxes. The United States levies the highest tax burden, among the eight nations in table 3.6, on dividend payments. The corporate income tax is not integrated with the investor-level tax, so dividends are paid from fully taxed corporate earnings and they are then subject to another round of taxation when the investor receives them. The United Kingdom, Germany, and France have tax codes that provide investors with a tax credit for the corporate tax paid on the earnings that underlie their dividend income. The other nations shown in table 3.6 have more modest, "partial integration" schemes that also reduce the tax burden relative to the "classical" system in the United States.

Finally, table 3.6 illustrates the variation across nations in the tax treatment of interest income. Both Japan and Italy apply a relatively low tax rate, 15 percent and 12.5 percent, respectively, to household interest income. In other nations the tax burden on interest income, and consequently the tax *disincentive* for high-tax-bracket investors to hold bonds or other interest-generating assets, is more substantial. The top marginal tax rate on interest income is 39.6 percent in the United States, 56.2 percent in France, and 60.0 percent in the Netherlands. These tax rates would play a key role in determining the tax incentives for investors to hold fixed-income assets rather than other securities in their portfolios.

3.3.2   Tax-Deferred Saving Opportunities

Just as marginal tax rates vary across nations, the opportunities for households to engage in tax-deferred saving also vary significantly. Table 3.7 sketches the current provisions for tax-deferred saving in the eight nations in table 3.6. Households in France and Japan do not currently have access to tax-deferred saving vehicles. Japan historically offered *maruyu* postal saving accounts to small investors, with favorable tax treatment, but these accounts were phased out in 1986. For the remaining six nations, households can contribute to retirement saving accounts using pretax dollars.

The amounts that households can accumulate through tax-deferred saving vehicles is a function of the amount that can be contributed to these accounts, and there is significant cross-country variation on this dimension. In Italy, households can contribute 2 percent of wages, and in Germany, the annual contribution limit is roughly $2,000. Canada, the United Kingdom, and the United States all allow more generous plans, with contribution limits in the range of $10,000 or above. In the United States, as in some other nations, the limit on the amount that a household can contribute to tax-deferred accounts may depend on the household's employment circumstances. All taxpayers can contribute $2,000 to either a traditional or a Roth Individual Retirement Account (IRA). In addition, an employee who works at a company that offers a 401(k) retirement saving plan can contribute annually up to $10,500 to this type of tax-deferred account. A self-employed person can make even larger contributions to a tax-deferred account known as a Keogh plan. This heterogeneity is not atypical for nations with tax-deferred plans; the United Kingdom also offers a range of different options for tax-deferred saving. Beginning in 2000, U.K. taxpayers will be able to contribute up to £5,000 to Individual Saving Accounts (ISAs) each year.

Table 3.7 does not capture the full richness of the cross-national differences in access to retirement saving plans, but it does illustrate the broad variation among nations with larger and smaller programs for tax-deferred accumulation. Issues such as the asset location problem are likely to be more serious concerns for households in the United States, the United Kingdom, and Canada, where higher contribution limits make it possible to accumulate substantial amounts of wealth in tax-deferred saving vehicles than elsewhere.

3.3.3 Tax Treatment of Interest Payments

A final source of tax variation across nations, with potentially important implications for portfolio structure, involves the tax deductibility of interest payments. Table 3.8 reports the tax rules the affect mortgage interest deductibility and the deduction of consumer interest in various nations. All of the countries considered here allow households to deduct interest on debt that is incurred in the context of portfolio investments. Only one of the eight nations, the Netherlands, currently allows any tax deduction for consumer borrowing, and there is a limit on such borrowing. Four of the eight nations allow households to deduct mortgage interest payments. In the United Kingdom, which has historically allowed a mortgage interest deduction for tax purposes, there has been gradual erosion of this

Table 3.7
Retirement saving incentives in major industrial nations

Country	Retirement saving accounts?	Contribution limit	Contributions deductible?	Special notes
Canada	Yes	$9,400 ($15,500 Canadian), indexed	Yes	Limits on foreign stock; carry forward unused contributions
France	No	—	—	—
Germany	Yes	Vermogensbildungs gesetz limit $2,200	Yes	Investment in "long-term funds"; other programs to accumulate housing down payments
Italy	Yes	2% of wages or $1,414	Yes	
Japan	No	—	—	Universal *maruyu* postal saving accounts were phased out in 1986
Netherlands	Yes	1,700 guilders, or approximately $850 per year for employee saving scheme	Yes	"Employee saving scheme" and "premium saving scheme"; four-year vesting period before withdrawal
United Kingdom	Yes	Personal pensions, contributions of 17.5–40% of earnings; Individual Saving Accounts (ISAs), limit of £5,000 per year contribution starting in 2000	Yes	ISAs face restrictions on investment choices; total contribution limits were higher in years before 2000
United States	Yes	$2,000 for Individual Retirement Accounts; $10,500 for 401(k) plans	Yes	Other variants include Roth IRAs and 403(b) plans

Source: American Council on Capital Formation (1998); comments from country chapter authors.

Table 3.8
Tax treatment of borrowing, major industrial nations

Country	Is mortgage interest deductible?	Tax treatment of consumer borrowing
Canada	No	Not deductible
France	Yes	Not deductible
Germany	No	Not deductible
Italy	Only for first-time home buyers	Not deductible
Japan	No, but tax credit for six years for new home buyers	Not deductible
Netherlands	Yes	Deductible subject to a cap
United Kingdom	No (effective April 2000)	Not deductible
United States	Yes, subject to rarely binding limit	Not deductible

Source: Poterba (1994) and information provided by country portfolio research teams.

deduction; it was eliminated in April 2000. Japan does not allow taxpayers to deduct mortgage interest, but it does offer a special tax credit to first-time home owners for six years after they purchase their home.

Three countries—the United States, the Netherlands, and France—allow relatively unrestricted deductions for mortgage interest, and a fourth, Italy, allows mortgage interest deductions for first-time home owners. In the United States, households cannot deduct interest on more than $1 million of mortgage debt, but this is a constraint that binds for relatively few households. In the light of this cross-sectional heterogeneity in tax rules, one should expect households to allocate a greater share of their portfolios to housing assets in the United States, France, and the Netherlands and to rely more on mortgage debt in these countries than in other nations.

3.4   Previous Studies of Taxation and Portfolio Choice

A number of empirical studies have tried to measure the impact of taxation on the structure of household portfolios. Most have relied on information from the United States, largely because of the historical availability of household-level information on balance sheets. This section provides a brief introduction to the existing literature on taxation and portfolio behavior. Poterba (2001) offers a more detailed review.

3.4.1   Asset Selection and Asset Allocation

The two issues in portfolio choice that have received the most attention in previous empirical research are asset selection and asset allocation. A number of studies have suggested important links between tax rules and the structure of household portfolios. We begin with a review of previous studies and then summarize the findings in Poterba and Samwick's (1999) analysis of taxation, asset selection, and asset allocation in the 1995 U.S. Survey of Consumer Finances.

Previous Research
The first major study to analyze how taxation affects household portfolios was Feldstein's (1976) paper using the 1962 Survey of Financial Characteristics of Consumers. At the time of this survey, the top marginal tax rate in the federal income tax code was 91 percent. Feldstein argued that net worth should be the key variable that influences a household's choice of portfolio structure and that parameters such as household risk tolerance were likely to be related to net worth but not to income. He therefore studied how portfolio structure was related to both household net worth and household income. He found that higher-income households were more likely than lower-income households to hold equity, conditional on wealth. Since equity is taxed less heavily than debt under the tax rules in the United States, this finding is consistent with the view that taxes affect portfolio structure. It is premised on the view that income does not affect portfolio choice except through its impact on tax rates.

King and Leape (1998) present related evidence on how marginal tax rates are related to portfolio choice. They find that tax variables affect which assets investors decide to hold, but they find very limited support for a link between tax rates and the fraction of the household's portfolio that is held in different assets. They analyze data from a 1978 survey conducted by SRI International. In addition to their findings on the patterns of asset holdings and taxes, they report that many investors have zero holdings of broad asset categories such as corporate stock, corporate bonds, and tax-exempt bonds. This study finds only weak evidence for the formation of tax-related portfolio clienteles.

A third study that investigates how taxes affect portfolio choice is Hubbard's (1985) analysis of data collected by the U.S. President's Commission on Pension Policy. Hubbard estimates the marginal tax rate facing different households and then relates these marginal tax rates to the structure of household portfolios. This study does not rely simply on the fact that income is related to marginal tax rates to investigate how taxes affect investor behavior, but it uses the detailed structure of the tax code to pin down the structure of marginal tax rates. Income, along with the marginal tax rate, is an explanatory variable that helps to account for the cross-sectional pattern of portfolio holdings.

Two more recent studies that examine the link between taxes and portfolio structure are Scholz (1994) and Samwick (2000). Both rely on data from the Survey of Consumer Finances, which has been carried out in the United States every three years since 1983. The 1983, 1986, and 1989 surveys were linked together to provide a panel data set, but a high rate of attrition between the surveys led to discontinuation of the panel component. (Detailed information on the structure of the surveys may be found in Kennickell and Starr-McCluer 1997.) Subsequent surveys have been cross-sectional. Scholz studies portfolio changes between 1983 and 1989, a period that includes the Tax Reform Act of 1986. He finds relatively small changes in portfolio structure between these two years, with the notable exception of some restructuring of household debt into the tax-favored mortgage category, in spite of the fact that marginal tax rates were changed substantially. Samwick (2000) is also concerned with changes that may have been induced by the tax reforms of the past two decades. Although there is a clear cross-sectional relationship between marginal tax rates and portfolio structure, the changes over time in portfolio structure are difficult to explain based on changes in marginal tax rates.

These studies leave two issues unresolved. One is whether three years is too short a time period over which to find major shifts in portfolio structure. What theoretical guidance we have with respect to taxation and portfolio structure provides little insight on the question of how portfolios adjust over time. Factors including the capital gains tax rate, the tax treatment of losses, and the trading costs associated with financial transactions can play a central role in determining these effects.

A second, and perhaps deeper, conceptual point arises in analyzing portfolio changes over time. The set of assets available in the economy is endogenous, and the amount of assets supplied by firms and other users of capital is affected by the required returns demanded by those who hold these assets. A major tax reform can have a wide range of consequences for the equilibrium structure of household portfolios. This can make it difficult to test a steady-state theory of portfolio structure with fixed asset supplies by analyzing a set of repeated portfolio cross sections.

Evidence from the Survey of Consumer Finances
Poterba and Samwick (1999) explore the relationship of household marginal tax rates, asset ownership decisions, and asset allocation using data from the Survey of Consumer Finances. Bertaut and Starr-McCluer (2000) present a related analysis with somewhat different empirical models. To motivate the analysis, recall that heavily taxed capital assets in the United States, such as bonds held outside tax-deferred accounts, dividend-paying common stocks, and many mutual funds, generate at least some of their income in a form that is subject to ordinary income taxation. Less heavily taxed assets—those that generate capital gains or tax-exempt interest, as some state and local government bonds do—provide investors with income flows that are not taxed at ordinary income tax rates. A household's marginal tax rate on ordinary income is the key factor that influences the relative attractiveness of various assets.

To test the hypothesis that taxes affect portfolio choices, Poterba and Samwick (1999) impute marginal tax rates to all of the households in the Survey of Consumer Finances. This is done by using the data on the survey households to construct as many items as possible from a household's tax return. These marginal tax rates are nonlinear functions of pretax household income and a variety of household characteristics, such as the number of dependents. This tax rate imputation algorithm tries to overcome one of the empirical difficulties: the lack of detailed sample survey information on household attributes that affect marginal tax rates.

The actual empirical tests consist of probit models for household ownership of assets in eight broad asset categories, along with tobit models for the share of household portfolios that are invested in each asset class. These reduced-form equations include a range of other covariates that are included to control for heterogeneity across households. These covariates include a set of indicator variables for seven different ranges of household income, five ranges of household net worth, five ranges for the age of the household head, and four indicators for the education level of the household head. The

Table 3.9
Estimated impact of a 10 percentage point change in a household's marginal tax rate on asset ownership probabilities

	1995	1992	1989	1983
Directly held equity	0.0130	0.2455	0.1414	0.1263
Equity mutual funds	0.4221*	0.3462*	0.6510*	0.0110
Tax-deferred equity	0.2196*	0.1934	0.4957*	0.3729*
Tax-deferred bonds	0.2571*	0.2720*	0.2087*	0.5693*
Tax-exempt bonds	0.3200*	0.4245*	0.6382*	0.2324
Taxable bonds	0.0331	0.2770*	0.1155	0.2546
Interest-bearing accounts	0.1716	0.3306*	0.3181	0.5638*
Other financial assets	0.0575	0.0689	0.0688	0.1480

Source: Poterba and Samwick (1999).
*Statistically significantly different from zero at the 95 percent confidence level.

reduced-form equations are estimated using single-year cross sections from the Survey of Consumer Finances.

Table 3.9 reports findings from probit models that explain which asset classes households own, and table 3.10 reports tobit models for the share of the household's portfolio that is held in each asset class. The results are reported in the form of derivatives of asset holding probabilities, or derivatives of asset shares, with respect to a ten percentage point increase in the marginal tax rate on ordinary income. These derivatives are calculated for each household in the sample, and the results are averaged to yield the entries in tables 3.9 and 3.10. Table 3.10 also reports the change in the portfolio share for various asset classes associated with a marginal tax rate increase, scaled by the initial portfolio share for the asset in question. This addresses the fact that some derivatives are small in part because the asset accounts for a relatively small share of the household sector's portfolio.

The empirical findings offer support for the view that taxes affect portfolio structure. In the spirit of King and Leape's (1998) results, the evidence for a link between tax rates and the set of assets households own (asset selection) is stronger than the evidence of a link between taxes and portfolio shares (asset allocation). Consider the results in table 3.9. The probability that a household owns tax-deferred assets, either equity or bonds, is a positive function of the household's marginal tax rate. The estimated effects are statistically significantly different from zero for most of the survey years, and

Table 3.10
Marginal impact of changes in marginal tax rate on portfolio ownership share

	1995	1992	1989	1983
Impact of tax rate change on portfolio share				
Directly held equity	−0.0219	0.0192	0.0048	−0.0151
Equity mutual funds	0.0495*	0.0177	0.0355*	−0.0010
Tax-deferred equity	0.0477*	0.0419	0.0509	0.0637*
Tax-deferred bonds	0.0396*	0.0720	0.0052	0.1080*
Tax-exempt bonds	0.0334*	0.0423*	0.0636*	0.0094
Taxable bonds	−0.0029	0.0279	−0.0148	0.0020
Interest-bearing accounts	−0.0926*	−0.0631	−0.0926	−0.1835*
Other financial assets	−0.0526*	−0.1579*	−0.0528	0.0165
Impact on portfolio share as a percentage of initial share				
Directly held equity	−5.3%	4.4%	1.1%	−3.1%
Equity mutual funds	17.2%	11.9%	42.1%	−4.0%
Tax-deferred equity	4.1%	5.2%	8.8%	11.2%
Tax-deferred bonds	3.7%	6.6%	0.5%	13.7%
Tax-exempt bonds	28.1%	24.4%	41.2%	13.8%
Taxable bonds	−0.8%	7.2%	−3.8%	0.6%
Interest-bearing accounts	−1.9%	−1.2%	−1.6%	−2.9%
Other financial assets	−3.3%	−10.4%	−3.3%	1.1%

Source: Poterba and Samwick (1999).
*Statistically significantly different from zero at the 95 percent confidence level.

the findings are substantively important. In 1995, for example, the results suggest that a ten percentage point increase in a household's marginal tax rate on ordinary income raises the probabilities of holding tax-deferred bonds or tax-deferred equity by 26 percent and 22 percent, respectively. There is also clear evidence of a link between marginal tax rates and the likelihood of holding tax-exempt bonds, which generate untaxed interest income.

The tobit results in table 3.10 are less consistent across years than the findings in table 3.9. There are also fewer statistically significant results in table 3.10. The evidence is clear that households with higher marginal tax rates are more likely to hold a significant share of their portfolio in the form of tax-exempt bonds. There is also some evidence, particularly for 1995, that higher-marginal-tax-rate households have a larger share of their portfolio in tax-deferred equities and tax-deferred bonds. High marginal tax rates are associated with lower shares of the portfolio in interest-bearing accounts, a heavily taxed asset.

These findings are generally supportive of a link between taxes and portfolio structure, although some results are surprising. One might have expected a stronger effect of tax rates on the portfolio share in directly held equity, since equity is a relatively tax-favored asset. The positive association between marginal tax rates and the portfolio share in taxable equity mutual funds is also surprising, since these funds are typically more heavily taxed than direct equity investments.

Non-U.S. Evidence on Taxes, Asset Allocation, and Asset Selection
The empirical studies just considered focus on taxes and portfolio choice in the United States. A small literature reports empirical results for other countries. For example, Hochguertel, Alessie, and van Soest (1997) find that the choice between holding risky and riskless assets for a large sample of households in the Netherlands is significantly affected by the household's marginal tax rate. Higher marginal tax rates are associated with a greater portfolio share for risky assets, which generate potential returns in the form of capital gains. Since capital gains are not taxed in the Netherlands, this is a natural asset selection effect to find. For Sweden, Agell and Edin (1990) present evidence that taxes influence the allocation of household portfolios across a set of relatively broad asset categories.

3.4.2   Taxes and Borrowing Behavior

The substantial tax wedge between the pretax and after-tax cost of borrowing provides a clear inducement for households to borrow when the tax system allows interest deductibility. In the United States, there have been substantial changes in the tax treatment of borrowing over time, and these provide an opportunity to study whether borrowing decisions are sensitive to investor tax rates. Both Scholz (1994) and Maki (1996) examine the response of household borrowing to the Tax Reform Act of 1986. These studies conclude that when nonmortgage debt became more expensive in after-tax terms after 1986, households responded by changing the character of their debt. These studies do not provide evidence of the overall interest elasticity of consumer borrowing.

Casual cross-national comparisons suggest that households in the United States, which offers relatively generous treatment of mortgage borrowing, hold more of their wealth in housing than do households in other nations. Firm conclusions of this type are difficult, however, because it is hard to control for all of the other factors that may vary across nations and affect the fraction of household wealth held in the form of housing. There are significant differences in down-payment requirements, for example, between many continental European countries and the United States. The availability of mortgage financing more generally is likely to be an important factor explaining cross-national differences in the share of housing wealth in household portfolios.

3.4.3 Taxes and Asset Location

Relatively little research has considered how investors decide whether to hold heavily taxed assets in their tax-deferred accounts. There is no consensus on the optimal asset allocation strategy for investors, and therefore on the "null hypothesis" that should be tested in this context.

The traditional analysis of how to allocate portfolio assets for investors with access to a tax-deferred account holds that if the investor is holding any bonds, heavily taxed assets that generate taxable interest income, they should be held in the tax-deferred account. Consider a situation in which stocks and bonds have the same risk-adjusted return. Assume that a household with access to a tax-deferred account is holding both stocks and bonds and that the household has all of its bond holdings in a taxable account. A simple asset reallocation, moving all of the bonds to the tax-deferred account and moving equities with an equal value to the taxable account, will increase the household's after-tax risk-adjusted return. This is a pure "tax arbitrage" in the sense that the household's after-tax return can be increased without changing its risk exposure.

Shoven (1998) has recently challenged the general applicability of this arbitrage argument to the asset location problem facing most households. He does not dispute the logic of the tax arbitrage claim, but notes that most households invest their tax-deferred accounts through mutual funds or other financial intermediaries. At least in the United States, the historical behavior of equity mutual fund managers has resulted in higher tax burdens on investors in these funds than in directly held equity portfolios. Shoven argues that the higher tax burden on equity mutual funds, relative to direct equity investments, reduces the gain from holding them on taxable account while bonds are held in a tax-deferred account. In addition, if households have access to lightly taxed alternatives to bonds that deliver similar return profiles in a less heavily taxed fashion, such as state and local government bonds that generate tax-exempt interest, then the standard analysis may overstate the benefits of holding bonds in the tax-deferred account. One clear lesson of Shoven's analysis is that the optimal structure of asset allocation between taxable and tax-exempt accounts is likely to be sensitive to the broad menu of assets that are available to households. This set of assets may vary across households, and it also may vary across nations, so that general prescriptions on optimal asset location may be an elusive goal.

There is relatively limited empirical evidence on the way households allocate assets between taxable and tax-deferred accounts. The most directly relevant study is Bodie and Crane (1997)'s analysis of the asset mix that U.S. households choose in their taxable and tax-deferred accounts. This study uses data from a sample of participants in a large pension system, the Teachers Insurance Annuity Association–College Retirement Equity Fund (TIAA-CREF). Survey participants reported information on the assets that they held in taxable accounts, and this information was matched to detailed records on their asset allocation in the tax-deferred accounts managed by TIAA-CREF. The general findings suggest modest differences, if any, between the asset allocations that investors choose in their taxable accounts and their asset allocations for tax-deferred assets. This finding may reflect a lack of investor sophistication in considering the optimal strategy for allocating assets when there are both taxable and tax-deferred habitats available.

There is some evidence that investors change their asset allocations in self-directed retirement accounts infrequently. Ameriks and Zeldes (2000) provide some evidence for this phenomenon among TIAA-CREF participants. Since there are substantial changes over time in the tax environment, and these changes may influence the relative attractiveness of different allocation strategies, this may provide further support for the notion that many investors are not considering the broad structure of their portfolios. It is possible that households think of their retirement accounts and their other (taxable) accounts in different ways, as the "mental accounts" literature would suggest. This may result in suboptimal asset allocation from the standpoint of maximizing after-tax returns.

3.4.4   The Choice of Financial Intermediaries

Relatively little research has focused on how investors choose between holding assets directly and holding them through a financial intermediary, such as a mutual fund or an insurance company. Several of the country chapters in Poterba (1994a) note that insurance companies offer attractive vehicles for asset accumulation, in part because of the favorable tax treatment of insurance assets. Yet there has been little attention to modeling these incentives in conjunction with data on household balance sheets, in order to estimate the elasticity of demand for insurance industry products as a function of the tax subsidy.

With respect to other financial intermediaries, such as mutual funds, there are both advantages and disadvantages to intermediary-based investment strategies. Intermediaries often provide greater portfolio diversification than the investor could achieve alone, given the scale of his or her own investments. In addition, the record-keeping and possible liquidity services that financial intermediaries provide may be valuable benefits from the household's standpoint. There are disadvantages, however, associated with investing through intermediaries. Most intermediaries charge for their services, and in many cases the asset management fee is substantial. The management services provided by the intermediary compensate the investor for these costs, but there is an active academic debate on whether active management offers returns that are higher by enough to offset its costs.

A tax-related disadvantage also is associated with holding assets through intermediaries, particularly mutual funds. Many fund managers, at least in the United States, appear to take decisions that are not optimal from the standpoint of maximizing a taxpayer's after-tax returns. This may be the result of general practices that are not tax efficient (see Dickson and Shoven 1995), or it may be due to the fact that individual taxpayers have idiosyncratic tax positions that are unlikely to be recognized when the investment manager makes decisions. Little evidence is available on the tax consequences of investing through equity mutual funds outside the United States; this probably reflects the greater importance of equity funds as investment vehicles in the United States.

A recent trend is toward investing through intermediaries, at least in the United States. The U.S. household sector has been a net seller of common stock for most of the past decade. More important, the number of households in the United States that own corporate stock directly fell in the early 1990s, while the number of households investing through equity mutual funds has risen for the last decade. Poterba and Samwick (1999) present some evidence suggesting that higher-marginal-tax-rate households are more likely to invest in equity mutual funds. This finding suggests that these investors are not focusing solely on the tax consequences of their investments when they decide whether to invest through a financial intermediary. Virtually no empirical research addresses the choice of direct rather than indirect financial investment and assesses the importance of taxes or other factors in such investment.

3.4.5 Taxes and Asset Trading Decisions

Although there is no consensus on why investors trade, there is general agreement that decisions about when to trade assets are quite sensitive to investor marginal tax rates. Most of the research on this issue comes from the United States, where there have been many substantial changes in capital gains tax rules. The evidence on trading and taxation in other nations is limited. Umlauf (1993) presents interesting evidence on how the location of trade may be affected by tax rates. He shows that volume on the Stockholm Stock Exchange plummeted after the Swedish government introduced a transaction tax on trades. Transactions volume rose again, and the trading of Swedish securities on the London Stock Exchange declined, when the tax was rescinded.

The empirical research on taxation and capital gain realizations takes two forms. There are time-series studies that document a large elasticity of total gain realizations with respect to the after-tax amount that investors receive when they realize gains. There are also studies using household-level data to estimate the realization elasticity; studies vary in whether they use simple cross sections or panel data for this purpose. Burman (1999) and Poterba (2001) review this large literature.

The first of the two primary findings in the capital gains tax literature is that the elasticity of capital gains realizations with respect to the after-tax price of capital gains is large, possibly large enough to result in an increase in total capital gains tax revenues when the capital gains tax rate is reduced. The estimates of this realization elasticity tend to be somewhat larger in time series rather than household data studies.

Second, there is an important difference between investor responses to anticipated tax changes, or to transitory changes in the capital gains tax rate, and those to permanent changes in the tax rate. In one household-level study of capital gain realizations (Auten and Clotfelter 1982), the elasticity of realizations with respect to a one-year change in the capital gains tax rate was three times as large as the elasticity with respect to a permanent rate change. This differential presumably reflects the relatively low cost that investors perceive when they consider retiming asset trades from one year to the next. An investor who is planning to sell an appreciated asset and knows that the capital gains tax rate next year will exceed that in the current year may try to move the asset sale into the current tax year. The difference between this year and next year's capital gains tax rates that will induce such a change may be much smaller than the tax rate change that will lead the investor to sell an asset that he had never considered selling before.

These results leave little doubt that taxation matters for asset trading decisions. What is not clear from previous research is whether the distortions in trading behavior that flow from tax incentives affect the welfare of investing households. Analyzing the efficiency cost of tax-induced trading requires a model of why investors trade in the absence of tax considerations, and at present there are no generally accepted models of trading. Balcer and Judd (1987) tackle part of this issue in studying how the timing of investments and liquidations over the life cycle will be affected by a realization-based capital gains tax. Kovenock and Rothschild (1987) explore the static portfolio distortions associated with capital gains taxes when they try to model the welfare cost of an undiversified portfolio. Further work along these lines may provide additional leads for modeling tax distortions and estimating their costs.

3.5   General Patterns and Directions for Further Work

To organize the analysis of taxation and household portfolio behavior, it is helpful to identify six margins on which taxes may affect investor behavior: asset selection, asset allocation, asset location, borrowing, asset trading, and the choice of whether to invest through financial intermediaries. After reviewing the tax rules affecting investors in a number of industrialized nations and the existing empirical evidence on taxation and portfolio structure, several conclusions emerge.

First, the evidence for a link between after-tax returns and whether households own particular assets seems to be stronger than the evidence of a link between after-tax returns and the amounts that households invest in different assets. This finding could be explained by the notion that investors are more attuned to questions about what they should invest in than they are to questions about precisely how much to invest in different assets. There may be an important element of history in the structure of household portfolios. Portfolio rebalancing may be something that investors do less frequently than asking if they are holding the right kind of assets; this suggests that asset selection may be more sensitive to taxation than asset allocation.

Second, asset trading appears to be affected by tax rules. There is clear evidence, from capital gains tax reforms in the United States and other policy changes, that asset trading behavior responds when investors perceive a tax-induced reward to trading at one point in time rather than another. There seems to be a similar effect on the geographical location of trades; when taxes make it expensive to carry out trades in one location, the trades may move elsewhere. It is not clear how much of the trading response to capital gains tax changes, for example, is the result of retiming of trades that would otherwise take place at a different point in time and how much is "new" trading.

Third, investors choose to invest through financial intermediaries, even when these intermediaries impose substantial tax costs or other expenses on their investors. The factors that explain the growth of financial intermediaries are not clear. It may be that investors value the asset-management services provided by mutual funds and other asset managers. It may be that they benefit from the record keeping and other services that such managers perform. There is an open question about the trade-offs among cost, after-tax return, expenses, and investor asset inflows in the market for financial services. This is an area that requires further study.

Fourth, the limited evidence on asset location decisions by investors in the United States suggests that relatively few investors are choosing markedly different asset allocation patterns in their taxable and their tax-deferred accounts. Whether this reflects lack of attention to the specialized tax benefits of investment through tax-deferred accounts or something else is not clear.

Finally, the evidence is relatively clear that when the tax code permits households to borrow and deduct their interest payments from taxable income, households try to structure their affairs to take advantage of this opportunity. It seems likely that overall borrowing is greater when borrowing is tax deductible, but the limited time-series variation in interest deduction rules within nations makes it difficult to assess this issue.

If there is a clear direction for further work on the subject of taxation and household portfolios, it probably involves the linkage between theoretical models of household portfolio structure and empirical evidence on household balance sheets. Unlike the analysis of how taxation distorts other margins of household behavior, such as hours of work, there is no agreement on the underlying theoretical model that drives investor behavior. This is particularly evident in discussions of asset trading decisions, but it is also clear with respect to the basic structure of household portfolios. Existing models require some assumptions, such as the possibility of short selling, that are probably not appropriate for a large set of households. Developing more realistic models of the institutional constraints confronting taxable investors, recognizing the importance of asset attributes as well as asset habitat for affecting after-tax returns, and finding the ultimate utility level that households can derive under different tax rules represents a substantial agenda for future work.

A related direction for further study concerns linking portfolio decisions about nonfinancial assets with choices concerning financial assets. The interconnections among home ownership, mortgage borrowing, and other borrowing are likely to be close. Recent research has just begun to explore the effect of other nonfinancial investments, such as direct investment in a self-employment venture or investment in nonresidential real estate, on the structure of financial portfolios. Yet Carroll (2000), Heaton and Lucas (2000a), and others have noted that such nonfinancial investments figure prominently in the portfolios of many high-net-worth households. Exploring the interactions between these assets and financial assets is a natural direction for future work.

Note

I am grateful to Michael Haliassos, Marco Ratti, Andrew Samwick, Martha Starr-McCluer, and Stephen Zeldes for helpful comments; to the editors and the authors of other chapters for providing me with detailed information on country-specific tax rules; and to Daniel Bergstresser for outstanding research assistance. Part of this chapter draws on previous joint work with Andrew Samwick. This research was supported by the National Science Foundation and the Smith Richardson Foundation.

4 Econometric Issues in the Estimation of Household Portfolio Models

Raffaele Miniaci and
Guglielmo Weber

This chapter addresses the methodological issues that arise in estimating portfolio choice models on survey data. Individual-level data are required, because under the assumption of incomplete markets, heterogeneity of preferences affects the actual portfolio composition (standard separation theorems will not generally apply).

The choice of topics covered reflects the belief that the key issue is participation: in most developed countries, a large fraction of households still do not own any risky financial assets, though this fraction is decreasing. Given panel data covering a reasonable number of time periods, we can seek to discover the nature of this dynamic participation problem. Limited participation may be due to state dependence, unobserved heterogeneity, serial correlation in shocks, or (time-varying) observable characteristics, including demographics. Given a specification for the participation equation, we can also specify an equation relating the share of risky assets in total or financial wealth to household wealth and characteristics. Estimation methods (both parametric and semiparametric) suitable for both types of equation are introduced, and an attempt is made at evaluating their potential advantages and drawbacks for the problem at hand.

Section 4.1 reviews sampling issues, which are especially relevant when questions concern sensitive topics, such as wealth and portfolio decisions. In section 4.2, we turn to econometric issues and estimation techniques: panel data techniques for discrete choice and for sample separation problems. In section 4.3, we illustrate some of these issues by estimating a participation probability equation on a small panel of Italian households (a subsample of the data used in chapter 7).

4.1 Sampling Issues

Financial data at the household level are typically found in banks'
and financial intermediaries' accounts and household survey data.
The first source provides an accurate picture of both stocks and flows
for each asset held by individual customers. The key drawbacks are
the unrepresentative, endogenous nature of the sample and the possibly incomplete coverage of individual portfolios (if the overall asset
position is split among financial institutions). The econometric techniques to correct for this type of nonrandom sampling are reviewed
by Cosslett (1981, 1993, 1997) and Manski and Lerman (1977). In
principle, given suitable information on the population at large, corrections for the choice-based sampling design are possible. These
data sources do not normally contain a great deal of information on
economically interesting household characteristics (family composition, income and age of adult members may be unknown), so they
are not often used.

The second source, household surveys, is potentially richer (questions can be asked on any aspect of household behavior, subject to
time constraints), but issues of nonrandom nonresponse, sample size,
and measurement error arise. This last point is particularly touchy
for asset and liability questions because of their sensitive nature and
complexity. Failure to respond to direct questions on asset holdings
may reflect an unwillingness to reveal overall wealth. Techniques
to deal with sensitive data problems have been devised, such as
randomized response, which may be used for both the intensive and
extensive margins. The randomized-response literature is summarized in Fox and Tracy (1986) and Chaudhuri and Mukerjee (1988). A
much more pervasive problem stems from the objective difficulty
of providing exact answers to questions on asset values. "First, the
respondent may simply not know the answer to the question, particularly if the answer requires adding several different accounts or
placing a value on hard-to-measure assets like a business. Second,
the respondent may have a rough idea of the amount but assumes
that the interviewer wants a very precise figure" (Juster and Smith
1997, p. 1268). A possible technique in such cases is that known as
unfolding brackets (reviewed in Juster and Smith 1997): respondents
who do not know exact amounts are asked if the asset value exceeds
a certain amount (normally a round number). If they answer yes, a
similar question is asked for a larger amount, until the respondent

replies in the negative. The resulting data points will suffer from nonstandard measurement error, similar in nature to the coarse data problems that can be tackled as in Hejitan and Rubin (1990).

4.2   Econometric Issues and Estimation Techniques

The econometric analysis of household wealth data is interesting if financial markets are incomplete (as Gollier stresses in chapter 1). Under incompleteness, the dynamic decision of how much wealth to accumulate is related to portfolio choice and is affected by uninsurable individual risks, such as labor income risk, longevity risk, and risk related to illiquid assets (such as housing). The econometric problems that arise in this area are therefore largely common to analysis of survey data in general. For instance, the household wealth accumulation process is likely to reflect age, time, and cohort effects, and many of the key components of wealth probably suffer from measurement error. Of particular interest in this context is the large number of zeros, which may be due to corner solutions or other reasons.

The portfolio-related questions that have been empirically addressed using household survey data can be broadly typified as follows:

1. How is financial wealth accumulated over the life cycle, and how does it relate to total net worth (including housing wealth, own business, human capital, and pension wealth)? Of particular interest is the behavior of the elderly, whose limited decumulation has been interpreted as evidence against the life cycle hypothesis: nontrivial corrections are needed for the effects of differential mortality by wealth before proper inference can be made.

2. How do households decide whether to invest in risky financial assets? Here the key open question is why so many households do not have direct holdings of risky assets (stocks, equity funds, and long-term bonds). This is known as the stockholding puzzle (Haliassos and Bertaut 1995) and is the micro analogue of the equity premium puzzle.

3. How do households allocate their (financial or total) wealth across asset categories? Are portfolio shares chosen in a manner consistent with the participation decision?

Question 1 has been widely investigated in the empirical literature (see, for example, Poterba 1994a; Sheiner and Weil 1992; Alessie, Lusardi, and Kapteyn 1995). Much of the analysis consists of plotting age profiles for some index (mean, median, upper quartile) of total net worth or financial wealth. These profiles can be drawn conditional on observable characteristics, and in this case regression techniques are used (either ordinary least squares [OLS] or least absolute deviations [LAD], depending on whether the moment under investigation is the conditional expectation or the conditional median; quantile regression techniques are reviewed in Buchinsky 1998 and Horowitz 1993). The most interesting problems in this area are the identification of cohort effects and the correction for nonrandom attrition (differential mortality by wealth).

As Shorrocks (1975) notes, a cross-sectional wealth age profile will give a misleading picture of individual age profiles for at least two reasons. First, if earlier generations are lifetime poorer, their wealth holdings will be lower than the wealth holdings of later generations: This may produce false evidence for decumulation. Second, if there is differential mortality by wealth (wealthy individuals live longer), the average wealth of survivors may increase with time even if each surviving individual is decumulating. This may therefore produce false evidence against decumulation. The first problem can be resolved (in the absence of pure trendlike time effects, as discussed in Deaton and Paxson 1994a) by pooling cross sections over a long time period and producing wealth-age profiles for year-of-birth cohorts (see Poterba and Samwick 1997 and Attanasio 1998, among others). The second is more complex, and its solution requires assumptions on the relation between mortality and wealth (see, for instance, Attanasio and Hoynes 2000).

Question 2 has been addressed in a number of recent articles. For identification, we require some theory on why the participation in financial markets for risky assets is limited. Informational problems have been cited by King and Leape (1998), liquidity trading has been emphasized by Allen and Gale (1994), and others have stressed the combined effect of transaction costs (Vissing-Jørgensen 2000) and the existence of indivisible risky consumer durable goods and undiversifiable own-business risk (Heaton and Lucas 2000a). The very existence of a large number of households that do not invest in any risky assets suggests that econometric analysis must address the issue of data censoring. This is a standard problem in the analysis of labor supply and of consumer demand for a number of goods (such as tobacco and motor fuel). The household portfolio literature has so far mostly used parametric techniques such as logit (Haliassos and Bertaut 1995) and tobit (Guiso, Jappelli, and Terlizzese 1996; see also Hochguertel, Alessie, and van Soest 1997 for an application of the two-limit tobit estimator) or probit (King and Leape 1998). However, censored quantile regressions could be fruitfully used to address this issue without reliance on strong distribution assumptions (Powell 1984; Fitzenberger 1997; Buchinsky 1998).

Question 3 is likely to become one of the most intensely investigated, given the increased stock market participation over the past two decades in the United States, United Kingdom, and many European countries. It is closely related to question 2 if the analysis concentrates on very broad asset categories (risky versus low-risk financial assets, say); if several assets are considered, it becomes more complex. A good, recent example where three financial assets are considered and the corresponding complete model of asset demands is estimated on a single cross section taking into account zero holdings is Perraudin and Sørensen (2000).

In this book, country studies mostly look at some very broad asset categories (human capital, housing wealth, and own business wealth for real wealth; stocks, other risky financial assets, and risk-free financial assets for financial wealth) and consider asset allocation among all of them or within financial wealth alone (conditional upon the chosen real wealth allocation). In this context, the most appealing strategy is first to estimate the probability of holding any given subset of assets, and then estimate the corresponding systems of asset share equations conditional on positive holdings of the assets. It is important to note that adding up and zero-one inequality constraints on shares for each asset have some consequences for all other assets in the portfolio. For this reason, it is easier not to estimate all possible systems of equations jointly. To exemplify, suppose we consider three assets: stocks, long-term bonds, and short-term bonds. We first estimate the probability of holding any (sensible) combination of the three. Then we estimate a two-equation asset share system for households that hold all three (the third equation is redundant), as well as single-asset-share systems of equations for the households that hold two of the three. In all these equations, the analysis is conducted conditional on participation, by introducing as an additional explanatory variable a suitable Heckman-style selectivity correction, provided that economic theory predicts that some variables should affect the participation decision but not the portfolio share allocation. If no such variables exist, strong parametric assumptions are needed to estimate participation and portfolio allocation decisions jointly.[1]

In what follows we concentrate on the key issue of estimating stock market participation and on how nonrandom participation affects the equation for risky financial assets. If the only available data are from a single cross section, the participation decision must be assumed to be static. Standard methods can then be applied to estimate both the participation equation and the continuous portfolio choice equation (these are reviewed in Maddala 1983). Given panel data covering a reasonable number of time periods, one can address the challenging question of the dynamic nature of the participation decision. Limited participation may be due to state dependence, unobserved heterogeneity, or serial correlation in shocks, as well as the effects of (time-varying) observable characteristics, including demographics. In the past two decades, progress has been made in establishing identification conditions and devising suitable estimation techniques to cope with dynamic discrete-choice problems.

4.2.1 Discrete-Choice Models

Let us assume our aim is to study if and when households own risky assets and that we have a longitudinal data set. We may or may not observe the value of the desired level (or share) of risky assets w_{it}^* for each household i at time t, but we know whether households hold risky assets and want to study the ownership (or participation) probabilities $\Pr(w_{it} = 1)$ where

$$w_{it} = \begin{cases} 1 & \text{if } w_{it}^* > 0 \\ 0 & \text{if } w_{it}^* \leq 0 \end{cases}$$

if short sales are not permitted.[2]

If we assume that ownership is independent over time, then the joint probability of $(w_{i1}, \ldots, w_{iT})$ is given by $\Pr(w_{i1}, \ldots, w_{iT}) = \prod_{t=1}^{T} \Pr(w_{it})$. Under these assumptions, ownership probabilities can be studied using standard cross-section discrete models where the number of observations is NT instead of N. But the independence assumption over time would imply that

$$\Pr(w_{it} = 1 | w_{i,t-1} = 1) = \Pr(w_{it} = 1), \tag{4.1}$$

that is, that current ownership is not affected by past ownership. There are two major reasons that equation 4.1 may fail to hold:

1. Heterogeneity. Households are characterized by unobservable variables that affect their risk aversion and their information set and, hence, their attitude toward investment in risky assets.

2. True state dependence. Some theoretical models suggest that due to transaction costs and cumulated experience, current ownership depends on past ownership.

Within this framework, ownership probability and its evolution over time can be properly investigated using Markov chain models (see Heckman 1981b). Different assumptions on the presence and nature of heterogeneity and state dependence will determine the specification of the model, its statistical properties, and computational burden.

Assume that the desired level (or share) of risky assets w_{it}^* is a linear function of a set of k strictly exogenous variables x_{it} and the actual ownership at time $t - 1$, $w_{i,t-1}$:[3]

$$w_{it}^* = \beta' x_{it} + \gamma w_{i,t-1} + \varepsilon_{it}, \tag{4.2}$$

where x_{it} is a $(k \times 1)$ vector of variables independent of ε_{it}, β is its associate vector of parameters, and γ measures the effect of past ownership on current ownership. If there is no true state dependence, $\gamma = 0$. Individual heterogeneity can be introduced assuming that the random variable ε_{it} can be decomposed as

$$\varepsilon_{it} = \alpha_i + u_{it},$$

where α_i is the individual effect related to any unobservable individual characteristic assumed to be time invariant, such as risk aversion, and u_{it} is a time-varying effect, such as individual income innovations or expectation errors.

If we also assume that unobservable individual heterogeneity is negligible, then equation 4.1 holds, and consistent estimates of β can be obtained from a single cross section. But what can we learn from a single cross section if we cannot rule out unobserved heterogeneity? If the x_{it} are strictly exogenous with respect to α_i, then the cross-sectional estimates of β give the partial effect of a change in x. If, instead, individual heterogeneity correlates with x_{it} at any point in time, then the cross-sectional estimates of β give the total effect of a change in x.

If we assume that unobservable individual heterogeneity is relevant but that u_{it} are serially independent and that there is no true state dependence, then we have a static model for discrete panel data. If u_{it} are serially correlated or there is true state dependence, we study ownership probability using some dynamic model.

Static Models with Heterogeneity
If there is no true state dependence, our model is given by

$$w_{it}^* = \beta' x_{it} + \varepsilon_{it}$$

$$w_{it} = \begin{cases} 1 & \text{if } \varepsilon_{it} > -\beta' x_{it} \\ 0 & \text{if } \varepsilon_{it} \leq -\beta' x_{it} \end{cases} \tag{4.3}$$

$$\varepsilon_{it} = \alpha_i + u_{it}.$$

Assume $F(\cdot)$ is the cumulative distribution function of the random variable ε. Therefore,

$$E(w_{it}|x_{it}) = \Pr(w_{it} = 1|x_{it}) = F(\beta' x_{it}).$$

We can treat the individual effect α_i as a fixed effect or a random variable. In the first case,

$$\text{Var}(\varepsilon_{it}|\alpha_i, x_i) = \text{Var}(u_{it}|\alpha_i, x_i) = \sigma_u^2,$$

where $x_i = (x_{i1}, \ldots, x_{iT})'$; when α_i is treated as random, we usually assume

$$E(\alpha_i|x_i) = E(u_{it}|x_i) = 0$$

$$\text{Var}(\varepsilon_{it}|x_i) = \sigma_u^2 + \sigma_\alpha^2.$$

In both cases, the scale factor cannot be identified, so we normalize the variance of u_{it} to 1.

It is important to notice that treating the time-invariant individual effect (α_i) as fixed does not necessarily imply that α_i must be a fixed constant: it can be either a fixed constant or a random variable. Often what in the literature is defined as a fixed-effects model can in fact be read as a random-effects model whose parameters are estimated on the basis of the conditional (on α_i) model. Thus, we use the terminology *fixed-effects estimators* instead of *fixed-effects models*.

Fixed-Effects Estimators   If α_i are treated as fixed, then we might be interested in estimating both α_i and β. When T tends to infinity, the maximum likelihood (ML) estimator is consistent, but for household panel data, T is usually small, and there are few observations to estimate each α_i. In other words, there is an incidental-parameter problem similar to the well-known problem that affects the fixed-effects linear model.

In the linear case, the ML estimators of α_i and β are independent of each other, and consistent estimates of β can be obtained independently of α_i. But for discrete-choice models, this does not hold, and when T is fixed, ML estimates of both slopes and fixed effects are generally inconsistent.

If we assume that $F(\cdot)$ is logistic and the x_i are strictly exogenous with respect to the time-varying effect u_{it}, we can circumvent the problem using the conditional ML estimator suggested by Chamberlain (1980). The idea is to condition upon a sufficient statistic for α_i, which is shown to be the sum of the w_{it} (i.e., the number of times it takes value 1).

Consider the case with only two time periods: we shall condition on $S_i = w_{i1} + w_{i2}$. Given that $w_{i1} + w_{i2} = 0$ or $= 2$ are not informative on β, the only interesting case is that in which some transition from nonownership to ownership (or vice versa) has been observed. Given the logistic assumption

$$\Pr(w_{i1} = 1 | x_{i1}, \alpha_i) = \frac{\exp(\beta' x_{i1} + \alpha_i)}{1 + \exp(\beta' x_{i1} + \alpha_i)},$$

define $A = \{w_{i1} = 0, w_{i2} = 1\}$; then:

$$\Pr(A | S_i = 1, \alpha_i, x_i) = \frac{\exp[\beta'(x_{i2} - x_{i1})]}{1 + \exp[\beta'(x_{i2} - x_{i1})]},$$

which does not depend on the individual fixed effect α_i (as is required for S_i to be a sufficient statistic). The conditional log-likelihood function is

$$\ln L = \sum_{i \,|\, S_i = 1} \mathbf{1}(A_i) \ln \frac{\exp[\beta'(x_{i2} - x_{i1})]}{1 + \exp[\beta'(x_{i2} - x_{i1})]}$$

$$+ (1 - \mathbf{1}(A_i)) \ln \frac{1}{1 + \exp[\beta'(x_{i2} - x_{i1})]},$$

where $\mathbf{1}(A_i) = 1$ if household i moved from nonownership to ownership. This is equivalent to the unconditional log-likelihood function of a cross-sectional logit model in which the two outcomes are

$(0,1)$ or $(1,0)$ and the explanatory variables are $x_2 - x_1$. Under mild regularity conditions on α_i, consistent estimates of β can be obtained using standard software for ML estimation of logit models, although for $\hat{\beta}_{CML}$ the ML estimates of the asymptotic covariance matrix are inappropriate (see Chamberlain 1980). This approach is therefore easy to implement, but it has the drawback that some variation in x_i from time 1 to time 2 is necessary to identify β, which precludes estimating the effects on ownership probability of such time-invariant characteristics as gender and education.

Full specification of $F(u_{it}|x_i, \alpha_i)$ is not necessary in a nonparametric context. Manski's (1987) conditional maximum score estimator does not impose any restriction on $F(\alpha_i|x_{it})$, thus allowing the individual effects to be correlated with the observables; it requires only the idiosyncratic term u_{it} to be stationary conditional on (x_i, α_i). But it does impose a substantive restriction on the x: for β to be identifiable (up to a scale parameter), there must be at least one continuous variable in x with nonzero coefficient. Given that β is identifiable up to a scale parameter, we shall assume that $\beta_1 = 1$. The estimation strategy relies on the observation that under the assumptions given,

$$\beta'(x_{it} - x_{it-1}) \gtreqqless 0 \Leftrightarrow E(w_{it} - w_{it-1} \mid x_i) \gtreqqless 0$$

and

$$H(b) \equiv E[sgn(b'(x_{it} - x_{is}))(w_{it} - w_{is})] \quad s < t$$

has its maximum in β. Estimates of β are thus obtained by maximizing the sample analogue of $H(\cdot)$: b is chosen in such a way that the sign of $b'(x_{it} - x_{is})$ equals the sign of $(w_{it} - w_{is})$ for as many observations as possible. The resulting estimates are $N^{1/3}$-consistent and have nonnormal limit distribution. To improve on these asymptotic properties, the sign function $sgn(b'(x_{it} - x_{is}))$ can be replaced by some smooth function $K(b'(x_{it} - x_{is})/\sigma_N)$ that converges to the indicator function as $N \rightarrow \infty$ (Horowitz 1992). Under appropriate values for the bandwidth parameter σ_N, the maximization of the smoothed $H_{NT}(b)$ results in estimates of β that are consistent and asymptotically normal, albeit not $\sqrt{N}$-consistent (Kyriazidou 1995; Charlier, Melenberg, and van Soest 1995). As in the fixed-effect logit conditional maximum likelihood (CML) estimator, the observations for which no transitions are observed convey no useful information, and the effects of time-invariant characteristics cannot be estimated.

Random-Effects Estimators   Consider model 4.3 in which both the individual effects α_i and the idiosyncratic effect u_{it} are independent of observable characteristics x_i, have normal distributions $u_{it} \sim N(0,1)$ and $\alpha_i \sim N(0, \sigma_\alpha^2)$, and u_{it} are serially uncorrelated. Then

$$\varepsilon_i \sim N(0, \Sigma)$$
$$\text{Var}(\varepsilon_i) = (\sigma_\alpha^2 + 2\sigma_{\alpha u})u' + I, \tag{4.4}$$

where $\varepsilon_i = (\varepsilon_{i1}, \dots, \varepsilon_{iT})'$. Under these assumptions, household i's contribution to the log-likelihood of this univariate probit model is:

$$\ln L_i = \ln \int_{-\infty}^{(2w_{i1}-1)\beta'x_{i1}} \cdots \int_{-\infty}^{(2w_{iT}-1)\beta'x_{iT}} \phi_T(\varepsilon_i)\, d\varepsilon_i, \tag{4.5}$$

where $\phi_T(\cdot)$ is the T-dimensional distribution function of ε_i. Although the model specified is a univariate probit, ML estimation requires the evaluation of NT-dimensional integrals, which is computationally cumbersome. Different approaches to cope with this problem are available: simulation methods can be used to approximate integrals (see Hajivassiliou and Ruud 1994), or restrictions on the process can be imposed (see Butler and Moffitt 1982 and Heckman 1981b). The most obvious restriction is to assume that the two error components are independent. In this case, $\varepsilon_{it} \mid \alpha_i \sim N(\alpha_i, 1)$, $\text{Cov}(\varepsilon_{it}, \varepsilon_{is} \mid \alpha_i) = 0$ and log-likelihood maximization requires only unidimensional numerical integration, which can be computed using the Butler and Moffitt (1982) procedure.[4] This result is granted by the assumption that u_{it} are serially uncorrelated. If this is not the case, then $\text{Cov}(\varepsilon_{it}, \varepsilon_{is} \mid \alpha_i) \neq 0$ and the evaluation of multidimensional integrals is necessary.

To avoid numerical integration altogether, we can adopt generalized methods of moments (GMM) estimators exploiting moment restrictions that do not depend on the intertemporal error covariance matrix. This class of estimators, which includes Chamberlain's (1984) minimum distance sequential estimator, is described in a unified framework by Bertschek and Lechner (1998), who also provide an efficiency ranking. Let $w_i = (w_{i1}, \dots, w_{iT})'$ be the sequence of w_{it} for household i, $x_i = (x_{i1}, \dots x_{iT})'(T \times k)$ the collection of the corresponding x_{it}. Thus, if we define the $T \times 1$ vector,

$$m_i(w_i, x_i; \beta) = w_i - E[w_i \mid x_i] = w_i - \Phi\left(\frac{x_i\beta}{\sqrt{1+\sigma_\alpha^2}}\right),$$

then under the foregoing assumptions, $E[m_i(w_i, x_i; \beta) \mid x_i] = 0$. All the m_i are orthogonal to the matrix of exogenous observable characteristics x_i and to any of their transformations $A(x_i)$. Thus, once we have defined the $q \times T$ "instrument matrix" $A(x_i)$ (with $q \geq k$), we can exploit the following unconditional moment restrictions for estimation:

$$E[A(x_i)m_i(w_i, x_i; \beta)] = 0. \tag{4.6}$$

In particular we can use the optimal instrument matrix derived by Chamberlain (1987) and Newey (1990) $A_i^*(x_i) = D(x_i)'\Omega(x_i)^{-1}$, where $D(x_i)(T \times k)$ has typical row d_{it}

$$d_{it} = -\phi(\beta' x_{it})x_{it}',$$

and $\Omega(x_i) = E[m_i(w_i, x_i; \beta)m_i(w_i, x_i; \beta)' \mid x_i]$. The resulting GMM estimate of β will be $\sqrt{N}$-consistent and asymptotically normal.

A similar estimator is suggested by Zeger and Liang (1986) who adopt a quasi-likelihood (QL) approach (McCullagh and Nelder 1983; Wedderburn 1974). The QL estimator is the solution of the score-like equation system derived from the following minimization problem:

$$\hat{\beta}_{QL} = \arg \min_{\beta} \sum_{i=1}^{N} m_i(w_i, x_i; \beta)'\Omega(x_i)^{-1} m_i(w_i, x_i; \beta). \tag{4.7}$$

This approach also does not require evaluating T-dimensional integrals, and the equation system derived from equation 4.7 can be solved iteratively. The estimator obtained is also $\sqrt{N}$-consistent and asymptotically normal (though generally less efficient than GMM).[5]

The proposed ML, GMM, and QL estimators require the observable characteristics to be uncorrelated with the unobservable heterogeneity component α and to be strictly exogenous. This clearly poses some problems when we want to relate asset ownership to income or wealth, for instance. Predetermined variables can be used in a GMM framework if the first moment restrictions (see equation 4.6) are suitably adapted (see Bertschek and Lechner 1998 and the two-step GMM estimator proposed by Arellano and Carrasco 1996 reviewed below).

In some cases, it is reasonable to assume that the observable characteristics are correlated with the individual effect α_i and that, conditional on them, the x's are strictly exogenous with respect to u_{it}, $E[u_{it} \mid x_i, \alpha_i] = 0$. Under these assumptions, Bover and Arellano (1997) extend Chamberlain's (1984) minimum distance estimator to the case at hand. This requires specifying the form of the correlation between observables x_i and individual unobservable heterogeneity as

$$E[\alpha_i | x_i] = \psi_1' x_{i1} + \cdots + \psi_T' x_{iT}.$$

The reduced form of the model then is given by

$$w_i^* = x_i \beta + \iota \alpha_i + u_i \tag{4.8}$$

$$= \begin{bmatrix} x_{i1}'(\psi_1 + \beta) + \cdots + x_{iT}' \psi_T \\ \vdots \\ x_{i1}' \psi_1 + \cdots + x_{iT}'(\psi_T + \beta) \end{bmatrix} + u_i \tag{4.9}$$

$$= \begin{bmatrix} (\psi_1 + \beta)' & \cdots & \psi_T' \\ \vdots & \ddots & \vdots \\ \psi_1' & \cdots & (\psi_T + \beta)' \end{bmatrix} \begin{bmatrix} x_{i1} \\ \vdots \\ x_{iT} \end{bmatrix} + u_i \tag{4.10}$$

$$= \Pi x_i^A + u_i \tag{4.11}$$

where $x_i^A = (x_{i1}', \ldots x_{iT}')' (kT \times 1)$. If we premultiply the reduced-form equation by $Q = I_T - \iota\iota'/T$, that is, we take the reduced-form equation in terms of deviations of the variables from their individual specific means (w_i^+, x_i^+ and u_i^+), we have

$$w_i^+ = x_i^+ \beta + u_i^+ = Q\Pi x_i^A + u_i^+,$$

which implies

$$\beta = \left(\sum_{i=1}^{N} x_i^{+\prime} x_i^+ \right)^{-1} \sum_{i=1}^{N} x_i^{+\prime} \Pi x_i^A. \tag{4.12}$$

Therefore, β can be estimated by replacing Π in equation 4.12 with a consistent estimate, $\hat{\Pi}$. If $\hat{\Pi}$ is consistent and asymptotically normal, then $\hat{\beta}$ will also be consistent and asymptotically normal. The estimator is easy to compute if we assume that $u_{it} | x_i^A \sim N(0, \sigma_t^2)$. In this case, the independent ML estimates of the T cross-sectional probit models give consistent estimates of the T rows of Π. The predicted index functions $\hat{\Pi} x_i^A$ can then be used as dependent variable in the OLS regression on x^+ as shown in equation 4.12. The estimated variance of β must be corrected to allow for the special nature of the dependent variable.[6]

Dynamic Models

If the idiosyncratic terms u_{it} are serially correlated or there is true state dependence, the ownership probability can be studied using dynamic models. But before introducing any estimation technique, it is necessary to consider two crucial problems.

Initial Conditions   The assumptions made concerning the initial conditions (i.e., on w_{i0}) are crucial to obtaining consistent estimators in a random-effects framework. There are typically two approaches to coping with this problem: assume either that the initial conditions are truly exogenous or that the process is in equilibrium at time 0. In both cases, the ML estimators are consistent if N (or N and T) goes to infinity.

Assuming that the initial conditions are exogenous is valid if the u_{it} are serially independent. Alternatively, we must assume that a new process is observed (with respect to the past) when we start to sample the individuals; otherwise the initial state is determined by the process generating the panel. An example could be the decision to invest in private pension funds: if the sampling period starts when private pension funds are introduced (by legislation), then we can treat initial conditions as exogenous.

On the other hand, the assumption that the process is in equilibrium requires that in any particular time (0, say) we can use the cross section to evaluate the (long-run) probability of ownership. This raises problems when the process is evolving and also when the x_{it}'s vary over time. As an example, consider the choice made by consumers whether to invest in Treasury bills. This asset has long been available to the general public and its market is mature, so we could reasonably assume that the underlying process is in equilibrium. However, if the proportion of individuals investing in such safe assets has been decreasing over time, because of innovations that decrease transaction costs in alternative asset markets, or if Treasury bill ownership depends on time-varying factors that are not themselves stable over time in the population, then the equilibrium condition is not met.

True State Dependence Versus Spurious State Dependence   Time dependence between observed events could depend on the fact that the actual experience of ownership has modified individual behavior, on the presence of unobserved components that are correlated over time, or both. That is why disentangling true and spurious state dependence is a problem. The unobserved individual effects persist over time, creating serially correlated residuals, so even if we observe that

$$\Pr(w_{it}|w_{i,t-1}, x_{it}) \neq \Pr(w_{it}|x_{it}),$$

we cannot say anything about true or spurious state dependence, because this inequality may be the result of past information on ownership yielding information on the unobserved effects. If the idiosyncratic components u_{it} are serially uncorrelated conditional on the individual effect, then a test can be run to check whether the following equality holds:

$$\Pr(w_{it}|w_{i,t-1}, x_{it}, \alpha_i) = \Pr(w_{it}|x_{it}, \alpha_i).$$

If u_{it} are serially correlated, Chamberlain (1985) suggests a simple method: as in continuous time models, if there is state dependence, there is a dynamic response even to variations in x_{it}. Therefore, we can base a test for the presence of state dependence on the equality

$$\Pr(w_{it}|x_{it}, \alpha_i) = \Pr(w_{it}|x_{it}, x_{i,t-1}, \ldots, \alpha_i),$$

which holds only if there is no state dependence.

Estimation   In what follows we review some of the estimation techniques proposed in the literature for dynamic discrete panel data. We start by assuming that terms u_{it} are serially correlated but that there is no true state dependence and x_{it} are strictly exogenous. Under these assumptions, we can use either simulated ML techniques (Lee 1997) or the GMM or QL estimators for static random-effects models. In the GMM approach, consistent estimates of $\Omega(x_i)$ can be obtained from $(T-1)T/2$ separate bivariate probits or using nonparametric methods (see Bertschek and Lechner 1998). With QL, given an initial estimate of the correlation matrix, consistent estimates are obtained as by-products of the iterative reweighted least-squares process, and consistency and asymptotic normality do not depend on the correct specification of the starting correlation matrix.

When there is true state dependence $(\gamma \neq 0)$, the appropriate estimation technique depends crucially on the fixed-random effects choice and on the nature of the observable characteristics x_{it}. If we consider α_i as fixed, we can use the estimator suggested by Honoré and Kyriazidou (2000b).

Let us assume that the initial state w_{i0} is observed and that the u_{it} are logistic independently and identically distributed (i.i.d.), independent of x_i, α_i, and w_{i0} in all time periods.[7] Then the conditional ownership probability at time t is

$$\Pr(w_{it} = 1 | x_i, \alpha_i, w_{i0}, \dots, w_{i,t-1}) = \frac{\exp(\beta' x_{it} + \gamma w_{i,t-1} + \alpha_i)}{1 + \exp(\beta' x_{it} + \gamma w_{i,t-1} + \alpha_i)}. \quad (4.13)$$

Chamberlain (1985) treats the special case in which $\beta = 0$, showing that in this case, $S_i \equiv \sum_{t=1}^{T} w_{it}$ is no longer a sufficient statistic for α_i, even conditional on w_{i0}, but that S_i and $\sum_{t=0}^{T-1} w_{it}$ are. Equivalently, the likelihood conditional on $(w_{i0}, \tilde{S}_i = \sum_{t=1}^{T-1} w_{it}$ and $w_{iT})$ does not depend on α_i. It is clear that the conditional estimator requires at least four observations (including 0): with three observations, the conditional event (w_{i1}) would be perfectly predicted by the conditioning set $(w_{i0}, \tilde{S}_i = w_{i1}, w_{i2})$.

When $\beta \neq 0$, we can consider the case where w is observed over four consecutive periods (from 0 to 3), while the explanatory variables are observed over periods 1 to 3 (so $T = 3$). As in the static model, once the initial (w_{i0}) and the final (w_{i3}) state are fixed, only the households with a transition from ownership at time 1 to nonownership at time 2 (or vice versa) are useful to identify the parameters in a conditional framework, that is, only consumers with $w_{i1} + w_{i2} = 1$. Define A as

$$A = \{w_{i0} = d_0, w_{i1} = 0, w_{i2} = 1, w_{i3} = d_3\},$$

where d_0 and d_3 are either 1 or 0. If the explanatory variables are discrete and $\Pr(x_{i2} = x_{i3}) > 0$, the conditional probabilities

$$\Pr(A | x_i, \alpha_i, d_0, d_3, w_{i1} + w_{i2} = 1, x_{i2} = x_{i3})$$

$$= \frac{1}{1 + \exp[\beta'(x_{i1} - x_{i2}) + \gamma(d_0 - d_3)]}$$

do not depend on the fixed effects α_i and can be used to draw inference on β and γ. Consistent and $\sqrt{N}$ asymptotically normal estimates of (β, γ) are obtained by maximizing the weighted log-likelihood function:

$$\sum_{i=1}^{N} \mathbf{1}(w_{i1} + w_{i2} = 1)\mathbf{1}(x_{i2} - x_{i3} = 0) \ln \frac{\exp[\beta'(x_{i1} - x_{i2}) + \gamma(w_{i0} - w_{i3})]^{w_{i1}}}{1 + \exp[\beta'(x_{i1} - x_{i2}) + \gamma(w_{i0} - w_{i3})]}.$$

If the identification assumption $x_{i2} = x_{i3}$ is not reasonable for the problem at hand, the indicator function $\mathbf{1}(x_{i2} - x_{i3} = 0)$ can be replaced by a kernel density function whose bandwidth shrinks as N increases and is such that it gives more weight to those observations for which x_{i2} is closer to x_{i3}. However, a trendlike variable such as the age of the household head cannot be included among the explanatory variables: the estimator cannot allow for the presence of state dependence and a deterministic trend.

The Honoré and Kyriazidou estimator, then, is an ingenious generalization of the conditional logit estimator: compared to the static case, two extra observations are required to disentangle unobserved heterogeneity and state dependence.[8]

If we consider the unobservable individual effects α_i as random, we can use the computationally intensive method of simulated ML estimators (Lee 1997; see also chapter 9, this volume). Alternatively, we can use the two-step GMM estimator proposed by Arellano and Carrasco (1996). Let us denote $x_i^t = (x_{i1}, \dots, x_{it})$, $w_i^t = (w_{i0}, \dots, w_{it})$, and $z_i^t = (x_i^t, w_i^{t-1})$, assume that w_{i0} is observed, and that

$$\varepsilon_{it}|z_i^t \sim N(E(\alpha_i|z_i^t), \sigma_t^2)$$

$$E(\alpha_i|z_i^t) = E[E(\alpha_i|z_i^{t+1}) \mid z_i^t].$$

With these assumptions, the individual unobserved heterogeneity term α_i can correlate with the observable characteristics x_{it} through the conditional mean of α_i, given the past and present value of $x_{it}(x_i^t)$ and ownership history (w_i^{t-1}) (i.e., through $E(\alpha|z_i^t)$). Predetermined variables can be included in the conditioning set, and this is particularly useful when asset ownership is studied. In fact, we can assume that wealth (or income) is correlated with unobservable individual effects α_i, as long as it does not depend on current or future values of the transitory shocks u_{it}, although there may be some feedback from lagged values of u_{it}. Furthermore, individual effects and idiosyncratic components are not required to be conditionally independent. Therefore, the following conditional first moment restrictions hold:

$$E(w_{it}|z_i^t) = \Pr(w_{it} = 1|z_i^t) = \Phi\left(\frac{\beta'x_{it} + \gamma w_{i,t-1} + E(\alpha_i|z_i^t)}{\sigma_t}\right)$$

$$= h_t(z_i^t). \tag{4.14}$$

Let us consider the case in which x_{it} contains only a random variable with a finite support of J points (e.g., J wealth or income classes). Therefore $z_{it} = (x_{it}, w_{i,t-1})$ has a finite support of $(2J)$ points, and z_i^t has $(2J)^t$ possible realizations, denoted ϱ_j^t $(j = 1, \ldots, (2J)^t)$. Let us also assume that $E(\alpha_i) = 0$. Inverting equation 4.14, we obtain

$$\beta' x_{it} + \gamma w_{i,t-1} + E(\alpha_i | z_i^t) = \sigma_t \Phi^{-1}(h_t(z_i^t)),$$

and by first differencing

$$\sigma_t \Phi^{-1}(h_t(z_i^t)) - \sigma_{t-1} \Phi^{-1}(h_{t-1}(z_i^{t-1})) - \beta' \Delta x_{it} + \gamma \Delta w_{i,t-1} = \eta_{it},$$

where

$$\eta_{it} = E(\alpha_i | z_i^t) - E(\alpha_i | z_i^{t-1})$$

$$E(\eta_{it} | z_i^{t-1}) = 0. \tag{4.15}$$

If we define a dummy variable $d_{ij}^t = \mathbf{1}(z_i^t = \varrho_j^t)$ that takes the value of one if the sequence of realizations of w_{it} and x_{it} for household i until time t is equal to the jth possible combination, then the unconditional moment restrictions,

$$E(d_{ij}^{t-1} \eta_{it}) = 0 \qquad j = 1, \ldots, (2J)^{t-1},$$

are equivalent to the conditional moment restrictions (equation 4.15). These are the conditions used in estimation and standard GMM asymptotic properties apply. An extension to the case of continuous x is also discussed in Arellano and Carrasco (1996).

4.2.2   Truncation, Censoring, and Sample Selection Models

Assume that information on the level (or share) of risky assets owned by households is available and that we want to exploit not only the dichotomous participation (or ownership) variable as in the discrete-choice models, but also the (continuous) variation of the level of risky assets across households. Given that not all the households hold risky assets, $w_{it} = w_{it}^*$ is observed only for participating families. As participation is correlated with the level of risky assets that the household would like to hold, then drawing inferences on the distribution of risky assets, $f(w_{it}^*)$, requires taking into account that the sample conveys information on the risky asset distribution conditional on ownership, $f(w_{it}^* | ownership)$. To understand the consequences of this and to keep the framework as simple as possible, consider the case in which w_{it}^* is independent across individuals and over time, and there exists a minimum amount c that the household has to invest in the risky asset to enter the market (fixed participation costs). Therefore, the desired level w_{it}^* is observed only if $w_{it}^* > c$ and

$$f(w_{it}^* | ownership) = f(w_{it}^* | w_{it}^* > c) = \frac{f(w_{it}^*)}{\Pr(w_{it}^* > c)}.$$

If the data are on owners only (as might be the case if data come from bank accounts), we have truncated models, where the individual contribution to the log-likelihood function is

$$\ln L_i = \sum_{t=1}^{T} \mathbf{1}(w_{it}^* > c)[\ln f(w_{it}^*) - \ln \Pr(w_{it}^* > c)].$$

If data on both owners and nonowners are available, nonowners convey information only on the probability of being below threshold c, which is the case of the censored regression models. In this case the individual contribution to the log-likelihood function is

$$\ln L_i = \sum_{t=1}^{T} \mathbf{1}(w_{it}^* > c)[\ln f(w_{it}^*) - \ln \Pr(w_{it}^* > c)]$$

$$+ (1 - \mathbf{1}(w_{it}^* > c)) \ln \Pr(w_{it}^* \le c).$$

But assume, for instance, that nonparticipation is primarily a problem of lack of information on the availability of the asset. If so, it would be reasonable to model the ownership decision on the basis of a different process from that generating w_{it}^*. A proper model could be

$$w_{it} = \begin{cases} w_{it}^* & \text{if } \mathbf{1}(y_{it}^* > 0) = 1 \\ \text{not observed} & \text{otherwise} \end{cases},$$

where y_{it}^* is a continuous latent variable, in general correlated with w_{it}^*. Models like this are usually referred to as sample selection models, and if ownership is independent over time, the individual contribution to the log-likelihood function is

$$\ln L_i = \sum_{t=1}^{T} \mathbf{1}(y_{it}^* > 0)[\ln f(w_{it}^* | y_{it}^* > 0)] + (1 - \mathbf{1}(y_{it}^* > 0)) \ln \Pr(y_{it}^* \le 0).$$

It is clear that from a statistical point of view, a censored regression model can be considered as a particular type of sample selection model.[9]

As in the discrete-choice models, under the independence assumption above, the distribution of risky assets can be studied using standard cross-section techniques where the number of observations is NT instead of N (see Amemiya 1985; Maddala 1983; Vella 1998). But the role played by individual unobserved heterogeneity is rarely negligible. Dependence on the past, in both the risky asset equation and the participation equation, is also likely to be important.

As with the discrete-choice model, we first illustrate static models, which are estimated with fixed- or random-effect methods, and then move on to dynamic models. In what follows, we do not consider truncated regression models.

Static Models with Heterogeneity

Fixed-Effects Estimators for Censored Regression Models

Consider the following censored regression model where $c = 0$ and individual unobserved heterogeneity is introduced:

$$w_{it}^* = \beta' x_{it} + \varepsilon_{it} \tag{4.16}$$

$$w_{it} = \max\{w_{it}^*, 0\} \tag{4.17}$$

$$\varepsilon_{it} = \alpha_i + u_{it} \tag{4.18}$$

The model is similar to the standard discrete-choice model, with the difference that the real value of the latent variable is observed if it satisfies the criterion 4.17. Thus, a possible estimation strategy is to extend to this case the estimators adopted for discrete-choice models. For instance, Chamberlain's (1984) minimum distance estimator has been adapted to this model by Bover and Arellano (1997), along the lines described above.

Another possibility is explored by Honoré (1992), who artificially censors the dependent variable in such a way that the individual specific effect can be differenced away. To convey the main idea behind Honoré's estimator, let us consider the case of $T = 2$ and $\beta' \Delta x_i \geq 0$ ($\Delta x_i = x_{i1} - x_{i2}$) (for more general cases, see Honoré 1992, Arellano and Honoré 2000, and Honoré and Kyriazidou 2000a). If u_{i1} and u_{i2} are i.i.d. conditional on x_i and α_i,[10] then the distribution $(w_{i1}^*, w_{i2}^* | x_i, \alpha_i)$ is symmetric around a 45-degree line through

$(\beta' x_{i1}, \beta' x_{i2})$, that is, the line $w_{i2}^* = w_{i1}^* - \beta' \Delta x_i$. But $(w_{i1}^*, w_{i2}^* | x_i, \alpha_i)$ is not observed, so the "trick" is to trim the observed counterpart $(w_{i1}, w_{i2} | x_i, \alpha_i)$ in such a way that the trimmed variables are symmetrically distributed around a 45-degree line. Under our simplifying assumption, it is sufficient to introduce the trimmed variable:

$$w_{i1}^T = \begin{cases} w_{i1} - \beta' \Delta x_i & \text{if } w_{i1} > \beta' \Delta x_i \\ 0 & \text{otherwise} \end{cases}.$$

The bivariate variable $(w_{i1}^T, w_{i2} | x_i, \alpha_i)$ is symmetrically distributed around the bisector, that is,

$$E[w_{i2} - w_{i1}^T | x_i, \alpha_i] = 0,$$

which implies

$$E[(w_{i2} - w_{i1}^T)\Delta x_i] = 0. \tag{4.19}$$

Equation 4.19 can be seen as the first-order condition of a convex minimization problem. Standard results on extremum estimators ensure that estimates of β satisfying a sample analogue of equation 4.19 will be consistent and $\sqrt{N}$ asymptotically normal.[11]

Under the assumptions of normality and serial independence of u_{it}, and strict exogeneity of the x (both conditional on α_i), a simpler GMM estimator can be used (Honoré, 1998).[12] In fact, under these assumptions,

$$E[w_{it}^2 - w_{it}(\beta' x_{it} + \alpha_i) - \sigma_u^2 \mid x_{it}, \alpha_i, w_{it} > 0] = 0,$$

and therefore

$$E[w_{it}^2 w_{is} - w_{it} w_{is}(\beta' x_{it} + \alpha_i) - w_{is}\sigma_u^2 \mid x_{it}, x_{is}, \alpha_i, w_{it} > 0, w_{is} > 0] = 0.$$

Taking differences between time t and time s and integrating out α_i gives

$$E[(w_{it}^2 w_{is} - w_{is}^2 w_{it}) - \beta'(x_{it} - x_{is})w_{it}w_{is} - \sigma_u^2(w_{is} - w_{it}) \mid x_{it}, x_{is}, w_{it} > 0,$$

$$w_{is} > 0] = 0,$$

which is equivalent to

$$(w_{it}^2 w_{is} - w_{is}^2 w_{it}) = \beta'(x_{it} - x_{is})w_{it}w_{is} + \sigma_u^2(w_{is} - w_{it}) + \zeta_{it}, \tag{4.20}$$

with $E[\zeta_{it} | x_{it}, x_{is}, w_{it} > 0, w_{is} > 0] = 0$. Thus, estimates of β and σ_u^2 can be obtained by IV estimation of equation 4.20 on the observations with positive asset holdings using functions of the x's as instruments.

Fixed-Effects Estimators for Sample Selection Models   Consider the following sample selection model:

$$w_{it}^* = \beta' x_{it} + \alpha_i + u_{it} \tag{4.21}$$

$$y_{it}^* = \delta' z_{it} + \mu_i + v_{it} \tag{4.22}$$

$$y_{it} = \mathbf{1}(y_{it}^* > 0) \tag{4.23}$$

$$w_{it} = \begin{cases} w_{it}^* & \text{if } y_{it} = 1 \\ 0 & \text{otherwise} \end{cases}, \tag{4.24}$$

where x_i and z_i are strictly exogenous with respect to u_{it}, v_{it} and μ_i. Consider three cases:

1. Both $\text{Cov}(\alpha_i, \mu_i)$ and $\text{Cov}(u_{it}, v_{it})$ equal zero.

2. $\text{Cov}(u_{it}, v_{it}) = 0$, but $\text{Cov}(\alpha_i, \mu_i) \neq 0$.

3. The individual effects α_i and μ_i are treated as constants and $\text{Cov}(u_{it}, v_{it}) = 0$.

In these special cases, as long as β is the full set of relevant parameters, the discrete-choice model in equation 4.22 can be neglected and β can be estimated on the subsample with positive w's.

In case 1, the standard linear random-effects estimator for an unbalanced panel (i.e., computed on the observation with $w_{it} > 0$) gives consistent estimates for β if x are strictly exogenous with respect to $\varepsilon_{it} = \alpha_i + u_{it}$ (see Wooldridge 1995). But to impose $\text{Cov}(\alpha_i, \mu_i) = \text{Cov}(u_{it}, v_{it}) = 0$ is rarely reasonable, because it is equivalent to assuming that sample selection is exogenous, that is, that being an owner or not does not depend on the level of risky assets desired, once allowance is made for the observables.

In cases 2 and 3, β can be consistently estimated with a simple within-group estimator for unbalanced panels. Thus, standard techniques are appropriate if we assume, for instance, that unobservable (time-invariant) risk aversion affects both the participation decision and the level of risky assets w_{it}, that is, that sample selection bias is due only to time-invariant individual effects. Although these assumptions are more reasonable than that underlying case 1, they rule out the possibility that time-varying unobserved effects play a major role in sample selection. If the decision to participate in the risky asset market and household portfolio shares depend on variation in transaction and information costs or liquidity problems that the econometrician is not able to control for, then the $\text{Cov}(u_{it}, v_{it}) = 0$ assumption is violated.

Different two-step procedures, as in Heckman (1979), have been proposed to correct for sample selection bias when $\text{Cov}(u_{it}, v_{it}) \neq 0$; they first compute the appropriate sample selection correction term and then estimate the "augmented" primary equation. The details of the appropriate estimators depend on the assumption concerning the correlations among the time-varying disturbances (u_{it} and v_{it}) and individual heterogeneity (α_i and μ_i), and on the form of their distributions (see Wooldridge 1995; Vella 1998; Vella and Verbeek 1999).

In general, given the sample selection model 4.21 through 4.24, the expected quantity (or share) of risky assets for household i holding risky assets at time t is

$$E[w_{it}|x_i, z_i, y_{it} = 1] = \beta' x_{it} + E[\alpha_i|x_i, z_i, y_{it} = 1] + \lambda_{it}, \qquad (4.25)$$

with

$$\lambda_{it} = E[u_{it}|\eta_{it} > -\delta' z_{it}, x_i, z_i],$$

where $\eta_{it} = \mu_i + v_{it}$. Equation 4.25 shows that the simple within-group estimator of β is not consistent because it would not eliminate the time-varying selectivity term, λ_{it}. For this reason, differencing the primary equation is not a solution to selection bias.

One possible solution is to make assumptions on the form of $E[\alpha_i|x_i, z_i, v_{it}]$ and $E[u_{it}|\eta_{it}, x_i, z_i]$ and on the distribution of η_{it}.[13] For instance, one could assume

$$\eta_i \sim N.i.d. \ (0, \sigma_\mu^2 u' + I_T)$$

$$E[u_{it}|x_i, z_i, v_{it}] = E[u_{it}|v_{it}] = \rho v_{it}$$

$$E[\alpha_i|x_i, z_i, v_{it}] = \psi' \bar{x}_i + \varsigma' \bar{z}_i + \varphi v_{it},$$

where $\rho, \psi, \varsigma,$ and φ are unknown parameters (see Wooldridge 1995). Then

$$E[w_{it}|x_i, z_i, y_{it} = 1] = \beta' x_{it} + \psi' \bar{x}_i + \varsigma' \bar{z}_i + (\varphi + \rho)E[\eta_{it}|\eta_{it} > -\delta' z_{it}, x_i, z_i],$$

where $E[\eta_{it}|\eta_{it} > -\delta' z_{it}, x_i, z_i]$ equals the inverse Mills ratio. At the first step, consistent estimates for δ and σ_μ^2 are obtained, as explained when discussing the random-effects probit model and the corresponding estimated inverse Mills ratio $\hat{\phi}(\cdot)/\hat{\Phi}(\cdot)$ is computed; at the second step, the following equation is estimated:

$$w_{it} = \beta' x_{it} + \psi' \bar{x}_i + \varsigma' \bar{z}_i + \theta \frac{\hat{\phi}_{it}}{\hat{\Phi}_{it}} + \varepsilon_{it} \qquad (4.26)$$

on the observations with $y_{it} = 1$. Equation 4.26 can be estimated by either pooled OLS or, if we are not interested in ψ and ς, with a fixed-effects estimator. Inference must take heteroskedasticity and the presence of a predicted regressor into account.[14]

In this framework, it is easy to introduce further flexibility, allowing θ and δ to be time specific. But two hypotheses are crucial: the normality of η_{it} and the independence of the individual effects in the selection rule (μ_i) from the observables.[15] These assumptions can be relaxed following Kyriazidou (1997), who suggests a two-step procedure similar to Powell's (1987) estimator. Consider the expected value of risky assets for a household that owns such assets in two periods t and s:

$$E[w_{it}|\zeta_i, y_{it} = 1, y_{is} = 1] = \beta' x_{it} + \alpha_i + \lambda_{i,ts}, \qquad (4.27)$$

where $\zeta_i = (z_{it}, x_{it}, z_{is}, x_{is}, \mu_i, \alpha_i)$ and

$$\lambda_{i,ts} = E[u_{it}|v_{it} > -\delta' z_{it} - \mu_i, v_{is} > -\delta' z_{is} - \mu_i, \zeta_i].$$

If $(v_{it}, u_{it}, v_{is}, u_{is})$ and $(v_{is}, u_{is}, v_{it}, u_{it})$ are identically distributed conditional on ζ_i, then for household i with $\delta' z_{it} = \delta' z_{is}$,

$$\lambda_{i,ts} = \lambda_{i,st},$$

and simple differencing of equation 4.27 eliminates the individual effects α_i and the sample selection term. On the basis of this observation, Kyriazidou (1997) proposes to estimate δ of the selection rule 4.22 to 4.23 using some of the fixed-effects estimation methods for static discrete-choice models previously described (e.g., Manski's conditional maximum score estimator or one of its smoothed versions), and then to estimate β by applying OLS to the differenced model, but giving more weight to those observations for which $\hat{\delta}'(z_{it} - z_{is})$ is close to zero by applying a kernel weight $K(\hat{\delta}'(z_{it} - z_{is})/h_n)$ where h_n is a bandwidth that shrinks to zero as the sample size increases. The resulting estimate is $\sqrt{nh_n}$-consistent and asymptotically normal.

Random-Effects Estimators   As in the discrete-choice case, maximum likelihood estimation of random-effects models is possible but computationally demanding, with flexible distributional assumptions. Restrictions on the distribution of time-invariant and time-varying error components can avoid the problem of multiple dimensional numerical integration in the same way as in the probit model.[16]

With sample selection models, the natural approach to reduce the computational burden compared to full ML is to adopt some limited information ML two-step procedure. Vella and Verbeek (1999), for instance, impose strict exogeneity of x_{it} and z_{it} with respect to ε_{it} and η_{it} and

$$\eta_i \sim N.i.d.\ (0, \sigma_\mu^2 u' + I_T)$$

$$E[\varepsilon_{it}|x_i, z_i, \eta_i] = E[\varepsilon_{it}|\eta_i] = \rho_1 \eta_{it} + \rho_2 \bar{\eta}_i,$$

where $\bar{\eta}_i = \sum_t \eta_{it}/T$ and ρ_1, ρ_2 are unknown parameters. These assumptions allow for heteroskedasticity and autocorrelation in the time-varying term of the primary equation, 4.21. In this framework, $E[\varepsilon_{it}|x_i, z_i, y_{it}]$ is a linear function of $E[\eta_{it}|x_i, z_i, y_{it}]$. The strategy is thus to estimate via ML methods the selection equation, to use $\hat{\delta}$ to compute $E[\eta_{it}|x_i, z_i, y_{it}]$ (i.e., to predict η_{it} and $\bar{\eta}_i$), and finally to estimate

$$w_{it} = \beta' x_{it} + \rho_1 \hat{\eta}_{it} + \rho_2 \hat{\bar{\eta}}_i + \varepsilon_{it}. \tag{4.28}$$

The computational advantage of this procedure is that at each step, only one-dimensional numerical integration is required.

Dynamic Models
The way in which dynamics are introduced in the previous models strongly affects the choice of the proper estimation technique. If it is only the assumption of no serial correlation of the u_{it} that is relaxed, then the Honoré (1998) IV estimator for the censored model and the Wooldridge (1995) and Vella and Verbeek (1999) two-step procedures for sample selection models can be simply adapted to the case. But if the lagged dependent variables appear in the primary equation or the selection rule, then the assumption of strict exogeneity of the observables no longer holds, and new estimators must be introduced. The dependence on the past can take different forms depending on whether the latent or the observed lagged endogenous variables enter the equations. In what follows, we present some of the possible cases that can be treated with estimation techniques that extend those proposed for the static models.

Fixed-Effects Estimators for Censored Models   If w_{it}^* is the process under examination, then the natural way to introduce the dynamics in censored models would be

$$w_{it}^* = \gamma w_{i,t-1}^* + \beta' x_{it} + \varepsilon_{it}$$

$$w_{it} = \max\{w_{it}^*, 0\} \tag{4.29}$$

$$\varepsilon_{it} = \alpha_i + u_{it}.$$

Let us follow Bover and Arellano (1997) and assume that

$$E[\alpha_i | x_i] = \psi' \bar{x}_i$$

$$E[w_{i0}^* | x_i] = \rho' \bar{x}_i.$$

Then the reduced form of the model is:

$$w_i^* = \Lambda x_i^A + u_i,$$

where $x_i^A = (x_{i1}', \dots x_{iT}', \bar{x}_i')'$. The dynamic equation, 4.29, can be re-written as

$$(I_0 - \gamma L) w_i^* = x_i \beta + \alpha_i \iota + u_i,$$

where $I_0 = (0, I_T)$ and $L = (I_T, 0)$ are $T \times (T+1)$ matrices and $w_i^* = (w_{i0}^*, \dots, w_{iT}^*)$. Taking differences from individual time means gives

$$QBw_i^* = x_i^+ \beta + u_i^+,$$

where $B = I_0 - L$, and, as above, $x_i^+ = Qx_i$ and $u_i^+ = Qu_i$ with $Q = I_T - \iota'/T$. Then, the reduced-form parameters Λ are related to β via

$$x_i^+ \beta = QB\Lambda x_i^A,$$

and estimates of $\xi = (\gamma, \beta')'$ are given by

$$\hat{\xi} = \left(\sum_i \hat{W}_i^{+'} \hat{W}_i^+ \right)^{-1} \sum_i \hat{W}_i^{+'} \hat{w}_{i0}^+,$$

where $\hat{W}_i^+ = Q\hat{W}_i$, $\hat{w}_{i0}^+ = Q\hat{w}_{i0}$, $\hat{W}_i = (\hat{w}_{i(-1)}, x_i)$, $\hat{w}_{i(-1)} = L\Lambda x_i^A$ and $\hat{w}_{i0} = I_0 \Lambda x_i^A$. We can see that consistent estimates of the parameters of interest can be obtained by regressing the predicted endogenous variable on the predicted lagged endogenous variable and the exogenous variables, all in mean-deviation form.

A different way to introduce dynamics into the censored regression model is to consider the following case (Honoré 1993):

$$w_{it}^* = \beta' x_{it} + \varepsilon_{it}$$

$$w_{it} = \max\{\beta' x_{it} + \gamma w_{i,t-1} + \varepsilon_{it}, 0\}$$

$$\varepsilon_{it} = \alpha_i + u_{it},$$

which can be estimated extending the trimmed least-squares estimator for the static model (Honoré 1992). To simplify the exposition, consider the case in which $t = 1, 2$, $w_{i0} = 0$, $\beta' \Delta x_i \geq 0$ ($\Delta x_i = x_{i1} - x_{i2}$), and $\gamma \geq 0$. Therefore,

$$w_{i1} = \max\{w_{i1}^*, 0\}$$

$$w_{i2} = \max\{w_{i2}^* + \gamma w_{i1}, 0\}.$$

Introduce the variable

$$w_{i2}(\gamma) = w_{i2} - \gamma w_{i1}$$

$$= \max\{-\gamma w_{i1}, w_{i2}^*\}.$$

$w_{i2}(\gamma)$ has a form similar to w_{i2} but with the difference that $w_{i2}(\gamma)$ is censored from below at γw_{i1} instead of zero. Similarly to the static case, w_{i1} and $w_{i2}(\gamma)$ will be trimmed in such a way that the resulting variables will be symmetrically distributed around the 45-degree line through $(0, \beta' \Delta x_i)$. The rationale of the approach is similar, but the dynamics imposes a more complicated trimming process even in the simplest case considered here.

Fixed-Effects Estimators for Sample Selection Models   In sample selection models, we can have dependency on the past in both the primary equation and the selection rule. In the primary equation, we can assume that the latent variable w_{it}^* depends on its past value $w_{i,t-1}^*$, while in the selection rule the dynamics is introduced on the observed values:

$$w_{it}^* = \gamma w_{i,t-1}^* + \beta' x_{it} + \alpha_i + u_{it}$$

$$y_{it} = \mathbf{1}(\rho y_{i,t-1} + \delta' z_{it} + \mu_i + v_{it} > 0)$$

$$w_{it} = \begin{cases} w_{it}^* & \text{if } y_{it} = 1 \\ 0 & \text{otherwise.} \end{cases}$$

An extension of Kyriazidou (1997) can be used to estimate this model. The strategy of Kyriazidou (1999) is to find orthogonality conditions for the dynamic sample selection model similar to those exploited to estimate the standard linear dynamic panel model. Assume w_{i0}^* and w_{it}^* are observed, x_{it} are strictly exogenous, and u_{it} are serially uncorrelated. It is well known that under these conditions, the following equalities hold:[17]

$$E[w_{i,t-j}^* \Delta u_{it}] = 0 \quad \text{for } t = 2, \ldots, T, \quad j = 2, \ldots, t \tag{4.30}$$

$$E[x_{is} \Delta u_{it}] = 0 \quad \text{for } t = 2, \ldots, T, \quad s = 1, \ldots, T. \tag{4.31}$$

Assume $(u_{it}, v_{it})|\zeta_i$ is i.i.d. over time for all individuals, where $\zeta_i = (x_i, z_i, \alpha_i, \mu_i, w_{i0}^*, y_{i0})$. To show how to find the analogue of the condition 4.30 for the sample selection model, consider first the case where $\beta = \rho = 0$. The analogue of the left-hand side of equation 4.30 is:

$$E[y_{it} y_{i,t-1} y_{i,t-2} y_{i,t-j} w_{i,t-j}^* \Delta u_{it}]$$

$$= E[y_{it} y_{i,t-1} y_{i,t-2} y_{i,t-j} w_{i,t-j} (\Delta w_{it} - \gamma \Delta w_{i,t-1})],$$

which is not zero (because $\text{Cov}(u_{it}, v_{it}) \neq 0$). However, given the stationarity of $(u_{it}, v_{it})|\zeta_i$ over time, similarly to the static case it is true that

$$E[y_{it} y_{i,t-1} y_{i,t-2} y_{i,t-j} w_{i,t-j} (\Delta w_{it} - \gamma \Delta w_{i,t-1})|\delta' \Delta z_{it} = 0] = 0.$$

For the general model, the orthogonality conditions analogue of equations 4.30 and 4.31 will be

$$E[y_{it} y_{i,t-1} y_{i,t-2} y_{i,t-j} w_{i,t-j} (\Delta w_{it} - \gamma \Delta w_{i,t-1} - \beta' \Delta x_{it})|\delta' \Delta z_{it} = 0] = 0$$

$$E[y_{it} y_{i,t-1} y_{i,t-2} y_{is} x_{is} (\Delta w_{it} - \gamma \Delta w_{i,t-1} - \beta' \Delta x_{it})|\delta' \Delta z_{it} = 0] = 0$$

for $t = 2, \ldots, T$, $j = 2, \ldots, t$, $s = 1, \ldots, T$. Kyriazidou's idea is to estimate first δ and then to do GMM exploiting the orthogonality conditions but weighing the observations with $K(\hat{\delta}' \Delta z_{it}/h_n)$ where $K(\cdot)$ is a kernel and h_n is a bandwidth that shrinks to zero as the sample size increases.

Random-Effects Estimators for Sample Selection Models   The procedure of Vella and Verbeek (1999) can be used for dynamic models. In particular, they consider a sample selection model with true state dependence in the selection rule (v_{it} must be serially uncorrelated), but without the lagged dependent variable in the primary equation ($\gamma = 0$). In their framework, it is sufficient to notice that if the selection rule is dynamic, then to correct for sample selection, it is necessary to condition on the complete (past and future) ownership history:

$$E[w_{it}|x_i, z_i, y_i, y_{i0}] = \beta'x_{it} + E[\varepsilon_{it}|x_i, z_i, y_i, y_{i0}].$$

The first step probit estimates must take into account the initial condition problem, either assuming y_{i0} is exogenous or specifying its distribution (conditional on x_i and μ_i; see Heckman 1981a). Once estimates of (ρ, δ') are obtained, then the augmented equation, 4.28 is estimated as in the static case.

4.3   An Illustration

In this section we illustrate some of the issues that arise in applying the presented techniques to a short panel. We take the specification adopted by Guiso and Jappelli in chapter 7 and estimate it in various ways using the subsample of households that participated in the Survey on Household Income and Wealth (SHIW) in 1991, 1993, and 1995. The reason for choosing this subsample is that at least one of the estimators we consider is very hard to implement when there is an unbalanced panel or even a rotating panel (this is the Bover and Arellano minimum distance estimator already described). Given that the emphasis of this section is on econometric issues, it is best to compare estimates using an identical sample. As we shall see, the qualitative nature of our results is in full agreement with Guiso and Jappelli's findings on a much larger sample.

We consider only the choice whether to invest in risky financial assets, to address how this decision is affected by wealth, income, and age, plus a few demographic and economic indicators (described in chapter 7). In this section, we treat all variables as strictly exogenous, even though in this context wealth could be predetermined or even endogenous (households that invest in risky assets could end up with higher wealth at the end of the period, that is, higher initial wealth at the beginning of the following period). In some preliminary work, we find that this issue is of minor importance in the sample chosen, in that estimates that allow for fixed effects are not greatly affected when wealth is treated as endogenous. The issue that we address here, instead, is the nature of unobserved heterogeneity.

Our sample is made up of 1,333 households, each appearing three times (in 1991, 1993, and 1995). Year of birth and the dummies for education and city size are constant over time; household head age is by construction a linear combination of year of birth and sampling year.

In table 4.1 we show results from estimating probit equations for participation. The estimates shown in the first column correspond to a specification in which individual heterogeneity is ignored and observations are treated as independent. This implies an assumption that the unobserved individual effect, α_i, is zero and the explanatory variables are independent of the time-varying component u_{it}, which is further assumed to be uncorrelated over time. Our estimates are quite close to those of Guiso and Jappelli and confirm that participation is concave in age and increasing in wealth. In column 2, we report estimation results when individual effects are treated as random. As we have pointed out, this implies assuming that the explanatory variables are independent of both the unobserved individual effect, α_i, and the time-varying component u_{it}. In both cases, the estimates change little when two-year dummies are introduced. Comparing columns 1 and 2, we see that parameter estimates are of the same sign and often of similar magnitude, but a formal Hausman test strongly rejects the null hypothesis that they are the same (it takes a value of 60 with 16 degrees of freedom). The likelihood ratio test for zero serial correlation within households reported at the bottom of column 2 rejects the null hypothesis even more strongly.

A fixed-effects probit model can be estimated using Bover and Arellano's minimum distance estimator. Here the dependence of the α_i on the observables is explicitly modeled by setting $E[\alpha_i|x_i] = \psi_0 + \psi'x_{i1} + \cdots + \psi'x_{iT}$, and reduced-form probit estimates are obtained for each cross section and then combined to obtain within-group consistent estimates for β.[18] For this reason, we need to observe individuals over exactly the same period of time.

We report the estimated parameters on time-varying regressors in column 3 of table 4.1. Here we find that all parameters are very poorly determined, even though the income and wealth parameters retain their signs. This could suggest that greater efficiency should be sought by searching for a better specification of $E[\alpha_i|x_i]$ (adding non-linear combinations of x_i) and using a GMM estimator at the second

Table 4.1
Risky financial asset ownership: Probit models

	ML pooled	ML random effects	Bover and Arellano fixed effects
Age	.0689755 (.0157758)	.1004041 (.0267395)	−.0548936 (.073805)
Age^2	−.0006939 (.0001475)	−.0009916 (.0002499)	.0006173 (.0005586)
Male	.3236662 (.1258394)	.5099218 (.2201663)	
South	−.1702247 (.1131982)	−.2341715 (.1870324)	
Married	−.1784394 (.123525)	−.2688552 (.21227)	
Education	.033786 (.007375)	.0589155 (.0127327)	
Disposable income	.0282562 (.0029365)	.0589155 (.0041822)	.0130741 (.4284517)
(Disposable income)^2	−.0000713 (.0000115)	−.0000886 (.0000157)	−.000058 (.003874)
Financial wealth	.0008722 (.0001794)	.0013964 (.0002721)	.0006587 (.0094926)
(Financial wealth)^2	−1.09e−07 (3.55e−08)	−1.76e−07 (4.65e−08)	−1.00e−07 (5.15E−06)
Family size	−.1146935 (.0369895)	−.1203103 (.0583214)	.0472207 (1.1479998)
Number of children	.0652896 (.0449664)	.0789333 (.0695918)	.1246956 (.9618887)
Unemployment rate	−.0266888 (.0077928)	−.0322399 (.0123217)	.0030726 (.0461745)
Number of ATMs	1.778919 (.2872766)	2.815325 (.4410536)	2.364737 (2.817425)
Credit/GDP	−.0002403 (.000722)	−.0001371 (.0012321)	.0022546 (.0246517)
Constant	−3.583943 (.4179343)	−5.404914 (.7260097)	
σ_α		.9979069 (.0718902)	
LRT $H_0 : \rho = 0$ (χ_1^2)		179.23	
Pooled vs. B.A. (χ_{11}^2)			115.07
Random vs. B.A. (χ_{11}^2)		33.41	

Source: Authors' computations on SHIW data.
Note: Standard errors in parentheses.

stage, but it is also consistent with the presence of a more serious identification problem of the age effects in particular (as we shall argue). Perhaps surprisingly, a formal Hausman test rejects the null hypothesis of parameter equality between columns 2 and 3 (and even more strongly between columns 1 and 3).

In table 4.2 we present logit estimates for the same specification. The first column corresponds to the standard logit estimator that treats the error term as independently distributed. As expected, parameter estimates are roughly rescaled by the same fixed factor (of approximately 1.8) compared to the corresponding probit estimates shown in table 4.1. The second column corresponds to a random-effects model where, conditional on a normally distributed individual effect, the time-varying disturbances are independently distributed according to a logistic cumulative density function. Column 2 in table 4.2 corresponds to column 2 in table 4.1, and the similarity between these estimates is striking, once allowance is made for a similar rescaling factor.[19]

In column 3 in table 4.2, we report conditional logit estimates. Here the sample size is reduced to the 1,002 cases in which there are transitions. The crucial difference with respect to the random-effects model is that here we allow α_i to depend on the explanatory variables. The difference with the Bover and Arellano estimator is that we do not explicitly model this dependence. Given that we do not exploit pure cross-section variability in estimation, the parameters of all time-invariant variables are not identified (and also the parameter of one more year dummy when these are allowed in the specification).[20] In this case we still find the same pattern of coefficients on income and wealth as in columns 1 and 2, and the precision of these estimates is reasonable. However, we find that the coefficients on the age terms are poorly determined and their signs differ from what one would expect (we have a negative coefficient on the age linear term and a positive coefficient on its square). This extreme lack of precision is likely to reflect the identification problem that Guiso and Jappelli noted: in a short panel, little age variability is left when fixed effects are removed. Finally, formal Hausman tests of parameter equality between columns 2 and 3 and 1 and 3 (reported at the bottom of the table) reject the null hypotesis. This unfortunately limits our ability to interpret coefficients in columns 1 and 2 as causal effects.

Table 4.2
Risky financial asset ownership: Logit models

	ML pooled	ML random effects	CML fixed effects
Age	.12633	.1786957	−.1308453
	(.0289633)	(.048154)	(.1822847)
Age^2	−.0012697	−.0017661	.0023295
	(.000273)	(.0004507)	(.0016589)
Male	.5622251	.9365492	
	(.2238208)	(.3966916)	
South	−.3656021	−.454399	
	(.2118589)	(.3396769)	
Married	−.3105582	−.4958084	
	(.219094)	(.3824534)	
Education	.0593103	.1057881	
	(.0131778)	(.0229011)	
Disposable income	.0492723	.0569984	.0692073
	(.0052779)	(.0075848)	(.0191042)
(Disposable income)^2	−.0001238	−.0001565	−.0006004
	(.0000191)	(.0000275)	(.0001785)
Financial wealth	.0015086	.0024564	.0034636
	(.0003126)	(.000483)	(.0013546)
(Financial wealth)^2	$-1.91e-07$	$-3.11e-07$	$-1.48e-06$
	$(5.95e-08)$	$(8.07e-08)$	$(1.01e-06)$
Family size	−.2049299	−.215104	.0299085
	(.0666116)	(.1053273)	(.2361482)
Number of children	.1126382	.1409757	.4670296
	(.0815525)	(.125723)	(.2275142)
Unemployment rate	−.0527695	−.0600871	−.0040395
	(.0149771)	(.0227064)	(.0493991)
Number of ATMs	3.120111	5.04526	4.595149
	(.5095193)	(.7872299)	(2.314526)
Credit/GDP	−.000487	−.0002588	.0098146
	(.001254)	(.0021848)	(.0096864)
Constant	−6.284394	−9.591793	
	(.7634376)	(1.308494)	
σ_α		1.758971	
		(.1278372)	
LRT $H_0 : \rho = 0$ (χ_1^2)		185.65	
Pooled vs. CML (χ_{11}^2)			51.22
Random vs. CML (χ_{11}^2)		64.05	

Source: Authors' computations on SHIW data.
Note: Standard errors in parentheses.

4.4 Conclusion

The aim of this chapter was to address some methodological issues that arise in estimating portfolio choice models on survey data. Particular attention has been devoted to the econometric consequences of limited participation in the risky asset market.

We have highlighted the difficulties of recovering causal effects in participation and portfolio share equations when there is unobserved heterogeneity. In the relatively simple case of a linear model for the desired risky assets share where unobserved heterogeneity affects only the intercept, important conceptual issues arise in a dynamic context (identification assumptions are required to disentangle true from spurious state dependence due to unobserved heterogeneity). Conceptual and practical problems also arise in a static model when age effects are estimated. We have shown that with a short panel, the effects of age on participation are imprecisely estimated if we allow for individual effects that correlate with observable variables. An interesting possibility is to explore why unobserved heterogeneity correlates with the explanatory variables. This exercise could lead to a rich enough specification where the remaining individual heterogeneity is uncorrelated with the explanatory variables. In this context, cross-sectional variability in age could be used to identify age effects.

The wealth of newly available estimators for panel data limited-dependent-variable models briefly reviewed in this chapter and the conceptual and empirical problems in interpreting as causal effects cross-sectional correlations both suggest that future econometric work on household portfolio choice should ideally be carried out on relatively long panels and that investigators will need to take a stance on the key identification issues discussed.

Notes

We are grateful for comments by Manuel Arellano, Ekaterini Kyriazidou, Steve Pischke, Enrico Rettore, and the editors of this book and for in-depth discussions with Loriana Pelizzon.

1. When more detailed asset categories are defined, the participation equations are hard to estimate jointly and may be even harder to interpret. Articles by King and Leape (1998), Gourieroux, Tiomo, and Trognon (1997), and Orsi and Pastorello (1999) are attempts in this direction.

2. This is the simplest way to generate zero holdings of risky assets. More interesting is Cragg's (1971) double hurdle model, which allows for zero holdings to be generated as either corner solutions or as a result of other considerations (e.g., lack of information). See also Pudney (1989, pp. 160–162).

3. Strict exogeneity requires that the expectation of the error term conditional on all the x_{is} is zero. Notice that the desired level of risky assets w_{it}^* (and therefore w_{it}) is a function of actual past ownership $(w_{i,t-j})$ and not the corresponding desired past level $(w_{i,t-j}^*)$.

4. These models can be estimated with STATA 6 using Gauss-Hermite quadrature procedures (xtprobit, re). This principle can be adapted to a logit specification if we are willing to assume that the ε_{it} follow a logistic distribution conditional on α_i, while the marginal distribution of α_i is normal (xtlogit, re in STATA 6).

5. QL estimates of the static probit model can be obtained in STATA 6.0. More specifically, in the command line xtprobit, one has to specify the "pa" option.

6. Bover and Arellano (1997) consider a more general form for $E[\alpha_i|x_i]$. They also show how to improve efficiency using GMM instead of a within-group estimator.

7. The fixed-effects models partly overcome the problems of the correct specification of the statistical relationship between the observed covariates and the unobserved permanent individual effect, and of the distribution assumption on the initial conditions.

8. The authors treat the case in which more than four observations are available and more than one lag of the dependent variable is included, and the semiparametric case in which the logit assumption is relaxed.

9. In some cases, a lower and an upper threshold must be jointly considered. An example of the application of a two-limit tobit model to portfolio analysis is given by Hochguertel, Alessie, and van Soest (1997).

10. This assumption is in fact stronger than necessary. Consistency of the estimator is ensured also by the weaker assumption of conditional exchangeability—that (u_{is}, u_{it}) is distributed like (u_{it}, u_{is}) conditional on (x_i, α_i).

11. Depending on the nature of the truncation or censoring rule, the trimmed variables used, and their (symmetry-preserving) transformation considered in equation 4.19, different estimators are defined. See Arellano and Honoré (2000) and Honoré and Kyriazidou (2000a).

12. The author shows how the orthogonality conditions change if there is heteroskedasticity or serial correlation in u_{it}.

13. Assumptions on the form of the distribution of u_{it} are not necessary. This is an advantage of two-step estimators, because standard ML estimators rely on the normality assumption of u_{it}, a hypothesis hardly defensible in household portfolio studies. Furthermore, heteroskedasticity and serial correlation of u_{it} are allowed.

14. Bover and Arellano (1997) can also be applied here. The reduced-form estimates $\hat{\Pi}$ are obtained by stacking T-independent cross-sectional estimates of the augmented primary equation.

15. This assumption is necessary to estimate the random-effect probit model at the first stage with a ML estimator.

16. Under the assumption that individual time-invariant effects (α_i) are uncorrelated with the time-varying disturbances (u_{it}), the random-effects censored regression model can be estimated using STATA 6.0 (xttobit command).

17. See Arellano and Bover (1995), as well as Ahn and Schmidt (1995).

18. With STATA 6, the reduced-form parameters π_t are obtained applying the probit command on each cross section. For each year, the set of conditioning variables includes $x_{i1}, \ldots, x_{iT}$. The estimates of β are then obtained regressing $\hat{\pi}'_t x_i$ on x_{it} using the fixed-effects estimator for linear panel data models (i.e., xtreg with the fe option). The correct covariance matrix of β (see Bover and Arellano 1997) must be computed using matrix algebra commands.

19. Models in columns 1 and 2 in tables 4.1 and 4.2 can be easily estimated with STATA 6. The pooled models are estimated using the probit and logit commands; random-effects models are estimated using the xtprobit and xtlogit commands with the random-effects option (re). Note that the QL estimator of the probit random-effect model (Zeger and Liang 1986) can be obtained specifying the population average option (pa) in the xtprobit command.

20. In fact, age and a full set of year dummies are collinear once fixed effects are conditioned on, even if no intercept is allowed. Age variability is exactly trendlike if fixed differences across individuals are removed. This highlights the difficulty of identifying age profiles in panel data models if time effects are thought to be at work.

II   Issues and Trends in
                          Household Portfolios

5

Household Portfolios in the United States

Carol C. Bertaut and
Martha Starr-McCluer

In deciding how to structure their assets and liabilities, U.S. households face a broad array of options. Savings can be allocated to a wide range of assets, from simple bank accounts to sophisticated assets like real estate investment trusts. Credit is available from many types of institutions—banks, credit unions, finance companies, credit cards—with all kinds of borrowing terms: loans versus lines of credit, fixed or variable interest rate, and secured or unsecured loans. Deregulation, easy entry, and developments in information technology have been important in the proliferation of financial products.

Given the relatively liberal U.S. financial environment, it is perhaps surprising that the portfolios of American households tend to be very simple and safe. In 1998, the typical household had three types of financial assets, most frequently a checking, savings, and tax-deferred retirement account. Less than one-half of all households had any type of investment in stock. There is also quite a lot of borrowing in costly forms like credit cards and from costly sources like finance companies. Even in the top quintile of the income distribution, portfolios tend to be fairly undiversified, with some borrowing in the form of high-cost debt. Understanding these puzzles may shed light on why households select the assets and liabilities that they do.

While there has been a considerable amount of research on household saving behavior, the portfolio decisions of households are less well understood. Some studies have examined the equity premium, borrowing constraints, and information and transactions costs (see King and Leape 1998; Haliassos and Bertaut 1995; Blume and Zeldes 1994). But there has been little systematic investigation of household portfolio behavior to date. There are several reasons that this gap needs to be filled. First, because returns vary across assets and costs vary across debts, portfolio decisions have important implications for the pace of wealth accumulation, and thus for such issues as the adequacy of precautionary saving and degree of retirement preparedness. Second, portfolio decisions play a key role in determining how changes in macrovariables—interest rates, stock prices, inflation, and unemployment—affect household spending and saving. Third, portfolio decisions also underlie the effects of fiscal policies, like the capital gains tax or social security reform, on personal and national saving. Fourth, the behavior of individual investors impinges directly on questions about the efficiency of financial markets (Shiller 2000). And finally, understanding households' portfolio decisions may provide richer insights into theories of consumption and saving behavior.

This chapter provides an in-depth review and analysis of household portfolios in the United States. It begins by describing trends in the structure of household portfolios in the past fifteen years, using both aggregate and survey data. We document the growth of tax-deferred retirement plans, the increased role of equity, and the shift toward home equity–based borrowing. We also update previous comparisons between the Federal Reserve Board's Survey of Consumer Finances (SCF) and aggregate data from the Flow of Funds. We next present evidence on the structure of household portfolios from the SCF and discuss previous research in the field. Then we estimate econometric models of the determinants of portfolio choice, including age, wealth, income risk, entry and information costs, and liquidity constraints. We focus on the role of risky assets in household portfolios, but also consider joint decisions to hold assets and liabilities; joint decisions are investigated using (for the first time, to our knowledge) a multivariate probit approach. The final section draws implications of our findings, especially those for understanding how household portfolios respond to changes in fiscal policy, macroeconomic variables, and financial innovations.

5.1 Data on Household Portfolios

Aggregate data on households' assets and liabilities are available from the Federal Reserve Board's Flow of Funds accounts (FFA). The FFA are compiled from institutional sources and provide a comprehensive view of households' holdings; they include both assets and liabilities held directly by households, as well as by pension funds held on households' behalf. Table 5.1 shows some broad trends in household portfolios from 1983 to 1998.[1] (Note that although published figures from the FFA on the household sector include the assets and liabilities of nonprofit organizations, the figures presented here remove the holdings of nonprofits).[2] Throughout this period, the most important item in aggregate household assets was residential property; nonetheless, its share of total assets slid from 28 percent in 1983 to 22 percent in 1998. For households overall, the relative importance of financial assets increased substantially over this period, rising from about 45 percent to 61 percent of total assets. The composition of financial assets also shifted appreciably, with the relative importance of time and savings deposits declining while the importance of pension funds, corporate equity, and mutual funds rose.

Several factors underlie these trends. The first and most important consideration is the sustained growth in stock prices over the period. As figure 5.1 shows, the Standard & Poor's (S&P) 500 stock price index rose from 165 in 1983 to 600 in 1995 and 1,100 in 1998.[3] With inflation subdued for most of this period, this represents an average real increase of over 10 percent per year. Second, whereas mutual funds represented a narrowly held specialty product before the 1980s, the industry grew dramatically after that time, with the number of funds rising from 564 in 1980 to 6,778 in 1998 (Investment Company Institute 1998). The large array of institutions offering mutual funds, the proliferation of types of funds available, and the rise of no-load funds have made it easier and less costly for investors to acquire a diversified portfolio of stock.

A third major trend during this period was the introduction of tax-deferred retirement accounts. Most households could make tax-deductible contributions to Individual Retirement Accounts (IRAs) between 1983 and 1986. Although broad deductibility was curtailed in 1986, IRA balances have continued to grow due to capital gains, rollovers from 401(k)-type accounts, and contributions from self-employed persons.[4] Additionally, following a Treasury ruling in the early 1980s, pension coverage started to shift away from traditional defined-benefit (DB) plans, in which employees receive a fixed payment based on salary and years of service, and toward 401(k)-type defined-contribution (DC) plans, in which employees or employers, or both, make contributions to retirement accounts. For employees, 401(k)-type plans have the advantages that both contributions and returns are tax deferred, vested balances are portable, employees

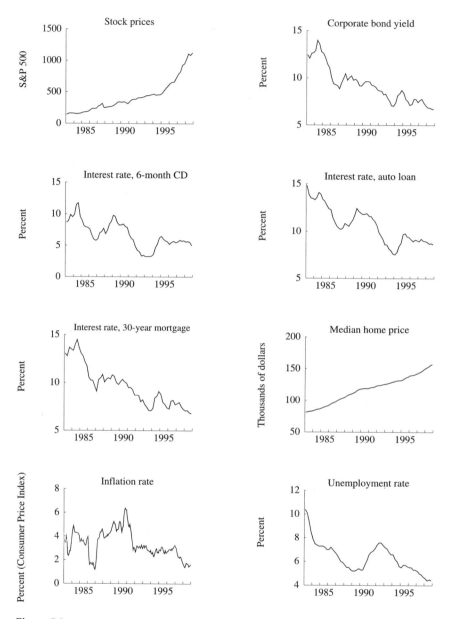

Figure 5.1
Asset returns and macrovariables, 1983–1998

often have investment options, and they may be able to borrow or make withdrawals from the account.

Fourth, the combination of rising stock prices and the growth of stock investment through mutual funds and retirement accounts has been associated with a significant increase in the equity share of households' financial assets. As shown at the bottom of table 5.1, the share of household sector financial assets invested in corporate equities, either directly or through a mutual fund, retirement account, other managed asset, or DC pension fund, rose from 15 percent in 1983 to 35 percent in 1998. In terms of total household assets, this rise put households' total stockholdings about on par with residential property at the end of 1998.

The final and related point concerns the role of equity in residential property. Equity in residential property dwindled in importance in the 1990s, with its share of total household wealth falling from 22 percent in the 1980s to about 15 percent in 1998. The decline partly reflects the relatively slow growth of housing prices: between 1983 and 1998, median home prices less than doubled, compared to the sixfold increase in stock prices (see figure 5.1). But factors on the liability side of the household balance sheet also contributed to this trend. Notably, whereas households used to be able to deduct all types of interest payments from their taxable income, the Tax Reform Act of 1986 limited deductibility to interest payments on debt backed by home equity.[5] This change increased the relative attractiveness of borrowing against the primary residence, contributing to a rise in the share of mortgage debt in total household borrowing and a rise in the ratio of mortgage debt to the value of residential property.[6]

While the aggregate data describe the portfolios of the household sector overall, they do not directly portray developments in the typical household portfolio. Ownership of some assets, notably stock and bonds, is quite concentrated at the top of the wealth distribution, so, for example, it is not necessarily clear whether the shift toward risky financial assets is broad-based. To examine trends at the household level, we look at data from the SCF. Conducted triennially since 1983, the survey collects detailed information on households' assets, liabilities, incomes, and other characteristics.[7] In recent years, the SCF sample has consisted of about 3,000 households drawn from a standard representative sample, supplemented by some 1,500 households drawn from a special high-wealth oversample based on tax records. In descriptive analysis, sample weights can be used to make

Table 5.1
Level and composition of household wealth: Aggregate data

	1983	1989	1992	1995	1998
Average net worth per household (thousands of 1998 dollars)	209.2	263.1	261.7	282.4	345.9
Assets and liabilities as percentage of total assets:					
Financial assets	44.5	48.8	53.0	56.3	60.8
Liquid assets[a]	3.5	3.6	3.5	3.4	3.4
Time and savings deposits	12.4	10.9	9.1	7.7	7.1
Savings bonds	0.6	0.5	0.6	0.6	0.5
Other bonds	2.7	3.7	4.3	3.8	2.5
Corporate equity[b]	6.7	8.1	10.4	12.4	14.3
Mutual funds	0.7	2.0	2.7	4.0	5.9
Pension reserves[c]	12.0	14.4	16.4	18.7	22.0
Life insurance	1.9	1.6	1.8	1.8	1.7
Bank personal trusts	2.5	2.4	2.6	2.6	2.4
Other financial	1.7	1.5	1.5	1.3	1.1
Nonfinancial assets	55.5	51.3	47.0	43.8	39.2
Residential property[d]	28.0	29.2	27.1	24.7	22.4
Noncorporate business[e]	19.1	14.1	12.1	11.6	10.4
Durable goods	8.5	8.0	7.8	7.5	6.3
Debts	13.0	14.1	14.6	15.0	14.1
Mortgage	8.5	10.0	10.8	10.5	9.8
Consumer debt	3.4	3.6	3.1	3.6	3.2
Other debt	1.1	0.6	0.6	0.8	1.0
Memo items					
Equity share of financial assets[f]	14.6	19.1	23.1	28.2	34.6
Equity in residential property as percentage of net worth	22.5	22.4	19.2	16.7	14.6
Mortgage debt as percentage of total debt	65.1	70.6	74.2	70.4	70.0
Mortgage debt as percentage of value of residential property	30.3	34.2	39.8	42.6	43.9

Source: Authors' computations, Flow of Funds Accounts, year-end values.
[a] Includes currency, checkable deposits, money market accounts, foreign accounts, and security credit.
[b] Includes equity in closely held businesses.
[c] Largely employer-sponsored plans; most IRA and Keoghs are included in the items in which they are invested, although those held in individual annuities at life insurance companies are included here.
[d] Residential property for 1 to 4 families.
[e] Equity in noncorporate businesses only.
[f] Published figure for the FFA household sector (i.e., includes nonprofits).

the data representative of the population as a whole. This dual-frame sample design provides adequate representation of both broadly held items, like homes and vehicles, and other items, like stocks and bonds, held disproportionately by the wealthy. The SCF's special sample and detailed information make it uniquely well suited for investigating the portfolios of U.S. households.[8]

Table 5.2 presents some basic descriptive statistics from the SCF. Because of concerns about nonreporting in survey data on wealth, it is of interest to know how the SCF compares to the Flow of Funds. As the table shows, estimates of average household wealth from the SCF have been about 10 percent to 20 percent below estimates for the same period from the FFA.[9] While it may be tempting to attribute the divergence to underreporting by households, there are a number of conceptual differences between the two data sources that at least contribute to the divergence. Notably, the FFA include some items not collected in the SCF (i.e., currency holdings, DB pension reserves, and durable goods other than vehicles), and these may well outweigh the items included in the SCF but not the FFA (nonresidential property and miscellaneous valuable assets such as artwork and antiques). A careful study by Antoniewicz (1996) found that after adjusting for conceptual differences between the FFA and SCF, the two data sources tend to square fairly well, although the SCF estimates of financial assets remained somewhat below comparable measures from the FFA.[10]

Tables 5.2 and 5.3 show trends in ownership and holdings of assets and liabilities using the SCF data. Many of the trends seen in the aggregate data are also apparent in the microdata. The share of liquid accounts, including checking, savings, money market, and call accounts, in total assets has edged down since 1989, although the share of households owning such accounts has remained above 85 percent. The period also saw declining ownership of several types of traditional investments—including certificates of deposit, U.S. savings bonds, other bonds, and cash-value life insurance—reflecting the relatively unattractive returns to these products and the proliferation of higher-return alternatives like mutual funds. Mutual fund ownership rose from some 5 percent of households in 1983 to over 16 percent in 1998, and although direct ownership of stock actually drifted down between 1983 and 1995, it moved back up in 1998. The share of households having a tax-deferred retirement account—

Table 5.2
Level and composition of household wealth: Survey data

	1983	1989	1992	1995	1998
Level of net worth:					
Median (thousands of 1998 dollars)	56.9	59.0	55.8	59.4	71.1
Average (thousands of 1998 dollars)	194.6	233.8	211.1	220.4	281.1
SCF average as percentage of FFA	93.0	88.9	80.7	78.0	81.3
Assets and liabilities as percentage of total assets:					
Financial assets	29.4	28.9	30.6	35.2	40.0
Liquid accounts	5.0	5.7	5.4	5.1	4.6
Certificates of deposit	3.3	3.0	2.5	2.1	1.7
Savings bonds	0.2	0.4	0.4	0.5	0.3
Other bonds	3.1	3.0	2.6	2.3	1.7
Stocks	7.9	4.5	5.1	5.7	9.2
Mutual funds	0.9	1.6	2.4	4.7	5.0
Retirement accounts	3.8	5.5	7.5	8.8	10.6
Cash-value life insurance	2.4	1.8	1.9	2.7	2.6
Trusts and other managed assets	2.6	1.9	1.7	2.2	3.6
Other financial	0.2	1.4	1.2	1.2	0.7
Memo: All equity	9.5	8.3	10.4	13.8	21.7
Nonfinancial assets	70.6	71.1	69.4	64.8	60.0
Primary residence	31.6	31.2	31.7	30.1	27.7
Investment real estate	15.3	16.2	14.9	11.4	10.6
Business equity	19.3	18.2	17.8	17.3	16.9
Other nonfinancial	4.3	5.5	5.0	6.0	4.8
Debts	12.9	15.3	16.2	16.1	15.4
Mortgage and home equity	7.4	8.4	10.4	10.8	10.3
Loans for investment real estate	2.7	4.0	3.2	2.4	2.1
Credit card balances	0.2	0.3	0.5	0.6	0.5
Other debt	2.6	2.6	2.1	2.3	2.4
Memo items					
Equity share of financial assets	n.a.	28.6	34.1	39.1	54.4
Equity in primary residence as percentage of net worth	27.9	26.9	25.4	23.0	20.6
Median share for home owners	59.6	58.4	54.1	49.3	43.4
Mortgage and home equity debt as percentage of total debt	57.2	54.8	64.2	67.4	66.8
Mortgage and home equity debt as percentage of home value	23.3	26.9	32.8	35.9	37.1

Source: Surveys of Consumer Finances, weighted data.

Notes:
Financial assets

Liquid accounts	Checking accounts, savings accounts, money market deposit accounts, money market mutual funds, and call accounts at brokerages.
CDs	Certificates of deposit (short or long term).
Savings bonds	U.S. savings bonds.
Other bonds	Federal government bonds other than U.S. savings bonds, bonds issued by state and local governments, corporate bonds, mortgage-backed bonds, foreign bonds, and other types of bonds.
Stocks	Directly held stock in publicly traded corporations.
Mutual funds	Directly held shares in all types of mutual funds, excluding money market.
Retirement accounts	Includes both individual accounts (IRA and Keogh) and employer-sponsored thrift-type retirement accounts.
Cash-value life insurance	Surrender value of life insurance policies that build up a cash value.
Trusts and managed assets	Equity interests in trusts, annuities, and managed investment accounts.
Other financial	Royalties; futures contracts; oil and gas leases; future proceeds from a lawsuit, estate, or lottery; deferred compensation; and others.
Memo: Equity	Includes directly held stock and shares held through mutual funds, retirement accounts, and trusts and other managed assets.

Nonfinancial assets

Primary residence	Single-family or other type of home (e.g., mobile home, apartment, town house).
Investment real estate	Includes residential and nonresidential property not owned through a business.
Business equity	Net equity in all types of privately owned businesses, farms or ranches, professional practices, and partnerships. The household may have an active management role in the business or may only invest in the business.
Other nonfinancial	Includes all standard passenger vehicles (cars, trucks, vans, minivans, sport utility vehicles) not owned by a business; all other types of personal-use vehicles (motor homes, recreational vehicles, planes, boats, motorcycles); and miscellaneous nonfinancial assets such as artwork, antiques, jewelry, furniture, and valuable collections (coins, stamps).

Debts

Mortgage and home equity	All borrowing secured by the primary residence, including first and second mortgages and home equity loans and lines of credit.
Investment real estate	All outstanding loans or mortgages on property other than the primary residence.
Credit card balances	Balances outstanding after the last month's payment on general-purpose (Mastercard/Visa) and other types of cards (store, gas, travel and entertainment, airline).
Other debt	Includes home improvement loans, student loans, vehicle loans, other installment loans, lines of credit other than home equity, and loans against pensions and life insurance policies.

Table 5.3
Ownership of assets and liabilities

	Percentage of households with holdings				
	1983	1989	1992	1995	1998
Net worth above 0	92.1	88.7	89.5	89.9	89.5
Financial assets	89.7	88.6	90.1	90.6	92.9
Liquid accounts	87.4	85.3	86.9	87.0	90.5
Certificates of deposit	20.1	19.9	16.7	14.3	15.3
Savings bonds	20.2	23.9	22.3	22.8	19.3
Other bonds	4.2	5.7	4.3	3.1	3.0
Stocks	19.1	16.8	17.0	15.2	19.2
Mutual funds	4.5	7.2	10.4	12.3	16.5
Retirement accounts	30.8	35.6	38.1	43.0	48.0
Cash-value life insurance	34.1	35.5	34.9	32.0	29.6
Trusts and other managed assets	4.0	3.6	4.0	3.9	6.0
Other financial	1.6	13.8	10.8	11.1	9.4
Memo: Any equity	n.a.	31.6	36.7	40.4	48.9
Nonfinancial assets	90.3	89.2	90.8	90.9	89.9
Primary residence	63.4	63.9	63.9	64.7	66.3
Investment real estate	21.0	20.2	19.3	18.0	18.6
Business equity	14.4	11.6	11.9	11.1	11.5
Other nonfinancial	7.4	12.4	8.3	9.0	8.5
Debts	70.0	72.7	73.4	74.7	74.3
Mortgage and home equity	36.9	39.5	39.1	41.0	43.1
Loans for investment real estate	8.2	7.3	7.8	6.4	6.6
Credit card balances	37.0	39.7	43.7	47.3	44.1
Other debt	53.8	56.0	54.0	54.3	48.5

Source: Surveys of Consumer Finances, weighted data.
Note: For detailed definitions, see notes to table 5.2.

either IRA or 401(k) type—rose from about 31 percent in 1983 to 48 percent in 1998.

As a result of the combination of broader ownership of equity and rising prices, the share of households owning publicly traded stock—either directly or indirectly through a mutual fund, retirement account, or other managed asset—rose substantially, from 31.6 percent in 1989 to almost 49 percent in 1998.[11] This expansion has been broad-based across income, age, and education groups, so that the composition of stockholders has changed somewhat; stock owners in 1998 were somewhat younger than stock owners in 1989, and their median income and wealth were lower (table 5.4).[12] None-

Table 5.4
Characteristics of households owning equity, 1989 and 1998

Characteristics	1989	1998
Average age of household head (years)	48.9	47.9
Education of household head (%)		
Below high school	7.7	8.4
High school diploma	45.3	44.7
College degree	47.0	46.8
Median income (thousands of 1998 dollars)	58.3	53.1
Median net worth (thousands of 1998 dollars)	184.3	156.1
Percentage of equity owners owning shares in one company only	14.6	4.5
Percentage of total household equity held by the top 5 percent of the wealth distribution	65.5	66.9
Millions of households	29.4	50.1

theless, stock ownership has traditionally been concentrated in the upper tail of the wealth distribution, and the recent expansion of ownership has not altered this picture; for example, the share of total household equity held by the top 5 percent of the wealth distribution essentially held steady between 1989 and 1998.

The broadening of stock ownership in the United States is an important change whose causes and implications are not well understood. Certainly declining information and transactions costs have had an influential role. Technological innovation substantially lowered institutions' costs of processing financial information; in the competitive, lightly regulated capital markets characteristic of the United States, this encouraged entry by mutual fund companies and discount brokerages and drove down fees and minimum investments.[13] Employer-sponsored retirement accounts introduced an easy way to acquire equity investments: employers preselect the investment options, choices must be described in a clear, jargon-free way, and there is no minimum investment, for example. More recently, the Internet has begun to facilitate significantly the collection of financial information and conduct of financial transactions, although only a small part of the population so far makes use of it.[14] But in addition to the role of declining information costs, the economic climate was unusually good in the 1990s, with declining unemployment, solid real income growth, and booming stock prices; no doubt these factors also made households feel more comfortable about investing in stock.

In addition to the broadening of stock ownership, the survey data document the declining relative importance of home equity in household wealth.[15] According to the survey data, for households overall, equity in the primary residence declined from 28 percent of net worth in 1983 to 21 percent in 1998. For the typical home owner, home equity represents a larger share of their total wealth than this overall share implies; for example, the median share among home owners was 43 percent in 1998. But the median share is also considerably lower now than it was in the 1980s, due to growth in retirement accounts and other stock-based assets in home owners' portfolios, along with the trend toward greater leverage associated with the home.

Finally, the share of households having credit card debt rose appreciably over the 1983–1998 period. Bank-type credit cards became widely available in the United States, especially in the first half of the 1990s when credit card solicitations filled households' mailboxes.[16] The widespread use of credit card debt in the United States is somewhat puzzling, considering the relatively high interest rates on this debt; even with the competition and low introductory rates, the average interest rate on bank-type credit cards remained above 15 percent in 1998, versus about 8 percent for a home-equity loan.[17]

5.2   Evidence on the Structure of Household Portfolios

In simple portfolio models, investors allocate funds across assets with different risks and returns; optimization results in diversified portfolios, with the relative importance of different assets reflecting investors' risk and time preferences. Of course, such simple models abstract from several important aspects of the household portfolio problem. In particular, (1) investors also face background risk associated with labor earnings and business income; (2) a key investment option, housing, yields consumption flows as well as investment returns, and its price may covary with income; (3) there may be information and transactions costs that vary across investments and across individuals; and (4) households' portfolio decisions may partly reflect a risk of facing liquidity constraints. This section describes evidence on the structure of household portfolios in the United States, using a format comparable to other studies in this book.

Table 5.5 provides some basic stylized facts on the structure of U.S. households' financial assets, using data from the 1998 SCF. The vast majority of households have only a few types of financial assets. Of the thirteen main categories of financial assets in the SCF, the average number per household was three.[18] Some 7 percent of households had no financial assets whatsoever; another 15 percent had only one asset, most commonly a checking account. Another 53 percent of households had two to four types of assets, typically a checking account along with a savings account, retirement account, or cash-value life insurance. The remaining 25 percent of households had five or more types of assets; items like directly held stock and mutual funds become common only among households having seven or more types of assets.

The incompleteness of the typical portfolio may partly have to do with entry, information, and transactions costs. Some items, like brokerage accounts and mutual funds, require minimum investments. For example, of the top-ranked mutual funds in a recent *Consumer Reports* review, the average minimum investment was $2,000 for nonretirement accounts; such funds would be inaccessible to the 32 percent of households with nonretirement financial assets below this level.[19] Also, whereas opening a checking account is fairly straightforward, it takes time to learn how to invest in other assets and to manage them over time.[20] King and Leape (1987) found that the probability of owning an asset rises with age, even after controlling for the life cycle profile in wealth; they interpret this finding as consistent with a model in which information about investment opportunities arrives stochastically over time. Using data from the Panel Study of Income Dynamics, Vissing-Jørgenson (1999a) documents appreciable costs of entry and participation in the U.S. stock market, with the latter on the order of $100 to $200 per year.[21] Haliassos and Bertaut (1995) and Bertaut (1998) also identify the role of information costs in deterring investment in stock.

As table 5.6 shows, there is a clear correlation between wealth and the structure of household portfolios.[22] Ownership of almost all types of assets and liabilities rises with wealth; the only exceptions are credit card balances and other consumer debt (left panel). As wealth rises, the shares of total assets held in homes and other nonfinancial assets (mostly vehicles) decline, while the shares in stocks, bonds, mutual funds, trusts and other managed assets, businesses, and other real estate rise; the share of all forms of publicly traded stock in total assets also rises (center panel). The variation in portfolio structure across the wealth distribution, combined with the

Table 5.5
Diversification of financial assets: Percentage of households owning different types of financial assets, by number of types held

	Percentage of households	Checking accounts	Savings accounts	Retirement accounts	Cash-value life insurance	Savings bonds
All households	100	80.9	56.0	48.0	29.6	19.3
Number of asset types						
None	7.1	0.0	0.0	0.0	0.0	0.0
1	14.5	68.0	15.0	2.7	5.7	0.3
2	16.9	85.3	50.3	21.6	13.8	4.1
3	19.6	92.0	68.7	52.7	24.9	12.2
4	16.5	92.5	71.4	67.3	39.6	23.7
5	12.1	90.0	79.5	83.1	51.0	40.0
6	6.9	92.2	78.6	92.6	61.6	51.2
7	4.1	93.5	77.1	94.7	72.0	55.6
8	1.6	96.3	79.1	90.4	64.9	58.6
9	0.6	93.0	83.3	93.8	84.0	87.2
10 or more	0.2	95.2	92.8	99.1	74.9	86.2

Source: 1998 Survey of Consumer Finances, weighted data.
Note: For detailed definitions, see notes to table 5.2.

concentration in wealth ownership, implies large differences in concentration across assets and liabilities. For example, households in the top 5 percent of the wealth distribution own 57 percent of total net worth, but their shares are considerably higher for stocks, bonds, trusts and other managed assets, business equity, and investment real estate (right panel). The only items where the distribution of holdings is anything close to proportionate are credit card balances and other consumer debt.

   Variations in asset composition imply differences in the riskiness of households' portfolios. To gain more insight into this question, we divide financial assets into three broad categories reflecting their degree of risk: (1) "safe" financial assets, including liquid accounts (checking, saving, money market, and call), certificates of deposit, and U.S. savings bonds; (2) "fairly safe" financial assets, including other government bonds, tax-free bonds, cash-value life insurance, and amounts in mutual funds, retirement accounts, and trusts

Money market accounts	Call accounts	CDs	Mutual funds	Stocks	Bonds	Trusts and man-aged assets	Median financial assets (thousands of 1998 dollars)
18.3	2.1	15.3	16.5	19.2	3.0	6.0	16.7
0.0	0.0	0.0	0.0	0.0	0.0	0.0	0.0
3.4	0.0	0.8	0.0	0.4	0.0	0.0	0.5
6.2	0.0	9.1	1.3	1.6	0.2	0.8	3.7
12.0	0.0	11.5	6.0	8.9	1.5	1.8	16.0
21.3	0.6	21.4	21.0	20.6	2.0	6.5	48.6
32.7	3.4	23.5	31.3	38.7	4.4	9.6	94.6
40.5	6.6	29.7	48.5	58.1	6.7	15.1	132.9
51.3	12.7	43.1	60.9	72.6	16.7	27.4	218.6
81.1	25.3	51.1	81.6	84.5	23.4	41.3	351.5
94.2	15.5	48.9	86.8	95.4	36.9	43.5	736.5
89.7	56.2	71.8	94.9	100.0	37.2	82.9	1059.6

and other managed assets that are not invested in stock; and (3) "fairly risky" assets, including stocks held directly or through mutual funds, retirement accounts, and trusts and other managed assets, and corporate, foreign and mortgage-backed bonds. While this categorization may have some arbitrary aspects, the main findings reported here are robust to minor changes in classification as long as liquid accounts are classified as "safe" and stock-based assets are classified as "fairly risky."

In the four most recent SCFs, about one-quarter of all households had safe assets only (table 5.7). About one-quarter of households had "safe" and "fairly safe" assets in 1989, with this category steadily losing ground over the 1990s. The categories into which households moved were "safe, fairly safe, and fairly risky" and "safe and fairly risky"; together these categories had almost half of all households in 1998, up from about one-third of households in 1989. Not surprisingly, these shifts, combined with the run-up in stock prices, boosted the share of households' financial assets held in risky forms to 55.3

Table 5.6
Ownership and holdings of assets and liabilities, by wealth quartile and top 5 percent

	Percentage of households with holdings					Item as percentage of group's total assets[a]					Group's holdings as percentage of total household holdings				
	0–24.99	25–49.99	50–74.99	75–100	Top 5	0–24.99	25–49.99	50–74.99	75–100	Top 5	0–24.99	25–49.99	50–74.99	75–100	Top 5
Net worth greater than 0	89.3	100.0	100.0	100.0	100.0	32.6	53.0	74.6	90.7	94.8	−0.2	3.1	11.3	85.7	57.2
Financial assets	79.9	95.6	99.2	100.0	100.0	18.1	19.4	30.0	43.8	43.6	0.5	2.6	9.4	87.5	58.1
Liquid accounts	74.1	92.5	98.8	99.9	99.8	5.9	4.4	5.4	4.4	3.3	1.6	5.3	15.0	78.1	42.5
CDs	3.8	11.6	21.7	28.7	24.7	0.6	1.5	2.8	1.6	0.8	0.3	4.2	19.3	76.2	29.5
Savings bonds	8.9	17.0	24.2	30.5	23.9	0.5	0.4	0.5	0.2	0.1	1.2	6.4	21.9	70.5	18.8
Other bonds	0.1	1.2	2.2	9.6	29.7	0.0	0.0	0.3	2.2	3.1	0.0	0.1	1.8	98.1	87.5
Stocks	3.8	10.7	20.0	47.3	72.8	0.5	0.9	2.0	11.2	15.8	0.0	0.5	2.5	96.9	81.6
Mutual funds	2.2	10.2	17.2	40.8	53.3	0.5	1.1	2.4	5.9	5.0	0.1	1.2	5.2	93.4	59.6
Retirement accounts	20.6	45.8	56.9	76.8	83.5	6.2	7.6	11.5	10.8	7.3	0.5	3.6	14.0	81.8	44.2
Cash life insurance	12.2	25.8	37.4	49.3	57.7	2.5	2.3	3.4	2.5	1.4	1.1	5.3	16.4	77.3	29.2
Trusts and managed assets	0.7	2.7	6.1	16.2	33.4	0.3	0.6	0.9	4.4	6.0	0.1	0.7	3.7	95.4	81.8
Other financial	8.2	9.7	8.9	11.1	24.0	1.1	0.7	0.9	0.6	0.8	1.8	6.5	16.6	75.1	49.9
Memo: Any equity	19.3	45.7	57.1	82.5	91.5	4.7	6.7	11.3	25.1	28.0	0.2	1.6	6.5	91.8	66.9
Nonfinancial assets	71.3	97.1	98.8	99.6	100.0	81.9	80.6	70.0	56.2	56.4	1.6	7.4	15.7	75.3	47.6
Primary residence	19.6	77.6	89.5	94.7	97.1	50.2	62.8	52.8	20.1	8.8	2.1	12.2	26.2	59.6	23.1
Investment real estate	1.8	10.6	20.2	47.1	75.5	2.4	3.9	5.4	12.2	13.3	0.4	2.0	5.9	91.7	62.0
Business equity	2.1	7.5	11.5	28.1	62.9	0.7	1.6	3.8	20.7	32.4	0.0	0.5	2.5	96.9	85.3
Other nonfinancial	69.1	87.8	91.1	92.5	93.0	28.6	12.3	8.1	3.2	2.0	6.8	16.0	23.6	53.7	25.0

Debts	56.0	83.4	74.8	73.9	76.7	67.4	47.0	25.4	9.3	5.2	8.4	18.3	23.6	49.7	21.9
Mortgage and home equity	14.5	54.1	55.6	57.6	54.3	42.0	36.4	19.8	5.8	2.3	5.1	20.7	27.7	46.5	16.9
Investment real estate debt	1.0	3.8	7.1	15.8	33.8	0.9	1.7	1.3	2.3	2.2	2.4	4.6	6.5	86.5	54.4
Credit card balances	35.9	56.1	45.9	33.1	14.8	6.0	2.4	0.8	0.2	0.0	22.8	29.3	24.7	23.2	5.4
Other debt	38.9	55.3	48.4	37.3	32.6	18.4	6.6	3.5	1.1	0.7	24.0	17.8	21.0	37.1	18.7

Source: 1998 Survey of Consumer Finances, weighted data.
Note: For detailed definitions, see notes to table 5.2.
[a] Calculated for households with positive net worth.

Table 5.7
Riskiness of household portfolios

Financial assets	1989	1992	1995	1998
Share of households with				
Safe assets only	25.9	26.5	24.4	25.4
Safe and fairly safe	28.2	24.5	23.2	16.8
Safe and fairly risky	2.9	4.4	—	12.9
Safe, fairly safe, and fairly risky	28.9	32.1	40.1	35.7
No safe, some other type	2.7	2.6	2.9	2.1
No financial assets	11.4	9.9	9.4	7.1
Percentage of households' total financial assets in				
Safe assets	37.4	32.5	25.6	19.0
Fairly safe assets	31.5	31.7	34.1	25.8
Fairly risky assets	31.1	35.8	40.3	55.3
Total	100.0	100.0	100.0	100.0
Percentage of households' total assets in risky items (risky financial assets, business equity, and investment real estate)	43.5	43.6	42.8	49.6

Note:

Safe assets	Liquid accounts (checking, saving, money market, and call), certificates of deposit, and U.S. savings bonds.
Fairly safe assets	Other government bonds, tax-free bonds, cash-value life insurance, and amounts in mutual funds, retirement accounts, trusts, and other managed assets that are not invested in stock.
Fairly risky assets	Directly held stock; stock held through mutual funds, retirement accounts, trusts and other managed assets; and corporate, foreign, and mortgage-backed bonds.

percent in 1998. Nonetheless, this figure overstates the relative importance of risky assets in the typical household's financial portfolio: for example, among all households, the median share of financial assets held in risky items was just 4 percent in 1998.

With financial assets comprising only one part of the portfolio picture, it may also be important to consider other risky assets held by households. Thus, table 5.7 also shows a more general measure of risk, including business equity and investment real estate, as well as risky financial assets. Here too the share of households having some type of risky asset rose between 1989 and 1998; by 1998, the share of total household assets held in risky forms reached almost 50 percent. But again, for the median household, risky assets represented only a small part of their total assets (5 percent in 1998).

A classic issue in portfolio studies concerns the tendency for risk to vary with age. As shown in table 5.8, the share of households having risky financial assets is generally highest in the prime-age years and drops off in the older age ranges. The share of risky assets in total financial assets was highest in the 45–54 group in the 1989 and 1992 surveys and in the 55–64 age group in 1995 and 1998. The measures of broader portfolio risk also show risk taking to be highest in the 35–64 age ranges. Of course, the patterns in the data may reflect both age and cohort effects, and it is not straightforward to separate these two.[23] Nonetheless, the survey data show that for virtually all age groups and for both risk measures, the percentages of households owning risky assets have risen substantially over time; only in the over-75 age group has ownership of risky assets held steady.

Several factors may underlie this age-risk profile. First, younger people face more background risk in their human capital, which could temper their demand for stocks. As they enter prime-age years and uncertainty about lifetime income declines, they may take on more financial risk (see chapter 1). Second, young and prime-aged people have greater labor supply flexibility than older people, so if the returns to their investments turned out to be low, they could work more or retire later (Bodie, Merton, and Samuelson 1992). In contrast, older people would have to reduce consumption in line with their income, and so may choose to limit their risk. A third factor concerns the fact that initial investment in housing is large and indivisible. For example, Flavin and Yamashita (1998) show that because younger households have highly leveraged portfolios typically dominated by housing wealth, they should use their cash flow to pay down their mortgages or invest in safe assets rather than buy stock. In contrast, older households have built up their assets and reduced their ratios of housing to net worth, and so can allocate higher shares of their financial assets to investments in stock. Finally, other sources of uncertainty in old age may also temper willingness to take risk, such as uncertainty about the length of life and the risk of large health or nursing care expenses.

5.3 Econometric Analysis

To gain further insight into the structure of household portfolios, we estimate models of portfolio structure as a function of age, wealth, and a number of household characteristics that may figure into

Table 5.8
Riskiness of household portfolios, by age of household head

| | Share of households having risky assets | | | | Risky assets as a share of the group's assets | | | | | | | |
| | | | | | Among households having risky assets | | | | Among all households in group | | | |
	1989	1992	1995	1998	1989	1992	1995	1998	1989	1992	1995	1998
Financial assets												
All households	31.9	37.2	40.6	49.2	38.1	43.4	47.1	60.5	31.1	35.8	40.3	55.3
By age of household head												
Under 35	22.6	28.5	36.6	40.8	29.2	37.0	40.3	51.0	20.4	26.2	30.1	44.0
35–44	39.3	42.5	46.6	56.5	44.3	40.7	47.5	60.9	34.1	32.5	40.3	55.9
45–54	42.3	47.0	49.0	58.9	43.0	48.0	47.9	60.8	38.3	42.6	42.9	57.8
55–64	36.4	45.4	40.0	56.2	35.8	45.5	51.1	64.2	30.0	39.9	44.8	59.7
65–74	27.1	31.8	34.5	43.3	35.4	42.5	41.9	57.4	28.3	33.8	35.8	52.7
75 and over	26.0	26.7	29.7	30.8	36.6	37.5	49.3	60.7	29.4	27.8	39.7	50.2
Total assets												
All households	46.4	48.6	51.6	56.9	50.0	50.3	49.2	54.4	43.5	43.6	42.9	49.6
By age of household head												
Under 35	33.3	36.5	44.3	45.2	37.5	37.9	31.5	42.5	28.1	29.0	24.0	36.0
35–44	55.0	54.7	56.7	64.6	46.5	44.5	43.9	48.3	39.8	38.0	37.6	44.4
45–54	57.6	57.6	61.0	67.2	54.5	54.6	50.0	55.9	49.0	49.4	45.6	52.7
55–64	54.4	62.8	54.1	64.5	53.5	54.5	57.4	60.3	48.8	51.0	51.5	56.8
65–74	44.3	45.7	50.3	55.0	51.0	53.9	50.7	55.2	44.9	46.3	45.1	50.4
75 and over	37.8	35.2	39.0	38.8	46.3	41.8	46.2	54.2	38.5	31.5	36.8	43.4

Source: Surveys of Consumer Finances, weighted data.
Note:
Risky financial assets   Directly held stock; stock held through mutual funds, retirement accounts, trusts, and other managed assets; and corporate, foreign, and mortgage-backed bonds.
Any risky assets   Risky financial assets, plus business equity and investment real estate.

portfolio decisions. With cross-section data, we have limited means of accounting for unobserved heterogeneity or dynamic aspects of asset ownership. However, we do have a large number of observations from the full distribution of wealth, carefully cleaned and edited data, and a rich array of background data on household characteristics. Thus, although our results are primarily suggestive of the effects of age and wealth on household portfolios, they nonetheless provide considerable insight into determinants of portfolio structure.

We first focus on the position of risky assets in household portfolios. Using limited-dependent variable specifications and pooled data from the 1989, 1992, 1995, and 1998 SCFs, we show that determinants of the decision to hold risky assets may differ from the determinants of the risky share; this is suggestive of differences in entry or information costs across households. We also show that, controlling for wealth, income, and other factors, the probability of having risky assets is significantly higher for prime-aged households than for households in the under-35 or over-65 age ranges; in contrast, age effects on the risky share are not always significant. We then take a broader approach to household portfolios, examining joint decisions to hold assets and liabilities. Here we take advantage of recent advances in simulation methods and estimate a multivariate probit model of such decisions. Broadly, the results suggest an important role of life cycle considerations in shaping household portfolios, as well as income risk, liquidity constraints, and differences across assets and households in information costs.

5.3.1   Holdings of Risky Assets

Econometric analysis of household portfolios must take into account the fact that many households have no risky assets at all. With cross-section data, this problem can be approached in three different ways. First, the household may hold the risky asset only if its optimal portfolio share exceeds some minimal level; then the optimal share is observed only if it is above this threshold, and data on nonowners convey only the probability of being below this level. This is a censored regression model and can be estimated using tobit. Second, the process underlying the decision to hold risky assets may differ from that determining the optimal share, for example, if participation reflects lack of information on the asset or its characteristics. In this case, the ownership decision should be modeled separately from the process generating the portfolio share. Here a sample selection approach is warranted if the ownership and share decisions are separate but have unobserved determinants that are correlated. We estimate and compare these two approaches, considering risky financial assets as a share of financial assets and total risky assets as a share of total assets.

To take full advantage of the SCF data, we pool the data from the 1989, 1992, 1995, and 1998 surveys, using time dummies to indicate the survey year (1995 is omitted). As discussed in Ameriks and Zeldes (2000), this approach assumes that cohort effects are equal to zero.[24] Excluded from the analysis are 1,029 households that have no financial assets whosoever on the grounds that, without assets, they face no decision about portfolio composition.[25] This leaves a sample of 14,618 households, of whom 8,310 have risky financial assets and 10,174 have risky assets more broadly defined.

As explanatory variables, we include dummy variables for the age range of the household head: under 35, 35–54 (omitted), 55–64, and 65 and over.[26] For wealth, we use the log of financial assets in the models for risky financial assets and the log of total assets in the models for total risky assets. In addition, a number of variables are included to reflect factors likely to shape portfolio decisions. As general household characteristics, we include the log of total household income; the household type (married couples, households headed by unmarried women, with households headed by unmarried men omitted);[27] whether the respondent was nonwhite or Hispanic; and the education of the household head (college degree, less than high school diploma, with high school diploma omitted). To capture possible differences in income variability, we include whether the head is self-employed, whether the head or spouse is covered under a DB pension plan, and the regional unemployment rate.[28] As a measure of labor supply flexibility, in addition to age, we include a variable indicating whether the household head is retired. To capture variation in risk preference, we include self-reported measures of willingness to take financial risks for commensurate returns (willing to take above-average or substantial risks, not willing to take financial risks, with willing to take average risks omitted).

The results are reported in Table 5.9. The tobit results for financial assets, shown in the left panel of the table, are consistent with the descriptive statistics: risky shares are lower in both the younger (under 35) and the older (55–64, and over 65) age ranges, compared to the 35–54 range, and tend to rise with wealth. Several of the other results are also consistent with expectations; for example, the risky share is lower among the self-employed and the retired and higher among those with DB pension plans, as would be expected from effects of income uncertainty and labor supply flexibility. However, the tobit assumes that the decision to hold risky assets directly reflects the optimal share, which may not be warranted if other factors, such as information or entry costs, affect the ownership decision also. In fact, a chi-square test based on the log-likelihood rejects the restrictions implied by the tobit model.[29] This suggests the decisions underlying ownership and portfolio share are not the same.

An alternative approach is Heckman's selection model, which models the ownership and risky share decisions separately while allowing for the possibility that unobserved determinants of the two decisions are correlated. To estimate this model, we include some variables that may affect the decision to hold risky assets but not the risky share. Assuming that variation in information and entry costs are important in this regard, we include the share of household heads employed in financial services in the region, the share of household heads in the region employed in firms with 500 or more workers (correlated with access to equity through tax-deferred retirement accounts), and a measure of how much a household shops around when making decisions about saving and borrowing.[30]

Results are shown in the middle panel of table 5.9. The coefficients on the extra information and entry variables have the expected signs and are generally statistically significant; also the correlation in error terms across the two equations is estimated to be positive and significant. Here we see similar mixed results for the coefficients on age; the probability of holding risky assets is significantly lower in the 55–64 and 65 and over age ranges, but the risky share is significantly lower for the 65 and over group only. Also, the under-35 households show no significant difference in ownership, but their risky share is lower, at a 10 percent level. Nonetheless, taken jointly, the age variables are significant in the ownership equation, significant in the share equation (albeit at a 10 percent level only), and significant in the selection model overall.[31] The coefficients on the year dummies also show uptrends in both ownership of risky assets and the risky share over time, and these are jointly significant.

Table 5.9
Models of risky financial assets: Ownership and risky share

	Financial assets						Total assets			
	Tobit		Heckman selection model				Heckman selection model			
	Share		Ownership		Share		Ownership		Share	
	Coefficient	S.E.	Coefficient	S.E.	Coefficient	S.E.	Coefficient	S.E.	Coefficient	S.E.
Constant	-.7721*	(.03)	-4.5803*	(.16)	-.0149	(.16)	-6.0648*	(.20)	-.8267*	(.07)
Married	.0326*	(.01)	.1885*	(.04)	-.0133	(.02)	.0013	(.04)	-.0681*	(.01)
Female headed	.0148	(.01)	.1523*	(.05)	-.0135	(.02)	-.0277	(.05)	-.0607*	(.02)
Age less than 35	-.0247*	(.01)	.0352	(.04)	-.0303+	(.02)	-.0008	(.04)	.0037	(.01)
Age 55–64	-.0398*	(.01)	-.1157*	(.04)	-.0091	(.01)	.0693	(.05)	.0144+	(.01)
Age 65 and over	-.1029*	(.01)	-.3652*	(.05)	-.0393*	(.02)	-.0879+	(.06)	-.0173+	(.01)
Log income	-.0076*	(.00)	.0385*	(.01)	-.0026	(.00)	.0819*	(.01)	-.0153*	(.00)
Log wealth	.0955*	(.00)	.3779*	(.01)	.0356*	(.01)	.4572*	(.01)	.1032*	(.00)
Nonwhite or Hispanic	-.0746*	(.01)	-.2471*	(.04)	-.0323	(.02)	-.1576*	(.04)	.0099	(.01)
Below high school	-.0793*	(.01)	-.1753*	(.04)	-.0194	(.03)	-.1378*	(.04)	-.0045	(.02)
College degree	.0372*	(.01)	.1194*	(.03)	.0285*	(.01)	.0970*	(.03)	-.0082	(.01)
DB pension	.0393*	(.01)	.1124*	(.03)	.0107	(.01)	.0223*	(.03)	-.0220*	(.01)
Self-employed	-.1292*	(.01)	-.4994*	(.04)	-.0642*	(.02)	.4914*	(.05)	.1333*	(.01)
Retired	.0936*	(.01)	-.3061*	(.05)	-.0419*	(.02)	-.1986*	(.05)	.0003	(.01)
No risk	-.1606*	(.01)	-.4477*	(.03)	-.0908*	(.03)	-.4381*	(.03)	-.0586*	(.01)
High risk	.0680*	(.01)	.1071*	(.04)	.0802*	(.01)	.2369*	(.04)	.0470*	(.01)

	(1)		(2)		(3)		(4)		(5)	
Unemployment rate	.0009	(.00)	-.0039	(.01)	.0019	(.00)	-.0139	(.01)	-.0026	(.00)
1989	-.1000*	(.01)	-.2377*	(.04)	-.0914*	(.02)	-.0790+	(.04)	-.0271*	(.01)
1992	-.0415*	(.01)	-.0749+	(.04)	-.0379*	(.01)	.0347	(.04)	.0177+	(.01)
1998	.0981*	(.01)	.1431*	(.04)	.1023*	(.01)	.0660+	(.04)	.0326*	(.01)
% FIRE employment	—	—	.0181+	(.01)	—	—	.0015	(.01)	—	—
% large employer	—	—	.0164*	(.00)	—	—	.0146*	(.00)	—	—
Shop around for best terms	—	—	.0114*	(.01)	—	—	.0142*	(.01)	—	—
Inverse Mills ratio	—	—	—	—	.1601+	(.10)	—	—	.2261*	(.06)
Estimate of ρ			.5374				.8354			
Joint significance of age variables	.0000		.0000		.0633		.0541		.0321	

Note: FIRE = finance, insurance, and real estate.
*Significant at 5 percent level.
+Significant at 10 percent level.

Also as expected, both ownership and share rise with the level of financial assets. Income raises ownership of risky assets but not the risky share. Conceivably, ownership may be lower among low-income households because their access to equity through retirement plans is more limited;[32] also, they may anticipate more problems with liquidity constraints, and so keep their assets in safer, more liquid forms. The probability of owning risky assets is also higher for households headed by college graduates and lower for those without high school diplomas. This finding, consistent with previous studies, may reflect lower background income risk faced by better-educated households (Hubbard, Skinner, and Zeldes 1995). Additionally, this group may have informational advantages that make it easier or less time-consuming for them to invest in stock (Haliassos and Bertaut 1995). We provide some evidence in favor of this interpretation.

Married couples and female-headed households have a higher probability of owning risky financial assets compared to unmarried men. The result for women differs from previous studies, which have suggested that women tend to have less risky portfolios than men (see, for example, Jianakoplos and Bernasek 1998). While this is a subject of open investigation, it should be noted that our specification controls for a number of factors that differ between women and men and contribute to observed portfolio differences between them (e.g., income, stated risk preference).[33] Conceivably, women may even favor risky investments compared to male counterparts, since their longer life expectancies imply longer investment horizons. Nonetheless, our finding on gender is somewhat sensitive to changes in specification; this suggests a need for caution in interpreting the result.

A final result of interest is the significantly lower ownership of risky assets among nonwhite and Hispanic households. Again, this may reflect greater income uncertainty or unequal access to credit, which could tilt the portfolio away from risky assets. Family background may also play some role here; for example, using data from the Panel Study of Income Dynamics, Chiteji and Stafford (1999) found that about 44 percent of young families whose parents owned stock held equities themselves, compared to 24 percent of those whose parents did not. Alternatively, it is possible that the lower incidence of stock ownership among minorities reflects some degree of differential treatment in the financial services industry (Loury 1998).

Results for the selection model using total risky assets are presented in the right panel of table 5.9. Most results are qualitatively quite similar to those for risky financial assets. The findings on age are somewhat weaker: ownership drops off in the 65 and over age group, as does the risky share, although both results are significant at a 10 percent level only. Both ownership and the risky share are strongly related to wealth. One notable difference from the financial asset model is that whereas risky assets were downplayed in the financial portfolios of the self-employed, this group was more likely to own risky assets overall (i.e., due to their business interests) and had a higher share of their assets in risky forms. This suggests that the safety of their financial portfolios may be hedging the risks associated with their other assets, although only partially.

5.3.2 Multivariate Probit Model

While decisions about risky assets are a central aspect of portfolio decisions, joint decisions about holding different assets and liabilities are also of interest.[34] In particular, households make decisions not only about financial assets, but also about home ownership and business interests. Also, their decisions about asset holdings may be taken with borrowing considerations in mind (Paxson 1990; Engen and Gale 1997).

To investigate joint decisions, we take advantage of recent advances in simulation methods and estimate a multivariate probit model of portfolio choice. Under the multivariate probit, we observe a 0-1 variable for whether a given household holds each asset or liability. We can also allow for correlation across the error terms resulting from unobservable household-specific factors. If the error terms are uncorrelated across assets, this results in a series of standard single-equation probits. However, if the error terms are correlated, it is preferable to model the asset-holding decisions jointly, as can be done with the multivariate probit.

The model we estimate contains four categories of assets: stock-based financial assets, safe investment assets, the primary residence, and business interests.[35] We also include one liability, consumer debt, due to interest in the puzzle of its widespread extent.[36] The explanatory variables are largely as before, although here we use the log of net worth as the measure of wealth. The model is estimated using Geweke, Hajivassiliou, and Keane's simulation method to approximate the multivariate normal distribution (Greene 1997).[37] Due to the computational intensity of the model, we use data from the 1995 SCF only. To our knowledge, this is the first application of the multivariate probit model to the analysis of portfolio choice. Results from the model are presented in table 5.10.

Age

The multivariate results show rather mixed effects of age on household portfolios. Age had no significant effect on the probability of having stock-based assets or on the probability of having safe investment assets. Under-35 households were significantly less likely to own a home than households in the 35–54 age range; this probably reflects the need to accumulate assets for a down payment or the lower attractiveness of home ownership to the young (or both). Our results do not show a tendency for home ownership to decline with age; the coefficient for the 65 and over range is positive and significant at the 10 percent level, although it is smaller than the coefficient for the 55–64 range. While this finding is interesting for the debate about whether the elderly spend down their housing wealth, it is unclear whether it should be interpreted literally, especially given that studies using panel data show a different result.[38] We also find that business ownership drops off significantly in the 65 and over age group, consistent with other research and suggesting that older households sell off business assets when they scale back work hours. The probability of having consumer debt drops off considerably in the older age ranges. However, the use of consumer debt is not higher in the younger age range, as might be predicted from a life cycle perspective. Conceivably this may not be the optimal choice of younger households, as some may be credit constrained. For example, the SCF asks whether households had been turned down for credit in the past five years or had not applied for credit in anticipation of being rejected. By this definition, in 1995, some 39 percent of under-35 households would be classified as liquidity constrained compared to 22 percent of households overall.[39]

Net Worth

Not surprisingly, higher net worth raises the probability of having all four types of assets and lowers the probability of having consumer debt. However, the same-size increase in wealth, other things

Table 5.10
Coefficient estimates from multivariate probit model of ownership of selected assets and liabilities of U.S. households, 1995 Survey of Consumer Finances

	Stocks		Safe assets		Homes		Businesses		Consumer debt	
	Coefficient	S.E.	Coefficient	S.E.	Coefficient	S.E.	Coefficient	S.E.	Coefficient	S.E.
Constant	−2.9947**	0.18	−0.6247**	0.19	−2.1538**	0.24	−4.0143**	0.23	1.7164**	0.18
Married	0.2825**	0.06	0.3853**	0.06	0.7059**	0.07	−0.0036	0.08	0.2464**	0.06
Female headed	0.1689*	0.08	0.0236	0.07	0.1268	0.08	−0.3958**	0.11	0.0671	0.07
Age less than 35	−0.0115	0.07	−0.0892	0.06	−0.4794**	0.07	−0.0294	0.09	−0.0163	0.06
Age 55–64	−0.0131	0.07	0.0143	0.07	0.4041**	0.10	−0.0676	0.08	−0.3404**	0.07
Age 65 and over	−0.0197	0.08	0.0765	0.08	0.1963+	0.10	−0.3286**	0.08	−0.8776**	0.08
Log income	0.1517**	0.01	0.0162	0.02	0.0695**	0.02	0.0249	0.02	−0.0372*	0.01
Log wealth	0.1174**	0.01	0.0835**	0.01	0.1981**	0.01	0.2541**	0.01	−0.0956**	0.01
Nonwhite or Hispanic	−0.2315**	0.06	−0.0623	0.06	−0.1638*	0.07	−0.1210	0.09	0.1215*	0.06
Below high school	−0.3073**	0.08	−0.2962**	0.08	0.0329	0.09	−0.0639	0.12	−0.1301+	0.08
College degree	0.3488**	0.05	0.0782	0.05	−0.0101	0.06	−0.0501	0.06	−0.2690**	0.05
DB pension	0.0885+	0.05	0.1895**	0.05	0.0615	0.06	−0.2094**	0.06	0.1795**	0.05
Self-employed	−0.3389**	0.06	−0.0792	0.06	0.0812	0.08	1.4926**	0.07	−0.1833**	0.06
Retired	−0.2075*	0.08	−0.1855*	0.08	−0.0757	0.10	−0.0718	0.09	−0.2810**	0.08
No risk	−0.6477**	0.05	−0.2957**	0.06	−0.0247	0.07	−0.1327+	0.08	−0.0773	0.05
High risk	0.1087+	0.06	−0.1771**	0.06	−0.0843	0.07	0.1359*	0.07	−0.0372	0.06
Unemployment rate	0.0359+	0.02	−0.0089	0.02	−0.0992**	0.02	−0.0428+	0.02	−0.0226	0.02
ρ with stocks	—	—	0.2658**	0.03	0.0488	0.04	−0.0162	0.04	0.0073	0.03
ρ with safe	—	—	—	—	0.0689+	0.04	−0.0058	0.04	0.0153	0.03
ρ with home	—	—	—	—	—	—	−0.1001*	0.05	0.1739**	0.03
ρ with business	—	—	—	—	—	—	—	—	−0.268	0.04

** Significant at 1 percent level.
* Significant at 5 percent level.
+ Significant at 10 percent level.
Log likelihood, −9064.6.

being equal, contributes more to the probability of stock ownership than ownership of safe investment assets. For example, for an otherwise typical household, an increase in net worth from about $9,000 to $59,000—equivalent to moving from the twenty-fifth to the fiftieth percentiles of the wealth distribution—increases the estimated probability of stock ownership from 28 percent to 36 percent, but increases the probability of owning safe investment assets from 65 percent to 70 percent. Both the higher probability of owning safe investment assets and the larger increase in the probability of stock ownership are consistent with the view that stocks should be added to a portfolio after a buffer of safe investment assets is in place.[40]

Income
As might be expected, higher income raises the probability of owning stock-based assets; it also raises the probability of home ownership. However, it has no significant effect on the probability of owning safe investment assets or a business, and it has a negative effect on the probability of having consumer debt.

Education
College-educated households have a significantly higher probability of owning stock-based assets, other things being equal. This may be a by-product of this group's lower income risk, which may make them feel more comfortable investing in stock. But it may also reflect some informational advantage characteristic of this group. Some evidence here is that, ceteris paribus, college-educated households are also less likely to have consumer debt, which is often at high interest rates and, unlike mortgage and home equity borrowing, is not tax advantaged; this may reflect a differential ability to gather and use financial information.[41]

Other Demographic Characteristics
Married-couple households are more likely to own stock-based assets, safe investment assets, and their own home; they are also more likely to have consumer debt. We find that female-headed households are more likely to own stock-based assets than households headed by single males. But interestingly, female-headed households are significantly less likely to own a business, suggesting that any greater willingness to take financial risk that they may have could reflect less need to hedge against business risks. Again, we find

nonwhite households less likely to own stocks, ceteris paribus; they are also less likely to own homes and more likely to have consumer debt. The lower probability of home ownership may at least partially reflect unequal access to mortgage debt (see Ladd 1998).

Correlation Across Equations

As shown at the bottom of table 5.10, the estimates of the ρ's from the multivariate probit are significant for many pairs of equations, rejecting the null hypothesis that the disturbance terms are uncorrelated. Since our models include a measure of risk preference, unobserved variation would be expected to reflect other factors, such as differences in income expectations, priors about asset returns, time preferences, and family background. The estimated correlations are positive and significant at a 5 percent level for stock-based assets and safe investment assets and for home ownership and consumer debt; the correlation is positive and significant at a 10 percent level for safe investment assets and home ownership. While a positive correlation between the various asset categories is perhaps not surprising, the positive correlation between home ownership and consumer debt is more puzzling, given that most home owners have access to lower-cost sources of borrowing. Perhaps those households more likely to own homes and have consumer debt than their observed characteristics would predict also have higher income expectations or higher discount rates. In contrast, the correlation is negative and significant for home and business ownership. Although the majority of business owners are also home owners, it is important to remember that these equations control for net worth and self-employment status. Thus, one possible interpretation is that, other things equal, business owners may be less willing to undertake the additional responsibilities associated with home ownership.

5.4 Conclusions and Policy Implications

Our econometric results highlight the important effects of age and wealth on the structure of household portfolios. Age has significant effects on the ownership of risky assets, although evidence of effects on the risky share is more mixed. Both ownership of risky assets and the risky share clearly rise with wealth, whether financial or total assets are considered. Factors associated with income risk and labor supply flexibility also have expected effects; for example, the financial portfolios of self-employed and retired households tend to be relatively safe, while college-educated households tend to take more risk. Our findings also suggest that differences across assets and across households in information and entry costs help explain the fairly simple and safe structure of the typical household portfolio in the United States. In particular, investing in stock-based assets requires time and ability to process financial information, with minimum investments often required for nonretirement accounts. For a sizable share of households, these features represent important deterrents to equity ownership. Nonetheless, as our descriptive statistics and econometric work show, this picture has changed considerably in recent years, as the ease of investing through employer-sponsored retirement accounts has put equity ownership within reach for a much broader segment of the population.

Our results suggest a number of policy implications. First, the finding about information and entry costs suggests that public and private policies affecting such costs are likely to have appreciable effects. The shift toward employer-sponsored retirement accounts has certainly been of major importance in this regard, converting to stock owners quite a lot of those who "should have" owned stock—based on such factors as income risk, labor supply flexibility, and time to retirement—but did not due to information and entry costs.[42] However, it is also true that even with low-cost access, some of those who do not currently own stock probably "should not" on these grounds, and need to be so advised. This suggests that, for example, any self-directed investment component of social security would require a strong informational component. This is all the more true because financial markets in the future may not be as beneficent as they have been in the past ten or twenty years.

Second, with age often a significant factor in portfolio choice, an important policy question concerns possible effects of demographic shifts on asset markets. For example, some have argued that the movement of the large baby boom cohort into preretirement saving years fueled the 1990s boom in stock prices, just as their movement into nesting years may have fueled an earlier boom in housing prices.[43] Of course, it is tricky to draw inferences for asset markets directly from household behavior. Theory does not suggest that life cycle aspects of portfolio choice would be fixed; rather, they would reflect expectations of a number of variables—such as real wages, unemployment, asset returns, and the generosity of public pensions—

that themselves may be influenced by demographics. This highlights the need for a general-equilibrium approach to analyzing asset-market effects of population aging. Understanding such effects would provide valuable insight for debates about retirement preparedness and retirement policy.

Finally, with portfolios differing considerably across the distribution of income or wealth, changes in key macrovariables, such as interest rates or stock prices, may have quite different effects on households of different types. For example, an increase in interest rates raises both households' debt payments and income from interest-bearing assets; however, because debt holdings tend to decline with wealth, the higher a household is on the wealth scale, the more likely it is that the income effect will dominate the effect on debt payments. Differential effects like this may have important implications for the behavior of aggregate consumption. Notably, if marginal propensities to consume vary across the wealth distribution, an increase in the value of a widely held asset (like housing) might have a much stronger effect on consumption than an increase for an asset held mostly by the rich (like stock).[44] This suggests that we may gain a richer view of consumption and saving by understanding household portfolios.

Notes

We are grateful to Dan Bergstresser, Diana Hancock, Arthur Kennickell, Dean Maki, Maria Perozek, Nick Souleles, participants at the European University Institute's Conference on Household Portfolios, and especially the editors of this book for valuable comments on earlier versions of this chapter. The views expressed in this chapter are those of the authors and not necessarily those of the Federal Reserve Board or its staff.

1. All dollar figures in the tables and text are adjusted to 1998 terms using the "current methods" version of the consumer price index for all urban consumers (Stewart and Reed 1999).

2. When we wrote this chapter, FFA estimates of nonprofit holdings were available through 1996 only due to lags in the availability of the source data. For 1998, we estimated holdings of nonprofits in 1998 by taking total (household plus nonprofit) holdings in 1998 and assuming that nonprofits held the same share of the total as in 1996. This assumption seems reasonable, given the small movements in the shares over the period for which separate estimates are available.

3. Year-end figures.

4. More recently, the 1997 tax bill introduced Roth IRAs, for which contributions are taxed but withdrawals are not.

5. The limits were phased in over a five-year period. See chapter 3 in this volume and Maki (1996) for further analysis of this subject.

6. Increased leverage may also reflect incentives to channel funds into retirement accounts rather than pay down tax-preferred debt (Engen and Gale 1997).

7. See Kennickell, Starr-McCluer, and Surette (2000) for an overview of the SCF. Because respondents often have incomplete information on their holdings or may be unwilling or unable to report details, the SCF data are carefully cleaned and edited, and missing values are systematically imputed.

8. The survey's scope for examining dynamic issues is limited by its cross-section design. This design is necessitated by the survey's main objective of providing representative information on household finances, along with the practicalities of the dual sample frame; for example, it is not possible to conduct regular reinterviews with the high-wealth cases. For analysis of SCF panel data collected in the 1980s, see Kennickell and Starr-McCluer (1997).

9. Although the surveys since 1992 have been about 20 percent below estimates of household wealth from the Flow of Funds, there is no clear reason that the 1990s surveys would capture a smaller share of FFA wealth than the 1980s surveys. The survey's sample design, questionnaire, and imputation methods were revised considerably in 1989, and in 1992 the area-probability sample frame was updated to reflect data from the 1990 census; if anything, these improvements would be expected to raise the share of aggregate wealth captured by the survey. One factor may relate to the composition of the 1983 oversample, which was based on income rather than estimated wealth; also, respondents had to volunteer to participate in the survey.

10. Two other issues are worth mentioning. First, in the FFA, households' holdings are computed as a residual, that is, by taking total holdings of a given asset or liability and subtracting out holdings attributable to other sectors. While there is no a priori reason to believe that this imparts a systematic bias to the household numbers, uncertainties in allocating funds across sectors may leave some scope for measurement error. Second, for practical reasons, the SCF does not sample households at the very top of the wealth distribution, such as those whose net worth would place them in the Forbes 400 range (for example, in 1998 the cut-off to make it into the Forbes 400 was a net worth of $500 million). This omission causes only modest understatement of total household wealth. For example, the total net worth of the Forbes 400 was $745 billion in 1998, compared to an estimate of $28,850 billion from the SCF, suggesting understatement in the SCF on the order of 2 1/2 percent.

11. This share cannot be directly computed for 1983, since that survey lacks information on the composition of investments in mutual funds, retirement accounts, and trusts and other managed assets. Using information on investment compositions in 1989 to impute compositions in 1983, Poterba and Samwick (1995) estimate that 33.2 percent of households held stock in some form in 1983.

12. Also note that in 1989, 15 percent of equity owners had shares in one company only; by 1998 this share had fallen below 5 percent.

13. According to the Investment Company Institute, the average cost of investing in equity mutual funds, including all major fees and expenses, fell by one-third between 1980 and 1997 (Rea and Reid 1998).

14. For example, only 8 percent of respondents to the 1998 SCF reported using the Internet or on-line services to make decisions about savings and investments. However, this share rose with household income, so that among households with incomes of $100,000 or more, about 22 percent said they used the Internet to this end.

15. The FFA series on residential property includes all homes with one to four units, not just the primary residence; other types of property are attributed to other sectors. The SCF distinguishes between the primary residence and other property owned by households (residential and commercial). According to the 1995 SCF, primary residences represented about 86 percent of the total value of residential property owned by households.

16. The share of households having at least one bank-type card (Mastercard, Visa, Optima, or Discover) rose from 43 percent in 1983 to 67 percent in 1998. Among households having cards, the share with balances outstanding after the last month's payments moved up from 52 percent to 55 percent.

17. The average credit card interest rate is from the Federal Reserve Board's G19 statistical release, and the home equity loan rate is from HSH Associates, Financial Publishers. For additional discussion, see Ausubel (1991) and Calem and Mester (1995).

18. The median was also 3.

19. See "Mutual Funds: Pieces of the Action," *Consumer Reports* (March 2000): 27–35. *Consumer Reports* limits its review to no-load mutual funds that have relatively low expense ratios and no 12b-1 fees. Minimum investments are often much lower for retirement accounts.

20. For example, in their study of tax compliance, Blumenthal and Slemrod (1992) found that filing the return for capital gains on investments increased total filing time by six hours.

21. Apparently in 1982–1984 dollars.

22. For early evidence on wealth and portfolio composition, see Uhler and Cragg (1971).

23. See Ameriks and Zeldes (2000) for a full discussion of this issue. Poterba and Samwick (1997) use a cohort approach to analyze data from the 1983, 1989, and 1992 SCFs.

24. In the period covered by our data, time effects seem likely to be more important than cohort effects, given the strong growth in stock ownership from the spread of retirement accounts, the boom in stock prices, and the reversal in the downtrend in direct stock ownership.

25. This avoids equating the decision not to have assets with the decision not to hold risky assets. Including households without assets affects the magnitudes of estimated coefficients, but with little qualitative effect on results.

26. We also tried the less flexible but simpler version of age and age squared, but found it yielded implausible results. In particular, the estimated coefficients suggested a very gentle rise and decline in risky holdings over the life cycle, but with a maximum at age 31–32, likely an artifact of the specification.

27. For purposes of this study, "married couples" means couples living together with shared finances.

28. Regional variables used in this study are for the nine census divisions (New England, Mid-Atlantic, South Atlantic, East South Central, West South Central, East North Central, West North Central, Mountain, and Pacific).

29. This test compares the likelihood of the tobit model with that of a model using a probit for ownership and a truncated regression for the risky share (Greene 1997). With log likelihoods of −6951.1 and −6196.2 respectively, the implied chi-squared test rejects the hypothesis that the assumptions of the tobit model are correct.

30. Note that the SCF's "shopping" questions have been asked somewhat differently in different surveys, with only one question asked in 1989 and 1992 and two asked thereafter; also, the responses are coded on different scales. We have standardized these measures by averaging the two questions asked in 1995 and 1998, and converting all measures to a scale of 1 to 10.

31. Our results differ somewhat from Ameriks and Zeldes (2000), who find a significant effect of age on ownership but not on the risky share, using pooled data from the 1989, 1992, and 1995 SCFs. Their regressions, like ours, include time dummies, but otherwise their specification differs from ours in a number of other respects (one age term, no controls for household wealth or other characteristics, OLS regressions). Running such regressions on our data yields similar results.

32. For example, in the 1998 SCF, only 12 percent of households in the bottom 25 percent of the income distribution were eligible to participate in employer-sponsored retirement accounts, compared to 42 percent of households overall.

33. Descriptive statistics from the SCF show the expected male-female gap: in 1998, about 33 percent of female-headed households owned stock in some form, compared to 42 percent of households headed by unmarried men and 58 percent of married couples. Nonetheless, female-headed households were considerably more likely to express unwillingness to take financial risks; well over one-half of female-headed households said they took no risks in their savings and investments, versus about one-third of male-headed and married-couple households. This difference in self-reported risk preference contributes to, but does not explain away, the different econometric result on gender.

34. Previous studies examining joint decisions include King and Leape (1998) and Dicks-Mireaux and King (1983).

35. As before, stock-based financial assets include directly held stock, and shares held through mutual funds, retirement accounts, and trusts and managed assets. Safe investment assets include safe financial assets other than liquid accounts: certificates of deposit, cash-value life insurance, savings bonds, other bonds, and nonstock amounts held through mutual funds, retirement accounts, and trusts and managed assets.

36. Here consumer debt includes credit card balances outstanding after the past month's payments, plus nonvehicle installment loans.

37. See also the November 1994 issue of *Review of Economics and Statistics*.

38. See chapter 11 and Kennickell and Starr-McCluer (1997). Note also that our use of 65 and over as the oldest age group may obscure a drop-off among the older old.

39. As in other studies using these variables, the "liquidity constrained" include households turned down for credit, and did not eventually get the amount they

requested by reapplying, and those that did not apply for credit because they thought they would be turned down. See, for example, Cox and Jappelli (1993).

40. The same increase in net worth for the otherwise typical household increases the estimated probability of home ownership from 86 percent to 93 percent and of business ownership from 4 percent to 9 percent, while it decreases the probability of holding consumer debt from 58 percent to 51 percent.

41. See, for example, Maki's (1996) work on household response to the elimination of the deductibility of interest on consumer debt.

42. Indeed, some evidence suggests that investing in equities through employer-sponsored accounts may increase equity ownership outside such accounts (Weisbenner 1999). Also, the shift to DC pensions has been accompanied by a general increase in workplace financial education, as discussed in Bayer, Bernheim, and Scholz (1996) and Bernheim and Garrett (1996).

43. Poterba (1998) investigates effects of population aging on stock and bond prices. For analysis of housing market effects, see Mankiw and Weil (1989), McFadden (1994), and Hoynes and McFadden (1997).

44. Dynan, Skinner, and Zeldes (2000) present evidence that marginal propensities to consume vary with permanent income. On wealth effects on spending, see Poterba and Samwick (1995) and Starr-McCluer (forthcoming).

6

Household Portfolios in the United Kingdom

James Banks and
Sarah Tanner

This chapter provides empirical evidence on the portfolios of U.K. households and their evolution in recent years. We argue that household portfolios in the United Kingdom share many features with those of other countries examined in this book. By far the most important items of measured household portfolios are housing and private pensions, jointly accounting for nearly two-thirds of total wealth. Within the group of financial assets, there are wide differences in ownership rates among households and relatively low levels of portfolio diversification in terms of both the proportion of households holding equity directly and the portfolio share of directly held equity. Age, income, and education are important factors in describing the level of financial wealth of households, and their degree of portfolio diversification. We estimate age and wealth profiles for the ownership of risky assets and conditional portfolio shares and show that, as in other countries, and the United States and Italy in particular, the ownership profile displays more of a pronounced hump shape across age groups than does the conditional share.

Several key episodes in the evolution of U.K. household portfolios are of particular interest in comparison to other countries. The first is the experience of the United Kingdom in the 1980s. This decade saw dramatic, and rapid, changes in the levels of ownership of different assets: private pensions, housing, and stocks and shares.[1] In all cases, government supply-side policies were fairly critical in driving the changes—through the introduction of personal pensions, the "right-to-buy" policy, which sold off public housing to tenants at considerably less than the market rate, and the privatization of nationalized industries. In the case of share ownership, for example, the proportion of households owning shares more than doubled during a four-year period in the mid-1980s coinciding with the privatization of

British Telecom and British Gas. The extensive advertising provided by the government for its privatization program appeared to have been successful in attracting new share owners from younger and less well-educated groups (although not typically from middle- or lower-income groups). There is some evidence that the privatization experience, as well as reductions in transactions costs, had the effect of raising the level of share ownership more generally. Households that were too young to have experienced privatization directly are more likely to own shares than older cohorts at the same age. But the argument that the privatization process may have played an educational role in teaching people about share ownership is limited by the fact that a large proportion of share owners at the end of the 1990s held shares only in privatized industries or the recently demutualized building societies.

A second key feature of the United Kingdom is the government's use of tax incentives to try to encourage saving—through private pensions and designated "tax-free" savings schemes such as Tax Exempt Special Savings Accounts (TESSAs), Personal Equity Plans (PEPs), and Individual Savings Accounts (ISAs). We provide a detailed discussion of the current tax treatment of different assets in the United Kingdom in the context of chapter 3 in this book and present some evidence on the importance of tax effects on household portfolios.

Most of this chapter focuses on analysis of microdata on saving and asset holding, and we provide descriptive evidence for comparison with the other countries represented in this book. For brevity, we do not describe the system or institutional factors in the United Kingdom in particular detail unless it is necessary. Useful summaries of these issues include Budd and Campbell (1998) on pensions and Banks and Blundell (1994) on savings institutions more generally.

6.1 Data Sources

For a country that has been typically at the forefront of microdata collection there is surprisingly little information on household portfolios in the United Kingdom. Ideally, we would like to know how much wealth is held in which different assets and by which people. Such an analysis is not possible using any of the official household surveys in the United Kingdom. Compared to the other countries represented in this book, the information available on wealth is poor, a situation that is not the case for, say, income or expenditure.

We can look at ownership by exploiting information on spending and income in the Family Expenditure Survey (FES) to identify whether households have particular assets (although not how much they have).[2] FES data on incomes and expenditures have been used extensively in analysis of consumption growth, both over time and by different types of households (see Attanasio and Weber 1993 and Banks and Blundell 1994, for example). The FES contains almost no information on individuals' stocks of wealth, but information on interest income received from interest-bearing accounts, dividend income from stocks and shares, and contributions made to private pensions and life insurance policies can be used to construct indicator variables for whether households in the FES have particular assets. This is not as rich a data source as if we had information on the value of each asset, but the big advantage of the FES is that it has been collecting consistent data on income, spending, and demographics every year since 1978. Thus, it is possible to set up a cohort (or pseudo-panel) data set to document changes for different generations over the past twenty years, a unique opportunity to study long-term trends in asset ownership using microdata. These pseudo-panel techniques have become common empirical approaches for the analysis of dynamic economic relationships when long-panel data are not available (see Deaton 1985).

To looks at amounts of wealth held, we draw on a privately collected survey: the Financial Research Survey (FRS) collected by National Opinion Polls. This is an ongoing survey collecting information on around 4,800 individuals each month. Information is obtained on all financial assets and liabilities held, with banded data on balances for most, as well as specific brand and product ownership information for almost all. The survey also has demographic variables relating to the household of which the individual is a member, some data on incomes, and summary information on other financial products, such as pensions, mortgages, and insurance. Two earlier years of this survey were used by Banks, Dilnot, and Low (1995) to document the distribution of wealth in 1987–1988 and 1991–1992,[3] but in the bulk of the analysis here, we use data covering the period January 1997 to June 1998, although we also draw on results from earlier years.[4]

The primary unit of observation in the FRS is the individual rather than the household, although some questions do refer to the household in which they reside and the characteristics of other household members. This makes it difficult to draw direct comparisons between the FRS and other surveys such as the FES where the primary unit of analysis is the household.

A further issue is that wealth values in the survey are collected in bands. For the purposes of this chapter, we use the midpoints of the bands and an imputed value for top-coded individuals to estimate holdings.[5] In cases where people say they have a particular asset but cannot recall or refuse to say the balance, we impute the median value of those of the same age band and education group who hold that asset.[6]

A final issue that arises with any household or individual survey of wealth is the degree to which they accord with aggregate measures. The FRS does not oversample the wealthy and, given the inequality in the distribution of wealth, this leads to grossed-up totals for total financial wealth, and individual components, substantially underrepresenting the aggregate wealth of the economy.[7] Banks, Dilnot, and Low (1995) and Banks and Tanner (1999) show that the FRS accounts for only around 40 percent of aggregate financial wealth. The underrepresentation of the wealthiest U.K. households in the FRS is confirmed in table 6.4, where it is clear that the top 5 percent of the FRS wealth distribution looks similar to the top quarter of the distribution, a situation unlikely to be the case given the large degree of inequality of financial wealth holdings. However, asset ownership rates and estimates of median wealth holdings will be largely unaffected by such undersampling.

6.2 Portfolio Structures

6.2.1 Macroeconomic Data

Table 6.1 reports portfolio shares for different assets calculated using aggregate data at five-yearly intervals between 1980 and 1995. It shows the importance of housing and private pensions in household portfolios. In reality, pension wealth will be even more important than these figures indicate, since accrued entitlements to unfunded state pension wealth are not included. These can be substantial for current retiring cohorts but will decline in the future following

Table 6.1
Composition of household wealth

	1980	1985	1990	1995
Financial assets				
Total financial assets	£273 billion	£646 billion	£1,160 billion	£1,973 billion
Proportion of total financial wealth				
Cash, transaction, and savings accounts	0.337	0.275	0.286	0.215
National savings	0.040	0.047	0.031	0.028
Bonds	0.046	0.033	0.006	0.008
Stocks	0.139	0.113	0.095	0.171
Unit trusts and investment trusts	0.010	0.015	0.014	0.028
Life and pension funds	0.348	0.450	0.506	0.494
Other	0.080	0.067	0.064	0.056
Total financial assets	1.000	1.000	1.000	1.000
Total assets	£717 billion	£1,316 billion	£2,512 billion	£3,134 billion
Proportion of total wealth				
Financial assets	0.382	0.464	0.434	0.551
Real estate wealth	0.431	0.395	0.456	0.352
Building trade, assets, and land	0.079	0.055	0.041	0.029
Consumer durables	0.107	0.086	0.069	0.068
Total assets	1.000	1.000	1.000	1.000
Debt (as proportion of total assets)				
Mortgages	0.070	0.092	0.109	0.121
Other debts	0.045	0.055	0.030	0.023

Note: Figures for financial assets are taken from the personal sector balance sheet. Figures for total assets are taken from official wealth statistics compiled by the Inland Revenue Statistics. The personal sector balance sheet includes assets of nonprofit organizations and is therefore not strictly comparable with the Inland Revenue Statistics series, which are computed for the household sector. This accounts for the discrepancy between total financial assets in row 1 and the product of total assets (row 10) and the share of total assets that are held in financial assets (row 11). We stick to both sources of data here because of the extra detail afforded on financial assets by the personal sector balance sheet.

reductions in the generosity of the basic state pension and state earnings-related pension scheme (SERPS). As some guide to the potential importance of this component of wealth, the Pension Provision Group (1998) estimated that government liabilities in state unfunded pensions, given announced policy changes, are currently £950 billion—of the same order of magnitude as the amount in funded pensions and life insurance reported in table 6.1.

These aggregate statistics also give an insight into some of the key changes that have occurred in wealth holding in the United Kingdom in recent years. As in other countries, there has been a reduction in the importance of cash, transactions, and savings accounts in household portfolios and an increase in the importance of pensions and other risky assets during the 1980s.

One category of financial assets, National Savings, is peculiar to the United Kingdom. National Savings is a government agency providing savings and investment vehicles that are used to finance national borrowing. But the agency provides a wide range of assets, most of which do not have the characteristics of traditional government bonds. For example, they provide short- and medium-term deposit accounts paying fixed rates of interest, some instant access products, and various types of bond.[8] In the official aggregate statistics reported in table 6.1, it is not possible to distinguish between the amount of wealth held in each of these forms; hence, this item represents a very heterogeneous part of the portfolio. In the microeconomic analysis that follows, we are able to distinguish among different forms of National Savings products and group them with assets of similar characteristics.

Within total wealth, there has been a shift toward financial assets—driven largely by the increase in life and pension funds—and a decline in the relative importance of housing wealth. Also noticeable, however, is the cyclicality of real estate wealth, due to large fluctuations in property values. Table 6.1 also shows an increase in household indebtedness over the period as a whole—from 11 percent of total assets in 1980 to 14 percent of total assets in 1995—although all of the increase occurred between 1980 and 1985. Perhaps surprisingly given the increased use of credit cards, other debt fell as a proportion of total assets over the period (and remained constant in nominal terms). However, there was an increase in mortgage lending following the deregulation of the mortgage market during the 1980s (see Muellbauer and Murphy 1990).

Aggregate portfolio shares do not reveal much about the asset holdings of the majority of people. Given the inequality in the distribution of wealth, only a relatively few people account for most of the total. For example, in 1995 the top 1 percent of the wealth distribution owned 19 percent of total personal sector wealth, the wealthiest 5 percent owned 39 percent of total marketable wealth, and the bottom half of the wealth distribution accounted for only 7 percent of total wealth (Inland Revenue 1999).[9] Although this distribution is equalized somewhat by the inclusion of occupational pension rights, it is still the case that the top half of the wealth distribution accounts for 89 percent; hence, changes in the aggregate statistics could be driven by changes in the behavior of a very few—and very wealthy—individuals. For a more representative guide to the portfolios of the majority of the population, we therefore turn to microdata sources.

6.2.2   Survey Data on Asset Holding

Table 6.2 presents ownership rates from the FRS for a variety of detailed asset classes. By far the most commonly held assets are liquid interest-bearing accounts, held by almost 90 percent of the population. Long-term deposit accounts and certificates of deposit are much more rarely held.[10] Government bonds appear to be more widely held, with one-quarter of the population reporting ownership, although much of this reflects the prevalence of National Savings bonds, which tend to be held in small quantities for long time periods. Such holdings make up a very small portion of the financing of government debt (typically less than 2 percent in any one year), but are held by a wide number of households. Around one-fifth of the population holds equities directly, and 11.5 percent hold unit and investment trusts, intermediated investment vehicles that almost always will have equity components of one form or other. We look at these holdings in more detail in later sections.

In addition to information on stocks of financial assets, the FRS contains limited information on the ownership of other financial products, including life insurance and pension policies. We include measures of these in table 6.2. Around 22 percent of adults have an occupational pension. This represents around one-half of employees, as is confirmed in other surveys and official statistics.[11] For personal pensions, there is some evidence of underreporting in the FRS. Table

Table 6.2
Detailed asset and debt ownership rates

	Proportion holding	Mean portfolio share
Transactions accounts	0.778	—
Savings accounts	0.617	0.568
Deposit accounts	0.154	0.128
Government bonds	0.253	0.065
Other bonds	0.036	0.023
Stocks	0.216	0.131
Investment trusts, unit trusts etc.	0.115	0.084
Personal pensions (defined-contribution plans)	0.080	—
Occupational pensions (predominantly defined-benefit plans)	0.223	—
Life insurance policy	0.376	—
Housing wealth	0.598	—
Business wealth	0.046	—
Mortgage/real estate debt	0.318	—
Loan	0.142	—

Source: Financial Research Survey, 1997–1998.
Note: Mean portfolio share computed for those with positive financial wealth only.

6.2 shows 8 percent of the FRS sample owning personal pensions, whereas other studies estimate ownership rates to be around 25 percent of employees, corresponding to 11 percent of adults. Finally, life insurance funds are also one of the more commonly held assets, with 37.6 percent of the population owning policies in 1997–1998. If anything this is an underestimate, particularly in comparison to the figures we present later from the FES data, because the FRS classification does not include life insurance policies held in association with endowment mortgages, which were particularly popular in the home ownership boom of the 1980s. As a proxy for the ownership of business wealth, we report the proportion of the sample who are self-employed. Similarly, to proxy the ownership of housing wealth, we use a dummy to capture whether the respondent lives in a house that is owner occupied.

Banks and Tanner (1999) present evidence from the FES to show how the prevalence of broader portfolio items has on average changed over time. They show that for the group of assets encompassing savings and deposit accounts (but excluding transactions accounts), the proportion of the population holding such assets has risen only slowly over the past twenty years (see table 6A.1 in the chapter appendix for a summary of their results in particular years corresponding to the other country chapters of this book). In contrast, ownership of life insurance policies has declined slowly over the same period, possibly as a result of the change in tax treatment in 1984. The biggest trends in households' asset ownership rates over the past twenty years have been in the proportion of households owning stocks, pensions, and housing.

Table 6.2 confirms that as in other countries, financial wealth is not predominantly held in a risky form. Of people who have positive wealth, more than half of total financial wealth is held in the form of savings accounts. And although government bonds are widely held (almost solely as a result of ownership of National Savings products), balances are typically low and represent only a small proportion of total financial wealth. Finally shares represent a fairly small fraction of wealth—just over 13 percent. Many holdings acquired as a result of privatization and demutualization are relatively small.

Table 6.3 presents evidence on the correlation between ownership of different types of assets, where the types are defined according to their risk. The first column considers only financial assets: completely safe assets—saving and deposit accounts and fixed-return National Savings; partially safe assets—diversified portfolios of risky assets (mutual funds, investment trusts and unit trusts and PEPs); and risky assets—undiversified holdings of risky assets (stocks and bonds). The majority of the population holds either just safe assets or a combination of completely safe and risky assets. Fewer than one in ten of the sample hold assets in all three categories.

In column 2 of table 6.3, we consider the risk properties of a broader portfolio that adds pensions, life insurance, and housing to the partially safe assets category since they are, at least in principle, diversified and adds business assets to the risky assets category. This reveals a greater degree of portfolio diversification. The proportion of the population with only safe assets falls from 49.9 percent to 12.7 percent, important information when considering the nature of household financial wealth portfolios. In particular, the degree to which pensions are (considered) to be safe or fairly safe assets will be an important determinant of other items of U.K. household port-

Table 6.3
Diversification of household portfolios, financial assets only

Completely safe assets[a]	Partially safe assets[b]	Risky assets[c]	Proportion of sample using narrow definition	Proportion of sample using broad definition
0	0	0	0.0950	0.0579
0	0	1	0.0013	0.0008
0	1	0	0.0003	0.0364
0	1	1	0.0003	0.0019
1	0	0	0.4990	0.1274
1	0	1	0.2901	0.0388
1	1	0	0.0281	0.3768
1	1	1	0.0859	0.3601

Source: Financial Research Survey, 1997–1998.
Note: Sample includes individuals with positive financial wealth only. The three left-hand columns describe all the possible permutations of different asset types in the portfolio, with a 0 representing no holdings of each asset type and a 1 representing some holdings. The two right-hand categories represent the proportions of the sample falling into each portfolio type category when risky assets are defined both narrowly and broadly (see text).
[a] Narrow definition: Saving and deposit accounts, fixed-return National Savings products. Broad definition: Same as narrow definition.
[b] Narrow definition: Mutual funds and investment trusts. Broad definition: Same as narrow definition, plus housing, private pensions, and life insurance policies.
[c] Narrow definition: Equity, bonds. Broad definition: Same as narrow definition, plus business assets.

folios, particularly given that private pension provision now covers around three-quarters of employees.

Table 6A.2 presents evidence on the evolution of portfolios over time using data from the FES and constructing a classification to correspond to the one presented here. There have been large changes in average portfolio types, particularly between 1978 and 1988. The substantial increases are in the proportion of households holding mixed portfolios, predominantly as a result of increasing ownership of shares, housing wealth, and pensions.

6.2.3   Variation by Age and Wealth

Univariate Analysis
Unconditional population averages conceal important variation in portfolio allocations. Other chapters in this book show important

Table 6.4
Composition of household financial assets, by wealth quartile

Proportion of total financial wealth held in ...	Wealth quartile				95th percentile
	I	II	III	IV	
Instant-access savings accounts	0.793	0.811	0.414	0.255	0.234
Deposit accounts	0.026	0.038	0.181	0.265	0.228
Government bonds	0.130	0.031	0.044	0.055	0.082
Other bonds	0.001	0.002	0.017	0.075	0.088
Stocks	0.042	0.103	0.238	0.142	0.171
Investment trusts, unit trusts, etc.	0.007	0.015	0.105	0.208	0.196

Source: Financial Research Survey, 1997–1998.
Note: Sample includes individuals with positive financial wealth only.

variations across household portfolios by wealth level and by age, and here we present comparable evidence for the United Kingdom.

Table 6.4 shows how portfolio shares vary according to total financial wealth (limited information on housing and pension wealth means that we cannot look at portfolio shares out of total wealth).[12] We divide the sample of people with positive financial wealth into wealth quartiles and also look separately at the portfolios of the wealthiest 5 percent (who are also included in the column for the top quartile). As expected, the concentration in risky assets increases further up the wealth distribution, although in the top quartile, risky assets are more likely to be held in the form of investment trusts, unit trusts, and PEPs as opposed to direct holdings of stocks. In the United Kingdom, the privatization of previously nationalized utilities and the demutualization of building societies brought share ownership down the wealth distribution into areas of the population that were not previously typically holding other forms of risky financial assets. The prevalence of government bonds in the bottom quartile reflects the importance of National Savings products for lower-income or lower-wealth households, possibly as a result of their being sold in post offices. These assets are not so important in the middle of the wealth distribution. What is also striking in table 6.4 is the degree to which the portfolios of the top 5 percent of the wealth distribution resemble those of the top quartile, pointing at the undersampling of the very wealthy in the FRS data. A priori, given the inequality in the wealth distribution, and particularly in the distribution of liquid financial wealth, one would expect this group to be holding substantially higher fractions of risky assets.

Table 6.5
Importance of risky assets, by wealth

Wealth decile	Unconditional portfolio share in risky assets	Proportion with risky assets	Conditional portfolio share in risky assets
1	0.133	0.228	0.582
2	0.219	0.452	0.484
3	0.127	0.286	0.445
4	0.156	0.399	0.393
5	0.194	0.371	0.523
6	0.418	0.775	0.541
7	0.409	0.758	0.539
8	0.397	0.752	0.528
9	0.457	0.845	0.542
10	0.526	0.925	0.569
All	0.304	0.579	0.525

Source: Financial Research Survey, 1997–1998.
Note: Sample includes individuals with positive financial wealth only. "Risky assets" include mutual funds and investment trusts, equity, and bonds. The unconditional shares are computed over all households in the decile. The conditional shares are computed only over those households in the decile that hold some risky assets.

Table 6.5 looks in more detail at portfolio shares held in risky assets across the wealth distribution, dividing those with positive financial wealth into deciles. The first column of the table gives the average portfolio share held in risky assets across all households in the decile.[13] This "unconditional" share rises with wealth, as would be expected. However, such an average compounds two effects: the probability of holding any risky assets at all and the amount held in risky assets by those who hold them. These two effects are separated out in columns 3 and 4. Column 3 shows that the proportion of each decile holding any risky assets rises with wealth, as expected. However, looking at the average portfolio share only for the households that have some risky assets (the "conditional" share), there is little variation by wealth level, indicating that entry costs may be important in determining portfolio choices, as outlined in other chapters in this book. On average, those who have any risky assets hold around half of their financial asset portfolio in risky assets, and this fraction does not vary substantially with size of the portfolio.

Table 6.6
Importance of risky assets, by age

Age	Unconditional share in risky assets	Proportion with risky assets	Conditional share in risky assets
Under 30	0.227	0.414	0.549
30–39	0.284	0.517	0.549
40–49	0.324	0.595	0.545
50–59	0.359	0.657	0.548
60–69	0.344	0.659	0.522
70 and over	0.263	0.586	0.449
All	0.304	0.597	0.525

Source: Financial Research Survey, 1997–1998.
Note: Sample includes individuals with positive financial wealth only. "Risky assets" include mutual funds and investment trusts, equity, and bonds. The unconditional shares are computed over all households in the age group. The conditional shares are computed only over those households in the age group that hold some risky assets.

Table 6.6 presents the results of a similar analysis of portfolio shares by age. Both the unconditional shares and the ownership rates of risky assets display a hump-shaped age profile, at least in cross section. The proportion of people with positive wealth who hold risky assets rises and peaks at ages 50 to 70 at almost two-thirds, before falling in the oldest age group. This downturn could be a result of trading out of risky assets as individuals age or could represent a cohort effect—that these older households were never as likely to own risky assets.[14] The hump shape in unconditional risky asset shares (for those with positive wealth) is more pronounced, with a fall of over 25 percent between the 50–59 and 70 and over groups. Once again, however, looking at the "conditional" shares, for only those holding risky assets, the profile is to a large extent flat. The one exception here is for the very oldest group of the population, who, if they hold risky assets, tend to hold less of their wealth in this form than their younger counterparts do.

Finally, drawing on the analysis of earlier years of the FRS data in Banks, Dilnot, and Low (1995), it is possible to look at how this age profile for ownership of risky financial assets has changed over time.[15] Table 6A.3 compares the most recent ownership profiles to those from earlier years of data (adjusting the group of risky assets slightly to get a definition that is comparable across years). It shows that, if anything, the age profile has become slightly less hump shaped (at least in relative terms) as a result of a disproportionate increase in risky asset holding among the youngest individuals in the sample.

Multivariate Analysis

Here we estimate age and wealth profiles for the ownership and importance of risky assets conditioning on other covariates and allowing for time effects. Interpreting a cross-sectional pattern across groups as an age profile potentially conflates age, cohort, and time effects. Hence, some identification strategy is required for such an interpretation to be valid. When considering either the likelihood of risky assets being held or their relative importance in the portfolio, cyclical asset returns ought to be important, and hence time effects (picking up movements in the profile from one year to the next) will be crucial. Therefore, in keeping with the other chapters in this book, we choose to allow unrestricted time effects and are required to assume away cohort effects to interpret differences across age groups as a true age profile.

Table 6.7 presents the marginal effects from two probit regressions relating the probability of ownership of risky assets to age bands and wealth deciles, with a number of other control variables, including income deciles, education, household composition, regional effects, ethnic group, and home ownership status.[16] The sample is restricted to individuals with positive financial wealth to facilitate the construction of wealth deciles and portfolio shares for risky assets. The age profile in ownership rates retains its humped shape, whether one controls for wealth levels or not, with the likelihood of ownership of risky assets rising until age 65 and then falling for retired households. The degree of hump shape in the profiles is reduced when one controls for the level of wealth; the difference between someone aged less than 30 and someone aged 60–64 falls from 23 percentage points to around 12 percentage points. The effect of education is also reduced but remains positive and significant. Ownership of risky assets increases with wealth, even controlling for these other factors, as would be expected.

Turning to the age and wealth profiles for the conditional portfolio share, the profiles look very different. The estimates for selectivity-adjusted regressions of the portfolio share on the same variables as above are presented in table 6.8. That is, the probits from table 6.7

Table 6.7
Probit estimation for ownership of risky assets

| Variable | Dependent variable: Whether individual has risky assets | | | |
	Marginal effect	Standard error	Marginal effect	Standard error
Age				
30–34	0.061	0.010	0.047	0.011
35–39	0.103	0.010	0.068	0.011
40–44	0.118	0.010	0.080	0.011
45–49	0.116	0.010	0.063	0.011
50–54	0.173	0.009	0.088	0.011
55–59	0.201	0.009	0.107	0.011
60–64	0.231	0.009	0.123	0.011
65–69	0.220	0.009	0.074	0.012
70 and over	0.208	0.008	0.088	0.010
Education				
Some postcompulsory schooling	0.075	0.005	0.043	0.005
Some college education	0.149	0.006	0.090	0.007
Wealth decile				
2	—	—	0.202	0.008
3	—	—	0.031	0.010
4	—	—	0.125	0.009
5	—	—	0.095	0.009
6	—	—	0.366	0.004
7	—	—	0.361	0.005
8	—	—	0.350	0.005
9	—	—	0.397	0.004
10	—	—	0.440	0.003

Source: Financial Research Survey, 1997–1998.
Note: The base group is a less than 30 year old with only compulsory schooling in the bottom wealth decile. Both specifications also include controls for income decile, number of adults and children in household, ethnic group, home ownership, a dummy to capture income nonresponse, and regional dummies. "Risky assets" include mutual funds and investment trusts, equity, and bonds.

Table 6.8
Age, education, and wealth profiles for conditional shares of risky assets

Variable	Parameter	Standard error	Parameter	Standard error
		Dependent variable: Portfolio share in risky assets		
Age				
30–34	−0.009	0.017	−0.020	0.017
35–39	0.001	0.018	−0.020	0.017
40–44	−0.010	0.018	−0.034	0.017
45–49	−0.010	0.018	−0.038	0.017
50–54	0.003	0.019	−0.049	0.017
55–59	0.026	0.020	−0.042	0.018
60–64	0.018	0.021	−0.059	0.018
65–69	−0.003	0.021	−0.087	0.018
70 and over	−0.054	0.019	−0.128	0.017
Education				
Some postcompulsory schooling	0.021	0.007	0.010	0.006
Some college education	0.071	0.011	0.044	0.008
Wealth decile				
2	—	—	−0.107	0.029
3	—	—	−0.175	0.027
4	—	—	−0.215	0.026
5	—	—	−0.090	0.025
6	—	—	0.003	0.042
7	—	—	0.002	0.041
8	—	—	−0.007	0.039
9	—	—	0.026	0.045
10	—	—	0.072	0.049
Mills ratio	0.133	0.038	0.129	0.049

Source: Financial Research Survey, 1997–1998.
Note: The base group is a less than 30 year old with only compulsory schooling in the bottom wealth decile. Both specifications also include controls for income decile, number of adults and children in household, ethnic group, home ownership, and a dummy to capture income nonresponse. The sample includes only individuals who own risky assets. The Mills ratio term for individual i is simply the selection correction term, computed by the ratio $\phi(X_i'\beta)/\Phi(X_i'\beta)$ where β are the probit parameters from table 6.7. "Risky assets" include mutual funds and investment trusts, equity, and bonds.

are used as first-stage regression in a two-step Heckman procedure where we omit regional dummies from the conditional share equation to identify the selection term (see Heckman 1979 or chapter 4, this book). When controls for wealth are not included, the age profile for the conditional share looks relatively flat (particularly for age 30 and above), with the only significant parameter being for those aged over 75, who are likely to hold less of their wealth in risky forms. The flatness of the age profile is in keeping with the univariate results in table 6.6 and is similar to the findings for other country studies in this book, particularly the United States and Italy. Although the differences by education (particularly higher education) are statistically significant, they are small in magnitude, with the most educated holding only 7 percentage points more of their portfolio in risky forms. Controlling for wealth, the conditional share falls more substantially by age (statistically significantly after age 40), and the educational differentials are less substantial, as one would expect. Finally, above the lowest decile, the conditional share broadly rises with wealth. This is in keeping with the simple theoretical predictions of classical portfolio theory, already outlined in this book.

Taken together, these results imply that most of the variation (across age or wealth) in the importance of risky assets in household portfolios measured by the unconditional portfolio shares is due to differences in ownership rates, as opposed to the proportion of the portfolio held in risky forms. This would suggest a possible role for entry costs or other fixed costs in explaining portfolio holdings. Were we to have data on conditional shares prior to 1987, we could test this hypothesis more directly, since there is some evidence that such costs fell in the mid-1980s during the period of privatization of large parts of the public sector industries and the deregulation of financial markets in the United Kingdom. It is to this episode that we now turn.

6.3 Share Ownership and the Privatization Episode

The 1980s was a period of enormous change in wealth ownership in the United Kingdom. The number of people with shares and private pensions and owning their homes increased dramatically during the decade (see Table 6A.1). In each case, government policies were important factors driving the changes—in particular the introduction of personal pensions, the right-to-buy policy that sold off public sector

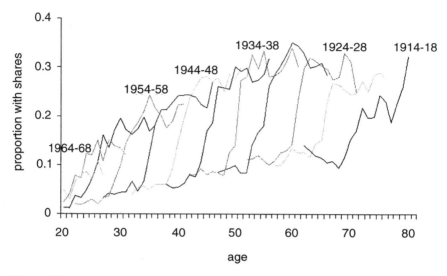

Figure 6.1
Cohort profiles of share ownership. *Source:* Family Expenditure Survey, 1978–1996.

houses to their tenants at below-market prices, and the privatization of nationalized industries. In this section we focus on the rise
in share ownership and use FES data to look at ownership rates of
stocks and shares since 1978. Although the information on share
ownership is imputed (from receipt of dividend income), it matches
well to all other sources of information on share ownership in the
United Kingdom over this period.[17]

Figures from the FES show that at the beginning of the 1980s,
fewer than one in ten households owned shares directly. By the end
of the decade, it was more than one in five. Most of the increase
occurred during a concentrated four-year period, from 1985 to 1988,
coinciding with the heavily advertised flotation of a number of public utilities, including British Telecom (1984) and British Gas (1986).
Cohort profiles of share ownership are plotted in figure 6.1. Share
ownership increased around the time of privatization across almost
all cohorts, but particularly among people who were in their 30s, 40s,
and 50s at the time. The cohort born between 1944 and 1948, for
example, experienced a rise in the level of share ownership from 6
percent in 1984 (when their average age was 38) to 28 percent in 1988.

As the level of share ownership has increased, the profile of a
typical shareholder has changed. Shareholders are, on average,

younger and relatively less well educated than twenty years ago. The average age of heads of households owning stocks and shares fell from 56.5 in 1978 to 51.7 in 1996 (while the average age of all household heads did not change significantly over the same period). And the proportion of share owners with higher education has fallen. In 1978, 63.7 percent of households with shares had a head with postcompulsory education, compared with 33.5 percent of all households. By 1988, the proportion of share-owning households with heads with postcompulsory education had fallen to 61.7 percent, while the proportion of all household heads with post-compulsory education had actually increased to 41.3 percent. However, while the differentials in share ownership between age and education groups have fallen, multivariate analysis shows that the differential effect of income actually increased over the period as a whole. These findings fit the conclusions of Haliassos and Bertaut (1995) in their analysis of low levels of share ownership in the United States. They attribute relatively low levels of share ownership, given the size of returns, to a lack of information. They conclude that an increase in share ownership may be brought about by extensive initial advertising plus a continuous flow of information, but that this may not be effective in drawing stockholders from lower-income groups. This is exactly what happened in the United Kingdom during the 1980s. Extensive initial advertising at the time of privatization resulted in higher levels of share ownership among younger and less well-educated households, but share owners were still predominantly drawn from those at the top of the income distribution.

Clearly a large part of the increase in share ownership is attributable to privatization and the fact that a number of people became shareholders for the first time by buying shares in privatized industries. An obvious question is whether people's experience of buying privatization shares had a knock-on effect, raising levels of share ownership more generally. If relatively low levels of share ownership reflect high transactions costs—and informational costs—then the increase in share ownership following privatization is likely to have resulted in higher levels of ownership of other shares as people learned about share ownership through privatization. In fact, even in the absence of privatization, we would expect falling transactions costs since the early 1980s, and in particular the reduction in stamp duty on share purchases, to have meant more widespread share ownership.[18]

The evidence on this issue is mixed. The cohort profiles show that the very youngest cohorts—those who were too young to experience privatization firsthand—have levels of share ownership that are higher than those of older cohorts at the same age. This suggests that the increase in share ownership since the early 1980s was not restricted simply to cohorts that could directly buy shares in privatized industries. But evidence on the types of shares that people hold shows that even by the late 1990s, a large number of share owners still owned shares only in denationalized industries or in a demutualized building society. In the latter case, the fact that someone owns shares arises not from any active decision to purchase shares on their part, but is a windfall to anyone with a mortgage or savings account with a building society at the time that it converts to a bank.[19] This form of share ownership is fairly widespread. For example, the British Household Panel Survey collected information on whether anyone had received a conversion share windfall in the twelve months prior to September 1997, a period that included the conversion of the Halifax, the largest building society in the United Kingdom. In total, one-quarter of the sample reported that they had received shares over this period. Of course, not everyone who received a windfall kept the shares, but only 17 percent of those who received a windfall said that they spent it (and therefore definitely cashed in their shares).

Table 6.9 summarizes equity holdings in the 1997–1998 FRS according to the type of shares that people have. It highlights the importance of denationalization and demutualization in explaining relatively high levels of share ownership in the United Kingdom. Nearly two-thirds of all shareholders (64 percent) own shares in a demutualized building society or a denationalized industry, and nearly 40 percent of shareholders own shares only in this form. The prevalence of mutual funds in share ownership is likely to reflect relatively high levels of ownership of Personal Equity Plans, which represent a tax-advantaged way to own shares (we discuss these in the next section).

Privatization in the United Kingdom clearly had a big effect on levels of share ownership, causing the number of households owning shares to more than double in the mid-1980s. But evidence that privatization played an educational role in encouraging share ownership more generally is limited. It is true that levels of share ownership among younger households are higher than they were

Table 6.9
Share ownership

Equity holdings	Percentage
No equity holdings	73.36
Denationalized/demutualized shares only	10.09
Other shares only	3.35
Denationalized/demutualized shares and other shares	1.74
Mutual funds only	5.07
Mutual funds and denationalized/demutualized shares	3.44
Mutual funds and other shares	1.15
Mutual funds, denationalized/demutualized shares, and other shares	1.80

Source: Financial Research Survey, 1997–1998.
Note: Denationalized shares are shares held in former nationalized industries. Demutualized shares are windfall shares given to savers in building societies when these converted to banks. Other shares refer to direct holdings of equity (i.e., not in mutual funds) other than those in demutualized building societies or former nationalized industries. Mutual funds include unit trusts, investment funds, and Personal Equity Plans.

twenty years ago, possibly reflecting more widespread knowledge about share ownership and lower transactions costs. But ten years after privatization, many people with shares have very limited shareholdings, often still holding shares only in denationalized industries or in recently demutualized industries. It is worth bearing in mind when considering the degree of portfolio diversification in the United Kingdom that a very large proportion of shareholders who acquired shares through privatization or demutualization own them in only one company.

6.4   Tax Incentives and Asset Holding

The final issue we deal with is that of potential tax effects on household portfolios. This is an important issue in the United Kingdom, where the tax treatment of different financial products varies considerably. This is a result of the introduction of several designated tax-free savings schemes introduced over the past twenty years specifically with the intention of promoting saving (either in aggregate or within certain groups) as well as successive reforms to the tax treatment of individual assets, such as housing and pensions.

In chapter 3 on taxation Poterba highlights six margins at which one might expect tax to matter in portfolio decisions: the selection of assets, the allocation of wealth into the various assets of the portfolio, the location of assets within broader tax envelopes, the use of borrowing, the frequency or timing of trading, and the use of intermediaries to hold portfolios. Of these margins, only the borrowing and frequency of trading margins are likely to be relatively unimportant given the current U.K. system. With the introduction of Personal Equity Plans in 1986 and Individual Savings Accounts in 1999, both of which allow individuals to earn tax-free returns on assets held within the scheme, the issue of tax envelopes has become a real one in the United Kingdom, as in the United States. Unlike the United States, however, there are no restrictions on when or how often capital can be withdrawn from the plan. Prior to the introduction of PEPs and ISAs, however, the selection and allocation margins will have been the most important, but estimating tax effects in this earlier period is complicated by the fact that there was little variation in tax treatments (over and above the individual's marginal tax rate) that was not also correlated with variation in the risk, return, or liquidity characteristics of the assets in question. Hence we focus on the decision to hold designated tax-exempt saving products. The incentives to hold savings in this form should be greater for individuals with higher marginal tax rates.

Table 6.10 presents a summary of the current tax treatment of different classes of assets according to whether tax is imposed on contributions, returns, or withdrawals.[20] The form of saving with the least favorable tax treatment is money held in an interest-bearing account. Not only is the income paid into such an account taxed at the marginal rate, but the full nominal interest income is also taxed—at 20 percent if the individual is a lower- or basic-rate taxpayer or 40 percent if the individual is a higher-rate taxpayer.[21] In the case of direct holdings of stocks and shares, both the contributions and returns are subject to tax, although tax is payable only on capital gains greater than an annual allowance (currently £7,100), which means that in reality, very few individuals pay capital gains tax. The important exceptions to this treatment of cash and equity are the specially designated tax-free savings schemes—before 1999 a PEP or TESSA and after 1999 an ISA. All three receive the same prepaid expenditure tax treatment. In other words, payments into the scheme are taxed but returns and withdrawals are tax free.

PEPs, introduced in 1987, provided tax relief for limited direct and indirect holdings of equity or certain unit or investment trusts (up to

Table 6.10
Tax treatment of different assets

Asset type	Tax treatment			
	Contributions	Income	Capital gain	Withdrawal
Interest-bearing accounts	Taxed	Taxed	—	Exempt
Stocks and shares	Taxed	Taxed	Taxed[a]	Exempt
ISAs, PEPs, TESSAs	Taxed	Exempt[b]	Exempt	Exempt
Owner-occupied housing	Taxed[c]	Exempt	Exempt	Exempt
Private pensions	Exempt[d]	Exempt[e]	Exempt	Taxed[f]

[a] Capital gains tax only on realized gains in excess of annual allowance (currently around $11,000 per year). This allowance exceeds the realized gains of the vast majority of households.
[b] Ten percent tax credit repaid on dividend income in ISA and PEP.
[c] Ten percent mortgage interest tax relief on interest on first £30,000.
[d] Employee contributions are exempt from income tax but are subject to employer's and employee's National Insurance. Employer contributions are exempt from income tax and from all National Insurance.
[e] Repayment of dividend tax credit (abolished in 1997).
[f] Individuals can withdraw 25 percent of accumulation (over and above NIC contributions) as a tax-free lump sum.

£6,000 a year in a general PEP and £3,600 in a single company PEP). The total amount of money held in PEPs by April 1999 (after which no new PEPs could be taken out) was £58.6 billion,[22] and they were held by more than one in ten individuals.

TESSAs, introduced in 1991, provided tax relief for interest income on funds held in designated bank and building society accounts, provided that the capital remained untouched for five years. Savers could invest up to £9,000 over the five years: £3,000 during the first year and £1,800 in each of the four subsequent years, up to the maximum. Approximately 2 million TESSAs were opened during the first three months that they were available. By March 1999, the total amount invested in TESSAs was just over £30 billion held in 5.7 million accounts.[23]

ISAs replaced TESSAs and PEPs from April 1999. They provide a single tax-free savings vehicle for holdings of cash, life insurance, and stocks and shares. They are subject to an overall annual investment limit of £5,000 (£7,000 in the first year) with separate limits of £1,000 on the amount that can be invested in life insurance and £1,000 (£3,000 in the first year) on the amount that can be invested in cash. This is a lower amount than could have been invested in a

Table 6.11
Ownership rates of PEPs and TESSAs, by tax status

	Proportion of sample with			
	Neither	TESSA only	PEP only	Both PEP and TESSA
Basic-rate taxpayer	0.8215	0.0517	0.1014	0.0254
Higher-rate taxpayer	0.6016	0.0492	0.2774	0.0718
Nontaxpayer	0.9434	0.0209	0.0301	0.0560
Total	0.8643	0.0388	0.0781	0.0188

Source: Financial Research Survey, 1997–1998.

TESSA and PEP. Also, the rate of the dividend tax credit has been reduced from 20 percent in a PEP to 10 percent in an ISA, making the total value of the tax relief less generous. However, ISAs offer an opportunity for tax-free saving to people who do not want to hold equity or tie their money up for five years—typically poorer savers.

Clearly, higher-rate taxpayers have the biggest incentive to hold TESSAs and PEPs instead of ordinary interest-bearing accounts or direct holdings of equity. Table 6.11 shows that, unconditionally, they are much more likely to own TESSAs and PEPs than basic rate taxpayers or nontaxpayers. Twenty-eight percent of higher-rate tax-payers hold PEPs only, 5 percent hold TESSAs only, and 7 percent hold both a PEP and a TESSA. The fact that 6 percent of non-taxpayers also hold at least one of these tax-free savings schemes might reflect previous savings decisions made when they were tax-payers. Also, both products offer rates of return that are competitive with similar non-tax-free savings vehicles, and both have been fairly heavily advertised.

Of course, the correlation between tax status and take-up of tax-free savings schemes could simply reflect the effect of other factors such as age, income, wealth, or education that are correlated with tax status. In table 6.12, we pursue an analysis corresponding to that of Poterba and Sandwick (1999) reported in chapter 3 in this book. The first four columns of the table report the results of a probit regression of PEP ownership on tax status and these other characteristics, both with and without controls for wealth.[24]

As in the United States, there is some evidence that tax has an effect on portfolio choices, as would be predicted by the theory. Be-

Table 6.12
Probit results

| | Dependent variable: Whether individual owns a PEP | | | |
	Marginal effect	Standard error	Marginal effect	Standard error
Nontaxpayer	−0.080	0.002	−0.059	0.002
Higher-rate taxpayer	0.123	0.008	0.061	0.006
Wealth	No	No	Yes	Yes
Other controls	Yes	Yes	Yes	Yes

| | Dependent variable: Whether individual owns an investment trust or a unit trust | | | |
	Marginal effect	Standard error	Marginal effect	Standard error
Nontaxpayer	−0.030	0.001	−0.021	0.001
Higher-rate taxpayer	0.035	0.004	0.007	0.003
Wealth	No	No	Yes	Yes
Other controls	Yes	Yes	Yes	Yes

Source: Financial Research Survey, 1997–1998.
Note: All specifications include controls for age, education, income decile, number of adults and children in household, ethnic group, home ownership, and a dummy to capture income nonresponse.

ing a nontaxpayer reduces the probability of having a PEP by 6 percentage points (compared to being a basic-rate taxpayer), while being a higher-rate taxpayer increases the probability of being a PEP holder by 6 percentage points, even conditional on age, education, wealth, and other demographic variables. However, there is always the possibility that unobservables, affecting both tax status and portfolio choices, are driving the correlation picked up in the top half of table 6.12. More striking, therefore, are the results presented in the bottom half of the table, where we perform the same analysis for ownership of unit trusts and investment trusts, which are similar investment vehicles to PEPs but subject to tax.[25]

There are still significant effects of tax status on the probability of ownership, suggesting that some of the observed effect of tax status on PEP ownership may have been picking up broader income effects, nonlinearities in the effects of other characteristics, or unobservables. However, the coefficients on tax status in the regressions for ownership of unit trusts and investment trusts are far smaller than they are for PEPs, suggesting that tax status has a much bigger effect for tax-free savings products, as we would expect. In particular, when controlling for wealth, individuals with high marginal tax rates are only 0.7 percentage points more likely to hold a unit trust or investment trust, compared with being 6 percentage points more likely to hold a PEP. The estimates therefore suggest evidence of tax effects, at least in the selection of assets within household portfolios, as found in the United States and documented elsewhere in this book.

6.5 Conclusion

This chapter provides empirical evidence on the portfolio holdings of U.K. households. Since household portfolios are diverse and the inequality in wealth holdings is high, aggregate figures are not necessarily good indicators of the portfolios of the majority of households. Additional data from surveys of individuals and households are therefore also used to look at portfolio patterns. A number of key patterns emerge, many of them shared with other countries examined in this book.

Large amounts of wealth are held in the form of pensions and housing. To get a true measure of the degree of portfolio diversification, it is important to take this into account, since pensions and housing are risky assets. Looking only at holdings of financial assets (not including pensions), most households do not hold large fractions of their financial portfolio in risky assets. A possible explanation is that transactions costs or information failures generate inertia in the demand for risky financial assets. Such a hypothesis is consistent with the finding that conditional portfolio shares of risky assets are typically large, even for those with low levels of wealth or for younger individuals. Even controlling for other characteristics, the conditional portfolio share for risky assets does not display as much variation as the ownership probabilities or as much as the classical theory (in the absence of such transaction costs or information failures) would predict.

The United Kingdom has experienced growth in holdings of risky financial assets over the past twenty years. During the 1980s, shares in newly privatized industries were taken up by many people who had not previously owned shares. By the end of the 1980s, the differentials in share ownership between age and education groups had fallen, although the differential effect of income actually increased over the period. This finding fits the analysis by Haliassos and Bertaut (1995) on the likely effects of increased information on patterns of share ownership. However, the argument that privatization played an educational role in teaching people about the process of and benefits from share ownership is limited by the fact that even by the 1990s, a large number of share owners owned shares only in privatized (or recently demutualized) companies.

Finally, we have analyzed the tax treatment of savings products in the United Kingdom and the potential effects on portfolio choice. Probit regressions for the ownership of tax-favored assets, in comparison to similar assets with the tax exemption, show that, controlling for other factors, marginal tax rates are important in determining asset ownership. These results are in accordance with those found by Poterba in the United States and discussed elsewhere in this book.

Although the United Kingdom has highly developed financial markets, a wide variety of financial products available, and considerable variation in the taxation of assets, ultimately we are limited in our ability to test rigorously the predictions of portfolio theory (either neoclassical or otherwise) by a lack of data. As in many other countries, there is very little information on household portfolios and no survey evidence on potential transactions costs, information failures, or other forms of rigidities that may lead to inertia in household portfolios. What data we do have in the United Kingdom, and the evidence from other countries examined in this book, suggest that such issues are important. A high priority for future research is to collect information on such variables, along with more detailed information on portfolios, including housing and pension wealth.

Appendix: Asset Ownership Rates over Time

Table 6A.1
Broad asset ownership rates over time

	Proportion of sample, by year					
	1978	1988	1990	1992	1994	1996
Savings accounts[a]	0.544	0.652	0.611	0.670	0.632	0.604
Bonds[b]	—	0.025	0.017	0.017	0.014	0.012
Stocks[c]	0.091	0.221	0.234	0.236	0.220	0.231
Life insurance[d]	0.781	0.735	0.724	0.708	0.683	0.655
Pensions[e]	0.388	0.437	0.471	0.443	0.414	0.419
Housing[f]	0.528	0.661	0.665	0.663	0.682	0.665
Mortgage	0.324	0.433	0.444	0.432	0.450	0.445

Source: Family Expenditure Survey, 1978–1996.
Note: Sample of households with head aged 20–80.
[a] Include National Savings Investment and Ordinary accounts. Ownership defined on the basis of receipt of interest income during previous twelve months.
[b] Bonds cannot be separated from stocks in 1978 and do not include National Savings products.
[c] Include unit trusts and PEPs. Ownership defined on basis of receipt of dividend income during previous twelve months.
[d] Includes fixed-term insurance, mortgage protection policies, death and burial policies, all endowment policies (including house purchase endowments), and annuities. Defined on the basis of current contributions.
[e] Include occupational and personal pensions, defined on the basis of receipt of private pension income or contributions made into an occupational or personal pension or payment of contracted-out rate of National Insurance.
[f] Includes ownership with a mortgage as well as outright ownership.

Table 6A.2
Diversification of household portfolios over time, financial and nonfinancial assets (broad definition)

Com-pletely safe	Par-tially safe	Risky	Proportion of sample, by year					
			1978	1988	1990	1992	1994	1996
0	0	0	0.0607	0.0722	0.0739	0.0862	0.0964	0.1096
0	0	1	0.0044	0.0054	0.0059	0.0041	0.0057	0.0041
0	1	0	0.3495	0.2172	0.2402	0.1950	0.2144	0.2213
0	1	1	0.0360	0.0477	0.0620	0.0398	0.0456	0.0539
1	0	0	0.0240	0.0277	0.0299	0.0341	0.0372	0.0378
1	0	1	0.0044	0.0055	0.0057	0.0078	0.0052	0.0073
1	1	0	0.4229	0.3783	0.3354	0.3694	0.3561	0.3195
1	1	1	0.0981	0.2459	0.2469	0.2636	0.2393	0.2465

Source: Family Expenditure Survey, 1978–1996.
Note: For definitions, see table 6.3. However, since the FES category for safe assets does not include transactions accounts that do not pay interest, the incidence of households with safe-only portfolios (1,0,0) is lower, and the proportion of "none" (0,0,0) is higher than in table 6.3.

Table 6A.3
Importance of risky assets, by age

Age	Unconditional portfolio shares, by year		
	1987/88	1991/92	1997/98
Under 30	0.049	0.078	0.165
30–34	0.082	0.110	0.217
35–39	0.092	0.123	0.264
40–44	0.107	0.138	0.264
45–49	0.112	0.160	0.274
50–54	0.124	0.168	0.299
55–59	0.107	0.181	0.311
60–64	0.096	0.131	0.295
65–69	0.095	0.140	0.257
70 and above	0.068	0.119	0.181
All	0.085	0.135	0.241

Source: Family Research Survey, 1987–1988, 1991–1992, and 1997–1998.
Note: Sample includes individuals with positive financial wealth only. In order to get a consistent definition over time, the definition of risky assets has been adjusted and is not directly comparable with that used in table 6.6. The unconditional shares are computed over all households in the age group.

Notes

This study forms part of the Institute for Fiscal Studies (IFS) research program into the changing distribution of consumption, economic resources and the welfare of households funded by the Leverhulme Trust, to which we are very grateful. Cofunding was provided by the Economic and Social Research Council (ESRC) Centre for the Microeconomic Analysis of Fiscal Policy at IFS. Many thanks are also due to National Opinion Polls (NOP) Financial for providing us with the FRS data used in this study and to Nick Watkins and Julia Beaver at NOP for helpful discussions during our subsequent analysis of the survey. Material from the FES made available by the Office for National Statistics (ONS) through the ESRC data archive has been used by permission of the controller of Her Majesty's Stationery Office (HMSO). Neither the ONS, the ESRC Data Archive, the Leverhulme Trust, nor NOP Financial bears any responsibility for the analysis or interpretation of the data reported here. Any errors are attributable solely to the authors.

1. For further discussion of these changes, see Johnson and Tanner (1998).

2. For a detailed analysis of the information in the FES, see Banks and Tanner (1999).

3. At that time, the survey was being conducted differently and as a result had much smaller sample sizes.

4. We pool data across the eighteen-month period. In total, there are over 75,000 individuals in the sample, distributed evenly over the eighteen-month period, with an average of 4,244 observations per month. Our sample excludes people who are aged 21 or under and those in full-time education. For a detailed analysis of the information in the FRS, see Banks and Tanner (1999).

5. One alternative would be to report minima and maxima for each asset or asset group, but when aggregating across assets, the banded estimates can very quickly become uninformatively wide, so we use midpoints instead. We have tried alternative estimators and confirmed that the results change little when using different assumptions or more flexible techniques such as grouped estimation. Primarily this is because the bands are very tight (within £10 or £100) wherever there is a large density of data and the number of assets held is typically low.

6. All in all, 25 percent of observations require some imputation, although only 4 percent of the sample (less than a fifth of those for whom some imputation is required) refuse all questions on asset values. Of those who refuse some but not all of the value questions they are asked, 52 percent (11 percent of the total sample) refuse only one, and a further 19 percent (4 percent of the sample) refuse only two.

7. A further problem arises because of top coding, which is likely to lead to an underestimation of the wealth held by the wealthiest people in the sample, in addition to the problem that the very wealthiest people in the population will not be sampled.

8. One of these types of bonds, premium bonds, offers a return in the form of a lottery. All premium bond holders are entered into a monthly draw with the chance to win from £50,000 up to £1 million, where the chance of winning depends on total premium bond holdings. Premium bonds are currently held by around one in five households in the United Kingdom.

9. For further discussion of the distribution of wealth in the United Kingdom and other countries, see Davies and Shorrocks (2000).

10. This includes long-notice accounts at the bank and building society, tax-exempt special savings accounts (minimum holding period five years), and National Savings certificates of deposit.

11. The 1996 General Household Survey shows that 64 percent of male adults and 50 percent of female adults work. Of these, 77 percent and 88 percent, respectively, are employees, of whom around one-half have occupational pension plans (Budd and Campbell 1998). This leads to an estimate of 23 percent of adults with an occupational scheme, confirmed in the FES data.

12. Even were such data available, they would be potentially difficult to interpret, particularly given conceptual difficulties in the valuation of public and private pension wealth and life insurance funds.

13. In this case we include the diversified risky assets classed as partially safe in table 6.4.

14. The effects of wealth-related differential mortality will work in the opposite direction to offset this.

15. Although the survey was very different in structure in these earlier years and had a much reduced sample (of some 6,500 observations per year), it is possible to get a broad definition of portfolio shares for equities, bonds and unit trusts, investment trusts, and PEPs from the earlier years. The definition of risky assets in the final column (for 1997–1998) has been adjusted to get comparability across years, and hence differs from that in table 6.7.

16. We have also estimated ownership probits using FES data pooled over the period 1978 to 1995 using the specification without wealth dummies but including a complete set of time effects, which yielded highly comparable results. These results are available from us on request.

17. For example, three other surveys—the 1987/88 General Household Survey, the 1987/88 Financial Research Survey, and Proshare (1990)—show the incidence of share ownership to be around 20 percent in 1988 for example. See Banks and Tanner (1999) for further information.

18. Stamp duty was reduced from 2 percent to 1 percent in 1984 and from 1 percent to 0.5 percent in 1986. Evidence on other costs of owning shares is limited. However, figures for the average annual management charges of pension funds, which are likely to be similar to those for mutual funds, show a fall during the 1990s from 150 basis points in 1989 to 124 basis points in 1998 (Press release from Money Management).

19. In fact, behavior by investors in anticipation of windfall shares caused many building societies to restrict shares to people who had mortgages or savings with them several years prior to their conversion.

20. For a detailed discussion of the taxation of pensions and tax-free savings schemes, see Emmerson and Tanner (2000).

21. The rate of tax on interest income is not the basic marginal rate of tax, but was set at the lower 20 percent rate of tax, which existed between 1992 and 1999. Since tax is taken off at source, the lower rate was imposed so that lower-rate taxpayers would not have to claim back the difference between the basic rate and the lower rate. However, from 1999, a new lower rate of 10 percent was set. Lower-rate taxpayers can claim back the difference between this lower rate and 20 percent.

22. Association of Unit Trusts and Investment Funds, press release, June 28, 1999.

23. *Inland Revenue Statistics*, 1999.

24. Unlike Poterba in chapter 3, we use broad marginal tax rate dummies rather than the precise marginal tax rate. A second important difference is that the marginal tax rates are self-assessed, since there is not enough income information in the survey to compute marginal tax rates.

25. In many cases, PEPs are just the envelope in which they hold a mutual fund such as a unit or investment trust.

7   Household Portfolios in Italy

Luigi Guiso and
Tullio Jappelli

The past decade witnessed significant developments in the composition of the portfolio of Italian households. Some of the changes parallel those in other countries, and others are specific to the Italian economy. The most significant changes are the increased participation in the equity market and the sharp increase in the share of stockholding, either directly or through mutual funds, and the parallel decline of transaction accounts and government bonds.

Until recently, the portfolio share of stocks was extremely low by comparison with other industrialized countries; most households held their financial wealth in the form· of transaction accounts or government bonds, and portfolios were poorly diversified. Capital controls, in place until 1989, effectively prevented international diversification. The thinness of the Italian stock market and its consequent volatility, even after the introduction of investment funds in the 1980s, discouraged the holding of equities. Other features were the relatively low level of household debt (mainly due to regulation, high enforcement costs, and lack of tax incentives to borrow) and the negligible role of life insurance and pension funds. Moreover, most financial assets featured short maturities, and long-term saving instruments had little importance. Although some of these features remain, it appears that Italian households are now in the course of a transition that will lead to a configuration more closely resembling other advanced industrial economies.

In this chapter, we document aggregate trends in the portfolio of Italian households and characterize portfolio differences across households, identifying the main variables that explain heterogeneity in the propensity to invest in financial assets. The Survey of Household Income and Wealth (SHIW), our main data source, is particularly well suited for this purpose. This survey, conducted by the Bank of Italy on a representative sample of about 8,000 households, is recurrent, so that from 1989 to 1998, we have five different cross sections; it has a panel component that allows us to address issues relevant to portfolio dynamics. Furthermore, the survey is a rich source of data on household portfolios, and for some years, it contains sections specifically designed to address selected issues, such as the relation between financial information and portfolio choice.

This chapter is organized as follows. Section 7.1 draws on the aggregate financial accounts and shows that in the past decade Italian households made a significant move toward riskier financial portfolios. In Section 7.2, using microeconomic data, we calculate that the increase in the aggregate share observed between 1989 and 1998 is to be attributed in almost equal parts to higher participation and to larger conditional shares. In section 7.3 we distinguish between safe and risky assets and characterize the wealth and age distribution of the household portfolio, two variables that are the focus of a large body of recent theoretical literature. We find the distinction between participation and conditional shares of paramount importance. Participation varies considerably with wealth and age, while asset shares, conditional on participation, are little affected by these variables. These results are confirmed by regression analysis in section 7.4. Section 7.5 explores different ways of reconciling the lack of participation with the presence of transaction and information costs. We first document the limited number of portfolio transitions of Italian households in panel data, which strongly suggests that adjustment costs in the form of brokerage fees and other transaction costs are important. We then explore the role of information costs and of background risk as additional factors helping to explain a low propensity to invest in risky assets. Section 7.6 summarizes the main findings.

7.1 Macroeconomic Trends

Before analyzing household-level data, we briefly describe the aggregate trends of the portfolio of Italian households. Because there are no official figures for aggregate real assets, we focus on financial wealth, drawing from the national financial accounts of the household sector. In the next section we document the time pattern of real asset holdings in microdata.

Table 7.1 reports the aggregate shares of financial assets in total financial wealth from 1985 to 1998. The table reveals that the composition of households' financial assets changed dramatically over the sample period. Currency and bank deposits (checking and saving accounts) plunged from 45.7 percent in 1985 to 25.0 percent in 1998. The weight of short-term government bonds was more than halved, and that of long-term bonds (government and corporate) increased. Stocks, mutual funds, and other managed investment accounts rose markedly, from 16 percent of financial wealth in 1985 to 47 percent in 1998. The importance of foreign assets increased steadily in the 1990s. Virtually nonexistent in 1985, they now account for more than 6 percent of financial wealth. Of these, 40 percent are stocks, 10 percent mutual funds, and 50 percent long-term bonds, suggesting that foreign assets are offering better opportunities to diversify risk. Although home-country bias is definitely a feature of the portfolio of Italian households, the trend suggests that the incidence of foreign securities in financial wealth is bound to increase still further. Finally, the indebtedness of Italian households increased steadily, if slowly. The share of debt (short and long term) was only 5.4 percent of total financial assets in 1985 but almost 9.0 percent by 1998.

In analyzing household portfolios, we find it useful to group financial assets into three categories according to riskiness: clearly safe financial assets include transaction accounts and certificates of deposit, fairly safe financial assets include Treasury bills and the cash value of life insurance, and risky financial assets include stocks, long-term government bonds, other bonds, mutual funds, managed investment accounts, and defined-contribution pension plans. The last rows of table 7.1 indicate that the share of clearly safe assets fell substantially, while that of risky assets—particularly stocks and mutual funds—rose sharply (from one-third to two-thirds of financial wealth). Thus, in 1998 the portfolio of Italian households was much more strongly tilted toward risky assets than it had ever been in the past. A number of factors contribute to explain the trends observed.

First, the nominal yield on transaction accounts and short-term bonds declined significantly over the 1990s, while the return on equities, mutual funds, and managed investment accounts was substantial. The 1990s also witnessed a remarkable development of mutual funds. Introduced in 1984, when only 10 were operating, they rose in number to 184 in 1990 and 459 in 1995. The market value of

Table 7.1
Composition of household financial wealth: Aggregate financial accounts

	Asset shares			
	1985	1990	1995	1998
Financial assets				
Currency	3.86	2.68	2.57	2.15
Transaction and savings accounts[a]	41.83	34.12	34.00	20.54
Short-term government bonds (T-bills)[b]	12.77	12.37	10.16	2.13
Long-term government bonds[c]	11.50	15.05	15.76	8.22
Other bonds[d]	2.82	3.16	5.85	9.53
Stocks	15.30	20.87	16.62	30.53
Mutual funds and managed investment accounts	0.85	2.30	4.07	16.42
Defined-contribution pension funds	6.74	5.93	5.74	4.54
Cash value of life insurance[e]	4.66	3.09	4.85	5.92
Other financial assets[f]	0.22	0.43	0.37	0.02
Total financial assets, of which:[g]	100.0	100.0	100.0	100.0
Foreign assets	0.32	2.32	2.08	5.80
Debt[g]				
Mortgage and real estate debt	3.73	4.65	4.86	6.12
Consumer credit	1.55	1.45	1.17	1.77
Other debt	0.15	0.31	0.80	0.82
Total debt	5.43	6.41	6.83	8.71
Clearly safe financial assets[h]	41.83	34.12	34.00	22.69
Fairly safe financial assets[i]	17.43	15.46	15.01	8.05
Risky financial assets, of which:[j]	37.21	47.31	48.04	69.24
Shares, mutual funds and managed accounts	16.15	23.17	20.69	46.95

Source: Annual Report of the Bank of Italy, various issues. In 1990 financial accounts were subject to major revisions, which led to a revaluation of the value of shares. Data for 1985 are imputed by rescaling the old series with the revised series (available from 1990).
[a] Include certificate of deposits.
[b] Up to one year or indexed to one-year maturity bonds.
[c] More than one-year maturity.
[d] Include bonds issued by private enterprises, special credit institutions, and foreign bonds.
[e] Includes assets held by domestic and foreign insurance companies as a counterpart to life insurance policies sold to residents.
[f] Reported as a share of total financial assets.
[g] Reported as a share of total assets (financial plus nonfinancial assets).
[h] Include currency, transaction accounts, and certificates of deposits.
[i] Include short-term government bonds and the cash value of life insurance.
[j] Include stocks, long-term government bonds, other bonds, mutual funds, and defined-contribution pensions.

the funds increased especially in recent years, from 7.2 percent of gross domestic product (GDP) in 1995 to 18.9 percent in 1997 (Cesari and Panetta 1998). Commercial banks massively entered the sector, increasing competition and reducing entry costs and management fees. Fierce advertising campaigns to acquire market shares helped to disseminate financial information. Financial innovation in terms of packaging of new financial products was substantial. By offering previously unavailable diversification opportunities and reducing minimum investment requirements, mutual funds enhanced Italian households' willingness to invest in risky financial assets, domestic and foreign alike.

A second factor has been the privatization of several large state-owned corporations and public utilities in the 1990s. Since 1992, over twenty-five state corporations, including public utilities and banks, have been successfully privatized, with a total revenue of about 71 billion euros. The privatization process and the number of firms going public have increased stock market capitalization.[1] These privatizations were accompanied by massive publicity, through which households became acquainted with stocks and their return and risk characteristics.[2] It is likely that this dissemination of information has permanently increased stockholding.

The reform of the social security system and the diminished expectations of pension benefits have prompted households to rely increasingly on their own savings for retirement. As a consequence, life insurance and private pension funds, historically negligible, have started to increase. Finally, the lifting of capital controls, which were in place until 1989, improved portfolio diversification through acquisition of foreign assets. The marked fluctuations in the exchange rate following the lira's exit from the exchange rate mechanism (ERM) in October 1992 slowed the process, which in fact accelerated again with Italy's return to the fixed exchange rate agreement in November 1996. With the single currency and the consequent elimination of intra-European exchange rates risk, and with regulatory standardization, we expect a further reduction in the home bias in the coming years.

These developments notwithstanding, the financial portfolio of Italian households—as it results from the financial accounts—retains several features of backwardness. The share of currency and transaction accounts remains high by international standards. Most financial assets have short maturities. Life insurance and pension funds still represent a small fraction. The breadth of the Italian stock market does not yet compare with other industrialized countries. In 1996 the number of listed firms was 3.8 per million inhabitants, against a European Union (EU) average of 13.5. Stock market capitalization was 21 percent of GDP, against 40 percent in the EU (Cecchetti 1999). Finally, household debt remains low, despite deregulation, which has prompted an increase in the supply of loans.[3]

Macroeconomic aggregates conceal crucial matters concerning household portfolio. For instance, the aggregate accounts cannot establish whether the change in asset shares in the past decade is due to a change in participation or to the amounts invested conditional on participation. Aggregate data are of no use in assessing whether the composition of household portfolios varies systematically with wealth or demographic characteristics (age, education, household composition). They also cannot address issues of portfolio transitions. Even when an aggregate asset share is constant over time, there could well be large but reciprocally offsetting movements into and out of the financial markets. The survey data to which we turn in the rest of this chapter provide answers to many of these questions.

7.2 The Microeconomic Picture

In this section we rely on a sequence of five waves of the SHIW, conducted in 1989, 1991, 1993, 1995, and 1998. This survey has collected detailed information on the composition of Italian households' wealth, both real and financial. Data are also available for 1987, but the 1987 survey has information only on highly aggregated asset categories, and the framing of the questions on financial assets was rather different from that of subsequent surveys. Accordingly, we start our analysis with 1989. Portfolio data are particularly rich in the 1995 and in the 1998 SHIW; special sections of the questionnaire address crucial issues in the analysis of household portfolios, such as knowledge of the various financial instruments, exposure to background risk, and attitudes toward risk. We use some of this information in section 7.5.

Alongside the portfolio data, the SHIW gives demographic characteristics of all household members. It has also a sizable rotating panel component; an increasing fraction of the sample is reinterviewed each time, and several households are interviewed three or four times. The panel component is particularly useful to address issues of portfolio dynamics, a subject explored in sections 7.4 and

7.5. The chapter appendix describes the content and sampling properties of the SHIW with particular focus on the variables related to
the household portfolio. Ample details on sampling, response rates,
processing of results, and comparison of survey data with macroeconomic data are provided by Brandolini and Cannari (1994). Here
we summarize the main characteristics of our data set.

Real asset values are reported at the end of each year and are
elicited directly, without use of bracketing. For real assets, the
SHIW reports information on primary residence, investment real
estate, business wealth, the stock of durable goods, other nonfinancial
assets (jewelry, gold coins, art objects, valuable furniture, and other
valuables), and debt. Debt is the sum of mortgage and other real
estate debt, consumer credit, personal loans, and credit card debt.
Each of these items is available separately, but because Italians
actually borrow very little, we focus on total indebtedness.

We define investment real estate and business wealth as risky real
assets. The residual category of safe real assets thus includes primary
residence, the stock of durable goods, and other nonfinancial assets.
These definitions allow us to define as total risky assets the sum of
risky real assets and risky financial assets (stocks, long-term government bonds, other bonds, mutual funds, managed investment
accounts, and defined-contribution pension plans).

Calculation of amounts held in financial assets requires a number
of imputations and assumptions. First, the list of financial assets on
which households report lengthens from thirteen in 1989 to twenty-
eight in 1995 and 1998. We group these assets into ten categories: (1)
currency, (2) transaction and savings accounts, (3) certificates of deposit, (4) Treasury bills, (5) long-term government bonds, (6) other
bonds, (7) stocks, (8) mutual funds and investment accounts, (9) cash
value of defined-contribution pension plans, and (10) cash value of
life insurance. This is the only way to make meaningful comparisons
across different surveys. It also avoids reporting data for assets
with very limited participation and amounts (such as certain types of
government bonds).

Second, in none of the surveys are households asked to report
actual financial asset amounts. In 1989, asset values are inferred in
two steps. Respondents first report the percentage share of financial
wealth in each asset. For cash and bank deposits, they are then
asked to report the share and the amount. One can then estimate the
amount invested in each financial asset, given that the portfolio

shares add up to one. In 1991, 1993, and 1995, respondents select from a list of fourteen possible asset brackets. The problem of bracketing from 1991 through 1995 can be handled by assuming that households own the midpoint of the interval or by applying more sophisticated imputation procedures (as in Stewart 1983). Imputation requires modeling the responses within each bracket, and its advantage diminishes when the number of brackets is relatively detailed, as in the case at hand. We thus proceed with the first alternative.

The cash value of life insurance policies and pension funds is not reported in the survey. From 1989 to 1993 we have information only on participation and annual contributions. In 1995 and 1998 we also have information on the year in which the household started to contribute. From this, we impute the cash value on the assumption that the average years of contributions remained constant over time and that contributions accumulate at the real interest rate of 3 percent.

It is worth pointing out that although this study uses the best available sources, survey data are contaminated by reporting and (unavoidable) imputation errors, so comparisons between the microdata and the aggregate data are somewhat problematic. For this reason, some of the dramatic developments in asset shares that we observe in the aggregate financial accounts are only partially revealed by the microeconomic data. As we explain, reporting errors and imputation affect asset amounts more than ownership; thus, we feel more confident about statements on the latter than on the former.

7.2.1 Participation

Table 7.2 reports the fraction of households owning financial assets, nonfinancial assets, and debt. In the sample period 1989 through 1998, there is relative stability in participation in real assets. Almost all households own durable goods, about 65 percent own their primary residence, and one-third have real estate other than the primary residence. The fraction with business wealth varies from 17 percent in 1989 to 13.6 percent in 1995 and in 1998 and is higher among the self-employed.

The fraction of households without transaction accounts (either checking or saving) is about 15 percent, a nonnegligible number. Attanasio, Guiso, and Jappelli (2001) argue that these households— mainly poor and less well educated—find it convenient to avoid the cost of acquiring and managing an account and hold only currency.

Table 7.2
Asset participation: Survey data, 1989–1998

	1989	1991	1993	1995	1998
Financial assets					
Transaction and savings accounts[a]	87.94	86.44	83.11	82.68	82.50
Certificates of deposits	2.55	4.44	4.64	5.25	3.16
Short-term government bonds (T-bills)[b]	25.16	27.31	25.72	29.92	14.64
Long-term government bonds[c]	2.44	2.94	3.14	5.14	2.80
Other bonds[d]	1.06	1.59	2.12	3.93	6.04
Stocks	4.48	4.24	4.72	3.95	7.29
Mutual funds and managed investment accounts	2.84	3.25	5.29	4.93	10.60
Defined-contribution pension funds[e]	5.43	6.07	7.31	7.77	7.72
Life insurance[f]	13.68	17.09	18.53	21.54	22.63
Nonfinancial assets[g]					
Primary residence	63.34	65.41	63.44	65.49	65.93
Investment real estate	33.74	25.82	32.27	32.03	26.12
Business	17.35	13.24	13.99	13.64	12.43
Stock of durable goods	100.00	99.96	98.84	99.07	100.00
Other nonfinancial assets	75.59	99.84	84.79	87.14	78.86
Debt[h]	8.55	12.75	15.09	27.16	21.16
Clearly safe financial assets[i]	87.94	86.48	83.14	82.72	85.57
Fairly safe financial assets[j]	33.56	38.54	37.56	43.23	33.79
Risky financial assets[k]	11.95	13.77	16.32	18.49	22.96
Total risky assets[l]	46.97	39.67	45.93	46.87	44.78

Source: All statistics use sample weights and are drawn from SHIW, 1989–1998.
Note: All statistics use sample weights.
[a] Include checking and saving accounts.
[b] Up to one year or indexed to one-year maturity bonds.
[c] More than one-year maturity.
[d] Corporate, foreign, and other types of bonds.
[e] Include employer-sponsored plans and personal retirement accounts.
[f] Refers to the cash value of whole life policies.
[g] Nonfinancial assets that could not be classified in any other category.
[h] The sum of mortgage and other real estate debt, consumer credit, personal loans, and credit card debt.
[i] Include transaction accounts and certificates of deposits.
[j] Include short-term government bonds and the cash value of life insurance.
[k] Include stocks, long-term government bonds, other bonds, mutual funds, and defined-contribution pensions.
[l] Include risky financial assets, business, equity and investment real estate.

The share declined by 4 percentage points between 1989 and 1998. One possible explanation is that the 3-percentage-point reduction in nominal interest rates on transaction accounts in the period made it less expensive to settle transactions in cash, inducing some households to close the account, thus saving on fixed cash management costs.

Short-term government bonds and bonds indexed to them are also popular assets, held by about one-fourth of the households until 1995. Long-term bonds are less widespread but show an increasing diffusion. Adding long-term government bonds with bonds issued by private corporations, which are mostly long term, the share of households holding bonds with longer maturities increased from 3.5 percent in 1989 to 9 percent in 1995. This major portfolio shift was dictated by the increasing spread between the long- and the short-term rate over the sample period. The trend reversed in 1998, partly reflecting the fact that direct holding of these assets was replaced by indirect participation through mutual funds.

By international standards, the share of households in Italy holding stocks directly is fairly low (between 4 and 5 percent, with a peak in 1998 of 7.3 percent). In 1998, over half of the total stockholders held shares of privatized companies. However, some households own stocks indirectly through mutual funds and investment accounts. Unfortunately, the SHIW does not report information on the specific types of mutual funds and investment accounts. On the assumption that at least one of these accounts is invested in the equity market, we place the upper bound of stock market participation (direct or indirect) at 6.4 percent in 1989, 7.7 percent in 1995, and 8.9 percent in 1998.

There are at least two reasons for the low participation in equity markets. First, entry and management costs have been historically high; second, the stock market has been extremely volatile, a consequence of a small and illiquid stock market. In the past four decades, the standard deviation of the real growth rate of stock prices was over 35 percent, as opposed to standard deviations ranging from 16 to 19 percent in France, Germany, the, United Kingdom, and the United States. The increased participation in mutual funds has been favored by the appearance of mutual funds, leading to lower transaction costs and better risk diversification. However, transaction costs remain high, particularly at low wealth levels, as we document in section 7.5.

The sample period also witnessed the growth in life insurance and private pension plan participation, from 17 percent in 1989 to 29 percent in 1998. The increased participation was prompted by two factors. First, the 1992 and 1996 reforms of the social security system reduced expected benefits and increased pension age, raising the incentives to find other instruments for retirement saving. Second, in 1986, the demand for life insurance was stimulated by tax incentives.

On the liability side, only 8.6 percent of the households reported being indebted in 1989. The share increased to 15 percent in 1993 and jumped to 27 percent in 1995. In that year, 11.1 percent reported having a housing mortgage, 9.1 percent borrowed to finance a car purchase and 3.9 percent to finance other durable expenditures, and only 1 percent had a personal loan. An additional 6.1 percent (33 percent of the self-employed) borrowed to finance a family business. Although household indebtedness is low in comparison with other industrial countries, the increase is noteworthy. Figures for earlier years show that the fraction with housing mortgages has remained fairly stable; the increased participation in credit markets is mainly due to expansion of consumer credit and personal loans.

In summary, in the 1990s the portfolio of Italian households underwent a number of important changes in participation in financial asset markets, while there was little change in the area of non-financial assets. Although a very large fraction of households holds mainly or exclusively transaction accounts, investment in long-term bonds and stocks (directly or through mutual funds), participation in life insurance and defined-contribution pension plans, and borrowing increased. Overall, the fraction of households holding fairly safe financial assets increased from 33.6 percent in 1989 to 43.2 percent in 1995 but declined to 33.8 in 1998. Those investing in risky financial assets increased steadily from 12 in 1989 to 23 percent in 1998.

Notice, however, that our classification of assets into clearly safe, fairly safe, and risky securities is likely to have changed in the most recent years. First, while including mutual funds among the risky assets category was probably a fair approximation until 1995, when most funds invested in stocks, the presence of a large number of money market and balanced funds in the late 1990s tends to blur our definition. Second, the riskiness of some instruments has likely undergone important changes in the recent years. Most notably, the inclusion of T-bills in the category of fairly safe assets rather than in the clearly safe group was motivated by the large and increasing government debt, leading investors to attach a nonzero probability of default even on short-term government bonds. But this changed after the strong fiscal 1996 contraction, so that today concerns for government solvency have diminished. These features should be borne in mind in interpreting the portfolio evolution after 1995, especially when we rely on grouped assets categories.

7.2.2   Diversification

The portfolios of Italian households span few assets. A large fraction of the sample hold very few types of financial instruments and tend to concentrate wealth in safe assets. Table 7.3 documents the allocation of financial wealth in greater detail. For each survey year, it reports the distribution of the eight possible portfolio configurations when financial assets are divided into clearly safe, fairly safe, and risky categories.

The table is interesting in a number of respects. First, the fraction of households holding no asset increased over time, from 11.6 per-

Table 7.3
Diversification of household financial portfolios: Fraction of households owning specific combinations of financial assets

Financial asset combination

Clearly safe[a]	Fairly safe[b]	Risky[c]	1989	1991	1993	1995	1998
0	0	0	11.64	12.18	14.63	14.86	13.17
0	0	1	0.11	0.08	0.35	0.22	0.15
0	1	0	0.52	1.16	2.15	1.61	1.08
0	1	1	0.01	0.05	0.14	0.09	0.03
1	0	0	50.96	44.83	36.47	41.33	42.71
1	0	1	3.44	4.10	5.32	· 5.83	10.17
1	1	0	24.65	27.70	28.26	25.77	20.08
1	1	1	8.65	9.90	12.67	10.28	12.61
Total			100.00	100.00	100.00	100.00	100.00

Source: SHIW, 1989–1998.
Note: 1 denotes that the asset is owned, 0 that it is not owned. All statistics use sample weights.
[a] Include transaction accounts and certificates of deposits.
[b] Include short-term government bonds and the cash value of life insurance.
[c] Include stocks, long-term government bonds, other bonds, mutual funds, and defined-contribution pensions.

cent in 1989 to 13.2 percent in 1998. Since currency is excluded from all asset categories and all households report holding some currency, this is the counterpart of the fall in participation in transaction accounts (table 7.2). Second, in each year, a large fraction of consumers allocated all of their financial wealth to safe or fairly safe assets. Third, the share of households investing only in clearly safe assets declined from 51.0 percent in 1989 to 42.7 percent in 1998. Fourth, the share with only clearly safe and fairly safe assets increased from 24.6 to 28.3 percent in 1993 and then declined to 20.1 percent in 1998 (reflecting the lower participation in short-term government bonds, which we have considered as fairly safe assets). Fifth, a small but increasing number of investors mixed clearly safe and risky assets (3.4 percent in 1989 and 10.2 percent in 1998), and very few combined fairly safe and risky assets. Finally, the relative weight of the group with complete portfolios (investing in all three types of assets) increased from 8.7 percent in 1989 to 12.6 in 1998.

The last three rows of table 7.3 represent portfolios with at least some degree of diversification, because they include clearly safe and fairly safe assets, or safe and risky assets. Adding up the three rows shows that the fraction of households with diversified portfolios increased by 10 percentage points, from 36.7 percent in 1989 to 43 percent in 1995 through 1998. This trend is largely due to increased participation in risky financial assets.

7.2.3   Portfolio Composition

Table 7.4 reports asset shares from 1989 to 1998, again distinguishing among financial assets, nonfinancial assets, and debt. Each type of financial asset is reported as a share of total financial assets, and nonfinancial assets and debt are reported as shares of total wealth (financial plus nonfinancial). Each share is computed as the ratio between the sample average value of the asset and the sample average value of the total, and is thus equivalent to a wealth-weighted average share. Table 7.4 is therefore comparable to the financial accounts data reported in table 7.1.

Underreporting of financial assets is more severe for risky financial assets than for transaction accounts or other safe assets. The reason is that the survey is not designed to describe the portfolio of the rich, who are likely to be largely responsible for the portfolio reallocations described in table 7.1. For instance, focusing on 1995, it appears that

Table 7.4
Composition of household wealth: Survey data

	1989	1991	1993	1995	1998
Financial assets[a]					
Currency	2.95	3.04	1.77	1.90	1.41
Transaction and savings accounts	50.15	41.46	34.52	29.23	38.08
Certificates of deposits	2.48	3.35	3.26	4.57	2.15
Short-term government bonds (T-bills)	27.80	26.84	26.13	28.35	9.70
Long-term government bonds	2.60	2.38	3.33	6.08	2.48
Other bonds	0.90	1.39	1.98	3.36	5.36
Stocks	2.78	6.17	9.52	4.96	7.45
Mutual funds and managed investment accounts	3.36	3.54	7.89	7.24	19.47
Defined-contribution pension funds	2.27	3.52	3.44	4.05	3.49
Cash value of life insurance	4.69	8.31	8.16	10.25	10.41
Total financial assets[b]	15.51	11.70	12.53	12.95	14.59
Nonfinancial assets[b]					
Primary residence	36.03	50.11	46.51	47.26	48.84
Investment real estate	25.80	16.80	19.95	21.22	16.97
Business	7.28	9.12	11.07	8.23	8.95
Stock of durable goods	12.82	9.64	8.24	8.42	8.87
Other nonfinancial assets	2.55	2.62	1.70	1.92	1.77
Total nonfinancial assets	84.49	88.30	87.47	87.05	85.41
Debt[b]	1.42	2.00	2.35	3.40	4.07
Clearly safe financial assets[c,a]	55.59	47.85	39.55	35.70	41.64
Fairly safe financial assets[d,a]	32.49	35.15	34.28	38.60	20.11
Risky financial assets[e,a]	11.91	17.00	26.16	25.69	38.25
Total risky assets[f,a]	34.93	27.91	34.29	32.78	31.50

Source: SHIW, 1989–1998.
Note: Asset shares are computed as ratio of averages. All statistics use sample weights.
[a] Reported as a share of total financial assets.
[b] Reported as a share of total assets (financial plus nonfinancial assets).
[c] Include transaction accounts and certificates of deposits.
[d] Include short-term government bonds and the cash value of life insurance.
[e] Include stocks, long-term government bonds, other bonds, mutual funds, and defined-contribution pension funds.
[f] Include risky financial assets, business equity, and investment real estate.

the survey understates stocks (5 percent against 16 percent in the aggregate financial accounts) and long-term government bonds (6.1 and 15.8 percent, respectively), and overstates the share invested in Treasury bills (28.4 and 10.2 percent). Comparisons for other years are qualitatively similar.

Overall, financial assets account for a small fraction of total assets (12 to 15 percent, depending on the survey year); the bulk of wealth is nonfinancial. Most of the nonfinancial assets consist of real estate, varying from 62 percent in 1989 (36 percent in primary residence and 25 percent in investment real estate) to 66 percent in 1995 (49 percent and 17 percent, respectively). This increase is largely accounted for by the rise in real estate prices in the early 1990s, not by any increase in home ownership rates. Business wealth accounts for about 10 percent of total assets and is relatively concentrated in the population, as suggested by the participation rates in table 7.2. Although the share of financial debt more than doubled between 1989 and 1998, it remains very low.

A closer look at the composition reveals that safe assets dominate financial portfolios. Nevertheless, the shift toward risky financial assets is remarkable, from 12 percent of financial wealth in 1989 to 38 percent in 1998. This shift is compensated by a 12-point decline in the share of fairly safe assets (from 32.5 percent in 1989 to 20.1 percent in 1998) and a 14-point reduction in the share of clearly safe financial assets (from 55.6 to 41.6 percent). Although the increase affects all risky financial assets, it is most evident for mutual funds and managed investment accounts (from 3.4 to 19.5 percent) and for direct stockholding (from 2.8 to 7.5).

The increase in the share of risky assets could be due to an increase in participation or in the relative amount invested by those who participate, that is, an increase in the conditional share. We thus decompose the change in the aggregate share in the sum of the change in participation, the change in conditional asset share, and a residual term that reflects shifts in the personal distribution of wealth.[4] We calculate that the increase in the aggregate share observed between 1989 to 1998 should be attributed almost equally to higher participation and to higher conditional shares. In fact, 60 percent of the 26.4 point increase in the share of risky assets in table 7.4 is explained by an increase in participation (particularly in mutual funds) and 40 percent by an increase in the conditional share. The ratio between the average wealth of investors and average total financial wealth has a negligible role.

7.3 Exploring the Portfolio Distribution

In the past decade, Italian households have made a significant move toward riskier financial portfolios, with an increase in long-term bonds and mutual funds. More households have acquired some sophistication in managing financial wealth, resulting in better diversification. Yet more than a third of the sample still concentrates all of its wealth in a few highly safe financial instruments with low expected returns. And almost half the sample has absolutely no risky assets, either real or financial.

Interpretation of the features of the households' portfolio is facilitated by a a brief summary of the predictions of the theoretical models. We focus on the relation between the portfolio and transaction costs, information, age, and wealth. Where applicable, we distinguish the effect of each on participation from its effect on conditional asset shares.

The preceding descriptive analysis makes it clear that the microeconomic data reveal substantial heterogeneity in portfolio choices. The first source of heterogeneity is nonparticipation and lack of diversification. Moreover, there is considerable portfolio heterogeneity even within the group investing in risky assets, not just in participation.[5] Nonparticipation is obviously inconsistent with the simple two-asset portfolio model without transaction costs in which risky assets yield a higher expected return than the safe asset. To reconcile theory with the evidence, we must therefore explore the possibility that transaction costs and financial information affect household portfolio choice. Furthermore, these costs vary across households and financial instruments, so that their presence affects portfolio choice much more than would be predicted by standard models in complete market settings and homogeneous agents. Lack of participation also suggests exploring the possibility that some consumers fail to invest in particular assets simply because they are unaware of their existence, hence the importance of variables correlated with financial sophistication, such as education. In fact, households differ considerably in terms of financial information, and education and information spillovers are strong predictors of financial sophistication (see section 7.5).

We document that participation varies considerably with wealth, while the conditional shares are little affected by this factor. As Gollier points out in chapter 1, the sign of the wealth-portfolio relation is one of the few cases where the theory offers clear-cut predictions. We then uncover a distinct pattern of participation over the life cycle. Several factors may affect the age-portfolio profile. King and Leape (1987) note that learning is correlated with age and that stock market participation and asset diversification should increase over the life cycle. Another potentially relevant factor is the greater importance of committed savings and borrowing constraints for people in the early stage of the life cycle. Paxson (1990) points out that households exposed to liquidity constraints and facing uncertain liquidity needs will tend to hold relatively liquid and safe assets. The model developed by Gollier and Zeckhauser (1998), with convex risk tolerance, predicts instead a negative relation between age and the share of risky assets. Bodie, Merton, and Samuelson (1992) predict a decline in risky asset shares in old age. They point out that the young are more willing to invest in risky assets because they enjoy greater labor supply flexibility. Investment in risky assets may decline with age because younger consumers have a better chance to diversify shocks over time. Finally, the portfolio also varies systematically with age in the model proposed by Cocco Gomes, and Maenhout (1999), simulating the choice between a risky and a safe asset in a multiperiod life cycle model. They argue that human capital is a better substitute for safe assets than for risky assets and find a concave profile of the share of risky assets over the life cycle. The intuition is that since the annuity value of labor income is low but increasing at young ages, and high but decreasing at middle ages, consumers substitute risky assets for abundant safe assets when young and rebalance the portfolio in old age, when the annuity value of labor income starts declining.[6]

In the rest of this section, we document portfolio heterogeneity and explore how the propensity to invest in risky assets and risky asset shares varies with household wealth, age, and education. A regression approach is taken up in section 7.4.

7.3.1   The Wealth-Portfolio Profile

The first four columns of table 7.5 report portfolio shares by wealth quartiles; the last column focuses on households in the top 5 percent

Table 7.5
Composition of household wealth, by wealth quartiles

	Below first quartile	Between first and second quartile	Between second and third quartile	Above third quartile	Top 5 percent
Financial assets					
Currency	9.39	3.45	2.33	1.09	0.52
Transaction and savings accounts	55.25	42.52	35.58	26.67	17.69
Certificates of deposits	1.34	3.30	5.81	5.58	4.04
Short-term government bonds (T-bills)	15.09	26.98	29.69	30.45	29.01
Long-term government bonds	1.01	2.57	2.50	7.39	7.19
Other bonds	1.08	3.12	1.59	2.58	8.32
Stocks	1.13	1.00	2.01	2.73	10.89
Mutual funds and managed investment accounts	0.46	2.22	3.78	7.70	11.92
Defined-contribution pension funds	3.37	3.50	5.44	4.21	3.21
Cash value of life insurance	11.84	11.33	11.28	11.57	7.19
Total financial assets	31.33	16.92	11.77	12.38	12.84
Nonfinancial assets					
Primary residence	11.87	53.75	60.52	51.55	34.38
Investment real estate	1.84	9.19	12.26	20.04	33.18
Business	1.44	2.21	3.95	7.48	13.29
Stock of durable goods	46.91	15.66	9.90	6.90	4.49
Other nonfinancial assets	6.60	2.26	1.60	1.65	1.82
Total nonfinancial assets	68.67	83.08	88.23	87.62	87.16
Debt	5.87	3.18	4.07	3.39	3.27
Risky financial assets[a]					
Participation	3.53	11.81	20.25	36.46	53.98
Share	7.07	12.41	15.32	24.62	51.80
Conditional share	61.97	44.72	41.09	43.50	53.37
Total risky assets[b]					
Participation	9.87	38.04	57.07	82.07	98.64
Share	5.50	13.50	18.01	36.79	41.54
Conditional share	36.24	33.70	30.87	36.37	52.35

Source: SHIW, 1995.
Note: The shares of risky financial assets and of total risky assets are scaled by financial wealth and total wealth, respectively. Conditional shares are computed in the group of those holding risky assets. Asset shares are computed as ratio of averages. All statistics use sample weights.
[a] Include stocks, long-term government bonds, other bonds, mutual funds, and defined-contribution pensions.
[b] Include risky financial assets, business equity, and investment real estate.

of the wealth distribution. The table refers to an intermediate year of our sample (1995). The qualitative patterns are similar in other survey years. Glancing through table 7.5, one sees that portfolio allocations are not independent of wealth. For instance, the relative weight of financial assets in total assets declines with wealth, in favor of investment real estate and business equity, while debt shares are slightly decreasing with wealth. Wealthier households tend to invest a much larger share of their wealth in risky assets—7.1 percent in the first wealth quartile and 24.6 percent in the fourth. This pattern is stronger still for investment real estate and business equity, whose share in total wealth rises from 5.5 percent in the bottom quartile to 36.8 percent in the top quartile.

The financial portfolio displays additional differences across quartiles as well. With the exception of defined-contribution pension funds, all risky financial assets (stocks, mutual funds, and long-term bonds) increase sharply with wealth. On the other hand, currency and transaction accounts decline from 65 percent in the bottom quartile (where currency represents almost 10 percent of the total) to 27.8 percent in the top quartile (where currency represents only 1 percent of financial wealth).

Households in the top 5 percent of the wealth distribution behave very differently from median households and even from top-quartile households as a group. We find that the rich invest most of their wealth in risky assets (51.8 percent, 33 percent of it in investment real estate and 13 percent in business). Stocks, held directly or through mutual funds and managed investment accounts, represent a large component of financial assets (22.8 percent), while transaction and saving accounts represent a relatively small share (17.7 percent). Durable goods account for almost half of the wealth of the bottom quartile but are a tiny portion of the portfolio of the top 5 percent (4.5 percent). Portfolio diversification too increases with wealth. The fraction of those with complete portfolios (holding clearly safe, fairly safe, and risky financial assets) or diversified portfolios (holding clearly safe and risky assets) is 0.6 percent in the bottom quartile, 6.0 in the second, 13.7 in the third, 26.3 in the fourth, and 40.9 percent in the top 5 percent. These patterns are even more marked for the top 1 percent.

The lower part of table 7.5 reports participation, asset shares, and asset shares conditional on participation in risky financial assets and total risky assets. There is a strong association between participation in risky assets and wealth. The relation between the conditional shares and wealth is much weaker and applies only to the upper 5 or 1 percent of the wealth distribution. The sensitivity of conditional shares to wealth only at high levels of the latter is broadly consistent with the standard theory of portfolio selection (see chapter 1, this volume) as well as with the computational findings surveyed by Haliassos and Michaelides (see chapter 2, this volume). Otherwise, the conditional share of risky financial assets is between 40 and 50 percent, and that of total risky assets around one-third. This implies that the relation between unconditional asset shares and wealth derives from the strong, positive association between participation and wealth rather than from an association between conditional shares and wealth. The relation between conditional risky asset shares and wealth is discussed further in section 7.4, with regression estimates of participation in risky assets and of conditional risky asset shares. At this stage we note only that the strong, positive association between participation and wealth is robust to the inclusion of a broad set of controls.

7.3.2   The Age-Portfolio Profile

Table 7.6 illustrates the age pattern of participation and of the share of risky assets separately for financial wealth and total wealth using pooled 1989–1998 data. As with wealth, the distinction between unconditional and conditional shares is quite important. Over the life cycle, the unconditional share of risky assets has a hump-shaped profile, resulting from the combination of a concave age profile of participation and a flat profile of the conditional share. Participation increases early in life (from 15 percent in the first age bracket to almost 20 percent in the 40–49 age bracket) and then falls considerably toward retirement, regardless of the definition of risky assets. By contrast, the conditional share is fairly constant through life at 45 percent, regardless of the definition of risky assets.[7] Overall, table 7.6 suggests that entry benefits or costs vary over the life cycle, possibly following the hump shape in wealth. This is what simulations of finite horizon consumption-portfolio models suggest (see chapter 2, this volume).

The profiles shown in table 7.6 are obtained by pooling all available cross sections and do not take into account the possible contamination of the age profiles by cohort effects. This issue may be of

Table 7.6
Cross-sectional age profile of participation and of the share of risky assets

	Risky financial assets[a]			Total risky assets[b]		
Age group	Partici-pation	Share	Condi-tional share	Partici-pation	Share	Condi-tional share
Under 30	15.12	18.95	43.69	35.93	37.90	55.48
30–39	19.07	21.49	47.50	47.21	30.79	42.74
40–49	19.89	21.42	45.15	52.28	31.45	41.96
50–59	17.30	22.06	44.47	53.07	35.62	45.92
60–69	10.52	18.27	44.83	41.46	31.67	44.50
70 and over	6.90	16.24	46.81	28.75	28.61	48.49

Source: SHIW, 1989–1995.
Note: The shares of risky financial assets and of total risky assets are scaled by financial wealth and total wealth, respectively. Conditional shares are computed in the group of those holding risky assets. All statistics use sample weights and pooled 1989–1995 data.
[a] Include stocks, long-term government bonds, other bonds, mutual funds, and defined-contribution pensions.
[b] Include risky financial assets, business equity, and investment real estate.

some relevance if, say, the increase in the number of investors in risky assets that we observe is more heavily concentrated in some cohorts. Furthermore, table 7.6 pools all observations and disregards time effects.

Given the collinearity of age, time, and cohort, we can identify only two of these effects with repeated cross-sectional data. In principle, there are two plausible identifying assumptions. One is to explain the raw data in terms of cohort and age effects. This decomposition disregards time effects or assumes that they reflect idiosyncratic macroshocks that sum to zero and are orthogonal to a time trend (Deaton and Paxson 1994). The other is to interpret the data as a combination of age and unrestricted time effects. The theory of portfolio choice provides no strong reason for including cohort effects in participation. Furthermore, financial innovations and increased competition among financial intermediaries point to the importance of time effects. So we believe that the description in terms of age and time effects is much more plausible. Accordingly, we aggregate the microeconomic data into five-year age cohort cells and compute the average ownership rate within each group. We then regress the ownership rate on an age polynomial and unrestricted time dummies.

In the left graph of figure 7.1, the solid line shows the estimated age profile of the participation rate in risky financial assets (the pattern is similar for total risky assets). The broken lines connect the raw data for each cohort, observed in five years between 1989 and 1998. Time effects are readily visible. For instance, participation increases for all cohorts from 1993 to 1998. Participation is clearly hump shaped. Confirming the pattern of table 7.6, at early stages of the life cycle, only a small fraction of consumers invests in risky assets. The age profile of participation again points to significant fixed costs in acquiring risky assets and suggests that people invest in risky assets only after they have accumulated enough wealth. This effect is amplified by the observation that the incentive to hold risky assets is not age independent. Theory indeed suggests that the young should have a greater incentive to invest in risky assets than the elderly, yet we observe a humped shape.

The right panel in figure 7.1 plots the age profile of the fraction investing in risky financial assets by education groups. We use compulsory schooling (eight years) to split the sample into two education groups. Both display a hump shape in the age profile of ownership of risky assets. But there are also interesting differences. At all ages, participation is about three times larger for the more educated (the gap is smaller but still substantial for ownership of total risky assets). Second, for the high-education group, the profile of ownership is steeper early in life and peaks later (around age 50) than for the less well educated (around age 40).

7.4   Regression Analysis

The preceding descriptive analysis shows that in Italy, the propensity to invest in risky assets increases strongly with wealth and education, while the age profile is hump shaped. However, conditional on ownership, risky asset shares are relatively flat over the life cycle and do not vary much with wealth, except at very high wealth levels (the top 5 percent). Because the descriptive analysis looks at the role of each variable in isolation and there could be other household characteristics that affect portfolio choice, in this section we supplement the evidence by regression analysis for the probability of investing in risky assets and for the share of risky assets. We present results from pooled cross-sectional data and panel data estimates controlling for the potential impact of fixed effects.

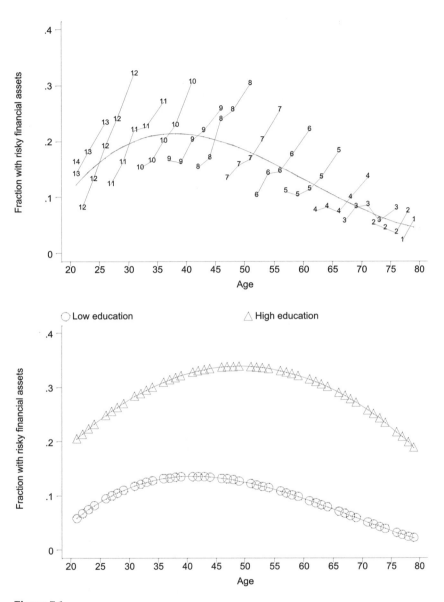

Figure 7.1
Participation by age, cohort, and education. (*Top*) Actual and estimated age profiles of the fraction investing in risky financial assets, defined as the number of financial assets in the portfolio. (*Bottom*) Plots by education the estimated age profiles of the fraction investing in risky financial assets. Low education = household heads up to compulsory schooling (up to eight years). High education = household heads with more than compulsory education (more than eight years).

For the regression analysis, we concentrate on the 1989–1995 period. As we have explained, the grouping of the various assets in our three categories is questionable after 1995. Since the analysis that follows is entirely based on the aggregate categories, in order to avoid using inconsistent definitions we do not include the 1998 data in our reference data set. In so doing, we gain in comparability and do not lose too much information, as the trends toward higher investment in risky assets is clearly apparent already in 1995. In addition, some crucial variables that we use in the estimation are not available to us for the most recent survey year.[8]

7.4.1   Cross-Sectional Data

We model the demand for risky assets as a two-stage decision process. Households first choose whether to hold risky assets; then they decide how to allocate wealth between safe and risky securities. Given that incomplete portfolios are the rule rather than the exception in our sample, the use of ordinary least squares (OLS) in asset shares equations would lead to inconsistent parameter estimates. Accordingly, we rely on a selection model.

The model requires suitable identification restrictions—variables that affect the participation decision but not the share of risky assets. We thus assume that a series of variables affecting the decision to invest in risky assets is correlated with entry costs and with fixed costs of managing a portfolio but not with asset shares. They are an index of bank diffusion (measured by the average number of automatic teller machine [ATM] locations in the city of residence), an index of financial development (the loan-GDP ratio in the province), and dummies for the size of the city of residence (which might be correlated with transaction costs in asset management).

In the participation and asset-share regressions, we also control for household income and wealth (linear and quadratic terms), household characteristics (family size, number of children, and region of residence), and variables related to the household head (age and age square, gender, marital status, and education). We add to the list of the regressors the average unemployment rate in the province of residence as a proxy for background risk (we comment on this variable in section 7.5). The sample uses the pooled surveys from 1989 to 1995, with a total of 30,881 observations. To account for the institutional developments mentioned in section 7.1 and for aggregate shocks, each regression includes year dummies.

The results of the participation equation for risky financial assets are reported in column 1 of table 7.7. The coefficients of age, wealth, and education are not only statistically different from zero but also economically important and confirm the descriptive evidence. At sample means, the predicted probability of investing in risky financial assets increases by 4 percentage points from age 25 to age 40 and declines by 8 percentage points between age 40 and age 70. Raising wealth from 25,000 to 200,000 euros (equivalent to approximately the twentieth and the eightieth percentiles of wealth) raises the predicted probability by 4 percentage points. Increasing education from compulsory schooling (eight years of education) to a university degree (twenty years) raises the predicted probability by 10 percentage points.

The regression coefficients also indicate that large households, women, and residents of southern regions are less likely to invest in risky financial assets. The provincial index of bank diffusion correlates positively with risky asset ownership. Dummies for city size have the expected sign, while the loan-GDP ratio is not significantly different from zero (these coefficients are not reported in the table). Time dummies indicate that the probability of owning increases steadily over time.

The second column of table 7.7 reports estimates of the share of risky financial assets. In general, we find the share harder to predict than the participation decision. The estimates signal that the conditional share is about constant up to age 60 and then declines during retirement. The relation between wealth and the asset share is positive in the relevant range of wealth. However, the effect is weak: increasing wealth from 25,000 to 200,000 euros raises the share of risky financial assets by only 3 percentage points. Education has a positive and significant coefficient, indicating that each year of education raises the predicted share by one percentage point. Finally, the demographic variables have the same sign as in the participation equation.

Like most other surveys, the SHIW uses a two-stage sample design, with first municipalities (or clusters) and then households. These clusters can induce neighborhood effects. This positive correlation between observations might inflate the standard errors, as

Table 7.7
Cross-sectional regressions for participation and the share of risky assets

Variable	Risky financial assets[a] Participation	Share	Total risky assets[b] Participation	Share
Age	0.032 (6.22)	0.009 (3.29)	0.018 (4.49)	−0.007 (−5.57)
Age squared/1,000	−0.364 (−7.53)	−0.112 (−4.41)	−0.234 (−6.49)	0.065 (−5.68)
Income	0.029 (24.40)	0.008 (8.89)	0.015 (12.01)	−0.004 (12.97)
Income squared/1,000	−0.093 (−15.24)	−0.022 (−6.23)	−0.088 (−8.91)	0.014 (9.17)
Wealth	0.0007 (11.50)	0.0002 (7.52)	0.006 (58.11)	0.0004 (24.82)
Wealth squared/1,000	−0.0001 (−7.94)	−0.00003 (−5.04)	−0.0006 (−28.24)	−0.00005 (−15.37)
Family size	−0.102 (−7.94)	−0.038 (−6.09)	−0.004 (−0.39)	−0.008 (−3.03)
Number of children	0.047 (2.90)	0.018 (2.37)	−0.001 (−0.09)	0.009 (2.68)
Married	−0.037 (−1.13)	−0.020 (−1.24)	−0.109 (−3.85)	−0.016 (−2.04)
Male	0.204 (6.17)	0.075 (4.60)	0.229 (8.38)	−0.038 (−4.73)
Resident in the south	−0.356 (−8.34)	−0.202 (−9.21)	0.231 (6.75)	−0.036 (−4.58)
Education	0.044 (17.60)	0.013 (7.83)	−0.005 (−2.47)	−0.005 (−8.52)
Average unemployment rate in the province	−2.298 (−8.16)	−0.470 (−3.06)	−1.639 (−8.09)	0.527 (9.17)
Index of bank diffusion[c]	0.331 (3.13)		−0.032 (−0.29)	
Mills ratio		0.409		0.027
Observations	30,834	4,558	30,834	13,489

Source: SHIW, 1989–1995.
Note: Income and wealth are deflated by the consumer price index (1995 base) and then expressed in euros. All regressions also include year dummies. The first-stage equations also include dummies for city size (between 20,000 and 40,000 residents, between 40,000 and 500,000, more than 500,000) and for the loan-GDP ratio in the province of residence. *t*-statistics are reported in parentheses.
[a] Include stocks, long-term government bonds, other bonds, mutual funds, and defined-contribution pensions.
[b] Include risky financial assets, business equity, and investment real estate.
[c] The ratio between the number of ATM points and population in each province.

Deaton (1997) explains. The individual cluster identification number is not released by the Bank of Italy. As a proxy for the clusters, we use a robust variance-covariance matrix, assuming that observations are independent across provinces but not necessarily within provinces (which might contain several clusters). In all cases the coefficients retain their statistical significance.

Table 7.7 also reports estimates of the determinants of participation and share of total risky assets, which include business equity and investment real estate. The coefficients confirm several of the patterns uncovered for risky financial assets. In particular, participation is concave in age, and there is a strong, positive association between wealth and participation and a small, positive correlation between wealth and the share.

There are, however, three important differences between the regressions for risky financial assets and total risky assets. Education and residency in the south (in the participation equation) change sign, while the index of bank diffusion is not significantly different from zero. The latter finding probably reflects the fact that banks are not a relevant channel of useful information on real estate and business investment, unlike financial assets. One possible explanation for the results concerning the education variable and the south dummy is that managing a financial portfolio is information intensive and requires a degree of intellectual ability, which is proxied by education. On the other hand, acquiring and managing nonresidential properties or running a small business (the other two components of total risky assets) is less demanding in terms of information and managing abilities. The dummy for the south might also pick up differences in financial development between areas of the country that are not accounted for by our controls.[9]

7.4.2   Panel Data

We also use the panel component of the SHIW to check whether the patterns uncovered by the descriptive and statistical analysis of pooled cross-sectional data are contaminated by unobserved heterogeneity. Each SHIW since 1989 has reinterviewed some respondents from the previous surveys. The fraction reinterviewed increased from 15 percent of the previous sample in 1989, to 27 percent in 1991, 43 percent in 1993, and 45 percent in 1995. Some households have been interviewed for more than two consecutive surveys, so the participation length differs across households. As explained, we neglect the newly available 1998 survey to preserve comparability. Dropping observations where the head has changed and those with inconsistent responses for age and education, we are left with an unbalanced sample of 11,549 observations on 4,609 households. Of these, 2,529 households were interviewed twice (in 1989–1991, 1991–1993, or 1993–1995); 1,515, three times (in 1989–1993 or in 1991–1995); and 565 households four times (from 1989 to 1995).

Table 7.8 reports two probit regressions with random effects for participation in risky financial assets and in total risky assets. Given the reduced sample size and the presence of random effects, the coefficients are generally estimated with larger standard errors than in table 7.7, but the results are quite similar, and we find qualitatively and quantitatively comparable effects on the predicted probability. Education has a positive effect on the probability of investing in risky financial assets but no effect on that of investing in total risky assets. The age profile is concave, while that of wealth is positive in the relevant range of this variable. The coefficient of the index of bank diffusion indicates that increases over time in the number of bank points raised households' incentives to invest in risky financial assets. As with the cross-sectional estimates, we find an insignificant effect of the index of bank diffusion on the probability of investing in total risky assets.

Probit models with random effects require that the observable characteristics be uncorrelated with the unobservable heterogeneity component of the error term and that they be strictly exogenous. In chapter 4, Miniaci and Weber note the importance of this point in the estimation of household portfolio models. As an alternative to the probit model with random effects, they experiment the fixed-effect conditional logit estimator. This estimator is consistent even if fixed effects are correlated with observable variables. The drawback is that individuals who do not change participation over the sample period do not contribute to the likelihood function, and so have no effect on the estimation. Thus, with conditional logit, one cannot estimate the effect of time-invariant characteristics (i.e., gender). In short-panel data, the problem is compounded because it is hard to identify the effect of variables, which are almost constant for each individual (such as education, family composition, or region of residence). Furthermore, the effect of variables that change in a predictable way at

Table 7.8
Panel data regressions for participation

Variable	Risky financial assets[a]	Total risky assets[b]
Age	0.052	0.065
	(3.29)	(4.42)
Age squared/1,000	−0.599	−0.680
	(−3.99)	(−4.98)
Income	0.038	0.028
	(13.07)	(8.29)
Income squared/1,000	−0.105	−0.150
	(−7.80)	(−7.71)
Wealth	0.001	0.009
	(11.78)	(26.75)
Wealth squared/1,000	−0.0001	−0.001
	(−5.46)	(−19.00)
Family size	−0.135	−0.033
	(−3.74)	(−0.98)
Number of children	0.091	0.015
	(2.08)	(0.36)
Married	−0.153	−0.169
	(−1.39)	(−1.58)
Education	0.079	0.001
	(9.99)	(0.15)
Average unemployment rate in the province	−3.244	−3.941
	(−4.14)	(−5.99)
Index of bank diffusion	1.855	−0.107
	(5.23)	(−0.29)
Observations	11,549	11,549

Source: SHIW rotating panel section, 1989–1995.

Note: Some households are interviewed from 1989 to 1995, others from 1989 to 1993 or from 1991 to 1995, and others in two years only. The regressions pool all data, a total of 11,549 observations on 4,609 households. Income and wealth are deflated by the consumer price index (1995 base) and then expressed in euro. Each regression includes also dummies for city size (between 20,000 and 40,000 residents, between 40,000 and 500,000, more than 500,000) and the loan-GDP ratio in the province of residence and year dummies. *t*-statistics are reported in parenthesis.

[a] Include stocks, long-term government bonds, other bonds, mutual funds, and defined-contribution pensions.

[b] Include risky financial assets, business equity, and investment real estate.

the individual level (such as age) is difficult to estimate because identification relies on only the nonlinear terms.

With conditional logit, the sample size drops dramatically (2,266 for ownership of risky financial assets and 3,367 for total risky assets). In these regressions, the effect of wealth on participation is qualitatively similar to that discussed in section 7.4.1, but the age coefficients and those of most other demographic variables are not statistically different from zero. In short-panel data, there is hardly enough information to identify the age effect; in other words, the fixed effects are correlated with age and other individual characteristics.

7.4.3 Summing Up

Let us summarize the main features of the data that emerge from the descriptive and regression analysis. First, ownership of risky assets is strongly increasing in wealth, exhibits a markedly concave age profile, and rises with education. Second, the conditional share of risky assets is also concave, but much less so than the ownership. Third, the share of risky financial assets increases with wealth. However, when account is taken of the other determinants, wealth exerts a mild effect on the portfolio: moving from low to high wealth raises the predicted share by only a few percentage points. The predictions are similar, but not identical, for total risky assets.

Overall, our findings reveal substantial differences between the determinants of ownership and those of asset shares conditional on participation. Age, wealth, and education—some of the main determinants of portfolio choice suggested by theory—affect portfolio decisions at the stage where households have to choose whether they should invest in risky assets. Once the decision is taken, the portfolio allocation is little affected by these factors.

How do these findings square with theoretical models of portfolio choice? The weak relation between the conditional share of risky assets and wealth suggests that preferences with linear risk tolerance may not be a bad characterization of reality, except perhaps at very high levels of wealth. The main problem in interpreting the empirical findings is that the theoretical models typically ignore the participation decision and focus on cases in which investors optimally choose to hold both safe and risky assets. Our results suggest instead that we need theoretical explanations for the concave age profile of participation in risky assets and for the strong, positive correlations between wealth and participation and between education and participation.

The only way to account for the lack of participation is to bring participation costs into the picture. There are essentially three sources of costs in the purchase of risky assets: minimum investment requirements, monetary transaction costs, and information costs. Since minimum investment requirements act as a barrier to entry at low wealth, they predict that participation increases with wealth. Monetary transaction costs lead to similar predictions, especially if these costs decrease with wealth.

In Italy, people pay substantial transaction costs when investing in a mutual fund. Entry fees vary with the amount invested and are generally between 3 and 4 percent for investment under 5,000 euros but can be as high as 6 percent. A significant reduction in costs applies only to very large investments, above 500,000 euros. Other mutual funds do not charge at entry but impose an exit fee that varies with the amount invested and the timing of disinvestment. These fees are between 2 and 3 percent for an investment of 5,000 euros withdrawn after one year.[10] The finding that the index of bank diffusion, which we regard as a good proxy for financial transaction costs, correlates positively with participation lends indirect support to the importance of these costs.

Participation costs, broadly interpreted, also help explain the correlation between participation and education. Education proxies for the ability to collect and process information. Participation costs are therefore lower for better-educated people, who will thus be more likely to participate. Information costs may also explain a puzzling feature of the data. If minimum investment requirements or fixed monetary costs were the only participation costs, we should find that the rich have complete portfolios, because entry costs vanish at high wealth levels. However, in table 7.5 we see that portfolios are poorly diversified even for the very rich. In the top 5 percent of the wealth distribution, only half of the households invest in risky financial assets. Information costs are not necessarily correlated with wealth and might therefore explain why so many rich households do not invest in risky financial assets.

Explaining why participation varies with age is more difficult because there is no obvious reason that participation costs vary with age. One may think that controlling for wealth and other relevant characteristics, the participation profile should be flat. But in reality we observe a concave profile. Calibration models of the sort discussed by Haliassos and Michaelides in chapter 2 suggest that participation costs—even when they are unrelated with age—could induce age-participation and wealth-participation profiles of the type that we observe in the data and potentially account for the correlation between education and participation. The reason that fixed costs can generate a hump in stockholding participation is that optimal policy functions for stockholding are upward sloping with respect to wealth and, with finite horizons, policy functions shift downward with age.

Another way to explain the results is that households differ in their liquidity needs and that these needs are correlated with age. Given the high transaction costs, it is clear that only investors who expect to hold assets for a relatively long time will acquire them. Those who have a high probability of needing to liquidate the asset will be more reluctant to buy, because the incidence of the costs decreases with the length of the holding period. For instance, if the entry or exit cost is 3 percent, the annual expected cost is only 0.3 percent if one expects to hold the asset for ten years but 6 percent if it is liquidated after six months.

This implies that households with short-term liquidity needs are less likely to buy assets that require fixed entry costs. Typically, households with liquidity needs are those that face liquidity constraints or with high income variability, such as the young, or those that face uninsured health risks, such as the old. They also include households that are accumulating assets to buy a house and are seeking a home to purchase. If housing prices are variable, there is a high chance of needing liquidity to take advantage of a good opportunity, and the corresponding incentive to pay the transaction cost to buy risky assets is low. More generally, households with limited access to credit markets (typically the young) are more reluctant to hold risky assets if these assets entail a liquidation cost. Income and health risk and credit market imperfections thus single out relatively young or relatively old households and are therefore consistent with the hump shape in participation.

In summary, the descriptive and regression results show that for many households, the main action in portfolio management is the decision to invest in risky assets. Once this decision is taken, the shape of the portfolio does not differ greatly from that predicted by standard models. These models, however, ignore investment costs and do not explain participation decisions and their relation with age, education, wealth, and other household characteristics.

7.5 Portfolio Transitions, Risk, and Financial Information

In this section we address a number of specific issues that are relevant for understanding the pattern of wealth allocation and have recently received attention in the theoretical and empirical literature. We focus on portfolio transitions, background risk, and information acquisition. Although each of these issues highlights important features of the behavior of Italian households, they are of broader interest and might be relevant for other countries as well. For brevity, here we summarize our main findings and refer readers to Guiso and Jappelli (2000) for further details.

At various points, we have cited fixed costs and management costs to interpret some of the patterns of household portfolios. These costs are indeed substantial, especially at low levels of wealth. One consequence of transaction costs is that they lead to inertia and lumpiness. In table 7.9 we report transition matrices of the participation rates in fairly safe and risky financial assets. We focus on the 2,926 transitions between 1993 and 1995. A similar picture would emerge using any other two consecutive surveys. Assets are grouped into three categories (safe, fairly safe, and risky). Each household in the transition matrix owns safe assets (which include currency), so the (0,0) cell identifies households with only safe assets, the (1,0) cell

Table 7.9
Financial portfolio transitions

1993		1995				
Fairly safe assets[a]	Risky assets[b]	1,1	1,0	0,1	0,0	Total
1	1	6.87	2.80	0.96	0.55	11.18
1	0	4.10	17.67	1.50	7.38	30.65
0	1	1.81	1.81	1.95	1.13	6.70
0	0	1.37	9.54	1.91	38.65	51.47
Total		14.15	31.82	6.32	47.71	100

Note: Portfolio transitions between period t and period $t + 1$ are computed on the basis of the panel section of the SHIW.
[a] Include short-term government bonds and life insurance.
[b] Include stocks, long-term government bonds, other bonds, mutual funds, and defined-contribution pensions.

those with only safe and fairly safe, the (0,1) cell those with only safe and risky assets, and the (1,1) cell those with all three types of assets. Each cell in the transition matrix reports the sixteen possible portfolio transitions. Complete persistence is found when all frequencies lie along the main diagonal, and portfolio transitions entail at least some positive off-diagonal elements.

The sum of the frequencies on the main diagonal indicates that over 65 percent of households did not change participation, evidence of substantial stickiness. The largest group is the lower left cell: almost 39 percent of households invested in only safe assets in both 1993 and 1995. Note also that the (0,0) group is the one with the least number of transitions: 75 percent did not invest in either fairly safe or risky assets between 1993 and 1995. The second most immobile group is the (1,1) group, where 61 percent did not change configuration. The third is the (1,0) group, where 58 percent experienced no transition. Analysis by education reveals that education correlates also with portfolio transitions. As noted, lack of portfolio transitions is consistent with the presence of large transaction costs.

Recent models of portfolio behavior proposed by Kimball (1992) posit that households' willingness to invest in risky assets and the amount held are affected not only by rate-of-return risk but also by independent sources of uncertainty. They imply that when people face risks that cannot be easily avoided or diversified (such as wage and unemployment risk), they are less willing to invest in risky assets. In order to reduce overall exposure to risk, people react to unavoidable risks by decreasing exposure to avoidable ones, such as a risky asset portfolio.

In table 7.7 the provincial unemployment rate has a negative and significant effect on the probability of holding risky assets, even controlling for age, wealth, and demographics only in the ownership equations. This negative correlation is noteworthy because the regressions also include a full set of city size dummies and a dummy for the south (where the unemployment rate is twice the national average). If one controls for random effects in the panel data probit regressions of table 7.8, the coefficients are negative and significantly different from zero in both ownership equations.

Managing a portfolio requires effort and knowledge of transaction costs, asset returns, volatility, and covariances with other assets. The 1995 and 1998 SHIW are a unique source of data on knowledge of financial assets and of current and past participation in financial markets. For instance, in 1995 about one-third of the sample did not know of the existence of equities; over 50 percent were ignorant of the existence of mutual funds; 10 percent, of all risky financial assets. Data for 1998 are similar, indicating that the privatization process increased participation, but not financial information per se, at least at the crude level recorded in the survey. In Guiso and Jappelli (2000) we construct a synthetic index of financial information, calculated as the number of assets that each household head knows about, divided by the number of potential assets known. We then use this index to provide insights into households' ignorance of basic facts of financial markets and on the determinants of financial information and sophistication. Investment in risky financial assets is strongly correlated with financial information and information externalities (as proxied by the average index in the province of residence), and conditional asset shares are relatively flat across the distribution of the index. This suggests that lack of financial information is an obstacle to entry into financial markets, but that once people start investing in risky assets, financial information plays no major role in shaping the portfolio.

7.6   Conclusion

In analyzing the structure of the portfolio of Italian households, we have uncovered several empirical regularities. The descriptive and regression analysis reveals substantial differences between the determinants of participation and those of asset shares conditional on participation. Participation in risky assets is strongly increasing in wealth, exhibits a marked concave age profile, and rises with education; on the other hand, the conditional share is quite flat at least until retirement, while the effect of wealth is relatively modest, as would be predicted by standard portfolio models with constant relative risk aversion preferences (see chapter 1, this volume).

In short, this chapter shows that most of the action in portfolio management concerns the decision to invest in risky assets. Once the decision is taken, the portfolio distribution accords reasonably well with that predicted by standard models. These models, however, largely ignore participation costs and their relation with age, education, wealth, and other household characteristics.

It is precisely the difference between participation decisions and conditional shares that calls for a close scrutiny of the relevance of participation costs. Minimum investment requirements act as a barrier to entry at low wealth and imply that participation increases with wealth. Monetary transaction costs imply similar predictions, especially if these costs decrease with wealth. Information costs, broadly interpreted, also help to explain the correlation between participation and education. Furthermore, information costs are not necessarily correlated with wealth and therefore might explain why so many wealthy households do not invest in risky financial assets. The extremely low number of portfolio transitions of Italian households supports models with large switching costs.

Further support for the importance of participation costs comes from a detailed analysis of the potential impact of background risk and financial information. We find strong evidence that participation depends on background risk. The evidence is weaker for asset shares, possibly because entry costs prevent poor households from investing in risky assets and because background risk is unimportant for the rich (who are more likely to participate). Direct indicators of financial asset knowledge suggest that financial information is of paramount importance in shaping households' portfolios.

Appendix: Data Sources, Financial and Real Assets

7A.1   The Cross-Sectional Data

The Bank of Italy Survey of Household Income and Wealth (SHIW) collects detailed data on demographics, households' consumption, income, and balance sheets. The data set used in this study has five independent cross sections of Italian households: 1989, 1991, 1993, 1995, and 1998. The regression analysis is performed using only data up to 1995. Each survey covers more than 8,000 households (with the exception of the 1998 survey, covering 7,147), for a total of 39,795 household-year observations. The SHIW surveys a representative sample of the Italian resident population. Sampling is in two stages—first municipalities and then households. Municipalities are divided into fifty-one strata defined by seventeen regions and three classes of population size (more than 40,000, 20,000 to 40,000, and less than 20,000). Households are randomly selected from registry office records. Households are defined as groups of individuals related by blood, marriage, or adoption and sharing the same dwelling. The net response rate (ratio of responses to contacted households net of ineligible units) is 38 percent in 1989, 33 percent in 1991, 58 percent in 1993, 57 percent in 1995, and 43 percent in 1998. The abrupt changes in the response rates in 1993 and 1998 could be partly due to the change in the firm collecting data in those years. A CD-ROM containing the entire historical SHIW can be obtained by writing to the Research Department, Banca d'Italia, Via Nazionale 91, 00186 Roma, Italy.

7A.2 Panel Data

Starting in 1989, each SHIW has reinterviewed some households from the previous surveys. The panel component has increased over time: 15 percent of the sample was reinterviewed in 1989, 27 percent in 1991, 43 percent in 1993, and 45 percent in 1995 (the 1998 survey is excluded from the panel estimation). Response rates increased in 1991 because in that year, households included in the panel were chosen among those that had previously expressed their willingness to being reinterviewed. There is a fixed component in the panel (for instance, households interviewed five times between 1987 to 1995 or four times from 1991 to 1995) and a new component every survey (for instance, households reinterviewed only in 1991 or in 1993). Brandolini and Cannari (1994) provide a detailed discussion of sample design, attrition, and other measurement issues.

7A.3 Financial Assets

Financial assets are the sum of transaction and saving accounts, certificates of deposit, government bonds, corporate bonds, stocks, mutual funds and management investment accounts, cash values of life insurance, cash values of defined-contribution pension funds, and foreign assets. In 1989, financial wealth is inferred with an accounting trick: households report fractions of financial wealth in total wealth, and then are asked to report the amount of checking accounts. Starting in 1991, respondents report each financial asset choosing one of fourteen brackets. The problem of bracketing can be handled either by assuming that all households own the midpoint of the interval or by applying more sophisticated imputation procedures, such as that suggested by Stewart (1983). The advantage of the second procedure falls with the number of brackets. Since we have fourteen brackets, we proceed with the first alternative. Asset categories become more detailed over the years, from thirteen in 1989 to seventeen in 1995 and 1998. Total financial assets come to only about half of the corresponding financial account aggregate. The items that are more seriously underestimated are corporate bonds, stocks, mutual funds, life insurance, private pensions, and foreign assets. This is partly due to underreporting by the wealthy, who own a disproportionate share of the more sophisticated financial instruments.

7A.4 Real Assets

Net real assets include real estate, business, valuables, and the stock of durable goods, minus liabilities. Liabilities are the sum of mortgage and other real estate debt, consumer credit, personal loans, and credit card debt. Respondents report a self-assessed value for each real asset and debt category.

Notes

We thank Angus Deaton, Michalis Haliassos, Raffaele Miniaci, Jim Poterba, Guglielmo Weber, and participants at the Conference on Household Portfolios. We acknowledge financial support from the European University Institute, the European Training and Mobility of Researchers Network Program, the Italian Ministry of Universities and Scientific Research, and the Italian National Research Council (CNR).

1. Between 1990 and 1997, seventy-one firms went public. An almost equal number delisted, so that the number of listed firms has remained unchanged at 244.

2. For instance, the privatization of ENEL, the national electric company, the last to take place in October 1999, featured 3.8 million bookings. To meet the request, the government raised the share of ENEL capital on sale from the initial allotment of 24 percent to 34 percent.

3. The relatively low indebtedness of Italian households reflects mainly supply factors (regulation and high enforcement costs) rather than low demand for credit (Guiso, Jappelli, and Terlizzese 1994). For instance, the process of repossessing collateral is extremely cumbersome in Italy, due to the length of the judicial process and various protections accorded to debtors.

4. The aggregate portfolio share of risky assets α can be written as $\alpha = P w_p \alpha_p$, where the three terms denote the participation rate (P), the ratio between average financial wealth of participants and average financial wealth in the population (w_p), and the participants' share invested in risky assets (α_p). The change in the aggregate share is then $d\alpha = (w_p \alpha_p)\, dP + (P w_p)\, d\alpha_p + (P \alpha_p)\, dw_p$.

5. For instance, there are considerable differences within the group of stockholders. In 1995, the only survey year for which this information is available, the average number of stocks in different companies is two, but 10 percent of stockholders hold equities of

more than four companies. Most stockholders hold equity of just one company, and almost invariably this is the company where one of the family members is employed.

6. This model does not require additional ingredients with respect to standard life cycle consumption models. Furthermore, since the lifetime profile of the annuity value of labor income differs in predictable ways between different population groups, the model suggests that portfolio composition shifts itself in predictable ways. For instance, if for some groups the path of labor income is steeper, then the portfolio composition is also more twisted toward risky assets at younger ages. Of course, the validity of this explanation rests on the assumption that human capital is a better substitute for safe than for risky assets.

7. The virtual irrelevance of age for conditional portfolio shares is inconsistent with financial advice given to older people to limit their exposure to stockholding.

8. A further reason for excluding the 1998 survey from the reference sample in the regression analysis is that in 1998, the company in charge of collecting the data and the collection methodology changed. Whether this has had any impact on the quality of the survey is still unclear, since at the time of the writing, the 1998 data were just released. The only noteworthy sign is that the traditional target sample size (over 8,000 households) has not been hit in the most recent survey, and that only 7,147 households have been interviewed.

9. An alternative explanation relies on the extent to which people trust each other. Guiso, Sapienza, and Zingales (2000) show that stockholding is positively affected by the level of trust in the province of residence. If, as in Putnam (1993), trust is lower in the south than in the north, the geographical variables may be capturing differences in trust.

10. On top of entry or exit costs, investors pay annual management fees on the order of 1.5 percent of the amount invested. Most funds include overperformance fees ranging from 0.2 to 0.8 percent of the amount invested or a retention of the overperformance ranging from 10 to over 35 percent.

8   Household Portfolios in Germany

Angelika Eymann* and
Axel Börsch-Supan

The saving behavior of German households has attracted the interest of a number of researchers.[1] Four features have been found to stand out, distinguishing the savings patterns of Germans from those observed in other industrialized countries. First, financial savings rates have been (and still are) fairly high by international standards, notwithstanding a very generous social security system. Second, home ownership rates are exceptionally low and have risen only very slightly during the past two decades. Third, consumer credit is rare compared to the Anglo-Saxon countries; debt financing of real estate increased to roughly two-thirds of the sales value of housing only in the 1990s. Fourth, financial portfolios are still dominated by relatively safe assets, notably checking and savings accounts and domestic bonds, and by illiquid assets, mainly life insurance policies. In 1993, only 12 percent of West Germans directly held stocks, while almost two-thirds of West German households owned a whole life insurance policy and about one-third held domestic bonds. Private pension funds are still uncommon.

The few empirical studies of the determinants of German households' portfolio choices focus exclusively on the impact of socio-economic characteristics on West German households' behavior.[2] The lack of a panel survey of financial behavior in Germany and the very restricted access to earlier waves of the Einkommens- und Verbrauchsstichprobe (EVS)—the Income and Expenditure Survey— have inhibited empirical researchers interested in the determinants of portfolio composition and its changes over time. The lack of panel data and regionally disaggregated time series of asset holdings has

---

* To our great sorrow, Angelika Eymann died three weeks after we finished this paper.

also impeded thorough studies of the financial adjustments of East German households after reunification.

This study seeks to set out the peculiarities of East and West German households' portfolios and to analyze how they can be traced back to financial institutions and sociodemographic characteristics of the households. In order to overcome the most severe data deficiencies, we combine several data sets. We use both macro- and microdata in order to present facts and recent trends in the households' portfolio composition. We then employ two microdata sets—the EVS and the Spiegel-Verlag survey Soll und Haben—to analyze the effects of various socioeconomic household characteristics that are posited as determinants in the theoretical section of this book[3] and have been found to influence portfolio choice significantly in Italy, the Netherlands, the United Kingdom, and the United States.[4] Finally, we exploit the information on assets provided by the German Socioeconomic Panel (GSOEP) to analyze the adjustment behavior of a balanced panel of East Germans from 1989 to 1996.

The following section presents facts and recent trends in ownership rates and portfolio composition of German households. Section 8.2 explores the effect of policy changes. Section 8.3 investigates the role of socioeconomic characteristics and financial knowledge. Section 8.4 analyzes differences in asset holdings between West and East German households and describes the financial adjustments of East German households during the transition. Section 8.5 concludes.

8.1 Portfolio Composition and Asset Ownership: Stylized Facts and Recent Trends

This section describes the structure of German households' portfolios in the 1980s and 1990s as reflected by national accounts and micro-survey data,[5] focusing on recent shifts between the portfolio shares of safe, illiquid, and liquid, yet risky assets.

Throughout, we use the following definitions of asset categories. Clearly safe assets are savings accounts and transaction accounts (if available). Fairly safe assets are building society savings contracts, life insurance contracts, bonds (if available, government bonds, savings certificates, and other domestic bonds), and other financial assets (including deposit accounts, options, futures, and tax-preferred financial investments in East Germany or Berlin). Risky assets are foreign bonds (if available), mutual funds (on stocks, if available), and stocks. Financial assets are savings and transactions accounts, building society savings contracts, life insurance contracts, government bonds, other bonds, other financial assets, mutual funds, and stocks. Nonfinancial assets are real estate (net worth). And debt refers to mortgage loans and consumer credit.

We used three databases:

• National accounts data for West Germany to describe the portfolio shares of financial assets held by households and nonprofit organizations[6] from 1975 to 1992, when the West German time series ended.

• Portfolio shares for both financial and nonfinancial assets that have been estimated by Deutsche Bundesbank (1999b) to describe trends in the portfolio composition of German households (excluding nonprofit organizations) after reunification.

• Waves 1978 to 1993 of the EVS to disentangle trends in ownership rates and conditional asset shares.

A detailed description of the data sets is provided in appendix 8A.[7] Our methods for computing average asset shares and ownership rates are described in appendix 8B.

8.1.1 Portfolio Composition

Both German national accounts data (table 8.1) and survey data (table 8.2) indicate that German households restructured their portfolios substantially during the 1980s and 1990s. According to the national accounts, the composition of the average financial portfolio changed from roughly 50 percent in clearly safe assets and 25 percent in fairly safe bonds and life insurance contracts (plus another 25 percent in stocks, building society savings contracts, and other financial assets) in 1975 to one-third in clearly safe assets and 40 percent in fairly safe bonds and life insurance contracts (plus 17 percent for stocks and mutual funds, and 10 percent for the remaining types of financial assets) in 1997. Similar to the trends in the other countries covered by this book, German households have decreased the share of safe assets and have become more willing (or, rather, somewhat less reluctant) to hold more risky assets in recent years. Three features seem most notable.

Table 8.1
Asset shares according to aggregate financial accounts

	West Germany: Households, including nonprofit organizations				Unified Germany: Households, excluding nonprofit organizations				
	1975	1980	1985	1990	1992	1990	1993	1995	1997
Financial assets									
Checking, deposit, and savings accounts	51.6	46.7	39.6	37.1	35.4	37.8	38.0	35.7	33.6
Bonds (including mutual funds on bonds)	12.0	17.3	21.5	22.8	26.2	n.a.	n.a.	n.a.	n.a.
Stocks (including mutual funds on stocks)	7.3	4.8	7.0	6.4	5.2	n.a.	n.a.	n.a.	n.a.
Bonds	n.a.	n.a.	n.a.	n.a.	n.a.	20.0	18.0	18.9	17.1
Stocks	n.a.	n.a.	n.a.	n.a.	n.a.	5.5	5.8	5.5	8.3
Mutual funds and managed investment accounts	n.a.	n.a.	n.a.	n.a.	n.a.	3.9	6.2	7.6	8.6
Building society savings contracts	7.8	7.3	5.5	4.1	3.7	4.1	3.7	3.4	3.4
Insurance and pension wealth	13.2	14.5	16.3	18.6	18.6	20.9	20.9	21.8	22.5
Other financial assets	8.1	9.6	10.0	11.2	11.1	7.8	7.4	6.9	6.6
Total financial assets	n.a.	n.a.	n.a.	n.a.	n.a.	37.5	39.2	40.4	42.8
Clearly safe financial assets	51.6	46.7	39.6	37.1	35.4	37.8	38.0	35.7	33.6
Fairly safe financial assets	41.1	48.5	53.4	56.5	59.4	52.8	50.0	51.2	49.5
Risky financial assets	7.3	4.8	7.0	6.4	5.2	9.4	12.0	13.1	16.9
Nonfinancial assets									
Real estate wealth	n.a.	n.a.	n.a.	n.a.	n.a.	83.0	82.4	82.7	81.9
Stock of durable goods	n.a.	n.a.	n.a.	n.a.	n.a.	17.0	17.6	17.3	18.1
Total nonfinancial assets	n.a.	n.a.	n.a.	n.a.	n.a.	62.5	60.8	59.6	57.2
Debt									
Long-term bank loans	57.4	65.2	63.0	68.0	69.0	n.a.	n.a.	n.a.	n.a.
Short-term bank loans	31.3	27.5	28.0	22.6	22.3	n.a.	n.a.	n.a.	n.a.
Other loans	11.3	7.3	9.0	9.4	8.7	n.a.	n.a.	n.a.	n.a.
Mortgage loans	n.a.	n.a.	n.a.	n.a.	n.a.	76.6	75.8	78.1	79.6
Consumer credit	n.a.	n.a.	n.a.	n.a.	n.a.	23.4	24.2	21.9	20.4
Total debt	n.a.	n.a.	n.a.	n.a.	n.a.	13.1	13.4	14.2	14.8

Source: Deutsche Bundesbank (1994b), Deutsche Bundesbank (1999b), and our own computations.

First, the decrease in safe assets almost matches the increase in bonds during the 1980s and early 1990s. Households reduced their holdings of savings accounts and building society savings contracts and increased their investments in bonds, bond-based mutual funds,[8] and, to a smaller extent, life insurance contracts. Stocks were largely unaffected by this restructuring; their share actually decreased slightly during the 1980s, unlike the pattern observed in the Anglo-Saxon countries. Not until the late 1990s did the portfolio shares of stocks start to increase.

Second, the share of housing wealth has decreased slightly while mortgage loans have increased. This pattern is matched by Deutsche Bundesbank (1999b) figures showing that the ratio of new mortgage loans and real estate formation rocketed from roughly 55 percent in the second half of the 1980s to almost 90 percent in 1993 before dropping to a still unusually high 75 percent in the late 1990s. The ratio of consumer credit to households' total net wealth remained roughly constant and is very low by international standards.

The third feature is the strong increase in the share of mutual funds, particularly pronounced between 1990 and 1993[9] and continuing throughout the 1990s. The very recent jump in the share of stocks is especially notable. The share of bonds decreased more slowly than mutual funds increased during the early 1990s. Thus, it appears unlikely that households merely reinvested domestic bonds in Luxembourg-based mutual funds until the introduction of a withholding tax on interest income in 1993. Instead, it seems that German households eventually—and still very reluctantly—followed the international trend toward riskier assets that started a decade earlier in such countries as the United Kingdom (see chapter 6, this volume). Nonetheless, stock-based mutual funds and stocks are still much less popular than in most of the other countries surveyed. Note that money market mutual funds were introduced only in 1994 and therefore do not appear in this description.

Neither national accounts data nor survey data can be expected to provide an unbiased estimate of households' asset holdings. The national accounts systematically exclude households' foreign assets (such as the proverbial Luxembourg-based mutual funds). The EVS systematically excludes, for confidentiality, the top 3 percent of German households by income.[10] Because there is no data set on the asset holdings of the wealthiest 3 percent of the population, it is impossible to judge whether average discrepancies between national

Angelika Eymann and Axel Börsch-Supan

Table 8.2
Portfolio composition according to survey data

	Ownership rates			Asset shares (conditional on ownership)			Asset shares			
	1983	1988	1993 West	1983	1988	1993 West	1983	1988	1993 West	1993 Unified
Financial assets										
Checking[a] and savings accounts	90.6	84.7	99.3	28.1	28.3	22.2	26.9	26.4	22.1	24.1
Government bonds	6.4	4.8	11.2	20.7	21.3	21.6	3.2	2.4	4.7	4.7
Other bonds	21.3	22.6	32.9	27.8	27.9	29.1	11.3	11.7	15.7	15.2
Stocks	9.7	11.4	12.0	17.6	19.2	18.5	3.8	4.7	4.6	4.3
Mutual funds and managed investment accounts	3.3	4.7	12.2	15.5	19.0	19.7	1.5	2.2	4.6	4.7
Life insurance contracts	67.2	64.6	61.6	44.8	48.1	41.3	36.3	39.1	31.4	29.1
Building society savings contracts	40.5	38.7	42.1	23.7	18.8	14.1	13.1	9.9	7.0	7.2
Other financial assets	5.8	5.3	19.9	27.9	27.7	26.8	4.0	3.5	9.8	10.7
Total financial assets	96.7	94.1	99.5	19.9	21.2	27.2	19.7	20.9	27.2	28.0
Clearly safe financial assets	90.6	84.7	99.3	28.1	28.3	22.2	26.9	26.4	22.1	24.1
Fairly safe financial assets	81.3	78.2	82.7	69.9	68.2	68.5	66.8	64.9	65.8	64.1
Risky financial assets	13.7	17.9	26.2	22.0	24.6	26.2	6.3	8.8	12.1	11.8
Nonfinancial assets										
Owner-occupied housing	43.9	45.7	46.7	n.a.	n.a.	n.a.	n.a.	n.a.	n.a.	n.a.
Total real estate	46.0	47.4	51.1	86.9	85.5	79.8	81.2	80.2	74.2	73.4
Business	5.5	n.a.	n.a.	n.a.	n.a.	n.a.	n.a.	n.a.	n.a.	n.a.
Total risky assets	17.8	n.a.	n.a.	n.a.	n.a.	n.a.	n.a.	n.a.	n.a.	n.a.

Debt

Mortgage and real estate debt	26.2	25.0	27.2	97.2	96.7	96.1	92.4	91.4	90.7	90.2
Consumer credit	17.3	19.1	22.5	27.5	27.2	24.7	7.6	8.7	9.3	9.8
Consumer credit in percentage of total net wealth (used as correction term[b])							1.0	1.1	1.4	1.4
Total debt	38.7	38.6	42.9	21.8	23.9	27.3	12.5	12.6	14.7	14.5

Source: Income and Expenditure Survey.

[a] Information on checking accounts is provided by wave 1993 only.

[b] The correction term equals the ratio of the average value of consumer credit to average total net wealth.

accounts and survey data are caused by undersampling or down-wardly biased responses.

National accounts and survey data reflect similar trends for all asset shares except life insurance contracts. However, the levels of asset differ markedly between macro- and microdata.[11] Within financial assets, underreporting is greatest for checking and savings accounts and for stocks and mutual funds. These are the assets likely to be preferred by persons at either end of the wealth distribution. The shares derived from survey data are too large for fairly safe assets and too small for clearly safe and risky ones (cf. tables 8.1 and 8.2). The average sales value of real estate is higher than estimated by the Deutsche Bundesbank. This result confirms Börsch-Supan et al.'s (1999) that home ownership rates reported in the EVS are substantially higher than those based on the National Housing Censuses.

8.1.2 Ownership Rates and Conditional Asset Shares

Previous empirical studies of portfolio choice have emphasized the need to disentangle the qualitative ownership choice from the quantitative share allocation once ownership has been decided.[12] This necessity of separate analysis is particularly apparent for assets that are held by a small percentage of the population, such as stocks and bonds.

The first columns of table 8.2 reveal that the most popular financial assets among German households are transaction and savings accounts, followed by life insurance policies. Building society savings contracts rank third and nongovernment bonds fourth. In terms of conditional asset shares, however, transaction and savings accounts rank only fourth, with less than a quarter of financial wealth invested in these assets in 1993. Conditional asset shares for life insurance contracts, nongovernment bonds, and other financial assets take the first three places with 40 percent, 29 percent, and 28 percent, respectively. Remarkably, even among the relatively few owners of stocks, the percentage of financial wealth invested in these assets is only two-thirds of the conditional asset share of nongovernment bonds.

Analyzing trends in households' portfolio composition on the basis of sample averages may yield grossly misleading results if trends in ownership rates and asset shares conditional on ownership diverge, because the aggregation lumps change on the extensive and the intensive margin. Table 8.2 shows that this problem is indeed relevant for several types of assets in Germany.[13] Throughout the period 1983 to 1993, ownership rates for real estate and building society savings contracts steadily moved in opposite directions to the corresponding conditional asset shares for owners of these assets. Comovement in ownership rates and conditional asset shares characterized total debt and mutual funds (both increasing) and life insurance contracts (decreasing). The ownership rates and conditional asset shares of stocks remained largely stable.

What seems most interesting and unusual from the international perspective, however, is the very strong increase in ownership rates of bonds and other financial assets during and shortly after reunification. This increase was not mirrored in conditional asset shares, which remained stable throughout the observation period. The increase in their unconditional asset shares, reflected in table 8.2, was thus clearly due to an increased willingness to hold such assets. Both old and new owners seem to have aimed at the same target level of these asset shares in their portfolio.

Table 8.2 suggests that ownership rates changed significantly during the observation period. However, both the timing of the restructuring and the assets involved differ from those observed in the country studies for Italy, the Netherlands, the United Kingdom, and the United States. Unlike U.K. households, Germans began accessing new types of assets only in the late 1980s and early 1990s. The rise in ownership rates affected essentially three assets: bonds, mutual funds, and other financial assets. Until 1993, the willingness to hold stocks remained constant at the very low level of roughly 10 percent of German households.

8.1.3 Diversification

Table 8.3 presents portfolio diversification in terms of clearly safe, fairly safe, and risky assets.[14] Households in the first three rows hold only one type of asset, those in the last row all three types. German households started to diversify their portfolios in the mid-1980s. The number of asset conglomerates held in the portfolio increased most sharply during the period of reunification, when risky assets (including foreign and private domestic bonds) attracted German households.

Unfortunately, the lack of German panel data on households' financial behavior precludes a more in-depth analysis of portfolio

Table 8.3
Diversification of household financial portfolios

| Percentage of households holding ... in their financial asset portfolio | | | | | | |
Clearly safe assetsª	Fairly safe assetsᵇ	Risky assets	1978	1983	1988	1993
No	No	No	3.5	3.2	5.9	0.5
No	No	Yes	0.1	0.1	0.2	0.0
No	Yes	No	5.0	5.7	8.4	0.2
No	Yes	Yes	0.3	0.4	0.9	0.0
Yes	No	No	14.3	14.2	14.2	15.0
Yes	No	Yes	1.3	1.2	1.5	1.8
Yes	Yes	No	63.2	63.2	53.6	58.1
Yes	Yes	Yes	12.4	12.0	15.4	24.4

Source: Income and Expenditure Survey, West German households only.
ª Checking accounts were included in the definition of clearly safe assets only in 1993. Previous waves neglected this asset.
ᵇ Information on other financial assets is unavailable for wave 1978.

mobility. Interpreting table 8.3, which uses independent cross sections, as longitudinal information, it suggests that only the previous owners of fairly safe assets (government bonds, savings certificates, life insurance contracts, and building society savings contracts) were willing to restructure and diversify their portfolios. They seem to have disposed of their clearly safe assets (mainly savings accounts) in the mid-1980s and gradually invested in riskier ones (other bonds, mutual funds, or stocks) in the late 1980s and early 1990s.

8.2   Policy Changes and Household Reactions

Financial regulations and tax policies were frequently revised in the 1980s and 1990s, leading to changes in the real returns on assets both before and after taxes. Here, we first describe these policy changes and their impact on yield structures. We then investigate whether and to what extent households reacted to these policy changes.[15] Since there is no German panel data set that would allow empirical analyses of policy changes and household behavior, this section must rely on comparisons of cross sections—that is, whether policy changes match the trends in asset shares and ownership rates reflected in tables 8.1 and 8.2. Clearly, we cannot rule out misinterpretations through the combination of cohort, time, and age effects, as well as lag and lead effects.

We first focus on the effects of financial market deregulation, privatization, and German reunification—that is, policy changes that by and large affect asset yields without discriminating among individuals. Then we look at changes in taxes and subsidies—that is, policy changes that are likely to have strong individual-specific effects.

8.2.1 Deregulation of Financial Markets and German Reunification

Bond Markets
During the 1980s, government and the universal banks in Germany typically relied on the domestic bond market to finance the budget deficit and refinance loans. Thus, bond issues by nonbank companies were nearly negligible until the late 1990s. Capital export restrictions hindering foreigners' purchases of domestic bonds were abolished in the mid-1980s. Bond market deregulation sought to widen the range of possible purchasers of domestic bonds, which consisted more or less exclusively of government and bank bonds. Deregulation was also supported by the Bundesbank, because it secured the role of the central bank's minimum reserve policy as a major instrument of monetary control. In hindsight, the deregulation process came just in time to permit German banks and several government agencies to attract international capital to issue bonds in order to finance the rebuilding of East Germany after reunification.

Bond yields and interest rates for short-term savings fell in real terms and moved largely in parallel during the second half of the 1980s. Real bond yields, however, jumped by 2 percent in 1990. Moreover, the spread between bond yields and short-term savings accounts rates widened to an unprecedented six percentage points. Only in 1992, when the inflation rate started to increase, did this spread return to its long-term average of about four points. Thus, German reunification implied a short-term rise in returns on bonds relative to savings accounts, yet eventually led to a sharp increase in the volatility of bond yields. These unexpected jolts to the yield structure of savings accounts and bonds seem to be a likely cause of the portfolio adjustments during and after reunification, when households replaced long-term savings accounts by bonds during the reunification period and then lost favor for bonds.

Stock Markets

Until recently, German stock markets were thin, decentralized, and comparatively neglected. In 1990, stock market capitalization amounted to just 23 percent of gross domestic product (GDP), compared with 42 percent in the Netherlands, 87 percent in the United Kingdom, and 55 percent in the United States.[16] Moreover, Wenger and Kaserer (1997) report that cross-holdings account for at least 27 percent of the gross capitalization; 46.8 percent of the stocks are held by banks and nonfinancial companies. Hence, only 11.4 percent of common stocks are held by private and institutional investors. Even after the soaring stock prices of the late 1990s, stock market capitalization has risen to only 39.4 percent of GDP in Germany as compared to 130 percent in the Netherlands, 155 percent in the United Kingdom, and 144 percent in the United States.

The deregulation of the German stock markets began only in 1989. It was initiated by the need to transpose European Union (EU) directives into German law in order to comply with the regulations of the single market in services. Unlike that of bond markets, stock market deregulation was initiated by foreign rather than domestic interest groups. At first, German authorities were not at all quick in transposing EU directives into law.[17] The process gained speed only when the regionally separated stock markets in Germany were centralized (1993) and the Frankfurt stock exchange was reorganized and expanded (1990, 1991, and 1997). Stock market deregulation gathered momentum with the privatization of some public sector industries, notably the initial public offering of Deutsche Telekom in November 1996. We expect that the process will accelerate when Germany's ailing pay-as-you-go social security system will be reformed by adding a new funded pillar to the pension system and further reducing the generosity of public health insurance.[18]

Major advances in stock market deregulation, whose purpose was to make the German stock market more attractive to domestic and foreign institutional investors, private investors with modest wealth, and smaller companies willing to issue stocks, were made in 1990, 1994, and 1998. These legal changes substantially lowered transaction costs (1990). Access for international and domestic institutional investors (especially mutual funds) was widened (1990, 1994, and 1998). Entry barriers for small corporations (discriminatory accounting and codetermination rules) and for private investors (minimal stock values) were reduced in 1994. In the end, stock market surveillance was tightened substantially (1994 and 1998). To foster widespread ownership, the corporate income tax code was revised in December 1999. This controversial change will eventually make capital gains tax free if they derive from sales of corporate reserves, which consist mainly in corporate cross-holdings valued at cost. Anticipation of the reform led to an 18 percent spurt in the Dentscher Aktienindex (DAX) performance index in just a month (December 1999).

For a person subject to the top marginal tax rate of 56 percent, Stehle (1999) shows that the average annual after-tax yield from German stocks was 4.6 percent from January 1969 to December 1997. From January 1988 to December 1998, however, it was 11.5 percent. The difference between the after-tax yield of government bonds and stocks, which averaged 4.8 percent for the whole period, was 11.1 percent in the 1990s.[19]

Recently the German stock markets appear to have gained in attractiveness only in the wake of the third wave of deregulation. We have four pieces of evidence. First, the number of initial public offerings started to increase in 1997 and then soared in 1999 to roughly ten times the previous average level.[20] Second, turnover on the stock market increased by roughly 30 percent in 1996, 1997, and 1998 and exceeded the growth rate of the DAX performance index in 1996 and 1998.[21] Third, the DAX performance index accelerated only in 1996. Fourth, table 8.1 shows that the share of stocks in household portfolios held largely stable during the first half of the 1990s and started to rise only after 1995.

The Bundesbank (1999b) estimates do not allow disentangling stock- and bond-based mutual funds. Deutsche Bundesbank (1994c) reports that the increase in mutual fund units in the early 1990s was accounted for almost exclusively by bond-based mutual funds. Presumably the increase in the late 1990s is due to stock-based funds, in both absolute and relative terms.

The example of mutual funds shows clearly that we cannot provide unambiguous causality. The data deficiencies in both the national accounts and the survey data mean that it remains unclear whether it was the gradual loosening of the regulations for mutual funds beginning in 1990 or the increased yields on both bonds and stocks that boosted the attractiveness of the funds.

8.2.2   Savings Subsidies and Taxation

Germany has a tradition of promoting the formation of household wealth. It rests on two pillars: favorable tax treatment of asset holdings and direct savings subsidies. Starting in the 1950s, German tax and subsidy policies were initially set up to foster the formation of industrial capital and housing in the early postwar years. In the 1960s and 1970s, the focus was gradually shifted to low- and medium-income earners with children.[22] In the wake of reunification, subsidies and tax exemptions were temporarily expanded to promote industry, infrastructure, and housing construction in East Germany, much in spirit of the policies of the early 1950s.

Savings Subsidies
Three different systems of subsidies for long-term saving plans were introduced in the late 1950s and 1960s: subsidies to undedicated long-term savings contracts (*Sparprämie*), subsidies to contributions to building society savings contracts (*Wohnungsbauprämie*), and subsidies to employer-sponsored savings plans (*Arbeitnehmer-Sparzulage*). Subsidy rates varied over time and were generally higher for dedicated savings plans.

The inflation of the 1970s seriously eroded the accessibility of the subsidies because income limits and contribution caps remained unadjusted. In the 1980s and 1990s, the scope of assets was narrowed to building society savings contracts, stocks, stock-based mutual funds, and loans to the employer, further reducing the attractiveness. The accessibility of *Wohnungsbauprämie* and *Arbeitnehmer-Sparzulage* was widened again during the 1990s, however. Subsidies to building society savings contracts were a key element in policies fostering housing construction in Eastern Germany. Germany may soon see yet another shift in the use of dedicated savings subsidies. It is now planned to funnel most savings subsidies to mutual funds dedicated to retirement income as an individual or employer-sponsored supplement to the public pension system.[23]

Although savings subsidies were available only to low- and lower-middle-income households and amounted to less than 200 Deutsche Marks (DM) per year during the 1980s and 1990s,[24] the successive policy changes have left their traces on households' portfolio choice. The decrease in long-term savings contracts in the 1980s (table 8.1) is most likely due to the decrease in real after-tax yields of long-term savings contracts compared with bonds. Another piece of evidence is the diverging trends in ownership rates and conditional asset shares of building society savings contracts between East and West Germany (see section 8.4). Tables 8.1 and 8.2 suggest that a growing number of eligible households took out building society savings contracts during the 1990s but held their investment to roughly 1,000 DM per year, the ceiling for these subsidies.

It is questionable whether policy shocks were the sole cause of changes in portfolio composition. Rather, changes in the relative yields on assets and savings policy shocks are likely codetermined by common underlying factors (notably the determinants of increasing budget deficits) and mutually reinforcing.

Taxation

The favorable tax treatment of rented and, to a lesser degree, owner-occupied housing[25] as well as of life insurance contracts forms the second and strongest pillar of German savings policy. Like the subsidies described above, tax exemptions generally favor low- and medium-income earner households with children.[26]

Stocks, mutual funds, and housing were also implicitly tax favored in that capital gains were not taxed if assets were held beyond the "speculation period" of six months and one year, respectively; these were lengthened to one year and ten years, respectively, in 2000, significantly reducing this incentive.

The attractiveness of owner-occupied housing is further reduced because interest payments for mortgages are not tax deductible. However, mortgage interest was made tax deductible in 1991 for a restricted period of three years. In line with a general expansion of the tax-favored treatment of housing in Eastern Germany, this measure was introduced in order to increase the incentives for housing construction. It seems likely that the increase in the ratio of new mortgage loans to real estate formation reported by Deutsche Bundesbank (1999b) for the early 1990s is related to this policy change.

Three major changes in the German tax code in the late 1980s and 1990s are likely to have substantially changed the after-tax yields of some asset categories.

In 1989, a 10 percent withholding tax on interest income (*Kleine Kapitalertragsteuer*) was introduced after prior announcement in 1988, reflecting political efforts to increase the tax base. It was abolished within a span of just six months.

In 1991, a ruling by the Supreme Court (Bundesverfassungs-gericht) forced the government to rule out tax discrimination between labor and capital income and to reinstate a withholding tax (*Zinsabschlagsteuer*) on interest, a 30 percent tax on interest income above 6,000 DM (12,000 DM for couples), in 1993.[27] In September 1994, this withholding tax was extended to interest income on foreign assets that are transferred to Germany (*Zwischengewinnbesteuerung*). The introduction of the withholding tax was accompanied by a drive to curb tax evasion. Audits of income tax statements were more frequent, and several major German banks were accused of helping their customers to evade tax payments illegally in the late 1990s. The income tax reform in 2000 further reduced the loopholes in the personal income tax code and reduce tax exemptions for interest income by 50 percent.[28]

In 1995, another Supreme Court ruling targeted the discriminatory favorable tax treatment of housing against financial assets. So in 1996, the government abolished the wealth tax, which favored housing and penalized stocks. This ruling also necessitated reform of the bequest and gift tax. The revised tax code, however, still allows for tax exemptions for housing up to the price of an average home if willed to children and an average townhouse if willed to grandchildren.

The wealthier German households have reacted sharply to changes in the tax code and the introduction of the withholding tax, although this is hard to see in the national accounts and the survey data (tables 8.1 and 8.2), since the macrodata sources do not include housing wealth by region and the survey data have only been collected at five-year intervals. However, the Bundesbank (1994a, 1994c) reports that the turnover rate of cash increased by 30 percent in 1992 and that investments in foreign mutual funds skyrocketed to 13 billion DM in 1988 and a total of 99.5 billion DM[29] between mid-1991 and November 1993. Shortly after the first withholding tax was abolished, net investment in foreign mutual funds turned negative. The same happened when the tax was extended to interest income from foreign mutual funds (*Zwischengewinnbesteuerung*) in the second half of 1993. Interestingly, and unlike the situation in 1988, the net capital outflow in the period 1991 to 1993 was small. Three-quarters of the

"foreign" investments consisted of investments in Luxembourg mutual funds, which were largely based on German bank bonds and (to
a smaller extent) German government bonds.[30]

8.3   Socioeconomic Determinants of Household Portfolio Choice

This section focuses on the socioeconomic determinants of households' willingness to hold risky assets and their portfolio composition. First, we present bivariate analyses of the determinants that are
at the focus of the theoretical section of this book and whose key role
is underscored by previous empirical studies.[31] Second, we sketch
the results of a multivariate analysis of the determinants' of households' willingness to hold clearly safe, fairly safe, and risky assets.

8.3.1   Bivariate Analyses

Risky Assets and Age
King and Leape (1987) suggest that age may affect the willingness to
hold risky assets, as older persons have acquired more information
on variance and yield than younger persons. The cross-sectional
ownership rates of risky assets do not really confirm this hypothesis,
however. We find that the cross-sectional age profile is essentially
flat from age 30 to 60 (cf. table 8.4). Ownership rates are lower only

Table 8.4
Cross-sectional age profile of asset ownership and share of risky assets

Age group	Ownership rates			Conditional asset shares (percentage of household wealth held in financial assets)			Asset shares (percentage of household wealth held in financial assets)		
	1983	1988	1993	1983	1988	1993	1983	1988	1993
Under 30	9.0	17.5	23.8	19.4	22.6	25.6	3.3	7.9	11.3
30–39	13.0	18.8	29.2	18.2	20.9	22.6	4.0	6.7	10.4
40–49	15.9	20.8	28.1	17.1	21.4	20.6	4.5	7.5	9.1
50–59	15.7	20.3	29.0	18.7	20.0	21.6	5.4	7.4	10.2
60–69	14.6	17.8	25.2	23.1	27.5	28.1	8.0	10.5	12.9
70 and over	12.3	12.6	20.4	33.6	38.4	41.4	12.2	13.4	19.5

Source: Income and Expenditure Survey; West German households only.

for the very young and the very old. Ownership rates have generally increased over time, and the rate of increase seems to be greater at the extremities of the age distribution. Growth rates are particularly high for the young and started to increase in the late 1980s. The very old do not seem to have invested in risky assets until the 1990s.

The cross-sectional age profile of the risky asset share conditional on ownership of such assets differs sharply from that of ownership rates. Conditional asset shares seem to be convex in age and highest for the retired. This profile suggests that households cut down their risky assets when they start taking out life insurance and invest in housing, and strongly increase their other investments when life insurance contracts mature around the age of retirement.

Cohort and Time Effects

Various studies have found that the age distribution of household wealth in Germany displays strong cohort effects for generations born during or before World War II.[32] Schnabel (1999) shows that these are particularly strong for housing wealth.

Figure 8.1 depicts average ownership rates of risky and fairly safe financial assets by cohort and age as well as predicted ownership rates by age.[33] Weighted empirical averages have been computed on the basis of the four samples of West German households interviewed in waves 1978 to 1993 of the EVS.

Figure 8.1 suggests that cohort and time effects are nonnegligible, but play only a minor role for financial assets, unlike owner-occupied housing. There is a weak hump-shape effect of age for risky assets and a strong one for fairly safe assets (which include building society savings and life insurance). Ownership rates of fairly safe assets remained remarkably stable, while those of risky assets rose substantially for all age groups.

Similar to table 8.4, figure 8.1a suggests that young households started investing in risky assets in the mid-1980s. For older cohorts, the willingness to hold risky assets seems to have increased only during or after German reunification. The respective rates of increase have decreased with age.

Wealth

Gollier (chapter 1, this volume) summarizes conditions under which wealth should correlate positively with the portfolio share of risky assets. Several studies have found wealth to be the major determi-

a. Risky assets

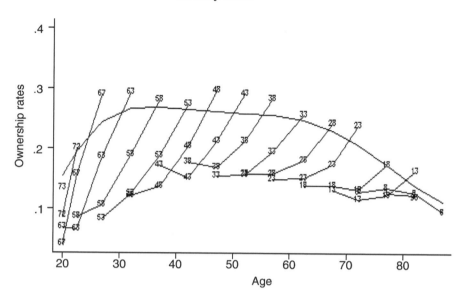

b. Fairly safe assets

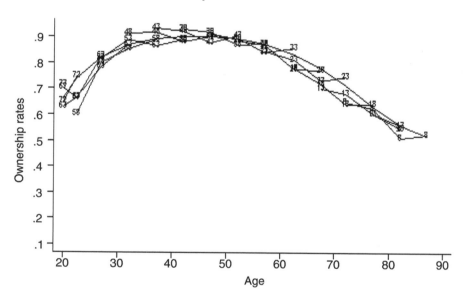

Figure 8.1
Cohort effects on ownership rates of financial assets. *Source:* Income and Expenditure
Survey 1978, 1983, 1988, and 1993 (West German households).

nant of households' willingness to hold risky assets.[34] Unfortunately, there is no German microdata set for the very wealthy. As noted, the EVS excludes the top three income percentiles. To examine the impact of wealth on portfolio choice, we split the sample of households participating in wave 1993 of the EVS into four (all-Germany) wealth quartiles.[35] We compute asset shares irrespective of ownership for each quartile as well as the top five percentiles in the EVS.

Table 8.5 reveals distinct jumps in several of the asset shares between quartiles. The lowest quartile in Western Germany seems to hold almost nothing but safe and fairly safe assets: life insurance contracts and building society contracts, but hardly any bonds. The second quartile also invests in bonds and mutual funds. Substantial real estate ownership appears only in the third quartile. Compared to these distinct jumps in bonds, mutual funds, and real estate, the increase in the portfolio share of stocks and life insurance with wealth is much smoother, although the share of stocks in the fourth quartile does rise notably.

The results in table 8.5 suggest that there are target levels for some asset shares. For instance, the shares of real estate and bonds are essentially stable for households that can readily obtain consumer credit and mortgage loans.

In order to analyze household heterogeneity with respect to the willingness to hold risky assets, we repeat the age cohort analysis by wealth quartile.[36] Again, we acknowledge that our interpretations could be distorted by the confounding of age, cohort, and time effects.

Figure 8.2 shows that both the timing and extent of changes in ownership differ by quartile. In the first two quartiles, ownership rates of risky assets rose only for the very youngest cohorts. In the third, all cohorts were increasingly willing to hold risky assets. The young started to invest in risky assets as early as the late 1980s; older cohorts followed in the 1990s.

The age-specific growth rates imply that ownership rates of risky assets generally decreased with age for the first three wealth quartiles in 1993; previously the age profile was flat. For the fourth quartile, the growth rates appear to have been stable over time across all cohorts, but growth rates were higher for the young, implying that a formerly rising age profile of the ownership rates of risky assets flattened out in 1993.

Table 8.5
Asset shares by wealth quartiles

	Below net worth quartile I	Between net worth quartiles I and II	Between net worth quartiles II and III	Above net worth quartile III	Top 5 percent
Financial assets					
Checking and savings accounts	47.2	29.6	24.2	17.0	11.3
Government bonds	1.5	4.9	4.3	5.0	5.2
Other bonds	6.2	14.6	15.2	17.1	17.2
Stocks	1.6	2.1	3.1	6.3	10.1
Mutual funds and managed investment accounts	2.0	3.8	4.4	5.1	5.4
Life insurance	26.7	27.1	30.7	33.4	35.8
Building society savings contracts	11.1	8.8	9.1	5.2	3.1
Total financial assets	217.6	90.2	27.3	21.2	21.0
Clearly safe financial assets	47.2	29.6	24.2	17.0	11.3
Fairly safe financial assets	47.9	62.4	65.9	68.2	68.9
Risky financial assets	4.9	8.0	9.9	14.9	19.8
Nonfinancial assets					
Total real estate	9.4	13.6	73.7	79.2	79.3
Total risky assets	4.9	8.0	9.9	14.9	19.8
Debt					
Mortgage and real estate debt	32.9	88.5	95.6	95.7	96.0
Consumer credit	67.1	11.5	4.4	4.3	4.0
Consumer credit in percentage of total net wealth	127.0	3.8	0.3	0.4	0.3
Total debt	189.2	33.0	5.7	9.1	8.7

Source: Income and Expenditure Survey, 1993, West German households only.
Note: "Total risky assets" include all "risky financial assets."

a. First quartile

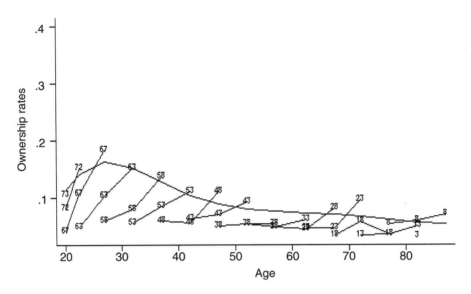

b. Second quartile

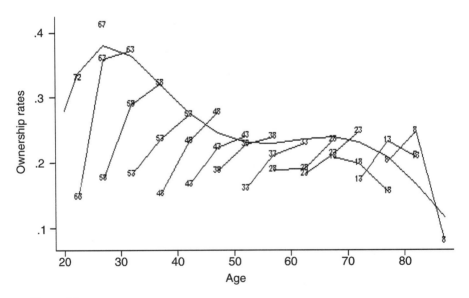

Figure 8.2
Ownership rates of risky assets by age, cohort, and net household wealth quartiles.
Source: Income and Expenditure Survey (waves 1983, 1988, 1993, West German households).

c. Third quartile

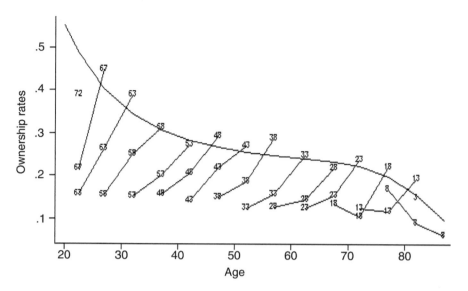

d. Fourth quartile

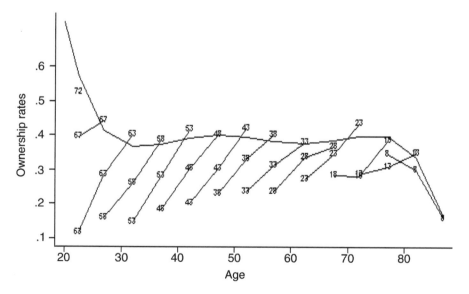

Figure 8.2 (continued)

Education

A number of theoretical and empirical studies of household portfolio choice have emphasized the role of education in willingness to hold risky assets and suggested that income uncertainty, income expectations, and financial information vary with schooling.[37]

Information on schooling is provided only in the 1993 wave of the EVS. We split the sample educational attainment. Figures 8.3 and 8.4 present predicted ownership rates of risky assets and the predicted number of financial assets by education segments.

Most notable is the distinct difference between household heads with and without postsecondary education. This difference applies to both level and cross-sectional age profile. Ownership rates of risky assets are much lower among household headed by persons with less than university or polytechnic education, in both Eastern and Western Germany.

Ownership rates of risky and fairly safe assets peak around the age of 50 for West Germans and around the age of 40 for East Germans with up to thirteen years of schooling (at most, upper secondary).[38] The hump shape of these households' age profiles seems to be slightly more pronounced than that in table 8.4. However, for Western Germans holding a university degree, ownership rates of risky assets rise up to the age of 70, then drop sharply.[39] The marked spread of the peak ages for persons with and without postsecondary education might explain why table 8.4 reflects a comparatively flat age profile for the full-sample ownership rates of risky assets.

Figure 8.4 suggests that the generally marked difference between the average number of financial assets held by households with and without postsecondary education increases with age. We presume that around the age of retirement, households with university education tend to reinvest the capital accumulated in life insurance contracts in risky assets.

Financial Information and Wealth Allocation

King and Leape (1987) report that more than a third of those who do not own risky assets in the 1978 Survey of Consumer Financial Decisions indicated that they had had too little knowledge to invest in these assets. Also, Kennickell, Starr-McCluer, and Sunden (1996) find that 1983 Survey of Consumer Finances respondents who are more likely to seek financial advice are also more willing to hold risky assets.

a. West German households

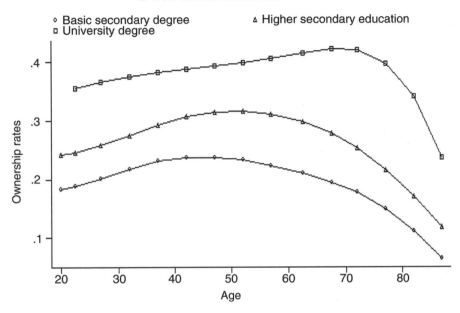

b. East German households

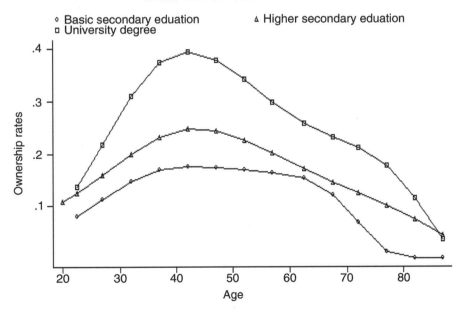

Figure 8.3
Ownership rates of risky assets by age, education, and region. *Source:* Income and Expenditure Survey, 1993.

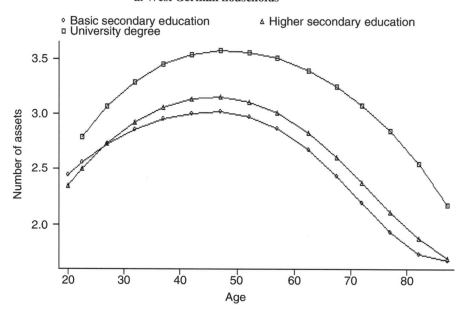

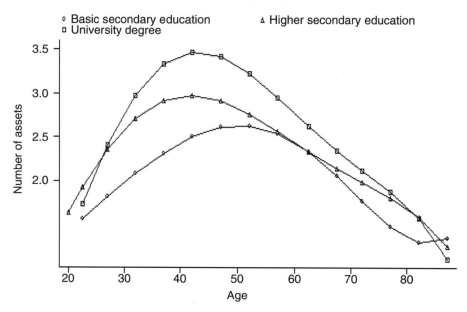

Figure 8.4
Number of financial assets by age, education, and region. *Source:* Income and Expenditure Survey, 1993.

Table 8.6
Individual assessment of information status and portfolio diversification

	Percentage of respondents describing themselves as ...			
	Very well informed	Fairly well informed	Not very well informed	Not at all informed
1980	19.6	31.7	35.0	13.7
1984	19.6	30.2	35.8	14.5
1989	17.3	32.1	37.5	14.1
1995	3.8	29.2	48.7	18.3

Percentage of respondents by composition of financial asset portfolio (1995)

Clearly safe assets	Fairly safe assets	Risky assets				
No	No	No	1.7	6.5	21.3	70.5
No	No	Yes	0	0	0	0
No	Yes	No	12.9	21.6	23.5	42.0
No	Yes	Yes	0	0	0	0
Yes	No	No	0.8	13.7	51.8	33.8
Yes	No	Yes	4.2	30.1	38.0	27.7
Yes	Yes	No	2.6	29.7	51.6	16.1
Yes	Yes	Yes	12.5	46.8	34.4	6.2

Source: Spiegel-Verlag (1980, 1985, 1989, 1996), West German households only.

Because the German EVS does not have information on the financial knowledge, we employ a marketing-oriented survey (*Soll und Haben*) on the financial behavior of households. The data set, collected by the publishing house Spiegel-Verlag, covers information search and status as well as, in part, on the individuals' socioeconomic background. The main purpose of the survey is to shed light on the web of portfolio choice, financial knowledge, and advice, while assessing customer satisfaction and the willingness to adopt new banking technologies.[40]

Judging from their self-assessments, more than half of German households consider themselves not "very well" or "at all" informed (see table 8.6). And, surprisingly, the self-assessed knowledge of financial affairs does not seem to have improved even in the late 1980s and early 1990s as portfolios diversified and got riskier.[41] Contrary to this finding—but in line with our expectations—cross-section results for 1995 suggest that those who describe themselves as well informed or actively searching for information from diverse banks are more willing to hold risky assets and have more diversified portfolios. Persons relying on the advice of family and friends or their own bank are most likely to have safe assets only.

8.3.2 Multivariate Analysis

The bivariate analyses have studied the effects of age, wealth, education, and information on households' willingness to hold risky and illiquid assets. These characteristics are clearly intercorrelated. To disentangle wealth, age, and education effects and to control for socioeconomic characteristics that affect the eligibility for favored tax treatment and savings subsidies for fairly safe assets, we now present the results of multivariate analyses of the determinants of ownership rates and portfolio shares of fairly safe and risky assets. Unfortunately, the EVS from 1978 to 1988 provides very little information on socioeconomic background. We thus confine ourselves to a cross-section analysis based on wave 1993 and acknowledge that we cannot disentangle age and cohort effects.

Table 8.7 presents estimation results for probit models of the decision to hold fairly safe or risky assets.[42] In order to analyze the cohort/age and wealth effects that have proved to be relevant, the set of explanatory variables includes third-order polynomials in wealth and age, dummy variables measuring education, and socioeconomic characteristics (such as employment status and number of children) that determine the households' tax treatment and access to savings subsidies. In order to analyze the differing age profiles of persons with and without university education, we also allow for education-specific slopes of the age polynomial.

The results by and large confirm our earlier findings. The willingness to hold fairly safe assets peaks at a net worth of 1.05 million DM. The willingness to hold risky assets, however, seems to increase at an almost constant rate throughout the entire range of wealth levels. The strongly nonlinear shape of its age profile, moreover, suggests that the composition of the portfolio of fairly safe assets changes strongly over the life cycle. Building society savings contracts appear to be popular among the very young, and life insurance contracts are favored by the middle-aged. The willingness to hold risky assets appears to be greatest for the very young and to decrease until age 50. Around retirement age, the willingness to hold risky assets increases again moderately until age 70. The estimation results suggest that education increases the willingness to hold risky assets, but—in contrast to the findings in figure 8.3—it does not shift the age profile of ownership rates.

Moreover, the estimation results show that the willingness to hold fairly safe and risky assets is convex in income, controlling for wealth, employment status, and family size. Being employed increases the willingness to invest in life insurance, building society savings, and other fairly safe assets. The same holds for larger family sizes. Unlike the self-employed, civil servants seem to be responsive to the tax advantages of life insurance contracts. The German tax and subsidy policy does not appear successful, however, in increasing the willingness of families with three or more children to invest in tax-favored assets or those eligible for subsidies.

Table 8.7 also presents two-step Heckit estimation results for the portfolio shares of fairly safe and risky assets. The impact of the respondents' socioeconomic characteristics on the conditional asset shares of risky and fairly safe assets differs notably from their impact on the willingness to hold these assets. Fairly safe assets and risky assets seem to be considered as substitutes for one another. Households that should have a higher incentive to invest in housing, save for retirement, or cover the risk of income losses due to the death of the breadwinner prove to hold higher shares of fairly safe assets and lower shares of risky ones. Also, persons with little education seem to hold smaller shares of risky and higher shares of fairly safe assets. Interestingly, income and proxy variables for income uncertainty seem to have no effect on the portfolio shares of risky or fairly safe assets. Net worth appears to affect the portfolio shares of fairly safe assets only.

8.4 Household Portfolios in Eastern Germany

The results of the previous section show that ten years after reunification, substantial regional differences in the households' portfolios persist even for households of the same age, wealth, and education level. Assigning causes to these differences is no easy task. Although reunification might appear as a welcome natural experiment at first sight, there are two reasons that such an analysis is likely to fail. First, we have virtually no data on East German households before

Table 8.7
Determinants of asset ownership and asset shares

	Fairly safe assets				Risky assets			
	Ownership (probit model: 1 = asset owned, 0 = not owned)		Asset shares (percentage of financial assets, Heckman two-step estimator)		Ownership (probit model: 1 = asset owned, 0 = not owned)		Asset shares (percentage of financial assets, Heckman two-step estimator)	
	Coefficient	t-ratio	Coefficient	t-ratio	Coefficient	t-ratio	Coefficient	t-ratio
Wealth Effect by Wealth Quartiles								
Net worth	**0.1695**	*20.49*	**1.3760**	*9.34*	**0.1213**	*19.38*	**0.2059**	*2.03*
Net worth squared	**−0.0112**	*−13.59*	**−0.0699**	*−7.27*	**−0.0056**	*−11.54*		
Net worth cubed	**0.0002**	*9.41*	**0.0008**	*6.22*	**0.0001**	*8.62*		
Age/Cohort Effect								
Age	**−1.2322**	*−5.97*	**11.3138**	*12.05*	**−0.8929**	*−4.74*	**−8.4788**	*−3.61*
Age squared	**0.2433**	*6.07*	**−1.1959**	*−12.26*	**0.1567**	*4.23*	**0.8827**	*3.60*
Age cubed	**−0.0158**	*−6.56*			**−0.0089**	*−3.93*		
Education								
University degree	−1.5091	*−1.67*	0.5329	*0.83*	0.4643	*0.64*	−2.2715	*−1.69*
10 years schooling	**0.1052**	*3.01*	**2.1990**	*3.45*	**−0.1023**	*−3.41*	**−3.2937**	*−2.29*
9 years schooling	**0.1493**	*4.43*	**2.7476**	*4.40*	**−0.2169**	*−7.42*	**−5.1376**	*−3.33*
No vocational training	**−0.0636**	*−2.46*	−0.8426	*−1.17*	**−0.1683**	*−6.02*	0.3731	*0.16*

Policy Effects

Self-employed	**-0.1225**	*-2.27*	**8.7031**	*12.33*	**-0.4583**	*-12.88*	*-0.3781*	*-0.21*
Farmer	0.1422	*0.94*	0.4008	*0.31*	-0.2642	*-3.07*	*-1.5502*	*-0.39*
Civil servant	**0.1321**	*2.19*	**0.9367**	*2.00*	**-0.2801**	*-7.86*	*-1.9284*	*-1.56*
Three or more children	**-0.4862**	*-5.51*	**2.5534**	*2.59*	**-0.1572**	*-2.74*		

Source: Income and Expenditure Survey, 1993, West German households only.

Note: Numbers in boldface type denote significance at the 1 percent level; numbers in italicized boldface type denote significance at the 5 percent level. The underlying regression equations also include variables measuring employment status, family status, household size, an income polynomial, and an age polynomial for university graduates (cf. table 8D.1 in the appendix).

unification. Second, while tax and subsidy policies are indeed different in the two parts of Germany, identification is confounded by the many other differences, notably strongly differing employment prospects, but also endowments of wealth and financial information, which were disseminated unequally already during reunification. This section must therefore remain largely descriptive.

On the basis of the results of the previous sections and those of the other country studies in this book, we expect that young Eastern German households are likely to hold less risky assets than their West German counterparts and that strong cohort effects should be visible for the middle-aged and older generations in Eastern Germany.

8.4.1   Net Worth and Portfolio Composition

The 1993 EVS, which covered all of united Germany, is the only data set that permits a detailed study of regional differences in households' portfolios and net worth. Three years after reunification, the net worth of East German households was still substantially less than that of West German households. The sixth decile of the Eastern German wealth distribution was roughly equal to the third decile of the Western. The same shift applies for all deciles up to the ninth. Wealth appears to be less equally distributed in the East, at least at the upper end of the scale. We speculate that this reflects the economic success of a very small part of the population in the transition process. Figure 8.5 shows that—at least on average—only the youngest East German cohorts had the chance to accumulate wealth comparable to their West German counterparts.

Table 8.8 only partly confirms our hypothesis that wealth is a key determinant of the willingness to hold risky assets. Instead, East Germans invested in those assets that were generally popular in the early and mid-1990s and particularly favored assets that could be purchased in small quantities. Ownership rates of mutual funds are higher in East than in West Germany, and stock, bonds, and real estate ownership rates are much lower.

Table 8.8 shows that East German households held less diversified portfolios in 1993. More than 40 percent of their wealth was in safe assets, almost twice the percentage for those in the West. Since whole life insurance did not exist in the former German Democratic Republic, it comes as no surprise that East Germans hold substantially

a. West German households

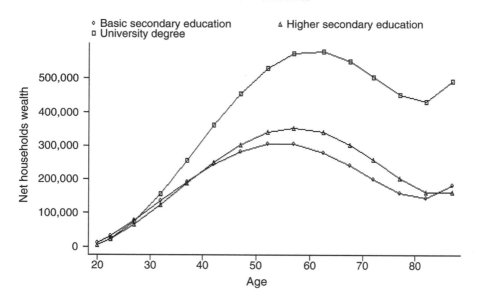

b. East German households

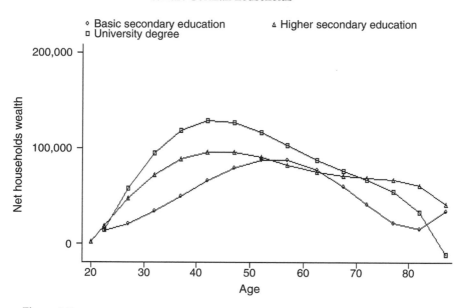

Figure 8.5
Net household wealth levels by age, education, and region. *Source:* Income and Expenditure Survey, 1993.

Table 8.8
Portfolio choice in East and West Germany, 1993

	Ownership rates		Conditional asset shares		Asset shares	
	West Germany	East Germany	West Germany	East Germany	West Germany	East Germany
Financial assets						
Checking and savings accounts	99.3	99.8	22.2	42.8	22.1	42.8
Government bonds	11.2	7.7	21.6	31.2	4.7	4.7
Other bonds (including savings certificates)	32.9	22.0	29.1	31.9	15.7	11.3
Stocks	12.0	3.1	18.5	17.0	4.6	0.8
Mutual funds and managed investment accounts	12.2	14.1	19.7	25.0	4.6	6.1
Life insurance contracts[a]	61.6	59.1	41.3	11.7	31.4	7.6
Building society savings contracts	42.1	33.9	14.1	20.2	7.0	9.0
Other financial assets	19.9	26.4	26.8	41.5	9.8	17.8
Total financial assets	99.5	99.8	27.2	34.9	27.2	35.0
Clearly safe financial assets	99.3	99.8	22.2	42.8	22.1	42.8
Fairly safe financial assets	82.7	80.4	68.5	53.4	65.8	48.2
Risky financial assets	26.2	19.8	26.2	27.3	12.1	9.1
Nonfinancial assets						
Total real estate[b]	51.1	27.4	79.8	84.9	74.2	67.2
Total risky assets[c]	26.2	19.8	26.2	27.3	12.1	9.1

Debt

Mortgage and real estate debt	27.2	10.3	96.1	95.8	90.7	78.1
Consumer credit	22.5	19.5	24.7	52.1	9.3	21.9
Consumer credit in percentage of total net wealth					1.4	2.1
Total debt	42.9	27.1	27.3	23.2	14.7	9.8

Source: Income and Expenditure Survey (1993).

[a] Waves 1978–1988 do not include the sales value of endowment life insurance contracts, only the insurance sum of life insurance contracts of any kind. The shares of life insurance contracts have been constructed on the basis of 1993 estimation results of regressing sales values of endowment life insurance contracts on insurance sums at various ages and employment characteristics of the respondent.

[b] Waves 1979–1988 do not include indications on the sales values of real estate. We have therefore predicted sales values of real estate on the basis of 1993 estimation results of a hedonic regression of sales values on unit values at various years of purchase and a number of housing characteristics.

[c] "Total risky assets" includes all "risky financial assets."

smaller percentages of their wealth in these assets, even though ownership rates are almost identical; the latter also mirror the huge marketing effort by the insurance industry.

8.4.2 Household Portfolios in Transition

Waves 1989 to 1997 of the German Socioeconomic Panel are the only data that can be exploited to analyze the gradual adjustment of East German households' portfolios. Unfortunately, this panel provides information on ownership of assets only, not on asset shares, and is suspected to be particularly prone to underreporting.[43]

In spite of these data problems, the adjustment pattern reflected by Figure 8.6 is surprisingly clear: East German households took just three years to adjust their portfolios to the newly available range of assets. After 1992, trends in East German ownership rates of financial assets by and large have followed West German ones. Moreover, the rates for life insurance and building society savings are almost identical for the younger cohorts in the two parts of the country. This confirms our thesis that East Germans have favored assets that allowed for small investment and that were either tax favored or eligible for savings subsidies.

8.5 Conclusion

Our study shows that the portfolio composition of German households has followed the general trends observed in the other countries surveyed in this book but that adjustment toward risky assets came five to ten years later. Significant differences in levels thus remain. Most notably, Germany has high rates of ownership of domestic bonds and life insurance contracts but low holdings of stocks and real estate. While levels are different, the impact of such household characteristics as wealth, age, education, and financial knowledge matches the findings of the other studies. Interestingly, most of these correlations are also visible in the comparison of East and West German portfolio choices.

The lack of panel data in Germany rules out any rigid econometric analysis of households' sensitivity to after-tax returns. We are therefore obliged to use policy case examples to shed light on the impact of the various tax and subsidy changes that have occurred during the past two decades. These examples strongly suggest that German

A. Stocks, bonds, mutual funds, savings contracts and other

West German households

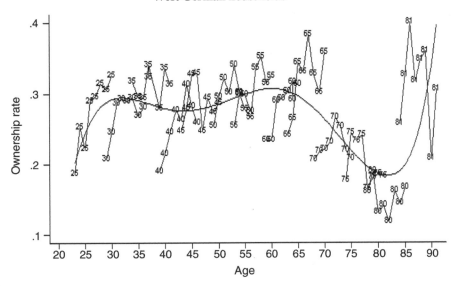

East German households

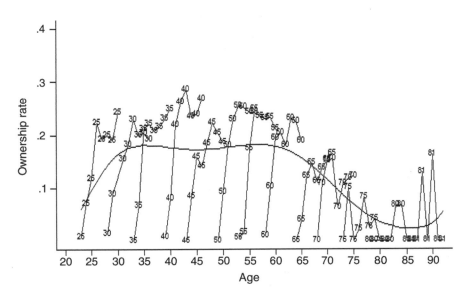

Figure 8.6
Age-cohort profiles of ownership rates by region. *Source:* GSOEP, waves 1990–1997.

B. Building society savings contracts

West German households

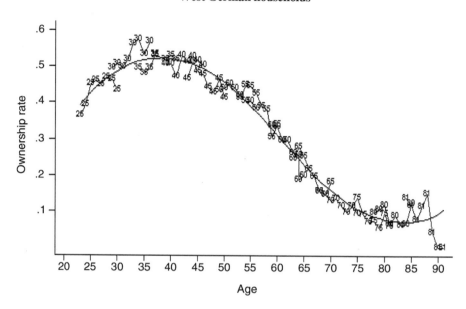

East German households

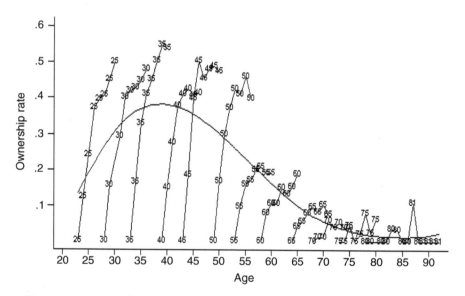

Figure 8.6 (continued)

C. Life insurance contracts (including whole life insurance contracts)
West German households

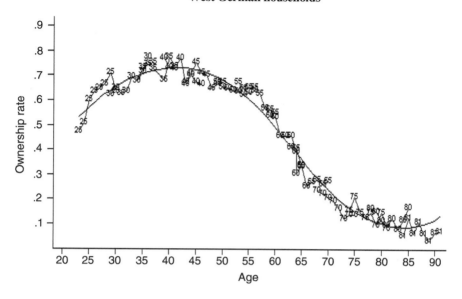

East German households

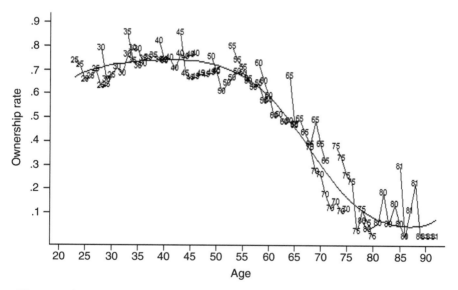

Figure 8.6 (continued)

D. Owner-occupied housing

West German households

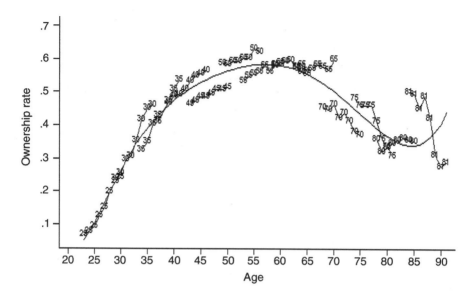

East German households

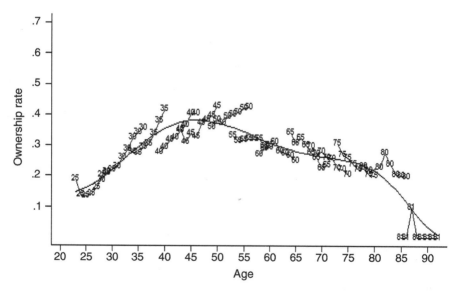

Figure 8.6 (continued)

households have been sensitive to changes in after-tax yields. Ownership rates of long-term savings contracts have decreased when the savings subsidies were abolished; ownership of bonds increased during the period of German reunification when bond yields rose and dropped when rising inflation rates reduced real-valued yields; investments in foreign mutual funds increased massively when the withholding tax on interest income was introduced; and ownership rates for stocks started to rise in the very late 1990s when the DAX performance index rocketed. The sensitivity of households to after-tax rates of return is an indication that after-tax returns were not equalized when before-tax returns or the tax wedge changed. We conclude that tax and subsidy policy still has a strong lever in Germany.

Germany will undergo substantial capital market changes in the fairly near future. Population aging will necessitate more private provision for old-age and health insurance. The stock market has only recently regained its status as an investment option for all households, including the large middle class. Institutional investors such as pension funds are appearing. Thus, the picture taken in this study is likely to change substantially over the coming decade. Judging by the past, the direction of change can be strongly influenced by tax and subsidy policy.

Appendix 8A: Description of Data Sets

National Accounts

Data source: Deutsche Bundesbank (1994b, 1999a).

Coverage: West Germany, 1975–1992; (Unified) Germany, 1990–1998.

Definition of households: Households and nonprofit organizations. Deposit/savings accounts of self-employed persons are not included.

Measurement concept for current sales value of asset holdings: Estimated sales values for foreign and domestic stocks and bonds.

Deutsche Bundesbank (Asset Holdings of Households)

Data source: Deutsche Bundesbank (1999b).

Coverage: (Unified) Germany, 1990–1997.

Definition of households: Households only.

Measurement concept for current sales value of asset holdings: Estimates for financial assets correspond to National Accounts figures but exclude asset holdings of nonprofit organizations. Estimated replacement values are used to assess the worth of households' housing property; other real estate is excluded.

Income and Expenditure Survey (EVS)

Data source: Statistisches Bundesamt.

Waves: 1978, 1983, 1988, 1993.

Coverage: Roughly 46,000, 43,000, and 44,000 West German households in waves 1978, 1983, and 1988.

• 98% subsamples, excluding households with more than six members, foreign households, and households with total net monthly income of over 20,000 DM (1978) and 25,000 DM (1983, 1988).

Roughly 32,000 West German households and 8,500 East German households in wave 1993.

• 80% subsample, excluding households with net monthly income of over 35,000 DM (1993).

Measurement concept of current sales value of asset holdings: No quantitative information on asset holdings (or total household wealth) is available in wave 1978. Self-assessed sales values of assets (life insurance sum rather than sales value, unit values of business property and real estate) in waves 1983 and 1988. Self-assessed sales value of assets (including real estate and endowment life insurance) in wave 1993. In waves 1983 to 1993, the upper limit of bracket substitutes for the true value of those who indicated asset brackets only.

Information on education and financial knowledge: Not available in waves 1978 to 1988.

Information on age: Birth cohorts only (youngest cohort, up to 21 years; oldest cohort, 80 years and older) in waves 1978 to 1988. Age in years in wave 1993.

Spiegel-Verlag Survey Soll und Haben

Data source: Spiegel-Verlag.

Waves: 1980, 1985, 1989, 1995.

Table 8A.1
Definition of assets and availability of quantitative information

	National accounts	Deutsche Bundesbank (1999b)	EVS, 1983–1993
Transaction accounts, savings accounts	Yes	Including savings certificates	Transaction accounts: 1993 only Savings accounts: Yes
Savings certificates	Yes—added to total bonds in table 8.1	Asset shares of savings certificates indicated in the national accounts subtracted from transaction/savings accounts and added to total bonds in table 8.2	
Government bonds	Included in total bonds	Included in total bonds	Yes
Other bonds	Included in total bonds	Included in total bonds	Yes
Life insurance contracts	Included in insurance and pension wealth	Included in insurance and pension wealth	1983–1988: Estimated sales value 1993: Yes
Pension wealth	Included in insurance and pension wealth	Included in insurance and pension wealth	Not available
Building society savings contracts	Yes	Yes	Yes
Stocks	Yes	Yes	Yes
Mutual funds	1960–1992: added to either stocks or bonds 1990–1998: Yes	Yes	Yes
Other financial assets	Yes	Yes	Yes
Owner-occupied housing	Not available	Included in total real estate	1993: Total real estate 1983–1988: Estimated total real estate
Other real estate	Not available	Rented and other housing included in total real estate	1993: Total real estate 1983–1988: Estimated total real estate
Business wealth	Not available	Not available	1983: Unit values
Other nonfinancial wealth	Not available	Yes	Not available
Mortgage credit	Long-term bank loans	Yes	Yes
Consumer credit	Short-term bank loans	Yes	Yes
Other debt	Other loans	Not available	Not available

Coverage: Roughly 4,000, 5,000, and 5,000 West Germans aged 14 years and older in waves 1980 to 1989. Roughly 6,500 West Germans and 2,300 East Germans aged 14 years and older in wave 1995.

Measurement concept of current sales value of asset holdings: No quantitative information on asset holdings (or total household wealth) available.

Information on education and financial knowledge: Education levels and self-assessed measures of information status.

GSOEP: Waves 1990–1997

Data source: SOEP-Gruppe, Deutsches Institut für Wirtschafts-forschung, Berlin.

Coverage: Balanced panels of 3,223 West German and 1,415 East German households who regularly indicated their asset holdings during the period 1990–1997.

Measurement concept of current sales value of asset holdings: No quantitative information on asset holdings (or total household wealth) available; definitions of assets refer to very high aggregation levels and neglect savings contracts, savings accounts, and other assets groups.

Appendix 8B: Definition of Asset Shares and Ownership Rates

Macrodata

$$\frac{\textit{Average share of asset}}{\textit{i of type } j} \equiv \frac{\text{Sum of sales values of asset } i \text{ for all households}}{\text{Sum of sales values of all assets of type } j \text{ for all households}}$$

Survey Data

$$\frac{\textit{Average share of asset}}{\textit{i of type } j} \equiv \frac{\text{Weighted average of sales values of asset } i}{\text{Weighted average sales value of all asset of type } j}$$

Ownership rate of asset i	$\equiv$ Percentage of households owning asset i

$$\text{Average share of asset } i \text{ conditional on ownership of asset } i \equiv \frac{\text{Weighted average of sales values of asset } i \text{ for all households owning asset } i}{\text{Weighted average sales value of all assets of type } j \text{ for all households owning asset } i}$$

Appendix 8C: Comparison of Macro and Survey Data

Table 8C.1
Comparison of aggregate and survey data, 1993

	Germany: Households excluding nonprofit organizations		
	Bundesbank (1999b) estimates (1)	Income and expenditure survey (EVS) (2)	Percentage of assets reported in EVS as compared to Bundesbank estimates (2)/(1)
Financial assets			
Checking, deposit, and savings accounts	41,222.7	14,157.6	34.3
Bonds	19,503.1	11,716.7	60.1
Stocks	6,295.9	2,522.4	40.1
Mutual funds and managed investment accounts	6,768.7	2,789.1	41.2
Building society savings contracts	6,765.1	4,214.5	62.3
Insurance and pension wealth	22,702.1	17,129.0	75.5
Other financial assets	8,067.9	6,320.6	78.3
Total financial assets	110,220.8	58,849.9	53.4
Nonfinancial assets			
Real estate wealth	167,132.2	181,939.4	108.9
Stock of durable goods	38,617.1	n.a.	n.a.
Total nonfinancial assets	205,749.3	181,939.4	88.4
Debt			
Mortgage loans	28,109.3	27,412.8	97.5
Consumer credit	8,951.1	2,990.4	33.4
Total debt	37,060.0	30,403.2	82.0
Total net wealth	277,253.6	210,386.1	75.9

Appendix 8D: Regression Results

Table 8D.1
Determinants of asset ownership and asset shares

	Fairly safe assets				Risky Assets			
	Ownership (probit estimation)		Asset shares (percentage of total financial assets, Heckman two-step estimator)		Ownership (probit estimation)		Asset shares (percentage of total financial assets, Heckman two-step estimator)	
	Coefficient	t-ratio	Coefficient	t-ratio	Coefficient	t-ratio	Coefficient	t-ratio
Age/10	-1.2322	-5.97	11.3138	12.05	-0.8929	-4.74	-8.4788	-3.61
Age/10 sq.	0.2433	6.07	-1.1959	-12.26	0.1567	4.23	0.8827	3.60
Age/10 cube	-0.0158	-6.56			-0.0089	-3.93		
Age/10, university degree	0.9176	1.63			-0.1247	-0.28		
Age/10 sq., university degree	-0.1869	-1.70			-0.0080	-0.09		
Age/10 cube, university degree	0.0121	1.77			0.0019	0.34		
Net worth/100,000 DM	0.1695	20.49	1.3760	9.34	0.1213	19.38	0.2059	2.03
Net worth/100,000 DM, sq.	-0.0112	-13.59	-0.0699	-7.27	-0.0056	-11.54		
Net worth/100,000 DM, cube	0.0002	9.41	0.0008	6.22	0.0001	8.62		
University degree	-1.5091	-1.67	0.5329	0.83	0.4643	0.64	-2.2715	-1.69
9 years schooling	0.1493	4.43	2.7476	4.40	-0.2169	-7.42	-5.1376	-3.33
10 years schooling	0.1052	3.01	2.1990	3.45	-0.1023	-3.41	-3.2937	-2.29
No vocational training	-0.0636	-2.46	-0.8426	-1.17	-0.1683	-6.02	0.3731	0.16
Income per capita/10,000 DM	0.2889	23.89	-0.1024	-0.75	0.2938	27.75	0.6169	2.19
Income per capita/10,000 DM, sq.	-0.0084	-15.65			-0.0098	-15.14		

	(1)		(2)		(3)		(4)	
	Coef.	t	Coef.	t	Coef.	t	Coef.	t
Double-income household	**0.1113**	*3.00*	**1.0265**	*2.47*	0.0087	*0.38*	*-1.9528*	*-2.07*
Self-employed	-0.1225	*-2.27*	**8.7031**	*12.33*	-0.4583	*-12.88*	-0.3781	*-0.21*
Farmer	0.1422	*0.94*	0.4008	*0.31*	-0.2642	*-3.07*	-1.5502	*-0.39*
Civil servant	**0.1321**	*2.19*	**0.9367**	*2.00*	-0.2801	*-7.86*	-1.9284	*-1.56*
Unemployed	-0.6651	*-15.53*	-0.2269	*-0.15*	-0.1790	*-3.68*	1.4764	*0.34*
Retired	-0.3764	*-9.57*	-4.9280	*-6.60*	-0.0234	*-0.69*	**5.4139**	*2.93*
Not employed	-0.4407	*-10.66*	-1.3796	*-1.08*	-0.0428	*-1.00*	**6.1580**	*2.10*
Single	-0.2727	*-6.40*	-4.3492	*-5.86*	-0.0056	*-0.17*	**4.9423**	*3.36*
Widowed	-0.1625	*-3.89*	-3.3969	*-3.72*	-0.1159	*-3.12*	3.6614	*1.67*
Divorced	-0.3905	*-9.47*	-3.4135	*-4.15*	-0.1660	*-4.54*	**5.7570**	*2.61*
One child	0.1155	*4.78*	0.2523	*0.51*	-0.0250	*-1.14*		
Two children	-0.0525	*-0.96*	**1.5166**	*2.44*	-0.0531	*-1.53*		
Three or more children	-0.4862	*-5.51*	**2.5334**	*2.59*	-0.1572	*-2.74*		
Household size	0.3130	*13.42*	0.1461	*0.46*	0.1441	*9.13*	-0.4001	*-0.83*
Constant	**1.7680**	*5.41*	**34.5642**	*13.68*	-0.0632	*-0.21*	**40.0172**	*6.05*
λ			**11.9331**	*4.74*			1.7542	*0.63*
ρ							0.0839	
Pseudo R²	21.34		0.4677		10.84			

Source: Income and Expenditure Survey (1993), West German households only.
Note: Numbers in boldfaced type denote significance at 1 percent level. Numbers in italicized boldfaced type denote significance at 5 percent level.

Notes

This chapter is an abbreviated version of a working paper that is available upon request. We gratefully acknowledge financial support from the Deutsche Forschungsgemeinschaft and the European Union (through Project B1 of the Sonderforschungsbereich 504 at the University of Mannheim, and through TMR-project ERBFMRXCT960016 "Savings and Pensions"). We thank Angus Deaton, Hans-Peter Grüner, Luigi Guiso, Michael Haliassos, Arie Kapteyn, Raimond Maurer, and Dirk Schiereck for their helpful comments; Mathias Sommer for excellent research assistance; and Ulrich Finke for improving our graphical skills.

1. Cf., e.g., Deutsche Bundesbank (1992, 1993b, 1999b), Euler (1985, 1990, 1992), Kim (1992), Börsch-Supan (1994a, 1994b), Schönig (1996), Börsch-Supan, Reil-Held, Rodepeter, and Schnabel (1999), and Schnabel (1999).

2. Schlomann (1992), Grimm (1998), and Lang (1998) have used waves 1983, 1988, and 1978, 1983, 1988 of the EVS, respectively, to analyze the socioeconomic determinants of household portfolio choice. Börsch-Supan and Stahl (1991), Brunsbach and Lang (1998), and Walliser and Winter (1999) have focused on building society savings (*Bausparverträge*) and life insurance contracts to analyze the effect of tax incentives and policy changes on asset choice. Himmelreicher (1999) has used the German Socioeconomic Panel for a cohort study of wealth and portfolio choice, but had to rely on reported income from interest and dividends and highly aggregated indications on asset ownership in order to determine household wealth levels.

3. Cf. Gollier (chapter 1, this volume). See also King and Leape (1987), Bodie, Merton, and Samuelson (1992), and Bertaut and Haliassos (1997).

4. Cf. Haliassos and Bertaut (1995), Guiso, Jappelli, and Terlizzese (1996), Bertaut (1998), Hochgürtel, Alessie, and van Soest (1997), and Eymann, Börsch-Supan, and Euwals (2000).

5. The time series of national accounts for West Germany ended in 1992 after a three-year overlap with the new time series for unified Germany. The EVS sampled East Germans only in 1993. Tables 8.1 and 8.2 include asset shares for both West Germany and unified Germany in the early 1990s in order to permit readers to analyze the series for West Germany as far as possible and to interpret the differences between the old and the new series. Section 8.4 uses survey data to analyze regional differences in the portfolio composition of households in greater detail.

6. Differences between the asset shares computed from national accounts data (which include nonprofit organizations; cf. Deutsche Bundesbank, 1999a) and the Deutsche Bundesbank (1999b) estimations (which refer to households only) are minor for the period 1990 to 1997. National accounts data underestimate households' asset holdings of transaction, deposit, and savings accounts, as well as insurance and pension wealth by roughly three percentage points. The current sales value of mutual funds and bonds is slightly overestimated, while estimates for the current sales value of stocks are surprisingly precise.

7. For our imputation methods, see Börsch-Supan and Eymann (2000).

8. Cf. Deutsche Bundesbank (1988).

9. Deutsche Bundesbank (1988) shows that the increase in bond-based mutual funds started as early as 1985 (when such funds still figured as "bonds" in the national accounts).

10. A more detailed description of the sampling frame is given in appendix 8A. See also Börsch-Supan et al. (1999). Lang (1998) and Schnabel (1999) have shown that the survey also underrepresents poorer households and thus generally oversamples middle-income households.

11. Table 8C.1 in appendix 8C shows that the coverage of financial assets and consumer credit is particularly poor in the survey data. The extent of underreporting varies with the individual wave of the EVS, however. The total net worth of financial assets reported amounts to slightly less than 50 percent of the total net worth reported by Deutsche Bundesbank in 1978 and decreased to slightly less than 40 percent in 1988 (Lang 1998). This trend has been reverted in the last wave (cf. table 8C.1). In 1993, the average value of financial assets per household amounts to 53.4 percent of the average financial wealth reported by Deutsche Bundesbank (1999b).

12. Cf., e.g., Haliassos and Bertaut (1995), Guiso, Jappelli, and Terlizzese (1996), Poterba and Samwick (1997), Cocco (1999), and Vissing-Jørgensen (1999a).

13. Savings accounts and life insurance assets were computed slightly differently in 1993 than in earlier years; see Börsch-Supan et al. (1999) and appendix 8A.

14. Checking accounts were not reported in the EVS before 1993, which should bias the figures in table 8.3 toward *less* diversification over time.

15. For a detailed survey of policy changes in Germany, see Börsch-Supan and Eymann (2000).

16. World Development Indicators, Table 5.2.

17. In the late 1980s, the average lag between the EC directive and the respective legal adjustments amounted to five years.

18. Cf. Börsch-Supan and Winter (2000).

19. The difference-in-difference is about the same for lower marginal tax rates.

20. Cf. Deutsche Börse (1999, table 2.3).

21. Cf. Deutsche Börse (1999, table 10.4).

22. For a detailed description of savings subsidies and taxation in Germany see Börsch-Supan (1994a). Recent policy changes are listed in Börsch-Supan and Eymann (2000).

23. These reforms have been enacted in 2000. Cf. Börsch-Supan and Winter (2000).

24. A maximum subsidy of 200 DM (£100) on a maximum contribution of 1,000 DM (£500).

25. Cf. Börsch-Supan (1994c).

26. Life insurance contracts are a noteworthy exception to this rule. The tax treatment of interest and capital gains favors the rich. Moreover, contributions to life insurance contracts are (partly) tax exempt for civil servants and the self-employed (cf. Brunsbach and Lang 1998).

27. The German Ministry of Finance estimated that the tax exemptions were high enough to free four-fifths of the German population from paying income tax on interest (cf. Deutsche Bundesbank 1994c). The tax-free amount was halved in 2000.

28. For a survey of the extent of income tax loopholes in Germany see Lang, Nöhrbass, and Stahl (1997).

29. Investments in Luxembourg-based mutual funds only.

30. Cf. Deutsche Bundesbank (1994c).

31. Cf. Haliassos and Bertaut (1995), Guiso, Jappelli, and Terlizzese (1996), Bertaut (1998), Hochgürtel, Alessie, and van Soest (1997), Poterba and Samwick (1997), or Eymann, Börsch-Supan, and Euwals (2000).

32. For example Börsch-Supan (1994b) or Schnabel (1999).

33. Predictions are based on estimation results for a probit model of households' possession of risky or fairly safe assets with a fifth-order age polynomial as the only explanatory variables and refer to the pooled cross-sections of waves 1978 to 1993. Cohort/time effects are captured by dummy variables.

34. Cf. Guiso, Jappelli, and Terlizzese (1996), Bertaut (1998), Hochgürtel, Alessie, and van Soest (1997), and Eymann, Börsch-Supan, and Euwals (2000).

35. Quartiles for the total net wealth of all households interviewed in the respective wave of the EVS. The first three quartiles are 23,048 DM, 120,188 DM, and 369,656 DM and the ninety-fifth percentile is equal to 849,332 DM.

36. The cohort study does not include 1978 since information on total net wealth is unavailable for that wave.

37. Cf., e.g., Guiso, Jappelli, and Terlizzese (1996), Bertaut and Haliassos (1997), or Bodie, Merton, and Samuelson (1992).

38. For a detailed discussion of the differences in East and West German households' portfolios, see section 8.4.

39. This drop is not significant because of the small cell size.

40. A detailed description of this data set is given in appendix 8A. For a comparison of the Spiegel-Verlag survey and the EVS, see Eymann (2000). Underreporting of risky assets seems to be greater in the Spiegel-Verlag survey, although respondents are generally younger and the two tails of the income distribution are underrepresented.

41. The wording of the question was changed in 1993.

42. The complete set of results is presented in table 8D.1.

43. Note that the GSOEP asset definitions differ from those used in the previous sections (cf. appendix 8A).

9   Household Portfolios in the Netherlands

Rob Alessie, Stefan
Hochguertel, and
Arthur van Soest

The composition of household portfolios in the Netherlands has changed dramatically in the past two decades. Twenty years ago, a common family typically put their savings into a risk-free savings account. Stocks and bonds were seen as playthings for the rich and adventurous. At some stage in life, the wealthier would buy their own house and take out a mortgage. The rest of their life, their savings would typically go to pay off the mortgage. In the 1990s this pattern no longer applied. As in many other Western countries, stocks, bonds, mutual funds, options, and other risky assets were no longer the exclusive domain of the rich and adventurous. Many more people invested in the stock market, and banks and other financial institutions offered a variety of products together with free advice for even the most modest purse. Special plans even permitted borrowing to finance purchasing stocks. The latest type of mortgage automatically invested repayments in a mutual fund instead of riskfree, to draw the greatest benefit from high stock market returns and the tax exemption of capital gains. While all this is clear from aggregate data, a closer look at the microlevel shows that there remains a very large group of families to which these trends do not apply. Many households have stuck to traditional saving instruments, in spite of the extraordinary returns, the enormous tax advantages of innovative portfolios, and the immense media play on this theme. This makes microlevel analysis of the determinants of ownership of certain types of and amounts of assets particularly useful.

There are two reasons that such an analysis is particularly interesting for the Netherlands. The first is the institutional setting. Financial markets are well developed compared to such countries as Germany and Italy, and the channels by which the common household can learn about all the existing possibilities are quite extensive.

More important perhaps, the tax system implicitly and explicitly offers strong incentives for various innovative types of saving and borrowing. We discuss some of these in detail and show, for instance, that investments with similar risk and return patterns get disparate tax treatment and sharply different after-tax returns. Although the complexity of the tax system precludes structural analysis in which the household maximizes some expected utility, we argue that the tax system has had clear effects on some of the diversification patterns observed.

The second reason for studying the Netherlands is the availability of rich, detailed panel data: the CentER Savings Survey (CSS). One of the stylized findings of the empirical work presented in this book is the enormous heterogeneity of portfolio behavior over time and across households. While repeated cross-section data are available for many countries, household panel data with detailed information on wealth and portfolio choice are scarce. An exception is the Survey on Household Income and Wealth data for Italy (see chapter 7, this volume, or Brandolini and Cannari 1994). The panel data allow controlling for household-specific effects and distinguishing state dependence from unobserved heterogeneity. Moreover, our data have information on consumer preferences that is not available in standard microdata.

The CSS data set has six annual waves, from 1993 through 1998, with information on wealth components, demographics, attitudes toward risk, time preference, and more for about 2500 households. Around 70 percent of these are a random sample, and the rest are chosen from high-income areas. The data allow for a distinction among various types of assets, such as traditional saving accounts, tax-favored employer saving plans, risky assets such as stocks, bonds, mutual funds, life insurance, pension plans, and housing wealth. Moreover, we have information on mortgage debt and consumer debt. We describe household portfolio ownership rates and diversification. We look at cohort and age patterns of ownership rates, which are important for the consequences of demographic trends such as population aging on portfolio structures (see, e.g., Poterba and Samwick 1997). We focus on financial assets, distinguishing among clearly safe, fairly safe, and risky assets. Although much of our analysis focuses on ownership of the assets, we also pay some attention to the amounts held and the shares of various types of assets in total wealth and financial wealth.

For external validation, we compare our survey microdata with two other sources: the Dutch National Accounts, which contain information on the stock of financial wealth and its composition, and the distribution and composition of household wealth published by Statistics Netherlands, mainly derived from administrative data.[1]

Using both static and dynamic discrete-choice models for panel data, we relate asset ownership to background variables such as the age and education of the head of household and household composition. Moreover, the rich set of subjective data on psychological and economic concepts allows us to investigate the relation between portfolio choice and income expectations, attitudes toward risk, and information about financial products. We analyze ownership of risky assets and ownership of a recently introduced asset type specific to the Netherlands: employer-sponsored savings plans (ESSPs). We also use a (static) panel data selection model to investigate the determinants of the shares of risky assets and ESSPs in total financial wealth.

Section 9.1 describes the aggregate stock of wealth data for the Netherlands. In section 9.2 we describe the CSS data set that we use in the rest of the chapter. We discuss the asset and debt types covered and how they are treated by the tax system. We compare statistics from our survey data with administrative data. We explain how we have aggregated the asset and debt types to the categories common to the country studies in this book. Section 9.3 presents ownership rates, asset shares, diversification of portfolios, and composition of household net worth in the common format. Section 9.4 shows age and cohort patterns of ownership rates for fairly safe and risky financial assets and for ESSPs. It also describes how the share of financial assets in total assets varies with age and cohort. In sections 9.5 and 9.6 we look at some results for binary choice models explaining asset ownership; section 9.5 uses static panel data models. Section 9.6 exploits the panel feature to consider dynamic models in which lagged ownership dummies are included among the regressors. In section 9.7, we use selection models to analyze the asset shares. Section 9.8 concludes.

9.1   Aggregate Data on the Stock of Wealth

In *National Accounts 1998* Statistics Netherlands presents for the first time the flow-of-funds statement of the households sector. This reports the size and composition of households' financial assets and liabilities for the years 1995 to 1998 (see table 9.1). Before discussing the figures, some observations are in order. First, the National Accounts do not provide data on the value of real assets (such as real estate). Second, "households" includes nonprofit institutions serving households (e.g. churches, consumer associations, labor unions) and the self-employed. Third, the classification of asset and liability categories is quite broad. For instance, no distinction is made between whole life insurance and pension or other annuity insurance.

Table 9.1 indicates that financial net worth (financial wealth) increased considerably: from 1,104 billion guilders at the beginning of 1995 to 1,520 billion guilders at the beginning of 1998, or by 37.7 percent.[2] Disposable household income grew much more slowly in this period, leading to an increase in the financial wealth-to-income ratio from 2.37 to 2.88. An interesting feature of the National Accounts data is that the changes in the stocks of assets and liabilities are decomposed into capital gains (or losses) and (net) transactions. Capital gains explain 77 percent of the increase in net worth. The remaining 23 percent is due to financial transactions, most of which are carried out by pension funds or life insurance companies. The reason is the extensive system of compulsory occupational pension plans in the Netherlands (see, e.g., Alessie, Kapteyn, and Klijn (1997) for details about the Dutch social security and pension systems).

The increase in financial wealth was accompanied by substantial portfolio transformation. The amount of money in transaction and saving accounts rose 22 percent, a smaller increase than that in financial net worth. This is due to the slow growth of saving accounts, since transaction accounts with growth of 44 percent, actually outpaced financial net worth. Similarly, the risk-free asset item certificates of deposit grew only modestly. The most obvious explanation for these findings is the low interest rates on saving accounts and CDs.

In these three years, the share of the risky asset category stocks, bonds and mutual funds increased from 21.9 percent to 25.1 percent, at the expense of the no-risk assets. In particular, the value of stocks rose considerably.[3] This reflects the increase in the CBS stock exchange index from 278 to 618 between the beginning of 1995 and 1998 (see the bottom panel of table 9.1). The effect of the stock market surge on relative asset shares was reinforced by the tax-free status of capital gains and the decline in interest rates on traditional risk-free savings instruments. Compared to other countries, Dutch house-

Table 9.1
Financial balances of the sector households and nonprofit institutions serving households (in billions of Dutch guilders)

	1995		Changes between 1995 and 1998		1998	
	Balance primo year	Asset share	Financial transactions	Capital gains (revaluation)	Balance primo year	Asset share
Assets						
Cash	36.8	2.5	−0.1	0.1	36.7	1.8
Transaction and saving accounts	269.2	18.1	58.7	−0.0	327.8	15.9
Transaction accounts	53.5	3.6	22.3	−0.1	75.8	3.7
Saving accounts	215.7	14.5	36.3	0.0	252.0	12.2
Certificates of deposits	43.8	2.9	2.4	0.0	46.1	2.2
Stocks, bonds, and mutual funds	325.1	21.9	34.1	157.8	517.0	25.1
Bonds	45.1	3.0	3.9	1.7	50.7	2.5
Stocks, mutual funds[a]	280.0	18.8	30.2	156.1	466.3	22.6
Defined-benefit and -contribution pensions and other life insurance	772.0	52.0	155.2	155.9	1,083.1	52.6
Other financial assets	5.1	0.3	−0.1	−0.5	4.6	0.2
Trade credits and residual	33.8	2.3	7.3	4.3	45.4	2.2
Total financial assets	1,485.8	100.0	257.5	317.5	2,060.7	100.0
Liabilities						
Short-term debt	33.3	2.2	13.2	0.4	46.9	2.3
Long-term debt	347.9	23.4	148.1	−2.5	493.5	23.9
Total debts	381.2	25.7	161.3	−2.1	540.4	26.2
Financial wealth	1,104.5	74.3	96.2	319.6	1,520.3	73.8
Financial wealth to income ratio	2.37				2.88	
CBS stock price index (1983 = 100)	278.0				618.0	
Mortgage interest rate	7.26				5.82	
House prices	228.0				293.0	

Source: The CBS (Statistics Netherlands) stock price index and the mortgage interest rate are from CBS Statline. House prices were provided by the Netherlands Association of Real Estate Agents (Nederlandse Vereniging van Makelaars, NVM). The balances and asset shares are from Dutch National Accounts 1998 (table R.4.B).
[a] Includes stocks from substantial holdings.

holds do not invest much in bonds (about 3 percent of total financial assets in 1995, compared to about 25 percent in Italy, 8 percent in the US, and 14 percent in Germany). Between 1995 and 1998 the share of bonds in total financial assets fell from 3.0 percent to 2.5 percent.

In the Netherlands, the asset category of defined-benefit pensions and defined-contribution pensions and other life insurance assets is an important part of the household portfolio: more than 50 percent of all financial assets are held in this form, very high by European standards. In Germany, the share of life insurance and pension plans in total financial assets is about 22 percent (see Deutsche Bundesbank 1999a) and in Italy only 11 percent. The high share in the Netherlands is largely due to the compulsory occupational pension system of the defined-benefit type, which covers most employees and former employees. Moreover, the category is rather broadly defined and also includes (non-compulsory) whole life insurance and annuities. These include assets that are popular because of their tax-preferred nature.

Since the National Accounts do not provide any information on the value of real assets, we rely on other sources. Statistics Netherlands annually publishes figures on the wealth distribution of households and its composition, drawn from the Income Panel Survey (IPO, Inkomens Panelonderzoek), a large sample survey (75,000 households) based on administrative records from the income and wealth tax register. The IPO statistics suggest that between the beginning of 1995 and 1997, the value of the housing stock grew by 30 percent, from 746 billion guilders to 913 billion guilders (see de Kleijn 1999). Most of this growth is explained by a surge in house prices (see table 9.1).

Table 9.1 shows that the long-term debt of households, mainly home mortgages, grew considerably over the period 1995–1998. This reflects increased mortgage borrowing due to the fall in interest rates (see table 9.1). Moreover, banks relaxed their rules, and the ratio of the maximum mortgage loan to household earnings was increased. Like long-term debt, short-term debt increased considerably, from 33.3 to 46.9 billion guilders, or from 7 percent to about 9 percent of disposable household income. The growth is presumably due to the decline in interest rates. The ratio of these liabilities to total financial assets held at about 2.2 percent.

We can conclude that the overall trend to more risky investment corresponds to that found elsewhere. Some specific findings are not in line with other countries, however. Some relate to the typical national features of the compulsory pension and tax systems. The clearest instance of an optimal use of the tax rules is the existence of special types of mortgages, combining interest deductions with untaxed capital gains. Other examples of specific asset ownership trends induced by the tax rules are discussed below, where the microdata not only allow study of different segments of households but also permit more detailed examination of types of assets. The macrodata are insufficient for this purpose due to their high level of aggregation and their definition of household.

9.2 Microdata

We use six waves of the CSS, 1993 to 1998. Nyhus (1996) describes this data set and its general quality. The panel consists of two samples. The first (REP) is intended to be representative of the Dutch population. It contains about 2,000 households in each wave with the sample replenished every year to adjust for attrition. The second sample (HIP) was drawn from high-income areas and should represent the top income decile. Initially, it consisted of about 900 families. It is available in all waves except the last one.

Due to nonresponse, the actual REP samples are not perfectly representative of the population. For our analysis, we combine the REP and HIP samples and use sample weights to adjust for the nonrandom sampling. The weights are based on income and home ownership. For observations with missing income, we predict income from background variables such as family size and education level and age of the head of the household. The weights are constructed using information from a much larger data set (WBO, Woning Behoefte Onderzoek, or Housing Needs Survey) collected by Statistics Netherlands, which is close to representative for the Dutch population.

The CSS data were collected by on-line terminal sessions, each family was provided with a PC and modem. The answers to the survey questions provide general information on the household and its members, the work history and labor market status of adult household members, health status, and detailed information on many types of income. The survey also includes many economic-psychological questions to elicit, for example, risk attitudes, time preference, expectations, and interest in financial matters. Important for our purposes are the questions on assets and liabilities. For most of the fourty asset and liability categories, respondents first indicate whether they have assets or debts of that type. If so, they are asked a series of questions on amounts and the precise nature of each asset. There is virtually no nonresponse to the ownership questions, but there is substantial nonresponse to some of the questions on amounts. For example, 25 percent of those who own shares do not know or refuse to state the value of their shares. Similar problems exist for the value of life insurance and defined-contribution plans (annuities), shares from a substantial holding, and business equity. Even for savings accounts, whose value would seem straightforward, about 10 percent failed to state the amount. Only for the value of house or mortgage is the nonresponse rate below 5 percent.

To deal with nonresponse, we have imputed the amounts for those whom we know own the asset but not the amount. The imputed values are based on amounts held in adjacent years and on regression models that relate observed amounts to household characteristics. We take account of prediction errors by drawing errors from the estimated error term distribution in the regression models, where full account is taken of the covariance structure of the error terms over time.

The asset and liability categories are listed in the right-hand panel of table 9.2. Checking accounts, deposit books, savings or deposit accounts, savings certificates, and savings arrangements linked to a Postbank account, are traditional risk-free savings, with varying withdrawal conditions (demand, fixed term, premium in case of withdrawal).[4] The interest income on saving and checking account balances is taxed above a threshold (2,000 guilders for couples, 1,000 for singles).[5]

ESSPs are an attractive new way of saving offered by most employers. They were introduced in the early 1990s in a political compromise by unions, employers and the government to stimulate labor force participation and wealth accumulation. As far as we know, no such assets exist in other countries. Interest income from these plans is treated separately from other interest income, and not liable to income tax up to a substantial threshold (2,000 guilders for couples, 1,000 for singles). Up to 1,670 guilders per year, contributions are tax deductible, and if the money is not withdrawn for four years, the withdrawals are not taxed. These provisions make the plans somewhat less liquid but much more tax-favored than ordinary savings accounts. The funds can also be used to purchase (illiquid) single premium annuities (which gives additional tax relief), or other assets, such as mutual funds. Thus, in terms of tax treatment, these plans have some similarities to Individual Retirement Accounts in the US, though the latter are much less liquid.

The CSS distinguishes two types of stocks: substantial holdings and other shares of private companies. The two are very different for tax purposes: the former are treated as business capital and the latter are not. Income from a substantial holding is subject to income tax (25 percent) insofar as this income exceeds the first tax bracket threshold. Dividends from other shares and from mutual funds or mutual fund accounts are taxable above the exemption threshold of 2,000 guilders for couples and 1,000 for singles. Capital gains on these are not taxed. The thresholds on dividends are separate from those on interest on savings, creating a tax incentive for diversification.

While mutual funds are typically portfolios of shares, growth funds are portfolios of nearly risk-free assets like bonds and deposits. The returns to growth funds (including capital gains) are liable to corporation tax at a flat rate of 35 percent, and not to income tax. Thus, growth funds are an attractive form of close to risk-free saving for households with high income and a high marginal tax rate whose interest income already exceeds the exemption limit. They are sometimes referred to as innovative saving (see Bovenberg and ter Rele 1998).

The premiums of single-premium annuity insurance policies (the only common form of defined-contribution pension plans) are tax-deductible with certain restrictions and up to an upper limit (normally 5,950 guilders for singles and 11,000 for couples and more if compulsory pensions are incomplete), but the remittances are taxed with other income. Thus, this instrument is most attractive for those who expect their income (and their marginal tax rate) to fall after retirement. The ownership rate of such pension plans is rather low, because most workers are covered by a compulsory pension plan. The amounts of compulsory pension wealth far exceed all discretionary financial wealth (see Alessie, Lusardi, and Kapteyn 1995). As pension wealth is a large part of total household wealth, it is unfortunate that our data do not provide reliable information on the size of compulsory pension entitlements. Noncompulsory defined-benefit pensions, a common asset in many other countries, hardly exist in the Netherlands.

The other type of life insurance asset, savings or endowment insurance policies, is taxed very differently: premiums paid are not tax deductible, but under some conditions concerning time span and amount, benefit payments are tax free. This type of life insurance is often combined with a mortgage (whole life insurance with mortgage on real estate, house, or second house).

Real estate ownership is taxed in various ways. Owner-occupied housing is mainly taxed through the income tax, by adding an imputed rent to income. Increases of the value of real estate are not taxed.

The survey also contains detailed information on various types of financial liability. By far the most important in size are home mortgages. Less common are mortgages on pieces of real estate and second home mortgages. Interest is fully tax deductible. Other types of financial debts referred to in the survey are private loans, extended lines of credit, outstanding debts on hire-purchase contracts, outstanding debts with mail-order firms, loans from family or friends, study loans, and loans not mentioned before. Since 1997, the deductibility of interest on these types of debt has been restricted, and it was phased out entirely by 2001. Finally, checking account overdrafts are included as a separate debt category.

Apart from the income tax and other taxes on income or imputed asset income, families whose net wealth exceeds a threshold (193,000 guilders for single taxpayers, 241,000 for married taxpayers in 1998), pay a flat-rate wealth tax of 0.7 percent on the amount above the threshold. In computing total wealth, owner-occupied housing is counted at only 60 percent of its market value and financial assets at 100 percent.

To illustrate the differences between tax treatments of various forms of (risk-free) savings, we discuss some results given by Bovenberg and ter Rele (1998), who follow the method of King and Fullerton (1984), and compute the after-tax return s from the pretax return r as

$$s = [(1 - m_w)/(1 - m_c)]^{1/dur}(1 + r) - 1.$$

Here dur is the duration of the investment, m_w is the marginal tax rate at which withdrawals are taxed, and m_c is the rate at which contributions can be deducted. Bovenberg and ter Rele (1998) posit an inflation rate of 2 percent and a nominal pretax return of 6 percent for each asset they consider. For households with average marginal tax rates, they find real after-tax returns of 1.2 percent for traditional saving accounts, 1.5 percent for (innovative) risk-free growth funds, and 20.8 percent for the tax-favored ESSPs. For high-income (high-marginal-tax-rate) households, the differences are larger still. Thus, ESSPs are extremely tax favored, though this is limited by ceilings that may make them not so important for the rich. Moreover, they are accessible only to employees of a participating employer. Although there are also advantages for the employers (they do not pay social contributions on the amounts so invested), some small employers do not offer them because of the administration costs. Bovenberg and ter Rele (1998) also compute the real after-tax returns of both types of life insurance: 4.0 percent for savings or endowment insurance policies (equal to the real pretax return) and 5.3 percent for pension plans. Thus, both types are tax favored compared to traditional or innovative savings.

The left-hand panel of table 9.2 shows how the asset types referred to in the survey are aggregated to obtain the classification common to all the country studies in this book, which will also be used in the remainder of this chapter. We include a separate category for employer-sponsored savings plans. To the common debt categories, we have added study loans and checking account overdrafts.

Table 9.2 also presents a classification of assets at a highly aggregated level. Growth funds are included under fairly safe assets, since they invest in bonds and deposits. Other mutual funds invest in shares and are viewed as risky assets.

The means of the amounts held and the ownership rates in the CSS can be compared with external data. The first source is the national accounts statistics, presented in table 9.1. The second is the IPO data set.[6] Comparison with the National Accounts data has some serious limitations, such as scanty information on business assets in the CSS, different definitions of the household, and different definitions of asset and liability types (see Alessie, Hochguertel, and van Soest 2000 for details). We therefore focus on the comparison with the IPO data.

Due to its partly administrative nature, IPO will not suffer so much from the typical measurement problems of survey data. This does not guarantee that these published data perfectly reflect national ownership rates or aggregate holdings. Underreporting to avoid

Table 9.2
Definition of asset and debt categories

Asset and liability aggregates	Asset and liability items in CentER Savings Survey
Assets	
Transaction and saving accounts and certificates of deposit	Checking accounts; savings arrangements linked to a Postbank account; deposit books; savings or deposit accounts; savings certificates
Bonds	Bonds and mortgage bonds (all types)
Stocks	Stocks and shares, including shares of substantial holding
Mutual funds, managed investment accounts	Mutual funds, mutual fund accounts; growth funds
Defined-contribution plans	Single-premium annuity insurance policies
Cash value of life insurance	Savings or endowment insurance policies, including whole life insurance linked to a life insurance mortgage (on all types of real estate)
Employer-sponsored savings plans	Employer-sponsored savings plans
Other financial assets	Money lent out to family or friends; savings or investments not previously mentioned
Total financial assets (sum of the above)	
Primary residence	Primary residence
Other real estate	Second house; other real estate not used for own accommodation
Real estate (sum of the above)	
Business equity	Business equity self-employed; business equity of independent professionals (lawyers, physicians, etc.) and freelance workers
Stock of durable goods	Cars; motorcycles; caravans; boats
Total nonfinancial assets (sum of the above)	
Total assets (total financial and nonfinancial assets)	
Debt	
Mortgage and real estate debt	Mortgages (on any type of real estate)
Study loans	Study loans
Checking account overdrafts	Checking account overdrafts
Consumer credit	Private loans; extended lines of credit; outstanding debts on hire-purchase contracts, debts based on payment by installment or equity-based loans; outstanding debts with mail-order firms, shops, or other sorts of retail business

Table 9.2
(continued)

Asset and liability aggregates	Asset and liability items in CentER Savings Survey
Other debt	Loans from family or friends; loans not mentioned before
Total debt (sum of the above)	
Total net worth (total assets less total debts)	
Asset categories according to riskiness	Included aggregates (and items)
Clearly safe financial assets	Transaction and saving accounts, certificates of deposit
Fairly safe financial assets	Defined-contribution plans; cash value of life insurance; employer-sponsored savings plans; growth funds; other financial assets
Risky financial assets	Stocks; bonds; mutual funds or mutual fund accounts
Total financial assets	
Risky total assets	Risky financial assets; business assets; other real estate

taxes might be as serious as measurement errors in surveys. For this reason, Statistics Netherlands has adjusted the IPO information on the value of the primary residence by making use of the Socio-Economic Panel. On the other hand, banks and other financial institutions must provide the tax authorities with details on customers' saving accounts balances, mortgage debt and mortgage interest payments, and interest income. Presumably, therefore, these asset items are measured rather accurately in the IPO at least for the households in the income or wealth tax register. IPO does not cover all assets, life insurance is not included, for example. IPO contains the same type of information on business equity as the CSS. These two data sets thus allow for a similar breakdown of assets and liabilities. The comparative results are summarized as follows:

· In the years 1993 through 1997 the IPO estimates of average net worth are 12 percent lower than the CSS estimates. This can mainly be attributed to the fact that home ownership rates are lower in IPO than in the CSS (43 percent versus about 48 percent). The CSS home ownership rate coincides with the Housing Needs Survey (WBO),[7] since rates from WBO were used to construct the sample weights of the CSS. It is unclear why the IPO figure is lower. The average value of the house conditional on ownership is somewhat higher in CSS than IPO. A comparison with the data from external sources in table 9.1 suggests that the IPO data on the value of the house are rather reliable.

• By comparison with the IPO, the CSS estimates of average checking and saving accounts balances are 20 percent lower.

• CSS finds a considerably higher ownership rate of stocks, bonds, and mutual funds (25.2 percent as against 12.8 percent for IPO in 1996). On the other hand, the unconditional means are similar. This implies that the CSS considerably underestimates the mean conditional on ownership. We suspect that the IPO estimates of the ownership rates of securities may be too low, due to, for example, nonreporting to the tax authorities. A comparison with the national accounts shows that IPO greatly underestimates aggregate share holdings (by 45 percent to 50 percent). In the CSS, the estimate of the average amount invested in shares from a substantial holding is considerably lower than its IPO equivalent. According to both IPO and CSS, very few households hold this type of asset, and these households are typically very wealthy.

• The difference between IPO and CSS estimates of the home ownership rates and average house value induces a difference in mortgage ownership rates and mortgage debt. Both data sources suggest that about 80 percent of home owner households have a mortgage.

• On consumer credit, the two surveys are quite similar.

Estimates of levels of wealth in survey data are often reputed to be unreliable. Our comparison is hampered by the fact that both macro and microdata have evident drawbacks. Still, the accuracy of the CSS estimates is no worse than other wealth surveys with the exception of the American Survey of Consumer Finances (see, e.g., Brandolini and Cannari 1994 for a useful overview).

9.3   Ownership and Composition of Household Assets and Liabilities: Survey Data

In this section, we describe ownership rates and the composition of asset portfolios of Dutch households according to the CSS survey data, using the common classification for all country studies (see table 9.2). All the results are weighted with the sample weights to make them representative for the Dutch population. The weighted ownership rates for assets are typically lower than the unweighted ownership rates, reflecting the fact that the rich are oversampled.[8]

Table 9.3 presents the ownership rates. Transaction and savings accounts are held by more than 95 percent of the households. The other 5 percent may be largely reporting error, since this category includes checking accounts, which are necessary for many financial transactions and are the usual channel for receiving income. Most households also hold at least one type of traditional saving account. Ownership of bonds is not common, the ownership rate never exceeds about 6 percent, with a decreasing trend. The ownership rate of stocks rose during the 1990s, from about 11 percent to more than 15 percent. Mutual funds and managed investment accounts were on average more popular than stocks, with an even higher growth rate over the sample period. Many financial institutions have been successful in introducing and marketing mutual funds as a low-threshold risky asset, available to many individual investors. Still, most households hold neither stocks nor mutual funds. This lack of participation can be explained by monetary transaction costs and information costs. In chapter 7, Guiso and Jappelli pay more attention to the nature of these costs. As in Italy, there is evidence that investing in a mutual fund has substantial transaction costs.[9]

Defined contribution pensions are less commonly held than in many other countries; the ownership rate hovers around 16 percent. The other type of life insurance assets, cash value of life insurance policies, has consistently higher ownership rates than the defined contribution plans, varying between 23 percent and 26 percent. These life insurance policies also include whole life insurance linked to a mortgage. The ownership rate of the new ESSPs rose rapidly on their introduction and has remained approximately constant since 1995.

The rates for primary residence show that the home ownership rate in the sample increased during the 1990s. Ownership of other real estate, however, declined somewhat. Business equity is held by about 6 percent, and the variation over the years does not reveal a systematic pattern. The stock of consumer durables covers only cars, motorbikes, boats, and caravans. Between 72 percent and 77 percent of all families own at least one of these. About 80 percent hold assets in at least one of the nonfinancial asset categories we consider.

Table 9.3
Asset and debt ownership rates: Survey data

	1993	1994	1995	1996	1997	1998
Assets						
Total financial assets	93.3	94.0	95.5	96.0	95.7	95.4
Checking and savings accounts	92.2	92.7	93.6	94.7	93.3	93.2
Bonds	6.0	4.8	4.2	4.6	3.5	3.5
Stocks[a]	11.4	10.0	11.5	13.5	14.4	15.4
Mutual funds	14.0	15.1	15.3	17.8	19.0	21.6
Defined-contribution plans	14.2	12.9	15.8	17.7	17.5	17.5
Cash value of life insurance	24.5	24.1	24.8	25.9	25.2	23.0
Employer-sponsored saving plans	18.1	17.2	36.1	39.9	36.6	35.8
Other financial assets	13.3	12.4	13.1	13.0	15.0	14.0
Total nonfinancial assets	78.4	79.4	80.0	81.4	83.2	79.2
Real estate	48.8	48.6	49.3	50.0	51.0	51.6
House	47.6	47.6	48.4	49.2	50.0	50.8
Other real estate	6.2	5.8	5.1	5.6	5.6	4.5
Business equity	4.8	5.9	6.3	6.8	7.1	5.1
Stock of durable goods	71.4	72.8	73.2	75.6	76.7	72.7
Total assets	95.9	96.4	97.2	97.4	97.4	97.1
Liabilities						
Total debt	64.5	63.9	63.9	65.3	65.7	65.7
Mortgage and real estate debt	39.7	38.9	40.9	41.8	43.0	42.6
Consumer credit	33.2	31.3	30.2	30.6	32.4	32.0
Other debt	7.4	8.1	7.3	7.0	7.0	5.6
Student loans	6.2	5.3	5.0	4.4	3.8	5.7
Checking account overdrafts	14.9	13.7	14.2	15.0	16.3	16.9
Net worth	97.7	98.1	98.8	98.6	98.6	98.9
Total assets	95.9	96.4	97.2	97.4	97.4	97.1
Clearly safe financial assets[b]	92.2	92.7	93.6	94.7	93.3	93.2
Fairly safe financial assets[c]	48.9	46.8	57.8	60.4	59.4	58.2
Safe financial assets[d]	93.2	93.8	95.3	95.9	95.7	95.1
Risky financial assets[e]	21.2	20.6	21.9	23.7	24.8	27.7
Risky total assets[f]	27.7	27.4	28.4	31.1	31.5	32.8

Source: CentER Savings Survey, sampling years 1993–1998.
Note: All statistics use sample weights.
[a] Include stocks from substantial holdings.
[b] Include transaction (checking) and saving accounts, and certificates of deposit.
[c] Include defined-contribution plans, the cash value of life insurance, employer-sponsored savings plans, growth funds, and other financial assets.
[d] The sum of clearly safe and fairly safe financial assets.
[e] Include stocks, bonds, mutual funds, and mutual fund accounts.
[f] The sum of risky financial assets and business assets and other real estate.

The majority of home owners also have one or more mortgages on their house or other real estate (mortgage and real estate debt). Like home ownership, mortgage ownership increased over time. Between 30 percent and 33 percent of all households have some form of consumer credit, and other types of financial debt are held by 10 percent to 13 percent.

There is a decreasing trend in holding of (subsidized) student loans. This is due to a political decision to introduce incentives to reduce the amount of time spent in school. Checking accounts overdrafts does not refer to the overall balance, but to checking accounts considered individually. 15 percent of households have at least one checking account with a negative balance (possibly in combination with other checking accounts with positive balances). The percentage of families with some type of financial liability, including mortgage debt, rose from 64 percent to 66 percent during the sample period.

Table 9.3 finally summarizes the ownership information at the higher level of aggregation defined in table 9.2. The percentage with fairly safe financial assets rose from 49 percent to 60 percent, largely due to the boom in ESSPs. Ownership of risky financial assets has also risen substantially, as in many other countries. In 1998, about 28 percent held some risky financial asset, and 33 percent held risky assets in general (that is, including business equity and investment real estate).

Table 9.4 gives the composition of financial and total wealth and of household debt. It gives the (estimated) amount of each asset and liability category held by the population as a whole, as a share of total financial wealth, total wealth, and total debt.[10] Missing values are imputed, as explained in section 9.2. A shortcoming of the table is that some large amounts may heavily influence the numbers, due to the skewed distribution of wealth and its components. This is probably why some of the time patterns are not very pronounced. It may also explain why the average amounts of total assets and total financial assets (also presented in the table) do not show the same high growth rates as in table 9.1. The mean amounts are strongly affected by a few very rich people, and there are simply too few of these in the CSS to capture the trend in the means. This problem does not affect the median values, which are insensitive to the outliers. The medians show much higher growth rates for the period 1993 through 1998, comparable to those in table 9.1: about 45 percent for financial assets and 50 percent for total assets.

Table 9.4
Asset and debt ownership rates: Survey data

	1993	1994	1995	1996	1997	1998
Assets	As a percentage of total financial assets					
Checking and savings accounts	35.9	36.4	32.7	30.7	30.5	35.1
Bonds	3.0	2.1	1.9	1.9	1.8	2.2
Stocks[a]	21.3	20.6	22.0	24.0	25.3	23.8
Mutual funds	10.9	12.0	10.6	12.2	11.7	13.3
Defined-contribution plans	9.7	11.5	11.4	10.3	8.7	7.9
Cash value of life insurance	12.9	12.0	14.4	13.9	12.1	10.4
Employer-sponsored saving plans	1.1	1.0	1.8	2.3	3.1	2.9
Other financial assets	5.3	4.3	5.2	4.7	6.8	4.5
Total financial assets (average amount in guilders)	74,893	70,416	74,969	84,803	85,060	81,563
	As a percentage of total assets					
Total financial assets	29.6	29.0	28.1	29.7	28.0	27.6
Total nonfinancial assets	70.4	71.0	71.9	70.3	72.0	72.4
Real estate	59.7	59.9	60.4	60.1	61.9	63.8
House	53.8	53.7	54.2	55.1	55.4	58.8
Other real estate	5.9	6.2	6.3	5.0	6.5	4.9
Business equity	5.0	5.8	6.4	4.9	5.0	3.7
Stock of durable goods	5.7	5.4	5.2	5.2	5.1	4.9
Total assets (average amount)	253,197	242,510	267,198	285,081	303,377	295,423
Liabilities	As a percentage of total debt					
Total debt (average amount)	74,311	66,562	73,876	77,178	78,373	71,676
Mortgage and real estate debt	87.9	88.5	88.4	89.2	89.0	88.5
Consumer credit	6.0	5.9	5.2	4.9	5.8	5.6
Other debt	4.7	4.3	4.9	4.4	3.7	3.7
Study loans	0.7	0.7	0.8	0.6	0.5	0.8
Checking account overdrafts	0.7	0.5	0.8	0.9	1.0	1.4
	As a percentage of total assets					
Total debt	29.3	27.4	27.6	27.1	25.8	24.3
Net worth	70.7	72.6	72.4	72.9	74.2	75.7
Clearly safe financial assets[b]	10.6	10.6	9.2	9.1	8.5	9.7
Fairly safe financial assets[c]	10.2	9.9	10.4	10.9	9.9	8.0
Safe financial assets[d]	20.8	20.5	19.6	20.0	18.5	17.7
Risky financial assets[e]	8.8	8.6	8.5	9.8	9.6	9.9
Risky total assets[f]	19.7	20.5	21.1	19.6	21.0	18.6

Table 9.4
(continued)

	1993	1994	1995	1996	1997	1998
	As a percentage of total financial assets					
Clearly safe financial assets[b]	35.9	36.4	32.7	30.7	30.5	35.1
Fairly safe financial assets[c]	34.4	34.1	37.1	36.5	35.3	28.9
Safe financial assets[d]	70.3	70.6	69.9	67.2	65.8	64.1
Risky financial assets	29.7	29.4	30.1	32.8	34.2	35.9

Source: CentER Savings Survey, sampling years 1993–1998.
Note: All statistics use sample weights.
[a] Include stocks from substantial holdings.
[b] Include transaction (checking) and saving accounts, and certificates of deposit.
[c] Include defined-contribution plans, the cash value of life insurance, employer-sponsored savings plans, growth funds, and other financial assets.
[d] The sum of clearly safe and fairly safe financial assets.
[e] Include stocks, bonds, mutual funds, and/or mutual fund accounts.
[f] The sum of risky financial assets and business assets and other real estate.

The first panel presents the shares of the various asset categories in total financial wealth. The share of risk-free financial assets is between 31 percent and 36 percent, and it declined between 1993 and 1997. The share of employer-sponsored savings plans rose but remained small, due to the low maximum amounts that are tax favored. The shares of stocks and mutual funds together exceed the share of risk-free financial assets and exhibit an increasing trend over time. The joint asset share of defined-contribution pension plans and whole life insurance policies ranges from 18 percent to 25 percent. The average share of financial in total assets has remained fairly stable, between 28 percent and 30 percent.

The two most important nonfinancial assets are primary residence and consumer durables (e.g. vehicles). The share of primary residence has risen, but not as much as one might expect given the enormous increase in house prices in the past decade.

The share of mortgage debt in total liabilities is large and hardly varies over time. Although many people have some form of consumer credit, the amounts are small: the total is no more than 5 percent or 6 percent of total financial debt. The total debt-to-asset ratio fell from about 29 percent to about 24 percent.

The table also presents the conditional shares for risky assets. These are computed as the ratio of the average amount of risky assets held by owners of risky assets to the average amount of total

Table 9.5
Diversification of households' financial portfolios

Asset combination								
Clearly safe[a]	Fairly safe[b]	Risky[c]	1993	1994	1995	1996	1997	1998
0	0	0	6.7	6.0	4.5	4.0	4.3	4.6
1	0	0	39.2	41.4	33.2	30.7	31.1	31.5
0	1	0	1.0	1.0	1.5	1.0	2.1	1.8
0	0	1	0.1	0.2	0.2	0.1	0.0	0.2
1	1	0	32.0	31.0	38.9	40.5	37.6	34.4
1	0	1	5.2	5.6	4.3	4.7	5.2	5.4
0	1	1	0.1	0.1	0.2	0.1	0.2	0.2
1	1	1	15.8	14.6	17.2	18.7	19.4	21.9

Source: CentER Savings Survey, sampling years 1993–1998.
Note: Ownership combinations of asset classes (portfolios) and their observed probabilities (summing to 100 percent in each year). 0 = not holding the asset category; 1 = holding the asset category. All statistics use sample weights.
[a] Include transaction (checking) and saving accounts, and certificates of deposit.
[b] Include defined-contribution plans, the cash value of life insurance, employer-sponsored savings plans, growth funds, and other financial assets.
[c] Include stocks, bonds, mutual funds, and mutual fund accounts.

assets of these households. These conditional shares are larger than the unconditional asset shares because the nil amounts of nonowners are not included. On the other hand, they are lowered because the total assets of risky asset owners are larger than those of nonowners (see table 9.7). The time pattern of conditional asset shares is similar to that in the unconditional shares.

Table 9.5 shows the ownership structure of financial asset portfolios. We consider the three categories clearly safe (i.e. risk free), fairly safe, and risky. This gives eight possible portfolio structures, depending on whether or not any of the three categories is held. The number of households reporting no financial assets fell in the first few years of the survey and has held at between 4 percent and 5 percent since then. In 1993, the largest group was households with risk-free financial assets only. This category has shrunk substantially, however. In the later years of the survey, the largest group is those with risk-free and fairly safe financial assets but no risky ones. About 5 percent hold clearly safe and risky but no fairly safe financial assets. This percentage has remained stable over time. The largest increase is found for the final group: almost 22 percent of all households held assets in each of the three risk categories in 1998, compared with less than 16 percent in 1993. Alhough this increase is similar to trends in other European countries, the degree of diversification is not. Dutch household portfolios are more diversified than those in the United Kingdom or Italy, though somewhat less diversified than in Germany. An explanation is the presence of several distinct tax exemptions up to certain thresholds (interest on traditional accounts, ESSPs, dividend payments), which creates incentives to invest in a number of different types of asset.

Table 9.6 reports the ownership rates for each quartile of total wealth and for the top five percentiles. Table 9.7 does the same for asset shares. We present the numbers only for 1997, the latest wave for which the high-income panel was available. There are enormous differences in the portfolio choices of households in the different wealth quartiles, and the differences are largely in line with the findings in the other country studies. While clearly safe financial assets are held by all quartiles, ownership of fairly safe and especially of risky assets is quite uncommon for low-wealth households. An exception is ESSPs which are common among employees in all wealth categories. This is what we should expect, given their favored tax treatment and the absence of transaction costs.

Table 9.6 shows that the wealth gradient of stocks is higher than that of mutual funds. This is due to the concentration of substantial share holdings among the very rich. The positive relation between wealth and home ownership is no surprise. The same holds for other nonfinancial assets. Somewhat unexpectedly, consumer credit and checking account overdrafts are not uncommon among the rich, though the rates are lower than in the lowest wealth quartile.

The portfolio shares in table 9.7 basically tell the same story. For the first wealth quartile, clearly safe assets and ESSPs together account for an average of almost 84 percent of total financial assets. For the top 5 percent of the wealth distribution, the figure is only 14 percent. In particular, the share of stocks is very large for the top 5 percent: 49 percent in 1997. The share of housing wealth (or other real estate) is quite large for the top two wealth quartiles but smaller for the top 5 percent. Again, this is presumably due to the impact of holders of substantial shares among the richest. The wealth gradient of business equity as a share in total assets is steep and positive, while the gradient of consumer durables is strongly negative.

Table 9.6
Asset and debt ownership rates by net worth quartiles, 1997

	Below quartile I	Between quartiles I and II	Between quartiles II and III	Above quartile III	Top 5%
Assets					
Total financial assets	87.1	98.1	98.9	98.8	99.0
Checking and savings accounts	83.1	95.7	96.8	97.7	96.6
Bonds	0.1	1.8	2.6	9.6	15.9
Stocks[a]	0.8	5.1	13.5	38.1	63.9
Mutual funds	1.3	14.8	19.9	40.0	49.6
Defined-contribution plans	6.3	11.7	20.0	32.0	37.3
Cash value of life insurance	5.6	12.8	44.3	38.2	32.0
Employer-sponsored saving plans	18.2	31.1	55.3	41.9	23.6
Other financial assets	9.4	12.9	15.3	22.4	36.2
Total nonfinancial assets	49.3	85.0	98.8	100.0	100.0
Real estate	5.0	18.2	85.9	95.2	100.0
House	5.0	16.9	84.6	93.5	96.1
Other real estate	0.0	2.2	3.2	17.1	35.1
Business	0.6	5.0	5.6	17.2	27.0
Stock of durable goods	48.3	80.8	87.5	90.4	90.6
Total assets	89.7	100.0	100.0	100.0	100.0
Liabilities					
Total debt	62.6	37.8	81.7	80.7	74.8
Mortgage and real estate debt	5.0	16.8	76.0	74.4	68.0
Consumer credit	47.7	23.3	34.2	24.3	22.6
Other debt	11.0	3.7	6.2	7.1	12.5
Study loans	7.8	4.7	1.4	1.4	1.1
Checking account overdrafts	27.2	9.1	14.7	14.2	15.3
Net worth	94.2	100.0	100.0	100.0	100.0
Clearly safe financial assets[b]	83.1	95.7	96.8	97.7	96.6
Fairly safe financial assets[c]	30.4	50.2	77.6	79.4	84.4
Safe financial assets[d]	87.1	98.1	98.7	98.8	99.0
Risky financial assets[e]	1.2	16.4	24.2	57.4	75.8
Risky total assets[f]	1.8	22.3	30.6	71.4	95.2

Source: CentER Savings Survey, sampling year, 1997.
Note: See table 9.4.

Table 9.7
Composition of assets by net worth quartiles, 1997

	Below quartile I	Between quartiles I and II	Between quartiles II and III	Above quartile III	Top 5%
Assets	As a percentage of total financial assets				
Checking and savings accounts	65.8	65.4	47.2	21.8	13.5
Bonds	0.0	0.6	0.7	2.2	2.3
Stocks[a]	0.6	3.1	6.0	32.9	49.2
Mutual funds	0.6	8.2	9.2	12.9	10.5
Defined-contribution plans	7.7	3.2	7.7	9.6	9.3
Cash value of life insurance	6.0	4.7	18.2	11.7	6.8
Employer-sponsored saving plans	16.2	6.2	6.1	1.8	0.6
Other financial assets	3.1	8.6	5.0	7.0	7.8
Total financial assets (average amount in guilders)	4,520	29,178	57,912	248,722	666,729
	As a percentage of total assets				
Real estate	58.3	46.8	74.6	58.5	46.8
House	58.3	44.6	72.9	49.5	33.3
Other real estate	0.0	2.2	1.7	9.0	13.4
Business equity	1.9	3.1	1.2	6.7	9.8
Stock of durable goods	17.7	14.6	5.9	3.5	2.3
Total nonfinancial assets (average amount)	15,947	53,021	258,400	546,169	954,009
Total assets (average amount)	20,467	82,200	316,312	794,892	1,620,738
Liabilities	As a percentage of total debt				
Mortgage and real estate debt	51.2	87.7	94.1	91.8	87.8
Consumer credit	30.6	8.3	3.7	2.4	1.9
Other debt	10.7	2.5	1.7	4.5	7.8
Study loans	4.3	0.7	0.1	0.0	0.0
Checking account over-drafts	3.1	0.7	0.4	1.3	2.4
Total debt (average amount)	24,920	34,605	118,393	135,660	190,468
	As a percentage of total financial assets				
Clearly safe financial assets[b]	65.8	65.4	47.2	21.8	13.5
Fairly safe financial assets[c]	33.6	25.5	39.2	35.6	30.0
Safe financial assets[d]	99.3	90.9	86.5	57.4	43.5
Risky financial assets[e]	0.7	9.1	13.5	42.6	56.5

Table 9.7
(continued)

	Below quartile I	Between quartiles I and II	Between quartiles II and III	Above quartile III	Top 5%
	As a percentage of total assets				
Total risky assets[f]	2.0	8.5	5.4	29.1	46.4
Conditional shares (shares for owners only)					
Financial risky assets (as a percentage of financial assets)	26.9	33.5	34.1	52.1	62.0
Total risky assets (as a percentage of total assets)	23.9	31.1	17.2	35.6	48.0

Source: CentER Savings Survey, sampling year, 1997.
Note: See table 9.4.

For the lowest wealth quartile, the share of consumer credit and the share of checking account overdrafts add up to almost 34 percent of total debt. For this quartile, total financial liabilities typically exceed total (gross) wealth. On the other hand, consumer debt plays a minor role for the higher wealth quartiles, where mortgage debt dominates the distribution of liabilities. In the top wealth quartile, some form of consumer debt is held by more than 24 percent, but the average amount is only 2.4 percent of total liabilities and less than 0.5 percent of average gross wealth.

The conditional shares of risky financial assets still increase with wealth, but less steeply than the unconditional asset shares. The main reason is that ownership of risky assets increases with wealth (see table 9.6). Still, these numbers suggest that total wealth does affect the conditional asset share, something we check formally in an econometric model in section 9.4.

Table 9.8 presents the same ownership rates as table 9.6, again for 1997, but now broken down according to age. The asset ownership rates for stocks, mutual funds, and bonds are much higher for the older age groups. King and Leape (1987) have a similar result. Their explanation is that, other things being equal, financial knowledge about assets such as stocks and bonds accumulates with age. We shall come back to this in section 9.5. Life insurance is typically held by people in their 30s and 40s. ESSPs are linked to employment and so are not held by people who retired before they were introduced.

Table 9.8
Asset and debt ownership rates by age of the household head, 1997

	Age class					
	Under 30	30–39	40–49	50–59	60–69	70 and over
Assets						
Total financial assets	95.3	96.9	94.9	96.9	96.8	91.7
Checking and savings accounts	94.8	92.6	91.8	95.2	95.3	90.5
Bonds	0.0	1.3	2.1	4.4	6.2	6.4
Stocks[a]	4.7	6.8	13.4	18.4	17.8	21.2
Mutual funds	10.0	14.5	14.3	24.3	23.1	25.1
Defined-contribution plans	7.2	15.8	22.9	23.6	15.6	4.0
Cash value of life insurance	13.8	33.1	34.3	30.0	14.3	3.8
Employer-sponsored saving plans	33.2	49.2	53.0	46.1	11.0	0.5
Other financial assets	15.2	11.5	15.7	14.7	16.8	17.4
Total nonfinancial assets	62.8	83.0	85.9	90.6	83.5	72.4
Real estate	16.7	48.3	57.6	62.3	51.5	34.3
House	16.7	47.0	57.4	61.3	51.0	30.4
Other real estate	0.7	3.0	4.9	9.5	4.8	7.7
Business	4.3	7.1	10.9	8.5	3.0	3.4
Stock of durable goods	59.9	75.8	78.5	84.3	77.9	65.7
Total assets	96.3	97.7	96.5	99.3	98.9	93.5
Liabilities						
Total debt	66.5	72.6	77.0	74.0	54.5	28.3
Mortgage and real estate debt	15.1	42.5	53.3	55.4	38.6	16.4
Consumer credit	26.9	38.8	40.1	37.0	24.2	9.8
Other debt	6.5	9.9	8.5	6.6	4.3	3.8
Study loans	24.8	8.1	1.7	1.4	0.7	0.7
Checking account over-drafts	31.8	20.3	18.9	16.2	10.8	4.9
Net worth	100.0	99.7	98.4	99.3	98.9	94.2
Clearly safe financial assets[b]	94.8	92.6	91.8	95.2	95.3	90.5
Fairly safe financial assets[c]	54.4	67.0	71.3	66.4	46.5	27.4
Safe financial assets[d]	95.3	96.8	94.9	96.9	96.8	91.7
Risky financial assets[e]	8.7	15.6	21.0	31.1	31.1	35.1
Risky total assets[f]	12.8	22.9	29.6	41.2	32.8	38.8

Source: CentER Savings Survey, sampling year, 1997.
Note: See table 9.4.

Home ownership rates are highest for people in their 40s and 50s and business equity is mostly held by people in their 40s and 50s.

The mortgage debt pattern follows that of home ownership, except for the oldest age groups. Many in this age group apparently now own their houses mortgage free. Between 1993 and 1998, the fraction of elderly households holding a mortgage increased, possibly because the fall in interest rates induced more elderly households to exploit tax arbitrage. Consumer debt is most common for people in their 30s, 40s and 50s and very low for the oldest group. Checking account overdrafts are particularly common for the youngest, which suggests that they may have limited access to other types of finance.

Table 9.9 presents the asset shares by age group. The share of risky assets rises with age, from under 10 percent to more than 50 percent. Stocks and bonds are particularly important for the two oldest groups and mutual funds less markedly so. The other age patterns for the asset shares are largely in line with the ownership rate patterns. In contrast to Italy, the conditional shares of risky assets also rise with age, although not as steeply as the unconditional.

9.4   Age, Cohort, and Time Patterns of Asset Ownership Rates

In figure 9.1, we present weighted age and cohort patterns of the ownership rates of some financial asset types, based on all six waves of the CSS. We use five-year cohorts (1915–1919 for the oldest cohort and 1970–1974 for the youngest). Cohorts are labeled by their middle year. Older and younger cohorts contain very few observations and are not included in the graphs. The three panels in figure 9.1 refer to ownership rates of fairly safe assets and risky assets, and ESSPs. (The clearly safe ownership rates are all close to one, making its graph not very interesting.) Note that ESSPs are also included in the fairly safe category. Each graph presents the raw ownership rates for each cohort in each wave; the six points for each cohort represent the average age level at the times of the interviews and form a "cohort curve." For each cohort, these six points are interconnected. The jumps between the cohort curves show that apart from age effects, there are cohort or time effects. The fact that cohort curves are not horizontal shows that there are time or age effects; the fact that not all cohort curves are the same shows that there is more than just time effects. As usual, however, the three effects cannot be disentangled without further assumptions.

Table 9.9
Composition of assets by age of the household head, 1997

	Age class					
	Under 30	30–39	40–49	50–59	60–69	70 and over
Assets	As a percentage of financial assets					
Checking and savings accounts	49.8	37.7	34.1	27.0	28.2	29.7
Bonds	0.0	0.3	1.3	0.5	1.8	5.5
Stocks[a]	4.4	13.1	13.7	21.3	36.4	37.7
Mutual funds	5.4	13.8	10.1	11.6	10.9	13.8
Defined-contribution plans	0.7	5.6	10.1	13.1	9.5	1.1
Cash value of life insurance	15.5	17.3	19.7	17.5	5.7	0.8
Employer-sponsored saving plans	8.9	6.7	5.7	3.9	0.6	0.0
Other financial assets	15.2	5.4	5.3	4.9	7.0	11.5
Total financial assets (average amount in guilders)	18,246	42,198	67,041	107,537	121,767	131,329
	As a percentage of total assets					
Real estate	59.1	69.1	66.0	64.4	55.2	48.2
House	57.4	66.1	61.9	52.6	52.1	40.0
Other real estate	1.7	3.1	4.1	11.8	3.0	8.3
Business equity	4.1	4.9	7.3	5.5	3.1	1.2
Stock of durable goods	7.8	5.7	5.1	4.4	5.9	4.6
Total nonfinancial assets (average amount)	44,887	165,814	242,595	311,354	218,464	154,205
Total assets (average amount)	63,133	208,012	309,635	418,891	340,231	285,534
Liabilities	As a percentage of total debt					
Mortgage and real estate debt	82.6	88.0	89.8	91.0	85.3	84.8
Consumer credit	8.3	7.5	4.9	4.4	8.8	3.6
Other debt	1.8	2.4	4.5	3.5	3.9	6.7
Study loans	6.0	1.3	0.2	0.1	0.0	0.3
Checking account over-drafts	1.3	0.8	0.6	0.9	2.0	4.6
Total debt (average amount in guilders)	28,622	81,168	99,643	112,275	55,152	18,285

Table 9.9
(continued)

	Age class					
	Under 30	30–39	40–49	50–59	60–69	70 and over
	As a percentage of financial assets					
Clearly safe financial assets[a]	49.8	37.7	34.1	27.0	28.2	29.7
Fairly safe financial assets[b]	41.1	42.1	44.2	42.5	27.9	20.0
Safe financial assets[c]	90.9	79.8	78.3	69.6	56.1	49.7
Risky financial assets[d]	9.1	20.2	21.7	30.4	43.9	50.3
	As a percentage of total assets					
Total risky assets[e]	8.5	12.1	16.1	25.1	21.9	32.6
Conditional shares (shares for owners only)						
Financial risky assets (as a percentage of financial assets)	32.1	40.0	37.0	43.2	56.6	64.0
Total risky assets (as a percentage of total assets)	24.2	27.1	28.0	34.8	32.3	44.7

Source: CentER Savings Survey, sampling year, 1997.
Note: See table 9.4.

Figure 9.1A shows that the ownership rates of fairly safe assets have a hump-shaped age curve. For the cohorts of working age, there is a steep increase between 1994 and 1996, reflecting the boom in ESSPs. Thus the jumps between the curves are better interpreted as time than as cohort effects.

The pattern for risky financial assets (figure 9.1B) is quite different: ownership rises continuously with age. For the younger cohorts, cohort and time effects do not seem to be important. For the older cohorts, there are clear downward jumps between cohort curves, reflecting either a cohort effect (older cohorts are less likely to own these assets, given age and calendar time) or a time effect (holding risky assets became more popular in the 1990s among the older age groups). The increase in the risky asset ownership rate is different from the pattern for some other countries. Italy and the United States, for example, have a hump-shaped pattern. Possible explanations for the increasing pattern are correlation between cohort and wealth or correlation between cohorts and knowledge about financial products. We analyze these explanations in the models in section 9.5.

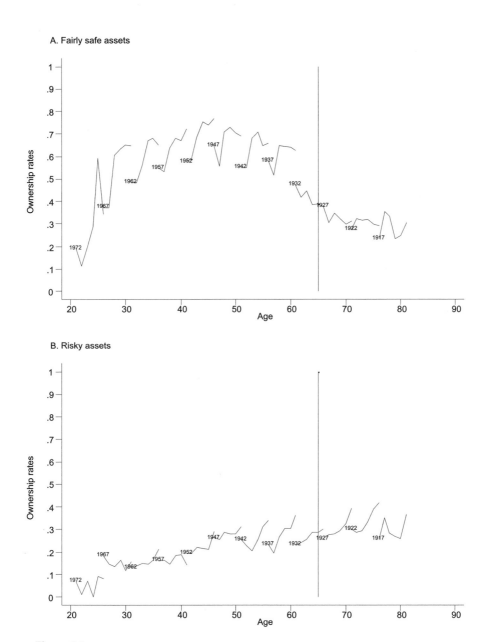

Figure 9.1
Ownership of assets, by birth cohort

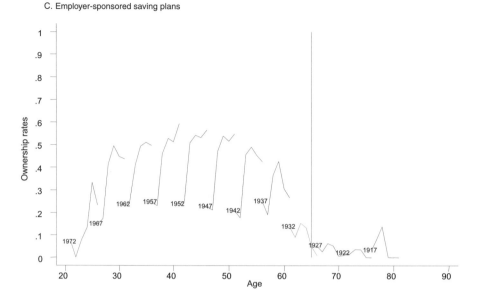

C. Employer-sponsored saving plans

Figure 9.1 (continued)

The ownership rates for ESSPs are presented in figure 9.1C. The differences between cohort curves stand out even more clearly than in figure 9.1A and reflect the time effects immediately upon the plans' institution.

Figure 9.2 gives the age patterns broken down by education. Four education levels are distinguished. Calendar time and cohort effects are ignored; the observations are simply pooled across all waves (each household is thus included as from one to six times). The curves are smoothed as functions of age, using a nonparametric kernel regression technique.[11] This is done to remove the noise in the raw ownership rates, particularly for the smaller cells. The age pattern of ownership of fairly safe assets (figure 9.2A) does not change systematically with education. The low rate for the well-educated young households could be due to the fact that they have only recently entered the labor market (or not). The pattern for risky assets (figure 9.2B) shows that ownership rises sharply with age for the highest education level. For the younger age groups, ownership of risky assets is almost equally likely for all education levels. On the other hand, for a 60 year-old head of household with high education,

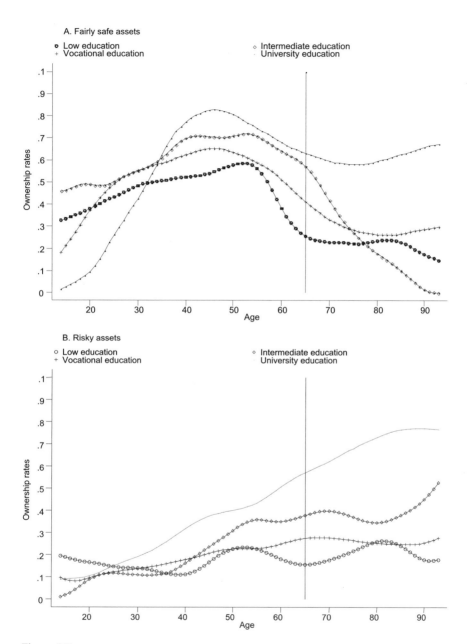

Figure 9.2
Ownership of assets, by education

ownership is much more likely than for a poorly educated head of the same age. Ownership of ESSPs displays no systematic correlation with education, so we do not graph this relationship.

9.5 Static Models for Asset Ownership

In this section we explain asset ownership with reference to various background variables. We focus on ownership of risky assets and on ownership of ESSPs. We have also estimated similar models for fairly safe assets, but the main conclusions coincide with the results for ESSPs.

As Miniaci and Weber note in chapter 4 there are various ways to model the binary choice of owning or not owning in a panel data context. Here we look at a static model; dynamics are added in the next section. We focus on random-effects models, because in fixed-effects models, many of the effects we are interested in are not identified, owing to insufficient time variation in some of the explanatory variables. The model we estimate is given by equations 4.3 through 4.5 in chapter 4. Both the individual effects and the error terms are assumed to follow a normal distribution and to be independent of the regressors. The errors are assumed independent over time. The model is estimated by maximum likelihood, using the complete unbalanced panel.

Instead of parameter estimates, we present estimated marginal effects, that is the changes in the ownership probability if explanatory variables change by one unit, ceteris paribus.[12] For most variables, these marginal effects are computed at the mean ownership probability. Exceptions are the effects for age, noncapital income, and total net worth. Specification tests show that we need a cubic wealth and (noncapital) income pattern and a quadratic age pattern. To interpret the estimated nonlinear patterns, we present the marginal effects for these variables at various values of the variable concerned, with the other regressors set to their means. For age, we consider a change by one year at ages 30, 45, and 65. For income and wealth, we consider changes by 1,000 guilders at the quartiles of the income and wealth sample distributions. We also present results of tests for joint significance of all the terms in the polynomials, and for groups of dummy variables. The results are presented in table 9.10.

Table 9.10
Static random-effects probit

Variable	Risky financial assets			Employer-sponsored saving plans		
	Marginal effect[a]	Standard error[b]	p-value[c]	Marginal effect[a]	Standard error[b]	p-value[c]
Number of observations/households	8,010/2,979			8,010/2,979		
Log likelihood	−3,065.73			−3,296.65		
Pseudo R^2	0.3834			0.4819		
Age						
At age 30	−0.00059	0.0018	0.072	0.01665	0.0035	0.000
At age 45	0.00105	0.0009		−0.01033	0.0019	
At age 65	0.00441	0.0024		−0.00920	0.0014	
Education						
Low education	−0.07645	0.0194	0.000	0.08218	0.0660	0.678
Intermediate/low education	−0.06115	0.0223		0.05359	0.0498	
Intermediate/high education	−0.06363	0.0210		0.07119	0.0485	
Vocational education, level 1	−0.10060	0.0156		0.03539	0.0506	
Vocational education, level 2	−0.08842	0.0179		0.06292	0.0459	
Vocational education, level 3	−0.03402	0.0213		0.04357	0.0330	
Noncapital income						
At 25 percent	0.00055	0.0002	0.000	0.00172	0.0002	0.000
At 50 percent	0.00053	0.0002		0.00138	0.0002	
At 75 percent	0.00050	0.0002		0.00111	0.0003	
Total net worth						
At 25 percent	0.00073	0.0001	0.000	0.00071	0.0001	0.000
At 50 percent	0.00083	0.0001		0.00030	0.0001	
At 75 percent	0.00071	0.0001		0.00017	0.0000	
Labor market status						
Unemployed	−0.07431	0.0282	0.000	−0.17542	0.0145	0.000
Retired	0.08767	0.0360		−0.25996	0.0216	
Disabled	−0.04510	0.0375		−0.18687	0.0140	
Other labor market status	0.04296	0.0446		−0.15784	0.0195	
Self-employed	0.14760	0.0506		−0.19139	0.0144	
High-income subpanel	0.06877	0.0255	0.003	0.04019	0.0304	0.175

Table 9.10
(continued)

Variable	Risky financial assets			Employer-sponsored saving plans		
	Marginal effect[a]	Standard error[b]	p-value[c]	Marginal effect[a]	Standard error[b]	p-value[c]
Household size						
Number of adults	−0.03461	0.0203	0.023	0.06686	0.0266	0.042
Number of children at home	−0.01356	0.0075		−0.00613	0.0101	
Financial interest						
Low	−0.22466	0.0201	0.000	−0.13060	0.0228	0.000
Medium	−0.13064	0.0189		−0.06628	0.0229	
Risk aversion						
Low	0.02212	0.0252	0.002	−0.01381	0.0271	0.657
Medium	0.04334	0.0131		0.00915	0.0164	

Note: The specification also controls for membership of the HIP subpanel, the number of adults and the number of children, year dummies, and degree of urbanization. See table 10 in Alessie, Hochguertel, and van Soest (2000) for detailed results. All regressors refer to the head of household, except noncapital income and total net worth. The latter variables were deflated using the CPI, 1995 = 100. The specification includes age as a second-order polynomial and noncapital income and total net worth as third-order polynomials of the log-transformed variable. The log transformation is of the form $y = \ln(x + 1)$ if $x \geq 0$, and $y = -\ln(-x + 1)$ if $x < 0$. Reference categories for dummy variable groups are university education; employment; financial interest: high; risk aversion: high.
[a] Changes in the ownership probability caused by marginal changes in regressors. For age, income, and net worth, marginal effects are based on the following discrete changes in the underlying variable: age: effect of an increase by 1 year, at ages 30, 45, and 65; noncapital income/total net worth: effect of an increase in noncapital income/total net worth by 1,000 guilders, at the 25, 50, and 75 percentiles of the noncapital income/total net worth distribution.
[b] Robust to heteroskedasticity.
[c] Refer to the (joint) test that all underlying coefficients are zero.

9.5.1   Risky Assets

We first discuss the estimates for ownership of risky assets. Income and wealth (net worth) patterns are strongly significant and positively sloped. The income pattern is close to linear; an increase of 1,000 guilders leads to a rise of between 0.05 and 0.06 percentage points in the probability of owning risky assets. The positive effect of income may be due to tax incentives: higher income means a higher marginal tax rate, hence a greater incentive to take advantage of the untaxed capital gains (see chapter 3, this volume).

The net worth pattern is also close to linear, with a wealth increase of 1,000 guilders leading to a rise in the ownership probability of between 0.071 and 0.083 percentage points. Chapter 1 shows, in a theoretical model, that the effect of wealth on the share of risky assets depends on the relation of wealth to risk aversion. The standard case is constant relative risk aversion and a constant risky asset share. Our finding is consistent with this theory if utility functions display decreasing relative risk aversion.

The labor market status of the head of household is significant. The retired and the self-employed are more likely to have risky assets than are employees. The household composition variables imply that larger families less frequently own risky financial assets.

We also used subjectively measured variables drawn from the psychological section of the survey, which is much richer than the typical household survey.[13] According to Gollier's theoretical model, expected utility models of portfolio choice predict that under plausible assumptions households with riskier human capital invest less in risky assets (see also Kimball 1993 for the impact of background risk on portfolio choice). We could not confirm this theoretical result; dummies concerning uncertainty over the expected income change are not significant at the 5 percent level.[14] These variables are therefore not included in the specification.

The head of household's interest in financial matters is summarized in two dummy variables. There is a strong, positive relationship between interest in financial matters and the probability of owning risky assets, with a difference of 22 percentage points between the very interested and the uninterested, ceteris paribus. Presumably the better-informed households are more aware of the advantages of risky assets and less hampered by fear of the unknown or initial costs than the less informed. Interest in financial matters serves as a proxy for information. Direct questions on respondents' knowledge of particular assets (see chapter 7 on Italy) are unavailable.[15]

The next variables reflect whether the head of household agrees with the statement that it is more important to have safe returns on financial investment than to take some risk to get an excess return. This can be seen as a proxy for risk aversion. As expected, the highly risk averse are the least likely to own risky financial assets.

Since the figures in the previous section suggest that age and time effects would be more important than cohort effects, we have not included the latter.[16] This implies that the age and time patterns are fully identified. The age pattern, ceteris paribus, is not very strong and significant only at the 5.3 percent level. The pattern is U-shaped, with a negative marginal effect of -0.06 percentage points per year at age 30 and a positive effect of 0.1 percentage point per year at age 45. Households headed by persons of retirement age exhibit the strongest propensity to hold risky assets (0.44 points per year) consistent with the steeply rising age pattern in figure 9.1. King and Leape (1987) get similar results. They stress the role of financial knowledge in making portfolio decisions, in particular when information-intensive assets (such as stocks and other risky securities) are involved, and attribute the age effect to the accumulation of information. Our finding that age plays a role even after controlling for interest in financial matters can be seen as evidence that the latter is an imperfect proxy for financial knowledge. A different interpretation might be that older people have more time to collect information and monitor their portfolios. The finding that risky asset ownership is significantly more likely for the universityeducated can again be interpreted as an effect of knowledge.

To save space, time effects and the effects of urbanization are not presented in the table (see Alessie, Hochguertel, and van Soest 2000 for full results). Controlling for all other variables, the pure time effect between 1993 and 1998 is an increase of more than 10 percentage points. Ownership of risky assets increases with urbanization. This may be a supply effect, since the density of banks, and hence the quantity and quality of financial information available, will be higher in urbanized areas, or a demand effect, since the information spillover between households is expected to be larger in densely populated areas. The finding is consistent with the evidence for Italy.

9.5.2 Employer-Sponsored Saving Plans

Dutch ESSPs are strongly taxfavored up to a limited amount, with an enormous real after-tax advantage compared to other assets of comparably low risk. Thus eligible savers who do not face serious liquidity constraints should absolutely invest in ESSPs.

Unfortunately, the available data do not provide direct information on who has access to ESSPs. The main proxy is labor market status, which is strongly significant and indicates that employees have a much larger chance of owning ESSPs than others. Since the labor market dummies reflect only the current status, not the employment history, they are incomplete proxies of access to ESSPs, and other proxies may help as well. This may explain the significant hump-shaped age pattern we find and the significant income and wealth patterns. The latter two are both monotonically increasing, indicating that higher-income households and the wealthy are more likely to have or to have had jobs that give access to ESSPs. The education variables, the risk-aversion variables, and the urbanization dummies are insignificant. On the other hand, if current or past access were all that matters, we would not expect interest in financial matters to play a role. The fact that the more interested more often own ESSPs suggests that there are people who are not interested or not informed about the advantages of ESSPs and do not buy them, even though they are eligible.

9.6 Portfolio Mobility and Dynamic Models of Asset Ownership

Our data are unique in the sense that they are genuine panel data, with the majority of the survey households followed for a number of years, so we can look at portfolio mobility. The upper part of table 9.11 presents a cross-tabulation of ownership of risky and fairly safe assets in two consecutive years, averaged over all pairs of years in the survey.[17] For example, 28.5 percent of the households have both risky and fairly safe assets in any given year, and 22.2 percent have both types of assets in two consecutive years. This means that more than one-fifth of the households with both types of assets dispose of one type in the course of a year. Similarly, the numbers in the upper part of the table imply that one in every six of the 34.6 percent of households that own risky assets in a given year no longer do the

Table 9.11
Ownership transitions between years: Fairly safe and risky financial assets

Short-term transitions		Year $t + 1$				
		00	01	10	11	all
Year t	00	16.46	0.73	5.19	0.73	23.11
	01	0.65	3.34	0.63	1.46	6.08
	10	4.07	0.57	32.57	5.11	42.32
	11	0.55	1.56	4.17	22.21	28.48
	All	21.73	6.20	42.56	29.51	100.00
Long-term transitions		Year 1998				
		00	01	10	11	all
Year 1993	00	19.71	1.44	13.46	1.92	36.54
	01	1.44	2.40	0.96	4.33	9.13
	10	4.81	1.92	14.90	12.98	34.62
	11	0.48	2.40	1.44	15.38	19.71
	All	26.44	8.17	30.77	34.62	100.00

Note: 00 = neither risky nor fairly safe assets; 01 = risky assets only; 10 = fairly safe assets only; 11 = both risky and fairly safe assets. All statistics are unweighted sample fractions. Fairly safe financial assets include defined-contribution plans, the cash value of life insurance, employer-sponsored savings plans, growth funds, and other financial assets. Risky financial assets include stocks, bonds, mutual funds, and mutual fund accounts. The upper panel of the table cross-tabulates adjacent years t and $t + 1$. Table entries are averages over all pairs of adjacent years, from 1993 to 1998; total sample size is 7,326 observations of 2,217 households. The lower panel cross-tabulates the first and last sampling year (1993 and 1998). Total sample size is 416 observations of 208 households.

next. About one in every nine households that have no risky financial assets in a given year acquire them in the following year. The lower part of table 9.11 shows the same cross-tabulation for 1993 and 1998, the first and last years, offering insight into long-term mobility. For example, one in every four households without risky financial assets in 1993 (71.2 percent of the sample) have them in 1998, and one in every seven with risky assets in 1993 no longer have them. The latter shift is surprisingly large: if knowledge of financial products is important and if such knowledge is acquired by owners, we would not expect so many people to dispose of risky assets when stock market returns are so high. Perhaps people saw the high returns as evidence of a speculative bubble and feared a stock market crisis.

The apparent positive correlation in table 9.11 between ownership in various years could have two different causes. There could be time-persistent differences in preferences (observed and unobserved heterogeneity). Alternatively, ownership may make it easier or more attractive to own in the future (true state dependence). An extensive discussion is given in chapter 4. Here we use a dynamic extension of the static model of the previous section to disentangle these two explanations. The model we use is one of the dynamic models analyzed by Lee (1997). The specification is

$$y_{it}^* = \beta' x_{it} + \lambda y_{i,t-1} + \alpha_i + \varepsilon_{it}; \quad \varepsilon_{it} = \rho \varepsilon_{it-1} + u_{it}$$

$$y_{it} = 1 \quad \text{if } y_{it}^* > 0; \quad y_{it} = 0 \quad \text{if } y_{it}^* > 0.$$

The observed dependent variable y_{it} is the ownership dummy (for risky assets or ESSPs). The regressors x_{it} are assumed to be strictly exogenous, that is independent of all u_{is}. The errors u_{it} are independently and identically distributed (i.i.d.) $N(0,1)$. The random effects α_i are i.i.d. $N(0, \sigma^2)$, independent of all x_{it} and all u_{it}. For $\lambda = \rho = 0$, the model is the same as the static model used in section 9.5. In general, the lagged effect $\lambda y_{i,t-1}$ reflects true state dependence, while unobserved heterogeneity enters through α_i.

The model can be estimated by (simulated) maximum likelihood. The initial conditions problem (due to the small number of waves) is treated as in Lee (1997). The results are presented in table 9.12.

9.6.1   Risky Assets

For risky asset ownership, the true state dependence effect is quite strong and significant. Having owned risky assets in the previous year increases the probability of current ownership by 28 percentage points, ceteris paribus. Explanations are transaction costs, habit formation, and the knowledge effect of previous ownership. The age pattern is totally insignificant. The other marginal effects largely reveal the same pattern and significance level as in the static model.[18] Further estimates, not given in the table but available in Alessie, Hochguertel, and van Soest (2000), show that allowing for true state dependence reduces the estimated importance of unobserved heterogeneity. The estimated variance of the random effects, σ^2, is about 57 percent less than in the static model. There is no evidence of autocorrelation in the error terms. The urbanization dummies are

Table 9.12
Dynamic random-effects probit

Variable	Risky financial assets			Employer-sponsored saving plans		
	Marginal effect[a]	Standard error[b]	p-value[c]	Marginal effect[a]	Standard error[b]	p-value[c]
Total number of observations/ households	7,197/2,166			7,197/2,166		
Log-likelihood	−2,713.20			−2,705.98		
Pseudo R^2	0.5232			0.8804		
Lagged endogenous (dummy) variable	0.28163	0.0460	0.000	0.53327	0.0338	0.000
Age						
At age 30	−0.00134	0.0027	0.520	0.00294	0.0024	0.000
At age 45	0.00035	0.0013		−0.00582	0.0011	
At age 65	0.00278	0.0025		−0.01367	0.0018	
Education						
Low	−0.09804	0.0396	0.002	0.06554	0.0487	0.851
Intermediate/low	−0.05940	0.0357		0.00815	0.0347	
Intermediate/high	−0.08258	0.0314		0.02722	0.0324	
Vocational education, level 1	−0.14695	0.0285		0.00649	0.0369	
Vocational education, level 2	−0.11282	0.0292		0.02443	0.0320	
Vocational education, level 3	−0.04183	0.0280		0.02160	0.0244	
Noncapital income						
At 25 percent	0.00070	0.0003	0.001	0.00133	0.0003	0.000
At 50 percent	0.00063	0.0002		0.00095	0.0002	
At 75 percent	0.00055	0.0002		0.00067	0.0002	
Total net worth						
At 25 percent	0.00134	0.0001	0.000	0.00053	0.0001	0.000
At 50 percent	0.00092	0.0001		0.00017	0.0000	
At 75 percent	0.00063	0.0000		0.00008	0.0000	
Labor market status						
Unemployed	−0.07499	0.0644	0.004	−0.25980	0.0375	0.000
Retired	0.12629	0.0424		−0.35543	0.0246	
Disabled	−0.02439	0.0635		−0.27930	0.0284	
Other labor market status	0.05377	0.0549		−0.23199	0.0308	
Self-employed	0.13883	0.0538		−0.28774	0.0214	

Table 9.12
(continued)

	Risky financial assets			Employer-sponsored saving plans		
Variable	Marginal effect[a]	Standard error[b]	p-value[c]	Marginal effect[a]	Standard error[b]	p-value[c]
Financial interest						
Low	−0.30434	0.0198	0.000	−0.11600	0.0231	0.000
Medium	−0.18032	0.0220		−0.06534	0.0216	
Risk aversion						
Low	0.04862	0.0362	0.002	−0.01400	0.0294	0.595
Medium	0.06179	0.0177		0.01228	0.0168	

Note: Risky financial assets include stocks, bonds, mutual funds, and mutual fund accounts. The specification also controls for membership of the HIP subpanel, the number of adults and the number of children, year dummies, and degree of urbanization. See table 10 in Alessie, Hochguertel, and van Soest (2000) for detailed results. All regressors refer to the head of household, except noncapital income and total net worth. The latter variables were deflated using the CPI, 1995 = 100. The specification includes age as a second-order polynomial and noncapital income and total net worth as third-order polynomials of the log-transformed variable. The log transformation is of the form $y = \ln(x + 1)$ if $x \geq 0$, and $y = -\ln(-x + 1)$ if $x < 0$. Reference categories for dummy variable groups are university education; paid employment; financial interest: high; risk aversion: high.
[a] Changes in the ownership probability caused by marginal changes in regressors. For age, income, and net worth, marginal effects are based on the following discrete changes in the underlying variable: age: effect of an increase by 1 year, at ages 30, 45, and 65; noncapital income/total net worth: effect of an increase in noncapital income/ total net worth by 1,000 guilders, at the 25, 50, and 75 percentiles of the noncapital income/total net worth distribution.
[b] Robust to heteroskedasticity.
[c] The p-values refer to the (joint) test that all underlying coefficients are zero.

now jointly significant at the 5 percent level; the positive relation between urbanization and ownership remains.

9.6.2 Employer-Sponsored Savings Plans

The true state dependence effect is even stronger for ESSPs than for risky assets: owners have a 53-point greater probability than non-owners of owning the next year. In fact, the tax system creates a strong incentive not to sell this asset during the first four years. Accordingly, the importance of unobserved heterogeneity is much smaller than in the static model. The effects of the other variables do not change much compared to the static results.

9.7   Models for Shares

In this section we analyze the shares of financial portfolios invested in risky assets and in ESSPs by the owners of those types of assets. Descriptive statistics on these conditional asset shares were discussed in section 9.3. To correct for the fact that owners are a selected sample, we use the sample selection model for panel data introduced by Wooldridge (1995). This is quite flexible, allowing for correlation between individual effects and regressors in the asset share equation but not imposing normality of the errors in the asset share equation (see chapter 4, this volume). The model is static and consists of two equations: one explains ownership, the other the share invested in the given asset. The selection equation is a static random-effects equation identical to the model estimated in section 9.5 and the estimation results in table 10 serve as the first-stage estimates. These are used to construct the inverse Mills ratio, which is then included as an additional regressor in the second step. To allow for quasi-fixed effects in the asset share equation, the means over all available time periods of the regressors in both equations are also added as additional regressors in the second step (this gives Miniaci and Weber's equation 4.25). Eicker-White-Huber standard errors are computed, correcting for heteroskedasticity. We do not correct for the estimation error in the first-stage regression, so our standard errors may slightly underestimate true standard errors. The results of the second stage regressions are presented in table 9.13.

9.7.1   Risky Assets

There are notable differences between the heteroskedasticity-robust significance levels and the levels computed in the standard way, implying that correcting for heteroskedasticty is of major importance here. The education variables are jointly significant, although none of the dummies is individually. Income and labor market status do not play a significant role, whereas they do have a clear impact on ownership. Wealth has a significant and positive impact. The same holds for the variables reflecting interest in financial matters, which sug-

Table 9.13
Selection model, second stage

Variable	Risky financial assets			Employer-sponsored saving plans		
	Marginal effect[a]	Standard error[b]	p-value[c]	Marginal effect[a]	Standard error[b]	p-value[c]
Total number of observations/ households	2,609/1,100			3,016/1,452		
R^2	0.1736			0.2648		
Age						
At age 30	−0.00338	0.0291	0.025	−0.00038	0.0361	0.421
At age 45	0.00086	0.0163		0.00044	0.0317	
At age 65	0.00652	0.0250		0.00155	0.0574	
Education						
Low education	−0.02253	0.0520	0.001	−0.03273	0.0267	0.069
Intermediate/low education	−0.01737	0.0360		0.04458	0.0183	
Intermediate/high education	−0.03795	0.0307		0.01720	0.0150	
Vocational education, level 1	−0.13107	0.0482		0.05863	0.0237	
Vocational education, level 2	−0.06699	0.0390		0.04266	0.0164	
Vocational education, level 3	−0.01955	0.0203		0.00020	0.0097	
Noncapital income						
At 25 percent	0.00023	0.0007	0.204	−0.00054	0.0003	0.013
At 50 percent	0.00008	0.0008		−0.00034	0.0010	
At 75 percent	0.00003	0.0010		−0.00022	0.0013	
Total net worth						
At 25 percent	0.00045	0.0006	0.039	−0.00059	0.0006	0.000
At 50 percent	0.00028	0.0003		−0.00028	0.0003	
At 75 percent	0.00018	0.0002		−0.00017	0.0002	
Labor market status						
Unemployed	−0.02498	0.0808	0.120	0.13339	0.0831	0.176
Retired	0.10646	0.0354		0.07276	0.0427	
Disabled	0.00652	0.0635		−0.02110	0.0433	
Other labor market status	0.10257	0.0487		−0.01793	0.0310	
Self-employed	0.22549	0.0401		0.06134	0.0372	

Table 9.13
(continued)

	Risky financial assets			Employer-sponsored saving plans		
Variable	Marginal effect[a]	Standard error[b]	p-value[c]	Marginal effect[a]	Standard error[b]	p-value[c]
Financial interest						
Low	−0.15138	0.0640	0.020	0.07746	0.0163	0.596
Medium	−0.10057	0.0296		0.03285	0.0117	
Risk aversion						
Low	0.05612	0.0306	0.023	0.02813	0.0191	0.946
Medium	0.07865	0.0203		0.00168	0.0102	

Note: First-stage estimates of the ownership equation are those reported in table 9.10. The specification also controls for membership of the HIP subpanel, the number of adults and the number of children, year dummies, and degree of urbanization (dummy variables). See table 10 in Alessie, Hochguertel, and van Soest (2000) for detailed results. All regressors refer to the head of household, except noncapital income and total net worth. The latter variables were deflated using the CPI, 1995 = 100. The specification includes age as a second-order polynomial and noncapital income and total net worth as third-order polynomials of the log-transformed variable. The log transformation is of the form $y = \ln(x + 1)$ if $x \geq 0$, and $y = -\ln(-x + 1)$ if $x < 0$. Reference categories for dummy variable groups are university education; paid employment; financial interest: high; risk aversion: high.
[a] Changes in the ownership probability caused by marginal changes in regressors. They are calculated conditional on ownership. For age, income, and net worth, marginal effects are based on the following discrete changes in the underlying variable: age: effect of an increase by 1 year, at ages 30, 45, and 65; noncapital income/total net worth: effect of an increase in noncapital income/total net worth by 1,000 guilders, at the 25, 50, and 75 percentiles of the noncapital income/total net worth distribution.
[b] Robust to heteroskedasticity.
[c] The p-values refer to the (joint) test that all underlying coefficients are zero.

gests that financial sophistication not only drives ownership but also affects the amount invested. The risk-aversion variables are jointly significant, but not very strongly and with no clear pattern.

Even after correcting for the other relevant variables, the age pattern is significant and U-shaped. This differs from the finding of Guiso and Jappelli in chapter 7 that the age profile is flat in Italy.

Finally, the inverse Mills ratio is positive and significant. This is what we could expect if unobserved preference heterogeneity affected the ownership decision and the amount in the same direction.

9.7.2   Employer-Sponsored Saving Plans

The tax-favored nature of ESSPs suggests that those who have access to them should hold the maximum amount, except in cases of severe liquidity constraints. The asset share should then depend on the number of years for which the household has been eligible and will be negatively correlated with total financial wealth.

The results are largely as expected. Age, education, labor market status, interest in financial matters, and risk aversion are insignificant. Total wealth is significant with the expected negative effect. Income has a positive effect, probably reflecting its negative relation to liquidity constraints. The asset share increases monotonically over calendar time, since the tax advantages hold for each new investment in each year. The inverse Mills ratio is insignificant, which may mean that unobserved preference heterogeneity does not play a large role. Again, this is as expected, if everyone just invests the maximum amount each year.

9.8   Conclusions

We have analyzed household portfolios in the Netherlands during the 1990s. Like those in other countries, Dutch households' portfolios have low diversification and low risk. Over the sample period, however, risky assets (stocks and mutual funds) and spreading wealth over more asset types have become more popular. This is found in both macro- and microdata, and in the raw statistics as well as in econometric models. The models exploit our rich panel data and allow us to disentangle true state dependence from unobserved heterogeneity. Dovetailing with the empirical evidence documented elsewhere in this book both ownership of risky assets and their proportions to wealth are increasing functions of the household's level of resources. This is consistent with utility functions that exhibit decreasing relative risk aversion.

We find powerful response to tax incentives. A strongly tax-favored asset, employer-sponsored saving plans, was introduced during our observation period and incorporated almost immediately into many households' portfolios, irrespective of wealth and income. Since these plans were introduced with an eye to labor supply, further research is needed to evaluate its political success. At any event, taxes definitely do matter for individual portfolio decisions.

Having analyzed the data in considerable depth, we find that some predictions of classical theory do not square with the empirical patterns in the Netherlands. The descriptive evidence shows that elderly households are more likely to own risky assets. This differs from the hump-shaped age profiles found in the raw data for Italy and the United States, for instance. Also, theory has stressed age patterns or their absence, but cannot give clear-cut predictions without knowledge of the shape of the utility function. Controlling for observable household characteristics and unobserved heterogeneity, the only remaining significant U-shaped age pattern is in a selection model for risky asset shares. Ownership does not have pronounced age effects. None of our models provides evidence for an important role of background risk, but confirms the predicted signs and significance of proxies for risk aversion and interest in financial matters.

Our results suggest several directions for future research. Our panel data could potentially be exploited even better if we had a theory generating unanimous predictions about an integrated approach to both portfolio choices and labor supply. We could also envisage much deeper understanding of the structural relations underlying observed portfolio patterns if our data were informative about relative asset prices and transaction costs or if some of the measurement problems associated with psychological background variables were overcome. There is a rich theory of consumer demand systems whose implications could be tested in a portfolio framework, and we might be able to attribute the aversion to diversification to either transaction costs or psychological factors.

Notes

This chapter was written while Alessie was at the European University Institute, whose hospitality is gratefully acknowledged. Hochguertel acknowledges financial support from the project "Finance and Consumption in the European Union." We also acknowledge financial support from the TMR Network on "Savings and Pensions" (grant number ERBFMRXCT960016). We are grateful to Tullio Jappelli, Martin Browning, other participants of the conference on Household Portfolios at the European University Institute, and seminar participants at the Free University of Amsterdam and Gothenburg University for useful comments. In this chapter, use is made of data of the CentER Savings Survey; we thank CentER of Tilburg University for supplying them.

1. More details on the comparison of micro- and macrodata and the Dutch institutional setting can be found in the working paper version of this study, Alessie, Hochguertel, and van Soest (2000).

2. The dollar-guilder exchange rate is about 2 ($1 = Dfl 2).

3. The asset item stocks includes the so-called stocks from substantial holding. A taxpayer is regarded as having a substantial holding in a corporation if he or she, either alone or with his or her spouse, holds directly or indirectly 5 percent of the issued capital. The aggregated value of substantial holdings is rather high; estimates from the Income Panel Survey (IPO) put it at 109 billion guilders at the beginning of 1997 (see de Kleijn 1999). Yet only 1.9 percent of the households own this type of stock.

4. The Postbank is a market leader in consumers' checking accounts; savings accounts are directly linked to a checking account.

5. All the tax rules that are described are valid for 1998. Substantial reforms have been implemented as of 2001.

6. Many low-income households are not required to provide information for income or wealth tax purposes, so that their wealth is not observed in IPO data. To correct for this, Statistics Netherlands has supplemented IPO with data from the Socio-Economic Panel, a household panel with limited information on assets and liabilities which is representative for the Dutch population.

7. Statistics Netherlands uses the WBO to construct the official home ownership statistics.

8. In 1998, there was no separate high-income panel (see section 9.2). Although the weights should in principle adjust for this, it may explain some of the unexpected changes in ownership rates or asset shares from 1997 to 1998.

9. There are explicit and implicit transaction costs. The explicit costs are typically low (about 0.5 percent of the investment). The implicit costs (entry and exit fees incorporated in the buying and selling price of the fund) are higher. The maximum entry fee is about 2.5 percent of the investment, and the maximum exit fee is about 1.5 percent (see Consumentenbond 1999). Apart from the transaction costs, the mutual funds charge a management fee of about 0.5 percent per year. Moreover, there are minimum investment requirements. In comparison to Italy (see chapter 7, this volume) transaction costs are sizable. It is not clear, however, whether Dutch people are aware of these implicit costs when they invest in mutual funds.

10. This is not the same as the average asset share due to different weighting. For example, the average asset share of stocks is lower than the share of stocks held by the population in total financial wealth of the population, since stocks are owned disproportionately by wealthy households. Table 9.4 gives the relevant numbers for comparing with aggregate data on total amounts, and can be referred to as "macro shares" (see Poterba and Samwick 1997 for similar calculations).

11. We used the quartic kernel and an adaptive bandwidth with weighting parameter set to 0.5; see, for example, Blundell and Duncan (1998) for an exposition.

12. To be precise, for continuous variables (like age or income), the derivative of the estimated probability is evaluated; for dummy variables (like education), the change from 0 to 1 is considered, and the corresponding change in probability is reported.

13. Das and Donkers (1999), Donkers and van Soest (1999), and Donkers, Melenberg, and van Soest (1999) use some of these variables for the earlier waves of the panel.

14. Likewise, Hochguertel (1997) found only weak support for the impact of background risk on portfolio choice, using the first three waves of the CentER Savings Survey.

15. It can be argued that the financial interest variables are endogenous. We cannot test or control for this due to lack of instruments. We also estimated the models in sections 9.5 through 9.7 without the financial interest variables and found that this did not substantially affect the estimates of the other parameters in the model. Thus, for example, significance levels and shapes of age and education patterns of ownership rates or asset shares hardly change.

16. An alternative would be to include cohort effects, age effects, and time effects restricted to sum to zero (cf. Deaton and Paxson 1994). This leads to results with a less plausible interpretation.

17. Since this table does not use the sample weights, ownership rates for one given year are higher than in table 9.3.

18. In particular, interest in financial matters is still significant with a similar order of magnitude. This is a counterargument against the conjecture that in the static models, interest in financial matters would be relevant only because owners become more interested (making it endogenous).

10 Portfolios of the Rich

Christopher D. Carroll

Since the pathbreaking work of Pareto more than a century ago, economists have known that wealth is extremely unevenly distributed. More recently, survey data have revealed that portfolio structures are also very different for households with different levels of wealth. While the portfolios of the rich are complex, the portfolio of financial and real assets of the median household (at least in the United States) is rather simple: a checking and savings account plus a home and mortgage, and not much else.[1] Overwhelmingly, the data tell us that if we wish to understand aggregate portfolio behavior, it is critical to understand the behavior of the richest few percent of households, both because they control the bulk of aggregate wealth and because their portfolio behavior is much more complex than that of the typical household.

Although the foregoing arguments may seem to provide a compelling rationale for studying the portfolios of the rich, there has been little recent academic work in this area. This chapter provides a summary of the basic facts about portfolios of wealthy households in the United States (and how the facts have changed over time) in a form that allows comparison of their behavior with the rest of the population in the United States and with portfolio behavior among other groups and other countries surveyed in this book. The chapter also makes a preliminary attempt to understand the characteristics that will be required of any model that hopes to be consistent with the observed behavior.

The principal conclusion will be that the most important way in which the portfolios of the rich differ from those of the rest is that the rich hold a much higher proportion of their portfolios in risky investments, with a particularly large concentration of net worth in their own entrepreneurial ventures.

After the empirical conclusions are presented, the chapter informally considers how these results relate to theoretical models of portfolio behavior. The starting point will be a standard stochastic version of the life cycle/permanent income hypothesis model. That model will prove inadequate, however, because it implies that the rich should look like scaled-up versions of everybody else. They should have neither the extreme wealth-to-income ratios observed in the data nor the unusual portfolio structures. The goal of the theoretical discussion will be to consider whether any of three potential modifications to the standard model might explain the observed combination of facts.

The first idea is that perhaps there is exogenous, immutable ex ante variation in risk aversion across households.[2] In that case more risk-tolerant households would take greater risks and on average would earn higher returns. If owning a private business is the form of economic activity that offers the highest risk and highest return, one might expect that the most risk-tolerant households would gravitate toward entrepreneurship and on average would end up richer (though the failures might end up poorer).[3] The chapter will argue that this story has several defects, ranging from the fact that the empirical evidence fails to find a correlation between wealth growth and initial (expressed) risk aversion to the fact that, taken alone, the story provides an explanation neither for the lack of diversification of entrepreneurial investments nor for the tendency of wealthy households to hold much of their net worth in their own entrepreneurial ventures.

These points lead to the second possibility: that the observed patterns are entirely a consequence of capital market imperfections, as suggested recently by Gentry and Hubbard (1998) and Quadrini (1999). Those authors argue that adverse selection and moral hazard problems require entrepreneurial enterprises to be largely self-financed. They further assume that there is a minimum efficient scale for private enterprises and that this minimum scale is large relative to the wealth of the typical household. The combination of these two assumptions can explain why households with low or moderate wealth or income are less likely to become entrepreneurs. Furthermore, this story requires no differences in tastes among members of the population and in principle can explain both the high saving rates of the rich and the high portfolio shares in their own entrepreneurial ventures. However, this story too has problems. The first is that in the absence of differences in preferences between the rich and the rest, the standard model implies that households that have invested heavily in their own entrepreneurial ventures should try to balance the riskiness of these investments by holding all other assets in very safe forms. Instead, the nonentrepreneurial investments of rich entrepreneurs are much riskier than the portfolios of nonrich nonentrepreneurs. A second problem with this story is that even the model with imperfect capital markets implies that as the rich get old, they eventually begin running down their wealth. In contrast, empirical data reveal no evidence that wealthy elderly households ever begin to run down their wealth.

The final possibility is that the model's assumption about the household utility function needs to be changed in a manner similar to that proposed by Carroll (2000), who simply assumes that wealth enters the utility function as a luxury good in a modified Stone-Geary form. Because Max Weber (1958) argued that a love of wealth for its own sake is the spirit of capitalism, Bakshi and Chen (1996) and Zou (1994) have dubbed such models "capitalist spirit" models. Carroll (2000) proposed this modification to the standard model as a way to explain the high lifetime saving rates of the rich and argued that many different kinds of motivations, ranging from philanthropic bequest motives to pure greed, would result in a formulation of saving behavior that would be well captured by the modified model. An unanticipated consequence of the model is that it implies that rich households have lower relative risk aversion than the nonrich, which could explain why the rich hold riskier portfolios than the rest and why high-wealth or high-income young households are more likely to begin entrepreneurial ventures.

The one feature of the data that the capitalist spirit model taken alone cannot explain is the tendency of entrepreneurs to invest largely in their own entrepreneurial ventures, which appears to require some form of capital market imperfection. The chapter thus concludes that the main features of the data can probably be explained in a model that combines capital market imperfections of the kind emphasized by Gentry and Hubbard (1998) and Quadrini (1999) with a utility function like that postulated in Carroll (2000).

10.1   The Data

U.S. survey data on the portfolios of the rich are the best in the world. The 1962–1963 Survey of Financial Characteristics of Consumers (SFCC) was the first wealth survey to heavily oversample the richest households. The next comprehensive wealth survey was the 1983 Survey of Consumer Finances (SCF), which was followed by a 1989 SCF consisting of a subsample of reinterviewed households from the 1983 survey, along with a fresh batch of new households. Since 1989 the SCF has been performed triennially (though with no further panel elements); the latest survey was completed in 1998.

The availability of data spanning such a long time period opens up the possibility of studying how portfolios change in response to changes in the economic environment. Before examining the data on portfolio structure, therefore, I present a summary of the taxation and legal changes that one might expect to have had a substantial impact on portfolio structure of wealthy households.

10.1.1 The Tax Environment

Table 10.1 summarizes the recent history of changes in the three aspects of U.S. taxes that are particularly important for the rich. (For information on broader changes in the U.S. tax code, see chapter 3, this volume.) The first two columns show the statutory top marginal federal tax rate, which declined from 91 percent in 1963 to 39.6 percent in 1993 and thereafter. The second column shows the actual taxes paid as a proportion of their incomes by the richest 1 percent of households. In spite of the dramatic decline in top marginal rates, the proportion of income paid in taxes has been fairly steady, varying between around 20 and 25 percent over the entire period. This reflects the fact that during the era of high top marginal rates, the tax code was riddled with tax shelters and loopholes that made it possible for almost all rich people to avoid paying the confiscatory top marginal rates on the statute books.

The estate tax is also highly relevant for the rich. The structure of the estate tax is rather complex, but that structure remained largely the same over the period in question. The first \$$x$ of an estate is free from estate taxation altogether, where \$$x$ is indicated by the column of the table labeled "exemption." Above that, taxes begin at a marginal rate of y percent and peak at a top marginal rate of z percent, where y and z are the first and second numbers in the column labeled "tax range."

The exclusion for closely held businesses is a mechanism that reduces the amount of the value of a closely held business that is taxable, under the condition that the heir plans to "actively manage"

Table 10.1
Major features of the tax code relevant for the rich

| Year | Top 1 percent by income | | Estate tax | | | | Gift tax |
	Marginal rate	Effective rate[a]	Tax range	Exemption	Exclusion for closely held business	Marital deduction	Annual exclusion[b]
1963	91%	24.6%	3–77%	$268,581	n.a.	50%	$13,429[c]
1977	70	27.8	18–70	295,971	$1,226,400	50% or $613,200	7,358
1980	70	23.9	18–70	312,071	965,790	50% or $482,895	5,794
1985	50	19.2	18–55	596,848	1,119,090	100%	14,921
1989	28	20.4	18–55	784,896	981,120	100%	13,081
1993	39.6	21.9	18–55	686,784	858,480	100%	11,446
1995	39.6	23.8	18–55	649,992	812,490	100%	10,833
1998	39.6	n.a.	18–55	638,750	766,500[d]	100%	10,220[e]

Sources: For marginal and effective rates prior to 1980, see Brownlee (2000). For marginal rates from 1980 to 1998, see Booth (1998). For effective rates from 1980 to 1993, see Slemrod (1994). For effective rates for 1995, see Kasten, Sammartino, and Weiner (1998). For estate and gift tax information, see Johnson and Eller (1998) and Joulfaian (1998).

Note: All dollar figures converted to 1999 dollars using the CPI All Urban, All Items Research Series. The adjustment factors used are 4.40, 2.42, 1.91, 1.48, 1.30, 1.14, 1.08, and 1.02 for 1963, 1977, 1980, 1985, 1989, 1993, 1995, and 1998, respectively.

[a] The effective individual income tax rate. This is calculated by dividing individual income tax by total income.

[b] Per donee.

[c] Since 1977 the gift tax range has been the same as the estate tax range. Prior to 1977, the gift tax range was 2.25–57.75 percent.

[d] Starting in 1998, the estate tax exemption increases yearly to $1 million in 2006, and the exclusion for closely held business is indexed for inflation.

[e] Starting in 1998, the annual exclusion is indexed for inflation.

the business rather than sell it. The marital deduction indicates how much of the estate is taxed when one spouse dies and the estate falls into the hands of the widow or widower. The 100 percent deduction since 1985 means that estates are taxed only when both members of a married couple have died.

The final kind of tax that is relevant to the rich is the gift tax exclusion amount $g, whose value is reported in the last column of the table. This is the amount that each member of the household (husband and wife) can give to any individual (son, daughter, son-in-law, daughter-in-law, grandchildren, and others) annually without incurring any additional taxes for the recipient or donor.

The table shows that there have been two big changes in the taxes specifically relevant for the rich over the period in question: the large increase in exemption levels for the estate tax in the early 1980s and the more gradual, but cumulatively very large, decline in top marginal rates. The most important change not captured in the table is probably the abrupt termination of a variety of tax shelters in the 1986 tax reform.

A final feature of the tax code that is relevant for the rich is the step-up in basis at death. The capital gains tax basis for an asset is normally defined as the nominal price at which the asset was bought. However, if the asset has been inherited, then the basis is the nominal valuation of the asset at the time it was inherited. The step-up in basis at death provides an incentive for individuals who anticipate leaving a bequest whose value is less than the exemption amount to hold their assets in forms that yield returns disproportionately in the form of capital gains, since capital gains that happen before death are untaxed. (Incentives for the very rich to hold their assets in forms that yield mainly capital gains are smaller because the capital gains do contribute to the valuation of the estate for tax purposes and thus are marginally taxed at the marginal estate tax rate for those who will leave bequests in excess of the exemption amount.)

Implications of the tax system for the portfolio structure of the rich are not always easy to determine by examining statutory provisions. For example, the incentive provided by the step-up in basis at death to hold assets in forms that yield capital gains depends importantly on the effective marginal rate of taxation on other forms of capital income, which is not very well proxied by the statutory top marginal rate. The exclusion for closely held businesses does provide an incentive to hold at least a limited absolute amount of the portfolio in the form of closely held businesses *if* the individual expects his or her heirs to continue to run the business. However, no marginal incentive to further business ownership is provided once the total amount of wealth held in this form exceeds the exclusion amount. (For a more detailed historical analysis of tax policies relevant for the rich in the postwar period, see Brownlee 2000.)

10.1.2 Detailed Portfolio Structure

The statistical summary of the portfolio structure of the rich (defined here and henceforth as the top 1 percent of households by net worth) begins with table 10.2, which provides data on the proportion of the rich who own any amount of various kinds of assets.

Perhaps the most dramatic change over time in the table is the sharp increase in the proportion of households with defined-contribution pension plans. In the 1962–1963 SFCC, only 10.1 percent of the rich had any such account; by 1983 the fraction had jumped to 65.6, and by 1995 the fraction had reached 78.6 percent. The low percentage in 1962–1963 reflects the fact that there was little tax advantage to such plans until the early 1980s, when Individual Retirement Accounts (IRAs) suddenly became available in principle to the whole population, and eligibility for company-based 401(k) pension plans was greatly expanded. What is interesting is the speed with which rich households availed themselves of these new options. In contrast, Bertaut and Starr-McCluer show in chapter 5 that only 31 percent of all households had acquired such accounts by the time of the 1983 survey.

Another notable change is that the proportion holding individual stock shares directly has fallen from 84.0 percent in 1962 to 65.0 percent in 1995, while the proportion holding mutual funds has risen from about 24 percent to about 45 percent. This reflects a broad pattern in which households have increasingly decided to hold shares in the form of mutual funds rather than individual stocks. This pattern has not been much studied by economists, although it is interesting because it reflects a convergence of actual behavior toward portfolio theory's recommendation for diversification.

Among the other categories of assets, the largest changes are seen in the holdings of other bonds (primarily corporate bonds), which declined sharply between 1962 and 1983 and fluctuated substantially between 1983 and 1995. Because nominal interest income is tax-

Table 10.2
Ownership rates of assets and liabilities

	Top 1 percent of households by net worth					Averages	
						Top 1 percent, 1962– 1995	0–99 percent, 1962– 1995
	1962	1983	1989	1992	1995		
Financial assets	*100.0*	*100.0*	*100.0*	*100.0*	*100.0*	*100.0*	*91.7*
Transaction and savings accounts[a]	91.6	99.6	100.0	100.0	99.9	98.2	84.6
Certificates of deposit	n.a.	38.7	32.7	31.5	24.6	31.9	14.0
U.S. savings bonds	36.7	23.2	18.1	18.9	28.0	25.0	23.3
Federal, state, and local bonds[b]	30.7	45.1	41.2	38.3	29.9	37.0	2.4
Other bonds[c]	30.3	9.6	16.2	21.2	12.8	18.0	1.7
Stocks	84.0	79.9	72.5	69.7	65.0	74.2	16.3
Mutual funds	24.0	33.8	39.1	46.0	45.0	37.6	7.5
Defined-contribution pensions[d]	10.1	65.6	71.3	76.1	78.6	60.4	28.7
Defined-benefit pensions	n.a.	24.3	13.7	20.1	10.6	17.2	20.3
Cash value of life insurance[e]	59.6	71.6	64.5	57.8	60.0	62.7	37.0
Other managed assets[f]	13.4	24.9	27.5	17.4	17.7	20.2	3.4
Other financial assets[g]	89.3	10.1	31.9	31.1	25.2	37.5	27.2
Nonfinancial assets	*96.7*	*100.0*	*99.3*	*100.0*	*99.8*	*99.2*	*89.3*
Primary residence	74.1	96.6	86.0	93.5	96.0	89.2	62.2
Vehicles	77.7	91.4	90.6	97.8	89.5	89.4	82.5
Investment real estate	44.0	74.2	76.6	75.4	61.3	66.3	16.3
Privately held businesses[h]	69.0	88.0	73.4	69.7	74.3	74.9	12.8
Other nonfinancial assets[i]	50.8	30.7	57.1	54.6	46.1	47.9	11.2
Debt	*50.2*	*77.9*	*77.3*	*80.3*	*70.5*	*71.2*	*71.5*
Mortgage[j]	30.7	54.5	35.8	53.4	52.5	45.4	37.6
Other real estate debt	12.8	45.2	48.3	53.6	35.1	39.0	6.6
Student loans	n.a.	n.a.	0.7	0.1	0.9	0.6	6.3
Other installment loans[k]	20.7	35.0	19.5	21.9	12.6	21.9	46.9
Credit cards	n.a.	9.6	14.8	17.0	12.2	13.4	33.8
Other debt[l]	17.6	15.2	20.2	30.8	17.2	20.2	9.4

Source: Survey of Financial Characteristics of Consumers and Surveys of Consumer Finances.

Table 10.2
(continued)

Note: Cells with an "n.a." indicate asset or debt categories not disaggregated in a particular survey year.

ᵃ Include checking, saving, money market, and call accounts.

ᵇ Include government bonds (not U.S. savings bonds) and municipal bonds.

ᶜ Include mortgage, corporate, foreign, and other types of bonds.

ᵈ Include employer-sponsored plans and personal retirement accounts.

ᵉ The cash value of whole life policies.

ᶠ Trusts, annuities, and managed investment accounts.

ᵍ Royalties, future proceeds from lawsuits, oil, gas, and mineral leases, and so forth.

ʰ Those in which the household has an active and/or passive interest.

ⁱ Such items as artwork and jewelry.

ʲ Any borrowing on home equity lines of credit.

ᵏ Vehicle loans, home improvement loans (not home equity loans), and other loans.

ˡ Other lines of credit, loans against pensions, loans against life insurance policies, margin loans, and so forth.

able annually while capital gains are taxable only on realization, the sharp increase in nominal interest rates caused by the acceleration of inflation in the 1960s and 1970s could explain a shift out of interest-bearing assets between 1963 and 1983. However, there is no obvious tax reason for the fluctuations between 1983 and 1995.

The proportion of the richest households owning equity in a privately held business has fluctuated substantially over the years, from a low of 69.0 percent in 1962–1963 to a high of 88.0 percent in 1983. To some extent, fluctuations in this variable may reflect stock market valuations, because after a large increase in stock prices, a higher proportion of the wealthy will be rich because of their stock holdings compared with the proportion who are rich because of their holdings of other kinds of assets. (The 1983 SCF was conducted before the bull markets of the 1980s and 1990s had boosted stock valuations.)

With respect to debt holdings, the proportion of rich households with any debt jumped sharply between the 1962–1963 SFCC, when it was 50.2 percent, and the 1983 SCF, when it was 77.9 percent, but exhibited no clear trend thereafter. Among debt categories, the most striking change is the increase in the proportion of households with mortgage debt, from 30.7 percent in 1962 to 52.5 percent in 1995. This likely reflects the fact that mortgage interest remained tax deductible after the 1986 tax reform, while other forms of debt lost their deductible status.

On the whole, the striking feature of this table is that the proportion of rich households owning various categories of assets has not changed greatly for most categories of assets, particularly considering that small sample sizes mean that there is inevitably some measurement error in the statistics for any particular year.[4]

Another useful comparison is of the rich to the rest of the population. Average values of ownership shares for the nonrich over the five survey years are presented in the last column of the table. The broadest observation to make here is that rich households are more likely to own virtually every kind of asset. Particularly striking is the discrepancy in the proportion owning equity in a privately held business, which averages about 75 percent for the rich but only 13 percent for the rest of the population. The contrast in ownership of shares in publicly traded companies is only slightly less dramatic: 74 percent versus 16 percent.

Table 10.3 examines the relative weight of various kinds of assets in the net worth of the richest households. The table shows that the shift in value from stocks to mutual funds was substantial, but even at the end of the sample in 1995, total net worth in individual shares still remained substantially greater than that in mutual funds. One of the largest shifts over time is in the role of investment real estate, which jumps from 7.4 percent of net worth in 1962–1963 to over 20 percent in 1983. Investment real estate continues to constitute more than 20 percent of the portfolio until 1995, when its share drops to 13.1 percent. The jump in investment real estate between the early 1960s and the early 1980s may reflect the prominent role of real estate in tax shelters until the tax reform act of 1986. One would have expected a decline in the value of investment real estate following the repeal of many of these tax shelters in the 1986 tax act, so it is surprising that no decline is manifest until 1995.

Another interesting observation from the table is the small amount of mortgage debt (only 1.1 percent of net worth on average) despite the fact that more than half the rich have positive amounts of such debt.

Comparing the rich to the rest of the population, again perhaps the most important difference is the importance of business equity for the rich. Such wealth accounts for about 40 percent of total net worth of the rich in 1983 and thereafter, vastly more than its share in the net worth of the typical household. Other differences include the lower total indebtedness of the rich and the much smaller proportion of total wealth tied up in home equity.

Table 10.3
Composition of net worth

	Top 1 percent of households by net worth					Averages	
						Top 1 percent, 1962– 1995	0–99 percent, 1962– 1995
	1962	1983	1989	1992	1995	1995	1995
Financial assets/net worth	57.4	36.6	32.0	32.0	40.8	*39.7*	*36.4*
As a fraction of total financial assets							
Transaction and savings accounts	6.5	7.6	18.4	14.6	14.6	12.3	22.4
Certificates of deposit	n.a.	2.3	3.9	2.5	2.7	2.9	9.4
U.S. savings bonds	1.0	0.3	0.4	0.4	0.2	0.4	2.8
Federal, state, and local bonds	7.3	12.4	12.8	13.4	11.5	11.5	3.7
Other bonds	1.2	0.5	4.0	3.1	2.1	2.2	1.0
Stocks	53.6	39.9	23.2	30.8	26.5	34.8	15.2
Mutual funds	3.4	3.1	7.0	7.6	15.7	7.4	6.6
Defined-contribution pensions	0.6	5.8	9.2	13.0	12.7	8.3	19.4
Cash value of life insurance	4.9	3.0	3.5	1.7	3.7	3.4	11.8
Other managed assets	21.5	24.5	12.6	8.0	7.9	14.9	4.8
Other financial assets	0.0	0.7	5.1	4.9	2.3	2.6	2.8
Nonfinancial assets/net worth	46.6	69.4	76.8	74.9	64.3	*66.4*	*86.7*
As a fraction of net worth							
Primary residence	5.2	7.8	7.8	8.9	7.1	7.4	49.6
Vehicles	0.4	0.3	0.8	0.7	0.7	0.6	6.3
Investment real estate	7.2	16.8	25.6	23.0	11.9	16.9	13.1
Net value of private businesses	30.6	39.3	38.5	39.0	41.4	37.7	14.8
Other nonfinancial assets	3.2	5.2	4.0	3.3	3.3	3.8	2.9
Debt/net worth	4.0	6.0	8.7	6.9	5.1	*6.1*	*23.1*
As a fraction of net worth							
Mortgage	0.6	0.8	0.9	1.6	1.6	1.1	15.5
Other real estate debt	1.5	3.1	6.7	4.4	2.6	3.7	3.2
Student loans	n.a.	n.a.	0.0	0.0	0.0	0.0	0.3
Other installment loans	0.7	0.8	0.3	0.2	0.1	0.4	3.1
Credit cards	n.a.	0.0	0.0	0.0	0.0	0.0	0.6
Other debt	1.2	1.3	0.8	0.7	0.7	0.9	0.5

Table 10.3
(continued)

	Top 1 percent of households by net worth					Averages	
						Top 1 percent, 1962–1995	0–99 percent, 1962–1995
	1962	1983	1989	1992	1995		
Memo items							
Median net worth (thousands of 1998 dollars)	1,841	4,291	4,720	4,138	4,748	3,948	51
Average net worth (thousands of 1998 dollars)	3,044	7,156	7,185	6,399	7,854	6,328	133
Median wealth to income ratio	15.4	14.9	18.8	20.8	20.0	18.0	1.5
Average wealth to income ratio	18.5	27.4	33.0	35.7	38.6	30.6	8.7

Source: Survey of Financial Characteristics of Consumers and Surveys of Consumer Finances.
Note: Cells with an "n.a." indicate asset or debt categories not disaggregated in a particular survey year.

10.1.3 Portfolio Structure and Portfolio Theory

The usual theoretical analysis of portfolio allocation considers the optimal proportion of net worth to invest in "risky" versus "safe" assets. This stylized theoretical treatment is conceptually useful but difficult to bring to data, because it is hard to allocate every asset to one of these two categories. Table 10.4 reflects an effort to find a compromise between the complexity of actual portfolios and the simplicity of theory.

Among financial assets, some are clearly safe (like checking, saving, and money market accounts) and some are clearly risky (like stock shares). But other assets are harder to allocate, either because the item itself has an ambiguous status (like long-term government bonds, which are subject to inflation risk but not repayment risk) or because the asset is a composite with unknown proportions of risky and safe assets (like mutual funds, which hold both stocks and government bonds). Consistent with the other chapters in this book, I have allocated all financial assets to one of three categories: clearly safe, fairly safe, and risky, which can be further aggregated into

Table 10.4
Composition of net worth by risk category

	Top 1 percent of households by net worth					Averages	
						Top 1 percent, 1962–1995	0–99 percent, 1962–1995
	1962	1983	1989	1992	1995		
Financial assets/net worth	*57.4*	*36.6*	*32.0*	*32.0*	*40.8*	*39.7*	*36.4*
	As a fraction of financial assets						
Safe	17.9	30.7	47.6	43.9	44.7	37.0	64.1
Clearly safe[a]	7.5	10.2	22.6	17.5	17.5	15.1	34.7
Fairly safe[b]	10.4	20.5	25.0	26.5	27.2	21.9	29.5
Risky[c]	82.1	69.3	52.4	56.1	55.3	63.0	35.9
	As a fraction of net worth						
Nonfinancial assets	*46.6*	*69.4*	*76.8*	*74.9*	*64.3*	*66.4*	*86.7*
Primary residence	5.2	7.8	7.8	8.9	7.1	7.4	49.6
Investment real estate	7.2	16.8	25.6	23.0	11.9	16.9	13.1
Business equity	30.6	39.3	38.5	39.0	41.4	37.7	14.8
Other nonfinancial assets	3.6	5.5	4.8	4.0	4.0	4.4	9.2
Debt	*4.0*	*6.0*	*8.7*	*6.9*	*5.1*	*6.1*	*23.1*
Mortgage	0.6	0.8	0.9	1.6	1.6	1.1	15.5
Other secured[d]	2.3	3.2	6.9	4.7	2.9	4.0	8.9
Unsecured[e]	0.7	2.1	0.9	0.6	0.5	1.0	2.5
Memo							
Risky assets—narrow[f]	30.8	14.6	7.4	9.8	10.8	14.7	5.4
Risky assets—broad[g]	84.9	81.4	80.8	80.0	75.8	80.6	41.2
Risky assets—broadest[h]	90.9	88.9	88.8	88.4	86.9	88.8	52.0
Mortgage debt/total debt	14.1	12.8	10.6	22.6	31.8	18.4	66.6

Sources: Calculations by the author using the Survey of Financial Characteristics of Consumers and Surveys of Consumer Finances.
Note: Calculations of fairly risky and fairly safe mutual funds and defined-contribution pensions are as follows.
1962 SFCC: Due to the lack of information on mutual fund investment strategies, all mutual funds are classified as risky and all defined-contribution pensions are classified as safe.
1983 SCF: The 1983 SCF did not ask about the investment strategy or risk characteristics of mutual funds or retirement accounts, so I had to make educated guesses based on other information. Tax-free mutual funds were allotted to the "fairly safe" category because such funds consist almost exclusively of state and local government bonds, direct holdings of which I put in this category. Taxable mutual funds were allotted to the "risky" category, because in the early 1980s these funds typically contained a mix of stocks and bonds. The calculation of risky and fairly safe, and

Table 10.4
(continued)

clearly safe defined-contribution pensions uses the institution that held the IRA/Keogh accounts as a proxy for investment direction. If a real estate investment company held the accounts, then those defined-contribution pensions were considered risky. If a commercial bank, savings and loan, or credit union held the accounts, then those assets were considered fairly safe. If a brokerage, insurance company, employer, school/college/university, investment management company, or the American Association of Retired Persons held the accounts, the defined-contribution pensions were split fifty-fifty between the fairly safe and risky. In the case that the household had no IRA/Keogh accounts but had a thrift pension account, the assets were considered fairly safe.

1989–1995 SCF: These surveys asked about the investment strategy for mutual funds and retirement accounts. Funds and accounts that consisted exclusively of one category of asset (such as stock or bond mutual funds) I allocated in the same way that I allocated direct holdings of that asset type. Mutual funds and accounts that contained a mix of stocks and bonds were allocated half and half to the "fairly safe" and "risky" categories. Accounts invested in real estate, commodities, or limited partnerships were put in the "risky" category.

[a] Includes transaction accounts (checking, saving, money market, and call accounts), certificates of deposit, and U.S. savings bonds.
[b] Includes state/local bonds, the fairly safe component of mutual funds, the fairly safe component of defined contribution pensions, and the cash value of life insurance policies.
[c] Includes stocks, bonds (all types but state/local and U.S. savings), other managed assets, other financial assets, and the risky component of mutual funds and defined-contribution pension accounts.
[d] Includes vehicle loans, loans against pensions and life insurance policies, investment real estate debt, and call account debt.
[e] Includes credit card balances, installment loans, other lines of credit, and other debt.
[f] Direct stockholdings.
[g] Risky financial assets, plus the net value of businesses and investment real estate.
[h] All assets in the broad definition and probably safe assets.

broad measures of safe and risky assets. I have divided nonfinancial assets into the primary residence, investment real estate, business equity, vehicles, and "other." With these definitions, we can construct three definitions of risky assets: a narrow definition, which includes only risky financial assets; a broad definition, which includes clearly and fairly risky financial assets, business equity, and investment real estate; and a broadest definition, which adds even the fairly safe assets.

It is apparent from the table that the portfolios of the rich are dramatically riskier than those of the rest of the population.[5] Across the five surveys, the proportion of their portfolios that consisted of broadly risky assets was about 80 percent, compared with an average percentage of only 40 percent for the nonrich households. Examining the data in more detail reveals two key differences be-

Table 10.5
Degree of diversification of portfolio structure

Asset combinations							
Clearly safe financial assets	Fairly safe financial assets	Risky financial assets	1962	1983	1989	1992	1995
0	0	0	0.0	0.0	0.0	0.0	0.0
0	0	1	0.0	0.0	0.0	0.0	0.0
0	1	0	1.1	0.0	0.0	0.0	0.1
0	1	1	1.8	0.0	0.0	0.0	0.0
1	0	0	0.0	2.5	1.6	6.5	2.4
1	0	1	4.4	1.6	10.8	5.1	9.4
1	1	0	10.9	12.8	9.1	9.4	10.7
1	1	1	81.8	83.2	78.5	78.9	77.4

Source: Author's calculations using the Survey of Financial Characteristics of Consumers and Surveys of Consumer Finances.
Note: 0 = no ownership of assets in the specified category; 1 = ownership.
   A description of the asset classifications appears in the notes at the end of table 10.4.

tween the rich and the rest: the rich hold a much smaller proportion of their wealth in home equity (7.4 percent versus 49.6 percent)[6] and a much larger proportion in business equity and investment real estate (the sum of these two categories is 54.6 percent for the rich versus 27.9 percent for the rest).

10.1.4 Portfolio Diversification and Age Structure

Another perspective on the portfolios of the rich is presented in table 10.5, which provides a census of the portfolio structure of the rich along the three dimensions corresponding to ownership or non-ownership of clearly safe, fairly safe, and risky assets, a total of eight different possibilities. In all five survey years, a majority or nearly a majority of the rich held some assets in each of these three categories. This is a sharp contrast to the behavior of the rest of the population, which is much more evenly distributed among the eight categories but is most heavily concentrated in the region with only safe assets. (See chapter 5, this book, for the data on the rest of the population.)

   Finally, table 10.6 presents data on ownership rates for risky assets by age of the household head for each of the survey years.[7] Interestingly, the patterns for ownership rates and for portfolio shares are

Table 10.6
Risk bearing by age

Survey	Age of household head					
	Under 30	30–39	40–49	50–59	60–69	70 and over
1962 SFCC						
Risky financial asset ownership	81.4	93.0	90.7	71.4	79.8	97.9
Risky financial asset/financial assets	85.5	96.7	73.7	83.1	75.1	77.5
Broad risky asset ownership	100.0	100.0	100.0	100.0	100.0	100.0
Broad risky asset/total assets	78.8	92.2	80.4	84.2	76.9	74.9
1983 SCF						
Risky financial asset ownership	47.4	72.6	65.3	96.9	100.0	84.0
Risky financial asset/financial assets	74.2	57.6	86.9	78.3	68.0	65.8
Broad risky asset ownership	100.0	100.0	100.0	100.0	100.0	100.0
Broad risky asset/total assets	67.8	74.9	87.8	85.2	72.1	74.8
1989 SCF						
Risky financial asset ownership	60.1	73.8	89.1	89.9	92.3	95.2
Risky financial asset/financial assets	92.5	47.3	61.6	51.2	51.0	51.8
Broad risky asset ownership	100.0	100.0	95.5	100.0	100.0	99.3
Broad risky asset/total assets	91.8	58.7	78.8	80.1	80.2	70.9
1992 SCF						
Risky financial asset ownership	64.1	89.0	77.2	89.5	88.1	84.3
Risky financial asset/financial assets	65.1	52.9	48.4	61.0	58.8	58.8
Broad risky asset ownership	92.0	100.0	100.0	100.0	100.0	100.0
Broad risky asset/total assets	76.4	72.7	79.0	75.6	78.9	73.6
1995 SCF						
Risky financial asset ownership	88.2	73.6	87.3	75.5	87.2	89.7
Risky financial asset/financial assets	27.2	60.1	59.1	50.7	51.2	57.9
Broad risky asset ownership	91.3	97.5	100.0	100.0	100.0	100.0
Broad risky asset/total assets	41.8	67.5	78.8	74.2	68.4	70.7
1962–1995						
Risky financial asset ownership	68.2	80.4	81.9	84.6	89.5	90.2
Risky financial asset/financial assets	68.9	62.9	65.9	64.9	60.8	62.3
Broad risky asset ownership	96.7	99.5	99.1	100.0	100.0	99.9
Broad risky asset/total assets	71.3	73.2	81.0	79.9	75.3	73.0

Source: Survey of Financial Characteristics of Consumers and Surveys of Consumer Finances.
Note: The definition of risky financial assets corresponds to the sum of clearly risky and fairly risky assets defined in table 10.4. The definition of broad risky assets corresponds to the "risky assets—broad" classification in table 10.4.

different. The probability of owning at least some amount of risky assets is monotonically increasing in age, but the proportion of the portfolio composed of broad risky assets rises through the first three age categories (up to age 49) but exhibits no clear pattern across the older age groups.[8] Ownership rates of risky assets show a similar monotonic increase (at least until age 70 and over), while the portfolio share shows some tendency to decline with age. As King and Leape (1987) argue, the monotonic increase in ownership rates may reflect the accumulation of experience with different assets as the household ages. The reduction in the risky share of the portfolio for the age groups 50 and over is interesting because it corresponds roughly to the common financial advice to shift assets away from risky forms as retirement approaches (though admittedly no such pattern is evident for the broad risky portfolio share). Note, however, that there is some debate about whether this advice is theoretically sound; furthermore, as several of the country chapters in this book show, there does not seem to be a consistent pattern to age profiles of the risky portfolio share across countries.

10.1.5   International Evidence on Portfolios of the Rich

Evidence about portfolios of the rich in other countries is presented in table 10.7. This table reflects data provided by the respective country experts for each of the country chapters examined in this book. Before describing the results, it is important to emphasize the problems associated with such international comparisons. Probably the greatest problem is that surveys in other countries generally have not made such an intense effort as the SCF does to get a large and representative sample of the very richest households; furthermore, little is known about exactly how participation rates for the wealthy vary across countries. As a result, a table merely presenting data from the top 1 percent of surveyed households across countries might well reflect differences in survey success and methodology more than actual differences in behavior across countries. My response to this problem is twofold. First, rather than focusing on the top 1 percent, where the variation in participation rates is likely to be very large across countries, I report information about the top 5 percent of households. Second, I strongly discourage direct comparison of portfolio statistics for the "rich" across countries. Instead, it seems likely to be more reliable simply to examine how the differences between the rich and the rest vary across countries.

Table 10.7
International comparison of portfolio structure

	United States, 1995		Netherlands, 1995		Italy, 1995		Germany, 1993		United Kingdom, 1997/98	
	Top 5 percent	Bottom 95 percent	Top 5 percent	Bottom 95 percent	Top 5 percent	Bottom 95 percent	Top 5 percent	Bottom 95 percent	Top 5 percent	Bottom 95 percent
Gross financial assets (GFA) per household	$1,120,583	$41,118	€278,778	€21,138	€122,507	€17,286	€155,623	€28,022	€175,427	€10,720
As a ratio to gross financial assets	100.0	100.0	100.0	100.0	100.0	100.0	100.0	100.0	100.0	100.0
Safe	37.0	54.1	21.8	47.8	52.7	81.2	68.3	79.5	54.5	77.2
Clearly safe	17.9	27.6	14.8	45.2	46.2	69.7	11.3	27.0	46.3	70.8
Fairly safe	19.2	26.5	7.0	2.6	6.5	11.5	57.0	52.5	8.2	6.4
Risky	50.7	29.9	52.9	14.3	30.6	9.2	19.7	10.0	25.1	15.0
Clearly risky	44.6	27.4	n.a.	n.a.	13.9	2.1	12.0	4.0	17.1	12.9
Fairly risky	6.1	2.4	n.a.	n.a.	16.7	7.1	7.6	6.0	8.8	2.0
Risk characteristics unknown	12.3	16.0	25.3	37.9	16.7	9.6	12.0	10.4	19.6	7.8
Nonfinancial assets per household	$1,626,405	$98,423	€432,098	€34,539	€905,204	€112,588	€661,115	€96,306	—	—
As a ratio to net worth	63.1	95.5	69.4	116.0	88.1	86.7	—	—	—	—
Gross value of primary residence	12.7	65.7	31.9	98.5	29.2	53.7	88.0	86.0	—	—
Net value of private business	32.0	6.5	19.1	3.1	37.0	15.6	—	—	—	—
Gross value investment real estate	13.5	9.9	16.8	4.2	16.0	5.5	—	—	—	—

Gross value of durables, of which	—	—	—	—	3.7	10.1	—	—	—
Vehicles	1.3	10.8	1.7	10.1	2.6	7.3	—	—	—
Other nonfinancial assets	3.6	2.7	n.a.	n.a.	2.1	1.8	—	—	—
Debt per household	$169,454	$36,479	€75,240	€16,197	€27,319	€4,753	€65,382	€15,111	—
As a ratio to net worth	6.6	35.4	14.1	51.5	2.7	3.7	8.7	16.4	—
Mortgage on primary residence	3.0	25.7	12.4	45.6	0.6	2.2	—	—	—
Other secured debt	3.1	5.9	—	—	—	—	—	—	—
Unsecured debt	0.5	3.8	1.7	5.4	—	—	0.4	1.8	—
Net worth per household	$2,577,534	$103,063	€622,933	€29,779	€1,027,711	€129,874	€750,592	€91,987	—
Memo									
Clearly risky financial assets/GFA	44.6	27.4	n.a.	n.a.	13.9	2.1	12.0	4.0	—
Broad risky assets/GFA	155.3	71.0	20.8	3.4	475.8	167.6	19.7	10.0	—
Very broad risky assets/GFA	174.5	97.5	52.2	8.2	482.3	179.1	76.7	62.5	—
Total household income	$216,142	$39,685	€59,958	€19,924	€64,012	€22,732	€80,655	€35,647	—
Total household non-capital income	$135,864	$37,985	n.a.	n.a.	€56,035	€21,864	€59,873	€32,306	—

Note: Households are sorted once, by the broadest measure of net worth available, to determine their classification into top 5 or bottom 95 percent. Asset shares are computed as a ratio of averages. All statistics use sample weights.

Definitions for United States. Data are drawn from the 1995 Survey of Consumer Finances. Figures are reported in 1999 dollars, converted from 1995 numbers using the CPI-U-RS.

Definitions of financial asset classifications:
   Clearly safe includes transaction accounts (checking, saving, money market), certificates of deposit, U.S. savings bonds, and mutual funds invested exclusively in these assets.

Table 10.7
(continued)

Fairly safe includes state/local bonds, mutual funds, and other managed assets invested in state/local bonds, and the cash value of life insurance policies.

Fairly risky includes bonds (all types except state/local and U.S. savings) and mutual funds invested in bonds (all types except state/local and U.S. savings).

Clearly risky includes stocks and financial assets invested in real estate, commodities, and private partnerships.

Risk characteristics unknown. The three largest components of this category are mutual funds whose investment direction is unknown, retirement accounts whose investment direction is unknown, and other managed assets whose investment direction is unknown. "Other financial assets" are also included in this category.

Mutual funds and retirement accounts invested in a single category of assets (for example, 100 percent stock mutual funds) are included in the corresponding category.

Other secured debt includes call account debt, vehicle loans, loans against pensions and life insurance policies, and loans for investment real estate.

Unsecured debt includes credit card balances, installment loans, other lines of credit, and other miscellaneous debts.

Broad risky assets consists of clearly risky and fairly risky financial assets, plus businesses and investment real estate.

Very broad risky assets consists of broad risky assets plus fairly safe assets.

Total household income includes all income to the household from any source.

Total noncapital income subtracts all capital income (e.g., dividends, interest, capital gains) from total household income.

Definitions for the Netherlands. Data are drawn from the 1995 CentER Savings Survey. For further information, see chapter 9. 1998 guilder are converted to euros using the rate 1 euro = 2.203 guilders.

Clearly safe—transactions and savings accounts and certificates of deposit.

Clearly risky—Stocks, bonds, mutual funds.

Risk characteristics unknown—The largest items are defined-contribution pension plans, cash value of life insurance, and employer-sponsored pension plans.

Definitions for Italy. All values are expressed in euro, obtained by converting 1995 lire to 1999 lire using the increase in the CPI from 1995 to 1999 (10.8 percent) and converting to euros using the 1999 fixed exchange rate between euros and lire: 1 euro = 1.936 lire. Data are drawn from the 1995 Survey of Household Income and Wealth, described in chapter 7.

Clearly safe includes currency, transaction accounts (checking, saving, and postal accounts), certificates of deposit, and short-term Treasury bills.

Fairly safe includes the cash value of life insurance policies.

Fairly risky includes bonds (all types except short-term government bills), mutual funds, and managed investment accounts.

Clearly risky includes only stocks.

Risk characteristics unknown include mutual funds and defined contribution pension funds.

Mortgage debt includes all mortgage debt, not just the primary residence.

Durables do not include art objects, jewelry, and so forth.

Broad risky assets consists of clearly risky and fairly risky financial assets, plus businesses and investment real estate.

Very broad risky assets consists of broad risky assets plus fairly safe assets.

Definitions for Germany. Data are drawn from the Income and Expenditure Survey wave 1993 covering 31,774 West German households and 8,456 East German households, 80 percent subsample, excluding households with total net monthly income of 35,000 DM (1993) or more. The data set is described in detail in the appendix to chapter 8. 1993 DM are converted to 1999 DM using the CPI index 1 DM (December 1999) = 1.054878 DM (1993), and then to euros by the fixed rate of 1.95583 DM = 1 euro.

Fairly safe includes the cash value of endowment life insurance, assets accumulated in building society savings contracts (*Bausparverträge*), municipal bonds, savings certificates, and government bonds.

Fairly risky includes other bonds and mutual funds invested in stocks or bonds.

Clearly risky includes stocks and mutual funds invested in real estate.

Risk characteristics unknown are "other" financial assets.

Nonfinancial assets. No data are available separating real estate into personal residence and other, so the number for personal residence reflects all real estate.

Definitions for United Kingdom. Data are drawn from the 1997–1998 Financial Research Survey. See chapter 6 for details. Figures were calculated in 1997 pounds, converted to 1999 pounds using the CPI inflation factor of 1.0726, then converted to euros using the 1999 euro/pound exchange rate of 1.7.

Clearly safe includes transaction accounts (checking, saving, money market), certificates of deposit, National Savings current accounts, Premium bonds, and TESSAs.

Fairly safe includes government and local bonds, plus National Savings Bonds.

Fairly risky includes all bonds (all types except government/local and National Savings).

Clearly risky includes stocks and shares.

Risk characteristics unknown. This is almost entirely mutual funds where investment direction is unknown and retirement accounts whose investment direction is unknown. "Other financial assets" are also included in this category.

Other secured debt includes call account debt, vehicle loans, loans against pensions and life insurance policies, and loans for investment real estate.

Secured and unsecured debt includes installment loans, other lines of credit, and other miscellaneous debts, agreed overdrafts, and vehicle or other secured loans.

Value of pension and life insurance assets not known in survey and hence not included in the definition of gross financial assets or in any subcomponent.

Other survey differences also hamper international comparisons. From the standpoint of comparing the results to the predictions of portfolio theory, we would like to be able to divide all assets between safe and risky categories. Unfortunately, the problems in making such allocations are even greater in most other surveys than they are in the SCF. In particular, most surveys collect little or no information about the investment strategies of mutual funds or defined-contribution pensions or about the risk characteristics of other financial assets. Given these problems, I concluded that the most informative feasible exercise was to allow individual country experts to determine, for each asset category, whether there was sufficient information about that category to allocate the asset unambiguously to one of the four levels of riskiness. If not, the analyst was asked to include the asset in the category "risk characteristics unknown." An example in the SCF would be a mutual fund that the respondent indicated invested in both stocks and bonds. Because the SCF does not collect any information about the proportion of the fund's value invested in each of these two categories, I included all such mutual fund assets in the "risk characteristics unknown" category.[9] Under this strategy, at least readers can be confident that the assets included in, say, the "clearly risky" category are indeed risky.

A final problem is in normalization. Portfolio theory yields predictions about the proportion of the portfolio that should be held in various kinds of assets. Accordingly, table 10.7 reports the ratio of various kinds of nonfinancial assets and debts to total net worth. It is very important to remember, however, that all of the measurement problems that affect the components of net worth also affect the total. For example, the net value of private business is not measured in the German survey data and consequently is not included in net worth. Furthermore, the German survey does not provide separate data for the value of the respondent's home and the value of all other real estate owned by that respondent, so the number reported in the table for private residence actually reflects all real estate. Since private business wealth constitutes at least 30 percent of total net worth of the rich in the three countries for which survey data on these components of wealth do exist, and investment real estate is around another 15 percent of net worth, the apparently surprising finding that the gross value of private residence constitutes 88 percent of net worth for the rich German households should not be taken at face value.

Keeping all of these problems in mind, a few conclusions still seem warranted. The most important is probably that in every country, the top 5 percent hold a substantially larger proportion of their financial assets in risky forms than do the rest. The difference is smallest in the United Kingdom, which may reflect the residual effects of the large-scale privatization of the Thatcher years and more recently the demutualization of many formerly cooperative financial enterprises.[10]

Another result common to all countries is that the ratio of debt to net worth is substantially smaller for the rich than for the rest, although the disparity is enormous in some countries (the United States) and rather small in others (Italy).

A striking difference across countries is in the breakdown of wealth between financial and nonfinancial forms. The two extremes are the United States and Italy. The ratio of nonfinancial to financial wealth for the top 5 percent in the United States is about 1.5, while that ratio in Italy is approximately 7. Similar, though less extreme, results hold for the bottom 95 percent of households (where measurement problems are probably somewhat smaller). The Italian country authors indicate that part of the discrepancy probably reflects systematic severe underestimation of financial assets in Italy. Nonetheless, while the magnitude of the difference may be mismeasured, qualitatively the observation that nonfinancial assets are much more important in Italy than the United States is probably true.

A final observation is that there are large differences in the levels of debt held by the bottom 95 percent across countries, ranging from a high of $36,000 in the United States to a low of only 4,753 euro in Italy. This observation reinforces existing research that has found that more highly developed financial markets in the United States have allowed much higher levels of borrowing.[11]

10.2   Analysis

It is now time to begin trying to understand the underlying behavioral patterns that give rise to the data reported above. We start by presenting a baseline formal model of saving over the life cycle, to which we will add a portfolio choice decision.

10.2.1   The Basic Stochastic Life Cycle Model

The following model is what I will henceforth characterize as the basic stochastic life cycle model. The consumer's goal is to

$$\max \sum_{s=t}^{T} \beta^{s-t} \mathcal{D}_{t,s} u(C_t), \tag{10.1}$$

where $u(C)$ is a constant relative risk aversion utility function $u(C) = c^{1-\rho}/(1-\rho)$, β is the (constant) geometric discount factor, and $\mathcal{D}_{t,s} = \prod_{h=t}^{s-1}(1-d_h)$ is the probability that the consumer will not die between periods t and s ($\mathcal{D}_{t,t}$ is defined to be 1; d_t is the probability of death between period t and $t+1$).

The maximization is, of course, subject to constraints. In particular, if, following Deaton (1991), we define X_t as cash on hand at time t, the sum of wealth and current income, then the consumer faces a budget constraint of the form

$$X_{t+1} = R_{t+1}S_t + Y_{t+1},$$

where $S_t = X_t - C_t$ is the portion of the last period's resources that the consumer did not spend, R_{t+1} is the gross rate of return earned between t and $t+1$, and Y_{t+1} is the noncapital income the consumer earns in period $t+1$.

Assume that the consumer's noncapital income in each period is given by his or her permanent income P_t multiplied by a mean-one transitory shock, $E_t[\tilde{\varepsilon}_{t+1}] = 1$, and assume that permanent income grows at rate G_t between periods but is also buffeted by a mean-one shock, $P_{t+1} = G_{t+1}P_t\eta_{t+1}$, such that $E_t[\tilde{\eta}_{t+1}] = 1$, where our notational convention is that a variable inside an expectations operator whose value is unknown as of the time at which the expectation is taken has a $\sim$ over it.

Given these assumptions, the consumer's choices are influenced by only two state variables at a given point in time: the level of the consumer's assets, X_t, and the level of permanent income, P_t. As usual, the problem can be rewritten in recursive form with a value function $V_t(X_t, P_t)$. Written out fully in this form, the consumer's problem is

$$V_t(X_t, P_t) = \max_{\{C_t\}} u(C_t) + \beta \mathcal{D}_{t,t+1} E_t[V_{t+1}(\tilde{X}_{t+1}, \tilde{P}_{t+1})] \tag{10.2}$$

such that

$$S_t = X_t - C_t$$

$$X_{t+1} = R_{t+1}S_t + Y_{t+1}$$

$$Y_{t+1} = P_{t+1}\varepsilon_{t+1}$$

$$P_{t+1} = G_t P_t \eta_{t+1}$$

10.2.2   The Saving Behavior of the Rich

Within the past decade, advances in computer speed and numerical methods have finally allowed economists to solve life cycle consumption and saving problems like that presented above with serious uncertainty and realistic utility (see, in particular, Hubbard, Skinner, and Zeldes 1994; Huggett 1996; and Carroll 1997). I have argued elsewhere (Carroll 1997) that the implications of these models fit the available evidence on the consumption and saving behavior of the typical household reasonably well, certainly much better than the old certainty equivalent (CEQ) models did.

However, another finding from this line of research has been that the model is unable to account for the very high concentrations of wealth at the top of the distribution.

How Rich Are They?
Figure 10.1 shows the ratio of wealth to permanent income by age for the population as a whole and for the households in the richest 1 percent by age category from the 1992 and 1995 SCFs.[12] Also plotted for comparison is the level of the wealth-to-income ratio at the top 1 percent implied by a standard life cycle model of saving similar to that in Carroll (1997) or Hubbard, Skinner, and Zeldes (1994). (Specifically, it is the Carroll model with HSZ baseline parameter values.) The richest 1 percent are much richer than implied by the life cycle model. In addition, the figure plots the age profile of the ninety-ninth percentile that would be implied by the HSZ model if it were assumed that households do not discount future utility at all. The figure shows that even with such patient households, the model remains far short of predicting the observed wealth-to-income ratios at the ninety-ninth percentile.[13]

This finding has been reconfirmed recently by Engen, Gale, and Uccello (1999), who do a very careful job of modeling pension

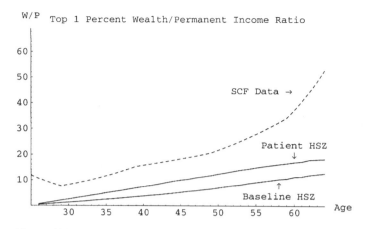

Figure 10.1
Wealth profiles for baseline and more patient households. *Source:* Reproduced from Carroll (2000)

arrangements, tax issues, and other institutional details neglected in Carroll (2000) and also find that the wealth-to-income ratios at the top part of the income distribution are much greater than predicted by a life cycle dynamic stochastic optimization model, even with a time preference rate of zero.

How Do They Spend It All?
In the 1989, 1992, and 1995 SCFs, households were asked whether their spending usually exceeds their income and whether their spending exceeded their income in the previous year. In order to run down their wealth, households obviously must eventually spend more than their income. Yet only 5 percent of the rich elderly households in the SCF answered that their spending usually exceeded their income.

More evidence is presented in figure 10.2, which shows the levels of wealth by age for the elderly in the 1992 and 1995 SCFs. There is no evidence in this figure that wealth is declining for this population; indeed, if anything, it seems to be increasing,[14] consistent with the answers that the rich elderly give to the questions about whether they are spending more than their incomes. The implication is that most of the wealth that we observe them holding will still be around at death. This is clearly a problem for any model in which the only purpose in saving is to provide for one's own future consumption.

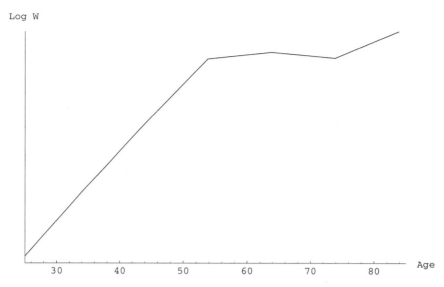

Figure 10.2
Age profile of log wealth for the 99th percentile, SCF data

This crude evidence is backed up by a study by Auten and Joulfaian (1996) that finds that the elasticity of bequests with respect to lifetime resources is well in excess of one (their point estimate is 1.3). (See Carroll 2000 for a summary of further evidence that, far from spending their wealth down, the rich elderly continue to save).

10.2.3   Adding Portfolio Choice

Recently a wave of articles (Bertaut and Halaissos 1997; Fratantoni 1998; Gakidis 1998; Cocco, Gomes, and Maenhout 1998; and Hochguertel 1998) has examined the predictions of stochastic life cycle models of the kind considered here when households facing labor income risk are allowed to choose freely between investing in a low-return safe asset and investing in risky assets parameterized to resemble the returns yielded by equity investments in the past.

The only modification to the formal optimization problem presented above necessary to allow portfolio choice is to designate R_{t+1} as the portfolio-weighted return, which will depend on the proportion of the portfolio that is allocated to the safe and the risky assets and on the rate of return on the risky asset between t and $t + 1$. Call the proportion of the portfolio invested in the risky asset ("stocks")

$w_{s,t}$ (where w is mnemonic for the portfolio weight), and $(1 - w_{s,t})$ is the portion invested in the safe asset. If the return on stocks between t and $t + 1$ is $R_{s,t+1}$, the portfolio-weighted return on the consumer's savings will be $R(1 - w_{s,t}) + R_{s,t}w_{s,t}$.

However, even without solving a model of this type formally, it is clear that such models will not be able to explain the empirical differences between the portfolio behavior of the rich and the behavior of the rest of the population, because when the utility function is in the constant relative risk aversion (CRRA) class, problems of this type are homothetic. That is, there is no systematic difference in the behavior of households at different levels of lifetime permanent income. Hence, such models provide no means to explain the very large differences between the rich and the rest in saving and portfolio behavior documented above.

10.2.4   Three Possible Modifications

There are at least three ways one might consider modifying the model in hopes of explaining the apparent nonhomotheticity of saving and portfolio behavior.

Heterogeneity in Risk Tolerance
The first is simply to allow for exogenous, immutable ex ante heterogeneity in risk tolerance across members of the population. Formally, rather than assuming that all households have the same value of ρ, we can assume that each household has an idiosyncratic, specific ρ_i.

The effect of this would be to allow households with low values of ρ (high risk tolerance) to choose highly risky but high-expected-return portfolios. On average, the risk-tolerant households would be rewarded with higher returns and would therefore end up richer than the rest of the population. Thus, the rich would be disproportionately risk lovers and would have riskier portfolios than the rest. As shorthand, I will call this the "preference heterogeneity" story henceforth.

Capital Market Imperfections
A second possibility is to follow Gentry and Hubbard (1998) and Quadrini (1999) in assuming that there are important imperfections in capital markets that require entrepreneurial investment to be

largely self-financed; imply that entrepreneurial investment has a higher return than investments made on open capital markets; and require a large minimum scale of investment. As those authors show, the combination of these three assumptions can yield an implication that portfolios of higher-wealth or higher-income households will be much more heavily weighted toward entrepreneurial investments and that rich households with business equity have higher-than-average saving rates (under the further assumption that the intertemporal elasticity of substitution is high, which means that they take advantage of the high returns that are available to them by saving more). I will refer to this theory as the "capital market imperfections" story.

Bequests as a Luxury Good
A final possibility is to change the assumption about the lifetime utility function. Carroll (2000) proposes adding a "joy of giving" bequest motive of the form $B(S)$ in a modified Stone-Geary form,[15]

$$B(S) = \frac{(S+\gamma)^{1-\alpha}}{1-\alpha}.$$

Carroll (2000) shows that if one assumes that $\alpha < \rho$, then wealth will be a "luxury good" in the sense that as lifetime resources rise, a larger proportion of those resources is devoted to S_T. In the limit as lifetime resources approach infinity, the proportion of resources devoted to the bequest approaches 1. The other salient feature of the model is that if $\gamma > 0$, there will be a "cutoff" level of lifetime resources such that households poorer than the cutoff will leave no bequest at all. Thus, the model is capable of matching the crude stylized fact that low-income people tend to leave no bequests and also captures the fact (from Auten and Joulfaian 1996) that among those who leave bequests, the elasticity of lifetime bequests with respect to lifetime income is greater than one.

In this chapter, the assumption is that one receives utility from the contemplation of the potential bequest in proportion to the probability that death (and the bequest) will occur. Thus, Bellman's equation is modified to

$$V_t(X_t, P_t) = \max_{\{C_t, w_{s,t}\}} u(C_t) + \beta(1-d_t)E_t[V_{t+1}(\tilde{X}_{t+1}, \tilde{P}_{t+1})] + d_t B(S_t),$$

and the transition equations for the state variables are unchanged.

While it is obvious how this model might help to explain the high saving rates of the rich, it is not so obvious why it might help explain the high degree of riskiness of their portfolios. It turns out, however, that precisely the same assumption that implies that bequests are a luxury good also implies that households are less risk averse with respect to gambles over bequests than with respect to gambles over consumption.[16] That assumption is that the exponent on the utility-from-bequests function α must be less than the exponent on the utility from consumption ρ. This implies that the marginal utility from bequests declines more slowly than the marginal utility from consumption, and thus as wealth rises, more and more of it is devoted to bequests rather than consumption. However, the traditional interpretation of exponents like ρ and α in utility functions of this class is as coefficients of relative risk aversion, so the assumption that bequests are a luxury good has the immediate implication of less risk aversion with respect to bequest gambles than consumption gambles!

Following Max Weber as recently interpreted by Zou (1994) and Bakshi and Chen (1996), I will henceforth call this the "capitalist spirit" model.

10.2.5   Distinguishing the Three Models

All of these theories can in principle explain the basic facts that the portfolios of the rich are disproportionately risky and that investments in closely held businesses are a disproportionate share of the portfolios of the rich. This section attempts to distinguish among the three theories on the basis of other kinds of evidence.

We begin with some direct evidence that there are substantial differences in the risk preferences of the rich compared with the rest of the population. Table 10.8 reports the results of a direct question SCF respondents are asked about their risk tolerance. Specifically, the respondents are asked

Which of the statements on this page comes closest to the amount of financial risk that you (and your [husband/wife/partner]) are willing to take when you save or make investments?

1. Take substantial financial risks expecting to earn substantial returns.
2. Take above-average financial risks expecting to earn above-average returns.
3. Take average financial risks expecting to earn average returns.
4. Not willing to take any financial risks.

Table 10.8
Risk aversion by income and net worth, 1992 and 1995 SCFs

	1992		1995	
Survey year	Mean	Percentage no risk	Mean	Percentage no risk
Permanent income percentiles				
99–100	2.5	3.8	2.6	6.2
80–98.9	2.8	16.9	2.8	16.1
0–79.9	3.3	48.7	3.2	40.1
Net worth percentiles				
99–100	2.6	11.5	2.5	6.5
80–98.9	2.9	21.6	2.8	17.6
0–79.9	3.3	48.4	3.2	43.8

Notes: The table summarizes answers to the following question: "Which of the statements on this page comes closest to the amount of financial risk that you (and your spouse/partner) are willing to take when you save or make investments? 1. Take substantial financial risks expecting to earn substantial returns; 2. Take above-average financial risks expecting to earn above-average returns; 3. Take average financial risks expecting to earn average returns; 4. Not willing to take any financial risks." To tabulate results by permanent income percentile, the sample was restricted to households that said that their income in the survey year was "about normal," and permanent income was defined as observed income for such households.

For 1992 and 1995, the table reports the mean values of the response and the percentage of households reporting that they are not willing to take any financial risks, by permanent income and net worth percentile.[17] The table shows that occupants of the highest permanent income and net worth brackets are notably more likely to express a willingness to accept above-average risk in exchange for above-average returns. Even more dramatic is the difference between the proportion of the rich and of the rest who express themselves as not willing to take any financial risks. Among the richest 1 percent by wealth, less than 10 percent express such extreme risk aversion; among the bottom 80 percent, nearly half express this sentiment.

Although economists have traditionally dismissed answers to survey questions of this type as meaningless, a recent literature (with contributions by Kahneman, Wakker, and Sarin 1997; Oswald 1997; Barsky, Juster, Kimball, and Shapiro 1997; and Ng 1997) has argued forcefully that answers to questions about preferences can provide reliable and useful information. Thus, these answers should be taken as serious evidence that the rich are more risk tolerant than the rest.

However, the table does not answer the question of the direction of causality between risk preference and wealth. It is possible, as the preference heterogeneity story would have it, that high risk tolerance leads to wealth, but it is equally possible that there is causality from wealth to risk tolerance.

One piece of existing evidence that is suggestive of causality from wealth to risk tolerance is the finding by Holtz-Eakin, Rosen, and Joulfaian (1994) that the receipt of an inheritance substantially increases the probability that the recipient will start an entrepreneurial venture. Their interpretation is that because the inheritors presumably knew that they would eventually inherit, their failure to start the entrepreneurial venture in advance of the receipt of the inheritance demonstrates the presence of liquidity constraints. An alternative interpretation is that the increase in disposable wealth increases the household's risk tolerance enough for them to become willing to take the risk of starting an entrepreneurial venture.[18]

The ideal experiment to answer the causality question would be to exogenously dump a large amount of wealth on a random sample of households and examine the effect on both their expressed risk preferences and their risk-taking behavior. The closest approximation to this ideal experiment in an available data set is the receipt of unexpected inheritances between the 1983 and 1989 panels of the SCF.

Table 10.9 presents the results of a simple regression analysis of the change in risk aversion between 1983 and 1989 on the size of inheritances received between the two surveys, using the numerical answer to the survey question about risk attitudes as the measure of risk aversion. That is, defining RISKAV83 as the 1983 answer to the risk aversion question and RISKAV89 as the 1989 answer, we define DRISKAV = RISKAV89-RISKAV83 and regress DRISKAV on a measure of the size of inheritances received and a set of control variables.[19] Specifically, LINH is the log of the value of inheritances, and the control variables in the weighted regression are the same as the variables used by Gentry and Hubbard (1998) in their extensive investigation of entrepreneurship using these data.

The coefficient on LINH is overwhelmingly statistically significant and negative, indicating that larger inheritances produce a greater decline in risk aversion. Recall that the simple preference heterogeneity story was one in which individuals enter the workforce with a built-in level of risk aversion, which is unchanging through the lifetime. If we interpret the RISKAV83 and RISKAV89 variables as

Table 10.9
Effect of inheritances on the change in risk aversion

| | Sample | |
	All recipients	Surprised
LINH	−0.186***	−0.199***
	(0.027)	(0.032)
MARRIED	0.220***	0.310***
	(0.077)	(0.103)
KIDS	−0.005	0.002
	(0.036)	(0.064)
A2	0.116	0.119
	(0.099)	(0.134)
A3	0.394***	0.495***
	(0.114)	(0.147)
UNEMP83	−0.214*	−0.422***
	(0.116)	(0.161)
UNEMP89	−0.408***	−0.468***
	(0.108)	0.120
OWNHOME	−0.149*	−0.209*
	(0.090)	(0.108)
EDUC	0.014	0.012
	(0.012)	(0.014)
CONSTANT	1.730	1.848
	(0.290)	(0.348)
Number of observations	491	357
R^2	0.132	0.159

Note: Dependent variable DRISKAV is the change in attitude toward financial risk for the household between 1983 and 1989, as described in the text. A negative change implies a reduction in risk aversion. Standard errors in parentheses. *denotes significance at the 90 percent level; **denotes significance at the 95 percent level; ***denotes significance at the 99 percent level. The first column ("All Recipients") reports results including all households that received an inheritance between 1983 and 1989. The second column ("Surprised") includes all households that received an inheritance between 1983 and 1989 but reported in 1983 that they did not expect ever to receive a substantial inheritance. The regression specification follows Gentry and Hubbard's baseline specification. Variable definitions:
LINH: Log of total value of inheritances received between 1983 and 1989
MARRIED: Dummy variable for household head married in 1989
KIDS: Number of children under 18 in the household in 1983
A2: Age dummy, household head between 35 and 54 in 1983
A3: Age dummy, household head at least 55 in 1983
UNEMP83: Dummy variable for household head unemployed in 1983 and employed in 1989
UNEMP89: Dummy variable for household head employed in 1983 and unemployed in 1989
OWNHOME: Dummy variable for household being a home owner in 1983
EDUC: Household head years of education in 1989

measures of this risk aversion, the results in table 10.9 constitute a direct rejection of this story. Indeed, almost half of households whose composition is unchanged report a different value of RISKAV89 than RISKAV83, and given that a large proportion of the change can be explained ex post via regressions like that reported in table 10.9, it is clear that these changes do not merely reflect measurement error.

One potential problem with this experiment is that inheritances may be anticipated. If so, the recipient might take the prospective inheritance into account in formulating risk attitudes even before actual receipt. However, if this were true, a regression of the change in risk preferences on the size of inheritances received would find a coefficient of zero, and so the fact that we found a highly significantly negative coefficient despite this bias only strengthens the case that changes in wealth affect risk aversion. Indeed, when we restrict the sample (in column 2) to those households that said in 1983 that they did not expect ever to receive a substantial inheritance (and presumably were surprised when they did), the coefficient estimate is a bit larger (though the difference is not statistically significant).

Unfortunately, there is a more serious problem with the experiment: the survey question cannot necessarily be interpreted as revealing the respondent's underlying coefficient of relative risk aversion. Instead, the question is about the respondent's willingness to bear financial risk, and economic theory informs us that willingness to bear financial risk should depend on a great many factors in addition to an agent's raw coefficient of relative risk aversion. In particular, what should matter is the expected coefficient of relative risk aversion for the future period's value function, which may depend, for example, on whether the consumer anticipates possibly being liquidity constrained in that future period. However, one conclusion from the recent work on portfolio theory is that the proportion of the portfolio invested in the risky asset should decline in the level of current-period cash on hand. The reason for this counterintuitive result is that when there is little financial wealth, virtually all of future consumption will be financed by labor income, and so adding a small financial risk has very little effect on overall consumption risk, so the agent is willing to invest a large proportion of her modest portfolio in the risky financial asset (this argument relies on an implicit assumption that the correlation between financial risk and labor income risk is low, as Cocco, Gomes, and Maenhout (1999) show it is). As wealth grows large, however, the proportion of future consumption to be financed out of that wealth also grows large, and thus willingness to bear additional financial risk declines (see Cocco, Gomes, and Maenhout 1999 for a fuller discussion of these issues). Thus, appropriately calibrated portfolio theory implies that we would expect to see a declining willingness to bear financial risk as wealth increased rather than the reverse, as indicated in the table.

Many economists remain uncomfortable with using survey measures like the SCF risk attitudes question. However, even if the results of table 10.9 are set aside, there are several other problems with the preference heterogeneity story as a complete explanation for the observed pattern of facts.

In principle, the preference heterogeneity story can indeed explain the large share of business equity in the portfolios of the richest households, under the assumption that private business investments bear the highest risk and the highest return among the categories of assets available. This assumption is plausible and therefore not problematic. However, several other features of the entrepreneurial investments of the rich *are* problematic for this theory.

First, entrepreneurial investments of the rich are highly undiversified. If the rich are even slightly risk averse, elementary portfolio theory under perfect capital markets implies that the optimal strategy is to invest a tiny amount in each of a large number of entrepreneurial ventures in order to diversify the idiosyncratic risk. Table 10.10 shows that instead, among the rich households with any private business equity, over 80 percent of that equity is in a single entrepreneurial venture, while the three largest entrepreneurial investments account for 94 percent of entrepreneurial wealth (a similar pattern holds for nonrich entrepreneurs). Furthermore, for rich entrepreneurial households, almost half of all income comes directly from business enterprises in which the household has an ownership stake. Failure of the business would wipe out not only the asset value of the business, but also the business-derived income; thus, the total riskiniess of business ownership is even greater than appears from the share of business equity in total net worth. This means the incentive for diversification is even stronger.

The next problem for the preference heterogeneity theory is that it provides no explanation for the fact that the great majority of entrepreneurial wealth is in enterprises in which a member of the household has an active management role. Table 10.10 shows that 85 percent of all entrepreneurial wealth is held in such actively man-

Table 10.10
Lack of diversification of business wealth. (Percent of first, second, and third largest businesses in total business equity and aggregate ratio of business-derived income to total income, for households owing some business equity, by net worth percentile, 1995 SCF)

	All house-holds	Percentile	
		0–99 percent	99–100 percent
Value of business			
Largest	0.88	0.89	0.82
Two largest	0.92	0.92	0.92
Three largest	0.92	0.92	0.94
Actively managed business assets	0.89	0.89	0.85
Ratio to total income			
Business income[a]	0.32	0.28	0.38
Business-derived income[b]	0.58	0.66	0.44

Source: Calculations by author using the 1995 Survey of Consumer Finances.
Note: Value in cells in the first four rows is the mean ratio of the value of the business(es) to total business equity.
[a] The income the household reported receiving from all the businesses the household owns, regardless of whether anyone in the household works in any of the businesses.
[b] Wages and salaries paid by the business to the household head or spouse plus retained earnings reported by the head or spouse from a business the household owns.

aged businesses. Again, with perfect capital markets, management should be completely detached from ownership to diversify idiosyncratic risk.

A final problem is that the preference heterogeneity story provides no explanation for the failure of the elderly rich to spend down their assets. Indeed, because risk tolerance is positively correlated with the intertemporal elasticity of substitution in models with time-separable preferences, we should actually expect the rich to be running down their wealth faster than the nonrich if the only difference in preferences between the rich and nonrich is in their degree of risk tolerance.

Given that several of the preceding arguments imply that the preference heterogeneity story also requires some form of capital market imperfections in order to explain the data, it is interesting to examine whether capital market imperfections by themselves might do the trick.

The central requirement of any story based purely on capital market imperfections is that business ownership must yield higher-than-market rates of return. Unfortunately, the economics and business literatures do not appear to contain credible estimates of the average rate of return on closely held business ventures. Suppose for the moment that we accept on faith the proposition that closely held business ventures earn a higher rate of return (in exchange for higher risk) than is available on open capital markets and that such ventures must be substantially self-financed for moral hazard or adverse selection reasons. By themselves, and in the absence of preference heterogeneity, these assumptions cannot explain the positive correlation between the level of initial labor income or initial wealth and the propensity to start businesses documented by Quadrini (1999) and Gentry and Hubbard (1998). The problem is that these arguments should apply with just as much force to very small business ventures (which can be financed without large initial wealth or income) as to larger ones. As anyone who has read John Kennedy O'Toole's novel *A Confederacy of Dunces* knows, there are principal/agent and moral hazard problems even for a hot dog vendor.

Gentry and Hubbard (1998) address this problem by simply assuming that there is a minimum efficient scale for business enterprises that is large relative to the resources of the median household, but this approach is insufficient to explain the data because the richest households would have wealth vastly greater than any fixed minimum efficient scale and therefore would have no need to tie up more than a trivial fraction of their total net worth in any single business enterprise. Quadrini (1999) deals with this problem by postulating a ladder of business opportunities at ever-rising minimum efficient scales, so that no matter how rich the household becomes, there is always an opportunity to jump up to an even higher rung on the ladder.

Even if we were to accept the story that there is a complicated ladder of minimum efficient scales of business operation à la Quadrini, the capital market imperfections story still faces three problems. First, it provides no explanation for the failure of the rich elderly eventually to begin running down their wealth. Second, if the risk preferences of the rich were similar to those of the rest, the extra risk associated with their entrepreneurial wealth should induce them to try to minimize the riskiness of the remainder of their portfolio. However, table 10.11 shows that the financial asset holdings of rich households that have a substantial fraction of their net worth tied up in business equity are actually considerably riskier than the financial

Table 10.11
Riskiness of financial assets in entrepreneurs' portfolios

	Average portfolio allocations for business owners and nonowners, 1995 SCF					
	Top 1 percent			0–99 percent		
	Bus = 0	0 < Bus < 33	33 < Bus < 100	Bus = 0	0 < Bus < 33	33 < Bus < 100
Financial assets/ net worth	*77.3*	*59.0*	*16.9*	*41.5*	*36.0*	*18.2*
	As a percentage of financial assets					
Safe	37.0	55.3	58.4	76.1	68.2	81.1
Clearly safe	13.0	18.8	26.7	47.5	37.0	55.3
Fairly safe	24.1	36.5	31.7	28.6	31.2	25.8
Risky	63.0	44.7	41.5	24.0	31.8	18.9

Source: Calculations by the author using the 1995 Survey of Consumer Finances.
Note: Only households with $1,000 or more in net worth are included in this table. BUS is defined as the ratio of noncorporate business equity to total net worth. For example, the leftmost column reports portfolio structure for households in the top 1 percent of the wealth distribution for whom the share of business equity in total net worth is 0. Definitions of financial assets, safe, and risky assets are as in previous tables.

asset holdings of the rest of the population (although less risky than the financial investments of the rich nonentrepreneurs). Finally, the results in table 10.8 strongly suggest that the rich, whether entrepreneurs or nonentrepreneurs, are much more risk tolerant than the rest of the population, and capital market imperfections alone can explain neither this nor the finding in table 10.9 that increases in wealth produce reductions in reported risk aversion.

It is now time to consider whether the capitalist spirit model can explain the overall pattern of facts. Recall that this model assumed that bequests are a luxury good, with the corollary implication that households are less risk averse with respect to risks to their bequests than with respect to risks to their consumption. Since the luxury good aspect of bequests implies that as a household becomes richer it plans to devote more and more of its resources to the bequest, the model also implies that risk aversion declines in the level of wealth. Thus, the capitalist spirit model is consistent with the results on self-reported risk attitudes, as well as with the risky portfolio structure for the rich, and with the evidence that receipt of inheritances reduces risk aversion (at least if we assume that those inheritances were not perfectly anticipated). It also can explain why higher-income or higher-net-worth households are more likely to invest in risky entrepreneurial ventures. Finally, it can explain the failure of the elderly rich to run down their assets before death (indeed, this is the empirical fact that the model was developed to explain; its ability to explain the other empirical patterns documented here was not anticipated in the original statement of the model).

However, if capital markets were perfect, rich households would still have every incentive to diversify the idiosyncratic component of their entrepreneurial investments by holding small shares of many entrepreneurial ventures. Their failure to do so is presumably explained by capital market imperfections.[20] Note, however, that one attractive feature of a model that combines capital market imperfections with the capitalist spirit utility function is that it is possible to dispense with the awkward assumption of a ladder of minimum efficient scales, which was necessary in the basic model of capital market imperfections in order to explain the data. This makes the analysis of such models considerably more tractable, transparent, and plausible.

10.3 Conclusion

The standard model of household behavior implies that the rich are just like scaled-up versions of everybody else, including in their portfolio allocation patterns. The data summarized in this chapter contradict that assertion for the United States since 1963 and for the other countries included in this survey.

The most important differences between the portfolios of the rich and the rest are the much higher proportion of their assets that the rich hold in risky forms and their much higher propensity to be involved in entrepreneurial activities and to hold much of their net worth in the form of their own entrepreneurial ventures. Several different features of the data point to a conclusion that relative risk aversion is a decreasing function of wealth. Other features, particularly the concentration of the wealth of the rich in their own entrepreneurial ventures, suggest that capita market imperfections are also important. But it appears that most of the features of the data can be explained by assuming both that bequests are a luxury good and that capital market imperfections require entrepreneurial enterprises to be largely self-financed and self-managed.

This is not to say that there could not also be exogenous differences in risk aversion across households, just that the case does not appear to be strong that such differences are necessary to explain the differences between the portfolios of the rich and the rest.

Notes

I am grateful to Kevin Moore for excellent research assistance and to Marco Pagano and other participants in the conference for numerous useful suggestions and ideas. An archive of all of the programs and data used to produce the tables, with extensive instructions, can be found at my web site, http://www.econ.jhu.edu/people/ ccarroll/carroll.html

1. Bertaut and Starr-McCluer in chapter 5 (this volume) find that the only kind of financial asset held by more than half of U.S. households is a checking/transactions account.

2. By ex ante, I mean a preference difference that exists prior to any saving or portfolio choice decision the household makes and is unaffected by the outcomes of such choices.

3. Surprisingly, it is not clear that classical theory supports the proposition that less risk-averse individuals will invest a higher proportion of their risky investments in the most risky activities. See chapter 1 for a discussion of the mutual fund separation theorem, which implies that the composition of risky assets should be similar whatever the level of risky asset holdings. I will assume that this reflects a limitation of classical theory rather than a plausible description of behavior.

4. One exception is "other financial assets," which had an 89.3 percent owernship rate in the 1962–1963 SFCC but much lower rates in the later surveys. This is almost certainly because holdings of cash were included in this grab-bag category in the SFCC but not in the SCFs. In any case, the next table shows that "other financial assets" constitutes a trivial proportion of net worth in all surveys.

5. One might wonder whether the differences in risky shares partly reflect age differences between the rich and the rest. However, when the age range for the rich and the rest is restricted to households aged 35–54, the divergence between the rich and the rest is, if anything, even greater. For example, the portfolio share of private business for the age 35–54 rich is 47.6 versus 17.9 for the age 35–54 nonrich, a greater discrepancy than the 37.7 versus 14.8 figures in table 10.4.

6. Home equity is calculated as the value of primary residence minus mortgage debt.

7. Portfolio shares are for the whole population of the rich, not just for those who own risky assets; the numbers are not conditional on participation.

8. It is important to recall that these figures may reflect the effects of both cohort and time effects as well as age effects, so the true age effects may differ from the reported numbers.

9. This contrasts with the strategy in table 10.4, where I divided such investments fifty-fifty between the fairly safe and fairly risky categories.

10. Shares were distributed to depositors, and thus many lower-income households that otherwise owned no shares became share owners. Research has shown that many

lower-wealth households have simply held onto the shares they obtained through demutualizations.

11. Italy is a particularly interesting case. Until recently, the minimum down payment on a home mortgage in Italy was on the order of 50 percent, while 5 percent down payment mortgages have been common in the United States for at least a decade. Furthermore, the legal system in Italy makes repossession of property extremely difficult and time-consuming. Thus, many Italians cannot afford to buy a house, and those who do buy end up borrowing much less. The high value of nonfinancial assets (mainly housing wealth) relative to financial is probably largely attributable to these features of the Italian financial system.

12. SCF respondents are asked whether their total income this year was above normal, about normal, or below normal. Following Friedman (1957), I define permanent income as the level of income the household would normally receive.

13. This figure is reproduced from Carroll (2000).

14. This is in effect a smoothed profile of wealth by age adjusted for cohort effects; see Carroll (2000) for methodological details.

15. It might seem that a "joy of giving" bequest motive and a "dynastic bequest motive" of the type considered by Barro (1974) would be virtually indistinguishable, but it turns out that there are several important differences. For example, the dynastic bequest model collapses to a standard life cycle model for households with no offspring, yet empirical evidence suggests that the rich, childless elderly continue to save. See Carroll (2000) for more arguments that the "joy of giving" bequest motive fits the data better.

16. The presence of the γ term in $B(S)$ implies increasing relative risk aversion as bequest gambles get larger. However, this does not alter the fact that risk aversion with respect to gambles over bequests is always less than risk aversion with respect to gambles over consumption.

17. My method of identifying permanent income is simple: I restrict the sample to households that reported that their income in the survey year was "about normal." Thus, I am employing Friedman's original definition of permanent income rather than modern definitions as the annuity value of human and nonhuman wealth.

18. Capital market imperfections or uncertainty about the timing or size of the bequest are still required; without either uncertainty or imperfections, the household's effective wealth would not change when a perfectly anticipated bequest was received.

19. The sample is restricted to households whose composition did not change between the two survey years, in order to ensure that changes in risk aversion really reflect changes in the attitudes of the same individual(s).

20. In discussing this chapter, Marco Pagano suggested that entrepreneurs may obtain utility directly from the ownership and consequent control over their entrepreneurial ventures. This would lead to a preferences-based theory of the nondiversification of entrepreneurial investment. However, in order to explain the overall pattern of facts, it would still be necessary to modify the utility function to put wealth in the utility function in some form, since not all of the rich are entrepreneurs. Because there is substantial independent evidence of capital market imperfections, it seems preferable to stick with a story that explains the facts using an assumption of capital market imperfections plus a single change in the utility function rather than with perfect capital markets plus two changes in the utility function.

11

Portfolio Holdings of the Elderly

Michael D. Hurd

As evidenced by the large public programs aimed at the elderly in the United States, Europe, and Japan, the economic status of the retired population has been and remains a matter of public concern. However, because of the demographic trends, it is likely that reductions in benefits will be made, so it is of considerable importance to understand the potential for the elderly to support themselves through their own savings. Although the elderly have substantial wealth, portfolio holdings have, for the most part, been rather restricted. For example, in 1992 in the United States, 67 percent of aged household units had some income from assets but just 20 percent of aged household units had income from dividends (Grad 1994).[1] Had the elderly invested more in common stocks, their assets today would be larger. Even now, were the newly retired to shift investments toward stocks and were the average rates of return over the past fifty years to be realized in the future, the capacity of the elderly to support themselves would be greater. Despite the higher rates of return in the long run, over time periods of several years investments in the stock market are at considerable risk. Therefore, it is questionable whether the retired elderly ought to invest substantially in the stock market. The study of portfolio choice will give evidence about the degree of investment risk undertaken by the elderly and the determinants of the investment choices they have made. Such a study could help understand the desirability of further stock market investment.

A second reason for studying portfolio choice by the elderly is the active discussion in the United States about investing some of the social security trust funds in the stock market. Depending on who will bear the risk, this investment could have the effect of causing the elderly to invest indirectly in the stock market, even though, as revealed by their own investment choices, they do not desire further stock investments. An extension is the proposal to privatize all or part of the social security system with either mandated portfolios or self-directed portfolios. As with investments of the social security trust funds in the stock market, the first case may require the elderly to invest more in the stock market than they wish. In the second case, one would like to understand what the likely portfolio choice would be so as to be able to predict the path of wealth.

A third reason for studying portfolio choice by the elderly is that as a group, they control a substantial fraction of the household wealth, so their investment choices could influence the future course of markets. In particular, the study of portfolio choice could illuminate the validity of the concern about "asset meltdown" as the baby boom generation retires. For example, if the elderly choose to hold their assets in money market funds, not only will they have less wealth on average but the effects on markets as they dissave will be different than if they held stocks.

According to finance theory, the portfolios of the elderly will differ from the portfolios of the nonelderly. The most obvious reason is that the elderly face substantial mortality risk, which increases sharply at advanced old age. Under the life cycle model, consumption and wealth will decline with age, at least for ages past a particular age that depends on rates of return and utility function parameters. Such declining consumption and wealth may influence portfolio choice. Because of high mortality risk, the elderly have a shorter time horizon than the nonelderly, and in the case of a couple, the time horizon for the couple as a unit is even shorter.

The great majority of the elderly have retired, and, particularly for the population that will be studied in this chapter (aged 70 or over), their ability to return to the labor force is very limited. This limitation eliminates a margin of adjustment to a financial loss that is available to those of working age, and it should reduce the willingness of the elderly to hold risky assets relative to the working-age population.

The elderly have large annuity income flows, and the risks associated with those flows are quite different from the risks of earnings. Social security is the most important income source for most elderly persons. Social security is indexed, and there is minimal risk that once an elderly person has retired, the social security benefit will be changed. In nominal terms, pension income is rather certain because of the funding requirements and guarantees of the Pension Benefit Guarantee Corporation. However, most pension income is not indexed, and so has inflation risk. This risk is quite different, and possibly smaller than the risk associated with the earnings streams of typical workers.

The elderly face a much a higher risk of health care consumption than the nonelderly, but a large fraction of the cost is covered by Medicare, and, in addition many of the elderly have medigap insurance that fills in most of the uncovered expenses. An exception would be the risk of nursing home admission and the associated costs.

An associated health risk, which is not discussed in the portfolio literature, might be called utility risk: health status is likely to affect the marginal utility of non–health care consumption. Therefore, when future health is uncertain, the marginal utility of wealth is uncertain, and this uncertainty should affect portfolio choice.

Both the elderly and nonelderly may desire to leave a bequest, but in the case of the nonelderly, the time horizon is so great that a bequest motive will not alter behavior. For the elderly, however, a bequest motive could extend the time horizon, reducing or eliminating any effects of mortality risk.

Because some elderly have substantial wealth, they may be better able to make risky investments.

In summary, it is not obvious whether the elderly should hold more or less than the nonelderly in risky assets. However, they face a substantially different environment from the nonelderly, and important features of that environment are more easily measured. For example, the most important asset of most of the nonelderly is human capital, which, because it involves future earnings, is not easily measured. Human capital of most elderly is zero. The implication is that we may be able to make empirical progress in validating portfolio theory by studying the portfolio holdings of the elderly separately from the portfolio holdings of the nonelderly.

Although the study of portfolio choice by the elderly is important from both the point of view of public policy and a scientific point of view, the study is complicated by life cycle effects that happen simultaneously with portfolio choice. Under the life cycle model, wealth will decline with age so that we should observe reductions in assets regardless of allocation (Yaari 1965). Thus, for example, a reduction in stockholdings as individuals age that is due to life cycle effects could be misattributed empirically to portfolio adjustments caused by mortality risk.

Several assets provide service flows as well as providing an investment vehicle. The most important of these is housing, which is held by the young elderly in greater concentrations than in any other age group. Another example is checking accounts, and even savings accounts and money market accounts because of the ability to write checks against them. The service flows will cause them to be held in greater concentrations than would be predicted by either the life cycle model or portfolio theory.

Some assets require personal attention such as a business and, in some cases, real estate. A declining ability with age to provide the personal input could cause these assets to be sold even though portfolio theory would say they should be retained.

Study of portfolio choice based on data from the 1990s is complicated by large changes in asset prices. To the extent that the price changes were unanticipated, total asset holdings and the change in asset holdings will not conform to a life cycle model; for example, the large increases in the value of stocks during the 1990s could lead to an increase in wealth even though the life cycle model calls for a decrease. Ex post portfolio allocation could differ from theoretical predictions if there are transaction costs associated with reallocation or simply inertia. There are surely large transaction costs associated with the buying or selling of housing, a business, and real estate.

A second complication is that expectations about future rates of return, as to both level and variation, are likely to have changed in the 1990s. This would cause a reallocation of assets even if the other observable determinants of asset allocation such as wealth level were unchanged.

A third complication is that the availability of financial instruments increased over the 1990s and the costs of acquiring some of the instruments decreased. If the availability and costs changed in an important way over the period of empirical study, observed portfolio reallocation could have been caused by these changes rather than by the factors discussed by finance theory, such as the level and variability of rates of return.

It is beyond the scope of this chapter to investigate all the possible causes of portfolio reallocation by the elderly. Rather I will focus on the main factors that are associated with the elderly but not with the nonelderly: mortality risk, pension and social security income, marital status, and indicators for a bequest motive. The frame of reference will be the life cycle model augmented with portfolio selection.

11.1 Data

The data for this chapter come from the study of the Asset and Health Dynamics among the Oldest-Old (AHEAD), a biennial panel survey of individuals born in 1923 or earlier and their spouses (Soldo, Hurd, Rodgers, and Wallace 1997). At baseline in 1993, it surveyed 8,222 individuals representative of the community-based population except for oversamples of blacks, Hispanics, and Floridians. Wave 2 was fielded in 1995. This chapter will be based on data from waves 1 and 2.

The main goal of AHEAD is to provide panel data from the three broad domains of economic status, health, and family connections. For this chapter, the most important variables are measures of asset holdings. In both waves, the financial respondent was asked for a complete inventory of assets and debts and about income sources.[2] Through the use of unfolding brackets, nonresponse to asset values was reduced to levels much lower than would be found in a typical household survey such as the Survey of Income and Program Participation (SIPP).[3] AHEAD has data on ten types of assets, mortgages, and "other debt." Housing wealth is house value minus mortgage value. Total wealth is housing wealth plus nonhousing wealth minus other debt.[4]

AHEAD queries about sources of income. This chapter uses measures of the annual social security income of a couple and of a single person, and measures of annual pension income and annuity income.

AHEAD has innovative questions about subjective probabilities, which request the respondents to give the chances of future events. This chapter uses observations on the subjective probability of survival. The form of the question is as follows:

[Using any] number from 0 to 100 where 0 means that you think there is absolutely no chance and 100 means that you think the event is absolutely sure to happen, . . . what do you think are the chances that you will live to be at least A,

where A is the target age. A is 80, 85, 90, 95, or 100 if the age of the respondent was less than 70, 70–74, 75–79, 80–84, and 85–89, respectively. The question was not asked of those 90 or over or of

Table 11.1
Wealth in wave 1 (thousands)

	Single			Married		
Age	Obser-vations	Mean	Median	Obser-vations	Mean	Median
70–74	1,060	135.4	51.2	1,713	254.1	142.0
75–79	1,008	116.3	51.0	1,064	245.5	120.0
80–84	857	93.9	42.5	662	211.3	112.6
85 or over	739	88.8	28.2	297	178.6	81.0

proxy respondents. Responses to this question vary appropriately with known mortality risk factors, and they predict actual mortality (Hurd, McFadden, and Merrill 2001).

The AHEAD data have advantages over other U.S. data sets. Most important, the study has many more observations on the elderly than, say, the Panel Study of Income Dynamics (PSID) or the Survey of Consumer Finances (SCF). It is panel data making it possible to study transitions in asset holdings. It measures a wide range of personal characteristics. Almost all of the respondents are retired, so one cannot study portfolio choices that accompany retirement. However, there is no uncertainty about future earnings, which simplifies the interpretation of portfolio choice results.

11.2 Results

Table 11.1 shows cross-section wealth in wave 1 of AHEAD. Wealth includes housing wealth, financial wealth, and other nonfinancial wealth.[5] In this table and in others except where noted, the observations are of persons. In the case of couples, if each spouse is age eligible, each will contribute an observation to the table. For example, if one spouse is 70–74 and the other is 75–79, the wealth of the couple enters the mean in each of the age bands 70–74 and 75–79. Therefore, the interpretation of the table is the wealth of the household in which a person lives.[6] This treatment of couples is appropriate for the AHEAD in that AHEAD is a survey of persons, not of households. Furthermore, when classifying wealth by household characteristics such as age, it avoids arbitrarily assigning the characteristics of one of the spouses to be the characteristics of the household.

The table shows that couples have somewhat more than twice the wealth of singles, whether measured by the mean or median. Wealth declines with age. The age profile is due to differences in the lifetime wealth of the cohorts, wealth change with age among survivors (life cycle effects), and the tendency of the more well-to-do in a cohort to have higher survival rates (differential mortality).

Table 11.2 shows for each of the assets the rate of ownership, which is the percentage of households that own each asset and the fraction of total wealth in each asset.[7] The headings in the table are in some cases shorthand for a more extensive list of assets. For example, "checking and savings" refers to "checking or savings accounts, or money market funds." The exact coverage can be found in the chapter appendix.

Among both singles and couples, the ownership rate of housing declines steadily with age. Because cohort effects are unlikely to be strong enough to produce such a decline, the ownership rate indicates that the rate of home owning declines with age, a life cycle effect. This conclusion is reinforced by a comparison of home ownership in the cohort of 1906–1911 as measured in 1979 in the Retirement History Survey (RHS) with the rate in AHEAD. In the RHS when the cohort was aged 68 to 73, 70.6 percent of households owned a home (Hurd and Shoven 1985); in AHEAD wave 1 when the cohort was aged 83 to 88, 64.1 percent of the cohort owned a home (not shown). This synthetic cohort comparison makes no correction for differential mortality—the tendency of the more well-to-do to have above-average survival rates. Because home owners have higher survival rates than those who do not own, the true life cycle reduction is greater than the synthetic cohort comparison suggests. The finding that home-owning rates decline with age is at odds with the literature on life cycle home ownership. For example, Venti and Wise (1989) conclude that the elderly do not reduce ownership or equity as they age. Their conclusions are based on the RHS, and likely differ from these because the RHS sample had not yet reached the ages at which asset reduction occurs.

Among singles, the ownership rates of real estate and businesses decline with age, as would be the case if their ownership required some level of personal input that becomes more difficult with age. However, the ownership rates of financial assets such as stocks, bonds, and CDs also decline with age, even though they can be held with little active personal input. The most obvious explanation is

Table 11.2
Asset ownership rate (percent) and fraction of total wealth

Asset type and age band	Singles		Couples	
	Owner-ship	Fraction	Owner-ship	Fraction
House				
70–74	66.1	0.447	90.2	0.381
75–79	62.7	0.480	87.3	0.382
80–84	58.5	0.473	82.8	0.405
85 or over	48.2	0.438	74.5	0.449
Real estate				
70–74	14.9	0.154	30.3	0.148
75–79	14.1	0.168	25.8	0.163
80–84	12.4	0.132	24.7	0.136
85 or over	10.3	0.106	15.2	0.075
Business				
70–74	3.8	0.034	9.9	0.047
75–79	2.0	0.019	7.0	0.042
80–84	1.7	0.013	3.6	0.030
85 or over	0.7	0.018	2.1	0.006
Checking and savings				
70–74	73.8	0.102	83.7	0.082
75–79	72.7	0.109	81.5	0.107
80–84	73.1	0.134	79.2	0.120
85 or over	68.0	0.137	71.5	0.133
Stocks and mutual funds				
70–74	16.6	0.086	30.4	0.123
75–79	14.3	0.096	26.5	0.126
80–84	14.3	0.107	24.3	0.126
85 or over	10.5	0.125	21.6	0.186
Certificates of deposit				
70–74	19.6	0.053	28.2	0.041
75–79	20.3	0.051	25.5	0.048
80–84	15.9	0.074	25.7	0.080
85 or over	16.3	0.105	19.6	0.080
Bonds				
70–74	4.8	0.023	8.8	0.034
75–79	4.4	0.019	9.0	0.027
80–84	3.4	0.027	7.5	0.027
85 or over	3.1	0.036	7.8	0.037

Table 11.2
(continued)

Asset type and age band	Singles Owner-ship	Fraction	Couples Owner-ship	Fraction
Individual Retirement Accounts				
70–74	18.1	0.053	38.6	0.088
75–79	6.0	0.015	18.2	0.034
80–84	2.1	0.004	11.0	0.020
85 or over	0.7	0.003	5.4	0.012
Transportation				
70–74	69.4	0.034	94.4	0.046
75–79	64.7	0.037	93.5	0.052
80–84	53.4	0.028	88.7	0.037
85 or over	37.4	0.018	74.9	0.029
Other				
70–74	9.0	0.018	15.7	0.020
75–79	7.1	0.011	15.0	0.017
80–84	5.7	0.011	11.2	0.023
85 or over	7.3	0.017	6.0	0.008
Debt				
70–74	17.6	0.003	17.6	0.009
75–79	14.4	0.003	14.7	0.003
80–84	10.0	0.003	8.0	0.003
85 or over	4.6	0.002	7.3	0.008
Number of observations				
70–74	1,062		1,698	
75–79	1,009		1,060	
80–84	856		660	
85 or over	740		289	

connected with the lower levels of wealth at advanced age. If there are indivisibilities of ownership or fixed costs, less wealth will be associated with fewer types of assets. If housing and checking provide service flows that most households require, ownership will be concentrated in those assets at lower levels of wealth. With respect to checking, this explanation is reasonably well supported by the data on the holdings of checking accounts by singles and somewhat less so for couples, although the magnitude of the wealth decline with age is considerably greater for couples than for singles. An additional factor is that especially among older singles, a considerable fraction are fairly recently widowed women who will retain checking accounts unless they take action. A final factor may simply be the highly selected sample of married people aged 85 or over: in wave 1 there were just 289 married people in that age group, or 7.7 percent of all age-eligible married people.

IRA ownership declines sharply with age, partly a cohort effect: IRAs were not widespread until the 1980s when the older persons of the AHEAD cohort were already retired. IRAs can still be acquired after retirement by rolling over a defined-benefit or defined-contribution pension plan into an IRA, or by having a younger spouse retire with a pension cash-out that is rolled into an IRA, but among the oldest cohorts, this would have been a rare event. The implication is that the current rate of IRA ownership by age is not a good guide to future ownership rates.

The fraction of wealth in each asset varies with age in a rather different manner from the rate of ownership. For example, the fraction in housing is almost constant with age, whereas the ownership rate declines steadily. The fraction in financial assets is constant or even increases with age. Apparently with increasing age, singles and couples sell housing, business, and real estate and transfer the receipts into financial assets. In addition, as the less well-to-do reduce their assets, they eliminate small holdings of financial assets, thus reducing the ownership rate.

A comparison of these results with those based on data from the other countries covered in this book is rather difficult because of differences in definitions of asset types, differences in wealth levels across the countries, and a lack of age detail in the data from the other countries. In AHEAD, the rate of ownership of stocks declines with age, and it is higher for couples than for singles. In the data from the Netherlands, the rate of ownership of risky financial assets

Table 11.3
Distribution (percent) of financial assets by risk characteristics

Age	Safe[a]		Fairly safe[b]		Risky[c]		Total	
	Singles	Couples	Singles	Couples	Singles	Couples	Singles	Couples
70–74	48.9	33.4	15.6	21.2	35.5	45.4	100	100
75–79	55.2	45.3	9.1	12.9	35.7	41.8	100	100
80–84	60.1	53.6	8.4	9.9	31.5	36.5	100	100
85 or over	59.6	47.5	9.2	9.6	31.2	42.9	100	100

[a] Checking and savings accounts and CDs.
[b] Bonds and half of IRAs.
[c] Stocks and mutual funds and half of IRAs.

is about 30 percent, and it is roughly flat in cross section and increasing in synthetic panels. The level is consistent with the level of stock and mutual fund holdings in the AHEAD data, but they show different age patterns. As we shall see in later tables, the increase in stockholdings in the AHEAD panel is consistent with the increase in synthetic panel in the Netherlands data.

In Italy the ownership rate of risky financial assets among those 70 or over is just 6.9 percent. This low rate is consistent with an overall low level of wealth, which makes comparison with the holdings in AHEAD rather tenuous.

Table 11.3 shows the allocation of financial assets by the risk categories of safe, fairly safe, and risky. The table shows that holding age constant, couples tend to have a greater share in risky assets and a smaller share in safe assets. With the exception of those 85 or older, the share in safe assets increases rather sharply with age: about 12 percentage points for singles and 20 percentage points for couples. The shares of both fairly safe and risky assets are reduced.

Because of differences in coverage and definition, the results in table 11.3 are not strictly comparable with the results from the SCF for the United States or for the other countries covered in this book. However, despite differences in definitions, the share in risky assets measured in AHEAD is broadly consistent with the share as measured in the SCF: among those 75 or over, the share in SCF was 27.8 percent in 1992 and 39.7 percent in 1995. In AHEAD wave 1 (1993), the shares are about 34 percent for singles and 42 percent for couples.

Table 11.4 shows real panel wealth by marital status transition. In this table, wealth in wave 1 is greater than wealth as shown in table

Table 11.4
Wealth in waves 1 and 2, panel (thousands of 1993 dollars)

Marital transition and age	Number	Mean		Median	
		Wave 1	Wave 2	Wave 1	Wave 2
Married to married					
70–74	1,433	262.1	334.2	150.5	167.6
75–79	817	258.5	323.5	129.5	158.6
80–84	484	224.1	346.5	119.5	164.8
85 or over	184	204.4	387.4	100.3	109.5
All	2,918	253.1	335.2	135.0	160.8
Single to single					
70–74	901	144.8	164.0	53.0	57.0
75–79	845	117.6	147.4	53.1	57.4
80–84	684	100.6	124.6	45.1	42.7
85 or over	542	96.4	122.0	31.5	38.0
All	2,972	117.5	142.1	47.5	49.4
Married to single					
70–74	101	212.9	214.7	90.5	116.8
75–79	90	148.7	189.9	86.6	86.0
80–84	68	177.0	214.8	82.3	99.7
85 or over	32	157.9	407.7	70.3	46.5
All	291	179.4	225.0	86.0	91.7
All					
70–74	1,961	205.5	245.8	95.0	106.7
75–79	1,392	172.7	217.8	75.1	86.0
80–84	1,074	138.4	188.7	65.0	64.4
85 or over	675	112.6	161.2	41.0	47.5
All	5,102	170.6	215.5	76.0	83.6

11.1 because of differential mortality: Table 11.4 only includes survivors to wave 2, and in wave 1 they had more wealth than those who died between the waves. The effect for couples can be seen by comparing the wave 1 wealth of couples that survived to wave 2 with wave 1 wealth of couples in which one spouse died. For example, among those aged 70 to 74, the surviving couple had mean and median wealth of $262.1 and $150.5, whereas the couples in which a spouse died had wealth of $212.6 and $90.5.

When calculating the wealth of "all," one of the spouses is chosen according to the following selection rule: if just one spouse is age eligible, that spouse is chosen; if just one spouse survives to wave 2, that spouse is chosen provided he or she is age eligible; otherwise one is chosen at random.[8] Therefore, the table represents the wealth of households in which at least one age-eligible spouse survives to wave 2. This selection rule will be followed in later tables, as noted.

The main feature of table 11.4 is that wealth increased between the waves, especially as measured by the mean. Among couples, mean wealth increased by 32 percent, and the median increased by 19 percent. Among singles, the increase was smaller, 23 percent at the mean. Median wealth among singles was small and showed little change between waves. These results are different from panel wealth change based on the RHS, SIPP, and other data. For example, in the RHS between 1969 and 1979, real wealth declined at an annual rate of 4.5 percent among retired singles and 1.6 percent among retired couples (Hurd 1987). The rate of decline in wealth was comparable in the 1984 and 1985 SIPP. An explanation of the difference is the large capital gains, especially in the stock market, between waves 1 and 2 of AHEAD. The wealth gains show the difficulty of studying life cycle behavior during periods when ex post rates of return on assets are substantially different from historical rates. The gains in wealth could not have been due to saving out of conventionally measured income; for example, total income over the two years of the panel was about $42,000, yet average wealth increased by $44,900. Among couples, the gap is even larger: wealth increased by about $73,000, yet total income was about $56,000.

The main unusual price change was in the stock market. Over the two years of AHEAD, a composite measure of the total return on stocks was about 32 percent real, with all of the gain in the second year of the panel.[9] The historical rate (since 1950) was about 10 percent per year. Corporate bonds also had a much higher return than historical averages: they had a real return of about 14 percent over the two years of AHEAD compared with a historical rate of about 1.6 percent per year. They were especially volatile, having a negative return of 13 percent in the first year between waves 1 and 2 and a positive return of 27 percent over the second.

A second finding is that wealth increased even when there was a widowing. For example, mean wealth increased by 25 percent. Results based on the RHS showed fairly large declines in wealth at widowing, and they were used to explain the high rate of poverty that accompanies widowhood (Hurd and Wise 1989). Whether this difference is due to the different ages of the RHS population, differences in rates of return on assets, or some other factor remains to be determined by further study.

Table 11.5 shows the panel change in wealth by asset type. Housing shows a decline in amount and as a fraction of total wealth. There was a large increase in the total in checking but a very stable fraction of wealth, both for "all" and for each marital status transition. The increases must have been the result of a rebalancing of portfolios because the real rate of return on this type of asset was about 1 percent; yet, say for couples, the increase in wealth was 34 percent.

The value of stockholdings more than doubled, and the share increased by about eight percentage points. The increase suggests either active additions to stocks and mutual funds or that the AHEAD population achieved above-average returns. Applying the observed rate of return on the S&P Composite would approximately increase wave 1 stock wealth to $29,000 rather than to the observed $49,000.

Wealth in CDs also increased substantially. The magnitude of the increase implies active additions because rates of return on CDs could not have accounted for the increase.

11.2.1 Rates of Asset Ownership

Because of volatility in asset prices, it is difficult to understand portfolio allocation by studying levels or changes in the value of each type of asset. For example, consider the simplest model of asset allocation: each person allocates a fixed amount of new savings to each asset type with no reallocation over time. Because of the historically greater rate of return on stocks, those of advanced age will have more wealth and a greater fraction of wealth in stocks than those of younger ages simply because they have been exposed to the higher rate of return for a longer time. Although there is no active asset management, we would conclude that age is associated with greater risk-taking behavior. If the model is modified to require that initially savings are used for assets that provide a service flow such as housing and checking, we would, in addition, find a positive correlation between wealth and the share in stocks: those with less income and, therefore, lower savings would have less wealth and a smaller share in stocks.

Table 11.5
Average wealth by asset type and fraction of total wealth in asset (thousands of 1993 dollars)

Asset and marital transition	Wave 1 Wealth in asset	Fraction	Wave 2 Wealth in asset	Fraction
House				
Married to married	94.8	0.375	90.2	0.269
Married to single	77.7	0.433	65.9	0.293
Single to single	53.4	0.454	50.4	0.355
All	74.1	0.402	69.8	0.294
Real estate				
Married to married	38.8	0.153	34.5	0.103
Married to single	21.6	0.120	42.1	0.187
Single to single	18.0	0.153	13.7	0.097
All	27.9	0.152	25.1	0.106
Business				
Married to married	11.5	0.046	26.9	0.080
Married to single	3.0	0.017	12.0	0.053
Single to single	2.3	0.020	6.9	0.048
All	6.7	0.037	16.5	0.070
Checking				
Married to married	24.7	0.098	33.1	0.099
Married to single	17.4	0.097	24.0	0.107
Single to single	13.1	0.111	15.6	0.110
All	18.8	0.102	24.5	0.103
Stock				
Married to married	31.8	0.126	71.5	0.213
Married to single	28.0	0.156	39.8	0.177
Single to single	12.1	0.103	28.1	0.198
All	22.1	0.120	49.0	0.207
Certificate of Deposit				
Married to married	12.5	0.049	24.4	0.073
Married to single	9.8	0.055	23.8	0.106
Single to single	7.6	0.065	13.5	0.095
All	10.0	0.054	19.2	0.081
Bond				
Married to married	7.7	0.030	19.8	0.059
Married to single	7.8	0.043	3.5	0.016
Single to single	3.2	0.027	4.9	0.034
All	5.5	0.030	11.9	0.050

Table 11.5
(continued)

	Wave 1		Wave 2	
Asset and marital transition	Wealth in asset	Fraction	Wealth in asset	Fraction
Individual Retirement Accounts				
Married to married	16.4	0.065	19.8	0.059
Married to single	5.2	0.029	6.2	0.028
Single to single	3.0	0.026	3.4	0.024
All	9.4	0.051	11.2	0.047
Transportation				
Married to married	11.9	0.047	10.5	0.031
Married to single	7.3	0.040	5.2	0.023
Single to single	3.5	0.030	3.2	0.023
All	7.6	0.041	6.8	0.029
Other				
Married to married	4.8	0.019	6.1	0.018
Married to single	2.7	0.015	3.5	0.016
Single to single	1.7	0.014	2.8	0.020
All	3.2	0.017	4.4	0.019
Debt				
Married to married	1.8	0.007	0.8	0.002
Married to single	0.6	0.003	1.4	0.006
Single to single	0.3	0.003	0.4	0.003
All	1.0	0.005	0.7	0.003

Note: Based on 2,918 observations married to married, 291 observations married to single, and 2,972 observations single to single.

An alternative to studying portfolio shares of total wealth is to study asset ownership because transitions in ownership represent behavior by the AHEAD respondents rather than being partially the result of price changes. We can observed portfolio rebalancing that involves the decision to introduce or eliminate different types of assets from the portfolio.[10] This strategy will be followed in the rest of this chapter.

Table 11.6 shows panel rates of ownership in waves 1 and 2. For example, the rate of home ownership in waves 1 and 2 among singles who survived from wave 1 to wave 2 was 66.1 percent and 64.8 percent. Among couples in which both spouses survived, the rates were 90.2 percent and 88.5 percent. The columns labeled "steady

Table 11.6
Rate of asset ownership (percent), waves 1, 2, and steady state

Asset type and age	Singles			Couples		
	Wave 1	Wave 2	Steady state	Wave 1	Wave 2	Steady state
House						
70–74	66.1	64.8	57.6	90.2	88.5	73.1
75–79	62.7	61.9	57.2	87.3	85.4	75.2
80–84	58.5	53.6	28.2	82.8	77.4	50.6
85 or over	48.2	46.5	39.0	74.5	71.6	55.0
Real estate						
70–74	14.9	12.9	10.1	30.3	23.3	15.9
75–79	14.1	11.3	8.3	25.8	18.7	12.1
80–84	12.4	8.7	5.9	24.7	18.6	13.0
85 or over	10.3	7.7	6.5	15.2	10.2	5.2
Business						
70–74	3.8	5.0	6.8	9.9	11.4	13.4
75–79	2.0	3.9	5.1	7.0	9.9	14.9
80–84	1.7	3.8	4.9	3.6	8.0	15.0
85 or over	0.7	3.1	9.9	2.1	2.5	2.5
Checking						
70–74	73.8	79.0	82.9	83.7	89.0	91.3
75–79	72.7	79.7	84.1	81.5	90.2	92.9
80–84	73.1	81.6	85.8	79.2	88.1	91.5
85 or over	68.0	77.0	80.1	71.5	83.9	88.4
Stock						
70–74	16.6	25.4	41.6	30.4	41.1	57.5
75–79	14.3	22.8	40.5	26.5	39.7	64.6
80–84	14.3	20.2	29.0	24.3	37.6	59.7
85 or over	10.5	20.6	40.9	21.6	28.8	44.1
Certificate of deposit						
70–74	19.6	26.5	34.0	28.2	34.1	38.6
75–79	20.3	28.5	36.3	25.5	41.0	50.4
80–84	15.9	25.5	32.4	25.7	40.6	48.4
85 or over	16.3	27.5	35.6	19.6	28.4	35.8
Bond						
70–74	4.8	8.2	12.0	8.8	13.0	17.6
75–79	4.4	6.3	7.8	9.0	12.7	15.2
80–84	3.4	5.7	8.2	7.5	12.4	16.2
85 or over	3.1	4.2	4.9	7.8	18.2	23.7

Table 11.6
(continued)

Asset type and age	Singles			Couples		
	Wave 1	Wave 2	Steady state	Wave 1	Wave 2	Steady state
Individual Retirement Accounts						
70–74	18.1	20.8	30.8	38.6	40.9	48.4
75–79	6.0	7.0	10.6	18.2	20.2	26.4
80–84	2.1	2.4	2.7	11.0	11.3	12.1
85 or over	0.7	1.8	1.8	5.4	4.1	2.2
Transportation						
70–74	69.4	64.3	33.1	94.4	92.2	87.9
75–79	64.7	57.0	25.2	93.5	88.8	63.6
80–84	53.4	45.1	12.6	88.7	81.8	60.1
85 or over	37.4	24.3	1.0	74.9	60.4	16.3
Other						
70–74	9.0	6.8	5.8	15.7	13.6	12.9
75–79	7.1	6.4	6.3	15.0	12.3	11.2
80–84	5.7	6.1	6.1	11.2	11.8	12.2
85 or over	7.3	4.7	3.8	6.0	6.1	6.1
Debt						
70–74	17.6	17.1	16.8	17.6	17.2	17.0
75–79	14.4	11.2	10.1	14.7	12.5	11.6
80–84	10.0	8.6	8.2	8.0	10.2	11.4
85 or over	4.6	4.4	4.3	7.3	5.7	4.4

state" show the steady-state rate of ownership that would eventually occur were the panel transition rates between waves 1 and 2 to remain constant. The steady-state rates are calculated as

$$\frac{T}{T+1}$$

and

$$T = \frac{1 - P_{00}}{1 - P_{11}},$$

where P_{00} is the transition probability from not owning in wave 1 to not owning in wave 2, and P_{11} is the transition probability from owning in wave 1 to owning in wave 2. For example among singles in wave 1 who survived to wave 2, 66.1 percent owned a house in wave 1, and among them 93 percent continued to own in wave 2. Among the 34 percent who did not own in wave 1, 7 percent became owners by wave 2. The ownership rate in wave 2 declined to 64.8 percent because more left the state of "owner" than entered that state. If the transition rates persist, the decline will continue, and eventually the ownership rate will reach 57.6 percent. Because the steady-state rates do not depend on the initial rates of ownership, they are independent of initial conditions.

Among singles, the pattern of housing ownership by age is approximately the same in cross section as in steady state: both show substantial declines with age. Because of variation in the steady state with age, which is caused by variation in the age-specific transition probabilities, the actual age path of 70- to 74-year-old singles will be determined by a sequence of the age-specific transition probabilities, but among those who survive well past age 85, the ownership rate will eventually reach 39 percent. This rate is somewhat lower than the observed rate of 48.2 percent, but the difference is to be expected because very old singles include a large number who were widowed in their 70s, and they entered widowhood with higher rates of home owning than did existing singles. For example, 10.4 percent of married people aged 75 to 79 at baseline died between the waves. Their rate of home owning was 87.3 percent in wave 1. Singles aged 75 to 79 had a rate of home owning of 62.7 percent in wave 1, so the newly widowed will tend to increase the rate of home owning among singles.[11] In steady state, the infusion of greater ownership would not matter, but the system takes many years to reach steady state, as evidenced by the rather small fraction of the gap between baseline and steady state that is covered by wave 2.

The age pattern among couples is similar to that of singles, but the levels are higher, and in cross section there is less variation with age. Because of differential mortality, a shallow age path among couples is to be expected: the persistent depletion from the population of couples of those households that have low rates of home owning will increase the average rate of ownership among the survivors. The steady-state age path, which represents the path that would be followed by survivors in steady state, is much steeper, declining by about 18 percentage points. The overall conclusion is that the observed housing transition rates are consistent with both the cross-section rates and the RHS cohort comparison and indicate declining home ownership with age.

The pattern of real estate ownership is similar to that of housing.

Among couples, the rate of business ownership is fairly high, and it increased between the waves. The change is consistent with a pattern of older workers or the recently retired switching to self-employment late in life.

Ownership rates of financial assets (checking, stocks, CDs, and bonds) decline with age, although there is some variation in the pattern depending on marital status and type of asset. For example, among singles, checking is almost constant with age, whereas it declines among couples. As discussed in connection with housing, the cross-sectional age pattern of ownership among singles is complicated by the constant infusion of the newly widowed, who have more assets than the existing stock of singles.

The most important aspect of the ownership rates of financial assets is, in distinction to nonfinancial assets, that they increased between the waves, and, as a result, the steady-state rates are higher than either the wave 1 or wave 2 rates. Unlike the situation with nonfinancial assets, the observed rates of transition are not consistent with the cross-section rates: the steady-state rates predict that ownership rates will increase as households age, yet financial asset ownership declines with age in cross section. For example, according to the steady-state rates, singles aged 70 to 74 would increase their rate of ownership of stocks from 16.6 percent to 41.6 percent were they to survive to advanced old age. Yet just 10.5 percent of singles aged 85 or over owned stocks in wave 1. The newly widowed could bring higher rates to the population of singles, but at baseline, their rates of ownership are not high enough to raise the rate among singles to such high levels. The steady-state ownership rates of stock among couples are also much higher than baseline rates and are not consistent with the observed levels in cross section. The obvious conclusion is that neither ownership rates nor the rates of transition have been constant.

The large increase in stockholdings between the waves is the result of a high rate of new ownership by the large fraction that did not own in wave 1: 80.2 percent of wave 1 households did not own stock in wave 1, and, as shown in the following table, 13.6 percent of them had become owners by wave 2. The rate of transition out of ownership was somewhat higher (16.1 percent), but the fraction of the wave 1 population with stocks (19.8 percent) was so low that the rate of stockholding increased substantially. An implication of these transition probabilities is that the elderly engage in a considerable amount of active portfolio management. The rate of movement into equities is high, possibly the result of an increasing availability of mutual funds with low management fees. The table also shows rather high differential mortality: the mortality rate among owners was 7.1 percent, but among nonowners it was 11.4 percent.

Rates of transition of stock ownership status (percent)

| | | Status in wave 2 | | | | |
Status in wave 1	Not owner	Owner	Died and single in wave 1	Died and married in wave 1	Attrition and other	Total
Not owner (80.2%)	69.0	13.6	6.6	4.8	5.5	100.0
Owner (19.8%)	16.1	72.9	3.2	3.9	3.9	100.0

The rate of ownership of IRAs increased somewhat in the younger age groups, and the steady-state rates predict further increases (see table 11.6).

Because the finding of a decline in home ownership with age is novel, I conducted further analysis to find the circumstances surrounding the transition from owning a home.[12] Table 11.7 shows the transitions by ownership status and living arrangements in wave 1 to ownership status and living arrangements in wave 2.[13] In wave 1, 74.7 percent of survivors to wave 2 were owners, and most of them lived alone as either a couple or a single person. The main changes between the waves were a decline from 62.0 percent to 57.8 percent in owning and living alone, and an increase of 4.0 percentage points in living in a nursing home.

There are rather large percentages along the diagonals of the transition matrix, indicating, as would be expected over just two years, considerable stability in living patterns. In absolute counts, the main transition from owning was from owning and living alone to not owning and living alone: the transition rate was 4.1 percent among the 62.0 percent who owned and lived alone in wave 1. The other main route from owning was from owning and living with others to not owning and living with others, where the transition rate was 6.4 percent. Thus, when the house was sold, the type of living arrange-

Table 11.7
Transition rates (percent) from home ownership and living arrangement status in wave 1 to home ownership and living arrangement status in wave 2

Wave 2 Status	Distri- bution	Wave 1 status			
		Owner		Not owner	
		Live alone (62.0%)	Live with others (12.4%)	Live alone (18.5%)	Live with others (7.1%)
Owner, live alone	57.8	89.1	12.6	5.1	0.7
Owner, live with others	12.4	3.3	78.1	0.4	8.2
Not owner, live alone	18.4	4.1	0.8	82.5	5.9
Not owner, live with others	7.5	1.0	6.4	3.9	74.7
Owner, nursing home	1.8	2.1	2.1	0.6	1.1
Not owner, nursing home	2.2	0.3	0.0	7.4	9.3
Total	100.0	100.0	100.0	100.0	100.0

ment tended to be preserved. The rate of entry into nursing homes was fairly small among owners, and even then, most remained owners. The greatest rate of entry into nursing homes was among nonowners, especially among those who lived with others at wave 1.

It is beyond the scope of this chapter to investigate the covariates such as health status and health change associated with these transitions. But the fact that selling a home is not predominantly associated with entry into a nursing home suggests that housing decumulation is part of life cycle decumulation, not just a response to a substantial health shock.

11.2.2 Analysis of Transitions

The transitions reported in table 11.6 do not control for influences on transitions that may be related to age; for example, according to portfolio theory, wealth itself may influence portfolio choice, and wealth declines with age. Analyzing all eleven assets is not practical and is likely not to be revelatory because some are held by few people and some make up very small fractions of the portfolios. Rather, the analyses will be restricted to the transitions of ownership of housing, checking, stocks, and CDs. These asset types are rather widely held, they have different rates of return and risk, and they have different service flows.

Housing is the most important asset for most of the elderly. It differs from most other assets in that it provides a service flow; the transaction costs in terms of money, physical effort, and personal attachment are substantial; ownership provides tax advantages; and health conditions may make ownership impractical. Checking accounts provide a service flow, and they carry very little risk in that the interest rate is short term and varies with the rate of inflation. Stocks have high average rates of return but with high variance over short or even medium terms. CDs have short maturities, which are adjusted to reflect variation in short-term interest rates, so to the extent that short-term rates vary with the inflation rate, CDs have little risk. From the point of view of portfolio theory, the comparison of holdings of stock with the holdings of CDs is most revelatory because the other assets have features that may obscure the pure portfolio choice. If the elderly dissave as called for by the life cycle model, people will reduce holdings of stocks and CDs, and the relative reduction should be determined by portfolio theory.

The analytical method will be to relate transitions in ownership to covariates that are thought to determine asset changes. The covariates are of two types: variables that under the life cycle model would cause variation in the rate of asset decumulation and variables that under portfolio theory would influence the relative balance between types of assets. According to a simple version of life cycle model (only one asset), decumulation, and therefore transitions into and out of ownership, will be influenced by mortality risk, the flow of annuities with some distinction between social security and pensions due to the differential indexing for inflation, wealth, marital status, and a bequest motive. The effects on wealth decumulation are signed under the life cycle model only for mortality risk and a bequest motive. The other variables could cause the rate of wealth decumulation either to increase or decrease depending on utility function parameters and, in the case of couples, on returns to scale in consumption (Hurd 1995). In addition, changes in the anticipated rate of return on assets will affect the consumption path, but the effects are uncertain: an increase in rates could cause either an increase or a decrease in the rate of dissaving.

Under portfolio theory, the same variables should affect portfolio balancing, although the effect of mortality is indirect, operating though the decline in consumption that is caused by mortality risk. Social security income is a riskless source of resources, allowing

households to take on more portfolio risk. Pension income is somewhat risky, so it is not a perfect substitute for social security income
in portfolio determination. The degree of substitution will depend on
perceived inflation risk and the correlation between inflation risk
and asset risk. Depending on the form of the utility function, wealth
itself can lead to greater risk taking. Married people and persons
with a bequest motive have a different time horizon from singles and
from people who lack a bequest motive, and this may cause variation
in portfolio choice.

An additional complication is that a number of assets have features that make them imperfect substitutes for other assets. Housing
and checking are examples, but real estate and businesses are likely
to be imperfect substitutes. IRAs have tax aspects, and they cannot
be established at advanced ages except under special circumstances.

Table 11.8 has results from the logistic estimation of the probability of the transition from owning housing to owning housing
and from not owning housing to owning housing. The own-to-own
transition is calculated over 3,541 observations on households that
owned housing in wave 1. Singles and couples are combined, but
only one observation on a couple is selected, following the selection
rule outlined earlier. Separate estimations by marital status produce similar results but with larger standard errors, so they are not
reported. The wealth quartiles are the quartiles of singles or couples
as appropriate. The average transition probabilities were 0.938 for
own-to-own and 0.070 for not own-to-own.

Consider first the transition from owning to owning. As in the
cross-tabulations, age effects are strong: among those 90 or over, the
probability of continuing to own is about 8 percent lower than
among those 70 to 74. Couples are about 6 percent more likely to
continue to own than singles. There is a positive association with
wealth, with the highest quartile about 4 percent more likely to retain housing than the lowest quartile.[14] The implication is that the
less well-to-do are more likely to sell a house, possibly to finance
nonhousing consumption. Neither pensions nor social security has
an effect among singles, but among couples, pension income of
$10,000 per year increases the retention rate by about 4 percent. If
the AHEAD respondents have children, the retention rate is reduced,
a result that is not consistent with a bequest motive. The subjective
survival probability increases the retention rate, which is consistent

with the life cycle model: variation from 0 to 1 increases the rate by 3 percent. The variables that indicate missing data or proxy interview often indicate poor health. Typically they are associated with dissaving, although in this table they have little effect.

The transition to ownership shows no age effects, but otherwise has the same general pattern as the transition from owning to owning: higher wealth is associated with greater ownership in wave 2, as is the subjective survival probability.

Table 11.9 has similar results for transitions involving checking accounts. With the exception of the top age band, age has little effect on the retention rate. The transitions increase sharply in wealth. Pension and social security income increase the transitions for singles but not for couples.

The transition from not owning to owning shows a small increase for those who are in their 80s. The effect at 90 is approximately zero: those aged 90 or over were not queried about the subjective survival probability, so the total "age 90 effect" is the sum of the coefficients on the indicator for age 90 and over and the indicator for missing subjective survival probability (0.67–0.71). Pension and particularly social security income increase substantially the transition to ownership; for example, $1,000 in social security income increases the rate by 18 percent. Generally the same variables that increase the retention rate increase the rate of new ownership.

Although the transition probabilities for stocks and mutual funds (table 11.10) show one significant age coefficient (age 75–79), it is hard to see any overall trend with age, particularly on the rate of new acquisition. As with housing and checking, wealth effects are substantial; for example, those in the highest quartile had about a seven-fold greater probability of new acquisition than those in the lowest quartile. Among singles, pension and social security income increase the probability of purchasing, and the effect of a high level of social security income is about as large as the wealth effects. Apparently with the growing availability of mutual funds in the 1990s, the reduction in transaction costs, and, possibly, the very large gains in the stock market in the year prior to AHEAD wave 2, a substantial number of the more well-to-do in the AHEAD cohort became new stock owners.

Table 11.11 has the logistic estimations for CD transitions. Age has no systematic effect on the retention of CDs. The wealth effects are weaker than for the other financial assets, and none is significant.

Table 11.8
Logistic estimation of transition probabilities: Housing

	Own wave 1 to own wave 2			Not own wave 1 to own wave 2		
	Estimate	Asymptotic t	Relative risk	Estimate	Asymptotic t	Relative risk
Constant	2.45	5.71	1.000	−3.87	8.16	1.000
Age 70–74	—	—	1.000	—	—	1.000
Age 75–79	0.09	0.45	1.007	0.18	0.64	1.192
Age 80–84	−0.58	3.06	0.941	−0.37	1.07	0.698
Age 85–89	−0.57	2.35	0.942	0.37	1.09	1.439
Age 90 or over	−0.71	1.76	0.924	−0.04	0.09	0.958
Single	—	—	1.000	—	—	1.000
Married	1.12	2.65	1.057	1.27	1.95	3.375
Spouse died between waves	−1.33	4.42	0.819	1.04	1.93	2.725
Lowest wealth quartile	—	—	1.000	—	—	1.000
Second wealth quartile	0.33	1.16	1.023	0.08	0.28	1.080
Third wealth quartile	0.40	1.41	1.027	0.65	1.88	1.883
Highest wealth quartile	0.75	2.49	1.044	0.40	0.90	1.473
Pension income (thousands)	−0.01	0.60	1.000	0.04	1.67	1.037
Social security income (thousands)	0.02	0.57	1.001	0.02	0.61	1.023
Married × pension income	0.05	2.15	1.004	−0.01	0.26	0.988
Married × social security income	−0.05	1.16	0.996	−0.15	1.86	0.861
Has children	−0.59	2.54	0.939	0.48	1.54	1.595
Subjective survival probability (0–1)	0.49	1.93	1.032	1.15	3.25	3.039
Spouse subjective survival probability	−0.10	0.24	0.992	−0.76	0.88	0.474
Proxy interview in wave 1	0.10	0.33	1.008	0.66	1.87	1.894

Spouse proxy interview in wave 1	0.40	0.96	1.027	−0.57	0.84	0.569
Subjective survival probability missing	−0.08	0.35	0.994	−0.12	0.30	0.887
Spouse subjective survival probability missing	0.12	0.25	1.009	−0.67	0.76	0.516
Average probability		0.938			0.070	
Average probability first wealth quartile		0.927			0.070	
Number of observations		3541			1415	

Table 11.9
Logistic estimation of transition probabilities: Checking and saving

	Own wave 1 to own wave 2			Not own wave 1 to own wave 2		
	Estimate	Asymptotic t	Relative risk	Estimate	Asymptotic t	Relative risk
Constant	0.83	2.96	1.000	−1.39	4.89	1.000
Age 70–74	—	—	1.000	—	—	1.000
Age 75–79	0.18	1.14	1.052	−0.07	0.43	0.943
Age 80–84	0.11	0.63	1.032	0.29	1.60	1.255
Age 85–89	0.02	0.07	1.005	0.38	1.74	1.340
Age 90 or over	−0.72	2.73	0.755	0.67	1.95	1.646
Single	—	—	1.000	—	—	1.000
Married	0.74	2.16	1.189	1.46	4.05	2.593
Spouse died between waves	−0.72	2.75	0.756	0.19	0.54	1.157
Lowest wealth quartile	—	—	1.000	—	—	1.000
Second wealth quartile	0.50	3.46	1.136	0.66	4.19	1.628
Third wealth quartile	1.40	7.91	1.298	1.18	6.21	2.241
Highest wealth quartile	1.68	8.65	1.330	1.19	4.24	2.258
Pension income (thousands)	0.05	2.35	1.016	0.09	2.77	1.071
Social security income (thousands)	0.05	1.99	1.015	0.21	7.78	1.178
Married × pension income	−0.04	1.59	0.987	−0.01	0.25	0.992
Married × social security income	−0.03	0.68	0.992	−0.13	2.95	0.903
Has children	0.04	0.27	1.013	−0.33	1.74	0.763
Subjective survival probability (0–1)	−0.25	1.22	0.922	−0.16	0.72	0.881
Spouse subjective survival probability	0.85	2.20	1.211	0.15	0.36	1.122
Proxy interview in wave 1	−0.48	2.30	0.841	−0.57	2.50	0.617

Spouse proxy interview in wave 1	−0.13	0.44	0.958	−0.65	1.78	0.575
Subjective survival probability missing	−0.27	1.36	0.915	−0.71	3.80	0.548
Spouse subjective survival probability missing	−0.20	0.59	0.938	−0.72	1.83	0.542
Average probability	0.906				0.539	
Average probability first wealth quartile	0.794				0.400	
Number of observations	3,701				1,255	

Table 11.10
Logistic estimation of transition probabilities: Stocks and mutual funds

	Own wave 1 to own wave 2			Not own wave 1 to own wave 2		
	Estimate	Asymptotic t	Relative risk	Estimate	Asymptotic t	Relative risk
Constant	−0.62	1.00	1.000	−3.99	15.14	1.000
Age 70–74	—	—	1.000	—	—	1.000
Age 75–79	0.52	2.27	1.357	0.06	0.47	1.056
Age 80–84	−0.00	0.01	0.999	0.02	0.17	1.023
Age 85–89	0.19	0.56	1.124	0.24	1.36	1.267
Age 90 or over	1.37	1.72	1.940	0.17	0.53	1.176
Single	—	—	1.000	—	—	1.000
Married	0.57	1.18	1.396	1.18	4.34	3.130
Spouse died between waves	−0.70	1.73	0.603	−0.17	0.70	0.848
Lowest wealth quartile	—	—	1.000	—	—	1.000
Second wealth quartile	1.19	2.48	1.825	0.78	4.53	2.143
Third wealth quartile	1.35	2.97	1.931	1.48	8.90	4.123
Highest wealth quartile	2.04	4.50	2.303	2.10	12.32	7.203
Pension income (thousands)	−0.01	0.25	0.997	0.03	2.40	1.030
Social security income (thousands)	0.03	0.98	1.023	0.11	5.72	1.114
Married × pension income	0.01	0.34	1.005	−0.02	1.04	0.985
Married × social security income	−0.01	0.13	0.996	−0.05	1.77	0.956
Has children	−0.30	1.23	0.813	−0.10	0.72	0.911
Subjective survival probability (0–1)	0.08	0.26	1.049	0.09	0.56	1.088
Spouse subjective survival probability	0.06	0.16	1.042	0.02	0.10	1.024
Proxy interview in wave 1	−1.17	2.79	0.408	−0.84	3.48	0.435

Spouse proxy interview in wave 1	0.15	0.33	1.103	−0.40	1.48	0.672
Subjective survival probability missing	−0.10	0.26	0.938	−0.57	3.05	0.571
Spouse subjective survival probability missing	−0.71	1.44	0.598	−0.30	1.00	0.747
Average probability	0.808				0.152	
Average probability first wealth quartile	0.519				0.048	
Number of observations	954				4,002	

Table 11.11
Logistic estimation of transition probabilities: Certificates of deposit

	Own wave 1 to own wave 2			Not own wave 1 to own wave 2		
	Estimate	Asymptotic t	Relative risk	Estimate	Asymptotic t	Relative risk
Constant	0.13	0.29	1.000	-3.27	14.59	1.000
Age 70–74	—	—	1.000	—	—	1.000
Age 75–79	-0.01	0.05	0.996	0.31	2.86	1.347
Age 80–84	-0.07	0.37	0.968	0.33	2.73	1.375
Age 85–89	-0.30	1.19	0.857	0.41	2.64	1.484
Age 90 or over	0.22	0.45	1.100	0.71	2.98	1.966
Single	—	—	1.000	—	—	1.000
Married	-0.03	0.09	0.985	1.36	5.77	3.519
Spouse died between waves	0.10	0.29	1.045	-0.11	0.50	0.904
Lowest wealth quartile	—	—	1.000	—	—	1.000
Second wealth quartile	0.10	0.26	1.045	1.06	7.22	2.705
Third wealth quartile	0.68	1.89	1.300	1.84	12.74	5.257
Highest wealth quartile	0.62	1.73	1.276	1.83	12.07	5.226
Pension income (thousands)	0.00	0.32	1.002	0.01	0.97	1.007
Social security income (thousands)	-0.01	0.48	0.994	0.08	4.94	1.085
Married × pension income	-0.00	0.16	0.999	-0.01	1.04	0.990
Married × social security income	0.02	0.54	1.009	-0.08	3.28	0.930
Has children	0.27	1.67	1.126	-0.25	2.18	0.783
Subjective survival probability (0–1)	-0.30	1.35	0.860	-0.46	3.20	0.642
Spouse subjective survival probability	-0.04	0.14	0.979	-0.32	1.47	0.731

Proxy interview in wave 1	−0.29	0.91	0.863	−0.80	4.10	0.458
Spouse proxy interview in wave 1	−0.06	0.19	0.970	−0.09	0.39	0.916
Subjective survival probability missing	−0.24	0.89	0.886	−0.54	3.59	0.591
Spouse subjective survival probability missing	−0.26	0.66	0.880	−0.08	0.31	0.926
Average probability		0.654			0.199	
Average probability first wealth quartile		0.512			0.068	
Number of observations		1,059			3,897	

The transition probabilities from owning to owning and from not owning to owning can be summarized by the steady-state ownership rates that the transition probabilities imply. The method is to calculate a baseline steady-state probability of owning from the estimated logistic transition models, and then successively alter the baseline transition probability models by the estimated effects of each covariate and recalculate the steady-state rate of ownership. The effect of a covariate can be summarized as the probability of ownership relative to the baseline probability.

Consider, for example, steady-state home ownership. The baseline steady-state depends on P_{11}, the transition rate from owning to owning, and on P_{00}, the transition rate from not owning to not owning. These transition probabilities are calculated for someone with baseline characteristics age 70 to 74, single, lowest wealth quartile, and so forth, and from them the steady-state ownership rate is found. Then a single characteristic such as age is altered; P_{11} and P_{00} are recalculated using the estimated effects in table 11.8; and the new steady-state ownership rate is found. The relative rate of ownership is the ratio of the second rate to the first.

Table 11.12 has the relative probability of holding housing, checking, stocks, and CDs in steady state as a function of the covariates. For example, those aged 75 to 79 are predicted to have a relative rate of owning housing that is 11.6 percent greater than those aged 70 to 74. In that the baseline-predicted steady-state probability is 0.533 (last row of table), the difference in rates is 6.2 percentage points. The probability is higher among 75 to 79 year olds because both the transition rates from owning to owning and the transition rates from not owning to owning are higher than they are for 70 to 74 year olds (table 11.8).

Housing ownership has a clear downward trend with age. Checking has no relation to age. Both stocks and CDs have higher ownership rates at ages 75 to 79 compared with 70 to 74, but at greater ages, there is no clear pattern. Couples will have higher ownership rates in steady state than singles. Under the assumption that the financial variables adequately control for wealth and income effects, these results indicate that couples hold more diversified portfolios than singles do. Higher wealth is associated strongly with greater rates of asset ownership, particularly for stocks and CDs. Among singles, pension income and social security income increase ownership rates; with one exception, the effects are smaller for couples.

Table 11.12
Relative probability of holding assets in steady state fitted from logistic estimation: Effects of characteristics

Explanatory variables and average values		Asset			
		House	Check-ing	Stock	CD
Age 70–74	0.39	1.000	1.000	1.000	1.000
Age 75–79	0.27	1.116	1.018	1.273*	1.154*
Age 80–84	0.21	0.604*	1.030	1.010	1.139*
Age 85–89	0.10	0.915*	1.024	1.200	1.082*
Age 90 or over[a]	0.03	0.607	0.832*	1.427	1.076*
Single	0.59	1.000	1.000	1.000	1.000
Married	0.41	1.714*	1.111*	1.713	1.593*
Lowest wealth quartile	0.26	1.000	1.000	1.000	1.000
Second wealth quartile	0.25	1.175	1.081*	1.825*	1.541*
Third wealth quartile	0.25	1.410	1.138*	1.998*	2.033*
Highest wealth quartile	0.25	1.448*	1.146*	2.153*	2.006*
Pension income (thousands)	3.47	1.014	1.013*	1.012*	1.005
Social security income (thousands)	7.24	1.017	1.019*	1.068*	1.038*
Married × pension income	2.25	1.018*	0.993	0.996	0.994
Married × social security income	3.00	0.912	0.987*	0.976	0.969*
Has children	0.84	0.949*	0.981	0.827	0.987*
Subjective survival probability (0–1)	0.33	1.568	0.952	1.075	0.675*
Spouse subjective survival probability (0–1)	0.14	0.629	1.093*	1.040	0.821
Proxy interview in wave 1	0.08	1.307	0.862	0.320	0.534
Spouse proxy interview in wave 1	0.05	0.924	0.918	0.877	0.928
Subjective survival probability missing	0.13	0.913	0.886	0.696	0.654
Spouse subjective survival probability missing	0.06	0.755	0.897	0.600	0.862
Baseline steady-state probabilities		0.533	0.853	0.436	0.360

[a] Includes the effects of "subjective survival probability missing" because those aged 90 or over were not asked that question, so they all have a missing value.
*One or both of the underlying coefficients significant at the 5 percent level. Not indicated for the last four variables.

Those with children have lower rates of ownership. The subjective survival probabilities show no consistent pattern.

11.2.3 Portfolio Theory and Portfolio Choice

The clearest test of the applicability of portfolio theory to the observed portfolio choices by the elderly comes from a comparison of the determinants of the holdings of stocks with the determinants of the holdings of CDs. Both types of assets have fairly small transactions costs; neither produces a flow of services, and neither requires an active involvement of the holder of the asset. The rate of return on stocks is high, and the variance is high over the short to medium term. The rate of return on CDs is low, and the variance is low.

Of the variables that explain the rates of asset ownership, portfolio theory gives the most straightforward prediction about the relative effects of social security income and a somewhat less straightforward prediction for pension income. Under the assumption that social security income is certain, those with relatively high levels should assume more risk. In that an increase in social security also increases resources, which as implied by the coefficients on wealth will, by itself, increase stock and CD ownership, the relevant comparison is the effect on stocks relative to the effect on CDs.

Table 11.12 shows that, indeed, increases in social security income are associated with higher stock ownership relative to CD ownership: for every $1,000 of social security income, stock ownership increases by 6.8 percent (relative to baseline) compared with 3.8 percent in CD ownership. Because baseline stock ownership rates are higher than baseline CD rates, the relative increase translates into larger percentage point differences: an increase of $1,000 in social security income is associated with a 3.0 percentage point increase in stockholdings and with 1.4 percentage point increase in CD holdings (not shown). Thus, for example, a single person with average social security income ($7,240) is about 21 percentage points more likely to hold stocks than a single person with no social security income and about 10 percentage points more likely to hold CDs, for a difference of 11 percentage points. Among couples, the effects of social security income are reduced relative to singles: it has almost no effect on the holdings of CDs and increases stock holdings by about 4 percent relative to baseline. In terms of percentage points, social security increases stockholdings by about 1.9 percentage points and CD holdings by 0.3 percentage points. This differential is almost the same as the differential for singles.

Portfolio theory predicts that risky income will cause less of a risky asset to be held, and the magnitude of the effect will depend on the correlation of the risk to the income with the risk to the asset. It is not clear whether the correlation is positive in the case of pension income and stocks. Most pension income is not indexed, so it is at risk from increases in inflation. Although in the long run, stocks are likely to be effectively indexed, over the short and medium terms they may not be, and at least over some historical periods, the stock market did not perform well when inflation was accelerating. If this were the case, pension income and stocks would have positively correlated risk; then we would expect smaller increases in stock holdings relative to CDs resulting from an increase in pension income than in the case of social security income. As shown in table 11.12 the data are not contradictory simply because pension income has almost no effect on either stock or CD holdings.

Greater wealth is associated with higher rates of ownership of all assets. This is consistent with the view that there are fixed costs of ownership, which could be monetary or informational; with such indivisibilities, those with little wealth will tend to hold only one type of asset. This view would explain the increasing rates of ownership of stocks as wealth increases. Portfolio theory would also predict increasing rates of ownership provided people exhibit decreasing absolute risk aversion (see chapter 1, this volume). However, the same theory would predict a decreasing rate of CD ownership as wealth increases. A comparison between CDs and stocks shows that the steady-state rate of ownership increased at about the same rate for each type of asset as wealth increased, lending support to a fixed-cost explanation.

The effect of the subjective survival probability is quite different for ownership of stocks versus CDs: both respondent and spouse subjective survival probabilities increase ownership rates of stocks, but both decrease rates for CDs. Conditional on the life cycle model, this finding is consistent with portfolio theory if there is decreasing absolute risk aversion. High survival probabilities flatten the consumption path, causing more wealth to be held, and the higher wealth will lead to holding more risky assets. However, this interpretation is rather tenuous in view of the lack of a differential wealth effect as directly measured by the constancy in the relative holdings of stocks and CDs.

11.3 Conclusion

Although not connected with the theory of portfolio choice, a notable finding is that home owning declined in the panel in both value and the rate of ownership. The finding is consistent across age groups and by marital status, and persisted after controlling for covariates by logistic estimation of transition probabilities. These results suggest that downsizing of home owning is the norm, and that prior contradictory findings were due to inadequate data.

A second notable finding is the large increase in bequeathable wealth in the panel. In view of the substantial increases in asset prices, an increase is not surprising. However, it is not obvious how to find desired or anticipated saving rates from the observed changes in wealth in the AHEAD panel.

A third finding concerns the high rate of active portfolio management, especially in the take-up of stocks between the waves. Active portfolio management seems to occur at all the ages in the AHEAD age group as the age effects were small. Holding stocks is becoming the norm for all ages.

The theory of portfolio choice received some support from the comparison of the steady-state rate of owning CDs versus owning stocks as a function of social security income. Other tests provided weak or little support. In particular, the relationship between wealth and the propensities to hold stocks and to hold CDs seems to be more consisted with a fixed-cost explanation. Some support for this view comes from additional estimates of the steady-state holdings as predicted by the same estimation methods as reported in tables 11.8 through 11.11, but where the covariates are augmented by education. Table 11.13 has excerpts from these estimations.[15]

Steady-state holdings of housing have no consistent pattern with education, and there are no significant coefficients. The steady-state holdings of checking are predicted to increase with education; for example, those with zero to eight years of education have a probability of owning checking or savings accounts that is just 0.82 of the probability of those with twelve years of education.

Education is significantly and highly related to the predicted propensity to hold stocks in steady state. The rate is about 3.3 times as great among those with more than twelve years of education than

Table 11.13
Relative steady-state ownership rates: Effects of education

	Asset			
Education level (years)	House	Checking	Stock	CD
0–8	1.064	0.822*	0.374*	0.483*
9–11	1.179	0.919*	0.592*	0.722*
12	1.000	1.000	1.000	1.000
12 or more	1.116	1.014	1.230*	0.903

Note: Based on logit estimation of transitions out of and into ownership. Other covariates as in tables 11.8 to 11.11 included but not shown.
*One or both of the underlying coefficients significant at the 5 percent level.

among those with zero to eight years. These estimations control for wealth, income, age, marital status, and the subjective probability of survival as well as the other covariates in tables 11.8 through 11.11. The likelihood of holding CDs increases in education, although at a smaller rate.

Housing offers a flow of services that all must have regardless of the level of education. To a somewhat lesser extent, the same is true of checking. Ownership of stock and CDs is purely a financial decision that seems to be informed by education, but even between stock and CDs, there are differences related to education. The largest part of the education effect on stock ownership rates comes from the take-up rate: the "risk" of the transition from not owning to owning is higher by a factor of 4.6 among those with more than twelve years of education than among those with zero to eight years of education; the retention rate is higher by a factor of 1.9 (not shown). For CDs, the relative risk of take-up is about 1.6, and the relative risk of retention is 2.4. Thus, as the culture of stock ownership was spreading through the U.S. population, encouraged by lower fees and a wider choice of mutual funds, the educated elderly moved into stock ownership at a much greater rate than the less educated elderly. For CDs, it is the higher retention rate that mainly leads to steady-state CD holdings by the more educated.

Appendix: AHEAD Survey Questions

Following are the survey questions that measured asset holdings in AHEAD. The words in all capitals are interviewer instructions. The letters "F," "K," and "J" reflect the numbering in the questionnaire.

AHEAD Wave 1

F25. Do you (and your (husband/wife/partner)) own your (house/apartment/home), rent it, or what?

K2. Do you (or your (husband/wife/partner)) have any real estate (other than your main home), such as land, a second home, rental real estate, a partnership, or money owed to you on a land contract or mortgage?

K4. What about the value of what you (or your (husband/wife/partner)) own for transportation, like cars, trucks, a trailer, a motor home, a boat, or an airplane—what are they worth altogether, minus anything you still owe on them?

K5. Do you (or your (husband/wife/partner)) own part or all of a business?

K7. Do you (or your (husband/wife/partner)) have any Individual Retirement Accounts, that is, IRA or Keogh accounts?

K10. (Aside from anything you have already told me about,) Do you (or your (husband/wife/partner)) have any shares of stock in publicly held corporations, or mutual funds?

K12. (Aside from anything you have already told me about,) Do you (or your (husband/wife/partner)) have any money in checking or savings accounts, or money market funds?

K14. (Aside from anything you have already told me about,) Do you (or your (husband/wife/partner)) have any money in certificates of deposit, government savings bonds, or Treasury bills?

K16. (Aside from anything you have already told me about,) Do you (or your (husband/wife/partner)) have any corporate, municipal, government, or foreign bonds, or any bond funds?

K21. Do you (or your (husband/wife/partner)) have any other savings or assets, such as jewelry, money owed to you by others, a collection for investment purposes, or an annuity that you haven't already told me about?

[INTERVIEWER: EXCLUDE THE CASH VALUE OF ANY LIFE INSURANCE POLICIES]

K23. And do you (or your (husband/wife/partner)) have any debts that we haven't asked about, such as credit card balances, medical debts, life insurance policy loans, loans from relatives, and so forth?

AHEAD Wave 2

F3. Do you (and your husband/wife/partner) own your home, rent it, or what?

J14. Do you (or your husband/wife/partner) have any real estate (other than your main home or second home), such as land, rental real estate, a partnership, or money owed to you on a land contract or mortgage?

J17. Do you (or your husband/wife/partner) own part or all of a business or farm?

J20. Do you (or your husband/wife/partner) currently have any money or assets that are held in an Individual Retirement Account, that is, in an IRA or KEOGH account?

J36. (Aside from anything you have already told me about ...) Do you (or your husband/wife/partner) have any shares of stock or stock mutual funds?

J40. (Aside from anything you have already told me about ...) Do you (or your husband/wife/partner) have any corporate, municipal, government or foreign bonds, or bond funds?

DO NOT COUNT GOVERNMENT SAVINGS BONDS OR TREASURY BILLS.

J44. (Aside from anything you have already told me about ...) Do you (or your husband/wife/partner) have any checking or savings accounts or money market funds?

J47. (Aside from anything you have already told me about ...) Do you (or your (husband/wife/partner)) have any money in Certificates of Deposit, Government Savings Bonds, or Treasury Bills?

J51. Do you (or your husband/wife/partner) own anything for transportation, like cars, trucks, a trailer, a motor home, a boat, or an airplane?

J52. Do you (or your husband/wife/partner) have any other savings or assets, such as jewelry, money owed to you by others, a collection for investment purposes, rights in a trust or estate where you are the beneficiary, or an annuity that you haven't already told us about?

EXCLUDE THE CASH VALUE OF ANY LIFE INSURANCE POLICIES

J81. And do you (or your husband/wife/partner) have any debts that we haven't asked about, such as credit card balances, medical debts, life insurance policy loans, loans from relatives, and so forth?

Notes

Financial support from the National Institute on Aging through grant 1P20-AG12815-05 to RAND is gratefully acknowledged. Many thanks to Angela Merrill for excellent research assistance.

1. An aged unit is a single person or couple in which at least one person is aged 65 or over.

2. For couples, the financial respondent is the spouse reported by the respondents to be more knowledgeable about the finances of the couple. For singles, the financial respondent is the (sole) respondent.

3. A nested composite imputation procedure was used to handle nonresponse to asset and total income questions. Asset ownership, unfolding brackets, and asset amounts were imputed sequentially. Dollar amounts are based on cross-wave imputation in which a reported value from one wave is used as a covariate in finding the nearest neighbor in the other wave.

4. The survey questions used in waves 1 and 2 are given in the chapter appendix.

5. The means and medians in this table and subsequent tables are weighted to reflect the oversamples and differential nonresponse.

6. In this chapter, a household is either a single person or a couple. The assets of other economically interdependent persons, whether related or not, are not included.

7. The fraction of total wealth is the total wealth in the asset divided by total wealth, not the average of the fractions.

8. The entries under "all" are meant to represent the average wealth in the cohort. Were each spouse to enter the calculations, couples could be given twice the weight of singles.

9. AHEAD wave 1 was fielded in October 1993 and completed in April 1994. For examples of rates of return in the stock and bond market, I use December 31, 1993, and December 31, 1995, as the approximate interview dates.

10. There will, of course, still be unobserved portfolio rebalancing, which involves marginal changes in the portfolio.

11. There may be an unusually high rate of home sales following widowing, which would reduce this effect.

12. Thanks to Angus Deaton for suggesting this line of inquiry.

13. The population represented by this table is somewhat different from that of table 11.6 because of missing values on living arrangements.

14. As shown at the bottom of the table, the rate in the lowest quartile is 0.927.

15. The estimated effects of the other covariates are not substantially different from those in tables 11.8 through 11.11, so they are not reported.

References

Abel, A. B. (1990). "Asset Prices Under Habit Formation and Catching Up with the Joneses." *American Economic Review Papers and Proceedings* 80, 38–42.

Abowd, J., and D. Card (1989). "On the Covariance Structure of Earnings and Hours Changes." *Econometrica* 57, 411–445.

Agell, J., and P. A. Edin (1990). "Marginal Taxes and the Asset Portfolios of Swedish Households." *Scandinavian Journal of Economics* 92, 47–64.

Ahn, S., and P. Schmidt (1995). "Efficient Estimation of Models for Dynamic Panel Data." *Journal of Econometrics* 68, 5–27.

Aiyagari, S. R. (1994). "Uninsured Idiosyncratic Risk and Aggregate Saving." *Quarterly Journal of Economics* 109, 659–684.

Alessie, R., S. Hochguertel, and A. van Soest (2000). "Household Portfolios in the Netherlands." Discussion Paper 55. Tilburg: CentER for Economic Research, Tilburg University.

Alessie, R., A. Kapteyn, and F. Klijn (1997). "Mandatory Pensions and Personal Savings in the Netherlands." *De Economist* 145, 291–324.

Alessie, R., A. Lusardi, and A. Kapteyn (1995). "Saving and Wealth Holdings of the Elderly." *Ricerche Economiche* 49, 293–314.

Allen, F., and D. Gale (1994). "Limited Market Participation and Volatility of Asset Prices." *American Economic Review* 84, 933–955.

Amemiya, T. (1985). *Advanced Econometrics*. Oxford: Basil Blackwell.

Amemiya, T., and T. MaCurdy (1986). "Instrumental Variable Estimation of an Error Component Model." *Econometrica* 54, 869–881.

American Council on Capital Formation (1996). *The Case for a Broad-Based Capital Gains Tax Cut*. Washington, D.C.: American Council on Capital Formation.

American Council on Capital Formation (1998). *An International Comparison of Incentives for Retirement Saving and Insurance*. Washington, D.C.: American Council on Capital Formation.

Ameriks, J., and S. P. Zeldes (2000). "How Do Household Portfolio Shares Vary with Age?" Paper presented at the Conference on Household Financial Decision-Making, University of Pennsylvania.

Antoniewicz, R. (1996). "A Comparison of the Household Sector from the Flow of Funds Accounts and the Survey of Consumer Finances." Federal Reserve Board Discussion Paper 96-26. Washington, D.C.: Federal Reserve Board.

Arellano, M., and O. Bover (1995). "Another Look at the Instrumental Variable Estimation of Error-Component Models." *Journal of Econometrics* 68, 29–51.

Arellano, M., and R. Carrasco (1996). "Binary Choice Panel Data with Predetermined Variables." Centro de Estudios Monetario y Financeros (CEMFI) Working Paper 9618. Madrid.

Arellano, M., and B. Honorè (2000). "Panel Data Models: Some Recent Developments." In J. Heckman and E. Leamer, eds., *Handbook of Econometrics*. Amsterdam: North-Holland.

Arrow, K. (1971). *Essays in the Theory of Risk Bearing*. Chicago: Markham Publishing Co.

Attanasio, O. P. (1998). "A Cohort Analysis of Saving Behavior by U.S. Households." *Journal of Human Resources* 33, 575–609.

Attanasio, O., L. Guiso, and T. Jappelli (2001). "The Demand for Money, Financial Innovation and the Welfare Cost of Inflation." *Journal of Political Economy*, forthcoming.

Attanasio, O. P., and H. Hoynes (2000). "Differential Mortality and Wealth Accumulation." *Journal of Human Resources* 35, 1–29.

Attanasio, O. P., and G. Weber (1993). "Consumption Growth, the Interest Rate and Aggregation." *Review of Economic Studies* 60, 631–649.

Auerbach, A. J., and M. A. King (1983). "Taxation, Portfolio Choice, and Debt-Equity Ratios: A General Equilibrium Model." *Quarterly Journal of Economics* 98, 587–609.

Ausubel, L. (1991). "The Failure of Competition in the Credit Card Market." *American Economic Review* 81, 50–81.

Auten, G., and C. Clotfelter (1982). "Permanent vs. Transitory Tax Effects and the Realization of Capital Gains." *Quarterly Journal of Economics* 97, 613–632.

Auten, G., and D. Joulfaian (1996). "Charitable Contributions and Intergenerational Transfers." *Journal of Public Economics* 59, 55–68.

Bakshi, G., and Z. Chen (1996). "The Spirit of Capitalism and Stock-Market Prices." *American Economic Review* 86, 133–157.

Balcer, Y., and K. Judd (1987). "Effects of Capital Gains Taxation on Life-Cycle Investment and Portfolio Management." *Journal of Finance* 42, 743–761.

Balduzzi, P., and A. W. Lynch (1999). "Transaction Costs and Predictability: Some Utility Cost Calculations." *Journal of Financial Economics* 52, 47–78.

Banks, J., and R. Blundell (1994). "Taxation and Savings Incentives in the UK." In J. Poterba, ed., *Household Saving and Public Policy*. Chicago: University of Chicago Press.

Banks, J., A. Dilnot, and H. Low (1995). "Patterns of Financial Wealth Holding in the UK." In J. Hills, ed., *New Inequalities: An Inquiry into the Link Between Income and Wealth*. Cambridge: Cambridge University Press.

Banks, J., and S. Tanner (1999). *Household Saving in the UK*. London: Institute for Fiscal Studies.

Barberis, N. 2000. "Investing for the Long Run When Returns Are Predictable." *Journal of Finance* 55, 225–264.

Barro, R. J. (1974). "Are Government Bonds Net Worth?" *Journal of Political Economy* 82, 1095–1117.

Barsky, R. B., F. T. Juster, M. S. Kimball, and M. D. Shapiro (1997). "Preferences Parameters and Behavioral Heterogeneity: An Experimental Approach in the Health and Retirement Study." *Quarterly Journal of Economics* 112, 537–579.

Baxter, M., and U. J. Jermann (1997). "The International Diversification Puzzle Is Worse Than You Think." *American Economic Review* 87, 170–180.

Bayer, P. J., B. D. Bernheim, and J. K. Scholz (1996). "The Effects of Financial Education in the Workplace: Evidence from a Survey of Employers." NBER Working Paper 5655. Cambridge, MA: National Bureau of Economic Research.

Bernheim, B. D., and D. M. Garrett (1996). "The Determinants and Consequences of Financial Education in the Workplace: Evidence from a Survey of Households." NBER Working Paper 5667. Cambridge, MA: National Bureau of Economic Research.

Bertaut, C. C. (1998). "Stockholding Behavior of U.S. Households: Evidence from the 1983–1989 Survey of Consumer Finances." *Review of Economics and Statistics* 80, 263–275.

Bertaut, C. C., and M. Haliassos (1997). "Precautionary Portfolio Behavior from a Life-Cycle Perspective." *Journal of Economic Dynamics and Control* 21, 1511–1542.

Bertschek, I., and M. Lechner (1998). "Convenient Estimators for the Panel Probit Model." *Journal of Econometrics* 87, 329–371.

Blume, M., J. Crockett, and I. Friend (1974). "Stockownership in the United States: Characteristics and Trends." *Survey of Current Business* 54, 16–40.

Blume, M., and S. P. Zeldes (1994). "Household Stockownership Patterns and Aggregate Pricing Theories." Mimeo. University of Pennsylvania.

Blumenthal, M., and J. Slemrod (1992). "The Compliance Cost of the U.S. Individual Income Tax System." *National Tax Journal* 45, 185–202.

Blundell, R., and A. Duncan (1998). "Kernel Regression in Empirical Microeconomics." *Journal of Human Resources* 33, 62–87.

Bodie, Z., and D. Crane (1997). "Personal Investing: Advice, Theory, and Evidence." *Financial Analysts Journal* 53, 13–23.

Bodie, Z., R. C. Merton, and W. F. Samuelson (1992). "Labor Supply Flexibility and Portfolio Choice in a Life Cycle Model." *Journal of Economic Dynamics and Control* 16, 427–449.

Booth, M. (1998). *Projecting Federal Tax Revenues and the Effect of Changes in Tax Law*. Washington, D.C.: Congressional Budget Office.

Börsch-Supan, A. (1994a). "Savings in Germany—Part I: Incentives." In J. M. Poterba, ed., *Public Policies and Household Saving*. Chicago: University of Chicago Press.

Börsch-Supan, A. (1994b). "Savings in Germany—Part II: Behavior." In J. M. Poterba, ed., *International Comparisons of Household Saving*. Chicago: University of Chicago Press.

Börsch-Supan, A. (1994c). "Housing Market Regulations and Housing Market Performance in the United States, Germany, and Japan." In R. M. Blank, ed., *Social Protection versus Economic Flexibility*. Chicago: University of Chicago Press.

Börsch-Supan, A., and A. Eymann (2000). "Household Portfolios in Germany." Discussion Paper 00-15, Sonderforschungsbereich 504, University of Mannheim.

Börsch-Supan, A., and K. Stahl (1991). "Do Savings Programs Dedicated to Homeownership Increase Personal Savings? An Analysis of the West German Bausparkassensystem." *Journal of Public Economics* 44, 265–297.

Börsch-Supan, A., and J. Winter (2000). "Pension Reform, Savings Behavior and Corporate Governance." Discussion Paper 99-48. Sonderforschungsbereich 504, University of Mannheim.

Börsch-Supan, A., A. Reil-Held, R. Rodepeter, R. Schnabel, and J. Winter (1999). "Ersparnisbildung in Deutschland: Messkonzepte und Ergebnisse auf Basis der EVS." *Allgemeines Statistisches Archiv* 83, 385–415. (The English version of this paper is available as Discussion Paper 99-02, Sonderforschungsbereich 504, University of Mannheim.)

Bovenberg, A. L., and H. ter Rele (1998). "Reforming Dutch Capital Taxation: An Analysis of Incentives to Save and Invest." Research Memorandum 142. The Hague: CPB Netherlands Bureau for Economic Policy Analysis.

Bover, O., and M. Arellano (1997). "Estimating Dynamic Limited Dependent Variable Models from Panel Data." *Investigaciones Economicas* 21, 141–165.

Brandolini, A., and L. Cannari (1994). "Methodological Appendix: The Bank of Italy's Survey of Household Income and Wealth." In A. Ando, L. Guiso, and I. Visco, eds., *Saving, and the Accumulation of Wealth: Essays on Italian Households and Government Behavior*. Cambridge: Cambridge University Press.

Brennan, M. (1970). "Taxes, Market Valuation, and Corporate Financial Policy." *National Tax Journal* 23, 417–427.

Brennan, M., E. Schwartz, and R. Lagnado (1997). "Strategic Asset Allocation." *Journal of Economic Dynamics and Control* 21, 1377–1403.

Brownlee, W. E. (2000). "Historical Perspectives on U.S. Tax Policy Toward the Rich." In J. B. Slemrod, ed., *Does Atlas Shrug? The Economic Consequences of Taxing the Rich*. Cambridge, MA: Harvard University Press.

Brunsbach, S., and O. Lang (1998). Steuervorteile und die Rendite des Lebensversicherungssparens. *Jahrbücher für Nationalökonomie und Statistik* 217, 185–213.

Buchinsky, M. (1998). "Recent Advances in Quantile Regression Models: A Practical Guideline for Empirical Research." *Journal of Human Resources* 33, 88–126.

Budd, A., and N. Campbell (1998). "The Roles of the Public and Private Sectors in the UK Pension System." In M. Feldstein, ed., *Privatizing Social Security*. Chicago: University of Chicago Press.

Burman, L. (1999). *The Labyrinth of Capital Gains Tax Policy*. Washington, D.C.: Urban Institute Press.

Burnside, C. (1999). "Discrete State-Space Methods for the Study of Dynamic Economies." In R. Marimon and A. Scott, eds., *Computational Methods for the Study of Dynamic Economies*. Oxford: Oxford University Press.

Butler, I., and R. Moffitt (1982). "A Computationally Efficient Quadrature Procedure for the One-Factor Multinomial Probit Model." *Econometrica* 50, 761–764.

Calem, P., and L. Mester (1995). "Consumer Behavior and the Stickiness of Credit Card Interest Rates." *American Economic Review* 85, 1327–1336.

Campbell, J. Y. (1987a). "Does Saving Anticipate Declining Labor Income? An Alternative Test of the Permanent Income Hypothesis." *Econometrica* 55, 1429–1473.

Campbell, J. Y. (1987b). "Stock Returns and the Term Structure." *Journal of Financial Economics* 18, 373–399.

Campbell, J. Y. (1991). "A Variance Decomposition of Stock Returns." *Economic Journal* 101, 157–179.

Campbell, J. Y. (1996). "Understanding Risk and Return." *Journal of Political Economy* 104, 298–345.

Campbell, J. Y., J. Cocco, F. J. Gomes, P. J. Maenhout, and L. Viceira (1998). "Stock Market Mean Reversion and the Optimal Allocation of a Long Lived Investor." Mimeo. Harvard University.

Campbell, J. Y., and J. Cochrane (1999). "By Force of Habit: A Consumption Based Explanation of Aggregate Stock Market Behavior." *Journal of Political Economy* 107, 205–251.

Campbell, J. Y., and H. Keun Koo (1997). "A Comparison of Numerical and Analytical Approximate Solutions to an Intertemporal Consumption Choice Problem." *Journal of Economic Dynamics and Control* 21, 273–295.

Campbell, J. Y., A. Lo, and C. MacKinlay (1997). *The Econometrics of Financial Markets*. Princeton, NJ: Princeton University Press.

Campbell, J. Y., and R. J. Shiller (1988). "Stock Prices, Earnings, and Expected Dividends." *Journal of Finance* 43, 661–676.

Campbell, J. Y., and L. Viceira (1999). "Consumption and Portfolio Decisions When Expected Returns Are Time Varying." *Quarterly Journal of Economics* 114, 433–495.

Campbell, J. Y., and L. M. Viceira (2000). *Strategic Asset Allocation: Portfolio Choice for Long-Term Investors*. Oxford: Oxford University Press.

Carroll, C. D. (1992). "The Buffer-Stock Theory of Saving: Some Macroeconomic Evidence." *Brookings Papers on Economic Activity* 2, 61–156.

Carroll, C. D. (1997). "Buffer-Stock Saving and the Life Cycle/Permanent Income Hypothesis." *Quarterly Journal of Economics* 112, 1–56.

Carroll, C. D. (2000). "Why Do the Rich Save So Much?" In J. B. Slemrod, ed., *Does Atlas Shrug? The Economic Consequences of Taxing the Rich*. Cambridge, MA: Harvard University Press.

Carroll, C. D., and A. Samwick (1998). "How Important Is Precautionary Saving?" *Review of Economics and Statistics* 80, 410–419.

Cecchetti, S. G. (1999). "Legal Structure, Financial Structure, and the Monetary Policy Transmission Mechanism." NBER Working Paper 7151.

Cesari, R., and F. Panetta (1998). "Style, Fees, and Performance of Italian Equity Funds." Bank of Italy, Temi di Discussione n. 325.

Chamberlain, G. (1980). "Analysis of Covariance with Qualitative Data." *Review of Economic Studies* 47, 225–238.

Chamberlain, G. (1984). "Panel Data." In Z. Griliches and M. Intriligator, eds., *Handbook of Econometrics*, Vol. 3. Amsterdam: North-Holland.

Chamberlain, G. (1985). "Heterogeneity, Omitted Variable Bias and Duration Dependence." In J. Heckman and B. Singer, eds., *Longitudinal Analysis of Labour Market Data*. Cambridge: Cambridge University Press.

Chamberlain, G. (1987). "Asymptotic Efficiency in Estimation with Conditional Moment Restrictions." *Journal of Econometrics* 34, 305–334.

Charlier, E., B. Melenberg, and A. van Soest (1995). "A Smoothed Maximum Score Estimator for the Binary Choice Panel Data Model with an Application to Labor Force Participation." *Statistica Neerlandica* 49, 324–343.

Chaudhuri, A., and R. Mukerjee (1988). *Randomized Response Theory and Techniques*. New York: Dekker.

Chiteji, N. S., and F. P. Stafford (1999). "Portfolio Choices of Parents and Their Children as Young Adults: Asset Accumulation by African-American Families." *American Economic Review Papers and Proceedings* 89, 377–380.

Cocco, J. (1998). "Owner Occupied Housing, Permanent Income, and Portfolio Choice." Mimeo. Harvard University.

Cocco, J. (1999). "Portfolio Choice in the Presence of Illiquid Durable Consumption Goods and Nontradable Income." Mimeo. Harvard University.

Cocco, J., F. J. Gomes, and P. J. Maenhout (1999). "Consumption and Portfolio Choice over the Life-Cycle." Mimeo. Harvard University.

Cochrane, J. (1999). "New Facts in Finance." *Economic Perspectives* (Federal Reserve Bank of Chicago) 23, 36–58.

Constantinides, G. M. (1984). "Optimal Stock Trading with Personal Taxes: Implications for Prices and the Abnormal January Returns." *Journal of Financial Economics* 13, 65–89.

Constantinides, G. M. (1990). "Habit Formation: A Resolution of the Equity Premium Puzzle." *Journal of Political Economy* 98, 519–543.

Constantinides, G. M., J. Donaldson, and R. Mehra (1998). "Junior Can't Borrow: A New Perspective on the Equity Premium Puzzle." Mimeo. University of Chicago.

Consumentenbond (1999). *Jaarboek Beleggen 1999*. Utrecht: Kosmos.

Cosslett, S. (1981). "Maximum Likelihood Estimators for Choice-Based Samples." *Econometrica* 49, 1289–1316.

Cosslett, S. (1993). "Estimation from Endogenously Stratified Samples'." In G. S. Maddala, C. R. Rao, and H. D. Vinod, eds., *Handbook of Statistics*, Vol. 11. Amsterdam: North-Holland.

Cosslett, S. (1997). "Nonparametric Maximum Likelihood Methods." In G. S. Maddala and C. R. Rao, eds., *Handbook of Statistics*, Vol. 15. Amsterdam: North-Holland.

Cox, D., and T. Japelli (1993). "The Effect of Borrowing Constraints on Consumer Liabilities." *Journal of Money, Credit, and Banking* 25, 445–454.

Cragg, J. (1971). "Some Statistical Models for Limited Dependent Variables with Application to the Demand for Durable Goods." *Econometrica* 39, 829–844.

Das, M., and B. Donkers (1999). "How Certain Are Dutch Households About Future Income? An Empirical Analysis." *Review of Income and Wealth* 45, 325–338.

Davies, J., and A. Shorrocks (2000). "The Distribution of Wealth." In A. B. Atkinson and F. Bourguignon, eds., *The Handbook of Income Distribution*. Amsterdam: North-Holland.

Davis, S., and P. Willen (2000). "Occupation-level Income Shocks and Asset Returns: Their Covariance and Implications for Portfolio Choice." NBER Working Paper 7905. Cambridge, MA: National Bureau of Economic Research.

Deaton, A. (1985). "Panel Data from a Time-series of Cross-Sections." *Journal of Econometrics* 30, 109–126.

Deaton, A. (1991). "Saving and Liquidity Constraints." *Econometrica* 59, 1221–1248.

Deaton, A. (1997). *The Analysis of Household Surveys*. Washington: The World Bank Press.

Deaton, A., and G. Laroque (1992). "On the Behavior of Commodity Prices." *Review of Economic Studies* 59, 1–23.

Deaton, A., and G. Laroque (1995). "Estimating a Nonlinear Rational Expectations Commodity Price Model with Unobservable State Variables." *Journal of Applied Econometrics* 10, S9–S40.

Deaton, A., and G. Laroque (1996). "Competitive Storage and Commodity Price Dynamics." *Journal of Political Economy* 104, 896–923.

Deaton, A., and C. Paxson (1994a). "Intertemporal Choice and Inequality." *Journal of Political Economy* 102, 437–467.

Deaton, A., and C. Paxson (1994b). "Saving, Growth, and Aging in Taiwan." In D. Wise, ed., *Studies in the Economics of Aging*. Chicago: University of Chicago Press.

den Haan, W. J. (1996). "Heterogeneity, Aggregate Uncertainty, and the Short Term Interest Rate." *Journal of Business and Economic Statistics* 14, 399–411.

Deutsche Börse (1999). *Deutsche Börse Information Products: Fact Book 1999.*

Deutsche Bundesbank (1988). "Investmentsparen im Aufwind—Zur Entwicklung des Investmentsparens in den achtziger Jahren." *Deutsche Bundesbank Monthly Report*, October, 32–39.

Deutsche Bundesbank (1992). "Die Entwicklung des Geld- und Sachvermögens westdeutscher privater Haushalte in den letzten zwanzig Jahren." *Deutsche Bundesbank Monthly Report*, April, 14–20.

Deutsche Bundesbank (1993). "Zur Vermögenssituation der privaten Haushalte in Deutschland." *Deutsche Bundesbank Monthly Report*, October, 19–32.

Deutsche Bundesbank (1994a). "Entwicklung und Bedeutung der Geldanlage in Investmentzertifikaten." *Deutsche Bundesbank Monthly Report*, October, 49–70.

Deutsche Bundesbank (1994b). "Ergebnisse der gesamtwirtschaftlichen Finanzierungsrechnung für Westdeutschland 1960 bis 1992." *Deutsche Bundesbank Monthly Report*.

Deutsche Bundesbank (1994c). "Aufkommen und ökonomische Auswirkungen des steuerlichen Zinsabschlags." *Deutsche Bundesbank Monthly Report*, January, 45–57.

Deutsche Bundesbank (1999a). "Changes in Households' Asset Situation Since the Beginning of the Nineties." *Deutsche Bundesbank Monthly Report*, January.

Deutsche Bundesbank (1999b). "Ergebnisse der gesamtwirtschaftlichen Finanzierungsrechnung für Deutschland 1990 bis 1998." *Deutsche Bundesbank Monthly Report*.

Deutsche Bundesbank (1999c). "Zur Entwicklung der privaten Vermögenssituation seit Beginn der Neunziger Jahre." *Deutsche Bundesbank Monthly Report*, January, 33–50.

Dicks-Mireaux, L.-D. L., and M. A. King (1983). "Portfolio Composition and Pension Wealth: An Econometric Study." In Z. Bodie and J. Shoven, eds., *Financial Aspects of the U.S. Pension System*. Chicago: University of Chicago Press.

Dickson, J., and J. B. Shoven (1995). "Taxation and Mutual Funds: An Investor Perspective." In J. Poterba, ed., *Tax Policy and the Economy*, Vol. 9. Cambridge, MA: MIT Press.

Donkers, B., B. Melenberg, and A. van Soest (1999). "Estimating Risk Attitudes Using Lotteries: A Large Sample Approach." *Journal of Risk and Uncertainty*, (forthcoming).

Donkers, B., and A. van Soest (1999). "Subjective Measures of Household Preferences and Financial Decisions." *Journal of Economic Psychology* 20, 613–642.

Duesenberry, J. S. (1949). *Incomes, Saving and the Theory of Consumer Behavior*. Cambridge, MA: Harvard University Press.

Dynan, K. E., J. S. Skinner, and S. P. Zeldes (2000). "Do the Rich Save More?" NBER Working Paper 7906. Cambridge, MA: National Bureau of Economic Research.

Eeckhoudt, L., and C. Gollier (1995). *Risk: Evaluation, Management and Sharing*. New York: Simon & Schuster.

Elton, E., and M. Gruber (1970). "Taxes and Portfolio Composition" *Journal of Financial Economics* 6, 399–410.

Emmerson, C., and S. Tanner (2000). "A Note on the Tax Treatment of Pensions and Individual Savings Accounts." *Fiscal Studies* 21, 65–74.

Employee Benefit Research Institute (1998). "U.S. Retirement Income System." EBRI Fact Sheet, December.

Engen, E., and W. G. Gale (1997). "Debt, Taxes, and the Effects of 401(k) Plans on Household Wealth Accumulation." Mimeo. Brookings Institution.

Engen, E., W. Gale, and C. Uccello (1999). "The Adequacy of Retirement Saving." *Brookings Papers on Economic Activity* 2, 65–165.

Epstein, L., and S. Zin (1989). "Substitution, Risk Aversion and the Temporal Behavior of Consumption and Asset Returns: A Theoretical Framework." *Econometrica* 57, 937–968.

Euler, M. (1985). "Geldvermögen privater Haushalte Ende 1983." *Wirtschaft und Statistik* 5, 408–418.

Euler, M. (1990). "Geldvermögen und Schulden privater Haushalte Ende 1988." *Wirtschaft und Statistik* 11, 798–808.

Euler, M. (1992). "Einkommens- und Verbrauchsstichprobe 1993." *Wirtschaft und Statistik* 7, 463–469.

Eymann, A. (2000). "Portfolio Choice and Knowledge." Mimeo. University of Mannheim.

Eymann, A., A. Börsch-Supan, and R. Euwals (2000). "Portfolio Choice with Behavioral Decision Mechanisms." Discussion Paper 1999-37. Sonderforschungsbereich 504, University of Mannheim.

Fama, E. F., and K. R. French (1988). "Dividend Yields and Expected Stock Returns." *Journal of Financial Economics* 22, 3–25.

Fama, E. F., and K. R. French (1989). "Business Conditions and Expected Returns on Stocks and Bonds." *Journal of Financial Economics* 25, 23–49.

Feenberg, D. R., and J. M. Poterba (1991). "Which Households Own Municipal Bonds? Evidence from Tax Returns." *National Tax Journal* 44, 93–103.

Feldstein, M. S. (1976). "Personal Taxation and Portfolio Composition: An Econometric Analysis." *Econometrica* 44, 631–649.

Fitzenberger, B. (1997). "A Guide to Censored Quantile Regressions." In G. S. Maddala and C. R. Rao, eds., *Handbook of Statistics*, Vol. 15. Amsterdam: North-Holland.

Flavin, M., and T. Yamashita (1998). "Owner-Occupied Housing and the Composition of the Household Portfolio Over the Life-Cycle." NBER Working Paper 6389. Cambridge, MA: National Bureau of Economic Research.

Flood, R. P., R. J. Hodrick, and P. Kaplan (1994). "An Evaluation of Recent Evidence on Stock Market Bubbles." In P. M. Garber and R. P. Flood., eds., *Speculative Bubbles, Speculative Attacks and Policy Switching*. Cambridge, MA: MIT Press.

Fox, J., and P. Tracy (1986). *Randomized Response: A Method for Sensitive Surveys*. London: Sage.

Fratantoni, M. C. (1998). "Income Uncertainty and the Equity Premium Puzzle." Mimeo. Johns Hopkins University.

Friedman, M. A. (1957). *A Theory of the Consumption Function*. Princeton, NJ: Princeton University Press.

Gakidis, H. (1998). "Stocks for the Old? Earnings Uncertainty and Life-Cycle Portfolio Choice." Unpublished Ph.D. dissertation, MIT.

Gentry, W. M., and R. G. Hubbard (1998). "Why Do the Wealthy Save So Much? Saving and Investment Decisions of Entrepreneurs." Mimeo. Columbia University.

Gollier, C. (1995). "The Comparative Statics of Changes in Risk Revisited." *Journal of Economic Theory* 66, 522–536.

Gollier, C., and J. W. Pratt (1996). "Risk Vulnerability and the Tempering Effect of Background Risk." *Econometrica* 64, 1109–1124.

Gollier, C., and R. J. Zeckhauser (1998). "Horizon Length and Portfolio Risk." Mimeo. University of Toulouse.

Gourieroux, C., A. Tiomo, and A. Trognon (1997). "The Portfolio Composition of Households: A Scoring Analysis from French Data." Centre de Recherche en Economie et Statistique (CREST) Working Paper 9706. Paris.

Gourinchas, P., and J. Parker (1999). "Consumption over the Life Cycle." Mimeo. Princeton University.

Grad, S. (1994). "Income of the Population 55 or Older, 1992." Washington, D.C.: U.S. Department of Health and Human Services, Social Security Administration.

Greene, W. H. (1997). *Econometric Analysis*. New York: Macmillan.

Grimm, M. (1998). "Die Verteilung von Geld- und Grundvermögen auf sozioökonomische Gruppen im Jahr 1988 und Vergleich mit früheren Ergebnissen." University of Frankfurt Discussion Paper 14.

Guiso, L., and T. Jappelli (2000). "Household Portfolios in Italy." Center for Economic Policy Research DP. n. 2549.

Guiso, L., T. Jappelli, and D. Terlizzese (1994). "Why Is Italy's Saving Rate So High?" In Albert Ando, Luigi Guiso and Ignazio Visco, eds., *Savings and the Accumulation of Wealth. Essays on Italian Households and Government Saving Behavior*. Cambridge: Cambridge University Press.

Guiso, L., T. Jappelli, and D. Terlizzese (1996). "Income Risk, Borrowing Constraints and Portfolio Choice." *American Economic Review* 86, 158–171.

Hajivassiliou, V., and P. Ruud (1994). "Classical Estimation Methods for LDV Models Using Simulation." In R. Engle and D. McFadden, eds., *Handbook of Econometrics*, Vol. 4. Amsterdam: North-Holland.

Haliassos, M., and C. C. Bertaut (1995). " Why Do So Few Hold Stocks?" *Economic Journal* 105, 1110–1129.

Haliassos, M., and C. Hassapis (1998). "Borrowing Constraints, Portfolio Choice, and Precautionary Motives." Mimeo. University of Cyprus.

Haliassos, M., and C. Hassapis (2000). "Equity Culture and Household Behavior." Mimeo. University of Cyprus.

Haliassos, M., and C. Hassapis (2001). "Non-expected Utility, Saving, and Portfolios." *Economic Journal* 110, 69–102.

Haliassos, M., and A. Michaelides (1999). "Portfolio Choice and Liquidity Constraints." Forthcoming in *International Economic Review*.

Haliassos, M., and A. Michaelides (2000). "Calibration and Computation of Household Portfolio Models." Mimeo. University of Cyprus.

Hansen, L., and J. Heckman (1996). "The Empirical Foundations of Calibration." *Journal of Economic Perspectives* 10, 87–104.

Harris, C., and D. Laibson (1999). "Dynamic Choices and Hyperbolic Consumers." Mimeo. Harvard University.

Heaton, J., and D. Lucas (1996). "Evaluating the Effects of Incomplete Markets on Risk Sharing and Asset Pricing." *Journal of Political Economy* 104, 443–487.

Heaton, J., and D. Lucas (1997). "Market Frictions, Savings Behavior, and Portfolio Choice." *Macroeconomic Dynamics* 1, 76–101.

Heaton, J., and D. Lucas (2000a). "Asset Pricing and Portfolio Choice: The Role of Entrepreneurial Risk." *Journal of Finance* 55, 1163–1198.

Heaton, J., and D. Lucas (2000b). "Portfolio Choice in the Presence of Background Risk." *Economic Journal* 109, 1–25.

Heckman, J. (1979). "Sample Selection Bias as a Specification Error." *Econometrica* 47, 153–161.

Heckman, J. (1981a). "Statistical Models for Discrete Panel Data." In C. Manski and D. McFadden, eds., *Structural Analysis of Discrete Data with Econometric Applications.* Cambridge, MA: MIT Press.

Heckman, J. (1981b). "The Incidental Parameters Problem and the Problem of Initial Conditions in Estimating a Discrete Time—Discrete Data Stochastic Process." In C. Manski and D. McFadden, eds., *Structural Analysis of Discrete Data with Econometric Applications.* Cambridge, MA: MIT Press.

Heitjan, D., and D. Rubin (1990). "Inference from Coarse Data via Multiple Imputation with Application to Age Heaping." *Journal of the American Statistical Association* 85, 304–314.

Himmelreicher, R. K. (1999). "Westdeutsche Haushalte und ihr Vermögen. Eine Längsschnitt-Kohortenanalyse auf Basis des SOEP (1985–1996)." Mimeo. University of Bremen.

Hochguertel, S. (1997). "Precautionary Motives and Portfolio Decisions." Mimeo. Tilburg University.

Hochguertel, S. (1998). "A Buffer Stock Model with Portfolio Choice: Implications of Income Risk and Liquidity Constraints." Mimeo. Uppsala University.

Hochguertel, S., R. Alessie, and A. van Soest (1997). "Saving Accounts versus Stocks and Bonds in Household Portfolio Allocation." *Scandinavian Journal of Economics* 99, 81–97.

Hodrick, R. (1992). "Dividend Yields and Expected Stock Returns: Alternative Procedures for Inference and Measurement." *Review of Financial Studies* 5, 357–386.

Holtz-Eakin, D., H. S. Rosen, and D. Joulfaian (1994). "Entrepreneurial Decisions and Liquidity Constraints." *RAND Journal of Economics* 25, 334–347.

Honoré, B. (1992). "Trimmed LAD and Least Square Estimation of Truncated and Censored Regression Models with Fixed Effects." *Econometrica* 60, 533–565.

Honoré, B. (1993). "Orthogonality Conditions for Tobit Models with Fixed Effects and Lagged Dependent Variables." *Journal of Econometrics* 59, 35–61.

Honoré, B. (1998). "IV Estimation of Panel Data Tobit Models with Normal Errors." Mimeo. Princeton University.

Honoré, B., and E. Kyriazidou (2000a). "Estimation of Tobit-Type Models with Individual Specific Effects." *Econometric Reviews* 19(3), 341–366.

Honoré, B., and E. Kyriazidou (2000b). "Panel Data Discrete Choice Models with Lagged Dependent Variables." *Econometrica* 68(4), 839–874.

Horowitz, J. (1992). "A Smoothed Maximum Score Estimator for the Binary Response Model." *Econometrica* 60, 505–531.

Horowitz, J. (1993). "Semiparametric and Nonparametric Estimation of Quantal Response Models." In G. S. Maddala, C. R. Rao, and H. D. Vinod, eds., *Handbook of Statistics*, Vol. 11. Amsterdam: North-Holland.

Hoynes, H., and D. McFadden (1997). "The Impact of Demographics on Housing and Non-Housing Wealth in the United States." In M. D. Hurd and N. Yashiro, eds., *The Economic Effects of Aging in the United States and Japan*. Chicago: University of Chicago Press.

Hubbard, R. G. (1985). "Personal Taxation, Pension Wealth, and Portfolio Composition." *Review of Economics and Statistics* 67, 53–60.

Hubbard, R. G., J. Skinner, and S. Zeldes (1994). "The Importance of Precautionary Motives for Explaining Individual and Aggregate Saving." In A. Meltzer and C. I. Plosser, eds., *The Carnegie Rochester Conference Series on Public Policy*, 40. Amsterdam: North-Holland.

Hubbard, R. G., J. Skinner, and S. Zeldes (1995). "Precautionary Saving and Social Insurance." *Journal of Political Economy* 103, 360–399.

Huggett, M. (1993). "The Risk-Free Rate in Heterogeneous-Agent Incomplete-Insurance Economies." *Journal of Economic Dynamics and Control* 17, 953–969.

Huggett, M. (1996). "Wealth Distribution in Life Cycle Economies." *Journal of Monetary Economics* 38, 469–494.

Hurd, M. D. (1987). "Savings of the Elderly and Desired Bequests." *American Economic Review* 77, 298–312.

Hurd, M. D. (1995). "Mortality Risk and Consumption by Couples." Paper presented at the IFS-Bank of Portugal Conference on the Microeconomics of Saving and Consumption Growth, Lisbon, November.

Hurd, M. D., D. McFadden, and A. Merrill (2001). "Predictors of Mortality among the Elderly." In D. Wise, ed., *Themes in the Economics of Aging*. University of Chicago Press.

Hurd, M. D., and J. B. Shoven (1985). "Inflation Vulnerability, Income, and Wealth of the Elderly, 1969–1979." In M. David and T. Smeeding, eds., *Horizontal Equity, Uncertainty, and Economic Well-Being*. Chicago: University of Chicago Press.

Hurd, M., and D. Wise (1989). "The Wealth and Poverty of Widows: Assets Before and After the Husband's Death." In D. Wise, ed., *The Economics of Aging*. The University of Chicago Press, pp. 177–199.

Inland Revenue (1999). *Inland Revenue Statistics*. London: Her Majesty's Stationary Office.

Investment Company Institute (1998). *Mutual Fund Fact Book*. Washington, D.C.: Investment Company Institute.

Jagannathan, R., and N. R. Kocherlakota (1996). "Why Should Older People Invest Less in Stocks Than Younger People?" *Federal Reserve Bank of Minneapolis Quarterly Review* 20, 11–23.

Jappelli, T. (1990). "Who Is Credit Constrained in the U.S. Economy?" *Quarterly Journal of Economics* 105, 219–234.

Jianakoplos, N., and A. Bernasek (1998). "Are Women More Risk Averse?" *Economic Inquiry* 36, 620–630.

Johnson, B., and M. Britton Eller (1998). "Federal Taxation of Inheritance and Wealth Transfers." In *Turning Administrative Systems into Information Systems 1996–1997*. Washington, D.C.: Internal Revenue Service.

Johnson, P., and S. Tanner (1998). "Ownership and the Distribution of Wealth." *Political Quarterly* 69, 365–377.

Joulfaian, D. (1998). "The Federal Estate and Gift Tax: Description, Profile of Taxpayers, and Economic Consequences." OTA Paper 80. Department of the Treasury, Office of Tax Analysis.

Judd, K. L. (1998). *Numerical Methods in Economics*. Cambridge, MA: MIT Press.

Juster, F., and J. Smith (1997). "Improving the Quality of Economic Data: Lessons from HRS and AHEAD." *Journal of American Statistical Association* 92, 1268–1278.

Kahneman, D., P. P. Wakker, and R. Sarin (1997). "Back to Bentham? Explorations of Experienced Utility." *Quarterly Journal of Economics* 112, 375–406.

Kasten, R., F. Sammartino, and D. Weiner (1998). "Estimates of Federal Tax Liabilities for Individuals and Families by Income Category and Family Type for 1995 and 1999." Washington, D.C.: Congressional Budget Office, Report to the House and Senate Budget Committees and the House Ways and Means Committee.

Kennickell, A. B., and M. Starr-McCluer (1997). "Household Saving and Portfolio Change: Evidence from the 1983–89 SCF Panel." *Review of Income and Wealth* 43, 1–19.

Kennickell, A. B., M. Starr-McCluer, and A. E. Sunden (1996). "Financial Advice and Household Portfolios." Mimeo. Federal Reserve Board.

Kennickell, A. B., M. Starr-McCluer, and B. Surette (2000). "Recent Changes in U.S. Family Finances: Results from the 1998 Survey of Consumer Finances." *Federal Reserve Bulletin*, January, 1–29.

Kim, S. (1992). *Sozialversicherungskapital und das Sparen der privaten Haushalte in der Bundesrepublik Deutschland von 1961 bis 1988*. Hamburg: Verlag Dr. Kovač.

Kimball, M. S. (1990). "Precautionary Saving in the Small and in the Large." *Econometrica* 58, 53–73.

Kimball, M. (1992). "Precautionary Motives for Holding Assets." In John Eatwell, Murray Milgate and Peter Newman, eds., *The New Palgrave Dictionary of Money and Finance*. London: MacMillan.

Kimball, M. S. (1993). "Standard Risk Aversion." *Econometrica* 61, 589–611.

King, M., and L-D. Dicks-Mireaux (1982). "Asset Holdings and the Life Cycle." *Economic Journal* 92, 247–267.

King, M. A., and D. Fullerton (1984). *The Taxation of Income from Capital.* Chicago: University of Chicago Press.

King, M. A., and J. I. Leape (1987). "Asset Accumulation, Information, and the Life Cycle." NBER Working Paper 2392. Cambridge, MA: National Bureau of Economic Research.

King, M. A., and J. I. Leape (1998). "Wealth and Portfolio Composition: Theory and Evidence." *Journal of Public Economics* 69, 155–193.

Kleijn, J. de (1999). "Vermogensverdeling 1997." *Sociaal Economische Maandstatistiek* 6, 24–27.

Kocherlakota, N. R. (1996). "The Equity Premium: It's Still a Puzzle." *Journal of Economic Literature* 34, 42–71.

Koo, H. K. (1995). "Consumption and Portfolio Selection with Labor Income I: Evaluation of Human Capital." Mimeo.

Kovenock, D., and M. Rothschild (1987). "Notes on the Effect of Capital Gains Taxation on Non-Austrian Assets." In A. Razin and E. Sadka, eds., *Economic Policy in Theory and Practice.* New York: St. Martin's Press.

Kreps, D. M., and E. L. Porteus (1978). "Temporal Resolution of Uncertainty and Dynamic Choice Theory." *Econometrica* 46, 185–200.

Krusell, P., and A. A. Smith, Jr. (1998). "Income and Wealth Heterogeneity in the Macroeconomy." *Journal of Political Economy* 106, 867–896.

Kydland, F. E., and E. C. Prescott (1982). "Time to Build and Aggregate Fluctuations." *Econometrica* 50, 1345–1370.

Kyriazidou, E. (1995). "Essays in Estimation and Testing of Econometric Models." Ph.D. dissertation, Northwestern University.

Kyriazidou, E. (1997). "Estimation of a Panel Data Sample Selection Model." *Econometrica* 65, 1335–1364.

Kyriazidou, E. (1999). "Estimation of Dynamic Panel Data Sample Selection Models." *Review of Economic Studies,* forthcoming.

Ladd, H. F. (1998). "Evidence on Discrimination in Mortgage Lending." *Journal of Economic Perspectives* 12, 41–62.

Laibson, D. I. (1997). "Golden Eggs and Hyperbolic Discounting." *Quarterly Journal of Economics* 62, 443–479.

Lamont, O. (1998). "Earnings and Expected Returns." *Journal of Finance* 53, 1563–1587.

Lang, O. (1998). *Steueranreize und Geldanlage im Lebenszyklus.* Baden-Baden: Nomos.

Lang, O., K. H. Nöhrbass, and K. Stahl (1997). "On Income Tax Avoidance: The Case of Germany." *Journal of Public Economics* 66, 327–347.

Leape, J. I. (1987). "Taxes and Transaction Costs in Asset Market Equilibrium." *Journal of Public Economics* 33, 1–20.

Lee, L. (1997). "Simulated Maximum Likelihood Estimation of Dynamic Discrete Choice Statistical Models: Some Monte Carlo Results." *Journal of Econometrics* 82, 1–35.

Lee, M. (1999). "A Root-N Consistent Semi-parametric Estimator for Related-Effect Binary Response Panel Data." *Econometrica* 67, 427–433.

Leland, H. E. (1980). "Who Should Buy Portfolio Insurance?" *Journal of Finance* 35, 581–596.

Lettau, M., and S. Ludvigson (1999). "Consumption, Aggregate Wealth and Expected Stock Returns." Mimeo. Federal Reserve Bank of New York.

Long, J. B. Jr. (1997). "Efficient Portfolio Choice with Differential Taxation of Dividends and Capital Gains." *Journal of Financial Economics* 5, 25–53.

Loury, G. C. (1998). "Why More Blacks Don't Invest." *New York Times*, June 6, 70–71.

Ludvigson, S. (1999). "Consumption and Credit: A Model of Time Varying Liquidity Constraints." *Review of Economics and Statistics* 81, 434–447.

Luttmer, E. G. J. (1999). "What Level of Fixed Costs Can Reconcile Consumption and Stock Returns?" *Journal of Political Economy* 107, 969–997.

MaCurdy, T. E. (1981). "The Use of Time Series Processes to Model the Error Structure of Earnings in Longitudinal Data Analysis." *Journal of Econometrics* 18, 83–114.

Maddala, G. (1983). *Limited Dependent and Qualitative Variables in Econometrics*. New York: Cambridge University Press.

Maki, D. M. (1996). "Portfolio Shuffling and Tax Reform." *National Tax Journal* 49, 317–329.

Malkiel, B. G. (1996). *A Random Walk Down Wall Street: Including a Life-Cycle Guide to Personal Investing*. 6th ed. New York: Norton.

Mankiw, N. G., and D. N. Weil (1989). "The Baby Boom, the Baby Bust, and the Housing Market." *Regional Science and Urban Economics* 19, 235–258.

Mankiw, N. G., and S. Zeldes (1991). "The Consumption of Stockholders and Non-Stockholders." *Journal of Financial Economics* 29, 97–112.

Manski, C. (1987). "Semiparametric Analysis of Random Effects Linear Models from Binary Panel Data." *Econometrica* 55, 357–362.

Manski, C., and S. Lerman (1977). "The Estimation of Choice Probabilities from Choice-Based Samples." *Econometrica* 45, 1977–1998.

Markowitz, H. (1952). "Portfolio Selection." *Journal of Finance* 7, 77–91.

McCullagh, P., and J. Nelder (1983). "Quasi-likelihood Functions." *Annals of Statistics* 11, 59–67.

McDonald, R. (1983). "Government Debt and Private Leverage." *Journal of Public Economics* 22, 303–325.

McFadden, D. (1994). "Demographics, the Housing Market, and the Welfare of the Elderly." In D. Wise, ed., *Studies in the Economics of Aging*. Chicago: University of Chicago Press.

Mehra, R., and E. Prescott (1985). "The Equity Premium: A Puzzle." *Journal of Monetary Economics* 10, 335–339.

Merton, R. C. (1969). "Lifetime Portfolio Selection Under Uncertainty: The Continuous-Time Case." *Review of Economics and Statistics* 51, 247–257.

Merton, R. C. (1971). "Optimum Consumption and Portfolio Rules in a Continuous Time Model." *Journal of Economic Theory* 3, 373–413.

Merton, R. C. (1973). "An Intertemporal Capital Asset Pricing Model." *Econometrica* 41, 867–887.

Michaelides, A. (1999). "Portfolio Choice, Liquidity Constraints and Stock Market Mean Reversion." Mimeo. University of Cyprus.

Michaelides, A., and S. Ng (1997). "Estimating the Rational Expectations Model of Speculative Storage: A Monte Carlo Comparison of Three Simulation Estimators." *Journal of Econometrics* 96, 231–266.

Miller, M. (1977). "Debt and Taxes." *Journal of Finance* 32, 261–275.

Modigliani, F., and R. Brumberg (1954). "Utility Analysis and the Consumption Function: An Interpretation of Cross-Section Data." In K. K. Kurihara, ed., *Post-Keynesian Economics*. New Brunswick, NJ: Rutgers University Press .

Modigliani, F., and R. Brumberg (1979). "Utility Analysis and the Consumption Function: An Attempt at Integration." In A. Abel, ed., *The Collected Papers of Franco Modigliani*, Vol. 2. Cambridge: MIT Press.

Mossin, J. (1968). "Optimal Multiperiod Portfolio Policies." *Journal of Business* 41, 215–229.

Muellbauer, J., and Murphy, A. (1990). "Is the UK Balance of Payments Sustainable?" *Economic Policy* 11, 345–383.

Newey, W. (1990). "Efficient Instrumental Variables Estimation of Nonlinear Models." *Econometrica* 59, 809–839.

Ng, Y. K. (1997). "A Case for Happiness, Cardinalism, and Interpersonal Comparability." *Economic Journal* 107, 1848–1858.

Nyhus, E. K. (1996). "The VSB-CentER Savings Project: Data Collection Methods, Questionnaires and Sampling Procedures." VSB-CentER Savings Project Progress Report 42. Tilburg University.

Orsi, R., and S. Pastorello (1999). "La composizione del portafoglio delle famiglie italiane: un modello a fattori per variabili qualitative." In *Ricerche quantitative per la politica economica—1997*. Rome: Banca d'Italia.

Oswald, A. J. (1997). "Happiness and Economic Performance." *Economic Journal* 107, 1815–1831.

Paxson, C. (1990). "Borrowing Constraints and Portfolio Choice." *Quarterly Journal of Economics* 105, 535–543.

Pension Provision Group (1998). *We All Need Pensions: The Prospects for Pension Provision*. London: Stationary Office.

Perraudin, W., and B. Sørensen (2000). "The Demand for Risky Assets: Sample Selection and Household Portfolios." *Journal of Econometrics* 97, 117–144.

Pischke, J. S. (1995). "Individual Income, Incomplete Information and Aggregate Consumption." *Econometrica* 63, 805–840.

Poterba, J. M. (1994a). *International Comparisons of Household Saving*. Chicago: University of Chicago Press.

Poterba, J. M. (1994b). *Public Policies and Household Saving*. Chicago: University of Chicago Press.

Poterba, J. M. (1998). "Population Age Structure and Asset Returns: An Empirical Investigation." NBER Working Paper 6774. Cambridge, MA: National Bureau of Economic Research.

Poterba, J. M. (1999). "Unrealized Capital Gains and the Measurement of After-Tax Portfolio Performance." *Journal of Private Portfolio Management* 1, 23–34.

Poterba, J. M. (2001). "Taxation, Risk-Taking, and Household Portfolio Behavior." In A. Auerbach and M. Feldstein, eds., *Handbook of Public Economics*. Amsterdam: North-Holland.

Poterba, J. M., and A. A. Samwick (1995). "Stock Ownership Patterns, Stock Market Fluctuations, and Consumption." *Brookings Papers on Economic Activity* 2, 295–372.

Poterba, J. M., and A. A. Samwick (1997). "Portfolio Allocations over the Life Cycle." NBER Working Paper 6185. Cambridge, MA: National Bureau of Economic Research.

Poterba, J. M., and A. A. Samwick (1999). "Taxation and Household Portfolio Composition: U.S. Evidence from the 1980s and 1990s." NBER Working Paper 7392. Cambridge, MA: National Bureau of Economic Research.

Powell, J. (1984). "Least Absolute Deviation Estimation for the Censored Regression Model." *Journal of Econometrics* 25, 303–325.

Powell, J. (1987). "Semiparametric Estimation of Bivariate Latent Variable Models." Social Systems Research Institute, University of Wisconsin—Madison. Working Paper 8704.

Pratt, J. (1964). "Risk Aversion in the Small and in the Large." *Econometrica* 32, 122–136.

Pudney, S. (1989). *Modelling Individual Choice: The Econometrics of Corners, Kinks and Holes*. Oxford: Basil Blackwell.

Putnam, R. (1993). "Making Democracy Work." Princeton: Princeton University Press.

Quadrini, V. (1999). "Entrepreneurship, Saving, and Social Mobility." *Journal of Economic Dynamics* 3, 1–40.

Quiggin, J. C. (1982). "A Theory of Anticipated Utility." *Journal of Economic Behavior and Organization* 3, 323–343.

Ramsey, Frank P. (1928). "A Mathematical Theory of Saving." *The Economic Journal* 38, 543–559.

Rea, J. D., and B. K. Reid (1998). "Trends in the Ownership Cost of Equity Mutual Funds." *Investment Company Institute Perspective* 4, 1–16.

Rea, J. D., B. K. Reid, and T. Lee (1999). "Mutual Fund Costs, 1980–1998." *Investment Company Institute Perspective* 5, 1–12.

Rietz, T. A. (1988). "The Equity Risk Premium: A Solution." *Journal of Monetary Economics* 22, 117–131.

Rios-Rull, J. V. (1996). "Life Cycle Economies and Aggregate Fluctuations." *Review of Economic Studies* 63, 465–490.

Ryder, H. E., Jr., and G. M. Heal (1973). "Optimum Growth with Intertemporally Dependent Preferences." *Review of Economic Studies* 40, 1–33.

Samuelson, P. A. (1963). "Risk and Uncertainty: The Fallacy of the Law of Large Numbers." *Scientia* 98, 108–113.

Samuelson, P. A. (1969). "Lifetime Portfolio Selection by Dynamic Stochastic Programming." *Review of Economics and Statistics* 51, 239–246.

Samuelson, P. A. (1989). "The Judgement of Economic Science on Rational Portfolio Management: Indexing, Timing, and Long-horizon Effects." *Journal of Portfolio Management* 16, 4–12.

Samwick, A. (2000). "Portfolio Responses to Taxation: Evidence from the End of the Rainbow." In J. Slemrod, ed., *Does Atlas Shrug?* Cambridge, MA: Harvard University Press.

Schlomann, H. (1992). *Vermögensverteilung und private Altersvorsorge.* Frankfurt am Main: Campus.

Schnabel, R. (1999). "Vermögen und Ersparnis im Lebenszyklus in Westdeutschland." University of Mannheim Discussion Paper 99-43. Sonderforschungsbereich 504.

Scholz, J. K. (1992). "A Direct Examination of the Dividend Clientele Hypothesis." *Journal of Public Economics* 49, 261–285.

Scholz, J. K. (1994). "Portfolio Choice and Tax Progressivity: Evidence from the Surveys of Consumer Finances." In J. Slemrod, ed., *Tax Progressivity and Income Inequality.* New York: Cambridge University Press.

Schönig, W. (1996). *Ersparnisbildung und Vermögensanlage privater Haushalte.* Frankfurt am Main: Peter Lang.

Segal, U., and A. Spivak (1990). "First Order versus Second Order Risk Aversion." *Journal of Economic Theory* 51, 111–125.

Selden, L. (1979). "An OCE Analysis of the Effect of Uncertainty on Saving Under Risk Independence." *Review of Economic Studies* 46, 73–82.

Sheiner, L., and N. Weil (1992). "The Housing Wealth of Aged." NBER Working Paper 4115. Cambridge, MA: National Bureau of Economic Research.

Shiller, Robert J. (2000). "Human Behavior and the Efficiency of the Financial System." In J. B. Taylor and M. Woodford, *Handbook of Macroeconomics.* Amsterdam: North-Holland.

Shorrocks, A. (1975). "The Age-Wealth Relationship: A Cross-Section and Cohort Analysis." *Review of Economics and Statistics* 57, 155–163.

Shoven, J. (1999). "The Location and Allocation of Assets in Pension and Conventional Savings Accounts." NBER Working Paper 7007. Cambridge, MA: National Bureau of Economic Research.

Shoven, J., and C. Sialm (1999). "Asset Location Arbitrage: What's Wrong with the Usual Story?" Mimeo. Stanford University.

Slemrod, J. (1994). *Tax Progressivity and Income Inequality*. New York: Cambridge University Press.

Soldo, B., M. Hurd, W. Rodgers, and R. Wallace (1997). "Asset and Health Dynamics Among the Oldest Old: An Overview of the AHEAD Study." *Journals of Gerontology Series B*, 52B. Special Issue, 1–20.

Spiegel-Verlag (1980). *Spiegel-Dokumentation: Soll und Haben—Eine Untersuchung über Einstellungen zum Geld und den Besitz von Konten, Wertpapieren, Lebensversicherungen und Bausparverträgen*. Hamburg.

Spiegel-Verlag (1985). *Spiegel-Dokumentation: Soll und Haben 2*. Hamburg.

Spiegel-Verlag (1989). *Spiegel-Dokumentation: Soll und Haben 3*. Hamburg.

Spiegel-Verlag (1996). *Spiegel-Dokumentation: Soll und Haben 4*. Hamburg.

Starr-McCluer, M. (2001). "Stock Market Wealth and Consumer Spending." *Economic Inquiry*, forthcoming.

Stehle, R. (1999). "Renditevergleich von Aktien und festverzinslichen Wertpapieren auf Basis des DAX und des REXP." Mimeo. Humboldt-University Berlin.

Stewart, K. J., and S. B. Reed (1999). "Consumer Price Index Research Series Using Current Methods, 1978–98." *Monthly Labor Review* 122, 29–38.

Stewart, M. B. (1983). "On Least Squares Estimation When the Dependent Variable Is Grouped." *Review of Economic Studies* 50, 737–753.

Storesletten, K., C. Telmer, and A. Yaron (1998). "Persistent Idiosyncratic Shocks and Incomplete Markets." Mimeo. Carnegie Mellon University.

Sundaresan, S. M. (1989). "Intertemporally Dependent Preferences and the Volatility of Consumption and Wealth." *Review of Financial Studies* 2, 73–89.

Tauchen, G. (1986). "Finite State Markov Chain Approximations to Univariate and Vector Autoregressions." *Economic Letters* 20, 177–181.

Tauchen, G., and R. Hussey (1991). "Quadrature Based Methods for Obtaining Approximate Solutions to Nonlinear Asset Pricing Models." *Econometrica* 59, 371–396.

Telmer, I. C. (1993). "Asset Pricing Puzzles and Incomplete Markets." *Journal of Finance* 48, 1803–1832.

Tobin, J. (1958). "Liquidity Preference as Behavior Towards Risk." *Review of Economic Studies* 25, 68–85.

Uhler, R. S., and J. G. Cragg (1971). "The Structure of the Asset Portfolios of Households." *Review of Economics and Statistics* 38, 341–357.

Umlauf, S. (1993). "Transaction Taxes and the Behavior of the Swedish Stock Market." *Journal of Financial Economics* 33, 227–240.

Vella, F. (1998). "Estimating Models with Sample Selection Bias: A Survey." *Journal of Human Resources* 33, 127–169.

Vella, F., and M. Verbeek (1999). "Two-Step Estimation of Panel Data Models with Censored Endogenous Variables and Selection Bias." *Journal of Econometrics* 90, 239–263.

Venti, S., and D. Wise (1989). "Aging, Moving, and Housing Wealth." In D. Wise, ed., *The Economics of Aging*. Chicago: University of Chicago Press.

Viceira, L. (1999). "Optimal Portfolio Choice for Long-Horizon Investors with Non-tradable Labor Income." *Journal of Finance*.

Vissing-Jørgensen, A. (2000). "Towards an Explanation of Household Portfolio Choice Heterogeneity: Non-Financial Income and Participation Cost Structures." Mimeo. University of Chicago.

von Neumann, J., and O. Morgenstern (1944). *Theory of Games and Economic Behavior*. Princeton, NJ: Princeton University Press.

Walliser, J., and J. Winter (1999). "Tax Incentives, Bequest Motives and the Demand for Life Insurance: Evidence from Germany." Discussion Paper 99-28. Sonderforschungs bereich 504, University of Mannheim.

Weber, M. M. (1958). *The Protestant Ethic and the Spirit of Capitalism*. New York: Charles Scribner and Sons.

Wedderburn, R. (1974). "Quasi-likelihood Functions, Generalized Linear Models, and the Gauss-Newton Method." *Biometrika* 61, 439–447.

Weil, P. (1990). "Nonexpected Utility in Macroeconomics." *Quarterly Journal of Economics* 105, 29–42.

Weisbenner, S. (1999). "Do Pension Plans with Participant Investment Choice Teach Households to Hold More Equity?" Federal Reserve Board Discussion Paper 1999-61.

Wenger, E., and C. Kaserer (1997). "The German System of Corporate Governance—A Model Which Should Not Be Imitated." American Institute for Contemporary German Studies, Working Paper 14.

Wilson, R. (1968). "The Theory of Syndicates." *Econometrica* 36, 113–132.

Wooldridge, J. (1995). "Selection Correction for Panel Data Models Under Conditional Mean Independence Assumptions." *Journal of Econometrics* 68, 115–132.

Yaari, M. E. (1965). "Uncertain Lifetime, Life Insurance, and the Theory of the Consumer." *Review of Economic Studies* 32, 137–150.

Yaari, M. E. (1987). "The Dual Theory of Choice Under Risk." *Econometrica* 55, 95–115.

Zeger, S., and K. Liang (1986). "Longitudinal Data Analysis for Discrete and Continuous Outcomes." *Biometrics* 42, 121–130.

Zeldes, S. (1989). "Consumption and Liquidity Constraints: An Empirical Investigation." *Journal of Political Economy* 97, 305–346.

Zou, H-F. (1994). "The 'Spirit of Capitalism' and Long-Run Growth." *European Journal of Political Economy* 10, 279–293.

Index

Absolute risk aversion, 31. *See also* Risk aversion
convex, 37
decreasing, 34
harmonic (HARA), 42
Age structure of portfolios, 12, 15, 21, 89–96, 199, 270–272
in Germany, 12–13, 307–308
in Italy, 12–13, 270–272
in the Netherlands, 12–13, 364–372
for the rich, 391, 403–405, 413–414, 424
in the United Kingdom, 12–13, 17, 219, 228–229, 231
in the United States, 12–13, 199, 207, 208, 211, 212
Asset. *See also* Wealth; Portfolios
allocation, 4, 112, 129
distinctive ownership patterns for the rich, 389–391, 395–400, 402–403, 423–424, 427
habitat, 108
international differences in ownership patterns, 405–407, 410–411
location, 115, 135
selection, 4, 110, 129
trading, 4, 117, 138
Asset shares. *See* Portfolios, shares in

Background risk, 3, 22, 35, 61–62, 74, 192, 199, 201, 206, 283–85, 375, 467. *See also* Uninsurable risks
Backward induction, 39, 90–92
Bellman
equation, 90, 417
value function, 40, 63–64, 90–91
Bequests, 391, 394, 415, 417–418, 425–427

Binary choice models, 372. *See also* Discrete choice models
Borrowing, 114, 126, 134
constraints, 62–63, 66, 77, 96, 181, 282. *See also* Capital market imperfections; Liquidity constraints; Short-sales constraints

Calibration, 64–65
Capital asset pricing model, 2, 105
Capitalist spirit model, 391, 418, 426–427. *See also* Bequests
Capital market imperfections. *See also* Liquidity constraints; Borrowing, constraints
differences across countries, 411
implications for portfolios of the rich, 390–391, 416–417, 424–427
Censored regression models, 161, 203
dynamic, 168–169
fixed effects, 162–163
random effects, 166
Conditional logit, 151, 158–159, 166, 174
Contraction mapping, 79, 93
Costs
entry, 56, 86, 203–204, 212–213, 230, 236
fixed, of asset ownership, 111
information, 22, 146, 164, 182, 244, 284–285, 317–318
participation, 56, 63–64, 85–86, 194, 281
transaction, 47, 67, 146, 156, 164, 181, 191–192, 220, 237, 239, 244, 281, 355

Data
Asset and Health Dynamics of Among the Oldest Old (United States), 435–436, 469–472

Data (cont.)
CentER Savings Survey (Netherlands), 342, 347–354
Family Expenditure Survey (United Kingdom), 221–222
Financial Resources Survey (United Kingdom), 221–222
Flow of Funds Accounts (United States), 182–183, 343
Housing Needs Survey (Netherlands), 347, 353
Income Panel Survey (Netherlands), 346, 351–354
Income and Expenditure Data (Germany), 332
measurement error in, 144–145, 351–354
nonresponse in survey, 144, 348
panel, 143–176, 208, 221, 238, 277–280, 343, 347, 372, 377
Spiegel Verlag Survey Holl und Haben (Germany), 332, 334
Survey of Consumer Finances (United States), 110, 113, 115, 116, 131, 185, 187–192
Survey of Household Income and Wealth (Italy), 256–258, 286–288
Discrete choice models, 148–160
static, 150–155, 372–377, 379–382
Discretization, 65
Deregulation, 301–303
Diversification. See Portfolios, diversification

Employer-sponsored Saving Plans (ESSP), 343, 348–349, 351, 355, 357, 361, 364, 366, 368–370, 377, 381–382, 385
Entrepreneurial ventures
and inheritance, 420, 422, 426
minimum efficient scale of, 390, 417, 425, 427
risk tolerance and, 389–391, 417, 420, 423, 425–427
self-financing of, 390–391, 398, 410, 417, 423–425, 427
Equity ownership. See Stock ownership
Equity premium, 35, 59, 65, 68–69, 82, 86, 93, 96–97, 181
Estate taxes. See Tax, code features relevant for the rich

Financial intermediaries, 116, 137
Fixed effects, 150, 372, 382. See also
Censored regression models;
Heterogeneity; Individual effects;
Sample selection models
censored regression models, 162–163, 168–169
discrete choice models, 150–152, 157–159
quasi-, 382
sample selection models, 164–166, 169–170

German reunification, 301–303, 319–322
GMM estimators, 153, 157, 159–160, 163, 170

Habit
formation, 50, 59
persistence, 82
Health risk, 433
Heterogeneity, 143, 149, 162, 171, 201, 379, 381, 384. See also Individual effects; Fixed effects; Random effects
in preferences, 416
in risk tolerance, 416
Housing, 185, 192, 219, 222, 224, 227–229, 239, 347, 353–355, 361, 366, 436–439
Hyperbolic discounting, 51

Individual effects, 154, 157. See also
Heterogeneity, Fixed effects; Random effects
Individual retirement accounts (IRAs), 220, 240–242. See also Retirement accounts
Information costs. See Costs, information
Interpolation, 65, 91

Liquidity constraints, 46, 182, 192, 201, 206, 208, 282, 385, 416–417. See also
Borrowing, constraints; Capital market imperfections
Life cycle hypothesis, 145, 390, 411–416
Logit model, 147, 151, 174

Maximum likelihood, 151–153, 156, 167, 379. See also Quasi-likelihood estimators; Simulated maximum likelihood

Maximum score estimator, 152, 166
Mean-reversion, 48, 86–89
Mills ratio, 165. *See also* Sample selection
  models
Minimum distance estimator, 153, 155,
  162, 168
Mutual funds, 8, 117, 183, 187, 255, 344,
  349, 351, 354, 355, 359, 361, 364, 366

Participation, 6, 8–14, 22, 55, 60–61, 63–
  64, 69, 81, 83–86, 88, 143, 145, 147, 171,
  193, 201–211, 258–262, 298–299, 372–
  382, 395–398, 444–452. *See also* Asset,
  selection; Costs, participation
Pensions, 183, 202, 212, 219, 222, 224,
  344, 346, 347, 349, 355, 466
  compulsory occupational, 344, 346, 349
  income, 90
  personal, 219, 225–226
  State Earning Related Pension Scheme
  (SERPS), 224
Personal Equity Plan (PEP), 220, 227,
  229, 240–242
Portfolios
  age structure of (*see* Age structure of
  portfolios)
  diversification, 2, 8, 10, 194, 219, 227,
  239, 244, 262–263, 299–300, 360–361,
  403–405
  dynamic model of, 66–67
  effects of education on, 8, 14, 206, 210,
  219–220, 222, 235, 237, 244, 273, 314,
  370–372
  effects of income on, 82, 206, 210, 222,
  232, 237
  effects of wealth on, 10, 193–194, 206,
  208–210, 228–230, 232–235, 267–270,
  310–313, 322–325, 361–364, 395–400
  of the elderly, 14, 431–472
  finite-horizon model of, 89–96
  infinite-horizon model of, 77–89
  puzzles, 55–56, 63–64, 69, 81–89, 93–96,
  145
  riskiness of, 194–199, 207–211, 227–228,
  390, 435
  shares in, 6, 14–18, 143, 147, 160–171,
  222–225, 229–231, 263–266, 293–298,
  357–360, 382–385, 398–400
  static problem of, 29, 32, 69–71
  theory of, implications for portfolios of
  the rich, 2, 229, 400, 422–424

transitions, 452–465
Precautionary effects, 74, 77, 182, 282
Privatization and share ownership in
  the UK, 219, 235–239
  Italy, 255
Probit model, 147, 153, 165, 172, 207–211
Prudence, 3, 82, 85, 93–95

Quadrature, 64–65, 91
Quasi-likelihood estimators, 154, 157

Random effects, 372, 379, 382. *See also*
  Censored regression models;
  Heterogeneity; Individual effects;
  Sample selection models
  in censored regression models, 166
  in discrete choice models, 153–155, 156,
  159–160
  in sample selection models, 167, 170
Randomized response, 144
Recursive utility, 50
Relative risk aversion, 31, 68, 79–80, 95,
  391, 412, 416–418, 420, 422, 427
  constant, 65, 67, 78, 90, 412
  decreasing, 34, 427
  measurement of, 32, 418–420
Retirement accounts, 182–184, 187–190,
  212, 349, 440
Risk aversion, 22, 31, 74, 82, 85, 149, 164,
  375, 376, 390–391, 404–405, 418–420.
  See also Absolute risk aversion;
  Relative risk aversion
  and bequests, 418, 426
  and business equity, 391, 417–418, 424–
  426
  heterogeneity in, 390, 416, 418–425, 428
  and inheritance, 420–422, 426–427
Risk vulnerability, 37

Sample design, 144
Sample selection models, 8, 161, 203,
  382–385
  dynamic models, 169–171
  fixed effects, 164–166
  random effects, 164, 167
Short-sales constraints, 78, 80, 82, 91. *See
  also* Borrowing, constraints; Capital
  market imperfections; Liquidity
  constraints
Simulated maximum likelihood, 153,
  157, 379

State dependence, 143, 149, 156–157, 379, 381
Stock ownership. *See also* Assets; Participation; Portfolios
  barriers to, 191 (*see also* Costs; Portfolios, puzzles)
  changes in, 190–191
  employer-sponsored retirement accounts, effect of, 191
  internet, effect of, 191
Strict exogeneity, 163–164, 167, 171

Tax
  on capital gains, 106, 122, 349
  code and effects on asset ownership, 229–244, 242–244, 304–307
  code features relevant for the rich, 392–395, 397
  deferred accounts, 108, 125, 135
  deferred retirement accounts (*see* Retirement accounts; *see also* Tax, deferred accounts)
  exempt Special Savings Account (TESSA), 220, 240–242, 243–244
  favored, 346, 349, 351, 385
  marginal rates, 106, 120
  risk, 120
Time consistency, 30
Time diversification, 28, 38, 42
Time-invariant distribution, 83
Tobit models, 147, 160, 201
Transaction costs. *See* Costs, transaction
Trimmed least squares estimator, 162–163, 169
Truncated regression models, 161
Two-fund separation theorem, 34

Unfolding brackets, 144
Uninsurable risks, 145, 146. *See also* Background risk
Utility
  aggregator function, 58
  Epstein-Zin form of, 58
  expected, 59, 65, 72–77
  homotheticity of function, 416
  Kreps-Porteus form of, 59, 65, 72–77
  Quiggin form of, 72–77
  rank-dependent, 60, 65, 68, 72–77
  recursive, 58
  Stone-Geary form of, 391, 417

Value function. *See* Bellman, value function

Wealth, 10, 77, 145–146, 193–194, 206, 222–225, 254, 390, 417, 423–427, 436–444. *See also* Asset; Portfolios